The Human Side of Managing Technological Innovation

W9-CEO-314

THE HUMAN SIDE OF MANAGING TECHNOLOGICAL INNOVATION

A Collection of Readings

Edited by **RALPH KATZ**

New York   Oxford
OXFORD UNIVERSITY PRESS
1997

Oxford University Press

Oxford   New York
Athens   Auckland   Bangkok   Bogotá   Bombay
Buenos Aires   Calcutta   Cape Town   Dar es Salaam
Delhi   Florence   Hong Kong   Istanbul   Karachi
Kuala Lumpur   Madras   Madrid   Melbourne
Mexico City   Nairobi   Paris   Singapore
Taipei   Tokyo   Toronto

and associated companies in
Berlin   Ibadan

Copyright © 1997 by Oxford University Press, Inc.

Published by Oxford University Press, Inc.,
198 Madison Avenue, New York, New York 10016

Oxford is a registered trademark of Oxford University Press

All rights reserved. No part of this publication
may be reproduced, stored in a retrieval system, or transmitted,
in any form or by any means, electronic, mechanical,
photocopying, recording, or otherwise, without the prior
permission of Oxford University Press.

Library of Congress Cataloging-in-Publication Data
The human side of managing technological innovation : a collection
    of readings / edited by Ralph Katz.
        p.   cm.
    Includes bibliographical references and index.
    ISBN 0-19-509693-2. — ISBN 0-19-509694-0 (pbk.)
    1. Technological innovations—Management.
  I. Katz, Ralph.
HD45.H84   1997   96-38714
658.5′14—dc20   CIP

9 8 7 6 5 4
Printed in the United States of America
on acid-free paper

This book is dedicated
to the loving memory of my parents
Ida and Myer Katz
and to my wonderful wife and family
Judy, Dan, and Elana.

CONTENTS

INTRODUCTION

Organizations competing in today's world of rapid technological and market changes are faced with the challenges of "dualism," that is, operating efficiently in the present while also innovating effectively for the future. Managers and leaders within these organizations not only have to focus on the market success and profitability of each of their established products and services, but they must also ensure their capability to introduce into next generation offerings those specific technical advances and product attributes that will sustain and even augment their continued global competitiveness. Technology-based companies, no matter how they are structured or organized, must develop and implement strategies that satisfy *both* of these sets of concerns. The surprisingly fast collapse or near-collapse of so many supposedly dominant, world-class, excellent organizations—especially over the last decade—gives ample testimony to the importance of managing this dualism.

Now, it would be somewhat straightforward if everyone working in an organization could agree on the strategies and means by which this dualism could be achieved, but such consensus is rare. Amid the diverse pressures of daily job requirements and rewards, managers representing different business units and departmental areas usually disagree on the relative merits of allocating already scarce resources and talents among the range of activities that might benefit "today's," versus "tomorrow's," products and services. Furthermore, most managerial practices and procedures cannot offer simple, ready-made solutions that are accommodating to what are essentially inherently conflicting demands and challenges. Classical management theory, for example, deals primarily with the efficient utilization and production of the company's existing assets and product offerings. The principles of high task specialization, unity of command and direction, high division of labor, and equality of responsibility and authority all address the problems of structuring work systems and information flows in clear, repetitive ways. They are geared toward the resolution of familiar problems and the facilitation of productivity and control through formal lines of positional and hierarchical authority or through job standardization. And organizations that are designed and managed for doing the same things well repetitively, as in manufacturing, are not particularly appropriate for doing something well once, as in R&D. Similarly, organizations designed and managed for doing something well once are not going to be appropriate for doing the same things well repetitively. Put simply, operating and innovating organizations represent *opposing* logics.

What is needed, therefore, is some comparable set of concepts and principles that would reveal how to organize Research, Development, and Engineering (RD&E) activities so that the outputs and creative ideas from innovating professionals are utilized effectively even as the organization deals with the pressures of meeting the everyday demands from its intensely competitive marketplace. How does one establish and manage an organizational RD&E setting such that new technical advances and developmental efforts not only take place but ultimately take place in a very timely, effective, and successful manner? If, in fact, "visionary" ideas and "stupid" ideas look the same at the earliest stages of the innovation process, then how does one manage, lead, allocate resources, or make the "right" decisions in the face of this dilemma?

The need to manage technology-based innovation and enhance the commercialization of new technical knowledge is not new. The ability to develop and incorporate research advances and technical know-how into new products and services has long been a cornerstone of economic growth and industrialization. According to recent U.S. National Science Foundation and National Research Council reports, leveraging the effective contributions of technical professionals through crossfunctional teams is one of the more important areas in the management of technological innovation. Organizations not only have to improve their abilities to assess, coordinate, and integrate alternative technical developments within their overall business strategies; but they must also be capable of implementing their plans through the leadership of their technical management and the efforts of their engineering and scientific personnel. Far more often than not, the frustrations identified in the management of innovation are simply not technical in nature, the problems being rooted more in the complex interplay among the many different priorities and motivational efforts of the technical professionals and their crossfunctional peers. The management of technological innovation has to take the human side of the equation into consideration!

In most industries today, a variety of economic, technical, and market-driven forces have coalesced to make these people-related problems even more salient. The diversification and decentralization of businesses, the growth of international alliances and competition, the faster rates at which new technologies are being generated worldwide, the increasing demands of more sophisticated customers, the growing use of computerized information and communication networking, and the dramatic reduction of lead times for new product development have all placed greater pressure on the firm to expand both its commitment to and its competence in managing technological innovation and organizational change. In particular, the ways in which a company's professional personnel and resources are allocated, positioned, and generally managed will have a strong bearing on the firm's ability to compete successfully in tomorrow's more global economy. As a result, decision makers in organizations today must have those managerial skills and perspectives necessary to enhance the innovation process and to bring technical advances successfully to the marketplace. They must acquire substantial knowledge and ability not only in managing and directing the technical and marketing developments themselves but also in utilizing and directing the professionals involved in these development efforts. They must be able to communicate, understand, inspire, and guide technical professionals and integrate them with other functional parts of the organization including finance, marketing, and manufacturing. The need for executive leadership in managing both innovation and people has never been greater.

The main objective of this readings book, *The Human Side of Managing Technological Innovation: A Collection of Readings*, is to provide a comprehensive picture of a variety of approaches and perspectives on issues critical to the effective management of technical professionals and crossfunctional teams throughout the innovation process. It is my hope to bridge the gap between theory and application by selecting those readings that contain concepts and empirical findings that will prove meaningful and useful to both students and practicing managers, executives, and professional staff personnel. The articles are not meant to span the entire gamut of issues involved in the management of technology and innovation. I have, instead, focused on readings that deal with the management and leadership of professional specialists and crossfunctional teams, as well as the structuring and coordination of organizational roles during the innovation process. For the most part, the papers discuss how internal work environments can be organized and structured to provide the kinds of opportunities, experiences, and managerial leadership that will enable professional specialists to innovate effectively through their organizational and team-based relationships. The articles included in this collection represent the thinking of a large number of researchers and practitioners seeking a richer understanding of the complex interplay between the specialized knowledge and skills of creative professionals and the realistic pressures and constraints required by successful business organizations. Readings that concentrate more on the complex interplay between business strategy and the management of innovation can be found in *Managing Strategic Innovation and Change*, a complementary volume of readings edited by my colleagues Michael Tushman and Philip Anderson and published by Oxford University Press.

The articles in this book can be used as a text for advanced undergraduate or graduate courses that focus primarily on how organizational managers, individual professionals, project teams, and/or functional groups deal with problems and issues related to the management of technology-based innovation. The collection can also be used as a complementary text for any course that emphasizes product, process, and organizational or technological innovation. It could be used in behavioral courses on issues of leadership, organizational behavior, organizational change, or general management; but more specifically, it could be used for courses broadly related to the management of innovation, courses such as R&D management, new-product development, project management, engineering management, managing professionals, and so forth. Another audience includes all of those managers and staff professionals working on innovative projects or dealing with product development activities, especially when they attend in-house company or university-based workshops and want to have background material on the kinds of problems and concerns included in the various articles. Finally, although many of the articles in this volume focus on technical professionals, the concepts and issues covered apply to a wide range of professionals including those involved in new products and services, consulting

services, organizational or technological change and uncertainty, or any situation involving the development or application of specialized knowledge and abilities.

The Human Side of Managing Technological Innovation is organized into six sections comprising a total of seventeen separate chapters. The sections range from issues related to the management and motivation of the individual technologist to more macro organizational and product development kinds of issues. Section I looks at problems associated with managing the performance and productivity of individual professionals. In Chapter 1, we examine the issue of motivation, emphasizing the importance of designing energizing and challenging work environments as well as the strong influence that organizational socialization can play in formulating such motivational conditions. Chapter 2 presents a variety of studies and methodologies for enhancing the creative performance of individual specialists within organizations. While Chapter 2 deals primarily with the contributions of individuals, the articles in Chapter 3 discuss several ideas and frameworks for measuring both the productivity and vitality of R&D environments.

Section II covers a number of important issues related to the management of professionals within groups and crossfunctional project teams. Chapter 4 deals with the formation and management of high-performing technical teams both through a case study of DEC's Alpha design team and through two empirical studies that summarize the characteristics of the high-performing teams within their respective samples. Chapter 5 next explores some of these same problems from a crossfunctional-team perspective and discusses how to maintain a team's performance over time, especially if the team becomes increasingly stable and insular. Chapter 6 rounds out the picture with its discussions of managing group and project performances within functional, project, or matrix types of organizational structures.

Section III examines the different technical, managerial, leadership, and entrepreneurial roles that professionals can and should play at particular stages of the innovation process. Chapter 7 investigates the role of the technical manager and describes many of the problems professionals encounter during the difficult transition from functional specialist to manager. The articles in Chapter 8 discuss and compare various leadership roles that technical managers have to carry out, especially as they try to initiate and implement critical organizational changes. Chapter 9 presents a general model for conceptualizing the innovation process and the critical roles that need to take place to support this process. The chapter also includes some empirical results on cultural differences surrounding the critical role of championing.

The papers in Section IV illustrate just how powerfully organizational structures and technical cultures influence the attitudes and behaviors of professionals within the innovation process. Chapter 10 cautions against generalizing across all types of professionals and R&D activities, pointing out critical differences between science and technology as well as between research and development activities. The chapter also shows the difficulty of communicating and transfering information effectively across different "technical cultures" but then goes on to reveal how the critical role of "technical gatekeeper" can help overcome this difficulty. Chapter 11 focuses on the strong effects that cultures have on professional performance and organizational innovation and illustrates these effects through a case study of the innovation of 3M's Post-it Notes. While Chapter 11 emphasizes the positive aspects of culture, Chapter 12 discusses some of the problems of sustaining innovative performance in organizations.

Section V discusses a variety of organizational processes and practices that influence an organization's ability to innovate in a timely and effective manner. Chapter 13 focuses on the decision-making process, stressing important differences in the management of routine, versus nonroutine, work as well as how managers who make "fast" decisions differ from those who are substantially slower at making key decisions. The last article in Chapter 13 illustrates how several outstanding companies are establishing much more relevant accounting and financial systems to *assist* rather than *control* their horizontal work processes. Chapter 14 discusses a number of important issues from a human resource management perspective, including issues of diversity, rewards, and dual ladder promotional systems. The issue of reducing product development cycle times is addressed directly in the articles of Chapter 15 by including the frameworks, experiences, and caveats from several well-known consultants and researchers.

The last section of the book, Section VI, deals with several key dynamics and interrelationships underlying the innovation process. Chapter 16 concentrates on the critical interface between marketing and R&D by including results from three different empirical studies. The chapter's first article investigates the characteristics that lead to more effective crossfunctional relationships; the second article examines many of the misunderstandings and unfortunate attributions that arise over time between marketing and R&D; and the third article summarizes the development activities and product attributes of those products that eventually win in the marketplace. Chapter 17 completes the volume by presenting three different perspectives on the innovation process. The first article portrays some of the limitations of trying to come up with new product ideas by identifying key market needs; it then goes on, however, to argue that organizations can enhance the management of new product developments by actively coopting ideas and solutions of "lead users." The second article discusses the innovation dilemma by comparing the patterns of product, versus process, innovation over the course of a product's life cycle and discussing how these patterns affect the dynamics between old and new technologies. And finally, the last article presents a broad overview of the management of technological innovation, summarizing what has been learned from many empirical investigations about staffing, structuring, and strategizing for improved innovation.

Clearly, no book could hope to cover every topic associated with the human side of managing technological innovation; nor could it possibly include all of the excellent articles related to the many issues and nuances involved in each of the sections and chapters. Nevertheless, it is my hope that the articles included in this collection will be relevant and useful to those readers who are part of an organization's innovation efforts and to those who have to manage the innovation or change process within their organizations. I hope the readings will increase their sensitivity to the kinds of problems and issues they will face and that they will have some new ideas, tools, and insights for handling these problems—or better yet—for their prevention.—R.K.

The Human Side of Managing Technological Innovation

THE MANAGEMENT AND MOTIVATION OF PROFESSIONAL PERFORMANCE

1

The Motivation of Technical Professionals

1

Motivating Your R&D Staff

George E. Manners, Jr.
Joseph A. Steger
Thomas W. Zimmerer

Ten basic tenets form a body of practical knowledge for generating the excitement that is the essence of motivation for technical people.

Over the years, we have found that research managers list "motivation" as the most perplexing requirement of the managerial role. This observation is true in many management situations. Motivation is one of the most critical ingredients in work performance as well as *the* most difficult to understand. There is a voluminous amount of literature on the topic, some of it quite valuable to the manager. However, this enormity of information lacks focus and, shall we say, a common body of practical knowledge.

We conceive of motivation simply as excite-

Reprinted with permission from *Research–Technology Management,* September–October, 1983.

George Manners is Professor of Management at Clemson University. *Joseph Steger* is Executive Vice President and Provost of University of Cincinnati. *Thomas Zimmerer* is an independent management consultant.

ment—an energizer that is reflected as excitement or arousal. This definition makes the concept of motivation more understandable and applicable. Most managers tend to conceive of motivation as a complex set of dimensions that in fact are not encompassed in our definition. Thus, performance is not motivation. Satisfaction is not motivation. Behaviors are not motivation. Results are not motivation. Too often these are in some confusing and ambiguous fashion encompassed in the concept of motivation when discussed by managers.

Another point: Because people are excited about work and are exhibiting lots of activity does not mean they are productively active. That is, the group could be highly motivated and running amuck because they are not managed to optimize the motivational spirit.

While the presence of motivation does not guarantee performance, the absence of motivation guarantees long-term performance problems. Obviously, a lack of arousal begets no effort and the precursor to *effort* is excitement or arousal. Edison's famous quote about genius being 99 percent perspiration and 1 percent inspiration is the essence of what motivation in our conception yields.

Thus, as long as one does not over-define motivation, we think that a focus—or common body of knowledge—is available to the practicing manager. This focus is contained in ten basic tenets which yield useful insight into how to generate work-group excitement without requiring the vocabulary of a clinical psychologist.

A tenet is an opinion which is held to be true— our opinion. These opinions, however, have been slowly articulated over a ten-year period by carefully observing successful motivational practices through our interactions with industrial and government R&D laboratories. We have come to view these tenets as fundamental truths of work excitement. We have found that the extent to which these tenets—and their prescriptions for managerial action—are understood by the practicing manager is the extent to which the capacity to motivate is understood. Some of these tenets may be viewed as simple platitudes, some not. Taken as a whole, however, they do form a common body of practical knowledge. The tenets are as follows.

DIFFICULTY

The first tenet of motivation is, quite simply, that generating incremental excitement about work is very difficult. On the other hand, most managers have observed that destroying excitement is relatively easy. Many young project managers find that the old excitement created by technical interactions while on the bench no longer works when they assume "power." Or, they agonize over how to rekindle work excitement in a bench scientist many years their elder.

It is interesting how many of these befuddled research managers blame "the corporation" for their motivational difficulties. Meanwhile, the effective motivators understand a fact of managerial existence: Do not expect much help from the larger organization. Many of the reasons why the larger organization (the laboratory *or* the corporation) will not necessarily aid the individual manager in the day-to-day motivations of researchers will become more clear once the other basic tenets are offered.

Difficult though this business is, the prize is worth the chase. We offer this advice, *Never give up*. The motivated work group is too important an antecedent to research success to stop trying. One can feel its effects simply by walking in the door of research offices. As the sage football scout once said: "I don't know what it is, but I know it when I see it."

FAT HAPPY RATS

Since so much of the literature on motivation emanates from experimental psychology, we should offer the observation that fat, happy rats never run mazes. They sit there. Now, this tenet should not lead to the conclusion that research managers should keep researchers deprived. On the contrary, keep the rewards coming to those who perform. And as the Japanese have so effectively pointed out, one must maintain a "positive tension." That is, an excitement that is directed toward answering, "How do we do it better?" Thus, no resting on one's laurels is allowed.

The other facet of the "Fat Happy Rat" tenet is that most "positive tension" is generated within the individual. Thus, *selection* of talent that are generators of their own excitement is critical and yet often neglected by R&D managers who focus on credentials.

The literature on achievement motivation reinforces this fact by concluding that those possessing the motivation to achieve (which is terribly difficult to "train"—thus the focus selection) tend to maintain that motivation to the extent that the desire to excel is given a climate to operationalize the desire. Thus, hungry researchers tend to stay hungry—given the manager's understanding of the other basic tenets.

An anecdote may serve to make the point about achievers: We once asked a research manager what he looked for in a young scientist or engineer. His response was "I will tell you what *not* to look for—'Soft Suburbanities.' They are never hungry enough!" While we all can observe some exceptions to this manager's rule, the work excitement of the hungry researchers in his laboratory was truly exceptional.

The observation of the achiever during the employment interview takes no special skill on the part of the manager. Thus, we are amused at how many R&D labs have dropped the practice of having prospective researchers make a presentation on their dissertation or other current research because "we do not learn much." Technically, this is probably true. But if a young researcher has just spent several years on a scientific/engineering problem and cannot communicate some excitement about it, that really tells you something about that candidate. We would argue that you reinstitute the presentation if you do not have one and consider the motivation impact of the candidate as well as his/her technical content.

LOW INTELLECTUAL CONTENT

A very interesting facet of motivation is the fact that emotion has almost no intellectual content. This creates problems for the research community because it is staffed by people of high intellect who believe you can intellectualize all motivational problems away. Thus, you will hear the argument

that if so-and-so only understood he would act differently. The research manager has missed the motivational point—intellectualizing doesn't handle emotion. And so-and-so acts the way she does not because of lack of understanding but in spite of understanding. The act makes him *feel good* regardless of the content.

The manager must understand that every managerial act has two principle components, namely, information and affect (or emotion). We observe that there is rarely much intellectual content in emotion but, where motivation is concerned, there is also very little intellectual content in information. A manager must be intellectually aware of his motivational objectives, but should not necessarily try to communicate it. Emotion gets in the way.

Even if a research manager possesses a Ph.D., he is rarely a clinical psychologist. Thus, *if it feels good, do not ask why, do it again.* We once had a manager say that you could not motivate adult researchers by sticking stars on poster paper the way they did in grade school. Meanwhile, his staff was falling all over themselves to get their names listed on the "patent award" plaque in the office foyer.

HEDONISM

As a fundamental determinant of motivation, we must observe that all individuals "seek pleasure and avoid pain." Although this may appear to be a worthless platitude, managers must first understand this to be absolutely true—because its implications for managerial thought and action are substantive.

First, hedonism implies *get to know your people.* What is pleasurable to person A may be quite unpleasant to person B. Especially where delegation is concerned, research managers tend to assume that a researcher will enjoy a task because the manager himself would enjoy it and yet it may threaten the researcher who is assigned to the task.

All individuals are different in what they like and what they fear. Thus, one of the most critical errors a manager can commit is to make broad generalizations about what people like—or what motivates them. This is extremely important if for no other reason than the fact that formal reward systems do imply such broad generalizations. Pay systems have become very standardized, even in the unlikely event that they are based only on performance. The individual manager in her day-to-day interactions has very little control over formal reward systems. She does, however, have considerable control over many informal rewards and these should be applied to specific individuals in terms of their specific likes and dislikes. Thus, for example, the manager can use job assignments, travel, equipment, and his time as important elements in his system to motivate his employees.

The key to hedonism as a tenet of motivation begins with the recognition of individual differences.

Second, hedonism requires the manager to *maintain control over (informal) rewards*. We find it interesting how many managers give up control over obvious rewards because they are an administrative headache. If the manager loses control over what a researcher likes (or, may like), he may lose the capacity to excite that individual about work. He must then rely on the employee's "self motivation"—which may be fine in some cases but we do not suggest that one rely solely on it.

PROTECTION OF SELF

All individuals have a certain desire for protection of self. Particularly in research work, the basic tenet of protection typically means protection from the possibility and consequences of failure. People who have spent their lives building self-esteem based upon technical competence will go to great lengths to avoid losing that fragile base. It is surprising how many managers cannot see through apathy, defensiveness, and aggression as a manifestation of the fear of failure.

In order to keep work excitement and openness high, the manager must communicate that you *take some risks and I will protect you if you fail*. This is an imperative step in a good motivational program. We once worked with an R&D manager who gave great inspirational speeches, always ending with: "you people must take more risks. The

future of the company and the country depends on it!" The people who then took risks and failed were handed their heads. Needless to say, risk taking and research performance in that company are very low.

Protection also implies a desire to "save face," a concept which American managers continuously ignore. This tenet simply requires that we *treat people with dignity*. Many researchers who tour an operating division—particularly blue-collar situations—have observed the pervasive attacks on simple human dignity and have commented, "no wonder the union is hostile." But some of the same researchers will return to the lab and exhibit the same attacks on the dignity of a technician. *Respect* and *dignity* are precursors to the generation of work excitement.

Given the contemporary economic climate, even well-educated employees work in a world of extreme uncertainty. This uncertainty is magnified by managers who feel that keeping subordinates "off-guard" keeps them "on their toes." These attacks can be quite subtle and when the desire for protection is aroused, the defenses can be very subtle. People find it difficult to respond openly to an injury to their self esteem although the damage, in fact, may be crippling to their capacity to perform.

ENHANCEMENT OF SELF

Managers must recognize the inherent conflict between the desire for protection and the desire for enhancement. By enhancement of self, we mean that all individuals seek some symbols of status. But in work, symbols of status should be associated with taking some risks—and succeeding. Thus, while a manager should communicate some protection from failure, she must also communicate that *incremental rewards should only be associated with success*. This is a difficult balancing act requiring a significant amount of self-discipline and consistency on the part of the manager. (It also assumes some control over rewards).

Aside from the distribution of rewards, an extremely simple corollary to this tenet is that *everybody wants to solo*. A researcher likes to be seen making an identifiable, perhaps singular, contribution to the group, however trivial this contribution may seem to an external observer. The emerging field of organization design seems to base its theory on this desire to solo.

We should also emphasize that soloing is not at all incompatible with teamwork. Our observation is that where effective team building has taken place, this tenet receives prime consideration. At one laboratory, a team-building exercise left us very impressed with the ability of each team to enhance its members—particularly the older professionals.

SOCIAL RELATIVITY

When a manager recognizes the first six tenets of motivation (i.e., he works hard at it, selects achievers, views excitement for excitement's sake, understands individual differences, provides a climate of dignity and protection, rewards incremental performance), he can still be perplexed at the level of dissatisfaction. Why? Because this tenet implies that all consequences in work are relative—relative to what other people are getting. This is one of the principal reasons why motivation, especially maintaining motivation, is so frustrating to many managers.

But satisfaction, as we have noted, is *not* motivation. Achievers are rarely satisfied. They want more. We have observed many managers who have gotten so tired of this "ingratitude" that they begin to believe that the only way to manage is to treat everybody absolutely equally. What the frustrated manager must realize is that *managing to motivate is incompatible with managing to minimize dissatisfaction.* The worst mistake a manager can make regarding motivation is to adopt a strategy to minimize dissatisfaction and yield a satisfied, complacent work group. Positive tension (by definition, lack of satisfaction) is a necessity.

Social relativity is also important as an input into how a manager allocates his time spent with those reporting to him. One must learn to distinguish between time spent on supervision and time spent on motivation. In general, low performers require disproportionate amounts of supervisory

time. You have to give them that time. Their excuse of not understanding the role requirements just might be true. But do not spend motivational time on low performers, "invest" it on the higher performers. One moves the group's mean performance to a new plateau by further motivating the high performers, not by rescuing the low performers.

This tenet also requires that the manager *make the recognition of performance very visible* to as many people as possible. Many have heard and agree with the principle of not publically punishing a subordinate. But rewarding a high performer should be as public as possible. Not only does this prescription work on the show-off phenomenon (i.e., enhancement) but it also communicates what constitutes performance to other group members. Everybody likes to have their work displayed for others to see. How many artists create a piece of work and hide it? This tenet, more than any other, forces the manager to recognize both the information and emotion of a motivational act.

SATIATION VERSUS VARIABILITY

We earlier defined motivation as excitement—the managerial act being the proper mix of information and emotion. Nowhere is this act more perplexing than in the trade-off between constancy and variability in work. Research managers may understand this concept somewhat better than most, but it is nevertheless perplexing. Consider the following three conclusions from Pelz and Andrews' *Scientists in Organizations* (New York: John Wiley and Sons, Inc., 1966):

1. In both research and development, the more effective professionals undertook several specialties or technical functions (p. 54).
2. Effective scientists reported good opportunities for professional growth . . . (p. 112).
3. As age increased, performance was sustained with periodic change in project . . . (p. 200).

In work, satiation on the job has a pejorative effect on motivation. Change is exciting. Change is developmental. Change shapes expectations about the future. As one R&D director related: "I reorganize my lab periodically whether it needs it or not."

Thus, this tenet implies that a manager should *create change, but not too fast*. In this regard, the time-honored principle that there should not be change for change sake is simply incorrect. We might even suggest that managers should engage in a form of "limited Trotskyism," implying a small dose of permanent revolution (or evolution). Continuous small change sensitizes researchers to the fact of change, and this in itself is exciting. (But not too fast—the protection tenet—or too equally as regards specific individuals—the hedonism tenet).

Small continuous change prevents the necessity of huge change which is too threatening.

The satiation versus variability tenet also implies that a manager should *vary the delivery of rewards*. Meaning, of course, that (1) no manager should reward incremental performance every time, or (2) no manager should use the same reward every time. Even if managers had an infinite pool of resources, a 100 percent reinforcement schedule has little information (it's redundant) and little emotion (it's boring).

Finally, this tenet implies that *career planning is not just for the young*. The aging technical specialist has too often been allowed to become obsolete. In this regard, dual-track systems have been a dismal failure. (We will re-address this question shortly). Hard work at team building is extremely important in this area. The research manager who can provide a work climate where coworkers are willing to provide others with growth support will find that they have a valuable motivational tool. The *Zeitgeist* of teamwork and mutual respect for the growth of others is what every manager, whatever their level in the organization, should seek to establish.

JUXTAPOSITION

One of the facts of organizational life that any manager must come to accept if he is to be an effective motivator is that most formal systems of rewards are inherently not motivational. We are not saying that money is not motivational, we are saying the *system* of delivering money is not motivational. This is because the basic tenet of the juxtaposition of act and consequence is invariably violated by pay systems. In essence the effectiveness of a reward is largely predicated upon the reward being tied to the act (to be rewarded) in time and space.

Rewards should be delivered in a timely manner. Although human beings have a greater capacity for memory than primates, it is surprising how short that memory span is where excitement about rewards and its association with appropriate behaviors is concerned. This is not an idle behavioral science concept, but too many managers treat it that way. One reason for this is that the juxtaposition concept requires a compulsion to observe the day-to-day performance of subordinates and provide something, anything, in the way of positive reinforcement to performers.

This returns us to an unavoidable conclusion: *a manager's motivational resources are rarely formal*. This is because the vast majority of managers have no control over the timely delivery of formal rewards. Ineffective managers translate this fact into the assumption that they have no power. Effective managers do not worry about it, and employ a continual stream of informal rewards to generate employee excitement. Moreover, we have observed how effective managers must keep coming up with new types of reward schemes; not only because their resources are not finite but because "higher" management will see a certain approach working, take control of it, routinize it, standardize it, and destroy it.

One of the more pleasing implications of this tenet is that performance *per se* is immediately exciting. In other words, if the manager can get the performance up, the excitement should go up. ("Eureka, I did it!"). Nevertheless, the rapid recognition must still be there. A beautiful golf shot may be exciting, but much less so if no one sees it.

EXPECTATIONS

As a final tenet of employee motivation, this is the most pervasive. Expectations are the essence of motivation. As such, this tenet is highly correlated with the other tenets.

First, this tenet implies that *the capacity to motivate is dependent upon managerial credibility*. If a manager has little credibility relative to his willingness or ability to deliver rewards, employees are not likely to be excited about the manager's requests for incremental effort. Credibility is hard to establish; easy to lose. If the subordinate does not believe in you, you cannot motivate him or her.

The demise of dual track systems in many research laboratories classically illustrates the role of expectations. In terms of the tenets of motivation, such systems are imperative. Over the years, however, the administration of the dual career path was such that the management track was perceived, usually correctly, as the only path to personal and professional growth. The director of research will say the system works, the researchers know better—they just saw an ineffective manager "moved" from the management track to high-up on the technical track to "save his face" because he was actually fired and ended up better than many on the technical track. The expectations are then changed and become very difficult to reverse.

Where expectations are concerned; establishing *an image of objectivity* requires a balance between information and emotion. A good research manager must draw a distinction between having a reputation for objectivity about research goals versus having a reputation for objectivity about people. Effective research managers are often viewed as somewhat lacking in objectivity in goal setting (they set very high goals, then orchestrate the motivation to achieve them), but are typically viewed as very objective (by high performers) in their evaluation of people.

In other words, the manager creates motivations about work goals by holding great expectations. He pushes for the three-minute mile and is seen as somewhat nonobjective in his expectations.

Yet his target is motivation and the ventilation by the researchers about such targets is in fact a reflection of excitement, be it, a bit frightening.

The expectations tenet certainly implies that *rewards are vastly superior to punishments* as a motivational device. Obviously we are not saying that ineffective research managers run around punishing technical professionals. What they resort to, however, are threats, subtle attacks on self-esteem, and so forth. These approaches have plenty of emotion, but little information. They only tell you what not to do. They generate minimal compliance and a desire to escape. Effective motivators recognize that attention to rewards provides both information and emotion. In short, they tell you what to do— and make you feel great doing it.

In summary, effective research managers have long ago learned that the recipe for success in motivating in a technical environment requires the careful formulation of an approach tailored to each individual. Successful motivation of employees begins with an in-depth understanding of the person in question. Blending these ten tenets into a conscious managerial style requires thoughtful consideration of the needs and expectations of the persons involved and the circumstances of the specific situation. It is obvious that if the manager cannot offer what the individual wants he cannot motivate that individual. This is an axiom that managers should never forget. The manager should strive to control rewards or access to those rewards and not let the rewards get lost in a bureaucratic system.

Employees' trusts and confidence in you as their manager will go a long way in forgiving a lack of skill in delivery, but a perception by subordinates of deceit and false manipulation will emasculate any plan. Never forget the emotional component of motivation. Blend these tenets of motivation with an honest and straightforward managerial delivery and we feel you will reap the rewards of your time and efforts.

2

One More Time:

How to Motivate Your Engineers

MICHAEL K. BADAWY

I. PROBLEM AND BACKGROUND

Engineering productivity is largely determined not by the efficiency of the factory worker, but by the effectiveness of the knowledge worker. As knowledge workers, engineers seem to be more productive when they are properly motivated. This poses significant challenges to engineering managers charged with the responsibility of effective utilization and motivation of these technical resources. Yet, while no single force will have a greater impact on the quality of life than engineers, there is substantial evidence derived from the author's own research studies and those of others that engineering resources are poorly managed and misutilized, and that understanding between management and these technical resources is lacking in industrial settings.[2–6,25]

Research has demonstrated that engineers' dissatisfaction and alienation in industry are mounting. Management's failure to reward engineers with motivations beyond those appealing to nonprofessionals has resulted in a higher rate of turnover among the former than among the latter group on comparable organizational levels.[17,19] Another reason relates to management's failure to recognize that engineering is intrinsically creative and cannot be managed like other labor, that engineers are professionals who demand special treatment, and that the engineering environment is characterized by unknowns and uncertainties which mitigate close control.[1] The net result is that engineers, as an expensive and scarce resource, very often are badly mismanaged. A third reason for engineers' dissatisfaction relates to the improper utilization of technical personnel, since as much as 30 percent of a professional's time is spent on work within the reach of a high school graduate.[14] Furthermore, the increasing tendency of engineers (and other professionals) to unionize is glaring evidence as to the tremendous discontent and alienation altogether felt by these groups in industry.[24,32]

It would appear that if management is serious about getting its "money's worth" and improving productivity and engineering performance, effective utilization of engineering resources is the key. Appropriate motivation and technical vitality of the engineering staff is, in turn, central to the question of utilization. The foregoing analysis, however, clearly suggests that engineers in industry generally are demotivated and largely dissatisfied. Changing the status quo calls for developing better styles for motivating engineers. This is the purpose of this paper. After developing a profile of engineers' job expectations and motivational styles, some of the myths and misconceptions in current motivational practices will then be discussed. Finally, some guidelines for better motivation and utilization of engineering manpower will also be presented.

II. MOTIVATIONAL STYLES OF ENGINEERS: A PROFILE

There are a number of theories that are relevant to engineers' motivation.[22,26,27] For space limitation,

Copyright © 1978 IEEE. Reprinted with permission from *IEEE Transactions on Engineering Management,* Vol. EM-25, No. 2, pp. 37–42, May 1978.

Michael Badawy is Professor of Management at Virginia Polytechnic Institute and State University.

it will suffice for our purposes here to briefly identify the most basic form of motivational need theories commonly known as "Maslow's hierarchy of needs." Maslow's theory (1954) postulates five general classes of needs arranged in levels of prepotency, so that when one level is satisfied, the next level is activated. The five levels are: 1) physiological needs, 2) security or safety needs, 3) social needs, 4) self-esteem needs, and 5) self-actualization needs.

From the standpoint of motivating engineers, it is quite important for engineering managers to keep the following points in mind in applying Maslow's need model[8]: 1) The view that people inherit most of their performance capabilities and are motivated only by reward and punishment has been proved inadequate. 2) Every person has multiple needs. Though the specific forms those needs take are highly individualized, the basic needs themselves are shared by everyone. 3) The emergence of needs does follow a specific rigid pattern. 4) A satisfied need is not a motivator of behavior. As one need is fulfilled, another higher need emerges. 5) It is not necessary to satisfy a "lower" need fully before a "higher" need may emerge and operate as a motivator. 6) There is no universal motivator for all people nor is there a single motivating force for any one individual. Rather, the significance of each need varies from one individual to another and varies for the same individual from time to time. 7) There are individual differences in the most appropriate ways for satisfying the same need. Two hungry individuals, for example, might choose different types of food to satisfy the hunger drive. Thus management should develop different motivational patterns to fit different employees' needs at different levels of administration. 8) Motivation is internal to the individual. A person is not motivated by what people think he ought to have, but rather by what he or she wants. It follows that management cannot really force or push people to produce. The most that can be done is to create a motivational environment by providing opportunities for people to satisfy their own needs. And 9) there are factors other than human needs that influence motivation. Among these other factors are the individual's evaluation of himself and his interpretation of his environment.

To sum up—needs are the keys to motivation. They initiate and guide the individual's actions until the goals that generated them are reached, at which time the tensions created by those needs are dissipated. It follows that, in order to motivate engineers, the manager must either act to create the feelings of need within the individuals involved or offer means for satisfying already existing needs.

Based on the foregoing analysis, what does current research tell us about engineers' motivation? The available research clearly demonstrates that there is a wide gap between what engineers want and what they actually get. This generally results in job dissatisfaction and alienation of engineers. Achievement, recognition, work assignments, and professional administration were found to be of overriding importance for professional personnel in general.[10] Freedom of action, increasing responsibility, and a high degree of autonomy and control over their own activities were reported to have significant value for knowledge workers.[18,31] Furthermore, a number of recent studies have shown that the top three motivating factors among knowledge workers are 1) salary or wages, 2) recognition, and 3) opportunity for growth.

The importance of money as a motivational incentive for engineers is controversial in the literature. It was reported that the amount of money an employee receives is only tenuously related to his actual or potential output.[21] This argument states that salary influences tend to move the individual from job dissatisfaction to no job dissatisfaction, as contrasted to the motivational factors which would move a person from no job satisfaction to job satisfaction. Once an adequate salary is attained, greater motivational mileage is gained from such factors as the awarding of advanced positions or titles.

However, in a study comparing motivational styles of engineers and scientists, salary was found to have more motivating value for engineers.[6] Financial considerations, in fact, emerged as the front-running incentives. Engineers, more than people in other professions, were found to value concrete material rewards. Salary has come to mean a great deal more than just money to the engineer. It represents to him the tangible evidence of how he rates in the organization. It has become to him a key symbol of status and recognition. In short, one cannot deny that salary increases embrace a nonfinancial measure of achievement, and as such can be useful motivators for engineers in that light.[16,19]

Another study shows that work itself has the greatest impact on engineers' motivation and yet, it is one least used by management.[29] Advancement in the company was also found to be a high motivating factor. The most commonly used motivation technique by management, according to this study, is the recognition of achievement.

To sum up—the above discussion and the available research suggest the following propositions concerning motivational styles of engineers: 1) Getting ahead and advancement within one's position within the company, pay, and working on challenging assignments are the basic features of the need system of the engineer.[6] 2) Engineers are particularly sensitive to what they regard as "unfairness," and they resent rewards based on any other basis but recognizable professional achievement. They also resent having their professional activities evaluated by those for whose professional judgment they have less than great respect.[17,32] 3) Technical personnel are neither going to be motivated through films or memorandums demanding that everyone look motivated, nor through the hiring of an outside consultant to make the "one and lasting" inspirational speech on motivation.[20] Rather, motivation of engineers tends to be internally generated.

III. CURRENT MANAGERIAL PRACTICES IN MOTIVATING ENGINEERS: SOME MISCONCEPTIONS

In this section the author will identify some problem areas relating to current managerial practices in motivating engineers.

A. Management's Image of the Engineer

A major source of tension and misunderstanding between management and engineers is management's concept of the "professional employee." Although engineers and scientists are professionals with extensive intellectual training and a high degree of specialization, there are important differences in work orientations, need systems, and career objectives between the two groups.[4,5] While most scientists are committed to the creation of new knowledge, most engineers are committed to the application of present knowledge.[32] In addition, the typical scientist might have a primary professional orientation characterized by a basic interest in advancing science, contribution to knowledge, and enhancing his professional reputation in his field. The typical engineer, on the other hand, might have an organizational orientation that manifests itself in a lesser commitment to the profession, but with a greater concern for the goals and approval of the organization with a focus on an organizational career.

The point is that the use of "professionalism" as an organizing concept is serious and misleading. For management to lump the two groups together in a professional stereotype and use that image as a basis for developing motivational practices is entirely wrong, because a policy based on an erroneous assumption cannot satisfy either group.

Another related source of problems in the engineer-management relationship is management's failure to differentiate between knowledge and nonknowledge workers. Current methods of engineering management are old, outdated, and were developed basically to manage production employees where physical labor was important. Now, when these techniques are used in managing knowledge workers, they get frustrated, dissatisfied, and altogether alienated. Examples include the traditional techniques of work organization, bureaucratic controls and authority systems, and excessive focus on organizational efficiency.

In addition, the small salary differential between engineers as professionals and skilled workmen who are not professionals (as seen by engineers), lends further support to the inappropriateness of management methods and policies. A small salary differential violates the professional engineers' sense of self-esteem, distorts their self-images, and causes dissatisfaction, particularly among the younger engineers at the bottom of the engineering salary range.[24]

Thus management's distorted image of engineers seems to emanate partly from the inappropriate practice of not differentiating between engineers as knowledge workers and nonknowledge workers. Furthermore, management does not usually take a truly professional attitude in treating engineers as "professionals" even when this is appropriately done, engineers are usually lumped in a large group with other professionals. Both practices are dysfunctional and thus lead to demotivational consequences. They also reflect a lack of management understanding of the particular needs of engineers. This has eventually led to the erosion of the engineer's sense of professionalism, identity, and status.

B. Inadequate Training of Engineering Managers

Managerial competency has three interrelated components: knowledge, skills (technical, administrative, and interpersonal), and attitudes. However, there is accumulated evidence suggesting that engineers are generally ill-equipped for careers in management.[8] While the training of the engineer typically emphasizes the reduction of all problems to terms that can be dealt with by objective measurement and established formulas based on predictable regularities, success in management is entirely based on different criteria. The world of management is far less exact, less regular, fuzzier, and less predictable than the world of engineering.

It follows that, because of the inadequate preparation of engineers for careers in management, many competent engineers may not become competent managers. Consequently, this has caused great dissatisfaction for many engineers who demand that managers be as competent at managing as the professionals are in their technical fields.[32] The fact of the matter, however, is that many engineering managers are promoted technical professionals who, without any additional training, do not qualify as management professionals

and are vastly less competent at managing than their subordinates are in technical work.

It would appear that the balance between technical and managerial competency is a delicate one, and those who are equally capable in both areas are "rare birds" indeed. I would also maintain that technical capability is hardly a sufficient prerequisite for success in management. Identification of managerial potential, it follows, is a must, as people should be appointed to management positions based on demonstrated or at least potential managerial skills.

In short, current practices of promoting good technologists to managerial positions are poor, inappropriate, and put engineering management in the hands of a group of engineers who were hardly trained for management in the first place. Therefore, they will not be able to manage or motivate others effectively.

C. Managerial Policies and Supervisory Practices

Management systems and policies in some areas do not reflect an adequate understanding of engineers' expectations as professionals. One example is the area of supervising engineers by administrative managers with engineering merely one of their functional responsibilities. Superior authority exercised by a nonprofessional engineer is resented by engineers, as it violates their professional pride. The working engineer feels himself downgraded by his company where this occurs, and the natural reaction is a disdain for company management.[24]

Another source of problems and tensions for engineers relates to criteria for promotion and professional advancement. These criteria are always vague and too general. Organizational policies regarding standards of performance, job descriptions, and professional recognition and promotions are not laid out clearly to career-minded engineers. This, combined with the minimum efforts made by superiors to develop subordinates' skills and potential, generates concern for professional advancement and dissatisfaction among engineers. Thus when subordinates' development becomes a key criterion for evaluating managerial performance, engineering managers will pay appropriate attention to this activity.

A third area of concern to engineers relates to management methods in measuring engineering productivity. Because the "mental component" of engineering is constantly increasing as more of the routine tasks are automated, new techniques and modified measures must be found to relate creative efforts to the traditional measures of productivity. It is noteworthy here that the difficulty to see or measure individual's achievement in most engineering activity, and the difficulty for the individual to relate himself to what happens, has "turned off" or demotivated some engineers. A much better way to increase the efficiency of the engineering department is to concentrate on improving its effectiveness.[11] This requires making the best use of creative abilities of engineering personnel.

D. Failure to Develop Task-Related Motivational Potential

The greatest motivational potential of engineers can be generated through the task itself where work must be considered as the prime challenge to the individual, and thus worthy of their effort. This means that through work designs containing strong elements of challenge, professional achievement, ingenuity, imagination, and flexibility, engineering managers can create significant opportunities with tremendous motivational potential for their subordinates. It is tragic, however, to note that one of the largest failings of American industry is the improper utilization of technical personnel.[16] There is also evidence, as mentioned earlier, that many engineers are handling assignments requiring many fewer skills and qualifications.[14]

Furthermore, the fact that many engineers are unable to see where their contribution fits into the total picture contributes significantly to their dissatisfaction, disappointed expectations, and consequent disillusionment. There is, in fact, a strong indication that engineers in general are underemployed, underutilized, and misutilized.[30]

E. Adoption of the Wrong Reward System

The value of a "dual ladder" as an advancement path for both technically and administratively ori-

ented personnel has been frequently questioned in the literature. The problem, basically, is that the rewards for both careers have never been equally attractive,[6] as will be discussed further below. In addition, scientists and engineers reported almost total reliance upon their supervisors for needed recognition rather than upon the organization itself, with very little faith in "so-called dual ladders" or other "structural gimmicks" designed to provide opportunity for financial and organizational advancement.[16] The major point here is that the major consideration in rewarding engineers is to reward achievement, not compliance or noncompliance with management's wishes.

Current reward systems for engineers are also inadequate for another reason. The higher compensation associated with administrative positions has caused a great many engineers and scientists to effectively abandon their profession.[31] In most organizations, the incentives are almost totally associated with hierarchical advancement (this, incidentally, is equally true in other functional areas).

F. Inadequate Motivational Systems for Older Engineers

The gap between the engineer's age and performance (the over-40 engineer) is a well-known problem in industry. Giving challenging assignments to younger persons creates obsolescence by depriving the senior person of chances to learn, change, and grow.[28] It also reflects a built-in bias for the youth. Furthermore, there is evidence attributing the growing trend toward earlier obsolescence to corporate management's establishment of rigid performance appraisal systems, inequitable job assignments, and insensitivity to the needs of older engineers.[12]

IV. TOWARD BETTER MOTIVATION OF ENGINEERS: SOME IMPLICATIONS FOR ENGINEERING MANAGEMENT

A. Treat Engineers as Professionals

As discussed above, the greatest source of tension and disappointment for engineers is that current management methods and policies do not reflect an adequate understanding of their need orientations and expectations as professionals. This needs to be changed. Responsibility, achievement, and contribution are very important ingredients of motivational systems for engineers. Engineering managers, in their quest for better productivity, should, therefore, stress these elements directing engineering efforts toward maximum contribution and judging them strictly on the basis of performance and quality of work.

Management methods and policies should also reflect an understanding and appreciation of the differences in work orientations and expectations between engineers, as knowledge workers, and non-knowledge workers. Engineers, for example, should be given the opportunity to review, appraise, and judge their own performance, and should be given the information and tools to do their job. Perhaps the most important rule, and the one to which few mangements pay much attention, is to enable the knowledge workers to do what they are being paid for. Not to be able to do what one is being paid for infallibly quenches whatever motivation there is.[15]

B. Enhancing Managerial Competency of Engineering Managers

The single most important factor in motivating engineers is the engineering manager, simply because he or she constitutes the linking pin between management, on the one hand, and engineers on the other hand. However, because of their inadequate preparation for careers in management, many competent engineers, as discussed above, may become incompetent managers. This suggests at least three possibilities to enhance managerial competency of engineering managers. First, the practice of promoting the most technically competent to an administrative position simply for their technical abilities should be abandoned, as strong evidence now suggests that these individuals make the poorest managers.[23] Supervisors should be technically competent, to command the respect of their subordinates, be desirous of a supervisory assignment, and be trained to bridge the gap from "technical orientation" to "management orientation".[16] In other words, management should look well beyond

the candidate's technical ability, searching for possible ingredients and characteristics that would make him or her a successful manager.

Secondly, better selection methods must be employed to identify those promising candidates who are likely to have the psychological prerequisites for managerial competency: a strong will to manage, a strong need for power, and a strong capacity for empathy.[8]

In addition to proper identification of managerial potential and sound selection, the third mechanism to promote and develop engineers' managerial skills is via changing the current educational orientation of industrial engineers. The present system erroneously overdevelops their analytical skills (as model builders), while their managerial skills (as decision-makers) remain highly underdeveloped. While changes in the formal education of engineers is obviously beyond management's control, continuing management education is not.[3] In fact, it provides an excellent vehicle for engineers' personal development and career growth. "In-house" programs have been undertaken by several companies, offering training and coaching activities to smooth the transition from engineering to administration.

C. Establishing Positive Motivational Climates

A powerful motivational mechanism is through job redesign. The meaning of meaningful work for engineers is changing due to changes in cultural values and social expectations. Engineers are changing their specifications for work satisfaction.[28] Meaningful work is not solely solving a technical challenge, and scientific progress for its own sake is under serious question. It follows that jobs need to be redesigned containing elements of challenge, achievement, and conveying the feeling that work has meaning and would make a positive contribution causing no ecological damages or future problems. In short, the concept of job enrichment is quite relevant here and should be used by engineering managers to enhance the motivational potential and productivity of engineers.

Reward systems appropriate for engineers are those emphasizing such factors as status, advancement to managerial positions, and authority and influence within the organization hierarchy.[8] Opportunities for participation and involvement in managerial and technical planning and decision-making are expected to enhance the engineer's status, influence, satisfaction, and productivity.[8,30]

In order to stimulate and reinforce creativity, appropriate organizational climates should be established. An organization with a more decentralized and less formal structure with variety of opportunities for communication, interaction, and participation should be designed.[3] More positive and enthusiastic responses to new ideas, less concern with personal "fitness" for an organizational pattern, and a reasonable degree of freedom and autonomy are some positive ingredients of a creative organizational climate.

Furthermore, a new set of criteria for evaluating engineering managers' performance is needed. These criteria should include not only performance goals (cost, product features, and efficiency), but also personal and subordinates' development efforts. This would encourage managers to help subordinates develop their skills and potential, and thus enhance subordinates' satisfaction and motivation. An excellent management system in this connection is management by objectives (MBO) which has been implemented by several organizations with impressive results.[7]

D. Better Personnel Management Policies

The human resource is certainly the only asset of significant worth in the engineering function. People are more productive when they feel they are a valuable part of the organization and that the organization cares about them as individuals. In addition, knowledge workers are a special kind of asset because they gain in value with time, especially when improvements and developments are made. This means that the future of the knowledge organization is dependent on recruiting good people, and personnel managers must, therefore, do a better job in this area.

Placement is another important area because placement of knowledge workers is the key to their productivity. Not only do opportunities have to be staffed with people capable of running with them

and of turning them into results, but knowledge workers must also be placed where their strengths can be productive.[15] Designing appropriate placement policies for engineers is thus a vital concern for personnel managers.

In view of the importance to engineers of salary and economic incentives, as discussed above, a sound scheme is a necessity. Salary ranges for various engineering classifications should be specifically spelled out, with recognition for extra schooling, personal development efforts, and attendance of technical and professional seminars.

Pension is a fourth related area where changes are needed. Engineers should not be "tied" to a particular company. An engineer should stay with a company because he is interested and challenged by his work and feels adequately compensated, not because of his pension plan, extended vacation, or other such "captive" fringe benefits. Engineers retained under the former set of circumstances are usually highly productive and represent minimal personnel problems, while those retained under the latter circumstances could, in fact, be far more expensive and may even constitute a bad investment. This argument suggests that companies should consider participation in portable pension plans which will allow an engineer to move from employer to employer without losing benefits. Vesting could either be immediate or after a very short period of employment.

Another mechanism that has considerable effect on engineers' motivation is the powerful communication content of incentives. If there is conflict between formal verbal communications and the implications of an incentive, it will always be resolved in favor of the message carried by the incentive.[31] Management actions actually speak louder than words.[28] For example, the engineer listening to top management talk about the need for technical vitality finds it hard to reconcile what he is hearing with overtime work requirements which cause him to drop educational activity. The point is that, although overtime work might be necessary under the circumstances, management somehow must show that it recognizes the impact on vitality; otherwise, management intentions will be misunderstood. Engineering managers, therefore, should understand that the design of the task environment can affect learning, growth, and motivation. Open communications, integrity, and positive reinforcement of company and professional values are certainly vital ingredients of an effective motivational climate.

E. Better Strategies for Career Planning and Motivation of Older Engineers

There is a need for improved management understanding of the concept of career planning for professional enrichment and growth of engineers. Management must also learn how to manage and motivate older engineers. This is because technological obsolescence, as discussed above, is partly caused by a built-in bias for the youth and the way work is organized.[28] Research on career planning shows that diversity is a vital ingredient in maintaining a productive and satisfying career, especially for older professionals.[13] However, most organizations do not provide the necessary opportunities for and encouragement of diversity. In short, there is strong evidence suggesting that pushing technical personnel in their late thirties and early forties into new fields will broaden their interests on and off the job, and will have a significant effect on motivation and productivity.[12,13]

From the standpoint of maintaining technical vitality and motivation of engineers, several strategies can be adopted. These include continuing education, retraining, sabbatical leaves, rotation programs, job transfers, and redesign. For these strategies to work, however, management must show its total commitment to the concept of continued learning throughout life as a powerful tool. That is, company policy and reward system must reinforce these learning behaviors and professional enrichment programs. It is noteworthy here that these mechanisms are particularly important for motivation and technical vitality of older engineers, as they can become bored with the same work after 5 or 10 years.

V. SUMMARY AND CONCLUSION

The purpose of this paper has been to develop a viable framework of motivational orientations of engineers, show some of the myths and misconceptions in current management practices in this area, and finally present some mechanisms and guidelines for better engineers' motivation and productivity. The theme of this paper is that motivation is intrinsic in nature, and that all the engineering manager can do is create the conditions and the appropriate environment conducive to engineers' motivation. While this is the responsibility of the engineering manager, the responsibility of the individual engineer is whether or not to take advantage of this environment and respond in such a manner to promote his or her personal as well as organizational goals.

Throughout the discussion, the author has tried to stay away from the conflicting theories and the controversial issues so persistent in the literature, simply because none of the available motivational theories has completely satisfied the test of empirical data. He has also tried to stay away from a "cookbook" approach to such a complex subject, as motivational schemes will work with varying degrees of success at different organizations and under different sets of circumstances. While the challenge for engineering management is to create the conditions for motivation, the challenge for industry is the creation of an atmosphere where emphasis can be placed on the motivational needs of the individual.

REFERENCES

1. D. C. Aird, "Improving the performance of engineers," in *Effective Management of Engineering Resources (Proc. 23rd Annu. Conf. of Joint Engineering Management Conf.).* The American Society of Mechanical Engineers, 1975, pp. 75–86.
2. C. Argyris, "On the effectiveness of R&D organizations," *Amer. Sci.,* vol. 56, no. 4, pp. 344–355, Winter 1968.
3. M. K. Badawy, "Towards better management of research organizations," *Soc. Res. Admin. J.,* pp. 9–15, Fall 1976.

4. —, "The myth of the professional employee," *Personnel J.,* pp. 449–455, Jan. 1973.

5. —, "Organizational designs for scientists and engineers: Some research findings and their implications for managers," *IEEE Trans. Eng. Manag.,* vol. EM-22, pp. 134–138, Nov. 1975.

6. —, "Industrial scientists and engineers: Motivational style differences," *Calif. Manag. Rev.,* vol. 14, no. 1, pp. 11–16, Fall 1971.

7. —, "Applying management by objectives to R&D labs," *Res. Manag.,* pp. 35–40, Nov. 1976.

8. —, "Motivating engineers: A little psychology goes a long way," *Machine Des.,* pp. 120–122, Oct. 16, 1975.

9. —, "Easing the switch from engineer to manager," *Machine Des.,* May 15, 1975.

10. W. Campfield, "Motivating the professional employee," *Personnel J.,* Sept. 1965.

11. T. Comella, "Engineering productivity formulating a plan of attack," *Machine Des.,* pp. 118–119, Dec. 11, 1975.

12. G. W. Dalton and P. H. Thompson, "Accelerating obsolescence of older engineers," *Harvard Business Rev.,* Sept.–Oct. 1971.

13. H. Dewhirst and R. Arvey, "Range of interests vs. job performance and satisfaction," *Res. Manag.,* pp. 18–23, July, 1976.

14. P. F. Drucker, "Management and the professional employee," *Harvard Business Rev.,* May/June 1952.

15. —, "Managing the knowledge worker," *The Wall Street Journal,* Nov. 7, 1975.

16. B. Evans and J. Whitten, "A critical reanalysis regarding the management of professionals," *Personnel Admin.,* pp. 35–40, Sept.–Oct. 1972.

17. W. Exton, "Optimizing professional performance with motivational leverage," in *Effective Management of Engineering Resources (Proc. 23rd Annu. Conf. of Joint Engineering Management Conf.).* The American Society of Mechanical Engineers, 1975, pp. 1–8.

18. S. Gellerman, *Motivation and Productivity.* New York: American Management Association, Inc.,1963.

19. A. Gerstenfeld and G. Rosica, "Why engineers transfer," *Business Horizons,* vol. 13, pp. 47–48, Apr. 1970.

20. E. Gomersall, "Current and future factors affecting the motivation of scientists, engineers and technicians," *Res. Manag.,* pp. 43–51, May 1971.

21. F. Herzberg, "Does money really motivate?" *Package Eng.,* May 1970.

22. —, *Work and the Nature of Man.* Cleveland, OH: World Publishing, 1966.

23. E. Hughes, "Preserving individualism on the R&D team," *Harvard Business Rev.,* Jan./Feb. 1968.

24. W. Imberman, "As the engineer sees his problem," *The Conf. Board Rec.,* pp. 30–34, Apr. 1976.

25. S. Marcson, "Utilization of scientific and technical personnel in industry," *Calif. Manag. Rev.,* pp. 33–42, Summer 1970.

26. A. H. Maslow, *Motivation and Personality.* New York: Harper & Row, 1954.

27. D. McGregor, *The Human Side of Enterprise.* New York: McGraw-Hill, 1960.

28. D. Miller, "Managing for long term technical vitality," *Res. Manag.,* pp. 15–19, July 1975.

29. S. Myers, "Who are your motivated workers?" *Harvard Business Rev.,* vol. 43, pp. 74–83, Jan./Feb. 1964.

30. R. R. Myers, "Under-employment of engineers," *Ind. Relations,* vol. 9, no. 4, pp. 437–452, Oct. 1970.

31. G. A. Roberts, "An approach to the management of knowledge workers," Basic Fluid Power Research Conf., Oklahoma State University, Annu. Rep. 9, 1975, pp. 1–8.

32. G. Rosica, "Organized professionals: A management dilemma," *Business Horizons,* pp. 59–65, June 1972.

The Subtle Significance of Job Satisfaction

DENNIS W. ORGAN

Imagine that Michael Jordan were to become dissatisfied with the Chicago Bulls organization. Suppose, for example, Jordan felt that the team's management had reneged on some promise, or violated some understanding, or sullied his reputation. How would Jordan act out his dissatisfaction? Would he deliberately turn over the ball, let an opposing player score an easy uncontested basket, commit silly fouls to exit the game early?

I submit that it is virtually unthinkable that Jordan or any other professional athlete would respond this way, for two reasons. First, to do so would severely compromise the player's own interests—the "stats" would suffer, and, with that, the bargaining wedge for future contracts. Second, and more important, true professionals cannot bear the intrinsic pain of deliberately botching their individual performance. Whatever grievance Jordan might have against the Bulls, he would inflict unbearable grief on himself as he mentally replayed episodes of shoddy workmanship.

So, given the prohibitive personal and psychic costs of betraying one's craft, how does a professional act out dissatisfaction—aside from merely voicing it? Perhaps voicing dissatisfaction is as far as some would go. But athletes, like other professionals—including those in the clinical laboratory—have some other options. They can choose to define their obligations and their roles narrowly; they will do what they contractually must do. They will do what redounds directly to their self-interests, but contribute only grudgingly (if at all) in other ways. They can choose not to help teammates improve their skills, not to sacrifice leisure hours to "rubber chicken" banquets for community groups, not to take part in (or not even to attend) informal discussions off the playing arena, not to make suggestions for improving the organization, not to sign autographs. They can tie up valuable management time by pressing every imaginable petty grievance, sour the whole atmosphere for players and staff, and undermine confidence in the organization.

Research now indicates that precisely these effects on Organizational Citizenship Behavior, rather than in-role performance or productivity as traditionally defined, are the casualty of dissatisfaction.

SATISFACTION CAUSES PRODUCTIVITY— AN APPEALING BUT DISCREDITED PREMISE

The notion that "a happy employee is a productive employee" lay for a long time at the center of one popular school of management thought. This concept of worker motivation, probably traceable to some distorted accounts of the legendary Hawthorne research of the 1920s and 1930s, certainly has its appeal. Most managers want productivity, and they prefer a satisfied work force over one that is dissatisfied. So practitioners espouse that whatever makes people happy is justifiable as "an investment in higher productivity." Not surprisingly, surveys have shown a strong tendency by human resource and line managers and union leaders to agree that an individual's job satisfaction translates into a corresponding level of productivity.[1,2]

Unfortunately, researchers began to discredit this theory almost from the start. Nearly 35 years

Reprinted with permission of Clinical Laboratory Management Association, Inc. From *Clinical Laboratory Management Review*, 1990, Vol. 4, pp. 94–98.

Dennis Organ is Professor of Management at Indiana University.

ago, Brayfield and Crockett[3] reviewed an already large body of empirical study of the relationship between job attitudes and productivity. They concluded that no "appreciable" relationships existed. Periodic updates have found no reason to modify this general assessment.

THE PENDULUM TURNS

Interestingly, the findings of "rigorous research" have not disturbed practicing managers. Well into the 1970s, possibly into the early 1980s, most managers—either because they did not know about the results of behavioral research, or perhaps because they chose to believe evidence from their own experience—held to the premise that satisfaction does significantly affect productivity. In retrospect, it is doubtful if management science research alone would have ever seriously undermined that premise.

A much more powerful stimulus to revising management opinion was the combined form of double-digit inflation in the late 1970s and the recession of the early 1980s. Malaise about the state of the "body economic" saturated the financial tabloids and the after-dinner speeches of corporate CEOs. We must wake up, it was argued, to the dawning of a new era—one of global competition, deregulation, and accountability. "Country-club-style" management led to creeping costs—costs that only begat more costs rather than increasing output. The ethos of the day was for organizations to hack away the dead wood, downsize to a lean and mean profile, and get more bang for the buck. That meant *every* buck, including the one spent on amenities to make people happy or put into their pay checks.

Tough-minded management came to the fore. Its rationale was the rigorous research showing no consistent or "appreciable" effect of satisfaction on productivity. The old model that a happy worker is a productive worker was rejected as simplistic, if not soft-headed. The new model emphasized performance; let satisfaction fall where it may. The important consideration was not *how many* people

were happy but *which* people. The underlying logic was to obtain results from those able and willing to supply them and to ensure that those people, and only those, had any reason for satisfaction.

The new, tough-minded management doctrine was evident in a variety of reforms in human resource practices. For example, many firms took steps to ensure that performance appraisals differentiated among people to a much greater extent. Supervisors could no longer rate a few people as, for example, a 5 on a 5-point scale and everyone else a 4. They had to use the 1s and 2s on the scale. Some programs required every manager to rank people from top to bottom. By definition every department had 50 percent of its people "below average." Moreover, performance measurement was not based on the subjective impressions of supervisors. Feverish activity went into the design of quantitative indicators of specific accomplishments. The message was clear and emphatic: "Let's see your stats as they relate to the bottom line." Merit-pay plans, although nominally in effect in most organizations for many years, acquired new and sharp teeth. Those in the top quartile of ratings and statistical categories received substantial raises; those in the bottom quartile were "zeroed out."

How did such reforms affect job satisfaction? For some, the effect was positive. Overall, as some research suggests (4,5), the effect was reduced satisfaction. But so what? Job satisfaction doesn't affect a person's productivity, so it doesn't matter. Or does it?

SATISFACTION AND ORGANIZATIONAL CITIZENSHIP BEHAVIOR

Research currently distinguishes between *in-role* performance and productivity and *extra-role* contributions in the form of Organizational Citizenship Behavior (OCB). Individual in-role performance consists of well-specified job requirements—what the person must do according to the job description—and accomplishments (such as meeting certain quotas or statistical norms) that contractually qualify the individual for incremental rewards, such as bonus pay or prizes. Such performance is to some degree a function of attitude, but also of aptitude, expertise, work flow, dependence on others, and resources (such as equipment, budget, staff). Positive attitudes can add little to a person's in-role performance once the limits of those other constraints are reached.

Negative attitudes that might otherwise cause reduced effort for this kind of performance often will not have this effect—people can be disciplined (even terminated) for unsatisfactory in-role performance. And, negative attitudes toward management notwithstanding, someone who needs bonus pay and qualifies for it will perform accordingly.

But for the professional—not only the Michael Jordans but also the highly skilled specialists in the laboratory—there is an even more compelling reason why in-role performance will not suffer because of dissatisfaction. The reason is ego-involvement. For the ego-involved professional, poor or even mediocre performance is intrinsically painful. It arouses feelings of guilt, embarrassment, and self-reproach.

So neither satisfaction nor dissatisfaction will necessarily manifest itself by effects on individual in-role performance.

The problem is that in-role performance is never enough. As Daniel Katz noted:

> An organization which depends solely upon its blueprints of prescribed behavior is a very fragile system. . . . The patterned activity which makes up an organization is so intrinsically a cooperative set of interrelationships, that we are not aware of the cooperative nexus any more than we are of any habitual behavior like walking. Within every work group in a factory, within every division in a government bureau, or within any department of a university are countless acts of cooperation without which the system would break down. We take these everyday acts for granted. . . .[6]

An effective organization depends on many forms of discretionary, voluntary contributions for which people seldom get direct credit. These contributions make up OCB. Satisfied people do more of these

things (because OCB is primarily a function of attitude and not very dependent on ability or resources); dissatisfied people can choose to do less of them without incurring the risk of sanctions or lost benefits. Because OCB includes many humble and mundane gestures, cutting back on OCB does not hurt the ego as would inferior task performance.

Characteristics of OCB

The concept of OCB becomes less abstract, and much more intuitively familiar to the practicing manager, by understanding some of its characteristics.

Altruism consists of those voluntary actions that help another person with a work problem—instructing a new hire on how to use equipment, helping a co-worker catch up with a backlog of work, fetching materials that a colleague needs and cannot procure on his own.

Courtesy subsumes all of those foresightful gestures that help someone else prevent a problem—touching base with people before committing to action that will affect them, providing advance notice to someone who needs to know to schedule work.

Sportsmanship is a citizen-like posture of tolerating the inevitable inconveniences and impositions of work without whining and grievances—for example, the forbearance shown by a technician whose vacation schedule must yield to unexpected contingencies, or by the programmer who must temporarily endure cramped work quarters.

Conscientiousness is a pattern of going well beyond minimally required levels of attendance, punctuality, housekeeping, conserving resources, and related matters of internal maintenance.

Civic virtue is responsible, constructive involvement in the political process of the organization, including not just expressing opinions but reading one's mail, attending meetings, and keeping abreast of larger issues involving the organization.

At Indiana University, we have developed reliable research instruments for rating people's contributions in these forms. Two other categories for which we do not presently have measures, but which logically relate to OCB, are *Peacemaking*—actions that help to prevent, resolve, or mitigate unconstructive interpersonal conflict—and *Cheerleading*—the words and gestures of encouragement and reinforcement of co-workers' accomplishments and professional development.

A key point is that the person who shows these characteristics of OCB seldom sees it register in his or her individual productivity or "stats" (an exception, perhaps, would be an outstanding attendance record). More often, OCB contributes either to a colleague's performance or to improving the efficiency of the system. A manager, for example, has more time and stamina for important business when not mediating protracted grievances by a staff lacking in sportsmanship. The operator who ignores matters of courtesy generally does not sacrifice his or her individual productivity but creates snafus farther down the line, eventually hurting other's work.

The experienced administrator may, as Katz suggested, take OCB for granted. But if, for whatever reasons, OCB diminishes, the perceptive manager either sees or foresees the eventual effects. As Max Depree, chairman of Herman Miller, Inc., observed,[7] one of the warning signs of a company in decline is a "general loss of grace and civility."

Research at Indiana University[8] and elsewhere confirms that OCB is where we must look for the effects of dissatisfaction. The effects are indirect and not generally visible in lower in-role performance. The loss is in those discretionary forms of citizenship on which effective systems depend.

Interdependence and OCB

Management theorists have always noted the essential condition of interdependence created by organization. Much of their creative energies have involved formulating principles, rules, and design structures that address this condition.

James D. Thompson[9] pointed out that formal structure suffices for only certain types of interdependence as they arise from the basic technology of organization. *Mediating technologies*—common to banks, telephone exchanges, libraries, and retail establishments—link clients or customers who

wish to be interdependent. This technology creates what Thompson termed "pooled interdependence," which can be managed by standardized rules and procedures. *Long-linked technologies,* of which the archetype is the assembly line, give rise to serial or "linear interdependence." Detailed plans and forecasts are needed to cope with long-linked technologies.

Thompson's third form, *intensive technology,* perhaps best describes the clinical laboratory. Thompson defines this form to "signify that a variety of techniques is drawn upon in order to achieve a change in some specific object; but the selection, combination, and order of application are determined by feedback from the object itself."[9] This type of technology breeds complex, often unforeseeable, reciprocal interdependence. Thompson argued that formal structure, standardized procedures, and elaborate plans are not sufficient to manage this dependence. It requires "mutual adjustment," spontaneous give-and-take, informal helping, teamwork, and cooperation—in other words, OCB. OCB always matters, but especially when intensive technologies breed complex reciprocal interdependence among people, managers, and departments.

SATISFACTION: FAIRNESS, NOT HAPPINESS

So job satisfaction is important after all. Does this mean reverting to country-club-style management, with all its attendant concern for making people happy? The answer is "no" because recent research[10] suggests that happiness has little to do with job satisfaction. When people answer questions about their satisfaction—with work, pay, supervision, promotion—they think about fairness. They compare what they might reasonably have expected and what they actually experience.

Fairness certainly is an inherently subjective and complex issue. People have different ideas about what makes an arrangement fair or unfair. One person will think in terms of visible accomplishments; another will think in terms of loyalty and commitment (e.g., seniority). Still others think of ability, effort, external markets (such as supply and demand for specific expertise), precedent (the fact that certain groups "have always rated a premium"), or education. Seldom is there consensus about the relative weights of these criteria. Fortunately, most people have a reasonably high threshold for perceiving inequity. A system need not match any one person's preferred formula so long as the rank and file understand that an array of relevant criteria have been considered. Most employees expect the technically excellent performer to command a differential in pay or status; they just don't want other criteria of worthiness to be totally ignored. When differentials become marked, and when they are determined by unduly narrow conceptions or measures of contribution, the threshold of unfairness is breached. Dissatisfaction mounts, OCB suffers, and eventually, so does the organization.

Any discussion of fairness at work must reckon with procedural and distributive justice. The process in which decisions are made and benefits determined can affect satisfaction just as much as the decisions and benefits themselves. Studies of employee personnel systems and managerial leadership point to four critical factors in perceptions of fairness:

- *Feedback*—ample and prompt.
- *Recourse*—the option of appeal.
- *Fundamental respect for human dignity*—Even the most incompetent and incorrigible subordinate has the right to be addressed civilly.
- *Some form of input*—We do not mean pure democracy, but simply the opportunity to be heard. As one CEO put it, "having a voice does not mean having a vote."

CONCLUSION

Management research and theory have taken a long time and a torturous path in catching up with the insights of Chester Barnard. More than half a century ago, Barnard[11] noted the essential condition of the "*willingness* of persons to contribute efforts to the cooperative system." This quality of willingness "is something different from effectiveness, ability, or value of personal contributions. . . . [it]means self-abnegation." Willingness is characterized by "[an] indefinitely large range of variation in its intensity among individuals" and, within individuals, "it cannot be constant in degree." Finally, this "willingness to cooperate, positive or negative, is the expression of the net satisfactions and dissatisfactions experienced or anticipated."

Barnard underscored the very nature of organizations as cooperative systems. Rules, structures, policies, job descriptions, sanctions, incentives—they all play necessary roles in collaborative endeavors, but as derivatives of, not as substitutes for, the underlying disposition to cooperate. Such a disposition can be sustained only by a sense of the organization as a microcosm of a just world. Occasional inequities can be tolerated if there is faith that the system works fairly over the long run, with self-correcting tendencies. When faith yields to a narrowly defined, *quid pro quo* contractual relationship, the disposition to cooperate ebbs. Surveys show that most of the nation's labor force begins work with a fairly high degree of job satisfaction and that most of the people, most of the time, will describe themselves as "all in all, satisfied." There is a generally prevalent inclination to give the employer the benefit of the doubt—"I'll assume you're treating me fairly until you persuade me otherwise." So the disposition is generally present to render a substantial contribution via OCB. A good-faith effort by managers to provide a "square deal" will do much to ensure the quality of OCB.

REFERENCES

1. Gannon, M. J., and J. P. Noon. "Management's critical deficiency." *Business Horizons* (1971) *14*, 49–56.
2. Katzell, R. A., and D. Yankelovich. *Work, productivity, and job satisfaction.* New York: The Psychological Corporation, 1975.
3. Brayfield, A. H., and W. H. Crockett. "Employee attitudes and employee performance." *Psychological Bulletin* (1955) *52*, 396–424.
4. Baird L. S., and W. C. Hammer. "Individual versus

system rewards: Who's dissatisfied, why and what is their likely response?" *Academy of Management Journal* (1979) **22,** 783–92.

5. Pearce, J. L. and L. W. Porter. "Employee responses to formal performance appraisal feedback." *Journal of Applied Psychology* (1986) *71,* 211–18.

6. Katz, D. "The motivational basis of organizational behavior." *Behavioral Science* (1964), *9,* 131–46.

7. Labich, K. "Hot company, warm culture." *Fortune* (February 27, 1989), 74–78.

8. Organ, D. W. *Organizational citizenship behavior.* Lexington, Mass.: Lexington Books, 1988.

9. Thompson, J. D. *Organizations in action.* New York: McGraw-Hill, 1967.

10. Organ, D. W., and J. P. Near. "Cognition vs. affect in measures of job satisfaction." *International Journal of Psychology* (1985) *20,* 241–53.

11. Barnard, C. I. *The functions of the executive.* Cambridge, Mass.: Harvard University Press, 1938.

4

Organizational Socialization and the Reduction of Uncertainty

RALPH KATZ

For many professionals, their first year of organizational employment is a very frustrating experience, full of stress, anxiety, and disillusionment. Their struggles to become accepted by others and to function as "true" contributing members within their new work settings are sufficiently dissatisfying that many switch companies within the first couple of years. In fact, it has been estimated that more than 50 percent of college graduates entering industrial corporations leave their initial firms within the first three or four years. Similar high rates of turnover were found in my own longitudinal studies of young technical professionals. Many of them even decided to abandon engineering or science as a career during this period of time. The end result, of course, is a very high rate of organizational turnover among new groups of professional employees—a wasteful outcome, not only economically but also in terms of lost promise and potential, especially if the turnover takes place among the most talented individuals.

For other professionals, however, the first years of work are seen as a marvelously satisfying and challenging experience, full of excitement, achievement, and personal development. Not only are these individuals more likely to remain with their organizations, but it is also likely that they will continue to perform effectively, developing strong commitments to both their project and their organizational settings.

Given this range of difference in the individual experiences of organizational newcomers, what is it that takes place during one's initial work years

that affects the amount of stress one feels and determines one set of outcomes over the other? One explanation lies in the perceptual accuracy with which individuals enter their new professional and organizational work environments. Generally speaking, the more that individuals begin their jobs with unrealistic views and expectations, the more they encounter "reality shock" as they confront the true demands of their everyday task activities. On the other hand, individuals who assume their new organizational positions with a more realistic understanding and perspective feel less surprised and disenchanted, because they possess, at least initially, more compatible relationships and interactions with supervisors, peers, and work-related expectations and pressures.

Based on this argument, if newcomers were given more accurate information about their prospective jobs, they would be able to undertake their new responsibilities with far less discomfort and frustration. They would be, in a sense, better innoculated against the idealistic hopes and expectations that so many young employees form about their upcoming organizational involvements. More "realistic previews" during recruiting, then, can play an important role in preventing disappointments from emerging and disillusioning professional newcomers as they begin to carry out their daily job assignments.

Although much can be done to educate and prepare new hires to meet the demands of their new world of work, one should also realize that the concerns, reactions, and accomplishments of new em-

Reprinted with permission from the author.

Ralph Katz is Professor of Management at Northeastern University's College of Business and Research Associate at MIT's Sloan School of Management.

ployees are eventually shaped by the structure of events and interactions taking place throughout their entire socialization experience within the organization (Katz, 1980; Schein, 1978). A "sink or swim" type of socialization process, for example, evokes considerably more tension and stress than a socialization process that is highly supportive and well structured, even though the actual task demands may be equivalent. If our ultimate objective is to learn how to provide new entrants with a better "joining-up" process—one that is not only less stressful but also more meaningful and personally developmental—then we need to understand more fully how individual needs and concerns should be met throughout this important introductory period of organizational careers.

CONTENT OF SOCIALIZATION

During the socialization phase of a new job, individuals are very uncertain insofar as organizationally relevant attitudes, behaviors, and procedures are concerned. It is in this early job state, therefore, that professionals learn not only the specific technical requirements of their jobs but also the socially acceptable attitudes and behaviors necessary for becoming effective organizational members. If new employees hope to direct and orient their own organizational performance in a meaningful and contributive manner, then they must develop a genuine understanding of the events and activities taking place around them. They must build a "situational perspective" within which ideas and assumptions can be tested, interpreted, and interrelated.

Creating this perceptual outlook is analagous to building a mental or cognitive map of one's organizational surrounding, including its particular cast of characters (Louis, 1980). To come to know a job situation and act within it implies that the professional hire has developed a sufficiently useful scheme for making sense out of the vast array of experiences associated with his or her participation in the new job setting. The newcomer must come to know what others in the organization are about, how they operate, and how he or she should per-

form on the job relative to these others. In time, these perceptions provide the new employee with a meaningful way of classifying events and organizing the many interrelationships that exist within the workplace.

In developing this local organizational perspective, every professional newcomer must accomplish over time at least three important tasks. They must build their own role identities within their new job contexts. They must discover how to deal with peers and certain influential authority figures, especially their boss or bosses, in addition to establishing a more informal network of information and support. And they must decipher the appropriate reward systems and situational norms of acceptable social and task-related behaviors.

1. Establishing One's Organizational Role Identity. As new hires start their organizational careers, they are faced with the problem of developing situational identities that will be viable and suitable both from their own perspectives and from the perspectives of other relevant organizational members. Whether one is aware of it or not, each new professional must find answers to the questions of "Who am I and what are my contributions going to be in this organization?"

This issue exists simply because all of us have a large repertory of possible roles and behavioral styles that can be enacted in any particular situation. The person who is viewed as influential, aggressive, and helpful in one organizational setting, for example, may be seen by others in a different situation as quiet, reserved, and uninvolved. To some extent, therefore, we can be different people in different situations, depending upon the particular sets of perceptions that come to surround and envelop us.

Newcomers are typically hired into their organizations as the result of some valued educational background or some highly specialized training program. But until they are actually working and participating in their specific job contexts, neither they nor their organizations can really be sure how they will fit into their new work environments. The socialization period, therefore, is a time of mutual discovery between the new employee and the employing organization, each learning more and more about the other. With increasing experience and organizational exposure, the new employee gradually acquires enough self-knowledge to develop a clearer image of his or her own strengths and weaknesses, assessing his or her own preferences, values, talents, and abilities. In a similar fashion, other organizational employees also develop their own perceptual views of the individual newcomer. And as these perceptions and expectations become more firmly established, they function to constrain the role behaviors that the individual is allowed to play within the overall work setting. Thus, it is the intersection among many sets of perceptions that eventually defines the specific role or situational identity of each individual employee. During socialization, then, every newcomer is testing his own self-image against the views and reactions of other organizational employees. The greater the fit between these developing perspectives, the less stress experienced by the new individual since the paths through which he is expected to contribute become increasingly well defined and mutually agreeable.

It is very possible, of course, that not everyone in the work environment will have the same reaction to or will develop the same impression of the new employee. Some may come to value and respect his or her particular skills and abilities; others may view such areas of expertise as unnecessary and irrelevant. Coworkers or project colleagues might also develop a picture of the new employee that is vastly different from the one constructed by his or her supervisor, the one formulated by his or her subordinates, or even the one held by those professionals, customers, or clients outside the organization. New professionals should realize that they are building different identities with different parts of the organization, depending on the kinds of interaction and contributions that take place during their socialization period. If there is no time for socialization to take place, then the identity that an individual will have will be based on some preconceived stereotype. Without socialization, all engineers are alike, all marketing people are alike, all Americans or Japanese are alike,

and so on. It is the relationships and identities that are built during the socialization process that break down and overcome such indiscriminate stereotypes.

In building these role identities, socialization must take place along both dimensions of interpersonal and task-related activities. The newcomer has a strong need to obtain answers to a number of important underlying interpersonal questions; while only some of these may be conscious, all need to be answered as quickly as possible. Having entered a strange and unfamiliar social arena, newcomers are strongly concerned with inclusion, that is, becoming a necessary and significant part of the overall organization. According to Schein (1978), Graen (1976), and Katz (1978), to become accepted and recognized as an important contributing member within one's work setting is one of the major obstacles with which new employees must struggle and which they must eventually overcome. To what extent, then, will they be considered worthwhile? Will they be liked, supported, and appreciated? Will they be kept informed, included, and be given opportunities to make meaningful contributions? These are some of the key interpersonal issues preoccupying employees as their new situational identities become progressively established.

From the technical or task-performance point of view, the newcomer must also figure out whether or not he or she can do the job effectively. To prove or test themselves on the job is another very important concern of new employees. Having spent most of their lives in an educational environment, which has kept them at arm's length from the "real," industrial world, young employees need to discover just what sort of persons they are and of what they are really capable. They need to see how they function on actual work tasks where the outcomes make a significant difference. For this reason the testing of one's skills and abilities is of critical importance.

An outstanding academic record may be indicative of a professional's willingness to work hard and accept responsibility in a well-structured environment, one in which the examinations, degree requirements, problem information, and schedules are laid out quite clearly. These same skills and abilities, however, may not be sufficient in a less certain and more complex work environment, one in which the professional must learn to work with others in order to define or clarify problems and their corresponding specifications, information needs, and schedule requirements. Much of a technologist's effort is often spent defining the problem in terms of the organization's capabilities, operations, constraints, interests, history of successes and failures, and so forth. This is not to say that educational achievement is not important but rather that there is not a direct mapping between how problem sets are presented and worked on in a classroom setting and how problems are formulated and solved in an organization.

Furthermore, new employees are not only concerned with using their present knowledge, but they also want opportunities that enable them to continue to learn and grow—to extend their talents and areas of expertise. One of the inevitable results of prolonged professional education is the expectation that one should continue to self-develop and be given the opportunities and freedom to do so. In short, what is really important to young employees during socialization is the opportunity to clearly demonstrate their work competence and future promise by being meaningfully utilized in some critical aspect of the organization's activities.

2. Learning to Deal and Network with One's Boss and Other Employees.   A first boss plays a disproportionate role in a young person's career. According to the results of many studies, one of the most critical factors influencing the professional and organizational career success of young employees falls within the mentoring domain of one's immediate supervisor. Despite the obvious importance of this supervisor-subordinate relationship, very few newcomers are entirely satisfied with their initial boss. One of the major tasks of socialization, then, is to learn how to relate and get along with this individual. He or she may be too Machiavellian, too unstructured, too busy, too fickle, too competent, or even relatively incompe-

tent in certain technical areas. Nevertheless, young employees must learn to cope with the reality of being dependent upon their particular supervisors.

The newcomer's immediate boss also plays a critical role in sponsoring or linking the new professional to the rest of the organization, in making sure his or her work priorities are consistent with organizational needs, in securing adequate resources, and in providing the additional information and expertise that are necessary to perform well. While some bosses do an excellent job of caring for their new subordinates in these ways, a more reasonable expectation is that only a modest amount of assistance and clarity will be forthcoming. In most instances, therefore, professionals have to assume primary responsibility for their own careers and development, seeking the kind of help, information, and sponsorship they need in order to complete their work activities more effectively. Simply wishing for supervisors to provide the kind of mentorship one would like to have, or simply waiting for stronger sponsorship to "walk through the door," will not work in today's more demanding and busy world.

This is not always an easy undertaking. It is often very stressful simply because of the high "psychological costs" that are involved in seeking help from supervisors who are in evaluative and more powerful positions. As summarized by Lee (1994), much research has shown that individuals tend to use information sources that have the least psychological risk instead of using the most effective sources of information. However, as in any negotiation or conflict situation, it becomes somewhat easier to approach the "other party" as one generates more meaningful information about those individuals. In a similar fashion it should become easier and less stressful for newcomers to deal with their boss as they acquire a more comprehensive picture of that individual. The more new employees gain insight into the characteristics and perspectives of their specific supervisor, the easier it will be for them to interact with him or her. Such insight typically requires a very good understanding of supervisors' goals, expectations, and work-related values; the personal and task-related pressures and demands that confront them; their areas of managerial strength and weakness; their preferences for different work styles, habits, and so on. In general, then, new employees will become less anxious and will have added control and predictability in dealing with their bosses as they generate increasingly more useful information about them.

In any interpersonal situation, individuals are also more likely to get along and work well together when they are more similar to each other and more compatible in their goals, values, and priority systems. Communication and interaction are always facilitated when individuals have common frames of reference and shared experiences. Accordingly, one can speculate that organizational socialization will be smoother for those new employees who have the most in common with their immediate supervisors. Lindholm (1983) for example, clearly demonstrated that the single most important determinant of a supervisor-subordinate mentoring relationship resided in the nature of their interpersonal relationship and attraction and not in the nature of their task association or performance.

It is also likely that the very idea of having a boss is inherently uncomfortable to young professionals who have recently left the autonomy of university student life. New employees, as a result, are likely to experience considerable conflict as they struggle to balance their desire for professional independence with their more immediate sense of dependence upon their new manager(s) for the definition of their work, their information, their resources, their rewards and promotions, and so forth. This conflict may be even more pronounced for the most creative young professionals who often have low tolerances for formal authority, structure, and procedures. Nonetheless, new hires must first clarify and then learn how to relate to the demands and expectations of their supervisors—how to keep them informed and how to seek their support and approval. At the same time, they must also begin to display an ability to function on their own, to take initiative, to define problems accurately by themselves, and to uncover relevant sources of new and useful information. One of the major accom-

plishments of socialization, then, in the ability to cope with the creative tension that stems from being dependent, on one hand, yet demonstrating one's independence on the other.

This trade-off between autonomy and control is often one of the major sources of tension between young professionals and their employing work organizations, according to the personal interviews conducted by Bailyn (1982). Quite often, organizations try to create an atmosphere for their young professionals that is very conducive to creative work; one in which professionals are given as much autonomy as possible in choosing problems. This high level of independence, however, is very frustrating to the relatively new professional. In the rapidly changing world of technology, it is not clear to the new employee just what problems or projects are most relevant to the organization's overall goals and objectives. What the young professional really wants is to be placed in a well-defined project that is central to the organization's mission. Having been given this kind of assignment, he or she then expects to be given the necessary resources, support, and decision-making discretion for carrying out the assignment. Too often, however, the opposite seems to take place. After giving the young professional the autonomous mandate to "be creative," the organization then places a great deal of control on his everyday problem-solving activities. In short, what becomes stressful to young professionals in the early years of work is to be given a very high level of freedom to choose which problems to work on only to be told *how* to work on these problems. In the industrial world of work, young professionals are more likely to welcome the reverse situation; otherwise, they would have remained in university-type settings.

In addition to gaining the acceptance of their boss, newcomers must also learn to deal with other members of the hierarchy and with other peer group members. For those entering with a clear group assignment, the only problem is how to mesh their own needs and abilities with the requirements of the group. For others, however, the problem is to locate the appropriate peer or reference groups with which to align themselves. Much of what goes on in an organization occurs through informal channels and associations that have evolved over time. Thus, one comes to understand and appreciate the political aspects of different reporting relationships and organizational undertakings primarily through the individual and group contacts one has made.

The building of relationships within the organization is also important, simply because they help us form the contacts and connections through which we are able to discover or gather key pieces of key information, make timely and important decisions, and implement project activities and decisions successfully. Very few organizations are ruled through omnipotent hierarchies, and very few function as pure democracies where all members have equal votes and the majority point of view dominates. Most organizations require the skillful building of interpersonal and political relationships, both formal and informal, in order to contribute effectively or to get new things done in new ways.

All too often, it takes much too long to finally convince new technical professionals that the organization is composed of many people with whom they must cultivate a work-related and/or personal relationship. They must build the communication network that not only keeps them informed but also allows them to draw upon the most useful knowledge and information embedded within the organization. Being relatively inexperienced, the new professional needs guidance and learning from more senior colleagues in order to carry out work activities in a more effective and timely manner. It should not be surprising, therefore, that studies of young technologists have consistently found that those professionals with the highest ratings of performance and contribution also have significantly broader information contacts within the organization than their technical counterparts (Allen, 1984). Unfortunately, what is surprising is just how hesitant and difficult it is for many new engineers to seek advice and information from other experienced professionals, especially those who are outside of their immediate work or project grouping. In studying the assimilation of young engineers going through their first six months of socialization,

Lee (1994) discovered that those engineers who reported having social activities with more experienced staff colleagues outside of the normal work context received the highest ratings of performance contribution in their initial appraisals. Such informal, after-work social contacts were even more strongly related to these engineers' performance ratings than their grade-point averages. Lee argues from his research findings that such informal social interaction makes it more comfortable and less threatening for the new technologist to approach and learn from her or his busy professional colleagues. It is also known that "friendlier" colleagues are more likely to provide more extensive background information and a richer context from which the new professional can learn more quickly, not only the organization's technical culture, but also its political one.

3. Deciphering Reward Systems and Situational Norms. As new employees learn to relate to other relevant individuals within the work setting, they must also unravel the customary norms of acceptable social and task related behaviors. If one truly hopes to become a viable, functioning member of the organization and pursue a long-term relationship, then one is required to learn the many attitudes and behaviors that are appropriate and expected within the new job setting. One must discover, for example, when to ask questions, offer new ideas or suggestions, push for change, take a vacation, or ask for a pay raise or promotion. Which work elements or requirements are really critical and which should be given the most attention. Newcomers must also align their own assumptions, values, and behavioral modes of conduct against parallel perspectives that are held by their peer and reference groups. Most likely, as employees are able to adopt the collectively held view of things during their socialization, they will be viewed more positively by the organization and will receive more favorable evaluations.

On the other hand, if the new employee finds it difficult to develop a situational perspective that is consistent with those that already exist within the work environment, a high level of stress is likely to result. This dilemma can come about in at least two ways. First, the new employee may strongly disagree with the collectively held view, operating under a very different set of assumptions, values, or priorities. The new assistant professor, for example, may be very excited about teaching and working with graduate students only to discover that his university colleagues value research output almost exclusively. Or there may be strong disagreement concerning the importance of different areas of research, the value of different research methodologies, or the merits of particular application areas. The specific sources of strain will certainly vary with each particular organizational and occupational setting; nevertheless, the more the individual sees oneself as having a "deviant" perspective within the workplace, the more he or she will experience stress in attempting to gain acceptance and prove oneself as a valuable, contributing member.

A second source of discomfort can occur simply when there is no collectively held view of things to guide the new employee. This situation can come about when there is little consensus within the environment, either because the individuals disagree among themselves, or because there has been insufficient time or insufficient stability to develop a collective viewpoint. In either case new employees who find themselves in these situations will experience considerably more stress because of the vast amount of uncertainty that still exists both within their own roles and within their relevant work environments. Each professional must discover what is *really* expected and what is *really* rewarded. To what extent can they trust the official formal statements of reward practices and policies? To what extent can they rely on information provided by older, more experienced employees, especially if the situation happens to be changing? New employees must determine for themselves how reward systems actually function so they can comfortably decide where to put their efforts and commitments.

Surprisingly enough, in most organizational settings, the criteria surrounding advancement and other kinds of rewards are very ambiguous especially to young employees in the midst of socialization. Moreover, different employees usually see very different things as being important in getting ahead, covering the full spectrum of possibilities from pure ability and performance to pure luck and politics. Part of the reason for all this ambiguity is that organizational careers are themselves highly variable in that one can succeed in many different ways. Nevertheless, as long as newcomers remain uncertain about the relative importance of alternative outcomes, they will experience considerable tension and stress as they execute their daily activities.

Much of the uncertainty that surrounds reward systems in today's organizations can be traced to the local-cosmopolitan distinctions originally discussed many years ago by Gouldner (1957). Having recently been trained in an educational or university-type setting, new professional employees usually enter their organizations with a relatively strong professional orientation. At the same time, however, they must begin to apply this professional knowledge for the good of the organization; that is, they must develop a parallel orientation in which their professional interests and activities are matched against the current and future demands of their functioning organization. This balancing act can lead to a great deal of tension and frustration, particularly if the young employee is forced to allocate his or her time and efforts between two relatively independent sets of interests and rewards. To what extent should they pursue task activities that will be well recognized and rewarded within their profession or within their organization? Can they, in fact, do both relatively easily? All too often, young employees face job situations in which there is too little overlap between the demands, challenges, and rewards of their profession and those of their actual work environments.

By trying to build an accurate picture of the reward system, the young employee is dealing, of course, with only a part of the overall issue. He or she must also begin to question the likelihood of achieving certain results and desired outcomes. An individual's willingness to carry out an action is greatly influenced by whether one feels he or she can perform the action, by one's beliefs concerning the consequences of doing it, and by the attractiveness of the outcomes associated with doing it. To answer these kinds of questions, a reasonable amount of critical performance feedback from supervisors and peers is required. Such feedback provides the newcomer with a clearer sense of how he or she is being viewed and regarded, helping each to find his or her particular "niche" in the overall scheme of things. Unfortunately, in most organizations this kind of useful feedback from supervisors is a rather rare occurrence. In fact, in my own research surveys on engineering professionals, performance feedback was one of the lowest rated behaviors attributed to engineering supervisors in over ten separate RD&E facilities. New employees, therefore, are faced with the problem of obtaining adequate feedback on their own individual performances which can be particularly difficult if one's work is diffused within a larger group or project effort. What becomes most distressing to new employees, then, is that they have entered the organization with an underlying expectation that they would be learning and improving on their first job, yet their supervisors fail to realize that they should act and feel responsible for teaching and helping the employees to accomplish this objective.

Employees need to determine how effectively they are currently performing, how difficult it might be for them to achieve desired outcomes, and how readily they could obtain or develop the various skills and knowledge necessary to meet the demands and expectations of the organization. As long as these critical concerns remain unmet and uncertain to the new professional, the amount of stress he or she experiences will escalate. One of the most important, yet most trying, learning experiences for the newly hired professional undergoing socialization is how to obtain valid feedback in those particular situations in which it does not automatically or effectively take place. And for many young professionals, the ultimate learning experience is to figure out how to become an excellent judge of one's own individual performance. Socialization, as a result, is facilitated to the extent that one's supervisor is able to: (1) make an accurate assessment of the new employee's performance and give useful and valid feedback on this performance; (2) transmit the right kinds of values and norms to the new employee in terms of the long-run contributions that are expected of him or her; and (3) design the right mix of meaningful, challenging tasks that permit the new employee to utilize and extend his or her professional skills and build his or her new situational identity.

PROCESS OF SOCIALIZATION

Underlying the tasks represented by the socialization process is the basic idea that individuals are strongly motivated to organize their work lives in a manner that reduces the amount of uncertainty they must face and that is therefore low in stress (Pfeffer, 1981; Katz, 1982). As argued by Weick (1980), employees seek to "enact" their environments by directing their activities toward the establishment of a workable level of certainty and clarity. As they enter their new job positions, they are primarily concerned with reality construction, building more realistic understandings of their unfamiliar social and task environments and their own situational roles within them. They endeavor, essentially, to structure the world of their experience, trying to unravel and define the many formal and informal rules that steer the workplace toward social order rather than toward social chaos.

One of the most obvious, yet most important and often overlooked aspects of new employee socialization is simply that it must take place. By and large, people will not accept uncertainty. They must succeed over time in formulating situational definitions of their workplace with which they can coexist and function comfortably; otherwise, they will feel terribly strained and will seek to leave the given work organization. Until the new employee has created a situational perspective on himself or herself, constructed guidelines regarding what is expected, and built certain situationally-contingent understandings necessary to participate meaningfully within the work setting, the individual cannot act as freely and as fully as he or she would like.

What is very important to recognize here is that stress does not come from the uncertainty itself; it comes from the individual's inability to reduce or lower it. As long as one is making progress in reducing uncertainty, that is, as long as socialization is being facilitated and the individual is making increasing sense out of his or her new work surroundings, stress and anxiety will diminish and satisfaction and motivation will rise. If, however, new employees are somehow prevented from accomplishing any or all of the broad socialization tasks previously discussed, then they are not succeeding in reducing as much of the uncertainty as they need to. This can become highly frustrating and anxiety producing, resulting eventually in higher levels of dissatisfaction and increased levels of organizational turnover. Just as the engineer is highly motivated to reduce technical uncertainty in his or her laboratory activities, the new employee is highly motivated to reduce social and interpersonal uncertainties within his or her new environments. Generally speaking, activity that results in the reduction of uncertainty leads to increasing satisfaction and reduced stress; whereas, activity or change that generates uncertainty creates dissatisfaction and higher stress. Thus, it is not change per se that is resisted, it is the increase in uncertainty that usually accompanies it that is so difficult for individuals to accept.

One must also realize that socialization, unlike an orientation program, does not take place over a day or two. It takes a fair amount of time for employees to feel accepted and competent and to accomplish all of the tasks necessary to develop a situational perspective. How long this socialization period lasts is not only influenced by the abilities, needs, and prior experiences of individual workers, but it also differs significantly across occupations. In general, one might posit that the length of one's initial socialization stage varies positively with the level of complexity of one's job and occupational requirements, ranging perhaps from as little as a month or two on very routine, programmed-type jobs to as much as a year or more on very skilled, unprogrammed-type jobs, as in the engineering and scientific professions. It is generally recognized, for example, that a substantial so-cialization phase is usually required before an engineer can fully contribute within the organization, making use of his or her knowledge and technical specialty. Even though one might have received an excellent university education in mechanical engineering principles, one must still figure out how to become an effective mechanical engineer at Westinghouse, Dupont or General Electric.

Socialization Is a Social Process

Another very important assumption about socialization is that it must take place through interaction—interaction with other key organizational employees and relevant clientele. By and large, new employees can only reduce uncertainty through interpersonal activities and interpersonal feedback processes.

Newcomers' perceptions and responses are not developed in a social vacuum but evolve through successive encounters with their work environments. Their outlooks become formulated as they interact with and act upon different aspects of their job setting. Their development cannot transpire in isolation, for it is the social context that provides the information and cues with which new employees define and interpret their work experiences (Salancik and Pfeffer, 1978).

One of the more important features of socialization is that the information and knowledge previously gathered by employees from their former colleges or other institutional settings are no longer sufficient nor completely appropriate for interpreting and understanding their new organization domains. As a result, they must depend on more-established professionals within their new situations to help them make sense out of the numerous activities taking place around them. The greater their unfamiliarity, the more they must rely on their new situations to provide the kinds of information and interaction by which they can eventually construct their own individual perspectives and situational identities. It is precisely this reliance on situational information and dependence on others for interpretation and meaning that forces new employees to be more vulnerable and more easily influenced during socialization.

Clearly, as employees become increasingly cognizant of their overall job surroundings, they become increasingly capable of relying on their own knowledge and experiences for interpreting organizational events and for executing their daily task activities. They are now freer to operate more self-sufficiently in that they are now better equipped to determine for themselves the importance and meaning of the various events and information flows surrounding them. On the other hand, as long as new employees have to balance their situational perspectives against the views of significant others within the workplace, frequent interaction with those individuals will be required.

New employees absorb the subtleties of local organizational culture and climate and construct their own definitions of organizational reality—and in particular their own role identities—through interactions with other individuals, including peers, supervisors, subordinates, and customers. Verbal and social interaction, in contrast to written documentation, are the predominant means by which new professionals acquire the most pertinent information about their new environments. Since multiple meanings are likely for any particular event, the more individuals with whom the new employee interacts, the more likely she or he is to put together a view that is both comprehensive and realistic. Different individuals will emphasize different aspects of the work setting and will also vary in the way they interpret events. Recent hires, as a result, formulate their concepts and guide their activities around the anticipated reactions and expectations of the many key employees with whom they are connected.

Of all the concepts that each individual newcomer acquires through the plethora of interpersonal contacts that takes place, perhaps the most important is one's self-concept. It has often been argued that one's fellow workers help to define for each newcomer many of the diverse aspects of the new job setting by the way they act and behave toward these aspects, for example, how they deal with absenteeism, budget overruns, schedule slippages, staff reports, or subordinate suggestions. Similarly, fellow employees help newcomers create perspec-

tives on themselves as particular kinds of individuals by the way the fellow employees act and respond toward these organizational newcomers. As a result, a new employee's self-image is largely a social product, significantly affected by the behaviors and attitudes of other employees within his or her organizational neighborhood. In essence the newcomer's situational identity is strongly influenced by the self-concept that is gleaned from the eyes of those significant others whom they come to know and with whom they interact.

If newcomers strive to reduce uncertainty by locating and orienting themselves relative to the views and expectations that emerge from those individuals on whom they are most dependent and with whom they are most interactive, then it should not be surprising that some of the most important and most satisfying experiences for new employees are those which attune them to what is expected of them. There is a strong need for newcomers to identify closely with those colleagues and supervisors who can furnish guidance and reassurance concerning such expectations. If on the other hand, the individual newcomer is precluded from reducing uncertainty and making increasing sense out of his or her organizational surrounding, then he or she will feel stressed and will be unable to act in a completely responsive and undistracted manner.

Many circumstances can arise in any work setting to delay a newcomer's socialization, circumstances that invariably prevent or inhibit the kinds of interpersonal interactions that are essential for uncertainty reduction. Consider, for example, the new employee whose boss is out of town, on vacation, has just quit, or is simply too busy to help with one's integration; or the new employee who is assigned to a job location or given an office far away from the boss or key reference groups. Chances are that the reduction of situational uncertainty under these kinds of conditions will be a much prolonged process, perhaps interfering with the newcomer's potential career success or even his or her willingness to remain in the organization. Research studies have shown, for example, that young engineers who are not well networked internally (so that their stronger communication links are with individuals outside their group or organization) are much less likely to receive a managerial promotion and are much more likely to leave the organization over time (Katz and Tushman, 1983).

Socialization Experiences Are Highly Influential and Long-Lasting

According to the law of primacy expressed by Brown (1963), early socialization experiences are particularly important because they greatly influence how later experiences will be interpreted. The early images and perspectives that are formed in the first year or two of one's organizational career have a strong and lasting influence on one's future task assignments, perceived performances and abilities, and promotional success.

What has become clear from a large number of studies (e.g., McCall and Lombardo, 1989; Bray and Howard, 1988; Lee, 1992) is that the degree to which an employee perceives his or her job as important and challenging by the end of the first year will strongly influence future performance and promotional opportunities. Such studies have shown that young professionals and managers who viewed their job assignments more positively or who were evaluated more positively by their supervisors after only one year of employment were also more likely to have received higher performance ratings and higher rates of promotion some five to ten years later. In their classic study of engineers and scientists, Pelz and Andrews (1976) reported that technical professionals who were able to utilize and demonstrate more diverse skills and abilities in accomplishing their tasks during their early career years were significantly more likely to advance within the organization than professional counterparts who were frequently rotated from project to project. General Electric even discovered from their own career-tracking studies of young professionals that the best predictor of career success at GE was the *number* of different supervisors who had personal knowledge of the task accomplishments of the young professional. Given the general consistency in the pattern of findings from these different studies, it is clear that the newcomer who gets widely known and comes to be seen and sponsored as a valued high performer gains a considerable long-term advantage over the newcomers not so fortunately viewed—the proverbial self-fulfilling prophecy.

In the process of interpreting their early work experiences, young employees begin to observe their colleagues as well as other members who have been labelled as successful or unsuccessful within the organization. They then begin to assess their own careers relative to these individuals. This process of comparison involves many factors, but temporal comparisons represent some of the most critical. By comparing one's progress against these other individuals, the new employee begins to form an implicit "career benchmark" against which both the individual and the organization can start to determine how well he or she is doing. In their studies of British and American managers respectively, Sofer (1970) and Lawrence (1990) show just how sensitive organizational members can become to their relative career progress. In another example Dalton et al. (1982) strongly argue from their study of R&D professionals that organizations have clearly defined expectations about the behaviors and responsibilities of their more successful engineers at well-defined age-related career stages.

All of these examples emphasize that soon after beginning work, employees gradually become concerned about how their progress fits within some framework of career benchmarks. Where are they—are they on schedule, ahead of schedule, behind schedule? The pressure from these kinds of comparisons can become extremely acute especially as the relative judgments become increasingly salient and competitive and their timing increasingly fixed and inflexible. Such events seem to occur in at least two different ways. First, the comparisons can become highly intense as employees enter an organization as part of a well-defined, well-bounded cohort but are then forced to compete amongst themselves for the best individual evaluations, as in the case of many law firms, public accounting firms, consulting companies, universities, and so on. The directness and clarity of these comparisons make the implicit aspects of the career benchmarking process more explicit and, in general, place the young employee under a great deal of stress as he or she competes for the next level of advancement.

For other young employees the occupation or other organization itself can present a fixed timetable for measuring success and career advancement. The tenure process in universities, standardized professional exams (e.g., registered engineer, CPA), or certain apprenticeship or associate periods are all examples of highly structured, well-defined timetables of career progress. These kinds of explicit benchmarks can also place the young employee under severe stress particularly if the employee loses control over the timing of the process or it becomes more like an "up or out" or a "pass/fail" type of system. While the climate that emerges from these more explicit models of career benchmarking may not be very supportive, they may "energize" a great deal of activity and long hours of work on the part of the new employee, at least during his or her early career years.

Because the employee's immediate supervisor influences and controls so many aspects of the communication, task, and career benchmarking factors during socialization, it becomes clear why so many studies have pinpointed the new employee's first boss as being so critical with respect to his or her successful advancements both organizationally and professionally (Kanter, 1977; Schein, 1978; Henning and Jardim, 1977). While supervisors play a critical role in linking their subordinates to other parts of the organization, they can also assume a broader role within their work groups, becoming actively involved in the training, integration, and socialization of their more recently hired members.

By building close working relationships with young subordinates, supervisors might not only improve their group's performance (Katz and Tushman, 1981), but they might also directly affect the personal growth and development of their young professionals. To the extent that supervisors help their new employees participate and contribute more effectively within their work settings, have clearer working relationships with other key organizational individuals, and communicate more easily with outside customers, clients, or profession-

als, these young professionals will experience less stress and will be less likely to leave the organization. Graen and Ginsburgh (1977) showed, for example, that organizational newcomers who built strong dyadic relationships with their immediate supervisors and who saw a strong relationship between their work and their professional careers were more likely to remain with the organization.

In a longer longitudinal study, Katz and Tushman (1983) found that young engineers who had high levels of interaction with their first and second level supervisors were significantly less likely to leave the organization over the next 5 years. These supervisors were seen as technically competent and were viewed as valuable sources of new ideas and information. As a result, they became more interactive simply because they were consulted and listened to more frequently on work related matters. At the same time, this high level of interpersonal activity allowed these supervisors to create close working relationships with their younger engineering subordinates, helping them become established and integrated during their early career years. Thus, it may be this high level of interpersonal contact with technically competent supervisors that not only facilitates socialization but also results in more accurate expectations, perceptions, and understandings about one's role in the job and in the larger organization—all of which are important in decreasing turnover and the anxiety levels of new employees.

It has been argued throughout this paper that becoming an integral part of the organization's communication and information processing networks and learning the organization's customs and norms are critically important for reducing stress and fostering more positive attitudes during the early stages of employees' careers. It has also been argued that supervisors play a very direct role in dealing with the initial concerns of young employees, allowing them to reduce uncertainty by helping them understand and interpret the reality of their new settings. In essence, supervisors operate as effective socializing agents and networks builders for their young employees.

In many cases, however, the supervisor is not

the only socializing agent of the new employee. The veteran group as a unit can also affect the attachment of new members to the organization. In line with the findings of Katz (1982) and McCain et al. (1981), for example, the larger the proportion of group members with the same group tenure and shared work history, the more distinct that cluster of individuals might become from other organizational members, in general, and from new entering members, in particular. Young employees, for example, might experience a great deal of stress and frustration in trying to integrate themselves into a well-established, older cohort or vice-versa.

Additional conflicts and power issues are also likely to result when there are larger gaps between cohorts within the overall work group. If the group has been staffed on a regular basis, then the new employee's integration is more likely to proceed in a smooth fashion since socialization can be nurtured through the existence of closer, linking cohorts (e.g., Ouchi and Jaeger, 1978). If there are large gaps between cohorts, however, then it is likely that perceptions and beliefs will differ more, resulting in considerable communication difficulty and impedance. The existence of well-differentiated cohorts, according to McCain et al. (1981), increases the possibility of different intragroup norms and expectations which can result in a group atmosphere that is characterized by severe intragroup conflict—a very stressful experience for new employees.

CONCLUSIONS

Perhaps the most important notion in this paper is that individuals undergoing a transition into a new organization are placed in a high anxiety-producing situation. They are motivated, therefore, to reduce this anxiety by learning the functional and social requirements of their new role as quickly as possible. What must be recognized and understood by organizations is that supervisors and group colleagues of new employees have a very special and important role to fulfill in inducting and socializing the new employee. The careful selection of

these individuals for young professionals should go a long way toward alleviating many of the problems that usually occur during the "joining-up" process. One must recognize that the problems and concerns of young professionals are real and must be dealt with before these young employees can become effective organizational members. Although organizations might want to develop specific training programs to teach managers how to "break-in" the young professional more effectively, an alternative strategy would be to make sure that young professionals are integrated and socialized into their job environments only through those particular groups and supervisors who appear especially effective in this function. Rather than allowing all supervisors and groups to recruit and hire new employees as additional staffing needs arise, a more centralized policy of rotating or transferring individuals to some areas in order to hire new employees through other key integrating areas might prove more beneficial to the organization as a whole in the long run. The careful assignment of groups and supervisors to new college recruits, combined with some training for these individuals, should go a long way toward utilizing the great potential in most young professionals, thereby reducing the high levels of frustration, stress, and dissatisfaction that so many of them experience during their initial career years.

REFERENCES

Allen, T. J. *Managing the flow of technology*. Cambridge: MIT Press, 1984.

Bailyn, L. Resolving contradictions in technical careers: or, what if I like being an engineer. *Technology Review*, 1982. November-December, 40–47.

Bray, D. W. and Howard, A. *Managerial lives in transition: Advancing age and changing times*. New York: Guilford Press, 1988.

Brown, J. A. C. *Techniques of persuasion*. Baltimore: Penguin Books, 1963.

Dalton, G. W., Thompson, P. H., and Price, R. L. The four stages of professional careers: A new look at performance by professionals. In R. Katz (Ed.), *Career issues in human resource management*. Englewood Cliffs, N.J.: Prentice-Hall, 1982.

Gouldner, A. W. Cosmopolitans and socials: Towards an

analysis of latent social roles. *Administrative Science Quarterly,* 1957, 2, 446–467.

Graen, G. Role-making processes within complex organizations. In M. D. Dunnette (Ed.), *Handbook of industrial and organizational Psychology.* Chicago: Rand McNally, 1976.

Graen, G. and Ginsburgh, S. Job resignation as a function of role orientation and leader acceptance. *Organizational Behavior and Human Performance,* 1977, 19, 1–17.

Henning, M. and Jardim, A. *The managerial woman.* New York: Doubleday, 1977.

Kanter, R. M. *Work and family in the United States.* New York: Russell Sage, 1977.

Katz, R. Job longevity as a situational factor in job satisfaction. *Administrative Science Quarterly.* 1978, 23, 204–223.

Katz, R. Time and work: Toward an integrative perspective. *Research in Organizational Behavior,* 1980, 2, JAI Press, 81–127.

Katz, R. The effects of group longevity on project communication and performance. *Administrative Science Quarterly,* 1982, 27, 81–104.

Katz, R. and Tushman, M. An investigation into the managerial roles and careers paths of gatekeeper and project supervisors in a major R&D facility. *R&D Management,* 1981, 11, 103–110.

Katz, R. and Tushman, M. A longitudinal study of the effects of boundary spanning supervision on turnover and promotion in research and development. *Academy of Management Journal,* 1983, 26, 437–456.

Lawrence, B. At the crossroads: A multiple-level explanation of individual attainment. *Organization Science,* 1990, 1, 65–85.

Lee, D. Job challenge, work effort, and job performance of young engineers. *IEEE Transactions on Engineering Management,* 1992, 39, 214–226.

Lee, D. Social ties, task-related communication and first job performance of young engineers. *Journal of Engineering and Technology Management,* 1994, 11, 203–228.

Lindholm, J. A study of the mentoring relationship in work organizations. Unpublished MIT Doctoral Dissertation. 1983.

Louis, M. Surprise and sense making: What newcomers experience in entering unfamiliar organizational settings. *Administrative Science Quarterly,* 1980, 25, 226–251.

McCain, B. R., O'Reilly, C. and Pfeffer, J. The effects of departmental demography on turnover. The case of a university. Working Paper, March 1981.

McCall, M. W. and Lombardo, M. M. *The lessons of experience: How successful executives develop on the job.* Lexington, Mass.: D.C. Heath & Co, 1989.

Ouchi, W. G. and Jaeger, A. M. Type Z organization: Stability in the midst of mobility. *Academy of Management Review,* 1978, 3, 305–314.

Pelz, D. C. and Andrews, F. M. *Scientists in organizations.* Ann Arbor: University of Michigan, 2nd ed., 1976.

Pfeffer, J. Management as symbolic action: The creation and maintenance of organizational paradigms. *Research in Organizational Behavior,* 1981, 3, JAI Press, 1981.

Salancik, G. R. and Pfeffer, J. A social information processing approach to job attitudes and task design. *Administrative Science Quarterly,* 1978, 23, 224–253.

Schein, E. H. *Career dynamics.* Reading, Mass.: Addison-Wesley, 1978.

Sofer, C. *Men in mid-career: A study of British managers and technical specialists.* London: Cambridge University Press, 1970.

Weick, K. E., *The social psychology of organizing.* Reading, Mass.: Addison-Wesley, 1980.

2

Creativity and the Management of Creative Professionals

5

Managing Creative Professionals

More than 30 years of research have provided answers to some of the questions technical managers ask about creativity in organizations.

The management of creative workers has become the most critical area faced by management in both the private and public sectors. Without a great deal of fanfare, creative workers, or, more strictly, professionals, have come center stage in the United States and the rest of the developed world. Quan-

titatively, professionals now surpass all other categories in the U.S. work force. Qualitatively, professionals have a disproportionate effect on all aspects of our society, as the researchers, designers, decision makers and managers who define and direct much of what is done in society. The quality and extent of what is accomplished in the foreseeable future has become a function of the ability of management to harness and channel the efforts of creative workers. The difference in success between one effort and another, one organization and another increasingly depends on whether manage-

Reprinted with permission from *Research-Technology Management,* March-April, 1985.
Albert Shapero is Professor of Management Science at Ohio State University.

ment understands the differences between the management of professionals and the management relevant to the assembly line.

In trying to evoke and develop creativity in an organization, managers are interested in such questions as: Can creative people be identified for the purpose of hiring? Are there valid and reliable tests that can predict who will be creative? Can creativity be developed or enhanced in employees? Are there creativity techniques that can be taught to employees that will increase creativity within the organization? What kinds of management actions help or retard creativity? What kinds of environments enhance or deter creativity? What differentiates the creative organization from those that aren't creative? Researchers on creativity have generated data that provide some answers to these questions.

From the beginning, much research on creativity has focussed on developing ways of predicting who will demonstrate high creativity in the future. One approach, based on biographical and autobiographical studies of individuals with demonstrated high creativity, attempts to develop predictive profiles. Included among the profile methods is factor analysis. Other attempts have produced psychometric instruments to measure intellectual capabilities considered by the researcher as central to creativity. Most of the latter have measured divergent thinking. Despite several decades of research effort on creativity and highly creative individuals, there is as yet no profile or test that reliably predicts who will be highly creative in the future. Efforts to develop tests to predict later creativity in students have borne little result. Longitudinal studies of the predictive strength of divergent-thinking tests given to students have been disappointing (Howieson, 1981; Kogan, 1974). So far, the only good indication that an individual will be highly creative in the future has been demonstrated high creativity in the past.

THE ENVIRONMENT FOR CREATIVITY

Two aspects of the environment for creativity have been examined by researchers: (1) the kinds of familial and educational environments in childhood that lead to creativity in adulthood, and (2) the kinds of immediate, organizational, and physical environments associated with high creativity. The effect of childhood environments in subsequent creativity is of little utility for managers, although one finding worth noting is that high creatives, unlike those with high IQs, came from families in which parents put little stress on grades (Getzels & Jackson, 1962).

The manager of professionals is concerned with organizational environments associated with high creativity and how they might be generated. Most of the organizational characteristics that appear to enhance creativity relate to the characteristics attributed to highly creative individuals (Steiner, 1965). For example, since nonconformity in both thought and action characterizes high creatives, the organization that is tolerant of a large variety of deviance from the norm is more likely to enhance creativity. It is not surprising to find many "high tech" companies, architectural firms, advertising organizations, and academic faculties are marked by unconventional dress and little rigidity concerning hours of work.

Characteristics of creative organizations (Steiner, 1965) include the following:

- Open channels of communications are maintained.

- Contacts with outside sources are encouraged.

- Nonspecialists are assigned to problems.

- Ideas are evaluated on their merits rather than on the status of their originator.

- Management encourages experiments with new ideas rather than making "rational" prejudgments.

- Decentralization is practiced.

- Much autonomy is allowed professional employees.

- Management is tolerant of risk-taking.

- The organization is not run tightly or rigidly.

- Participative decision making is encouraged.

- Employees have fun.

THE PROCESS OF CREATING

In spite of the apparent uniqueness of the creative process in each individual and the idiosyncratic patterns followed by many creative individuals, studies of the process are in fair agreement that it follows a recognizable overall pattern. The creative process has been variously described, but most descriptions include a series of steps, varying in number, that can be subsumed within the following four steps: (1) preparation, (2) incubation, (3) illumination, and (4) verification.

Preparation. The creative process begins with a problem perceived or experienced. Whenever humans have a problem, and don't know how to solve it by direct action, they resort to thinking, problem-solving, and creativity. The problems that lead to creative responses arise from many sources. They can be thrust upon one or assigned from the outside, be perceived as a threat or opportunity, be encountered, or be sought out because humans are dreaming, restless creatures who enjoy the creative process. Once a problem is perceived, the creative process begins.

Research shows that the conscious "creative" moment comes only after intensive preparation and a period of subconscious incubation. Louis Pasteur put it succinctly: "Chance only favors the prepared mind." Helmholz described his own creative process: "It was always necessary, first of all, that I should have turned my problem over on all sides to such an extent that I had all its angles and complexities "in my head" and could run through them freely without writing" (McKellar, 1957). In a study of highly productive inventors, Rossman (1964) found that they all started the process by "soaking themselves in the problem." Though Rossman reports that some inventors reviewed all previous efforts to solve the problem and others avoided being influenced by previous attempts, all spent time thoroughly exploring the problem to be solved.

The preparation process can include literature searches, talking to many people about aspects of the problem, experimentation, and doodling. Some-

times the preparation process can appear as unplanned, unfocused meandering through a variety of materials. McKellar (1957) considers it as almost a form of "overlearning" to the point where some of the materials become "automatic" in one's consciousness. The gathering of information is a critical part of the process in which the individual examines the materials critically, but not negatively. The creative process requires discriminating criticism that does not reject, but builds upon the materials examined.

Incubation. This is a process that goes on below the level of consciousness. It cannot be commanded. Incubation appears to be a gestation period in which the process goes on subconsciously, and it works best when the individual is inactive with regard to the problem or working on something else. A passage of time, vital to the process, varies with the problem and individual (McKellar, 1957). The philosopher Nietsche spoke of a period of 18 months, and the poetess Amy Lowell spoke of six months. It can be a period of frustration for the individual working against a deadline, for it cannot be pushed or rushed. It is a period when apparently nothing is happening.

One soaks oneself in the problem and then waits. The passage of time is often accomplished by sleep. It is as if sleep provides the time and the opportunity to abandon consciousness of the problem and let the unconscious work. Some great creative discoveries have surfaced in sleep. Kekulé realized his discovery of the benzene ring as the result of a dream of the image of a snake that seized hold of its own tail. Many of Descartes' basic notions of analytical geometry formed in his dreams. Everyone has had the experience of "fighting" a problem to an impasse, and having the solution suddenly crystallize while visiting with friends or discussing other things. The need for a period of incubation may explain why professionals who work on more than one project at a time are more productive than others. Having more than one project permits a person to switch to another project when apparently at an impasse. Switching from one project to another permits the first project to incubate until it is ready, while one is still doing something productive.

The incubation process is recognized but not understood. One plausible explanation is that it is a period in which the mind tests different associations, matches different frames of reference and different conceptual elements to see if they make sense. This explanation fits with the most accepted view of creativity as a process of association.

Probably the most widely held psychological conception is that creativity is the ability to call up and make new and useful combinations out of divergent bits of stored information (Guilford, 1964). The more creative the individual the greater the ability to synthesize remote bits of information. The likelihood of a solution being creative is a function of the number and uncommonness of associative elements an individual brings together (Mednick, 1962). The latter notion has been incorporated into a test for creative ability, The Remote Associations test (Mednick & Mednick, 1964). The test taker is asked to "make sense" out of each of 30 sets of three, not obviously related, terms by providing a fourth term related to them (e.g., the fourth term related to "cookies," "sixteen," and "heart" would be "sweet"). Another associationist view is Koestler's "bisociation of Matrices," expressed by the metaphor of creativity as a "dumping together on the floor the contents of different drawers in one's mind" (Koestler, 1964).

Illumination. The Gestalt psychologists refer to illumination as the "aha!" phenomenon. It is that sudden insight, that flash of understanding, in which the solution appears. The mathematician Polya describes it as entering an unfamiliar room in the dark, and stumbling around, falling over pieces of furniture, looking for the light switch. When the switch is found and activated, everything falls into place. All historic examples of the incubation process end with that moment of illumination.

Verification. After the exhilaration of illumination comes the tedious, time-consuming stage of verification. The creative idea must pass the tests of validity, reality, utility, realizability, costs, time, and acceptance in the marketplace.

CREATIVE PROBLEM SOLVING

Rules for creative problem solving can be derived from the data available on the process. They include the following:

1. Soak yourself in the problem. Read, review, examine and analyze any material that you can find on the problem. Talk to people who know about the problem. Look at every side of the problem. Saturate yourself in the subject. Be critical in the positive sense. Don't accept authority. Question the premises. However, insist on finding a way to solve the problem, and do not accept that it cannot be solved.

As a manager, do not easily accept the conclusion that "it can't be done." On hearing all the reasons from his group why something wouldn't work, one successful manager of professionals counters, "I agree it can't be done, but if we had to do it or be shot what could we do?" It always changes the atmosphere, and turns the group to finding ways to attack the problem rather than judge it. Push the people in your organization to soak themselves in the problem. Provide them with all the information you can. Err on the side of overload. Encourage them to contact a wide variety of sources for information.

2. Play with the problem. Stay loose and flexible in dealing with the problem. Try different assumptions. Leave out one of the conditions that affects the problem, and see what that suggests. Approach the problem from different directions. Turn it over and inside out. Assume different environments. Shift parts of the problem around, physically and spatially. Change the time sequence. Change the order of events. Change the situation.

As a manager, you can help by encouraging your people to explore the problem from every kind of viewpoint. You can do this by discussion, by questioning, by encouraging "wild" approaches in the early stages of a project.

3. Suspend judgment. Fight any tendency to draw early conclusions. You will only lock yourself in, and lose several degrees of freedom. Early fixation on even part of a problem definition keeps you from seeing larger parts of the problem. It foreshortens your perception. Even worse is to get an early fix on part or all of a solution. It cuts you off from a great many possibilities, since you begin to justify your early solution. Suspension of judgment keeps you open to new information, and enables you to see new possibilities as the problem unfolds. If solutions keep suggesting themselves to you, write them down in a notebook, and deliberately put them aside until later in the project. Get them out of your mind.

As a manager, help your people suspend judgment. The manager is probably the biggest obstacle to suspensions of judgment. The manager represents deadlines and budgets, and they must not be forgotten. However, it is important not to push for immediate judgments. Don't pressure your people to come up with solutions in the early stages of a project. Encourage them to note and file any early conclusions as suggested above.

4. Come up with at least two solutions. When you start out with the objective of coming up with two different solutions, it keeps you from fixating on a solution and keeps you thinking about the problem. Studies have shown second solutions tend to be more creative, and trying for two solutions results in more creative solutions. It was found, experimentally, that asking people for two solutions, as compared to one, increased the number of "creative" solutions from 16 percent to 52 percent. When pushed to the limit by being asked for three different solutions, it was found not all responded, but there was an increase by 25 percent in very good, creative solutions (Hyman and Anderson, 1965).

As a manager, insist on two independent solutions to a problem. It is not necessary to work them out in detail, but make sure they are significantly different. The first solution seems to catch all the anxieties and stiffness of an individual, while the second is more free flowing.

5. When stuck. Try more than one way of picturing the problem and solution. Go from a word description to a drawing. Many creative scientists, mathematicians and writers use sketches and diagrams to put the problem into a different perspective. Go from a drawing to abstraction.

Try your problem out on other people. When you discuss your problem with others, you see it differently. You have to make sense out of it.

What the other people say is less important than your own presentation, though unexpected questions can help hook different parts of your brain together.

Give your subconscious a chance to work. Take a break. When you are really up against it, do something else for a while. Remember! It is a ripening process, and you can't force it. Spending round-the-clock sessions will only exhaust you, rather than solve the problem.

As a manager, put yourself in the way of being the person on whom the problem can be tried. Ask your people to "draw you a picture" of the problem to help you understand it. When they get too intense and are not making progress, give them another short assignment to pull them away for awhile, to let their subconscious work.

CREATIVITY FROM THE VIEWPOINT OF THE MANAGER

Can anything systematic be done to increase creativity in individuals and in an organization? Does management really want creativity and the somewhat less controlled conditions necessary to foster it?

To individuals, more creativity carries an implication of special, personally gratifying experiences. To managers, more creativity means new ideas, inventions, and solutions that will do wonderful things for the organization in the marketplace. Few, however, have thought through the consequences of having more creative people and of allowing the conditions that enhance creative behavior in their organizations.

Trying to answer the converse of the question, "Can anything be done to increase creativity?" quickly illustrates how much is generally known about conditions for creativity. Pose the question

"Can anything be done to kill creativity in an individual or an organization?" and the mind immediately fills with answers:

- Discourage and penalize risk-taking.
- Discourage and ridicule new ideas.
- Reject and discourage attempts to try unusual methods.
- Make sure all communications follow formal organizational lines and all employees cover themselves.
- Discourage reading and communications with people outside the immediate organization.
- Discourage nonconformity of any kind.
- Discourage joking and humor.
- Provide no recognition.
- Provide no resources.

We easily intuit what it takes to minimize creative behavior, which suggests that it must be possible to improve creativity or, at least, to minimize barriers to creativity. The available information strongly indicates that it is possible to improve one's own creativity and the creativity of employees. It is possible to increase the creative activities and products of an organization. Increasing creativity in an organization is achievable, but it takes a lot more effort than preventing it from occurring. Continuity and stability are important attributes in society, and, of necessity, the dice are loaded against divergence and change.

Highly creative people are attracted by the work, by the problem being worked on, which is good from an organizational viewpoint, but they don't respond in satisfactory ways to the political or organizational constraints that are involved in every problem. Creative people are nonconformists. They are jokers. They have little reverence for authority or procedures. They are short on apparent "loyalty" to the organizations they work for. They don't respond to the kinds of incentives that stir others. They are not moved by status. High creatives don't seem to care about what others think, and they don't easily become part of a general consensus. (Could a preference for consensus

management be why the Japanese have recently expressed concern about a lack of creativity in Japan?) In short, creative people can make most managers very uncomfortable. (Teachers and even parents are far more comfortable with students and children with high IQs than with those who are highly creative.)

A case can be always made for creativity, but managers should carefully and honestly think about whether they truly need more creativity and can live with it. If successful at hiring and retaining high creatives, and at generating the conditions needed to keep them creative, management may be creating conditions that make it difficult for its own natural style of doing things. New methods, processes and products can be purchased, copied, and stolen. According to one ironic maxim, it doesn't pay to be first— pioneers get killed. Some years ago, the head of a metal machining company producing thousands of metal fasteners picked through his catalog and fondly indicated product after product that had been invented by other companies. "You know," he said, "we don't know anything about managing creative people, but we're very, very good at designing around other people's designs. What we're really competent at is production and marketing, and we beat the hell out of the creative companies. I can't wait for their next products." Cynical? Perhaps, but it highlights the questions raised here. Many can benefit from the creativity of a few, and there are industries, companies, and fields where creativity is far less needed than in others.

ON THE ROAD TO MORE CREATIVITY

If desired, creativity can be consciously and systematically enhanced in an organization through hiring, motivation, organization, and management actions.

Hiring.   The number of highly creative people in an organization can be increased by a hiring policy that deliberately attempts to identify, locate, and hire them. The only valid and reliable way to identify individuals with a high probability of future creative performance is through evidence of past creative performance. The more recent and continuous the past creative performance, the more likely there will be future creative performance.

Where examples of a professional's work are not as easily demonstrated as in the arts and architecture, the task of determining past creative performance is harder. It is difficult to tease out evidence of the individual creative contributions of an engineer or scientist who has worked on a project that employed scores or hundreds of professionals. One way to tackle the problem is to put the questions directly to the individual: "What are the most creative things you have done on the job in the past three years? What are the most creative things you have ever done?" Similar questions about the individual's work can be asked of others who are familiar with it. In some fields patents, in others publications, may serve the purpose, though they should be examined for their content.

Tests, profiles of traits, and checklists are neither valid nor reliable. No available test can determine who will perform creativity in the future with any reliability. (One may be tempted to follow the example of the author who tried to hire on the basis of the apparent relationship between a good sense of humor and creativity. The rationale was, "If they don't turn out to be creative, at least they'll be a barrel of laughs.")

Motivation. Creative behavior can be maintained and enhanced through incentives that reward creative output and encourage risk-taking, and the use of new methods, processes, and materials. For those who are already highly creative, incentives can maintain and encourage their creative efforts and help retain them in the organization. For other professionals, incentives and positive feedback from management can encourage them to overcome some of the natural blocks to creativity and to take more risks and be more curious. As with any other desired behavior, feedback from management, the performance evaluation system, and the example of management can help stimulate creativity. If a manager smiles on "far out" ideas when they are ven-

tured, lets them be tried (even when he or she is personally sure they won't work), and will even express some extravagant ideas himself, others may feel freer to think and act creatively.

Providing the necessaries. The availability of resources for initial creative efforts is a powerful indicator of management support for creative activities. The resources required to give an idea a preliminary investigation are seldom of any magnitude. Direct provision of resources, or turning a blind and benevolent eye on the inevitable "bootlegging" of an unauthorized project, both serve the purpose of support for creative experimentation. Providing resources for preliminary explorations of ideas without requiring exhaustive justification is a form of intellectual overhead and should be treated as such, formally or informally. (Remember that time is one of the most important resources required for creative activities.)

Some boost to creativity can be obtained through educational programs, though management should be wary of "patented" techniques. All creativity-enhancing techniques have some limited value in terms of stirring up new ideas for a short time. An inherent limitation in almost all of the techniques is that they purport to provide *the* way to the generation of creative ideas or to problem solving. The overall process follows a broad general pattern, but individuals must find their own personal approach.

Managing. Managers should assign tough deadlines but stay out of the operating details of a project. There is no conflict between a deadline and creativity. Creative people resist closure because they see new possibilities as the project unfolds. For all the complaints, deadlines are necessary. Without deadlines few creative projects would ever finish.

Both productivity and creativity can be enhanced by assigning more than one project to a professional. Not all the projects have to be of equal weight, or size, or value. The ability to switch to a second project and let the first project incubate in the subconscious is important to creativity. With only one project and a tough deadline, there is a tendency to try to force the project at times when it can't be forced. Having other projects provides a legitimate (forgivable) and productive way to back off from a stymied project when a pause is needed.

New projects need fresh, unchanneled thinking. Managers might make up project groups to include people of different backgrounds, and refrain from always assigning projects to the individuals who have done that kind of work before and are apparently most suited to it.

Each professional's assignments should provide diversity for that individual. And highly productive groups of five or more years duration should be made more diverse through the addition of new people and by making certain that the individuals in the group get occasional assignments to work with other groups.

Organizations. Organizational mechanisms to assure that new ideas don't get turned down for the wrong reasons (such as middle-management cautiousness) are important. One company set up a new products committee to which any employee, and not just professionals, could submit ideas. The committee, made up of senior scientists, product development people, and a patent lawyer, investigated and discussed each idea and wrote up a decision stating why the idea was accepted, rejected, or recommended for more research. By taking a positive and encouraging stance the company developed a strong flow of ideas from throughout the organization.

There should be a legitimate (nonthreatening) means for taking an idea up the management line if it is rejected by first-line management. The means may be a new product committee, of the type described above, or a procedure for periodic review of ideas people feel strongly about. After many attempts to correlate creativity with personal characteristics, General Electric found that a key variable was the ability not to be dissuaded from their intuitions. The former director of technical systems

and materials Jerome Suran believes that high creatives are stubborn types, "because you don't get past the first level of management in a big company unless you feel strongly about your ideas" (Cullem, 1981).

A periodic review of organizational procedures and forms, with a view to identifying and removing those that cannot pass a test of necessity, is often a good idea. Too many required administrative procedures and forms sop up time and energy and impede creative activity. Procedures and forms are pervasive forces for conformity, and the more there are, the less space and time is left for nonconforming, creative thought and effort. Professional organizations should follow the rule that for every procedure or form that is added, at least one should be removed.

REFERENCES

Cullem, T., "Stimulating Creativity," *Electronic Engineering Times,* July 20, 1981.

Getzels, J. W. and P. W. Jackson, *Creativity and Intelligence,* New York, John Wiley and Sons, 1962.

Guilford, J. P., *The Nature of Human Intelligence,* New York, McGraw-Hill, 1964.

Howieson, N., "A Longitudinal Study of Creativity: 1965–1975," *Journal of Creative Behavior,* April-June, 1981.

Hyman, R. and B. Anderson, "Solving Problems," *International Science and Technology,* September 1965.

Koestler, A., *The Act of Creation,* New York, Macmillan, 1964.

Kogan, N. and E. Pankove, "Long Term Predictive Validity of Divergent Thinking Tests. Some negative evidence," *Journal of Educational Psychology,* 66 (6), 1974.

McKellar, P., *Imagination and Thinking,* New York, Basic Books, 1957.

Mednick, S. A., "The Associative Basis of the Creative Process," *Psychology Review,* 69 (3), 1962.

Mednick, S. A. and M. T. Mednick, Remote Associates Test, Boston, Houghton Mifflin, 1964.

Rossman, J., *Industrial Creativity,* New Hyde Park N.Y., University Books, 1964.

Steiner, G. A., *The Creative Organization,* Chicago, University of Chicago Press, 1965.

6

How Bell Labs Creates Star Performers

ROBERT KELLEY AND JANET CAPLAN

It's a given that today's companies must keep new products and services coming—and respond quickly to continually shifting customer demands. To maintain this competitive pace, managers need to improve the productivity of their knowledge professionals. But while many have expected new technologies like companywide computer networks to boost performance, the real promise lies elsewhere. Changing the ways professionals work, not installing new computers, is the best way to leverage this intellectual capital.

Yet managers have been loath to tackle this kind of productivity improvement. For good reason, companies in high-tech and other creatively driven businesses often avoid direct exhortations to be more productive. Professionals such as engineers, scientists, lawyers, programmers, and journalists already work hard, perhaps 50 to 60 hours a week. To demand more of them is counterproductive because, unlike many manufacturing or service workers, these professionals have options. When pushed, they may withhold their best ideas or simply leave the company.

Although managers know that some professionals excel, few people, including the "stars" themselves, can describe exactly how they do it. But we believe that defining the difference between top performers and average workers is essential for improving professional productivity. For the past seven years, our research has focused on the engineers and computer scientists at AT&T's prestigious Bell Laboratories. This study has led to a successful training program based on the work strategies of star performers. The program has dra-

matically improved productivity, as evaluated by both managers and engineers.

In fields like computer programming, an eight-to-one difference between the productivity of stars and average workers has been reported. As one of the Bell Labs executives observed, "Ten to fifteen percent of our scientists and engineers are stars, while the vast majority are simply good, solid middle performers." When asked why this is so, most managers come up with a variety of plausible explanations. Top performers, they say, have higher IQs. Or they're better problem solvers, or driven by an enormous will to win. In other words, stars are better people in some fundamental sense, while middle performers lack the inborn traits that are necessary for more than solid plodding.

Since such traits are exceedingly difficult to change, a job-training program to become a "better person" sounds hopeless. Our research, however, has revealed a basic flaw in this reasoning. None of the above explanations for the difference between stars and middle performers stands up to empirical testing. Based on a wide range of cognitive and social measures, from standard tests for IQ to personality inventories, there's little meaningful difference in the innate abilities of star performers and average workers.

Rather, the real differences turn up in the strategic ways top performers do their jobs. While it's impossible to get in the door of Bell Labs without technical competence and high-level reasoning abilities, these cognitive skills don't guarantee success. But specific work strategies like taking initiative and networking make for star performance *and* are trainable. When companies promote such

Reprinted by permission of *Harvard Business Review*. From "How Bell Labs Creates Star Performers" by Robert Kelley and Janet Caplan, Vol. 71, 1993, pp. 128–139. Copyright © 1993 by the President and Fellows of Harvard College, all rights reserved.
Robert Kelley is an Adjunct Professor of Management at Carnegie Mellon University. **Janet Caplan** is an independent management consultant in Minneapolis, MN.

strategies systematically, individual professionals not only improve but also pass along the benefits to their colleagues and the company's bottom line.

DEMYSTIFYING HIGH PRODUCTIVITY

Let's consider the first major hurdle to a training program: defining productivity for a particular job. Some software companies, for example, use lines of computer code as their productivity measure, based on the assumption that good programmers generate more lines than others. This measure, however, ignores the fact that 4 lines of elegant computer code are better than 100 lines that accomplish the same objective. In addition, few professionals do the exact same job. Two computer-code testers may have the same job title, yet one may test 50 small computer programs in a single day, while the other spends as long as 3 weeks testing 1 large program.

Peter Drucker has discussed the apparently impossible task of understanding the productivity of knowledge professionals. In particular, he has pointed to the difficulties of analyzing the process that produces high-quality results in knowledge work. The best we can do, Drucker says, is ask, "What works?" Implicit in this question is the reality that the work of knowledge professionals happens inside their heads. And managers can't directly observe, let alone accurately evaluate, these mental processes or strategies.

That leaves asking workers to disclose their mental secrets. This is no simple task, however. First of all, many people have a hard time describing what goes on in their minds when they work or even determining whether or not they've been productive (see the box "How Do Professionals Define Their Productivity?"). Second, researchers can fall for nonsensical productivity recipes if their methods aren't sufficiently focused.

In the early 1980s, for example, much ado was made about peak performance. Many researchers interviewed Olympic champions, who dutifully recounted this typical daily regimen: they woke at dawn, stretched out, ate their Wheaties, spent an hour visualizing their success, and practiced their sport for three hours. After enough champions had described the same regimen, a spate of books hit the market on how to become a peak performer in sports, sales, or management.

But what about the Olympic contenders who didn't win? Chances are these athletes also woke at dawn, stretched out, ate their Wheaties, spent an hour visualizing success, and practiced their sport for three hours. In other words, it's not enough to ask the stars what works; researchers must compare the regimens of star performers to those of the also-rans and then target the differences.

In fact, no one has come up with a generally accepted definition of productivity in any knowledge profession, let alone across these professions. In our research at Bell Labs, rather than grappling with a broad definition of productivity, we focused on the practical ways managers can distinguish stars from middle performers. And when it came time to evaluate the training program, we asked managers to tell us what practical changes, such as spotting and fixing problems or pleasing customers, they expected to observe in the engineers whose performances had improved.

When we began our study in 1986, the Bell Labs Switching Systems Business Unit (SSBU) was feeling the pinch of competition from companies like Northern Telecom. Before the breakup of AT&T's Bell system, the Labs felt as much like a university research center as a corporate entity. Top-flight engineers went there for a combination of reasons: the opportunity to work on leading-edge telecommunications projects, the outstanding reputation of Bell Labs as an applied R&D think tank, and the job security that came with working for AT&T.

But Bell Labs executives watched market share drop sharply during the 1980s, and these managers soon realized that recruiting the best and brightest computer engineers and scientists wasn't enough. As it turned out, academic talent was not a good predictor of on-the-job productivity. As in other companies, applied R&D at Bell Labs now means fast, cost-effective product cycles. And job security is tied to value-added contribution, not scholarly performance.

How Do Professionals Define Their Productivity?

While a company's performance-rating system may not identify all high achievers, don't expect individual professionals to have a clearer or more consistent view of their own work. In 1990, for instance, we asked 40 engineers at Bell Labs and 25 engineers at another high-tech telecommunications company to evaluate themselves. Using a short e-mail survey, we queried the engineers every day for two weeks. The four questions in the survey were:

- How productive were you today?
- How did you measure your productivity?
- What caused you to be either productive or unproductive today?
- Did you get feedback about your productivity?

Although you might expect individual workers to rate their own productivity more positvely than their bosses would, the engineers actually turned out to be quite hard on themselves. On average, these self-doubters rated their daily productivity at a rather low 68% given the performance needs of a technical environment like Bell Labs.

One reason for such uncertainty could be unclear performance standards. For instance, the most popular method for measuring personal productivity turned out to be checking off items on a to-do list, which engineers cited 41% of the time. A gut feeling of being productive came in a distant second at 16%, and the actual amount of time spent working trailed at 14%. Only one engineer on one day cited "amount of my work making a direct contribution to the company" as a measure of personal productivity.

Indeed, our work with expert engineers indicates that many of the assumptions about what makes for high productivity in an organization are tacit. More often than not, such measures aren't explicitly or specifically enunciated by top managers. Although the engineers we surveyed preferred concrete accomplishments as personal gauges of productivity, they also complained about having a tough time deciding whether or not the tasks on their to-do lists added any value to the company. And on a day-to-day basis, managers don't seem to help with this problem. Of the 65 engineers, 44% said they received absolutely no productivity feedback from their managers during the period of the survey.

But what interfered with productivity? The engineers cited meetings, meetings, and more meetings. When they weren't in meetings, our survey respondents complained, they were being interrupted. These two factors accounted for 45% of the cited obstacles to productivity on any given day. However, while most professionals, especially top managers, would agree that meetings are the bane of their existence, we suggest there are also other reasons for reduced productivity. Organizations would do well to examine their performance expectations, clearly outlining which activities add value to the company and providing the feedback necessary to keep people on track.

Consider the actual work of an engineer at Bell Labs. The SSBU creates and develops the switches that control telephone systems around the world. These switches entail substantial computer hardware and millions of lines of software code. SSBU engineers spend considerable time simply maintaining the lines of code that run a switch. The jobs of SSBU engineers also call for creativity. For example, engineers write software programs for switching systems in response to customer requests for services like caller ID, which displays an incoming caller's name and phone number on a telephone set before the call is answered.

These engineers usually work in teams because the scale of the work is beyond any one person. It can take anywhere from 5 engineers to 150 to complete a software application, in 6 months or as long as 2 years. According to one experienced engineer, "No one engineer can understand the entire switch or have all the knowledge needed to do his or her job." Individual productivity at the SSBU, then, depends on the ability to channel one's expertise, creativity, and insight into work with other professionals—a formidable job assignment, even for the smartest knowledge worker.

TARGETING THE RIGHT STRATEGIES

To specify how a star engineer does his or her work, we developed an expert model, but we turned the usual approach on its head. Expert models were invented by artificial intelligence researchers in an effort to get computers to mimic the skills of human beings. Researchers have created such models by interviewing expert welders, for example, and asking them to explain in concrete detail how they go about their job. Researchers then used the interview data to construct a computer program that reproduced the experts' skills in the form of a robotic welder. But based on our interviews with the SSBU experts—in this case, star performers in software development—the expert model for engineers was one people could use, not computers.

First we had to identify the experts. Initially, we relied on managers to point out star performers. We looked for those who had received the highest performance ratings and merit awards. We also asked managers, "If you were starting a new company and could hire only ten knowledge professionals from your present staff, whom would you hire?" There was surprising consensus among managers about who these software engineers were.

Yet once we started interviewing the engineers themselves, the picture grew murkier. As we discovered, managers sometimes overlook important components of star performance, like who originates an idea and who helps colleagues the most when it comes to solving critical problems. Being closer to the action, however, knowledge professionals certainly consider these skills when rating their peers.

In addition, the engineers believed that the Bell Labs performance evaluation system was flawed because it turned up too many false negatives, that is, people who were outstanding performers but for reasons of work style or modesty received low ratings from managers. (Later on, we found only a 50% agreement between peer and manager ratings.) The experts selected for our study, therefore, had to be highly valued performers in *both* their managers' and peers' eyes.

What Star Performers Said. We asked each of the expert engineers to define productivity, how they knew when they were productive, and what exactly it was that they did to be productive. For example, one expert told us that networking was crucial to getting his job done. We then asked him how he went about networking with other experts. He explained that networking was a barter system in which an engineer needed to earn his or her own way. From his perspective, that meant first becoming a technical expert in a particularly sought-after area, then letting people know of your expertise, then making yourself available to others. Once an engineer has developed his or her bargaining chips, it's possible to gain access to the rest of this knowledge network. But once in the network, you have to maintain a balance of trade to stay in.

After we met with the experts in groups, they came to a consensus about the two categories—cognitive skills and work strategies—that influence high productivity. Since all Bell Labs engineers score at the top in IQ tests, cognitive abilities neither guarantee success nor differentiate stars from middle performers. However, the Bell engineers identified nine work strategies that do make a difference: taking initiative, networking, self-management, teamwork effectiveness, leadership, followership, perspective, show-and-tell, and organizational savvy (see Figure 6.1 "An Expert Model for Engineers").

Moreover, the engineers ranked the work strategies in order of importance. Taking initiative is the core strategy in this expert model. An engineer must be able to take initiative upon arriving at Bell Labs or develop the ability for doing so soon after. In a competitive technical environment, it's just not possible to survive otherwise. Yet taking initiative is also one of the most elusive strategies and therefore difficult to quantify. As one engineer explained, "I go into my supervisor's office for a performance evaluation, and she tells me that I should take more initiative. I say to myself that I'm already taking initiative, so what exactly is it that she wants me to do?"

Clearly, any training program for improving the productivity of professionals must first target taking initiative. During our discussions with the Bell Labs experts, one proposed creating practical checklists to detail each work strategy. The "Checklist for Taking Initiative" outlines a sample of specific actions and behaviors that define this core strategy.

The second layer of the expert model includes work strategies like networking and self-management. Although the Bell Labs engineers thought these were critical for high productivity, they acknowledged that they could be acquired at a slower pace. The third and final layer contains show-and-tell and organizational savvy, which these star performers considered "icing on the cake." Professionals who develop these work strategies have a leg up for managerial promotions, but giving riveting presentations and playing the correct political games aren't essential to getting the technical job done.

What Middle Performers Said. At the same time that we were defining the expert model with star engineers, we were also interviewing middle performers at the Bell Labs SSBU. When we first compared the interviews, it appeared that stars and

The Nine Work Strategies

Taking initiative: accepting responsibility above and beyond your stated job, volunteering for additional activities, and promoting new ideas.

Networking: getting direct and immediate access to coworkers with technical expertise and sharing your own knowledge with those who need it.

Self-management: regulating your own work commitments, time, performance level, and career growth.

Teamwork effectiveness: assuming joint responsibility for work activities, coordinating efforts, and accomplishing shared goals with coworkers.

Leadership: formulating, stating, and building consensus on common goals and working to accomplish them.

Followership: helping the leader accomplish the organization's goals and thinking for yourself rather than relying solely on managerial direction.

Perspective: seeing your job in its larger context and taking on other viewpoints like those of the customer, manager, and work team.

Show-and-tell: presenting your ideas persuasively in written or oral form.

Organizational savvy: navigating the competing interests in an organization, be they individual or group, to promote cooperation, address conflicts, and get things done.

Figure 6.1. An expert model for engineers

Checklist for Taking Initiative

Going Beyond the Job

- I make the most of my present assignment.
- I do more than I am asked to do.
- I look for places where I might spot problems and fix them.
- I fix bugs that I notice in programs or at least tell someone about them.
- I look for opportunities to do extra work to help the project move along more quickly.

New Ideas and Follow-Through

- I try to do some original work.
- I look for places where something that's already done might be done better.
- I have ideas about new features and other technical projects that might be developed.
- When I have an idea, I try to make it work and let people know about it.
- I try to document what my idea is and why it's a good idea.
- I think about and try to document how my idea would save the company money or bring in new business.

- I seek advice from people who have been successful in promoting ideas.
- I construct a plan for selling my idea to people in the company.

Dealing Constructively with Criticism

- I tell colleagues about my ideas to get their reactions and criticisms.
- I use their comments and criticisms to make my ideas better.
- I consult the sources of criticisms to help find solutions.
- I continue to revise my ideas to incorporate my colleagues' concerns.

Planning for the Future

- I spend time planning what I'd like to work on next.
- I look for other interesting projects to work on when my present work gets close to the finish line.
- I talk to people to find out what projects are coming up and will need people.

---

middle performers gave similar answers. For example, both groups identified taking initiative as a useful work strategy. But closer inspection revealed that the answers of stars and average engineers differed in two critical ways: how they ranked the strategies in importance and how they described them.

To begin with, middle performers inverted the expert model's ranking of the nine work strategies. According to these engineers, show-and-tell and organizational savvy were the core strategies and were largely responsible for high performance ratings from managers. It's easy to understand why these nonexpert engineers came to this conclusion. One of the few times senior managers see knowledge professionals in action is when they give pre-

sentations. And in some cases, mediocre professionals with a flair for showmanship are rewarded by top management. But in general, executives use such public presentations to infer the skills and strategies that produce good technical work. Picking up on only the superficial aspect, the Bell Labs middle performers were overly focused on impression management rather than critical strategies like networking.

As for describing the work strategies, the differences between stars and middle performers were even more striking. One middle performer at the SSBU, for instance, told us of gathering and organizing source materials, including documents and software tools, for a project he was beginning with his group. Another described writing a memo to his supervisor about a software bug. Both engineers believed they showed a great deal of initiative in taking it upon themselves to do this work.

Yet when we described these examples to the Bell Labs experts, they were critical. They thought these engineers were barely doing their jobs, let alone taking initiative. For example, one expert explained that by the time a software bug is documented, it is often impossible for the software developers to re-create the problem in order to fix it. For the experts, fixing a bug yourself or preparing for a project is what's expected of you in your job. Real initiative means going above and beyond the call of duty. In addition, such actions must help other people besides yourself and involve taking some risks.

Discussions about networking surfaced equally revealing differences, since both stars and middle performers said networks of knowledgeable people are critical for highly productive technical work. For example, a middle performer at Bell Labs talked about being stumped by a technical problem. He painstakingly called various technical gurus and then waited, wasting valuable time while calls went unreturned and e-mail messages unanswered. Star performers, however, rarely face such situations because they do the work of building reliable networks before they actually need them. When they call someone for advice, stars almost always get a faster answer.

In fact, we found similar differences between stars and middle performers in their definitions of all the work strategies. In particular, some middle-performing engineers clearly lacked perspective. One engineer described the many hours he had spent mastering a software tool for organizing files, which ended up delaying the delivery of a customer's product. From an expert's perspective, of course, the customer comes first. Although star performers agreed that upgrading their knowledge of current software tools is useful, they also emphasized the need to set priorities. And these experts stressed the need to "shift gears" between the narrow focus required for certain tasks and a broad view of how their project may fit into a larger one.

TRAINING KNOWLEDGE PROFESSIONALS

Not surprisingly, knowledge workers don't like off-the-shelf productivity training programs. Our discussions with engineers at Bell Labs and elsewhere show that these people like to make their own choices. Such professionals readily admit that they could do their jobs better, but they're also wary, as at least one Bell Labs participant put it, of "becoming a clone."

Knowledge professionals value the real experts on productivity in their laboratory or law firm, not trainers who breeze in, teach a day-long workshop, and then breeze out. Therefore, once the Bell Labs SSBU training program got underway, respected engineers led the training sessions. In fact, the process of developing the expert model became the foundation for the training program itself. The Bell Labs experts we interviewed reported increases in their own productivity because they had picked up valuable tips from listening to their star colleagues.

The expert model also has a clear advantage over a system like mentoring. While many professionals are experts about their own productivity, no single star performer knows everything. Unlike a mentoring program in which one senior professional advises a junior staff member or a group of new workers, an expert model pools the strategies of many stars. And a training program based on such a model makes those strategies explicit.

Developing the Curriculum. In the spring of 1989, top managers at Bell Labs agreed to a pilot training program for the SSBU. Sixteen engineers chosen by managers participated in two groups that met once a week over the course of ten weeks. These groups included a mix of stars and middle performers but were weighted more heavily with stars, since we wanted them to become trainers later. After the initial pilot sessions, we reversed the ratio of stars to middle performers in the groups.

The training program's primary task was to make the critical work strategies concrete, accessible, and learnable. Each week of the pilot program focused on one of the nine strategies, and the last week was used for a wrap-up. But despite this neat schedule, the first engineers to participate revised the curriculum as they went along, testing ideas out in real time, keeping what worked, and discarding what didn't.

For example, the engineers developed a teamwork exercise based on work-related issues at the SSBU. The group formed a mock task force to focus on a pressing company issue like whether or not the software development process should be standardized. Participants decided to spend part of each remaining session in this mock task force. A few weeks into the exercise, however, one engineer complained that while this was more realistic than most training activities, it still had no real impact on her day-to-day work or that of the company. Within a week, top managers at Bell Labs told the pilot group that they would read and respond to a written report from this no longer "mock" task force. Suddenly, this particular teamwork exercise became more compelling than anything the group had done before.

By the end of the pilot program, the 16 engineers had created a detailed curriculum for each of the 9 work strategies. Each piece of that curriculum included frank discussion, work-related exercises, ratings on the work strategy checklists, and homework that required participants to practice while they learned. As the box "A Day in the Life of Productivity Trainers" indicates, a Bell Labs workshop session involved not only specific case studies and exercises but also active disagreement among all participants.

Eventually, the Bell Labs training program was streamlined to six weeks, with the sessions facilitated by expert engineers who had previously participated. Yet continually reshaping the curriculum in response to critical events on the job is still the current program's most important feature.

For example, during one of the later sessions, top management issued a memo on company quality initiatives. Engineers at the SSBU thought the memo blamed them for poor quality. So participants in the training program decided to respond directly to the memo as part of that session's work.

Up to that point, it was quite unusual for engineers to take such a step because most believed that top managers would not appreciate, let alone respond to, a direct approach. But as it turned out, the engineers got a quick and constructive response. Top managers sent e-mail messages and talked to some of the participants about their concerns.

In addition, if professionals try to analyze their own productivity, they need a clear idea of how others, especially managers, view their performance. Bell Labs trainees received feedback from peers, managers, customers, and fellow participants. They also rated themselves on the work strategy checklists and filled out several other self-evaluations. With such a range of feedback, most participating engineers knew what their strengths were and where they most needed to improve by the end of the program.

Measuring the Bottom Line. Since 1989, more than 600 of the 5,000 engineers at the Bell Labs SSBU have participated in what is now called the Productivity Enhancement Group (PEG). Since these engineers were scattered across many projects and departments, it's difficult to demonstrate the program's effectiveness through measures like fewer person hours spent on a particular project. In their self-evaluations, however, participants reported a 10% increase in productivity immediately after the sessions ended, which grew to 20% after 6 months and 25% after a full year. This steady upward curve is the opposite of what follows most training programs. Typically, effectiveness is greatest on the last day of the program and falls to zero after a year.

But even if PEG participants reported substantial productivity increases, this doesn't prove that the performance of these engineers actually changed. The corporate goal for PEG was not, for example, taking initiative for initiative's sake but adding value to the company. Therefore, we met with managers again, asking them, "What would you look for as indices of increased productivity in a person who worked for you?" Figure 6.2 "What Managers Thought: The Real Test of Productivity" shows that the productivity of PEG participants improved twice as much as nonparticipants over an eight-month pe-

A Day in the Life of Productivity Trainers

7:30 A.M. The engineer-facilitators, who train in pairs, meet their partners to get ready for a class on taking initiative. They review the agenda, organize notes, decide who's going to do what, and worry.

8:00 Class begins with a discussion of taking initiative, based on a case study that was part of the homework assignment. The case describes an engineer who volunteered to organize a technical project assigned to her department. Discussion is heated. Did organizing the project go beyond what was expected of this engineer? Did it involve taking any risks? An argument breaks out about whether the definition of initiative should include risk taking. One participant, a recognized technical guru, describes how he recently took initiative by letting his department head know that a technical project was floundering. He ruffled department feathers but succeeded because of how he strategically documented ideas, built a network of allies, and took calculated risks.

9:05 Facilitators sit back and observe the 30-minute mock task force meeting. The task force agrees that today's goal is to concentrate on soliciting input from all members, especially the quiet ones. The task force is working on recommendations for revamping the recognition and reward system at the Labs. There's disagreement over whether or not performance evaluations should be scrapped, and the task force gets bogged down. Members use a round-robin approach to solicit suggestions. Deadlock is broken by addressing the deeper issue of how to define the bottom-line goals of reward systems. Facilitators give feedback about the meeting. Task force members exchange feedback.

10:15 Coffee break. Facilitators huddle briefly to make changes in the next portion of the program based on participants' reactions to the first part.

10:30 The group discusses the checklist for taking initiative, another part of the homework assignment. Almost all the participants rated themselves on the list, but some are clearly overwhelmed: for example, one says, "I never knew I could have been doing these things. What an eye-opener."

11:45 Facilitators summarize the session and go over the new homework assignment. Each participant is expected to use his or her networks to find an answer to the same tough technical question. Next week, participants will compare their networking strategies by discussing how long it took them to get the answer, whether they received the right answer, and how many people they had to contact.

Noon Lunch with ten facilitators from other groups. Some sample comments and questions:

- "What did you do when that initiative discussion bogged down?"
- "We had an engineer who hated the checklists!"
- "I think we had the group from hell. Everybody was quiet except for this one engineer who thought he had the answer to everything. He wouldn't let go of this one idea about initiative, so we took a poll of the other group members. It turned out they disagreed with him, and that diffused it."
- "After this group, I'll never be afraid to run a meeting again."
- "What changes should be made to the program for the groups that will meet this afternoon?"

riod. According to the SSBU managers, these engineers improved in seven areas, including spotting and fixing problems, getting work done on time with high quality, pleasing customers, and working well with other departments. And star performers were not alone in benefiting from PEG training. Star and middle performers improved at similar rates.

We also compared our manager surveys with the company's standard performance ratings, which are routinely collected at Bell Labs and are the basis for salary adjustments and promotions. We looked at these ratings before participants began PEG and then eight months after they had finished the program. Interestingly enough, the performance ratings of PEG participants improved at twice the rate of nonparticipants, mirroring the results of our manager surveys.

In addition, PEG had an especially strong impact on women and minority engineers (see the Box "Women and Minorities at Bell Labs"). In traditional organizations, these groups are often excluded from the expert loop. But creating an expert model that demystifies certain productivity secrets, particularly the importance of key work strategies and how to acquire them, makes the loop explicit and accessible to all.

Ultimately, of course, such productivity increases for individual professionals fall to the company's bottom line. If the total compensation package for a knowledge professional is about $62,500 (salary plus fringe benefits), the ROI is $625 each year for every 1% productivity increase. Thus a

10% increase yields $6,250 for each participant, while a 25% productivity increase would pay back $15,625, and so on.

But these ROI numbers don't include the more indirect productivity benefits. PEG participants improved dramatically in the ways they assisted colleagues. These engineers also built stronger ties to customers. While such positive changes are hard to measure, they are essential to a highly productive work team.

MAKING A COMMITMENT TO STAR PERFORMANCE

Some managers still wonder whether high productivity is due only to individual work style and motivation. In many cases, they're searching for a jus-

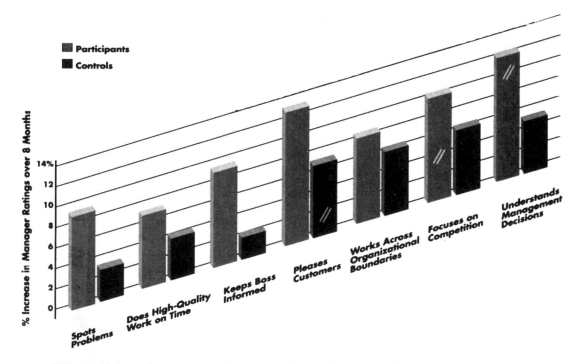

This chart is based on a survey that was used to evaluate the effects of the training program. The study compared 300 participants with 300 nonparticipants (controls). Managers of each group completed the survey before the training sessions began and then again eight months later.

Figure 6.2.   What managers thought, the real test of productivity

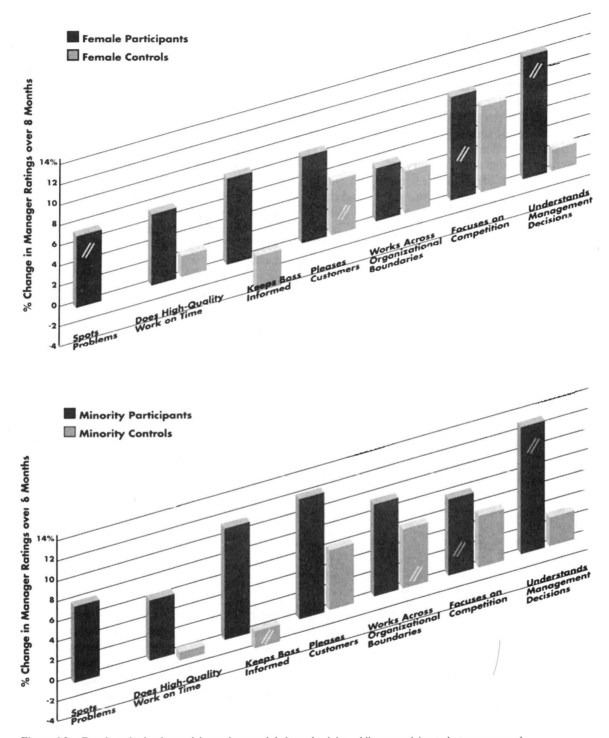

Figure 6.3. Female and minority participants increased their productivity, while nonparticipants lost some ground

Women and Minorities at Bell Labs

At large companies like AT&T, which employ many women and minority professionals, there are often separate support groups for women and each minority. Such groups do foster the sharing of problems and success stories; yet they may also limit the contact of women and minorities with a wider range of company experts.

The effectiveness of an expert-model approach in no way dismisses the fact that women and minorities have traditionally been excluded from productivity secrets in engineering or other high-tech environments. But since the Productivity Enhancement Group (PEG) program focuses on improving individual productivity, it can sidestep some of these organizational barriers, particularly stereotypes about the productivity and work styles of women and minorities. In fact, teaching professionals expert work strategies may be the most pragmatic form of affirmative action.

As the graphs in Figure 6.3 based on the manager surveys show, the productivity of women and minority PEG participants improved at four times the rate of comparable nonparticipants. On the dimensions that most directly affected managers—"does high-quality work on time" and "keeps boss informed"—the productivity of women and minorities who didn't participate in PEG actually *decreased* during the eight-month survey period.

The fact that managers reported that some women engineers lost ground in the crucial area of keeping their bosses informed is particularly telling. Men and women may indeed communicate with their bosses differently. But in PEG, everyone learns the necessity of regular communication with managers.

But we've found no such relationships. Rather, training programs like PEG can help professionals discover the strengths and weaknesses of their individual work styles. Managers gain little by foisting a time-management system, complete with scheduling book and to-do priority tabs, on someone who prefers to keep such information in his or her head. Helping this worker to develop a better strategy for storing information mentally and setting priorities makes more sense.

Motivation, however, is another matter. At Bell Labs, most of the engineers we worked with were eager for productivity tips. They knew their success was tied to high performance, and they saw how easily the work piled up. Since the PEG sessions focused on developing individual work strategies, motivated professionals benefited by improving their own productivity.

But when workers aren't motivated to improve, a program like PEG is of little help. In surveys done outside of Bell Labs, we've found that about one-third of knowledge workers don't feel tied to their company's destiny, nor do they feel that their productivity and good ideas are sufficiently rewarded. For example, teamwork is often touted by corporate headquarters as critical to both individual and company success; however, an employee's ability to work with others often has little to do with annual performance ratings or rewards. Many professionals know this and are right to resent it.

Yet such resentment can lead to serious drops in productivity. A company with unproductive and actively resentful professionals, then, may need to address additional organizational issues, such as revising the reward system or treating its professionals as individuals with individual needs.

Clearly, it's not possible to turn every average worker into a star. Despite PEG or any other training program, there are differences among professionals, must as there are among athletes who follow the same training regimen. It's probably not even desirable or cost-effective to put all professionals through a training program, since not everyone enjoys or is compelled by intense workshop sessions.

However, the PEG participants at Bell Labs

tification for their own style. "Clean desk" people want to believe that being organized leads to higher productivity. "Sloppy desk" managers, however, view their style as evidence of the creativity that translates into high performance.

have not only improved their own productivity but also positively affected the productivity of nonparticipating coworkers. The checklists and other materials derived from the expert model have been photocopied, passed around, and incorporated into the everyday functioning of the SSBU. Once such informal dissemination happens on a wide scale, formal training is no longer necessary.

Developing an expert model can provide a powerful platform for leveraging intellectual capital in many professions. The PEG program at the BELL Labs SSBU, however, isn't a blueprint for another company, even a research laboratory with a similar environment. The mix of work strategies may differ from profession to profession; a marketing department, for example, may find that show-and-tell is a core strategy for star performance, along with taking initiative. Yet, regardless of profession, top managers need to focus on people when they address productivity improvement. In the new knowledge economy, it's the performance of knowledge professionals, not just complex technologies, that will make or break a business.

7

The Idea Makers

THOMAS KIELY

Employees of Du Pont use dreams and metaphors to solve manufacturing problems and develop new products. At Eastman Kodak, Hoechst Celanese, and Amoco, scientists and engineers shake up their thinking with imagination-enhancing games that would have been familiar to surrealist artists in the 1920s. Managers at Texas Utilities, a Dallas-based power company, solve an expensive capital planning problem by imagining themselves as a kilowatt traveling through the company's systems.

Fantasy, games, and dream analysis are the kind of inspiration-kindling strategies that poets might practice in their search for novel expressions. But these are just a few of the creativity techniques used by employees at a growing number of companies. Managers promoting use of these activities hope to spark creative thinking throughout the corporate ranks, from maintenance workers to CEOs. Ultimately, they see creativity as a means to enhance quality, performance, and innovation within the company.

"Employing creative people is necessary in today's competitive world, but absolutely not sufficient," says Sheldon Buckler, vice-chairman of Polaroid, in Cambridge, Mass. "You also need an environment that values and encourages what employees do, and they need tools to help them to keep renewing creativity. That is what creativity techniques do."

Some companies have plunged headlong into creativity training. Frito-Lay, a subsidiary of PepsiCo, trained all 25,000 of its employees during the 1980s, Corning trained 26,000 employees in several countries, and Exxon has trained nearly 7,000 employees in its sales, exploration, and chemicals divisions since 1988. Texas Utilities trained its top 400

executives to use an array of creative thinking techniques, and is now offering similar instruction to other employees. In fact, more than one-fourth of all U.S. companies employing more than 100 people offer some kind of creativity training to employees, according to surveys conducted by *Training* magazine, a Minneapolis-based trade publication.

Despite this growing popularity, some critics dismiss creativity training as a flaky management fad. There is a danger, they say, that managers will apply these methods as Band-Aids for problems that require more serious attention. Moreover, critics charge, the focus on generating new ideas misses the point of what is really wrong with most businesses. "Ideas come rather easily," says Thomas Kuczmarski, president of Kuczmarski & Associates, a Chicago-based innovation consulting firm. "The real problem companies face is in transforming those ideas into products"—and that bespeaks organizational obstacles, not deficient thinking skills.

Even most proponents of creativity training agree that invention—coming up with a new idea—is only the first step. The real goal is innovation—in other words, turning an idea into something of value to the business. But they contend that creativity techniques help prime the idea pump and coax employees to strive for the original and the unexpected. Moreover, innovation is not just the business of new-product or marketing departments. Companies like Du Pont and Kodak want assembly line workers to discover novel solutions to shop floor problems; want sales employees to think up new ways to woo customers when tried approaches fail; and want managers to gain insight into how they budget, plan, and strategize.

Reprinted with permission from Kiely, Thomas, "The Idea Makers," *Technology Review,* January, 1993, pp. 33–40.
Thomas Kiely is an Associate Editor at Harvard Business Review.

At Kodak, for example, maintenance workers used a creativity technique to reinvent the way they tend a film-processing machine. The machine, which is the size of a football field and is used to deposit the emulsion coating on photographic film, must be shut down periodically for preventive maintenance and for capital improvements. Too often, these shutdowns had occurred during large production runs.

A dozen maintenance employees, working with one of the corporation's creativity trainers, imagined that they were at a party, celebrating their ability to reduce the job from seven days to four without interrupting production runs. They imagined who was at the party and what was said—and began to draw out real solutions from the imagined party banter. By standing the problem on its sequential head, the team looked at the dilemma from a fresh perspective. Ultimately, they refined their ideas (which included developing modular equipment and making creative use of production schedules) and successfully completed their charge.

While creativity techniques won't create an organization full of Picassos and Edisons, these thinking methods do nudge people to stretch beyond the familiar. Du Pont, for instance, was searching for additional markets for fire-resistant Nomex fibers, which the company sold for use in protective clothing worn by firefighters. There was one problem: the fiber's tight structure was impervious to dyes. Potential customers (it could be used in the interior of aircraft) would not buy the material unless Du Pont could manufacture a version that could be colored at a reasonable cost.

A solution eluded researchers—until one scientist, who had been taught creativity techniques, began to dabble with a problem-solving method called metaphoric thinking. The idea, says Charles Prather, director of Du Pont's Center for Creativity and Innovation, is to liken a problem to processes that are completely unrelated; the mind then leaps to make connections, occasionally discovering something clever along the way.

The Du Pont scientist, who grew up in coal country in West Virginia, compared his problem to a mine shaft. To excavate minerals, miners dig a hole into the earth and use props to keep the hole from collapsing. Expanding on the idea, the researcher figured out a way to chemically prop open a hole in the Nomex structure as the material is being manufactured so it could later be filled with dyes.

THE MANY PATHS TO CREATIVITY

Most of the creativity techniques being used in business fall into one of four groupings: *Fluency* techniques help stimulate the generation of ideas; *excursion* sessions push the mind to grope for illuminations; *pattern breakers* force thinkers to restate problems in novel ways; and *shake-up exercises* (such as games) help loosen up groups and make them more receptive to unusual ideas.

Fluency techniques are the simplest and most widely used. Creativity proponents claim that fluency techniques help individuals or teams develop flexible habits of mind, and suspend judgment and analysis in favor of sheer flow of ideas.

One of the most formidable barriers to creativity is criticism. The possibility that the boss or colleagues will attack an idea inhibits employees from offering their thoughts—especially novel ones. And managers do often focus so intently upon the flaws of an employee suggestion or new product idea that they lose sight of the potential, says Robert Johnston, a partner at Idea-Scope, an innovation consulting firm in Cambridge, Mass. Creativity, says John Seeley Brown, director of the Xerox Palo Alto Research Center (PARC), demands openness, interaction, and collaboration, a willingness to try to bridge differences in disciplines and methodologies, and a willingness to listen for glimmerings of useful ideas, however raw.

This insight underlies the oldest fluency technique—brainstorming. Developed by creativity guru Alex Osborn in 1938, brainstorming has become primarily a group activity in which participants fire off as many ideas as possible. The premise is that a group will produce a far greater number of ideas, from different perspectives, than an individual can. In an ideal brainstorming session, all thoughts are treated as welcome guests; judgment is deferred. Criticism is forbidden until afterward, when ideas are evaluated and prioritized.

Unfortunately, brainstorming rarely achieves its nonjudgmental ideal. In fact, most creativity consultants and many companies have abandoned brainstorming as ineffective. The Center for Creative Leadership (CCL), a management research and consulting organization in Greensboro, N.C., has found that there is often little difference between the production of ideas by individuals and teams.

"There are a lot of pressures that inhibit group performance," explains Jim Shields, manager of innovation programs and products at CCL. Brainstorming sessions can be undercut by group uniformity pressures and perceived threats from senior managers in attendance, he says. Personality differences also come into play; some people are naturally willing to talk, while others tend to remain silent, and the best ideas do not necessarily come from the loudest people, he points out.

To avoid the shortcomings of brainstorming, some companies have adopted instead the fluency technique called brainwriting. During a group brainwriting session, employees write down their ideas on slips of paper, usually in a manner that protects their anonymity. Then they exchange papers and try to build upon each others' insights. That way the loudest voices don't necessarily prevail, and employees feel less pressure to perform for the boss.

"Brainwriting is popular with scientists and researchers," says Jeff Felberg, director of Amoco Chemical's New Ideas Process, a program to foster new business development. "They tend to judge ideas strongly. Brainwriting helps get them beyond self-censorship."

Brainwriting can be easily adapted to work over a computer network. Employees at Electronic Data Systems, the computer systems management arm of General Motors, maintain automated brainwriting facilities in Cambridge, Mass., and Ann Arbor, Mich. The facilities include a bank of networked Macintosh computers occupying the conference table. Brainwriters type their thoughts anonymously into the network, then consolidate ideas onto a "public" computer screen that all can view together.

Two other fluency techniques are mind-mapping and storyboarding—both methods for visualizing ideas and associations. With mind-mapping, individuals or groups draw a primary idea in the center of the paper, then depict new or related ideas as vines growing in all directions. "It's an organized brainstorming method," says Michael Stanley, a logistics engineering manager at Boeing. "Without mind maps we could get lost in the minutia."

Boeing engineers have used mind maps to get a better understanding of the internal process for developing technical manuals—and to pinpoint ways to improve work flow by eliminating redundancies. They also used a mind map to explain quickly and cogently to a customer a complicated maintenance program for a Boeing-made weapon system. In both instances, says Stanley, mind maps proved an effective way to condense a lot of information into a single image.

With storyboarding, participants in a group jot ideas down on index cards, which are then displayed on large bulletin boards or conference room walls. This technique is especially handy for thinking about processes. Each step in a process is a frame in a narrative. Employees readily reshuffle, rewrite, or even eliminate cards, with an eye toward improving the efficiency of the flow.

Allstate Business Insurance, General Electric, and Bell Atlantic all use variations of storyboarding. At Xerox PARC, researchers sketch ideas onto a large white wall in a common area, opening up a discussion of their ideas to other researchers from all disciplines. The technique invites group commentary and multiple perspectives, all of which can be considered and reconsidered over time. At Bell Atlantic, departments hang large swaths of brown wrapping paper up on hallway or conference room walls. Employees use pens, markers, and post-its to change the diagram, adding boxes and arrows and an abundance of comments. The group slowly redesigns a process, such as how to move an idea from laboratory to market.

WALKS ON THE WILD SIDE

Techniques such as storyboarding and brainwriting, while useful, often help people hatch more or less conventional ideas. Fluency techniques "are like business trips," says CCL's Shields: "They are goal focused, straight line, efficient, and usually predictable." A second set of thinking stimuli, by contrast, inspire employees to crawl out onto mental limbs. These "excursions," Shields says, are "wandering, unpredictable, novel." Excursion techniques take the individual or group away from the problem so that the unconscious can work on it from a different perspective—metaphoric and non-sequential—and then prompt the imagination to pull out ideas.

One excursion technique, called a forced relationship, works this two-cycle magic using a wholly unrelated stimulus such as photographs, objects, or paintings. This past summer, for instance, a group of Polaroid managers from various departments (including sales, design, research, manufacturing, and marketing) met to seek ways to better mesh different functions. The company's senior creativity specialist, Suzanne Merritt, asked the managers to look at a couple of paintings and describe what they saw. Merritt then asked the managers to force-fit their impressions from the paintings—which she picked at random from a large collection—to their original task of figuring out how to improve interdepartmental harmony.

One painting showed crows in a tree beside a fish-populated pool of water. To some in the group, it seemed as though the fish were vainly trying to communicate to the unhearing birds—and as they discussed this impression, both marketing and R&D realized that they saw themselves as the unheard fish. Researchers speak a technical language, preoccupied with scientific rather than commercial matters, marketers felt; while R&D believed that marketing was deaf to new technical insights. As a result of this meeting, teams of marketing and research employees will now meet quarterly to "learn how to talk to each other," Merritt says.

Randomly selected words can similarly serve as problem-solving stimuli. This technique is pop-ular at meetings of the International Creative Forum, a consortium of companies (including IBM, Nestle, and Prudential Insurance) that use creativity techniques to mediate upon common business problems. At a forum gathering last spring, for instance, upper-middle managers from member companies tried to envision customer demands in the year 2000. The managers first discussed general demographic forecasts and market trends, then broke up into sub-groups to try to identify future opportunities.

One sub-group, looking at the aging population, used the word "window," randomly selected from a list of words to focus their thoughts. Seeing a senior citizen's mind as a window opening onto a landscape of desires, the group came up with a concept for a suite of services that would go directly to the customer to fulfill a variety of everyday needs—from taking out the garbage and delivering groceries to paying bills and fixing the car.

Excursions can also be dreams. Three years ago, Floyd Ragsdale, a section engineer at Du Pont's polymers plant in Richmond, Va., was part of a team that had struggled for weeks to solve a problem with collapsing vacuum hoses at a fibers production facility. Trained to review his problem before dropping off to sleep, the engineer woke with an image of a child's slinky toy still vivid in his mind. He jotted down a note about his dream on a pad he kept beside the bed, then realized that the image suggested a remedy. The research team soon verified his dream-produced idea, which essentially was to strengthen the vacuum hoses by inserting slinky-like springs.

Despite its new-age flavor, the use of dreams to augment creative thought has a venerable history. The nineteenth century Flemish chemist August Kekulé dreamed of a snake biting its own tail—and realized he had found the ring-like molecular structure of benzene, a problem he had worked on for years. And the 1936 Nobel Prize—winning physiologist Otto Loewi claimed that his insight that the nerve impulse is both an electrical and a chemical process originated in a dream.

Other excursion techniques teach workers to dream while they are awake. By imagining themselves inside products or processes, for instance, employees use mental images summoned from the unconscious. A Du Pont researcher, trying to find ways to control colors in one product, visualized himself inside the material. He imagined light penetrating it and reflecting off individual particles— and saw a solution (which, for proprietary reasons, Du Pont won't yet disclose).

And Texas Utilities managers used a visualization technique to dramatically reduce the company's capital equipment costs. Huge power-generating machinery such as turbines, generators, and boilers have an average life expectancy of 35 years, says Texas Utilities executive vice-president Robert Gary; replacement costs for large equipment is typically $3,000–5,000 per kilowatt.

A team of managers, engaged in a three-month study to shave these costs, visualized itself as a kilowatt traveling through the company's various fossil fuel and nuclear power systems. As they imaginatively traveled through each stage of the process, they began to understand the complex and diverse levels of durability within systems—and saw a way to take advantage of it. Rather than continue to replace whole systems, they proposed, the company should adopt a maintenance plan that called for replacing key constituent parts. Gary claims that the redesigned maintenance plan will drive the company's equipment costs down tenfold or more during the decade ahead.

STRETCHING AND RELAXING

A third set of techniques, known as pattern breakers, force the mind to stretch to find patterns between dissimilar concepts, in the hope of discovering unusual ideas in odd associations (a notion promulgated by surrealist poets and artists in the 1920s). The metaphorical thinking strategy that the Du Pont researcher used to find a way to make dyeable Nomex is one example of a pattern breaker.

Pattern breakers differ from excursion techniques in a subtle but important way. Excursion exercises are intended to take a person's mind away from a problem temporarily so the unconscious can mull it over. Metaphorical thinking and other pattern breakers, in contrast, keep the problem in focus but in a different light, jarring people out of their mental ruts and sparking fresh insights. The imagined party conjured up by Kodak maintenance workers is a good model of a pattern-breaking exercise.

Other random stimuli also can be used. Synectics, a Cambridge, Mass., innovation consulting firm, asks clients to take a stroll with an instant film camera, and then uses the snapshots as prompts. One such client was a large management consulting firm trying to develop a program of services aimed at corporate R&D units. The camera-toting group returned to Synectics with images of a glass jar, a household wash product, and a Federal Express package, among others.

The picture of the glass jar, which was surrounded by colorful trinkets, led to a discussion about how to sell a service that seemed practical to the consultants who devised it but that was lost in a crowd of business services. The image of the Federal Express package prompted comments about how the package delivery company had concocted a successful business system (speedy delivery) that helps other business systems to work—a discussion that helped the consulting company to design a new service to help clients accelerate their R&D. As is the case with most pattern breakers, this activity is more goal-directed than an excursion exercise. Throughout the examination of the photos, participants kept their objective in mind and focused their comments accordingly.

Just as an open attitude toward new ideas and a taste for alternative solutions are preconditions for creativity, so are risk-taking and a willingness to "fail" or embarrass oneself. In the fourth class of creativity techniques—shake-up exercises—employees engage in games or team activities intended to help them relax, laugh, and fumble. "Humor breaks the self-censoring mechanism," says Jeffrey Mauzy, a principal at Synectics. "It's hard to come up with ideas; it's harder to say them. But when we're laughing, we're less inhibited."

Companies like First Chicago bank have used role-playing games—replete with funny costumes—and outdoor activities to shake employees up. Ditto Kodak: Deborah Nicklaus, a creativity specialist from the company's management services department, has a collection of about 30 hats that she uses in relaxation games. She might ask a participant to don a Santa Claus cap and describe a proposed product from the point of view of Father Christmas: How could the company market the product to a customer who will use it only once a year? Will a camera capture an image using only the light from Rudolph's nose? Should it be able to work in the freezing temperatures of the North Pole? The point is not to actually devise a product or a marketing strategy but rather to loosen up the imagination in preparation for the business tasks at hand. Other shake-up exercises involve group fantasies: Invent a western town, or a city block, in detail; imagine suspending the laws of nature; create a product line for Napoleon. One Kodak game asks participants to imagine they are in a hot air balloon and to describe what they see behind them as the balloon carries them across an unknown landscape.

Kodak also maintains a "humor room" stocked with games, objects (such as toy robots and juggling balls) creativity books, and Monty Python videos. A financial planning group, working on new corporate performance measures, has used the humor room as a conference site. "People relax in the room, and open up," says group member Thomas Dabrowski. In one instance, the group convened to brainstorm how to measure the company's effectiveness in distributing goods to customers. Like most companies, Kodak monitors delivery time, distribution costs, and customer satisfaction. The group was seeking unconventional yardsticks that might provide new information to the company's top decision makers. Inspired by the humor room, Dabrowski says, the participants tossed out a few off-the-wall ideas, one of which eventually led to a new method for visualizing these costs and their relationships.

At Texas Utilities executives have invited children to participate in business meetings. In one of these sessions, the children—fifth and sixth graders recruited from a local school's gifted and talented program—listened as executives complained about time wasted in meetings. One little girl pointed out that the way they described meetings made them sound important. Maybe, she suggested, managers needed to use meetings differ-

ently rather than have fewer of them. Prodded by the children, the managers devised solutions that included a "buddy system" (for sharing meeting attendance) and the use of tape recordings.

Executives from other Dallas-area companies have done tours of duty in playgrounds. "We ask them to notice how kids play," explains Ann McGee-Cooper, a consultant who also helped to bring children into the company. "Kids discover, and when they tire of their own rules, they change them," she says. The executives then try to look at their own problems as games where the rules can be changed, where nothing is set and all alternatives are possible.

Groups will often use a combination of creativity techniques, depending on how experienced and tolerant of offbeat activities the participants are. "You can't go into a room with people and start up with excursion techniques," says Houston-based creativity consultant Rolf Smith, the former head of the U.S. Air Force Office of Innovation and a codeveloper of Exxon's innovation program. "They'll throw you out the door. It gets higher-value ideas, but it's loosey-goosey stuff. You have to start with the basics, then introduce these techniques slowly."

When a Du Pont creativity facilitator works with a research or business group, the day usually begins with a brainstorming session, which gets the usual thoughts out. In hindsight, these are usually the most commonplace ideas spawned that day. But "you have to allow people to get out the ideas they came to the meeting with—let them be heard and honored—before you can go on," says Du Pont creativity center director Prather. When the group exhausts its first wave of ideas, Prather says, "then we bring out the more advanced techniques, like forced relationships—and this brings on a new avalanche of ideas."

A CREATIVE CULTURE

To some innovation experts, creativity training is loopy nonsense. "Creativity is not predictable, and it can't be measured," says management consultant and experimental psychologist Joseph Harless, president of the Atlanta-based Performance Guild. Many employees are uneasy with the exercises as well: "Some people see these creative experiences as something magical or mystical, or tied to mental illness," says innovation consultant Shields. "You can't ask people to do something that is uncomfortable for them."

Creativity researchers admit that the benefits of creativity training are hard to pin down. "We make assumptions that training works," says William Shephard, director of programs at the Creative Education Foundation in Buffalo, "but we don't know enough about it yet. All of this is still in its infancy." There is no definitive way to evaluate whether creativity training improves workplace performance; the "proof," such as it is, remains anecdotal. That is not enough for many executives. "Senior managers often say that creativity is alright for research or advertising or marketing but not for them," says Edward de Bono, an author and consultant who is considered the father of creativity training.

Polaroid vice-chairman Buckler contends that senior managers who stand aloof from creativity training are making a mistake. "We have a responsibility to create a climate in which real creativity is welcome," says Buckler, who says that he uses the techniques in his own work. "You can't delegate that. We want to make a strong statement in the company that we value creativity and that it's a priority."

But merely providing creativity training is not enough. True innovation requires that the organization be receptive to new ideas. "Corporations that are training researchers to be more creative "are focusing on people as the problem," says Ranganath Nayak, senior vice-president at the Cambridge, Mass., consulting firm Arthur D. Little. "But the problem is not the people," he says. "There are lots of good ideas out there. The problem is the system for managing research and development."

"If all you're doing is creativity training, you'll be disappointed," adds Gifford Pinchot, a consultant based in Brandford, Conn., who has shifted his focus from creativity training to the innovation process. He recently surveyed 200 client companies that had produced new ideas at his creativity sessions during the last decade and found that "few of these companies had implemented the ideas." The reason, says Pinchot, is that "often there is no one person within the company willing to work to drive the idea through the inevitable corporate barriers." Ideas cannot make their own cases in busy organizations; to succeed, they need champions or sponsors with the passion or the power to push them.

A study of creativity among corporate research scientists in the late 1980s suggests that the work environment itself is a critical factor in stimulating or blocking creativity. Study co-author Teresa Amabile, a psychology professor at Brandeis University, says that the challenge of the work, a sense of ownership in it, autonomy, stimulating co-workers, and management encouragement all seem to nurture creativity—and that scientists, when defining what it takes to be creative, rate these factors as more important than individual traits.

Xerox PARC, for one, eschews creativity training but takes considerable pains to create an environment that encourages researchers to reach for new ideas. Managers expect researchers to grapple with problems that are risky and adventurous and to pursue cross-disciplinary work. Scientists who dwell on status quo problems are asked to leave, says center director Brown. Staff are encouraged to visit universities, other parts of the company, and research institutes to keep up with new trends—and even to work directly with customers.

A few companies have taken dramatic steps to reshape the climate for both invention and innovation. Hoechst Celanese, for example, opened an Office of Innovation to help research employees take ideas and run with them. It is not merely a suggestion box but a vigorous support operation that offers creativity training, helps entrepreneurial researchers focus and refine ideas, ensures that they have the time to work, and provides funding and other resources.

In another twist to foster creativity and innovation, Medtronics, a medical devices company in

Minneapolis, invites its elite researchers (generally those who have the most patents) to help top managers set the technical direction of the company. Allstate Business Insurance is seeking to change compensation programs to reward team performance as well as individual achievement. Hewlett-Packard, Texas Instruments, and 3M encourage select groups of employees to spend on-the-job time thinking about new products or ways to improve the business. 3M has committed itself to earning 25 percent of its revenues from products that are less than five years old—a goal that makes creativity a corporate imperative.

Because the kinds of products that companies must deliver today often involve diverse specialties, companies could tailor incentive programs to encourage teams to operate like small entrepreneurial outfits within the larger organization, say innovation experts like Kuczmarski and Pinchot, with team members investing some of their own capital and also receiving a share of any profits.

Even ardent creativity boosters echo the charge that creativity alone isn't enough. Lindsey Collier, an engineer who brought creativity training and the humor room to Kodak, says that while top managers laud creativity training, they do little to push it. Now a consultant, he charges that Kodak's "innovation network," a program aimed at collecting and fostering new ideas from employees and customers, is mired in red tape. Industry watchers and former executives have leveled similar criticism against Du Pont and Exxon.

But creativity champions like Polaroid's Merritt say that if teams are to be the heart of restruc-

tured research programs, as the critics suggest, creativity techniques can help. When companies throw together employees from research, marketing, and manufacturing—and sometimes even include customers and suppliers in the mix—pattern-breaking and excursion exercises could help these teams become more cohesive. "Creativity techniques help a group to find a common bond," she says.

Much corporate interest in creativity still focuses on departments that are already strong on this count, such as R&D and marketing. But it would be a mistake to confine creativity efforts so narrowly; why carry coals to Newcastle? Besides, measures that cut costs or improve quality—which often are suggested by shop-floor workers or customer-service staff—usually can be implemented much more quickly than ideas for new products. "Most of our successes with creativity are in continuous improvement," says Dennis Carter, a resource training manager at a Du Pont fiber-making plant in Buffalo.

In the long run, argues Xerox PARC's Brown, corporations and their employees need to learn how to "reinvent innovation, not reinvent invention." Dramatic changes in markets—like the shift from minicomputers to microcomputers—are occurring more frequently and more rapidly, washing away companies that cannot adapt fast enough. Organizations ought to be thinking—creatively—about how to understand and exploit rapid change.

"If we can understand how to do that," Brown says, "then we may be better positioned to tap the inherent genius of invention in the American spirit."

8

Managing Creativity:
A Japanese Model

MIN BASADUR

Dr. Min Basadur visited several major companies in Japan to conduct comparative research on organizational creativity. Unexpected insights emerged during interviews with Japanese managers and are the basis for this article. These managers knew a great deal about North American motivational theory and how to implement it. Employee creativity is managed through deliberate structural means, not to effect direct economic outcomes, but to develop motivation, job satisfaction, and teamwork. Contrasts to North American suggestion systems are made.

The rapidly accelerating rate of technological and environmental change demands much greater organizational adaptability than in the more stable past. Attempting behavioral change has turned out to be very difficult for many North American organizations because they have, by and large, developed along bureaucratic, non-flexible, and non-adaptive lines. Recent research has indicated that people at all organizational levels in North American business and industry can learn to think more creatively, to discover and solve important interfunctional problems, and to innovate new products and new methods faster, all of which results in greater organizational adaptability.[1] Simply put, creativity in organizations is a continuous search for and solving of problems and a creating and implementing of new solutions for the betterment of the organization, its customers, and its members.

Much has been written about the recent business success of Japanese corporations. It is often implied that superior management methods are the key. At the same time, the Japanese are viewed as not being truly creative. They are accused of being very good at copying and nothing more. For example, it is pointed out they have not produced many Nobel laureates, nor have they made many basic science discoveries. It could be argued that this is because they have not yet had the world class training needed by their scientists. Some observers believe the Japanese will soon begin producing Nobel laureates by making world-class training available. This belief is based on the fact that Japanese students are being sent to top North American institutions to learn mathematics and science from the current "masters," much like North American students went to learn from the European masters in the 19th century.

The Japanese may already be better students of creativity than North Americans. They appear to be ahead of North Americans in implementing new ideas about management from the behavioral sciences which our own managers find difficult to accept. These new ideas include improved manufacturing and service management methods for higher quality, efficiency, and flexibility, such as "Just in Time" (J.I.T.), "Statistical Process Controls" (S.P.C.), and "Quality Circles" (Q.C.C.).

Many of these ideas originated in North America in the 1940s and 1950s but have never really caught on and were left in the classroom. Attempts to ap-

Reprinted with permission from Basadur, Min "Managing Creativity: A Japanese Model," *Academy of Management Executive,* Vol. 6, 1992, pp. 29–40.

Min Basadur is a Professor in the College of Business at McMaster University.

ply them in the workplace have often failed. Rather than admit we just don't want to change, North American managers have found it easier to assume that there is something mysterious about Japanese culture that permits new approaches to management to work over there but not here. This article examines the ways in which management ideas that originated in North America are being applied in Japan.

FINDING OUT ABOUT JAPANESE CREATIVITY

A bilingual Japanese colleague of mine set up open-ended interviews with five major Japanese companies including second and third visits in cases when it was necessary to probe more deeply. Comparisons were made with North American firms on emerging themes. To facilitate comparisons, data were gathered during the same time period from eleven leading North American companies. These data were obtained by a combination of questionnaire, in-depth interviews, and shop floor visits. The data from the Japanese and North American companies were organized along emerging themes, similarities, and contrasts. For example, would Japanese styles of creativity favor problem finding activity more than their North American counterparts? Another purpose was to see if Japanese organizations understood creativity as the process pictured in Figure 8.1 and do they try to implement the model.

The model in Figure 8.1 provides a framework for speculation about Japanese management practices. Creativity in organizations is a continuous finding and solving of problems and a creating and implementing of new solutions. *Problem finding* activity means continuously identifying new and useful problems to be solved. This may include finding new product or service opportunities by anticipating new customer needs, discovering ways to improve existing products, services, procedures, and processes or finding opportunities to improve the satisfaction and well-being of organizational members. Finally, problem finding includes defining such new problems and opportunities accu-

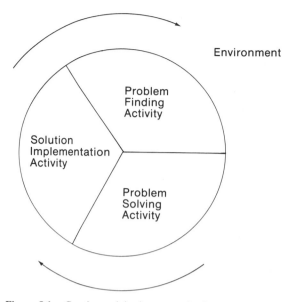

Figure 8.1. Creative activity is an organization.

rately and creatively. *Problem solving* activity means developing new, useful, imaginative solutions to found problems. *Solution implementing* activity means successfully installing such new solutions into the ongoing life of the organization.[2]

Problem finding may be the key to Japanese management success. The more emphasis placed on problem finding, the less is needed for solving and implementation. Solutions are more on target and successful implementation is facilitated. This is especially true when hierarchically lower level employees are invited to participate in the problem finding phase. Ownership and commitment are increased by early inclusion in change making. It takes less time to implement solutions when those affected have been permitted to participate from the beginning in finding and defining the problem and developing the solution.

Trained by traditional business schools in the "scientific management" approach originally identified by Frederick Taylor, most North American managers do not understand the importance of involving employees in early problem finding activities. They assume they are the only ones who know what needs to be done or that they can solve problems faster or better on their own. When these managers attempt to impose their solutions on their subordinates, there can be resentment and subordinates are often left uncommitted. Solutions fail either due to inadequate problem definition or lack of ownership. The same managers are likely to repeat the cycle over and over again hoping to find one solution that will finally be accepted and do some good. Such haphazard problem solving activity wastes human resources and detracts from managerial productivity. Training in creative problem solving is designed to improve upon these inadequate attitudes and behaviors but it is difficult to get many North American organizations to provide such training and to get it used on the job.

Organizations often view training as a luxury to be initiated only when business is good and the pressure is off. It is regarded as an educational experience serving as a reward for people having done a good job, rather than to change attitudes and behaviors. The training is not seen as something that can genuinely change and improve the way work is done. As a result, many management methods are rejected after a short trial period even when they have worked well elsewhere, notably in Japan. The real reason for rejection is often a lack of desire or willpower to make significant changes. Since change is the essence of creativity, the ability to foster change is a major indicator worth observing when comparing management practices in Japan and North America.

PROBLEM FINDING IS EMPHASIZED

The first Japanese company visited was a large international consumer electronics firm. Discussions were held with several senior R&D managers about managing this function. While there were many similarities to North American R&D management, one major difference that emerged was that newly hired R&D scientists and engineers always start their careers with six months in the sales department. The company wants them to learn first hand at the beginning of their careers about the needs and problems of their customers. In the long run,

their jobs will focus on meeting those needs and solving those problems. For the next eighteen months, the new hires gradually work their way back to R&D through stints in various other functions including manufacturing and engineering. This suggests an interesting organizational emphasis on inducing problem finding behavior (anticipating and sensing customer needs) through structural means (job placement and rotation).

The remaining four companies visited were world-class manufacturers of car parts and scale measurement instruments. This time the interviews were with manufacturing and personnel managers and centered on the nature of their Employee Suggestion Systems (E.S.S.). It is not uncommon for employees of top Japanese companies to conceive and implement between forty and one hundred new suggestions per person, per year on average. This figure might amaze most North American managers since leading U.S. companies consider themselves lucky to obtain an average of about two suggestions per person, per year (see Table 8.1). The rest of this article explains not only how it is possible to achieve the Japanese levels, but also the theoretical rationale and comprehensive organizational benefits.

The interviews were in-depth, open-ended question and answer sessions; and shop floor visits. The collected data reveals that the primary objectives of the E.S.S. are motivation, job satisfaction, and group interaction. There is an infrastructure which guarantees that all three phases of creativity are completed. Individuals are encouraged to find problems with their work and improve their own jobs. Suggestions are submitted only after the solution has been demonstrated to work successfully. All suggestions are accepted and given credit. Monetary awards for most ideas are small.

Quality circle activity provides a reservoir of problems to aid individual problem finding activity, and smart managers learn how to get individuals to select problems of strategic importance to solve. Employees are trained that suggestions desired include new and improved products as well as methods. Individuals are encouraged to ask co-

TABLE 8.1
Leading Japanese Companies

Company	# of suggestions	# of employees	per/employee
MATSUSHITA	6,446,935	81,000	79.6
HITACHI	3,618,014	57,051	63.4
MAZDA	3,025,853	23,929	126.5
TOYOTA	2,648,710	55,578	47.6
NISSAN	1,393,745	48,849	38.5
NIPPON DENSO	1,393,745	33,192	41.6
CANON	1,076,356	13,788	78.1
FUJI ELECTRIC	1,022,340	10,226	99.6
TOHOKU OKI	734,044	881	833.2
JVC	738,529	15,000	48.6
TYPICAL LEADING U.S. COMPANY	21,000	9,000	2.3

Reference: Japan Human Relations Association, April, 1988: "The Power of Suggestion"

workers for help in problem solving. If individuals or informal teams cannot solve certain problems, they are referred to a quality circle team or the engineering department for help.

Group-oriented quality circles work supportively with the individually oriented Employee Suggestion System in other ways as well. The team gets credit every time one of its members submits a suggestion. Major celebrations are held by top management each year-end honoring teams and individual members of teams who have performed well in their suggestion work. All new employees are trained the first day on the job about the importance of the E.S.S. and how it works. Managers and supervisors are trained to work closely with subordinates to help them find and solve problems, implement their solution, and provide plenty of positive feedback throughout.

R&D IS EVERYBODY'S BUSINESS

In all four companies, suggestions for improving both procedures and products are encouraged. Employees are trained from the first day on the job that "R&D is everybody's business." For example, in one company of 9,000 employees, 660,000 employee suggestions were received in one year. Of these, 6,000 were suggestions for new products or product improvements and the remainder were suggestions for new methods. New methods are improvements to the work itself—simplifying jobs, accelerating procedures and work flow, and so on.

PROBLEMS ARE GOLDEN EGGS

In the companies studied, creative activity is deliberately induced on the job in a manner that is consistent with Figure 8.1. On the first day on the job, new employees are trained that problems (discontents) are really "golden eggs." In other words, it is good to identify problems. One should be constructively "discontented" with one's job and with company products and seek ways to improve them. In some of the companies, the "golden eggs" are posted on large sheets of paper in the work area. Employees are then encouraged to interact with their co-workers to solve such problems and demonstrate that their solutions can be implemented.

In North America there is a real reluctance to identify problems. Employees, especially managers, often don't want anybody to know they've got problems because they are seen as a sign of weakness and poor performance. Subordinates soon pick up this attitude and adopt a problem avoidance approach to their work ("it didn't happen on my shift" and "that's not our problem").

This leads to neglect of important interfunctional opportunities for improvement and customer needs.

> In these Japanese firms not only are people taught, but there is also a structured mechanism for causing problem finding activity. Workers are provided with problem finding cards. If dissatisfied with something about one's job, the worker writes the discontent on the card and posts it up on a wall poster in the column marked "problems." Workers post their problems, their "golden eggs," their discontents, so other people can see them. If others notice a problem posted which is of interest to them, they will join forces to help solve it.

Group interaction is stimulated and people work together on the problems they select. Later they can write their solutions in the second column beside the problem on the wall poster. There is a third column for implementation documentation. When all three columns are complete, and the individual or small team has done the problem finding and the problem solving and has shown that the solution works, then it can be said that a suggestion has been completed, but not until then. This suggestion can now be submitted.

IMPLEMENTATION BEFORE SUBMISSION AND ALL SUGGESTIONS ACCEPTED

Although not all suggestions are actually implemented, all of them are accepted. In other words, when all three phases of the creative process are completed (problem found, problem solved, solution shown to be implementable) by the employees themselves, a suggestion has been created and is accepted. About ninety-six percent of the suggestions end up being put into practice.

An "idea" is not a "suggestion" until it has gone through all three stages of the creative process modelled in Figure 8.1. Every suggestion receives a monetary award. The vast majority of the suggestions are small $5 (500 yen) ideas. These are accepted and assigned the award by the supervisor on the spot. The suggestions that are more creative and significant are evaluated by a committee against multiple criteria including creativity and contribution to goals; they receive bigger awards of up to $10,000 and more.

The main objective is to accept all ideas and encourage the little ones as well as the big ones. It is the *process* of getting involved in one's work that counts, not the quality of any single idea. The goal is to have thinking workers and a spirit of never-ending improvement. Of the small ratio (about four percent) of accepted suggestions that do not get implemented right away, most are the kind that require skills beyond the scope of the suggestors. The team leader or the supervisor can get additional help from other departments for these ideas. Also, it may be found that the implementation of a suggestion is not timely or is inappropriate in the bigger picture. In this case, the idea is not implemented, but is given credit anyway. This is the way the system is supposed to operate and works very well in actual practice.

Employees are told they are expected to create new ideas. Some companies even establish informal goals per person per month. Each formal work group has a team leader who ensures that daily production is met and new ideas keep flowing at the same time. The team leader communicates, coordinates, and gets help across the organization as needed. This prevents the work group from worrying unduly about maintaining daily production and saying "we don't have time to work on new ideas." Workers are given overtime as needed to complete their suggestions. The overtime is usually aimed at implementation work. Much of the problem finding and problem solving work is done continuously in people's minds off the job as well as on the job. When people are creatively involved in their work, ideas about new problems and solutions can occur to them at any time.

COACHING, POSITIVE FEEDBACK, AND FACILITATOR SKILLS EMPHASIZED FOR MANAGERS

The secret to making this process work begins with getting people to take ownership of problem finding as well as evaluation and implementation. Employees learn to accept evaluation and implementation of their ideas as part of their jobs. Their supervisors and managers support them and help them to be successful throughout the process. This includes helping the employee evaluate a potential suggestion's worthiness and how to make it work.

The boss is trained to be an encourager and coach, providing positive feedback at every opportunity. The system is structured to make sure such coaching and feedback occurs. A supervisor will help a new employee find a "golden egg" and develop a suggestion as part of the orientation process. Employees are given coaching on the appropriateness of "golden eggs" to be posted and positive feedback on all contributions.

On larger projects, the team leader and supervisor make sure that additional time (including overtime) and other resources are made available to workers as needed. Also, teams routinely make presentations to the rest of the organization during working hours, typically in the company cafeteria. The plant manager acts as a master of ceremonies, giving praise, recognition, and expert commentary as each project is presented. Suggestions which require higher level consideration for awards or implementation enter a formal system of evaluation and feedback. The suggestors are given feedback and positive recognition by design at several stages of this formal process.

Managers are not permitted to submit suggestions—that is, to get directly involved in the Employee Suggestion System; however, they are trained to get indirectly involved. For example, if a manager happens to think up an idea, rather than submit it, he or she is trained to figure out what problem that idea is trying to solve. The manager then goes down into the ranks and seeks out someone willing to post that problem. The group, or anybody in the group, can solve it themselves, probably with a different solution. This is how problem ownership is built.

Managers learn how to "dump problems into the fray" and let the ownership grow. This contrasts with the old-fashioned scientific management approach which designates management as "thinkers" and labor as "doers," which is not very scientific at all because thinking is done from the top down and wastes the minds of the workers. Worse yet, changes are usually sprung on the work force suddenly and are resisted.

First line supervisors find themselves stuck in the middle—expected to support the change but facing an unwilling, untrusting, and unaccepting group of subordinates who feel no ownership for the change. According to this research, Japanese managers are trained to facilitate change, not impose it. The Employee Suggestion System provides an excellent tool to accomplish this facilitative approach.

MOTIVATION IS THE OUTCOME

When the top managers of these leading companies were asked what the primary objective of their Employee Suggestion System was, none of them said new products or new methods. Furthermore, none of them said lower costs, or higher profits. In fact, none of them mentioned any final economic outcomes. In contrast, all of them said *motivated people*.

These Japanese organizations believe that workers get motivated when they get a chance to be creative on the job. Employees enjoy coming to work. This is what the Japanese call "cheerfulness" and we call "job satisfaction." This creative activity also stimulates group interaction. People help each other solve problems which provides the opportunity for genuine team building.

People find real reasons to work together and feel good about their accomplishments, monetary awards, and the fact that their work team gets credit for their individual suggestions. Individual awards, especially larger ones, are shared with the team. The team decides how much the individual gets and how much they keep for their "activity fund." The activity fund is accumulated by the work teams to fund personal development, recreation, physical education, and other growth activities. The fund grows from quality circle awards and employee suggestion awards. Individuals get recognition and the team gets recognition.

All of the companies said they have found that when people are given the opportunity to engage in creative activity (as it has been described here), they become very motivated. This causes them to want to participate even more in creative activity. It also causes them to work harder on performing their normal routine jobs better—more quality, more quantity, and lower cost. This is consistent with increasing organizational efficiency and short-term organizational effectiveness. Figure 8.2[3] models this simple management process.

CONSISTENCY WITH MOTIVATION RESEARCH

Organizational research conducted by P.E. Mott showed that effective organizations have three major simultaneous characteristics: efficiency, adaptability, and flexibility.[3] Efficiency is the ability to organize for routine production. Every organization is turning out some kind of product (a needed good or service).

Efficient organizations are customer focussed; they know their customer and product. Over the years they have developed good routines for making their product the best they can with current technology. They produce a high quantity, quality product, and maintain a high output over input ratio (low cost) during production.

Effective organizations are also able to respond and react to sudden temporary changes or interruptions. They can deal with unexpected disruptions and get back quickly to their normal routine without getting stuck in red tape. Flexibility is a way of preserving efficiency. Flexibility and efficiency are both necessary in the short run.

Adaptability is a longer range characteristic and refers to an organization's capacity to continually and intentionally change its routines and find new and better ways to do the work. Adaptable organizations anticipate problems and develop timely solutions. They stay abreast of new methods and technologies that may be applicable to the organization. The organization's members accept good, new ideas and make sure new solutions and techniques get installed and maintained. Acceptance of new ideas is widespread across all organizational departments.

The creative process of problem finding, problem solving and solution implementation becomes more vital as the amount of change confronting the oganization increases. Up until recently, many or-

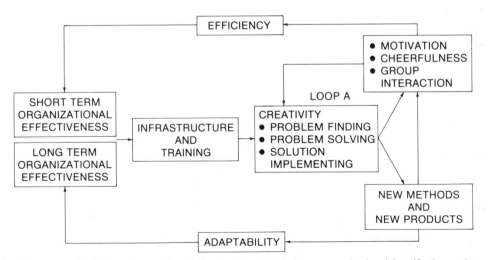

Figure 8.2. Japanese model for fostering problem finding and creativity to increase motivation, job satifaction, and teamwork.

ganizations could be effective by concentrating only on efficiency and flexibility. Today, adaptability is equally important because of the rapidly accelerating rate of change. Adaptability is crucial for long-term effectiveness.

Motivating people by providing the opportunity for creative activity is consistent with the motivation literature in industrial and organizational psychology. One major category of motivational theories are the *need* theories. Two important motivational need sets are the need for competence and the need for curiosity and activity. These two needs and related motives provide the most direct explanation of how creativity is a means for motivating people.[4]

> People have a desire to master their environment. Such mastery is intrinsically pleasurable and independent of outside rewards. This need for competence is aroused when people are faced with new challenging situations and dissipates after repeated mastery of the task. The concept of intrinsic motivation is also consistent with the notion that curiosity, activity, and exploration are enjoyed for their own sake. This was discovered in early animal research and in later studies in humans.

People develop negative attitudes toward repetitive tasks and report experiencing fatigue and boredom. Berlyne suggests that people adapt to certain levels of stimulation and take action to reduce discrepancies from these levels. The implication is similar to Herzberg's notion that challenging jobs are motivating in themselves.

Other motivation theories are also consistent with what is being practiced in the companies in this study. Herzberg proposes that the way to motivate most people is by redesigning their jobs so the work itself provides opportunity for growth, challenge, stimulation, learning, and recognition.[5] McClelland has advanced the need for achievement as the primary driving force motivating organizational members.[6] By giving employees the opportunity to find challenging problems, solve them, and implement solutions, the Employee Suggestion System taps into both the forces of intrinsically re-

warding work and the need for achievement. According to Maslow, offering employees the opportunity to satisfy their higher level needs for self-esteem and for self-actualization through work accomplishment is the best way to motivate them.[7]

The Japanese Employee Suggestion System is a straightforward example of how these two highest level needs can be met. People are provided with the opportunity to use their creativity. They seek out work-related challenges of interest to themselves, then find success and recognition in developing implementable solutions that are welcomed and celebrated by the organization.

Motivation theory has not remained static since the 1950s and 1960s. Deci and Ryan provided a comprehensive review of intrinsic motivation.[8] Locke and Latham showed that when people are given a chance to set their own goals (the problem-anticipating aspect of problem finding) and the more specifically they state those goals (the problem definition aspect of problem finding), the more motivated they are to achieve those goals.[9]

The Japanese may not yet be at the forefront of initiating theoretical research, but their ability to apply motivation theory is impressive and far more than simple copying. As Japanese students continue to learn from the "masters," the time will come when their research informs our practice.

The vast majority of North American business and industry is still organized and managed on the scientific management concept made popular by Frederick Taylor in 1911.[10] One of the main premises of scientific management is that people at work are motivated by one dominant factor—money. This is the concept of "economic man." In spite of research showing that most people at work are multi-motivated (money does play a role but in a complex way), most managers continue to manage by simplistic, economic formulae.

The motivating factor in most North American employee suggestion systems is extrinsic, usually money. A few employees suggest a few big ideas that save the company large sums of money and win major cash awards for themselves. Most people don't participate.

In contrast, Japanese employee suggestion

TABLE 8.2
Contrasting Elements Summary Employee Suggestion Systems

	New (Japanese)	Traditional (North American)
Culture	• Group & individual synchronized	• Individual
Core objectives	• Thinking workers • Never ending improvement • Individual growth • Communications • Decision making	• Breakthrough • Produce savings
Management	• Primary responsibility	• Secondary at best
Area of suggestion	• Within your job & your workplace	• Outside of your job or your workplace
Evaluation	• Simple • Quick answers • Supervisor responsibility • Lots of suggester involvement • Most accepted	• Very structured • Slow answers • Evaluator responsibility • Little suggester involvement • Most rejected
Communication	• Employee to supervisor • Employee to employee	• Employee to evaluator to supervision to management
Awards	• Intrinsic	• Extrinsic

systems emphasize a large number of small ideas and everyone participates. There are small monetary awards for each implementable suggestion shared by the participating members. Larger awards are given for ideas of greater scope, but the vast majority of suggestions win small awards. The real awards, as far as employees are concerned, are the feelings of accomplishment, recognition, and growth.

TOP DOWN IMPETUS AND STRATEGIC ALIGNMENT

In the Japanese companies interviewed, training and a well-developed infrastructure are used to make creative activity important. They are also used to align creative activity strategically with important organizational goals as an every day routine. Managers are trained to help their employees find, solve, and implement problems and solutions.

As clear company goals are articulated by top management and specific departmental objectives

and subgoals are developed, these are communicated downward to guide individuals and teams in their selection of problems. This results in a close alignment of E.S.S. activity with strategic corporate needs. Managers who are skillful in the E.S.S. learn how to influence their subordinates toward including problems which are related to specific goals and objectives for their departments.

The reward system reinforces the importance of creative activity to the company. Not only does the E.S.S. provide extrinsic and intrinsic rewards for employees, but their managers' performance appraisals are also based in part on their ability to get their subordinates to perform well in the E.S.S.

In the Japanese companies I visited, Management by Objectives (M.B.O.) is integrated with the Employee Suggestion System. Typically, the manager's objectives will include helping people create and implement suggestions. This emphasis on getting subordinates involved in creating new ideas is part of the long-range process of management. The belief is that if people are encouraged to use their thinking power on a habitual daily basis, major tangible benefits will accrue to the organization in the long run.

Quality circle (Q.C.C.) group activity also serves to help align E.S.S. activity with strategic goals. Q.C.C. work is a concentrated attack on major "theme" problems identified by upper management. These themes are assigned about every six months. A bonus of Q.C.C. activity is that it also provides a regular forum for spontaneous discussion of spinoff problems during Q.C.C. team meetings. The Q.C.C. infrastructure serves as a deliberate reservoir for problem finding to fuel the Employee Suggestion System program. Both the group-oriented Quality Circles and the individually oriented Employee Suggestion System are sparked by top management involvement. Not only is top management instrumental in setting direction and relevant goals, it also works hard insuring that such goals are followed up. Celebrations are hosted at the end of the year by presidential level management for teams which have performed well in Q.C.C. and E.S.S. activity.

JOB REDESIGN, ENRICHMENT, AND ADAPTABILITY

Proactive creative activity leads to a continuous supply of new methods and new products. This is synonymous with Mott's definition of organizational adaptability. Not only are new problems deliberately anticipated and solved, but also acceptance of the new solutions by employees is virtually assured because the employees are finding and solving their own problems and implementing their own changes. They have high ownership of the solutions and are redesigning their own jobs. This is consistent with a well-documented axiom of organizational psychology: "People don't resist change; they do resist being changed."

Herzberg's research on job satisfaction suggests that motivation can be achieved best by factors intrinsic to the work itself, such as responsibility and opportunity for growth and achievement. The validity of job enrichment, which is based on Herzberg's dual factor theory is supported by the findings reported in this article. Many companies have tried to redesign employee jobs to make them more intrinsically rewarding, however, evaluation of research results have been inconsistent. This may be because employees do not participate in it. The Japanese model goes one step further by letting employees be creative and allowing them to enrich their own jobs. Perhaps this is the missing link for North American companies who have tried other approaches to job enrichment and failed.

TEAMWORK AND INDIVIDUAL WORK HARMONIZED

When individuals start working together on problems of common interest, solve them, and implement solutions together, group cohesiveness develops. Cohesiveness is an important factor in group productivity. The E.S.S. encourages small, informal teams to develop. People who want to work together on problems of common interest join up. The attraction contributes to cohesiveness. Group cohesiveness is also built more formally through the Quality Circle approach. Even though Q.C.C. activity is, in theory, voluntary, in actual practice everybody is a member of a quality circle team because it is the same as their functional work unit team.

One of the firms stressed that in their experience Q.C.C. didn't work well alone and neither did E.S.S., but together they worked very well. The firm recommended that both be used for best results.

The Quality Circle (Q.C.C.) system provides opportunities for group performance, recognition, and initiative. The Employee Suggestion System (E.S.S.) adds opportunities for individual performance, recognition, and initiative. Q.C.C. activity is highly structured and uses analytical problem solving tools such as fishboning and root cause analysis. The team must stick to the theme and not pursue other problems or ideas. Prior to the introduction of E.S.S., this restriction bothered many people. If one were sitting in a Quality Circle working on the assigned theme and suddenly thought up an idea to solve a totally unrelated problem, it would be frustrating to not be permitted to voice the idea.

The Employee Suggestion System provides an outlet for finding, solving and implementing solutions to off-theme problems. The team gets credit for every suggestion that one of their team members submits individually and there is little conflict between the E.S.S. and Q.C.C. systems.

In contrast, attempts by some North American companies to install group-based Q.C.C. systems have run into conflict with long-established individual-based suggestion sytems. These companies have not yet figured out how to integrate the two systems.

HOW DO NORTH AMERICAN SYSTEMS COMPARE?

One key to the success of the Japanese Employee Suggestion System is the emphasis on problem finding. In North America, promotions and rewards go more often to people who appear not to have many problems. Managers don't feel they have enough time for problem finding. They feel they are too busy doing their "regular work" which often means fire-fighting activity and meeting short-term cost and profit goals. They want their people feeling the same way, and put focus on solutions, not problems. While the term "constructive discontent" is something that is often given lip service in North American organizations, the Japanese companies studied in this research are promoting and implementing it through simple structural methods.

Most North American suggestion systems use the suggestion box approach. Employees dump ideas in the suggestion box without the responsibility of evaluating them first or explaining just what the problem is that they are trying to solve. Managers evaluate the ideas and the employee waits to hear the judgment. Usually, the wait is long and most ideas are rejected. Managers find it onerous to judge so many suggestions and worry about the amount of change they represent. Many sug-

gestions are difficult to understand since they have neither been discussed, nor shared with other employees. There is no incentive to share an idea with anybody for reasons such as the boss may not want to hear about new changes, other employees will want to share in the award, or someone may claim it as their own idea. The main incentive is to make lots of money for the individual submitting the suggestion. Small ideas are not worth the effort.

> Teamwork, job satisfaction, and motivation are all secondary. In addition, many employees of North American companies do not receive awards for suggestions to improve their own job. They are rewarded only for ideas that are outside their own job. This goes against all the rules of motivation theory.

Finally, in many traditional North American companies, new product ideas are considered the job of R&D departments exclusively. Suggestion systems are concerned only with methods and procedures to save money or increase efficiency. New product ideas are not encouraged from employees of other departments and usually there are no organizational mechanisms to facilitate their emergence or development.

DISCOVERING HOW AND WHY JAPANESE ORGANIZATIONS INDUCE CREATIVITY

The major discovery of this research is that Japanese organizations demonstrate a great deal of knowledge about inducing employee creativity through deliberate structural means. They believe they derive important benefits in doing so. This study indicates that top Japanese organizations recognize, emphasize, support, and induce problem finding which is elevated to at least equal priority as problem solving and solution implementation. They recognize all three as separate important activities which is consistent with research that suggest that all three activities need to be nurtured and managed to achieve organizational creativity. They have devised structural means through the way they place R&D hires and their Employee Suggestion Systems to induce creativity throughout the organization.

Through managing the Employee Suggestion System, the Japanese companies in our study implement what theory and literature suggests needs to be done to induce creative behavior, to get creative output in the organization, and to motivate members of the organization. By doing so, they get tangible creative output like short-term costs savings and new products and procedures. They also reap other important benefits, the most important being motivated, committed people who enjoy their jobs, participate in teamwork, and get fully involved in advancing the company goals.

NOTES

The author would like to acknowledge Professor Mitsuru Wakabayashi, associate professor, Dept. of Educational Psychology, Nagoya University, Dr. Bruce Paton, vice president, Internal Consulting, Frito-Lay, Inc., and Jim O'Neal, present of Northern European Operations. Pepsi-Co Foods International for their help in laying the groundwork for this research.

1. For discussion and supporting data on organizational creativity see the author's following research. M.S. Basadur, G.B. Graen, and S.G. Green, "Training in Creative Problem Solving: Effects on Ideation and Problem Finding and Solving in an Industrial Research Organization," in *Organizational Behavior and Human Performance, 30,* 1982, 41–70; M.S. Basadur, "Needed Research in Creativity for Business and Industrial Applications," in S.G. Isaksen (ed.) *Frontiers of Creativity Research: Beyond the Basics* (Buffalo, N.Y.: Bearly, 1987); M.S. Basadur, G.B. Graen, and T.A. Scandura, "Training Effects on Attitudes Toward Divergent Thinking Among Manufacturing Engineers," in *Journal of Applied Psychology,* Vol. 71, No. 4, 1986, 612–617.

2. For more information concerning the creative process in organizations, see M.S. Basadur, G.B. Graen, and M. Wakabayashi, "Identifying Individual Differences in Creative Problem Solving Style" in *Journal of Creative Behavior,* Vol. 24, No. 2, 1990, 111–131; M.S. Basadur, "Managing the Creative Process in Organizations," in M.J. Runco (ed.) *Problem Finding, Problem Solving and Creativity* (New York: Ablex, 1991, in press). The latter is also available from the author as McMaster University Faculty of Business Research and Working Paper Series, No. 357, April 1991.

3. See P.E. Mott, *The Characteristics of Effective Organizations* (New York, NY: Harper and Row, 1972); M.S. Basadur, "Impacts and Outcomes of Creativity in Organizational Settings," in S.G. Isaksen, M.C. Murdock, R.L. Firestein, and D.J. Treffinger (ed.) *The Emergence of a Discipline: Nurturing and Developing Creativity,* Volume II (New York: Ablex, 1991; in press). The latter is also available as McMaster University Faculty of Business Research and Working Paper Series. No. 358, April 1991.

4. For more discussion on human needs and related motives see D.E. Berlyne, "Arousal and Reinforcement" in Nebraska Symposium on Motivation, D. Levine, ed. (Lincoln, NE: University of Nebraska Press, 1967) and R.W. White, "Motivation reconsidered: The concept of competence," *Psychological Review,* 66(5), 297–333.

5. For further discussion on motivation see F. Herzberg, B. Mausner, and B. Snyderman, *The Motivation to Work* (2nd ed.) (New York, NY: Wiley, 1959).

6. See D.C. McClelland, *Personality* (New York, NY: Dryden Press, 1951).

7. See A.H. Maslow, *Motivation and Personality* (New York, NY: Harper and Row, 1954).

8. See E.L. Deci and R.M. Ryan, *Intrinsic Motivation and Self-determination in Human Behavior* (New York, NY: Plenum Press, 1985).

9. See E.A. Locke and G.P. Latham, "Work Motivation and Satisfaction: Light at the End of the Tunnel," *Psychological Service,* Vol. 1, No. 4, July 1990, 240–246.

10. For review of scientific management see F.W. Taylor, *Principles of Scientific Management* (New York, NY: Norton, reprinted 1967, originally published in 1911).

3

The Management of Technical Productivity and Vitality

9

Assessing the Value of Your Technology

JAMES W. TIPPING, EUGENE ZEFFREN, AND ALAN R. FUSFELD

R&D's role in the innovation process can be meaningfully represented by a hierarchy of managerial factors (The Technology Value Pyramid) that provide the foundations, links to strategy and financial outcomes for the corporation. The recognition of these TVP factors, together with an assembled menu of metrics, allows the model to be used to track the contribution to innovation performance at different levels of the TVP. The TVP model can be used to track the performance both prospectively and retrospectively, to diagnose weaknesses in the R&D organization and to plan for improvement in R&D contribution to the corporation. The various R&D stakeholders have different interests and perspectives

Acknowledgment: The authors recognize and appreciate the contributions from the members of the R&D effectiveness subcommittee of the IRI's Research-on-Research Committee.

Reprinted with permission from *Research-Technology Management*, September-October, 1995.

James Tipping is an independent consultant. Previously, he was responsible for corporate R&D at ICI America. *Eugene Zeffren* is President of Helene Curtis U.S.A. *Alan Fusfeld* is President of the Fusfeld Group, a management of technology consulting firm.

on the innovation process, and these are accommodated by the TVP model and the menu of metrics.

Management's most serious responsibility is to account for, and to use as effectively as possible, the corporate assets with which it has been entrusted. To date, R&D management has not devised a methodology through which it can satisfactorily discharge this responsibility in any way other than in a passive fiduciary sense, and this often has little or no relationship to agreed business goals. Consequently, top corporate executives have no mechanism with which to either judge or participate in what is potentially the corporation's best competitive weapon—its technology!

Even though they possess some of the world's best-equipped R&D facilities, staffed by the most talented scientists, it is doubtful that U.S. corporations are deriving anything like the competitive advantage possible from their R&D efforts. Despite the recognized importance of technology it would appear that many corporations are finding it easier to look elsewhere for competitive advantage—for example, from marketing, acquisition, capital investment, and so on. Even those world-class corporations that do look seriously to technology for competitive advantage are frustrated in their attempts to couple their R&D effectively into their businesses, in part because of the absence of an accepted methodology to measure effectiveness (value) and continuously improve their R&D. We believe it is the responsibility of R&D management to develop this methodology.

Accounting for, and in turn improving, R&D performance and effectiveness to produce value calls for a shared understanding with the stakeholders of the role that R&D plays in that corporation, to agree to that role, and to be partners in the R&D process. This partnership may well be different for different stakeholders. It calls for R&D to clearly communicate with the stakeholders so that the stakeholders become truly involved with R&D; this involvement must be at a level which to date is rarely seen in U.S. corporations. It is only through this high level of interaction that a partnership can be established that both allows leading and lagging indicators of value-producing R&D performance to be credibly established, and ultimately allows leverageable value to be created by R&D.

The true value from R&D becomes apparent only when one looks closely at the role that R&D plays throughout the creation and development of the innovations necessary to both defend and grow the corporation's businesses. One cannot judge the value of an R&D organization to a corporation simply by looking at the new products it has produced recently, just as one cannot judge the value of a house by looking at the exterior brickwork. R&D protects and supports the day-to-day operations of businesses every day of the year but rarely accounts for these activities and therefore rarely receives credit for doing so. Furthermore, would it be worthwhile to put a value on the know-how that, say, a Du Pont or a General Electric has built up over the past 100 years? Certainly one wouldn't do this by simply counting patents or measuring recent achievements; this would miss the tremendous technology platform of potential value these companies have built up, and any worthwhile measurement of R&D value must provide a way of giving credit for this value and, in particular, changes in the value from year to year. While, arguably, the value of R&D is reflected in the share price of a corporation, it is our contention that curent approaches do not allow a true assessment of this value to be made.

We have developed an approach to these important considerations whereby the technology development and innovation processes are described in a pyramid of values which derive from R&D. This Technology Value Pyramid (TVP) model (Figure 9.1) allows the stakeholder to be easily involved with factors important in these processes in the most direct and relevant manner, and to be presented with simple measurement tools that can be used in both a leading and lagging manner.

CEOs, business heads, board members, the financial community, and leaders and managers of R&D will benefit most from use of the TVP model. All businesses will find the TVP model to be rel-

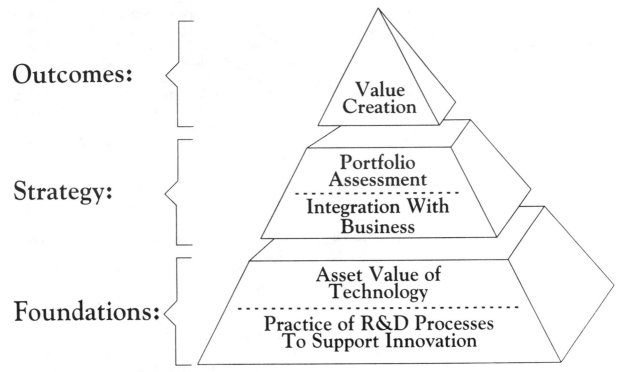

The Five Managerial Factors

1. *Value Creation (VC).—Demonstrates the value of R&D activities to the positioning, profitability and growth of the corporation and to the creation of shareholder value.*

2. *Portfolio Assessment (PA).—Communicates the total R&D program arrayed across various dimensions of interest, including time horizon, level of risk, core competency exploitation, and new/old business. This allows optimization of the total program for the corporation's benefit.*

3. *Integration With Business (IWB).—Indicates the degree of integration, the commitment of the business to the R&D processes and programs, teamwork, and ability to exploit technology across the organization.*

4. *Asset Value of Technology (AVT).—Indicates the strength and vitality of the firm's technology (e.g., proprietary assets, know-how, people, etc.) and foreshadows the potential of the R&D organization to create future value for the firm.*

5. *Practice of R&D Processes To Support Innovation (PRD).—Indicates the efficiency and effectiveness of R&D processes in producing useful output for the firm. The processes include project management practices, idea generation, communication, and other "best practices" in managing R&D.*

    Figure 9.1.   Technology value pyramid.

evant but its precise use will vary from business to business, depending on the balance of the research within individual portfolios. (Although the TVP approach can be applied to the public R&D measurement area, this article focuses on the private sector and only makes reference to the public sector for comparison purposes.)

FIVE MANAGERIAL FACTORS

As shown in Figure 9.1, the Technology Value Pyramid represents the hierarchical integration of the five managerial factors that describe the innovative capability of the firm. Metrics associated with each factor allow the TVP to be used to analyze the performance of the R&D organization, and to guide improvement efforts. Used prospectively, the TVP can be a "leading indicator" of R&D's contribution to the firm. The TVP is based on the beliefs that in order to create and sustain technological advantage for the corporation:

- The R&D effort must defend and enhance the value of the corporation.
- There must be a linkage of R&D and the strategic aims of the corporation.
- R&D must be able to sustain its capability to produce useful output over the long term.

These beliefs imply that not only will one have to assess the ability of an R&D organization to create value for the corporation, but also, one must be able to assess how well R&D is linked to the business goals, and how well it actually carries out its R&D functions. Effective measurements in these areas are both the key to understanding and the basis for improvement.

Two managerial factors, *Practice of R&D Processes To Support Innovation* and *Asset Value of Technology,* are the core operational elements of the R&D enterprise, the nuts and bolts of the operation. Effective management at these levels is characterized by high technical output and efficient technology management practices. Metrics to assess the adequacy of the foundation would be those that allow measurement of parameters relevant to those R&D practices that help spur innovation, that allow an assessment of the value of the technology development capability of the organization (its asset value), and that allow the assessment of the likelihood of sustaining or enhancing that value over time. This level is the foundation of the pyramid.

The next level in the pyramid relates to business and technology strategy. The managerial factors at this level are *Integration with Business* and *Portfolio Assessment.* These factors reflect on how well a firm's technology strategy is linked with its business strategy, from both a corporate and a business unit perspective. Using the appropriate metrics, one can define how the various steps in a firm's process or product creation activity link to

the various levels of the model that show how the business creates value for its customers. Measurements in this area also allow an assessment of the portfolio of projects, both from the point of view of how well they will accomplish the firm's business objectives and how well they allow the developed competitive advantage to be sustained. Thus, measurements here deal with such issues as a quantitative assessment of strategic alignment as well as the extent of investment in a firm's core technical competencies.

Value Creation is the managerial factor at the top of the pyramid, and is the overarching goal of every R&D program. The TVP's foundations are linked to Value Creation through strategy. Measurements of Value Creation demonstrate how the technology development effort has contributed to the growth of the firm and the growth (if any) of its profitability. Thus, these metrics lead to an assessment of R&D's contribution to shareholder value. Used prospectively with respect to the current project portfolio, they can also indicate the potential of the R&D program to create future value for the firm.

The TVP model rests on three basic assumptions:

- *Wealth creation stems from the innovation process.* Hence, the output of R&D is directly linked to enhancing the value of the firm.
- *The various stakeholders in R&D have different interests.* Hence, measurements key to one group will be secondary to others.
- *The time scale of interest of the various stakeholders will vary.* Therefore, measurements must allow different stakeholders to address their particular period of interest for measuring the R&D activity.

Our research tells us that the primary stakeholders and the TVP factors expected to be of greatest interest to them vary as follows:

- The stakeholders most interested in value creation will be the board, financial community, and the CEO.

- Business management will be keenly interested in metrics that assess the degree of integration of R&D with the business and the balance within the project portfolio relative to business unit needs.
- R&D management will be appropriately concerned with all levels of the pyramid but will likely be most concerned with both portfolio assessment and the value of the technology assets within the firm.
- Finally, the R&D staff is likely to be most keenly interested in measurements of the practice of R&D to support innovation.

THE MENU OF METRICS

In building the model, we focused on those measurements relevant to both the building and sustaining of the firm's competitive advantage. The particular set of measures appropriate for a firm will vary by industry type, and within an industry by a firm's competitive strategy (e.g., cost, differentiation, combinations of cost and differentiation). The menu of metrics that forms the substance of the Technology Value Pyramid provides a broad selection of measures; firms can select those that make sense for them based upon their individual business strategies and their industry type. The menu of metrics is presented in Table 9.1.

The menu was derived from almost two years of discussion and debate within IRI's Research on Research Subcommittee on the Measurement of the Effectiveness and Productivity of R&D, with input from the Quality Directors Network. The metrics chosen represent those considered to be the most generally relevant and useful set of measurements considered for the various factors. Information on more than one factor can sometimes be gleaned from a single metric.

UTILITY AND APPLICATION

Previous attempts to deal with the measurement of R&D value have been dissatisfying in many ways.

Those that treated only sales or profit generation often did not address the needs of the technical community. These needs include the need to protect the longer-term future of the firm (addressed in the TVP through selection of relevant measures of Portfolio Assessment and Asset Value of the Technology), the need to assess development of the organization (using metrics of the Asset Value of Technology and Practice of R&D Processes To Support Innovation factors) and the need to assess how well the firm's core technical competencies are being developed and protected (Portfolio Assessment, Asset Value of the Technology, and Practice of R&D Processes To Support Innovation factors).

Previous measurement proposals that focused on R&D practices and ignored value creation gave some business managers the sense that R&D was parochial and myopic. The TVP makes it clear that a holistic view is the only comprehensive way to measure and appreciate R&D's contribution to a company. It provides the flexibility for a firm from any industry to assess R&D's true value to that firm.

A powerful feature of the model is its applicability to various organizational formats for managing R&D—centralized, decentralized and hybrid. The centralized format has one laboratory organization, usually a corporate lab supporting all technical activities in the firm, from upstream applied research and technology development (including basic research) to product and process development and technical service. Decentralized formats have no corporate lab and all technical work is carried out by business unit labs. Hybrids will have a corporate laboratory, usually handling upstream work and new business technology development needs, and perhaps new technical competency development, with business unit labs handling product development, process development and technical service.

By using the TVP model, R&D and business unit leaders can understand the broad responsibilities of R&D and can jointly decide which measures will be appropriate for that business unit. The chief technical officer must work with the CEO and gen-

TABLE 9.1
Technology Value Pyramid Menu of Metrics

Metric/Factor	Definition	Comments
1. Financial return/VC		
a. New Sales Ratio (NSR)	The ratio of sales revenue in year i from product developments commercialized in years $i - j$ to $i - l$ to total sales revenue in year i, or: $$NSR = (1/Sales) \times \sum_{N=i-j}^{N=i-l} (NP\ Sales)$$ where: NP Sales = sales revenue in year i from product developments commercialized in year N; Sales = total sales revenue in year i.	Metrics for determining the value of the investment in R&D require a system for identifying and tracking over time the cost and commercial outcomes of R&D activities, by programs or by individual projects as well as on a total basis. In this category, three basic metrics are needed to determine the value-creation benefits of R&D: New Sales Ratio (NSR, 1a); Cost Savings Ratio (CSR, 1b), and R&D Intensity (RI, 1d). Most other useful financial metrics can be derived from these three basic metrics. NSR is essentially the fraction of sales derived from new products, with the time frame being chosen as appropriate for the company and/or industry. Since technical effort is usually the source of cost savings from process developments and for formula modifications, CSR is an attempt to capture that in a reliable manner. As seen in Metric 5, Gross Profit Margin, the gross profit number used in CSR represents the revenues minus cost of goods sold, including product cost and direct manufacturing cost. The latter are those costs that can be reduced by technology development efforts, and to the extent they are, they represent contributions from R&D.
b. Cost Savings Ratio (CSR)	The ratio of savings in the cost of goods sold in year i from process developments or product changes adopted in years $i - k$ to $i - l$ to average gross profits in year i, or: $$CSR = (1/GP) \times \sum_{N=i-k}^{N=i-l} (CG\ Savings)$$ where: CG Savings = reduction in cost of goods sold in year i from process developments or product changes adopted in year N; GP = average gross profit for business unit in year i.	
c. R&D Yield	The gross profit (GP) contribution from the sale of new and improved products (NP) and from the lower cost of goods from new and improved processes or new formulations (CR). R&D Yield = NP + CR, where: NP = GP × NSR CR = GP × CSR, or: R&D Yield = GP (NSR + CSR)	The time frame is important for proper use of these metrics. When i = current year or earlier, the metrics are retrospective; when i = next year or later, the metrics are prospective. In these definitions, j and k are constants which reflect the strategic emphasis and/or industry characteristics of the business enterprise. To utilize these metrics, appropriate values must be selected for j and k, and operational definitions must be established for product development, process development and R&D expenditures. This should be straightforward in most firms.
d. R&D Return	The ratio of R&D benefits to R&D investment. R&D Return = R&D Yield/ R&D Effort = (GP/Sales) × (NSR + CSR)/RI where: R&D Effort = Annual expenditure on R&D. RI = R&D Intensity $$= \frac{R\&D\ Effort_i}{Sales_i}$$	

Table 9.1—*Continued*

Metric/Factor	Definition	Comments
2. Projected value of the R&D pipeline/VC, PA		
a. Projected Sales Value from Pipeline	Fraction of future sales by year projected from projects in the R&D pipeline, incorporating probability of attaining objective for each project.	Most companies attempt to project future sales and income from projects in the pipeline; the cumulative value of these projects represents the projected value of the pipeline in total. Such projections must always be done with a careful understanding of the assumptions behind the probability determinations. Care must be taken not to let biases for or against individual projects influence the assignment of probabilities of sucess for the various projects
b. Projected Income Value from Pipeline	Fraction of future net income (and/or return) by year projected from projects in the R&D pipeline, incorporating NPV times probabilitiy of attaing objective for each project.	
3. Comparative manufacturing cost/VC, AVT	Benchmarked manufacturing cost data vs. competition for substantially identical manufacturing steps or for producing substantially the same product (eliminating factors unrelated to technology-based differences).	While most firms have accurate data on their own manufacturing costs, the generation of accurate manufacturing cost data for the competition is considerably more difficult. Therefore, when using this measurement, the firmness of the estimate of the competitive manufacturing cost should be identified.
4. Product quality and reliability/VC, AVT		
a. Customer or Consumer Evaluation	Relative quality (as evaluated by the customer/consumer) vs. competitive product in blinded product evaluation by techniques appropriate to the industry segment.	The two measures provided here are best used together. Each firm will generally have a preferred technique for evaluating with customers or consumers how well their products perform versus competition.
b. Reliability/Defect Rate Assessment	At the firm level, fraction of company's product output that meets or exceeds the established quality standards. At the product level, fraction of a given product's quarterly output that meets or exceeds the established quality standards.	
5. Gross profit margin/VC, AVT	Gross Profit as a percentage of sales, where gross profit equals net sales minus cost of goods sold (product costs plus direct manufacturing costs). Value assessment should be based on *change* in gross profit margin from period to period. (Periods should be appropriate to an industry and may be in excess of 1 year.)	Gross profit margin is used in assessing the value of the technology assets of the firm and R&D's contribution to value creation, since beyond direct manufacturing costs and costs of goods sold, other activities of the firm have significant influences on profit margin. In any event, users of this metric must be sure of the connection to the R&D enterprise.

Table 9.1—*Continued*

Metric/Factor	Definition	Comments
6. Market share/VC, AVT		
a. Direct Market Share	Company (or business unit) market share in various categories measured as appropriate for the industry or category. As with gross profit margin, changes should be assessed at least annually to determine rate of progress or decline.	Market share determinations need to be approached cautiously. While product advances should have a beneficial impact on market share and can be representative of value creation for the firm, there can be many confounding factors in a market share determination. These would include such things as the size and quality of the marketing effort, the competitive response, the relative state of the economy, etc. One should also be sensitive to share data in related markets, since market transformation is often created by unexpected competitors.
b. Related Market Share	Share data in related markets for indication of threats or opportunities.	
7. Strategic alignment/ PA, IWB, AVT		
a. Corporate and Business Unit	Fraction of total R&D portfolio which is consistent with corporate goals and, where applicable, for each major business unit. Should also include specific identification of the corporate or business goal with which a project is identified.	While it seems unlikely that much, if any, of the R&D portfolio would not be consistent with corporate goals, this question needs to be explicitly addressed. If the number of projects not consistent with corporate or business unit goals is substantial, explanations need to be given. For goal coverage, serious questions must be asked if major business goals are not addressed by the R&D portfolio. In particular, either the total size of the R&D effort or its distribution must be questioned.
b. Goal Coverage	Fraction of corporate or business unit goals requiring technology development that are addressed by the R&D portfolio.	
8. Distribution of technology investment/PA, AVT	Analysis of the fraction of the total R&D investment along various dimensions. Each company should describe its portfolio of technical activities along dimensions that are important to decision making and communication between stakeholders. Some of the more common dimensions are: A. Dimensions potentially of greater interest to the CEO (and to business management): • Categorization of reward vs. risk • By product line or business unit • For maintenance of current business, expansion of current business, or creation of new business • Environmentally driven vs. non-environmental	This measurement area provides much texture for the analysis of how well a firm's R&D program is protecting the technology investment and technical position of the company. Important output from assessments of technology investment distribution are the questions that are the analysis causes to be asked regarding what distribution is desired. This helps set the direction for modifying the R&D portfolio.

Table 9.1—*Continued*

Metric/Factor	Definition	Comments
	• Distribution according to time of commercialization B. Dimensions potentially of greater interest to business management (and some CEOs): • For cost reduction, applications development, or performance differentiation • For technical service, basic research, applied research, product development and process development • For current markets, markets new to the company, or markets new to the world • For current technology, technology new to the company, or technology new to the world C. Dimensions potentially of greater interest to R&D management: • Distribution by project stage • Distribution by technical discipline • External R&D vs. Internal • Base, key or pacing technology • Core vs. new competencies • U.S. vs. non-U.S.	
9. Number of ways technology is exploited/PA, AVT	Assessment of the number of different product types or business segments utilizing or planning to utilize a given technical asset (the exploitation of functional competencies).	Measurements in this area cause a firm to stretch the limits of application of its technology. By conscious examination of this, market opportunities beyond one's current markets can be created. While such opportunities may or may not be pursued, this examination allows R&D to maximize the possible output from its creative endeavors.
10. Number of project definitions having business/marketing approval/IWB	Fraction (or percent) of projects in the total R&D portfolio with explicit business unit and/or corporate business management sign-off.	Ideally, all projects except "skunk works projects" would have either corporate or business unit sign-off. In practice, exploratory feasibility determination work is likely not to; such work would be expected, however, to be aimed at areas of known interest.
11. Use of project milestone system/PRD, IWB	Fraction of projects in the total portfolio going through a defined project management system with defined milestones.	The ideal value for this measurement must be determined by each firm for itself, as it will depend on a number of aspects of the Distribution of the Technology Investment (Metric 8). Firms with a larger percentage of exploratory projects would be expected to have a lower fraction going through a defined project management system. Once feasibility has been demonstrated, most

Table 9.1—*Continued*

Metric/Factor	Definition	Comments
		firms would have a fairly high percentage of their projects going through a defined system.
12. Percent funding by the business/IWB	Fraction (or percent) of the R&D budget from business unit sources.	This measurement has most utility for corporate labs or for centralized R&D organizations. Again, the ideal value for this measurement will depend on the individual firm's circumstances. The number will also depend on the strategic intent of the firm; if R&D is being asked to break ground in a new business area for which no revenues currently exist, one would expect the fraction of the R&D budget from business unit sources to be lower.
13. Technology transfer to manufacturing/ IWB, PRD	Semi-quantitative assessment (e.g., an interval scale from 1 to 5) of the effectiveness of the transfer with ratings obtained from both R&D and manufacturing sides of the interface.	This measurement is important for its reflection on the closeness of the working relationship between R&D and manufacturing. As with several other measures described later, the suggested measurement technique involves an interval scale, with ratings from 1 to 5. Such a scale must be carefully created with proper anchoring descriptions for the ends of the scale, and for the middle.
14. Use of cross-functional teams/IWB, PRD	Fraction of projects in the R&D portfolio with specific cross-functional teams assigned. This analysis can be further subdivided by project types; e.g., short-term development, long-term development, process development, applied research, etc.	Current assessment of best practices of technology management includes the use of cross-functional teams to ensure alignment of research with the other functions and with the business strategy. Research has shown it to be one of the more useful leading indicators for financial success and R&D output. Metrics should evaluate not only the number of teams but also their composition and role. Internal trend analysis is more important than absolute benchmarking against competitors.
15. Rating of product technology benefits/AVT, VC		
a. Customer Rating	Numerical ranking of a firm's product by a given customer divided by that customer's ranking of the best competitive product. This ratio can be averaged across customers and/or market segments using the product to obtain an average ratio value.	Ideally, this metric will measure the customers' perceptions of how each competitor delivers value. A customer survey should be used to determine how the products from each competitor rank on a numerical scale in delivering benefits. To handle the individual opinions, a ratio should be made of the firm's numerical rating to the

Table 9.1—*Continued*

Metric/Factor	Definition	Comments
b. Economic Evaluation	{Price differential per unit obtained by virtue of quality feature(s) derived from technical effort minus the cost per unit of providing the feature(s)} times unit sales volume for products containing the feature(s).	competitor. The ratios can be averaged across many customers and different market segments to obtain an average ratio value. The Economic Evaluation measure provides an estimate of the commercial value of a technology benefit in the firm's products, based on the proposition that the benefit allows a premium price relative to the competition. The Market Share evaluation assumes that competitive pressures may prevent the firm from gaining a price premium for the technology benefit, but for the benefit to be worth the cost in this situation, market share gains should provide the economic gain that is desired.
c. Market Share Evaluation	Differential share gain(s) at a constant price for product(s) containing the quality feature(s).	
16. Response time to competitive moves/AVT,PRD	Time required for the firm to match competitors' newest product benefit(s) divided by time required for competitor to match firm's newest product benefit(s).	This metric relates to the ability of the firm to either maintain a leadership position or to match technology moves by the competition. It is a part of Customer Satisfaction.
17. Current investment in technology/AVT	Current annual expenditures for R&D staff and equipment ratioed to best competitor, to industry average, and to industry total.	This metric measures the rate of current activity in developing the technology of interest with the intent of predicting whether the firm is expected to gain or lose ground in the technology. It should be kept separately for the key and pacing technologies most critical to the strategy. It is best used as a ratio of investment by the firm compared to the best competitor. Ideally, quality of the research staff should also be factored into the metric, since output of the investment will be determined not only by the effort but by the abilities of the researchers.
18. Quality of personnel/ AVT, PRD	Several measures are possible; the ones chosen should be appropriate for the firm's technology development strategy.	Research has shown this metric to be a leading indicator for many intermediate factors, but only a weak leading indicator of new products. Quality of personnel relative to the competitors is a difficult metric to evaluate in most cases. In some cases, it is clear that one competitor considers one competitive area more strategic than another competitor and consequently puts the best resources there. In using this metric it is
a. Internal Customer Rating	Interval rating scale (e.g., a scale from 1 to 5) from R&D's internal customers, such as marketing, manufacturing, etc.	
b. External Customer Rating	Interval rating scale from the firm's major customers.	

Table 9.1—*Continued*

Metric/Factor	Definition	Comments
c. External Recognition	External awards and invited lectures by the professional staff over a relevant time period.	important to decide whether one is addressing the quality in a specific arena or the general overall quality of the research group.
d. Published Works	Publications and patents by the professional staff over a relevant time period.	
19. Development cycle time/ AVT, PRD		
a. Market Cycle Time	Elapsed time from identification of a customer product need until commercial sales commence.	The literature suggests that short cycle time will greatly influence financial return, other factors being equal. However, there is also an
b. Project Management Cycle Time	Elapsed time from establishment of a discrete project to address an identified customer product need until commercial sales commence. For both (a) and (b) the end point can be the time when manufacturing feasibility is established for those cases where no commercialization occurs. Compare to historical values and benchmark vs. competition, if possible. Group by categories of projects (e.g., major new product, minor product variation, etc.). Can also be used to track milestone attainment rate for firms using a stage gate management process.	indication that shortening the cycle time may result in shortcuts and poor quality work which will more than overpower the positive gains. Another concern is that the metric could cause a firm to move to short-term, faster projects which inherently do not have the impact of longer, more strategic projects. The metric is probably most useful as an internal standard for continual improvement, since obtaining competitor information for comparison is likely to be very difficult. The cycle time that should be measured and charted is the interval between the first indication of a customer need or opportunity to the time that a successful solution, by an appropriate measure for the industry, is available for general use by the customers.
20. Customer rating of technical capability/AVT	Average customer rating (internal or external) of overall technical capability of the firm (interval rating scale) in providing technical service and/or new product innovations. Can be ratioed to ratings for relevant competitors for benchmarking purposes.	This metric relates to Quality of Personnel and Customer Rating of Product Technology Benefits, but is more future-oriented. It attempts to measure the customers' perceptions of the ability (not willingness) of the firm to bring value to the customers' future problems. Assuming that a technology is used in a variety of markets, the metric should integrate over the different needs and wants of the customers. A competitor with a strong technology position having broad value will be the most successful at meeting the customer needs in many markets, rather than only a few. A competitor's indifference to a market niche should not be equated with its inability to bring technical strength to bear when desired. Consequently, this

Table 9.1—*Continued*

Metric/Factor	Definition	Comments
		metric probably should not be a weighted average across markets, but an evaluation of the breadth of capability across the entire range of opportunities. A customer survey focused on the competitor's ability to use technology to solve new problems should be used with quantitative rankings.
21. Number and quality of patents/ AVT, PRD		
a. Percent Useful	Percentage of active patents from the company's total patent estate which are incorporated into or used to defend the firm's commercial products or processes.	There is considerable debate about the validity of using the number of patents as an indicator of the strength of the technology or the management of technology for a firm. Research indicates some negative correlation to financial performance and patent volume. Also, some firms do not patent extensively as a matter of strategy, and patents are not particularly valuable in other industries. This metric should only be used if patents are considered especially valuable in the industry and competitors follow a vigorous strategy of creating a patent "forest."
b. Value Ratio	Interval rating (1 to 5) for potential strategic value times rating (1 to 5) for strength of protection divided by 25 (maximum attainable value). Yields a number between 0 and 1.	
c. Retention Percent	Percent of granted patents maintained.	The number of high-quality patents is probably a more useful metric. Internal assessment of value is one method of determining quality of the patenting activity, which does not require the lag time of citations or sales development, and which should relate to success of the firm's strategy.
d. Cost of Invention	Number of patents from R&D/R&D effort. One can also calculate this just using the number of useful patents from R&D.	The metric should be kept for patents in the key technologies of greatest strategic value and in the relevant pacing technologies. All patent metrics should be benchmarked against competitors and compared to exploitation of the current technology position.
22. Sales protected by proprietary position/AVT, VC		
a. % Patent Protected Sales	Percentage of sales protected by patents owned by the company.	Sales of products under patent is another means of assessing the value of the patenting activity. Rigor is required to count only patents that truly protect the sales, and not background patents. This assumes a strategy of first-filing in the U.S. and ignores the potential for protection of sales by longer-lived counterparts in other countries. The assumption is useful for tracking the turnover of the patent portfolio
b. % Proprietary Sales	Percentage of sales protected by patents plus trade secrets and/or other exclusive company know-how or arrangements.	

Table 9.1—*Continued*

Metric/Factor	Definition	Comments
		The % Proprietary Sales metric allows inclusion of proprietary positions achieved by means other than patents.
23. Peer evaluation/ AVT, PRF		
a. External	Numerical rating (interval rating scale) from 1 to 5 by a panel of external experts on the merits of the firm's technology positioning and technology management practices. Panel selections critical; must be capable and objective. Could include outside directors from technology companies or university science/engineering departments, consultants in technology management, professors, venture capitalists, etc.	Peer evaluation is another method of assessing the strength of the technology of a firm and the management of technology. A variant of this metric (b) is to use an internal panel of experienced scientists, probably technical ladder rather than management people, whose responsibility is to form overall judgments on the technology positioning and management of the firm. In either case, consistency of the panel over time is important in identifying and making improvements.
b. Internal	Same rating scale applied by internal experts; probably staff on company's technical ladder.	
24. Customer satisfaction/ AVT, PRD		
a. External	Average rating by key external customers using a 1 to 5 interval rating scale to evaluate various dimensions regarding product technology or process technology benefits and technical service provided.	Customer ratings of Quality of Personnel, Technical Capability, and Product Technology Benefits speak to external customer satisfaction. Recognizing that the first customer for technology management is internal, customer satisfaction surveys should be used to determine satisfaction from engineering, production and marketing along axes that are important to them:
b. Internal	Same rating approach along dimensions important to key internal customers such as marketing, engineering, manufacturing etc.; dimensions would include, for example, timeliness of developments, competitiveness of solutions, etc.	on-time delivery of technology developments and packages; competitiveness of solutions developed; general satisfaction with the job being done.
25. Development pipeline milestones achieved/PRD		
a. Percent of Project Milestones Achieved	Percent of project milestones achieved within three months of projected achievement date (or within that time appropriate for an industry). Plot as histogram to reveal actual performance, showing percent that beat the target as well as those that miss it.	Reaching milestones in the time predicted is a measure of effective planning and management. Use of milestones correlates with shorter cycle time. A consistent management system is required to track this metric so that variability of the number/quality/ difficulty of the milestones does not cause random fluctuation in the metric.
b. Performance Level at Each Milestone	Percent completion of objectives expected by a milestone date at the milestone date.	

Table 9.1—_Continued_

Metric/Factor	Definition	Comments
26. Customer contact time/PRD	Average hours per researcher spent in direct contact with external (or internal) customers.	One of the best practices identified for technology management is customer contact time by the scientists. This metric provides a quantitative measure; management must also ensure that the time is well spent.
27. Preservation of technical output/PRD	Percent of research project outcomes captured in technical reports.	The value of counting reports and publications is debatable. Positive correlations have been seen with items relating to communications, cross-functional activities, and use of milestones; however, they have shown no relation to financial outputs or to creation of value.
28. Efficiency of internal technical processes/PA, PRD		
a. Project Assessment	The total cost of all commercially successful projects divided by the number of commercially successful projects.	There are many metrics of this type that relate to the efficiency of the daily processes by which research is conducted. Examples are turnaround time for customer service requests and dollars spent per customer service request. Internal services such as analytical service, computer services, or library services can be measured in the same way.
b. Portfolio Assessment	The total R&D budget divided by the number of projects with commercial output. Subdivide by projects of similar type (technical service, short-term, long-term) and use in conjunction with project value assessment.	
29. Employee morale/PRD	Quantitative ratings of key aspects of employee satisfaction and morale as shown by direct employee survey.	Employee morale or job satisfaction are generally thought to be a direct input to motivation and productivity. The level or extent of motivation may be a more useful metric since it is closer to productivity. Motivation can be measured by a direct survey, or more qualitatively through focus group discussions.
30. Goal clarity/PRD	Interval rating scale assessing the extent to which project performance objectives are clearly identified and understood by all participants on the project team.	Internal research in some companies has shown this measurement to be significantly related to successful innovation. Low rankings here would point to a need to improve communication regarding project objectives between R&D and key internal and external customers.
31. Project ownership/ empowerment/ PRD	Interval rating scale assessing the extent to which participants feel they have the support and freedom they need to be successful in the project.	This measurement has also been reported to correlate positively with successful innovation from R&D. It is also likely related to employee morale on a project team.

Table 9.1—*Continued*

Metric/Factor	Definition	Comments
32. Management support/PRD	Interval rating scale assessing the extent to which participants feel they have management's backing and an understanding that failure while learning will not be punished.	This support is also critical to successful innovation. Low ratings in this area point to a breakdown in relations (and perhaps in credibility) between R&D management and the project team and, perhaps, between R&D management and business management.
33. Project championship/ PRD	Percent of projects for which an effective project champion can be identified on the project team.	As with metrics 30–32, the project championship measure has been correlated in some companies with successful innovation. Project champions, whether or not they are identified as project leaders, lend an air of enthusiasm, optimism and urgency to a project that tends to permeate the team.

eral management to determine which measure will be used to assess broader corporate responsibilities. For corporate labs whose customers are business unit labs, both laboratory managements must agree on the measures they will use to evaluate the productivity and effectiveness of their organization, and this must be understood by both business unit and corporate management.

The TVP model can be used either retrospectively or prospectively, with the time frame that is pertinent to the particular firm. In using the model prospectively, however, one must remember that the projections will only be as good as the assumptions about the probabilities of technical and commercial success that led to them. Thus, prospective measures must always be used cautiously.

Not all measurements are right for all companies, or at all times, for describing or tracking the most important aspects of R&D. However, each company should be able to select a small set of metrics that are appropriate for assessing the value received from R&D and the likelihood of being able to sustain that value. From an R&D perspective, the *critical factors of the moment* are dependent on the situation of the company, the perspective re-

quired and the basic dynamics of the model. Let's start from the top.

1. Top Down and Output-Oriented

The TVP model provides a top-down perspective that is output-oriented. Value Creation is the prime driver of overall business returns that are derived from technology-based new products/processes. Metrics that track value are predictors of business growth and (implicitly) a critical input for strategic business reviews. These metrics are used to answer such critical questions as:

- Are we spending the right amount on R&D?

- Are we getting good returns on our R&D?

If the metrics associated with Value Creation are being maintained or going up:

- The corporation has the likely substance to extend a technology-based or innovation-based growth program;

- The investors can expect an extended stream of positive returns from the accumulation of financial payoffs from technology-based innovations; and

• The R&D units enjoy the likelihood of consistent funding to reinvest in technology applications for the near term and base-building for the future.

The key words here are "likely" or "possible." Value Creation is a necessary but not sufficient condition for growth. It is also only a measure of the moment, whether it is looking to the past or to the future. And, any downward movements will predict the difficulties the business will have in achieving solid gains against the competition. These indicators are crucial to assessing the total returns from R&D investments, whether enough is being spent on R&D, and what the likely future value is to the company from a technology perspective.

2. Drivers of 'Value Creation'

Value Creation is the result of an accumulation of effort by R&D and the business to produce new ideas and to put the best ones into practice. Due to all of the factors that are involved, momentum is built into these factors over time. They will change, but not rapidly. Change is caused by the drivers of Value Creation. These drivers are strategies that transform the R&D foundations of competencies, know-how, etc. into specific projects and implementation. These are the strategies that are represented and measured by metrics associated with the Portfolio Assessment and the Integration with Business factors. In other words, the portfolio of R&D programs, when reviewed in total, represents the technical strategy of the company, and measures of how well the R&D program is integrated with the business give insight into how relevant the technical strategy is to the business strategy.

When Value Creation is positive, these strategies are most likely working well. When Value Creation is going in the wrong direction, look first to these areas for the cause.

Given this importance to Value Creation, it is no surprise that companies have routinely focused in recent years on methodologies and activities dealing with Portfolio Assessment and Integration with Business issues. These are correctly perceived

as the means to the ends that improve the future stream of results from R&D.

Metrics that track Portfolio Assessment describe the state of the various pipelines that run through the R&D enterprise, as well as the targets that are being pursued. They provide a view of how the R&D dollars are being spent in terms of timing, risks and possible returns. Portfolio Assessment is a prime place to look for answers if there are problems with Value Creation, with competitive or market share issues, or with internal satisfaction.

Unlike metrics that track Value Creation, which tend to have modest levels of momentum associated with them and provide significant underpinnings to the business returns, metrics associated with Portfolio Assessment can vary quickly and have little immediate effect on the business. Major effects are cumulative. This dynamic often leads to short-term, risk-averse behaviors that over time undermine Value Creation. Thus, when used properly, measurement of Portfolio Assessment can alert companies to this trend and point to corrective measures before Value Creation turns down. Maintaining an aggressive monitoring of the Portfolio Assessment is extremely important to the long-term support for Value Creation.

Similarly, when problems within the portfolio are corrected, it is necessary to give the solution enough time to work.

If metrics that can be associated with Portfolio Assessment show strategy by *which* categories of R&D and targets are being developed, the metrics associated with integration with Business show a strategy for *how* it is being done, and, consequently, with what level of quality and execution.

Measurements of Integration with Business focus on process, culture, teamwork, and organization. They also touch on many of the aspects of cycle time. The issues addressed by these metrics change slowly and are probably the true pacing items that are applied by the organization to the Portfolio Assessment which, in turn, puts limits on the realizable Value Creation.

When there are difficulties attributable to barriers, for example, that can be removed, then the metrics and the results can be changed relatively rapidly. However, when there are difficulties due to lack of cooperation, lack of contact with the market, lack of good competitive intelligence, or with a lack of risk taking, then new attitudes and new behaviors are required. This takes time to build into the culture, and the measurements and the results will be slow to change.

3. Business and Technology Leadership

The dynamics of metrics associated with Integration with Business depend on organizational matters, in contrast to those of the Portfolio Assessment, which depend on investment decisions. And, a consideration of organizational *and* investment matters quickly brings the matters of business and technology leadership into the model.

The underlying dynamics do not permit converting management desires for immediate gratification (at low risk) into sustained profitable growth. Presuming a management commitment to doing the right things, there must be allowances made for the application of enough time to link all of the elements on an ongoing basis. Over time, all of the measurements should point to a consistent improvement in the transformation strategies and to the attendant output in Value Creation.

Conversely, monitoring the transformation strategy factors of an otherwise healthy technology-based enterprise will show the early warning signs of any degradation and, to the degree possible, allow timely correction action to be taken before a sound technology foundation begins to crumble.

4. Foundations

The foundations for the strategies represented by the Portfolio Assessment and the Integration with Business factors are built on the Asset Value of Technology and the Practice of R&D Processes To Support Innovation factors. Some of the critical questions regarding these dynamics are:

- Are we becoming more or less productive with our R&D?
- Are we building a strong enough future base of competencies?

- Are we getting an early warning of any declining capability?

Foundation factors have the most momentum of any category. They are very slow to change and provide the real rate limitations to growth through technology-based innovation. However, they are also very vulnerable to neglect. They represent significant elements of the culture of the R&D organization, and like most cultural issues, can *deteriorate rapidly* but *improve only slowly*. They need nurturing, leadership and the execution of well-focused technology strategies to become strong elements of a company's growth foundation. And, just as weak transformation strategies degrade Value Creation, they also degrade the foundations.

External Technological Change is the other major dynamic that affects foundations. In these cases, technological breakthroughs undermine traditional technical competencies, bringing in new competitors, toppling current competitors and even redefining the structure of an industry. Although the resulting paradigm shifts take time to develop, R&D and the business are usually both entrenched in the traditional areas and either don't see the changes coming or insist on devaluing the importance until it is too late. The foundations which, if strong, took considerable time to build, must nonetheless be constantly extended and rebuilt to provide options that are the logical growth paths for the business's future. Otherwise, over time, they will erode significantly. Thus, certain of the metrics associated with the Practice of R&D Processes To Support Innovation factor ask for an assessment of either competitors or companies in related markets. Such measures alert R&D leadership to both threats and opportunities within and outside the industry.

Thus, the dynamics of the foundation factors are that they are slow to build and relatively easy to degrade in spite of strong momentum. They are also fundamental to a strong competitive strategy (based on technical core competencies), to R&D creativity, and to productivity. They are a significant contributor to cycle-time reduction, and a rate-limiting source for the options to be taken up by

How Useful Is the TVP?

The approach advocated in this article was first presented at the Industrial Research Institute Fall Meeting, October 1994 in Williamsburg, Virginia. Following the presentation, workshops explored the acceptance and utility of the Technology Value Pyramid. Two hundred twenty-four attendees from 165 companies completed pre-workshop questionnaires, and 213 attendees from 161 companies filled in post-workshop questionnaires.

Eighty-five percent of the respondents were either R&D directors or chief technical officers. Slightly over half of the respondents were from firms with hybrid R&D organizations, with 32 percent from firms with centralized R&D and 15 percent from firms with decentralized R&D. Except for the engineering/construction industry segment, all segments had at least 10 companies repre-

sented, with chemicals leading with 58. The companies were predominantly product oriented (85 percent), with the balance equally split between process and service orientations.

Eighty-five percent of the respondents to the post-workshop questionnaire agreed that the TVP was a useful technique for selecting metrics for managing R&D and communicating with stakeholders.

Respondents considered all managerial factors highly important, with average ratings going from 3.8 to 4.3 (out of 5). No factors of importance were thought to be omitted. There was no significant difference between industries regarding which factors are important, nor which individual metrics are important.

The top 11 metrics from table 9.1 are listed below in rank order (the rating is not monotonic), and it is interesting to note that all five TVP factors are represented by these top 11 measures.

Rank*	Metric menu number	Avg. score	Metric
1	1	3.7	Financial Return to the Business.
2	7	3.5	Strategic Alignment with the Business.
3	2	2.6	Projected Value of R&D Pipeline.
4	9	1.9	Sales or Gross Profits from New Products.
5	11	1.7	Accomplishment of Project Milestones.
6	8	1.7	Portfolio Distribution of R&D Projects.
7	24	1.6	Customer Satisfaction Surveys.
8	6	1.6	Market Share.
9	19	1.5	Development Cycle Time.
10	4	1.4	Product Quality & Reliability.
11	5	1.4	Gross Profit Margin.

*Respondents were asked to identify metrics in use, to rank order the top five, and to rank order those thought to be the top five for the firm's CEO.

There was unanimous agreement that is is necessary to consider the interests of different stakeholders in selecting metrics for R&D. While 55 percent of the respondents felt the list of stakeholders was not complete, most suggested modifications were for specific identification of stakeholders that are included in the broad classes already identified. For example, marketing and manufacturing managers can be included in the

broad class of "SBU Managers" and, in fact, the menu of metrics does allow one to deal specifically with their interests. Additional stakeholder suggestions worthy of further consideration include both external customers and the public/community. This latter group is of particular concern regarding the environmental performance of the firm and R&D's role in that regard.

the transformation strategies. The drivers of these factors are the R&D leadership.

GUIDELINES FOR USE

The principal use of the model is for communication and control. This includes communication about, and control of, the overall R&D program, the research program, the business technical programs, and the development of external relationships. The model is not intended to aid project evaluation except as a project would contribute to the improvement of various factors.

Depending on particular needs of stakeholders or of decisions to be taken, different categories and factors should be examined. In addition, time periods should be adjusted for different industries, technologies and types of R&D.

Each of the primary stakeholders will tend to concentrate their attention on different parts of the model. And, while that is logical, it is important to note that all of the factors are connected with time lags by the basic dynamics. It remains for R&D and, in particular, the CTO to make sure that there is awareness of all the factors of the menu, that each stakeholder is reminded of their interconnectedness, and that a consistency is maintained (or that corrective action is taken to achieve consistency) between the collective expectations of the stakeholders and the realities of the model represented by the Technology Value Pyramid.

A HOLISTIC APPROACH

The TVP provides a holistic approach to assessing the value of R&D to the corporation and for guiding improvement efforts when such are deemed necessary. Implementation will require close interaction with the firm's accounting function in order to obtain appropriately detailed sales and cost information. This information is important for developing meaningful calculations of the Value Creation factor. With this information, and with accurate data tracking mechanisms for various R&D activities, the TVP is a powerful tool. By working at the Value Creation level, one can assess value delivered by working retrospectively; prospectively, one can estimate future value creation potential. If the results of these analyses are dissatisfying, one can use the deeper layers of the pyramid to examine potential sources of problems (diagnosis) and to develop appropriate action programs for involvement (prescription). Thus, wise use of the model should allow R&D organizations to improve their innovative output and to develop a means of sustaining innovative output over time.

Use of the model, in and of itself, will not improve an R&D organization; measurements only provide data. We do believe that the set of measurements in the TVP will allow most organizations to select a subset for themselves that can meaningfully report on the effectiveness and productivity of their R&D organization, and the value that it brings to the corporation. Improvement depends on R&D management action consciously taken to improve various measures of performance within the selected set of measurements.

The TVP as currently developed also does not provide a technique for R&D managers to automatically select the measures appropriate for a firm. The ongoing work of the Industrial Research Institute's Subcommittee on Measuring the Effectiveness and Productivity of R&D will provide such a technique. This work is focusing on the development of an expert system-based program that would allow users of the TVP to easily select an appropriate set of measures for their particular circumstances. Future work will also address the utility and validity of the model through use of the TVP concept.

10

Measuring R&D Effectiveness

ROBERT SZAKONYI

Compare your department's performance of ten basic activities with the performance of an "average" R&D department.

Improving the effectiveness of R&D is the most important issue in R&D management. It sums up the major concerns of R&D managers such as: Are we selecting the right R&D projects? Are we managing our projects well? Are we contributing as much as we should to the company's businesses? Although R&D managers and researchers have attempted to measure R&D effectiveness for over 30 years, there are still no methods that are widely accepted for doing this. The crux of the problem seems to lie in the great difficulty in measuring R&D *output*. R&D managers have sensed correctly that any quantitative measures would focus, not on the quality of the R&D and its contribution to the company's businesses, but on countable items such as patents or citations in technical journals. Consequently, even though R&D managers have wanted to measure R&D effectiveness, they have not had an acceptable method for doing so.

As summarized in my review of the literature (see *Research-Technology Management,* March–April, 1994), methods for linking R&D to profits, sales, or other financial benefits, even given their shortcomings, can be helpful, provided everyone recognizes (1) that there are major limitations in any method for translating R&D output into financial payoffs, and (2) that there is a certain artificiality in isolating the contributions of R&D to profits, and so on. The methods have been useful in providing a common frame of reference for how and how much R&D influences a company's busi-

nesses. Methods for evaluating R&D output that are based on judgments about the success of individual R&D projects also can be useful. As long as the people involved are aware of (1) problems of converting qualitative judgments into rankings and (2) problems related to the relative weights of different variables, these methods can help clarify how much various R&D projects have accomplished. Measuring R&D output in terms of how many patents, publications, or citations to publications were produced is not very useful. Although such measures may at times reveal interesting patterns regarding the progress of technical work, they cannot be thought of as legitimate indicators of R&D output.

Where all the methods for measuring R&D output fall short, however, is that they really do not measure R&D effectiveness. *R&D output and R&D effectiveness are not the same thing.* As a result, the purpose of this article is to present a new approach to measuring R&D effectiveness, an approach that overcomes major shortcomings of past efforts. Such a system should require as little qualitative judgment as possible. Evaluators should be able to identify the presence or absence of particular features, rather than trying to judge their performance. It should also provide a logical set of benchmarks so that a company can compare itself against the experiences of others.

The framework of my approach to measuring R&D effectiveness consists of the following ten R&D activities: (1) selecting projects; (2) planning and managing projects; (3) generating new product ideas; (4) maintaining the quality of the R&D process and methods; (5) motivating technical people; (6) establishing cross-disciplinary teams; (7)

Reprinted with permission from *Research-Technology Management,* May–June, 1994.
Robert Szakonyi is Director of the Center on Technology Management at Chicago's IIT Center.

coordinating R&D and marketing; (8) transferring technology to manufacturing; (9) fostering collaboration between R&D and finance; and (10) linking R&D to business planning. The substance of this new approach consists of 60 examples of how an R&D department performs at each of six levels with regard to these ten R&D activities. The examples are drawn from my experience in consulting or doing research from 1978 to 1992 at over 300 companies in 27 different industries. In the tables that follow, each R&D activity level is scored from 0 to 5. These scores could be used to derive overall benchmark scores, so that R&D departments can measure themselves against my "average" as a whole rather than against each individual activity.

Although more than just the R&D department must be effective for a company to do well in these activities, the *focus* in this approach to measuring R&D effectiveness is on the R&D department's operations. Obviously, a department cannot link its R&D effectively to business planning if there are no business plans. Similarly, an R&D department's relations with the marketing, manufacturing, or finance department are not one-way. If the other department refuses to cooperate, then the R&D department is hampered. A low score on these activities, therefore, does not necessarily mean that an R&D department is operating poorly. What it definitely does mean is that the company needs improvement with regard to the effectiveness of R&D. Finally, although all 10 activities are important, they do not necessarily carry the same weight. Each company can choose the relative weight it wants to place on each activity as well as how such weights might vary over time for any particular business.

1. SELECTING R&D

Level A: Issue is not recognized. Although every R&D department recognizes that the projects it selects should serve the company's interests, some R&D departments have their own unique perception of what those interests are. For example, the R&D department at one aerospace company

picked projects to build up the technical skills of its engineers instead of picking projects that the company needed.

Level B: Initial efforts are made toward addressing issue. An R&D department of an automotive company recognized that its projects should serve the company's needs, but it lacked the skills to select projects in a particular technical area. Although it had skills in mechanical engineering and selected well in this area, it lacked skills in electronics engineering. In this area, the department picked projects that were more appropriate for a university than an industrial laboratory.

Level C: Right skills are in place. An R&D department of an instrument company that had traditionally been oriented toward mechanical engineering had weaknesses in electronics engineering, but gradually built up skills in this area until it was able to select projects competently in both areas. The department had other problems, however, because it lacked methods for clarifying priorities among projects.

Level D: Appropriate methods are used. A telecommunication comapny's R&D department developed methods for selecting projects competently for its service businesses and for its businesses that sold products. It also had methods for clarifying priorities among these two sets of projects. Nonetheless, this R&D department still had difficulties integrating its projects into company businesses because it picked these projects on its own; i.e., without the help of the marketing department.

This is the level at which the *average R&D department* operates. The average department has the technical skills to pick projects in the required areas; it also has developed reasonably workable procedures for selecting projects. However, the average department usually picks its projects with inadequate input from the managers of the other functions in the company.

Level E: Responsibilities are clarified. An R&D department of a consumer products company overcame the difficulties of the average R&D department by working with its company's operating divisions. Over a couple years, the department worked out ways of sharing responsibility for selecting projects. A few years later, however, relations with the operating divisions returned to their previous state. After defining their responsibilities clearly, the managers of R&D and of the operating divisions had allowed their relations to stagnate.

Level F: Continuous improvement is underway. An R&D department of a pharmaceutical company and the operating divisions had exceptional working relations in selecting R&D projects. They also worked hard at maintaining those relations. For example, both parties were committed to having the company undertake a significant amount of exploratory research. Together they looked for better ways of evaluating how much exploratory research to support, such as models for determining the optimal amount of long-range research.

2. PLANNING AND MANAGING PROJECTS

Level A: Issue is not recognized. In order to plan and manage projects, they must first exist;

yet, this was not the case at the R&D department of a steel company. Technical work was done by the technical people more or less as they saw fit, except when they had to do it in response to requests from the operating divisions for technical services. R&D done in this company seldom had clear objectives; it also was not evaluated in terms of meeting technical milestones, which did not even exist.

Level B: Initial efforts are made toward addressing issue. An R&D department of a consumer products company had projects with objectives, but it still had major difficulties in executing them. This was because the members of the R&D department did not understand planning and tracking of projects. In this company, R&D project planning was done poorly, if at all. Furthermore, the project plans that did exist were not taken seriously.

Level C: Right skills are in place. In an R&D department of a pulp and paper company, the technical people had the skills to plan, but project planning was still poor. The reason for this was that the technical people did not use the methods for project planning that had been worked out. Even though there was a manual on project planning, they chose to ignore it.

TABLE 10.1
Activity 1—Selecting R&D

		Points
Level A (Not recognized)	R&D department blindly picks projects to build up technical skills instead of selecting projects that are needed (*aerospace*).	0
Level B (Initial efforts)	Has skills in mechanical engineering, but lacks skills to select in electronics engineering (*automotive*).	1
Level C (Skills)	Has skills in mechanical and electronics engineering, but lacks methods to clarify priorities of projects (*instruments*).	2
Level D (Methods)	Develops methods to select projects for service businesses as well as businesses that sell products, but picks projects on own without marketing (*telecommunications*).	3
Level E (Responsibilities)	R&D department works with operating divisions to compare priorities and jointly select projects, but after a couple of years both parties lose their sense of mission (*consumer products*).	4
Level F (Continuous improvements)	R&D department and operating divisions look at various models for evaluating payoffs from exploratory research so as to find better ways of determining how much far-out research to do (*pharmaceutical*).	5

☐ = Average R&D department.

Level D: Appropriate methods are used. In an R&D department of an instruments company, projects were planned well in terms of objectives, schedules, and costs. Difficulties still arose in the execution of these projects, however, because the company lacked "rules of the road" concerning who was responsible for a project. In this company, the role of a project manager was unclear. In addition, there were no guidelines on how conflicts between projects should be resolved.

The *average R&D department* operates at this level with regard to planning and managing R&D projects. Over the last 30 years, most R&D departments have realized how important project planning and management is and have established procedures for planning and managing projects. The average R&D department, however, has not worked out clearly what the respective responsibilities of a project manager and of a line manager in R&D are for carrying out projects.

Level E: Responsibilities are clarified. An R&D department of a metals company planned projects well and defined the responsibilities of its project managers clearly. Although successful, this R&D department still had weaknesses. One weakness was that it did not seek further improvements in how projects were managed, such as in how well the senior business managers understood project results.

Level F: Continuous improvement is underway. An R&D department of a computer company not only mastered the challenges of project planning and management, but also took initiatives to improve the capabilities of its technical people. It fostered training to sharpen their planning and technical skills, and it developed better tools for planning projects, thereby shortening the duration of its projects significantly.

3. GENERATING NEW PRODUCT IDEAS

Level A: Issue is not recognized. Although technical people are not the only ones who should be responsible for generating new product ideas, they certainly should be among the leaders in this area. In the R&D department of a food processing company, however, the technical people had to be led to develop new product concepts. These people could handle the technical work required after a new project concept was developed, but they were not aware of their responsibility for developing these concepts.

TABLE 10.2
Activity 2—Planning and Managing Projects

		Points
Level A (Not recognized)	Projects do not exist; technical work is done without clear objectives; milestones, or accountability (*steel*).	0
Level B (Initial efforts)	R&D wants to plan, but does not understand what planning and tracking of projects consists of (*consumer products*).	1
Level C (Skills)	Has skills to plan, but cannot get planning methods accepted (*pulp and paper*).	2
Level D (Methods)	Projects are planned, but responsibilities of project managers within a project and coordination between projects are lacking (*instruments*).	3
Level E (Responsibilities)	Projects are planned well, but improvements, such as improving senior business management's understanding of projects, are not sought (*metals*).	4
Level F (Continuous improvements)	Training is fostered in the R&D department to sharpen technical people's planning and technical skills in order to shorten projects (*computer*).	5

☐ = Average R&D department.

Level B: Initial efforts are made toward addressing issue. In a steel company's R&D department, people wanted to generate new product ideas but lacked experience with the company businesses, so that they were not able to generate relevant ideas. These R&D people also lacked the skills to think creatively about businesses outside the company's traditional interests.

Level C: Right skills are in place. In an R&D department of a chemical company, the technical people had the skills to develop new product concepts and developed new ideas, but most of these ideas were lost because the department did not have procedures for collecting and evaluating suggestions about new products.

This is the level at which the *average R&D department* operates. Many of the technical people have the skills to develop new product ideas and they do develop new ideas, but the average R&D department has poor methods for capturing and evaluating these ideas. As a result, many promising new product ideas are lost.

Level D: Appropriate methods are used. In an R&D department of a tire and rubber company,

mechanisms were developed to instill an innovative climate, including procedures to capture and evaluate new product ideas. However, the department still had major problems in getting new product ideas utilized because: (1) The individual suggesters did not understand their responsibilities, and (2) The staff responsible for fostering innovation did not understand its duties. The individual suggesters did not realize that they would need to take certain steps to ensure that their ideas were practical, while those responsible for fostering innovation did not know how to develop support for new ideas.

Level E: Responsibilities are clarified. An R&D department of a building materials company developed a system for effectively integrating the generation of new product ideas into mainstream activities. It did this by incorporating the process of generating ideas into the planning process. New product ideas were elicited and then evaluated within the context of defining the direction for the company. Although this process worked well at the conception of a product, this company still had problems because it was not fully committed to innovation. It reached the level of fostering new

TABLE 10.3
Activity 3—Generating New Product Ideas

		Points
Level A (Not recognized)	Technical people have to be led to develop new product ideas (*food processing*).	0
Level B (Initial efforts)	R&D people want to generate new ideas, but lack the business experience to generate new ideas applicable to new businesses or the skills to think creatively (*steel*).	1
Level C (Skills)	R&D department has new ideas, but not the methods to capture and evaluate them (*chemicals*).	2
Level D (Methods)	Has mechanisms to instill a new innovative climate, but does not understand duties of the innovation staff or responsibilities of individual suggesters (*tire and rubber*).	3
Level E (Responsibilities)	Develops a system for integrating suggestions about new product concepts into the planning process, but cannot maintain a commitment toward new ideas (*building materials*).	4
Level F (Continuous improvements)	Pushes not only to develop new product ideas, but looks at them from the perspective of the customers; studies customers' behavior (*office equipment*).	5

☐ = Average R&D department.

ideas, but it did not maintain a commitment to supporting the ideas.

Level F: Continuous improvement is underway. An R&D department at an office equipment company not only developed new product ideas but also worked on improving how it handled new ideas. This department took actions to look at its customers' needs from the perspective of the customers. It also conducted studies of the behavior of people who work in offices so that it could identify customer needs that were not even apparent to the customer. Finally, it made conscious efforts to explain all of its new ideas to key customers.

4. MAINTAINING QUALITY OF R&D PROCESS/METHODS

Level A: Issue is not recognized. Engineers in an R&D department of a petroleum equipment company were unaware of how the poor quality of their designs contributed to problems in manufacturing products. Rather than using analytical tools to test the quality of their designs, they passed the designs on as they saw fit. Design flaws were found by manufacturing people, who then sent a flood of engineering change requests back to the R&D department.

Level B: Initial efforts are made toward addressing issue. At a household products company, the technical personnel wanted to improve the quality of their R&D but lacked detailed knowledge of the company's products. Without this knowledge, they found it difficult to design experiments and tests so as to meet the required quality standards.

Level C: Right skills are in place. At a photographic equipment company, the technical personnel had the training to do quality work. The problem was that they did not use quality tools (e.g., fishbone diagrams or quality function deployment) for increasing the rigor of R&D, except when these tools were absolutely required. Typically, these technical personnel felt that because they were under so

much pressure to meet deadlines they did not have the time to use the quality tools.

This is the level at which the *average R&D department* operates. Most of the technical personnel in the average department have the skills to do quality work and have had some training in tools for improving quality. In practice though, they do not use these tools. The pressures to meet schedules usually seem so large to them that they do not believe they can afford the extra time required to use quality tools.

Level D: Appropriate methods are used. An R&D department of a chemical company overcame many of the problems in getting quality improvement methods used. Still, although these methods were used, they were not always used as effectively as they should have been. One of the reasons for this was that no one in the R&D department was designated as being responsible for seeing that such methods were used regularly.

Level E: Responsibilities are clarified. An R&D department at another chemical company made major progress in getting quality tools used. A knowledgeable and experienced technical person was assigned the tasks of: (1) Finding the best quality tools available within and outside the company, and (2) Teaching technical personnel how the tools could be used. Many of the people began using these tools regularly. However, the person who was responsible for quality was still not successful in inducing the technical people to make these tools their own. For instance, he was not able to persuade them to improve the tools by modifying them to fit the purposes of their work.

Level F: Continuous improvement is underway. The technical people in an R&D department of one semiconductor company took the lead in seeking ways to improve R&D. For example, they looked for commonalities across the designs produced in various engineering groups, so that fewer designs would need to be done from scratch. By finding common building blocks across designs, they were able to eliminate many errors, to develop more robust designs, and to save time.

TABLE 10.4
Activity 4—Maintaining Quality of R&D Processes and Methods

		Points
Level A (Not recognized)	Technical people do not understand that their own designs have flaws (*petroleum equipment*).	0
Level B (Initial efforts)	Wants to improve, but lacks detailed knowledge of the products (*household products*).	1
Level C (Skills)	Has the technical training to do quality work, but does not use the methods (e.g., fishbone diagram) for ensuring quality (*photographic equipment*).	2
Level D (Methods)	Working at improving quality within the lab, but has not designated anyone to see that it happens (*chemical*).	3
Level E (Responsibilities)	Quality tools are used, but technical people have still not made them their own (*chemical*).	4
Level F (Continuous improvements)	Technical people take the lead in looking for commonalities across designs so that fewer designs need to be done from scratch (*semiconductors*).	5

☐ = Average R&D department.

5. MOTIVATING TECHNICAL PEOPLE

Level A: Issue is not recognized. R&D managers at a chemical company lacked an understanding of how to manage technical people. Instead of recognizing that technical people need to be motivated to do good work, they managed their staff autocratically, telling people what they wanted done and how to do it. Consequently, the creative output of the staff suffered.

Level B: Initial efforts are made toward addressing issue. At an automotive company, the R&D managers recognized that they needed to motivate their staff better. Specifically, they knew that they had to get the staff to understand how they fit in the company. These R&D managers believed that when the tecnical people understood this, they would be more inspired to do creative work and understand better what they should contribute. Although these managers recognized what was needed, they did not find ways to accomplish this.

This is the level at which the *average R&D department* operates. The managers understand that they must motivate their staff, and, in general, they carried out technical projects earlier in their careers. However, understanding that something needs to

be done is not the same as knowing how to do it. R&D managers, on the whole, are more capable in technical areas than in management. Usually their entire education and most of their working experience have involved mainly technical issues. Therefore, the challenge of motivating other people is often something with which they have had little experience and about which they are either uncomfortable or unsure of themselves.

Level C: Right skills are in place. At an appliance company, the R&D managers made progress in motivating technical people. They were able to get them to be more creative and more proactive in seeking out new opportunities. What these managers still needed to find were methods of performance evaluation to solidify the progress they had made in motivating their staff. In other words, they needed formal procedures to reinforce their own personal initiatives to motivate people.

Level D: Appropriate methods are used. At an oil company, the R&D managers put in place procedures for motivating technical people and for achieving technical excellence. Although major progress was made, further progress was hampered by the practice of middle-level R&D managers

TABLE 10.5
Activity 5—Motivating Technical People

		Points
Level A (Not recognized)	R&D managers manage technical people autocratically (*chemical*).	0
Level B (Initial efforts)	R&D managers recognize that technical people do not understand how they fit in the company, but have not found ways to correct this (*automotive*).	1
Level C (Skills)	Has made progress in encouraging technical people to be more creative and proactive, but still needs methods of performance evaluation to solidify progress (*appliances*).	2
Level D (Methods)	Has procedures in place for achieving technical excellence, but middle-level R&D managers hamper progress by making too many of the technical decisions involving projects themselves (*oil*).	3
Level E (Responsibilities)	Has succeeded in instituting a new system of rewards revolving around R&D project management, but still needs to deal with "political" problems in the lab related to authority to certain R&D groups (*pharmaceutical*).	4
Level F (Continuous improvements)	Develops a culture that makes R&D managers push responsibility downward, thus allowing technical people to expand their jobs (*instruments*).	5

☐ = Average R&D department.

making too many of the technical decisions about projects. Although these R&D managers supported the idea of giving technical people more authority to take initiatives, they found it difficult to trust their judgment about project issues.

Level E: Responsibilities are clarified. At a pharmaceutical company, the R&D managers motivated technical personnel by instituting a system of rewards revolving around project management. Project managers were given the authority to make major decisions regarding their projects, and they were rewarded for doing this. As part of this system, the responsibilities of middle-level R&D managers were also clarified so that they did not interfere too much with projects. Although this system was effective, other issues still needed to be addressed and were not. One issue was that some of the middle-level managers still did not accept giving certain R&D groups or project managers authority and thus created "political" problems in the laboratory.

Level F: Continuous improvement is underway. The R&D managers at an instrument com-

pany developed a culture that made middle-level R&D managers want to push responsibility downward, thus allowing technical people to expand their jobs and seek out opportunities on their own. In order to maintain a culture such as this in the laboratory, the R&D managers had to continually seek ways of improving everyone's understanding of what was required to get creative technical work done.

6. ESTABLISHING CROSS-DISCIPLINARY TEAMS

Level A: Issue is not recognized. A food processing company's R&D managers had great difficulty in getting cross-disciplinary—more accurately, cross-functional—teams accepted. Allegiance to the R&D department was so strong that many technical people did not appreciate the benefits of teams. The same held true for members of other functions. Therefore, even though efforts at establishing teams were continually made, these teams almost always floundered.

Level B: Initial efforts are made toward addressing issue. At a computer company, there were many cross-disciplinary teams involving technical people. However, these teams were usually only moderately successful because the technical people lacked training in what being a representative on a team involved.

This is the level of development at which the *average R&D department* operates with regard to both cross-disciplinary and cross-functional teams, although the average R&D department has somewhat more success with the former. Technical people—and people in the rest of the company—usually do not have much knowledge about how one participates on a team. Often, they do not understand the purpose and benefits of a cross-disciplinary or cross-functional team and make only half-hearted commitments when involved with team activities.

Level C: Right skills are in place. At a health care products company, cross-functional teams were manned with competent people—people who understood how to participate on a team. Nevertheless, teams still had problems because the company lacked "rules-of-the-road" regarding the managing of teams and the running of projects. There were no guidelines on how teams should be run or on what was expected from projects, nor was there a common understanding of how more than one team could draw upon common resources. Therefore, even though the people themselves were capable of executing well, the teams often did not produce the results desired.

Level D: Appropriate methods are used. At a photographic equipment company, there were teams that functioned well. People who were knowledgeable about how to work on teams had good procedures for coordinating their actions. The limitations of teams in this company stemmed from senior managers not giving teams enough authority to take actions. Therefore, even though the teams were capable of being very successful, they were handicapped in what they could do.

Level E: Responsibilities are clarified. At a health care products company, teams were very effective when the company was small. These teams were manned by capable people and were given sufficient authority. When the company grew larger, however, many of the conditions that led to well-functioning teams disappeared. From then on, team members cooperated less and the authority of the teams diminished.

TABLE 10.6
Activity 6—Establishing Cross-Disciplinary Teams

		Points
Level A (Not recognized)	Has difficulty getting the idea of cross-disciplinary teams accepted (*food processing*).	0
Level B (Initial efforts)	Wants to have teams, but technical people need to be trained to participate on teams (*computer*).	1
Level C (Skills)	Has teams manned with competent people, but lacks "rules-of-the-road" regarding the running of projects (*health care products*).	2
Level D (Methods)	Has teams that function well, but is handicapped because teams are not given enough authority (*photographic equipment*).	3
Level E (Responsibilities)	Had effective teams in the past, but does not know how to make them effective since the company has grown larger (*health care products*).	4
Level F (Continuous improvements)	The idea of cross-disciplinary teams is inculcated in everyone; many models for teams are available in company, and each team can choose its own model (*aerospace*).	5

☐ = Average R&D department.

TABLE 10.7
Activity 7—Coordinating R&D and Marketing

		Points
Level A (Not recognized)	R&D department does not think that it needs to work with marketing in developing new products (*aerospace*).	0
Level B (Initial efforts)	Technical people want better coordination with marketing, but lack the skills to analyze the business applications of a technical idea (*petroleum equipment*).	1
Level C (Skills)	Technical people know how to develop applications of a technology, but lack methods for working backward from a customer need to selecting technical projects (*chemical*).	2
Level D (Methods)	Works closely with marketing, but has difficulties in sorting out where responsibilities lie between technical concept and product concept (*food processing*).	3
Level E (Responsibilities)	Close coordination between R&D and marketing departments, but has not figured out how to develop new products effectively (*chemical*).	4
Level F (Continuous improvements)	Close coordination, with a former technical person in charge of marketing and taking the lead in technical marketing and new market development (*industrial equipment*).	5

☐ = Average R&D department.

Level F: Continuous improvement is underway. At an aerospace company, everyone understood cross-disciplinary teams, and the teams remained effective as the company grew. In this company, there were many models of what teams could be like. Members of a team could choose a model, (e.g., "Skunk Works"), adapt this model to their circumstances, and then modify their own model as a project progressed.

7. COORDINATING R&D AND MARKETING

Level A: Issue is not recognized. The R&D department at an aerospace company did not understand that it needed to work with the marketing department in developing new products. The senior technical managers of this company believed that their businesses were strictly technology-driven. Therefore, they ignored whatever input the marketing department tried to make regarding which technical projects were needed.

Level B: Initial efforts are made toward addressing issue. At a petroleum equipment company, the technical people recognized that their

R&D had to meet market needs. However, because many of these people lacked the skills to analyze the business applications of their technical ideas, they had great difficulty in communicating with the marketing people.

Level C: Right skills are in place. At a chemical company, the technical people knew how to develop applications of a technology. They could also communicate effectively with marketing people concerning the benefits of a technology they had developed. Where these technical people had problems, however, was in working backward from a customer need to selecting technical projects. They lacked methods for choosing the right technical work to do.

The *average R&D department* operated at this level. The technical people usually have the skills to communicate to marketing what the results of R&D can lead to. Their problem is in communicating with marketing people regarding how a market need could be filled. In other words, the average R&D department has not found methods of matching technical capabilities and market needs, except for those cases in which it can demonstrate the market advantages of a technology it has developed.

Level D: Appropriate methods are used. In a food processing company, the technical people and the marketing people worked out methods for communicating effectively. Nevertheless, problems still occurred in new product development. Many of these problems involved an unclear definition of responsibilities regarding the overlap between developing a technical concept and developing a product concept. There was a gray area between the conclusion of an R&D project that was technically successful and the start of a commercial development whose business prospects were promising but uncertain. The technical people and the marketing people in this company had difficulties sorting out who should deal with development issues.

Level E: Responsibilities are clarified. At a chemical company, the R&D and marketing departments worked in close coordination. R&D groups were responsible for the technical issues related to new product development; marketing groups were responsible for the long-term marketing issues. Both sides agreed on their responsibilities; yet, they still had difficulties. Although they worked together effectively, they had not figured out how to develop new products effectively. They had excellent communications, but they needed to improve the content of what they communicated.

Level F: Continuous improvement is underway. At an industrial equipment company, the communication between R&D and marketing was excellent. The person in charge of marketing was a former technical person who was as knowledgeable about the company's technologies as the person in charge of R&D. Together they developed new products for new markets; the senior R&D manager took the lead in developing the technology, while the senior marketing manager took the lead in technical marketing and in market development.

8. TRANSFERRING TECHNOLOGY TO MANUFACTURING

Level A: Issue is not recognized. At a telecommunications company, engineers did not consider manufacturing when they were doing their technical work, except at the end. During a project, they were preoccupied with a product's technical performance. Eventually, these engineers did seek input from the manufacturing people regarding producibility of the product. By then, however, it was too late to redesign the product so that it could be produced more easily and cheaply.

Level B: Initial efforts are made toward addressing issue. At a power generation equipment company, the R&D department wanted to have a better transfer of technology to manufacturing, but it lacked process engineering skills. Traditionally, the R&D department neglected issues related to manufacturing. Almost all of the technical people were oriented toward developing new products or conducting field services. Consequently, when the department transferred technology to manufacturing, it passed on designs that could not be manufactured easily.

Level C: Right skills are in place. Although the technical people at an automotive company had the skills to transfer technology, major problems remained in transferring technology. These technical people could not get manufacturing people to agree to the procedures for managing a technology transfer; e.g., one stage for prototype development, one stage for testing, etc.

This is the level at which the *average R&D department* operates. It is committed to transferring technology and it has the necessary skills. However, the average R&D department lacks the procedures for transferring technology to the manufacturing department, and a stalemate often occurs: The R&D has not been tested enough under manufacturing conditions, and the manufacturing people are reluctant to introduce a new technology into a plant until it has been tested enough.

Level D: Appropriate methods are used. A computer company's R&D department had the skills and methods for transferring technology, but problems still existed because the R&D and manufacturing departments disagreed about their responsibilities for testing and for documentation.

TABLE 10.8
Activity 8—Transferring Technology to Manufacturing

		Points
Level A (Not recognized)	Engineers do not consider manufacturing when doing technical work (*telecommunications*).	0
Level B (Initial efforts)	Wants better technology transfer, but lacks process engineering skills in the R&D department (*power generation equipment*).	1
Level C (Skills)	Technical people have the skills to transfer technology, but cannot develop methods with manufacturing to manage a phased transfer (*automotive*).	2
Level D (Methods)	Has methods for transferring technology, but there are disagreements about responsibilities for testing and documentation (*computer*).	3
Level E (Responsibilities)	Has a technical services group in the plant that is responsible for handling technology transfers, but this group normally focuses on current operations (*steel*).	4
Level F (Continuous improvements)	Not only has a group between R&D and manufacturing that aids technology transfer, but also tries to find new ways of integrating designs in order to link engineering and manufacturing more effectively (*semiconductors*).	5

☐ = Average R&D department.

Their differences of opinion concerned what kinds of tests should be conducted, when those tests should be conducted, what kinds of data were needed, when the data should be provided, and who was responsible for conducting tests and providing data at various stages during a transfer of technology.

Level E: Responsibilities are clarified. At a steel company, these problems of responsibility for a technology transfer were solved. The R&D department worked closely with a technical services group in the manufacturing plant, which was responsible for handling technology transfers. This group conducted the tests and made sure that all of the required data were provided. Although this group functioned very competently, it normally focused on maintaining the current operations of the plant. Thus, it did not seek better ways of transferring technology.

Level F: Continuous improvement is underway. At a semiconductor company, there was a group that worked with the engineering and manufacturing departments in transferring technology. This group not only aided technology transfers, but

also tried to find new ways of integrating designs in order to link engineering and manufacturing more effectively. This group consisted of design engineers from the engineering department, and test and manufacturing engineers and manufacturing workers from the manufacturing department.

9. FOSTERING COLLABORATION BETWEEN R&D AND FINANCE

Level A: Issue is not recognized. At a health care products company, the R&D department did not recognize how poor were its relations with the finance department. Although the R&D department naturally was concerned about its budget and about the financial payoffs from its R&D, it understood little about finance and communicated with the finance department only when required to. In return, the finance department had grave doubts about the value of the R&D.

This is the level at which the *average R&D department* operates. Researchers know that finance is important because there are continually questions regarding the size of the R&D budget and because questions about the return on investment from R&D are inescapable. Nonetheless, most members of the average R&D department do not know much about the financial affairs of their company and have few interactions with members of the finance or accounting department. The finance department, on the other hand, knows little about what is going on in the R&D department.

Level B: Initial efforts are made toward addressing issue. At a food processing company, the R&D managers were interested in working better with finance managers, but lacking knowledge about discounted cash flow, depreciation rates, capital projections, corporate taxes, etc., they conducted their R&D in a partial vacuum. They also had great difficulty in explaining the value of R&D to finance managers and to financially oriented business managers.

Level C: Right skills are in place. The R&D managers at an aerospace company understood financial matters, but they had difficulty communicating with finance people because they sought, but could not find, methods for determining the financial benefits of R&D. Although these R&D managers understood concepts such as discounted cash

flow and depreciation rates, they could not translate technical results in a way that would reveal the financial benefits of R&D. In other words, they understood the technology and they more or less understood financial matters, but they could not bridge the gap.

Level D: Appropriate methods are used. At a chemical company, there were technically knowledgeable economic analysts who worked with R&D people in bridging this gap between technology and finance. These analysts had training in engineering economics and other financial disciplines, but also had worked with R&D for many years. Nevertheless, although R&D managers found the analysts to be helpful, there still were disagreements about when they should get involved in evaluating the worth of an R&D project and about what their responsibilities were for the evaluation of R&D.

Level E: Responsibilities are clarified. At a consumer products company, a finance person was transferred to the R&D department to serve as a bridge between R&D and finance. He worked closely with R&D managers to improve the financial management of the laboratory and he explained

TABLE 10.9
Activity 9—Fostering Collaboration Between R&D and Finance

		Points
Level A (Not recognized)	R&D department does not recognize how poor its relations with the finance or accounting department are (*health care products*).	0
Level B (Initial efforts)	R&D managers are interested in working better with finance, but lack knowledge about the financial affairs of the company (*food processing*).	1
Level C (Skills)	Understands financial matters, but lacks methods for determining the financial benefits of R&D (*aerospace*).	2
Level D (Methods)	Economic analysts work closely with R&D people, but there are disagreements about involvement and responsibilities (*chemical*).	3
Level E (Responsibilities)	A finance person is transferred to R&D to serve as a bridge with finance, but company's accounting procedures short-change benefits of technology (*consumer products*).	4
Level F (Continuous improvements)	R&D managers have option of discussing with finance manager how economic analyses of technology are conducted if it looks like strategic benefits of technology are neglected (*defense electronics*).	5

☐ = Average R&D department.

the value of R&D to finance managers. Nonetheless, even with these improvements the value of R&D was not always appreciated in this company because its accounting procedures shortchanged the benefits of technology.

Level F: Continuous improvement is underway. A defense electronics company solved this problem of shortchanging the benefits of technology by giving R&D managers the option of discussing with the finance managers how economic analyses were conducted, if they thought that these analyses neglected the strategic benefits of technology. For example, if an R&D manager thought that a benefit such as the capability for providing better field services to existing customers, or for making quicker deliveries of products, or for improving quality, would not be taken into account, he or she could discuss with finance managers how these benefits could be reckoned with when decisions about technology were made.

10. LINKING R&D TO BUSINESS PLANNING

Level A: Issue is not recognized. The R&D department of a pulp and paper company took a completely unstructured approach to managing technology. It did not plan its own R&D, and it did not try to integrate its R&D into the company's short- and medium-range planning. Instead, the R&D department pursued long-term research based on its own ideas about what the business would need in the future. Because the company did not have long-term plans, the research was almost never linked to the business goals.

Level B: Initial efforts are made toward addressing issue. At a food processing company, the R&D department did want to have technology plans and to integrate them into the business plans. It set up a group of planners that was assigned the responsibility of developing technology plans for the laboratory as a whole. Because the planners knew far more about data collection than about developing plans and getting planning accepted and

implemented, they failed in their mission and the group was eventually disbanded. This group of planners was committed to planning, but it did not know how to plan.

The *average R&D department* operates at this level. It wants better planning of overall R&D goals and use of R&D resources, but it does not know how to develop technology plans. The selection of individual projects in the average R&D department is done without reference to technology plans. The budgeting of R&D resources consists of funding the projects that are selected. Rather than having a clear overall direction, the average R&D department has merely a collection of diverse projects.

Level C: Right skills are in place. At an instruments company, the R&D department had the skills to plan but it lacked the methods for analyzing technologies. Without techniques for evaluating the company's technical strengths and weaknesses, for assessing the potential of new technologies, and for translating technical capabilities into business applications, it was not able to develop the kind of technology plans it wanted to.

Level D: Appropriate methods are used. In a natural resources company, the R&D department developed its own techniques for analyzing technology. Consequently, it was able to develop technology plans that delineated where the laboratory was going. However, disputes arose between company business planners and the R&D planners about what part technology planning should play in business planning. The business planners had their own plans and did not want technology incorporated into them. They felt that it was not the responsibility of the R&D department to get its technology plans incorporated into company plans.

Level E: Responsibilities are clarified. At a telecommunications company, the R&D department and the business units developed plans and coordinated those plans with each other. Although this company made significant progress in planning, each year the planners had to revive interest in planning. The R&D managers and business managers developed plans when required, but they did

TABLE 10.10
Activity 10—Linking R&D to Business Planning

		Points
Level A (Not recognized)	R&D department takes a completely unstructured approach to managing technology (*pulp and paper*).	0
Level B (Initial efforts)	R&D planners want better planning, but know more about data collection than about developing plans and getting planning accepted and implemented (*food processing*).	1
Level C (Skills)	R&D department has the skills to plan, but lacks methods for analyzing technologies (*instruments*).	2
Level D (Methods)	Although there is planning in both R&D and in the businesses, there are disputes about what part technology should play in business planning (*natural resources*).	3
Level E (Responsibilities)	Technology and business planning are accepted and done, but the planning process is taken as a given (*telecommunications*).	4
Level F (Continuous improvements)	An R&D planning group orchestrates technology audits, but also tracks planning decisions about technology and sponsors an audit of its own activities (*specialty materials*).	5

☐ = Average R&D department.

not embrace the ideas of planning or look for ways of improving the planning process.

Level F: Continuous improvement is underway. At a specialty materials company, planning was fully embraced within the R&D department and in the rest of the company, where it was part of the mainstream of company activities. For example, there was an R&D planning group that orchestrated audits of various technical groups' technologies. This planning group helped technical groups and business groups to make assessments of the strengths and weaknesses of the technologies in their businesses, and to plan the development of new technologies. In addition, this planning group worked at improving the planning process, by for example, helping technical and business groups track their planning decisions about technology, and by sponsoring an audit of the planning group's own activities.

THE AVERAGE R&D DEPARTMENT

In reviewing all ten R&D activities, one can see the "average" R&D department operates at various levels, depending upon the activity. The average score for the average R&D department on all ten activities is 1.7, somewhat below the mid-point of 2.5. The average R&D department operates best when selecting R&D and planning and managing projects. In these two activities, the average department uses appropriate methods but has not clarified the responsibilities of various groups. It operates fairly effectively in these two areas for two reasons: First, all R&D managers continually try to find better ways of selecting R&D; second, most R&D managers now accept that in order to accomplish technical objectives on time and within budget an R&D department must have effective methods for planning and managing projects.

In four of the ten activities—generating new product ideas, maintaining quality of the R&D processes and methods, coordinating R&D and marketing, and transferring technology to manufacturing—the average R&D department does somewhat less well: It has the right skills in place, but it does not use the appropriate methods. There are three reasons for this:

1. Finding and implementing good methods of generating new product ideas requires a different kind of management talent than selecting R&D or planning and managing projects does. To generate new product ideas, an innovative environment must exist; otherwise, methods for stimulating creativity will not work well. The managers of the average R&D department are much better at, say, selecting projects than in creating an innovative environment.

2. Until five or ten years ago, the average R&D department did not pay much attention to the quality of the R&D processes and methods. This is illustrated by the dearth of articles about quality in R&D before the early 1980s. Currently, the average R&D department is looking for methods of improving quality within R&D and, on the whole, has just started implementing them.

3. The average R&D department has the skills to work with the marketing and manufacturing departments but has not developed the right mechanisms for improving coordination with them. To develop such mechanisms, R&D departments need to establish common goals with marketing and manufacturing—which, of course, requires improved coordination. In other words, the average R&D department is caught in a vicious circle as it tries to improve its relations with the marketing and manufacturing departments—it cannot develop the right mechanisms until it improves coordination, and it cannot improve coordination until it develops the right mechanisms.

In three of the four remaining activities—motivating technical people, establishing cross-disciplinary teams, and linking R&D to business planning—the average R&D department has made initial efforts toward addressing the issues, but does not now have the right skills in place to be effective. With regard to motivating technical people and establishing cross-disciplinary teams, the main reason for the average R&D department's weakness is the managers' poor skills in dealing with people. R&D managers, on the whole, are technically trained and oriented much more toward technical than management issues. To motivate technical people, an R&D manager must first understand what technical people want and value. To establish cross-disciplinary teams effectively, the manager must appreciate the interests of many potentially conflicting individuals or groups. In general, managers in the average R&D department fall short in these areas.

With regard to planning, the average R&D department does not do well, partly because the average company does not do planning well. Long-range planning requires a dedication to asking tough questions about future possibilities, and to making a solid commitment to take actions in accordance with one's plans. Neither the average R&D department nor the average company knows how to do this effectively.

With regard to the remaining activity—fostering collaboration between R&D and finance—the average R&D department does very poorly. Very few technical people have an appreciation of financial matters or close contact with members of the finance department. To the average technical person, the finance department seems like a distant operation that is preoccupied with numbers. People in the average R&D department also do not understand how much their lack of understanding about financial issues hampers company support for technology.

11

How Good Is Our Research?

WALTER L. ROBB

Four measurements help the GE R&D Center determine whether its research is as productive as it should be.

In June, 1990 the *Wall Street Journal* presented a very flattering—and accurate—picture of the efforts of the GE R&D Center to, as it put it, "move ideas from lab to market." The reporter summed it up succinctly: "Research thrives, and sells." I couldn't have said it better myself.

The theme correctly reflected the current dual emphasis at the R&D Center: internally, to increase the freedom and initiative of researchers to come up with more new ideas and do more exploratory research; externally, an increased emphasis on effectively marketing R&D to the company's businesses. That means both marketing the capabilities of researchers to produce unique, strategically important forefront technology to meet challenges and problems the businesses already know about, and also marketing the results of our own explorations beyond the current scope of those businesses' technical efforts.

For an impressionistic survey of this emphasis and its success I direct you to the article. But a more critical audience of R&D professionals deserves a more searching look at a particular aspect of this new emphasis that impressionistic accounts tend to overlook: namely, how do we know it is working? In particular, how can an R&D Center, while becoming more exploratory and better at marketing its skills and its results, meet critical scrutiny from the company's top management? As R&D gets viewed more critically from the corporate office, the need grows to give straight answers to the question: "How do we know our research is as productive as it should be?" In today's era of intense global competition, we can't rely on history or sentiment. We are living at a time when sudden changes breed short memories. One day the corporate lab is praised as the "lab that never lets you down." The next day its damned as the lab that hasn't had a really good new idea in 30 years.

In this era, lab directors aren't going to get away with qualitative assertions about productivity. I recall a conversation I had with one of my contemporaries, the director of a corporate lab. He told me, "My predecessor used to say that the best measurement of R&D is inversely proportional to the number of times that you're asked to measure R&D." Then that contemporary of mine paused for a moment and said, "Come to think about it, maybe that's how the guy who said that *became* my predecessor."

One sure way to become a predecessor is to blithely tell the CEO that good research is too mystical to be measured. It's one thing to recognize that all measurements of research are imperfect. But it's quite another thing to say that because they are imperfect, we shouldn't measure at all. It's also important to recognize that the measurement process shouldn't become so intense that it wastes the time of the researchers and leads to second-guessing and acrimony among the management. We need measures that indicate productivity without themselves having a negative effect on productivity. With that in mind, I describe here four ways of measuring the impact of our renewed approach to R&D. Each of them is incomplete in itself. But each adds an important dimension to the total picture. I'll start with

Reprinted with permission from *Research-Technology Management,* March–April, 1991.

Walter Robb is Senior Vice President for Corporate R&D at the General Electric Company. He is also a member of GE's Corporate Executive Council.

the roughest and most impressionistic, and work my way to more quantifiable, definite measures.

THE "JIMMY STEWART TEST"

The first is what I call the "Jimmy Stewart test," after the actor. One of his most famous roles was in a movie called "It's a Wonderful Life." In it, he plays a man who runs a small-town savings and loan. A sudden setback has left him discouraged and considering suicide. At that point, his guardian angel comes down from heaven and figures out a way to cheer him up and save his life. The guardian angel shows Jimmy Stewart how much worse the world would have been if he *hadn't* lived.

In much the same way, we can ask ourselves a similar question. What would our companies look like today if a central research laboratory had *not* existed? What businesses would the company *not* now be in? What profits would be foregone? In GE, that's pretty easy. GE Medical Systems—a $2 billion business—would not have existed without inventions from the R&D Center. And, more recently, it could very well have been put out of business—been sold or traded off, even possibly shut down—if it hadn't been for continuous innovation from the R&D Center.

The breakthrough technology in medical diagnostics in the 1970s was computed tomography. In GE, only the corporate laboratory had the range of skills and the inventiveness to create a leadership product for the company. And the story was repeated in the 1980s for magnetic resonance imaging. The impact can be easily measured. At GE Medical Systems, we had between $1–5 million net income from 1950–1974. Starting in 1974, with the marriage with Corporate R&D, net income shot up to $150 million in the 1980s.

GE Plastics, a $3 billion business, again, would not have made it into the modern age without the corporate lab. It was originally based on mature and non-proprietary products and processes, like phenolics, glyptal and plastics molding—businesses GE has long since exited. It was the connection with corporate R&D that produced the series of new and proprietary polymers—such as Lexan® polycarbonate resin, Noryl® resins, and Ultem® polyetherimides—that enabled GE to become the world leader in engineering plastics. So without in any way minimizing the importance of such elements as marketing and manufacturing, we can conclude that the corporate lab was an absolutely critical reason why GE Plastics not only escaped obsolescence, but is now producing hundreds of millions of dollars of net income for the company.

A third major example is GE Lighting. Again, the story goes way back to a crisis that threatened GE's role as a leader—the development of tungsten filaments for incandescent lamps. Again, in addition to making the invention that solved that problem, the corporate lab went on to make a series of major lighting inventions that broadened the product line—such inventions as the Lucalox and Multivapor lamps. Again, the result was hundreds of millions of dollars of net income that might have been threatened without the continuing technology edge.

Add up the income from these three businesses alone and you're in the range of several hundred million dollars. Giving the R&D Center only a fraction of the credit for it puts us pretty far along in justifying our existence in hard dollars–and–cents terms. More important, our relationship with these three businesses is not a one-shot historical event. It's an ongoing story. By 1989, major new products and processes were being either newly announced or solidly launched for each of these businesses to continue the story.

But this kind of analysis has another side to it. At the GE R&D Center we must be honest and modest and recognize that there are 11 other major GE businesses where we have *not* in the past been on the critical path. The businesses are power systems, appliances, transportation, construction equipment, credit, broadcasting, motors, automation, aerospace, aircraft engines, and communications. We have made contributions to almost all of these businesses, and substantial contributions to most of them. But we can't claim to have been critical for their survival and growth. So this first kind of measure—looking for your role as a critical path resource—not only makes it possible to justify the existence of the corporate lab. It also helps point out where improvement is needed. And that's an important role for any measurement of productivity.

Right now, getting on the critical path of more of the company's businesses is a crucial part of our dual emphasis on more exploration and better technology transfer. We have initiatives underway with many of those 11 businesses that go far beyond our impact in the past. We will measure ourselves in the future in part by how well we are able to bring these initiatives off.

COUNTING OUTPUTS

That "Jimmy Stewart test" I've just described—estimating what the company would have foregone if you hadn't been there—is only one part of the story. A second type of measure that we have found useful is counting outputs. Over the years, our laboratory has tried counting just about everything—counting liaison reports, counting memos and counting papers, for example. We've come to believe that the best thing to count, even though it only imperfectly reflects the output of the lab, is patents. I'm familiar with all the disadvantages of patents as a measure. But as Winston Churchill said about democracy, it's a bad system—the only thing worse is all the others. Patents at least correspond to one important thing we're supposed to be doing—invention—and are subjected to an external validity check, at the Patent Office.

One rough measure we've found illuminating is cost per patent. To get a first indication of the bang corporations get from their own R&D buck, we've estimated patents obtained per million dollars of own-funds R&D spending. We've used one patent per "megabuck" as a kind of benchmark. We were pleased to see that our figure stood at substantially better than that, at about 1.25 patents per megabuck. Most of our major advanced technology competitors in the U.S. were substantially below that one patent-per-megabuck figure. To be complete, we didn't beat all our U.S. competitors. One scored the remarkable figure of three patents per megabuck. But we think that's the consequence of a cutback in R&D spending coinciding with the reaping of previous years' work as patents. That's the trouble with using ratios of output to input as measures. A high score can reflect decreases in input rather than increases in output.

Another objection to the use of patents as a measure is that it measures not the productivity of researchers, but the productivity of patent attorneys. We're quite proud of the productivity of ours. In fact, we've got them on an incentive system where their pay is partly determined by the number of patent applications they complete and ship off to Washington. That system is so successful that the Patent Office itself is copying some of our plan's features. But we don't believe that the attorneys' productivity explains away all the differences in patent figures between companies. It especially doesn't explain away the performance at the Patent Office of the Japanese. Patenting in the U.S. is the single best measure of the remarkable surge in Japanese technology in the past couple of decades. For example, Japan now gets more U.S. patents than the United Kingdom, France and West Germany *combined*. In terms of other measures—for example, scientific publications and citations—Japan lags far behind those countries.

We've tried to look more closely into the patent numbers, particularly in comparing ourselves with our Japanese competitors. We've looked at the number of times a patent is cited, and find that the Japanese patents hold up well in this regard—in some high-tech areas Japanese patents are cited more than American ones. (See, for example, Francis Narin and J. Davidson Frame, "The Growth of Japanese Science and Technology," *Science,* 14 August, 1989, for a discussion of this and other patent-related issues in the open literature.) Again there are problems—for example, tighter communities tend to reference their own patents back and forth.

Another measure is the number of fields or subfields the patent attorney indexes. The more basic the patent, the more fields it will be indexed to.

Here, the Japanese tend to focus their work more on target fields, rather than looking for basic inventions outside their previous realm of interest, as U.S. firms are more prone to do.

Within GE, another of the measures we've found useful is foreign filings. In our company the operating department decides how many countries in which to file. We find that GE businesses tend to file patents from the corporate lab in more countries than they file their own. This is another indicator that we are doing our job of providing GE businesses with a significant technological edge worthy of patent protection.

Yet another measure is licensing income. This is an area where we learned a lot from RCA. In GE, in the past, licensing wasn't taken as seriously as it should have been, in part because each business was given responsibility for the patents it owned—including technology that had been created on its behalf by the R&D Center. The last thing the business wanted to do was tell the chairman it was making its net income from licensing. That's not a macho thing to do. However, when you sum up all the licensing income of GE in 1989 it added up to $359 million. That's beginning to sound pretty macho.

At the R&D Center, we've used licensing as one more measure of our effectiveness. We've looked at the license agreements that the company businesses signed that generated licensing revenue. The total licensing revenue in that category was in the tens of millions of dollars. It included a wide range of technology—from flat panel liquid crystal displays, to technology for large steam turbine generators, CT scanners and HVDC transformers. In one area alone, which the company had largely neglected before the RCA people encouraged us to look more closely, we found we owned key patents on technology used in camcorders and facsimile machines. Those patents now bring in licensing income in the neighborhood of $10 million a year.

Another important patent-related issue for measuring the value of R&D is how much royalties GE businesses are avoiding paying because of patents. What is the business paying versus what the competition is paying? GE Medical, for example, looks good in this regard. It has been able to swap patents to get the rights it needs. Some of its competitors have had to pay top dollar for those rights because all they had was money. Also, GE Aircraft Engines recently had a patent issue with its major competitor, and was able to settle it as an exchange of patents rather than paying out money. The technology that made this possible came out of the corporate laboratory. To sum up my views on counting outputs as a measure, all counting gives an incomplete picture. But of all the candidates, patents, and related areas like patent citations and licensing, are the best things to count.

ANALYZING TECHNOLOGY TRANSITIONS

But what really counts is dollars and cents. How much is the technology generated by the R&D Center worth to the company? To get a better handle on this issue, we tried a third type of measurement—a rigorously-carried-out discounted rate of return analysis of transitions. By that word transition, we are talking about a technology advance that originated in the R&D Center and was moved to a business operation. Here we do not restrict ourselves to the critical path innovations but look at a broader spectrum of our work. In doing so, we followed the old saying that "only the Almighty is qualified to look upon His own work and declare that it is good." So we asked an outside organization, Booz, Allen & Hamilton, to carry out the analysis.

Here's how they did it. Booz, Allen made a full list of the transitions of technology that the R&D Center attempted to make to GE businesses in the mid-1980s. They performed a discounted cash flow analysis, based on inputs from the receivers of the transition—how much did it really cost? Was it successful? How much of the credit belongs to the R&D Center? How much benefit will result, in dollars and cents? Using those inputs, they computed the payback, present value of the investment in the R&D, and the rate of return on the investment.

The Booz, Allen consultants sat down with people from the R&D Center and compiled a list of transitions that occurred in the 1982–1987 period. After looking at some 240 candidates from the 1980s, they settled on 190 transitions that fell fully within the time period and for which we had enough information. For each one, the team prepared a one-page summary that included the time of starting the program, the date the transition was started and the success status of the program—did it provide the business with a technology edge that translates into measurable financial benefits? What is the amount of those estimated benefits and their time frame? How much is in hand already, and how is the rest expected to be distributed over the years ahead?

Next, how much credit does the R&D Center deserve for those benefits? What is the Center's role in the technology? Sometimes that role is as a leader and enabler—we get the idea for an innovation and sell it to an initially reluctant product department. More frequently, our role is that of partner and collaborator. In these cases the business comes to us with a problem or opportunity, or we work together to define it.

The next and most tricky part of the procedure is to translate the R&D Center's credit into a percentage. Does our role entitle us to 10 percent of the credit for the benefits of the project, for example, or 50 percent or 90 percent? To arrive at this number the Booz, Allen consultants talked to the receivers of the transition, the people in the operating departments. Their estimates of the credit to go to the R&D Center were generally in pretty close agreement with those made by the Center's own people. In some cases they were more generous. I recall one example where an engineering manger of a business credited us with 110 percent of the benefits. When we asked him what he meant by that, he replied, "Well, we told the researchers to stop working on that project, but fortunately they didn't listen to us!"

Taking the numbers for the stream of costs and of benefits over time, the Booz, Allen consultants carried out some fairly standard accounting calculations to arrive at the present value of the expenditure on the R&D—that is, the amount of today's dollars for which it would make sense to exchange the stream of projected benefits. They used that to figure the payback on the R&D expenditure, expressed as a ratio of present value to investment, and the rate of return on investment expressed as a percentage. That gives the corporate office a way to compare its investment in R&D with other types of investments, such as new manufacturing plant, or acquisitions. The consultants carried out this analysis for all 190 of the transitions, and did an intensive analysis for three GE businesses, doing in-depth interviews with the receivers of the technology in order to make sure that the numerical results really reflected what was happening. In selecting these businesses, we made a point of *not* choosing Plastics or Medical, two where we knew in advance the results would turn out highly positive.

Here's how the study turned out. For the entire sample of 190 transitions, the consultants calculated a 20 percent rate of return, which translates into a present value ratio of nearly 2—that is, *the value of the output of the R&D Center is about twice the cost*. That compares very favorably with alternative uses of the money. For the three businesses looked at in detail the results looked like this:

	Present Value	Rate of Return
Business A	5.5	40%
Business B	2.0	22%
Business C	1.8	19%

Incidentally, I mentioned that we deliberately chose the ones to look at in detail so they wouldn't be ones where we were obviously on the critical path. But in the case of Business A, an invention we made has turned out to be a critical path achievement, even though it was not initially expected to be one. The nature of the business changed—in the direction that made the technology absolutely crucial. So we were able to add one more to the list of businesses where we have provided a crucial strategic advantage—a list that we'd eventually like to see encompass all of GE's 14 businesses.

We don't take those present value and rate-of-return numbers to be more than an approximate measure. For one thing, a lot depends on present estimates of future return. Of that overall 20 percent rate of return, 2 percent was "in the bank" at the time of the study, 8 percent was "in the mail"—that is, it represented firm orders or savings that were in place and will continue—and the other 10 percent represented "in progress, or potential" returns—estimates that tracked with the business plan for the years until the benefits of this innovation are fully reaped. Nothing has occurred in the two years since the study to suggest the returns were overrated.

As I indicated earlier, for measurements of productivity to be useful they must be more than disembodied numbers. They must give you understanding you previously lacked about how you are doing, and how you can do better. The Booz, Allen study did these things. It clarified for us, for example, how much of the return on technology transitions is tied to a very small number of transitions. In this case, over 50 percent of the return is driven by only five transitions.

It also clarified how widely the payback varied over different projects. A small number of transitions have a very high payback and a substantial number have a very small payback. Only about half the transitions yielded paybacks above breakeven. In the three businesses which we looked at intensively, for example, there were 7 very high payback-ratio transitions ("very high" meant more than 15), 5 moderate (payback ratio 2–15), and 22 with a payback ratio less than 2. It is natural for company executives to look at these numbers and say, "If only you'd gotten rid of those 22 dogs—those low payoff programs—think what a terrific overall rate of return you would have!" And it's a natural reaction of R&D people to laugh at that objection and accuse those executives of not understanding what R&D is all about. If you knew in advance what the payoff would be, then its not R&D!

But we can use studies like this to get clues for recognizing the reason programs that initially sound promising turn into dogs. In the case of the ones we looked at, the list of reasons projects were not successful reads like this: "Inability to meet market timing requirements. . . . market changed . . . product late to market . . . mismatch between technology and market life cycles . . . product cost performance not in line with market requirement . . . GE got out of the business." As you look at that kind of list, you see that purely technical success or failure rarely plays the decisive role in transition success. Usually the technologists are able to meet or exceed the technical goals that have been set. But this is far from guaranteeing the success of the transition. In some cases we poured millions of dollars into programs that, while meeting one technical goal after another, became less and less valuable to the intended customer.

VOTING WITH DOLLARS

Such considerations further sensitized us to the need to monitor the business aspects of a transition as closely as we have always monitored the technology aspects. That in turn led us to the fourth kind of measurement, which might be labeled the "free market measurement." This, quite simply, is a method where our customers, the people in GE businesses, vote with their dollars. In the past, we had an R&D Center funding system under which we got only about one-third of our funding from contracts with GE businesses and external agencies. We got about two-thirds of our money in the form of what we called "assessed" funds. This was money assessed by Corporate headquarters from GE businesses according to a formula that took the sales, profitability and technology-intensiveness of the businesses into account. The money was then shipped to us. We worked hard to use it to benefit the businesses it came from, but there was no direct accountability on a business-by-business basis.

In 1988, a task force of GE technical leaders came up with a new funding system. Under it, we now raise some three-fourths of our annual funding through contracts with individual businesses, and one-fourth is assessed funds. That one-fourth is deliberately ticketed for exploratory work above and beyond the identified needs of GE's current businesses. This new system serves as both a measurement process and a funding system. Our ability to raise funds for future work from GE's businesses is a direct measurement of their satisfaction with our past work and expectations for the future. This method of dividing our support between contract and assessed funding is at the very core of our dual approach to more exploration and better marketing.

The current split of one-quarter exploratory/assessed, three-quarters contract is not set in concrete. But the basic idea is now well established. The most effective marketing of most of our effort is done up front—in working with the businesses to understand their strategies, determine how technology fits in and get our contract programs on their critical path. We need to do that not only as a way of raising money but as a way of getting the full attention and involvement of the people who will bring the technology to customers. If we supported our work entirely by contracts, we would be letting down on the other important responsibility of a corporate R&D Center: gaining the knowledge and trying out the imaginative ideas that the company's businesses don't even know they need yet.

This system doesn't yet provide a method of measuring the value of our exploratory work. By the very nature of the work, it takes a long range measurement—if the work had a payoff within two years, then it wouldn't be exploration. But the long time scale does not absolve us of the need to measure—it merely makes that need more long term, in order to truly capture the full benefits of exploratory work. It might be, for example, that even if our explorers did not bring back a single big-hit project, they still might pay their way by maintaining a laboratory climate that would help attract the kind of excellent people needed to make our

contract projects pay off. So the measurement of exploratory work remains a major challenge. Some people claim that exploratory work can only be justified on faith. I answer that, in this case, having faith is just another name for having a good memory. The payoff for exploratory work is by its nature long term and unpredictable, but the payoff is there. I am confident that with enough memory and patience, that can be demonstrated with measurements.

Such measurements will complement the four I've discussed. To sum up, they are (1) Estimating where the company would be without the lab, in terms of entire business areas foregone; (2) Counting things—we believe the best things to count are patents; (3) Transition analysis—what is the worth of the technology you undertake, measured with the help of people in the businesses that actually use it in their products and processes? (4) The free market measurement, making the level of support for the laboratory directly reflect the decisions of the businesses that will make and sell the resulting technology.

I have presented my discussion of the GE R&D Center's current dual emphasis on exploration and marketing in terms of measurement to make an important point. That emphasis is not simply a matter of exhortation or image, but it is something we are willing—indeed eager—to stand up and be measured on. No one measurement suffices by itself; all measurements are imperfect. But these four, taken together, tell a very positive story of productivity and contribution to the Company's performance. We're not afraid of being measured. We're confident that the more we are measured, the more evident it will be that in an era of global competition, the most productive place a company can invest its money is in the brains of its brightest people—that is, in supporting corporate level R&D.

MANAGING INNOVATIVE GROUPS
AND PROJECT TEAMS

4

The Management of High Performing Technical Teams

12

Building High Performing Engineering Project Teams

HANS J. THAMHAIN
DAVID L. WILEMON

Team building is the process of taking a collection of individuals with different needs, backgrounds, and expertise and transforming them into an integrated, effective work unit. In this transformation process, the goals and energies of individual contributors merge and support the objectives of the team. The basic concept of team building goes back in history a long time. However, the onset of modern team building came with the evolution of mul-

tidisciplinary management techniques and contemporary organization forms such as matrix. With these developments, traditional bureaucratic hierarchies declined and horizontally oriented teams and work units became increasingly important.

Today, team building is considered by many management practitioners and researchers to be one of the most critical leadership qualities that determines the performance and success of multidisci-

Copyright © 1987 IEEE. Reprinted with permission from *IEEE Transactions on Engineering Management*, Vol. EM-34, No. 3, pp. 130–137, August 1987.

Hans Thamhain is Professor of Management at Bentley College. *David Wilemon* is Professor of Management at Syracuse University.

plinary efforts. The outcomes of these projects critically depend on carefully orchestrated group efforts, requiring the coordination and integration of many task specialists in a dynamic work environment with complex organization interfaces. Therefore, it is not surprising to find a strong emphasis on team work and team building practice among today's managers, a trend which, we expect, will continue and most likely intensify for years to come.

ENGINEERING TEAM BUILDING TODAY

Team building is important in any environment which requires the coordination and integration of multidisciplinary activities. It is especially crucial in a technical environment where projects are often highly complex and require the integration of many functional specialties in an often unconventional organizational setting such as the matrix. To manage these multifunctional activities, it is necessary for the managers and their lead engineering personnel to cross organizational lines and deal with resource personnel over whom they have little or no formal authority. Yet another set of challenges is presented by the contemporary nature of the engineering organization with its horizontal and vertical lines of communication and control, its resource sharings among projects and task teams, multiple reporting relationships to several bosses, and dual accountabilities.

Managing technical projects effectively in such dynamic environments requires the understanding of organizational and behavioral variables and their interaction. It is further necessary to foster a climate conducive to multidisciplinary team building. Such a team must have a capacity for innovatively transforming a set of technical objectives and requirements into specific products, system concepts, or services that compete favorably against other available alternatives.

BASIS OF THIS REPORT

The team building concept is not entirely new, it's been around for thousands of years, but its application to systematic efforts within a permanent organizational framework—rather than temporary work setting—is relatively recent. Starting with the evolution of formal project organizations in the 1960's, managers in various organizational settings have expressed increasing concern and interest on the concepts and practices of multidisciplinary team building. Responding to this interest, many field studies have been conducted investigating work group dynamics in a general context contributing to the theoretical and practical understanding of team building.[2–4, 6, 13, 14, 18, 20, 38] However, few studies specifically focus on the process and criteria of building effective high-performing engineering teams.[18, 19, 24, 37] Because of this special need and interest the authors have organized and conducted a series of studies over the last four years. These field studies analyzed some 30 companies involving over 500 engineering professionals including 37 managers. All of these companies were U.S. based and were managers of high-technology businesses. The data were gathered primarily by means of interviews augmented by short questionnaires. The results are documented in five research papers listed below:

1. skill requirements for engineering program managers[30],

2. professional needs analysis of engineering personnel versus performance[29],

3. analysis of barriers to teamwork and potential effects on project performance[35],

4. determination of team performance measures and their drivers and barriers, some performance correlates[31],

5. a model for developing high-performing project teams.[37]

This article is an attempt to summarize and integrate the findings from our research and to establish a conceptional framework for effective team building in an engineering/technological work environment.

Originally, a broadly stated proposition was defined to guide our research. It is restated here to focus this paper and to help in guiding the discussion:

P: Engineering team performance is associated with drivers and barriers related predominately to 1) leadership and 2) a professionally stimulating work environment.

MODEL FOR TEAM BUILDING

The characteristics of a project team and its ultimate performance depends on many factors. Using a systems approach, Figure 12.1 provides a simple model for organizing and analyzing these factors. It defines three sets of variables: 1) *inputs* such as resources and objectives, 2) *outputs* of the workgroups such as the team results or the team characteristics, and 3) *influences* toward effective team work such as leadership, job content, personal goals, and work environment. All of these variables are likely to be interrelated in a complex, intricate form. However, using the systems approach allows researchers and management practitioners to break down the complexity of the team work process which transforms resources into specific results under the influence of managerial, organizational, and other environmental factors. Furthermore, the model can provide a framework for studying team characteristics and performance at various phases of a project life cycle. Such an investigation has

been initiated by the authors. It will include the following project phases: 1) Project Definition and Planning, 2) Project Start-Up, 3) Main Phase, and 4) Project Phase-Out.

FACETS OF TEAM PERFORMANCE

Obviously, each organization has their own way to measure and express performance of a project team. However, in spite of the existing cultural and philosophical differences there seems to be a general agreement among engineering managers on certain factors which are included in the characteristics of a successful technical project team. In fact, over 90 percent of the 500 engineering professionals interviewed over the last four years mentioned three measures as the most important criteria for measuring team performance:

1. technical success,
2. on-time performance,
3. on-budget/within resource performance.

Further, over 60 percent of those who identified these three measures, ranked them in the above order.

When describing the characteristics of an ef-

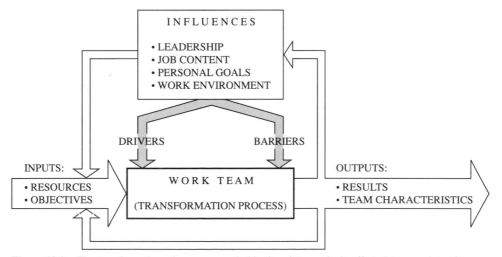

Figure 12.1. The transformation of resources and objectives into results is affected by a variety of drivers and barriers.

fective, high-performing engineering team, managers point at the factors summarized in Figure 12.2. These managers stress consistently that a high-performing engineering team not only produces technical results on time and on budget but is also characterized by *specific task* and *people-related qualities* as shown below.

Task-Related Qualities	People-Related Qualities
• oriented toward technical success; • committed to the project; result-oriented attitude; • innovative and creative;	• high involvement, work interest, and energy; • capacity to solve conflict; • good communication;
• concern for quality; • willingness to change project plan if necessary; • ability to predict trends; • on-time performance; • on-budget performance.	• good team spirit; • mutual trust; • self-development of team members; • effective organizational interfacing; • high need for achievement.

In fact, some quantitative analysis, performed during previous studies[31,32], shows a statistically significant association between the above team qualities and team performance at a confidence

JOB/RESULT-ORIENTED CHARACTERISTICS (DIRECT MEASURE OF PROJECT PERFORMANCE)

PEOPLE-ORIENTED CHARACTERISTICS (INDIRECT MEASURE OF PROJECT PERFORMANCE)

TECHNICAL SUCCESS — R.1

ON-TIME, ON-BUDGET PERFORMANCE — R.2

COMMITTED, RESULT-ORIENTED — R.3

INNOVATIVE, CREATIVE — R.4

CONCERN FOR QUALITY — R.5

WILLINGNESS TO CHANGE — R.6

ABILITY TO PREDICT TRENDS — R.7

THE EFFECTIVE ENGINEEREING TEAM

P.1 — HIGH INVOLVEMENT, HIGH ENERGY

P.2 — CAPACITY TO SOLVE CONFLICT

P.3 — GOOD COMMUNICATIONS

P.4 — GOOD TEAM SPIRIT

P.5 — MUTUAL TRUST

P.6 — MEMBERSHIP SELF-DEVELOPMENT

P.7 — EFFECTIVE ORGANIZAT'L INTERFACE

P.8 — HIGH NEED FOR ACHIEVEMENT

Figure 12.2. Characteristics of an effective engineering team.

level of $p = 95$ percent or better. Specifically, these measures yielded an average rank order correlation of $\tau = 0.37$. Moreover, there appears to be a strong agreement between the two professional groups, 1) managers and 2) project team members, on the importance of these characteristics, as measured via a Kruskal-Wallis analysis of variance by ranks at a confidence level of $p = 95$ percent.

The significance of determining team performance characteristics is in two areas. First, it offers some clues as to what an effective team environment looks like. This can stimulate thoughts of how to foster a work environment responsive to the needs of the people and conducive to team building. Second, the results allow us to define measures and characteristics of an effective team environment for further studies such as the subsequent discussion on drivers and barriers toward team performance.

DRIVERS AND BARRIERS OF HIGH TEAM PERFORMANCE

In 1983 and 84, additional management insight was gained by an investigation of drivers and barriers to high team performance (see 31 and 35). Drivers are factors associated with the project environment that are perceived to be enhancing team effectiveness, while barriers are perceived to be impeding team performance. A listing of the principal drivers and barriers, as perceived by project professionals is shown below:

Drivers, Enhancing Project Performance

- Professionally stimulating and challenging work;
- Professional growth potential;
- Freedom to choose, decision making;

Barriers, Impeding Project Performance

- Different interests and priorities among team members;
- Unclear project objectives;
- Role conflict and

Drivers, Enhancing Project Performance

- Good overall direction and leadership;
- Tangible rewards;
- Mutual trust, security, and open communications;
- Proper experience and skills;
- Sense of accomplishment;
- Good interpersonal relations among team members and with management;
- Proper planning;
- Sufficient resources;
- Low interpersonal conflict.

Barriers, Impeding Project Performance

power struggle among team members;
- Excessive changes of project scope, spec, schedule and budget;
- Lack of team definition and structure;
- Wrong capabilities, poor selection of project personnel;
- Lacking commitment from team members or management;
- Low credibility of project leader;
- Poor communications;
- Poor job security.

Furthermore, studies conducted by Gemmill, Thamhain, and Wilemon between 1974 and 1985[29, 31-33] showed significant correlations and interdependencies among work-environmental factors and team performance. These studies indicate that high team performance involves four primary issues: 1) managerial leadership, 2) job content, 3) personal goals and objectives, and 4) work environment and organizational support. In addition, a recent follow-up study by Thamhain (in part reported in[33]) used the above typology to collect data and categorize over 60 influence factors which were mentioned by engineering managers as drivers or barriers toward high team performance. The actual correlation of these influence factors to the project team characteristics and performance* provided some interesting insight into the strength and effect of these factors. One of the important findings was that only

*Kendall Tau rank-order correlation was used as a measure of association. For method and references to statistical models see Appendix.

12 of the 60 influence factors were found to be statistically significant. All other factors seem to be much less important to high team performance. Specifically, the findings, summarized in Figure 12.3, indicate that the *six drivers which have the strongest positive association with project team performance are:*

- Interesting and stimulating work,
- Recognition of accomplishment (of individual or team),
- Experienced engineering management personnel,
- Proper technical direction and leadership,
- Qualified project team personnel, and

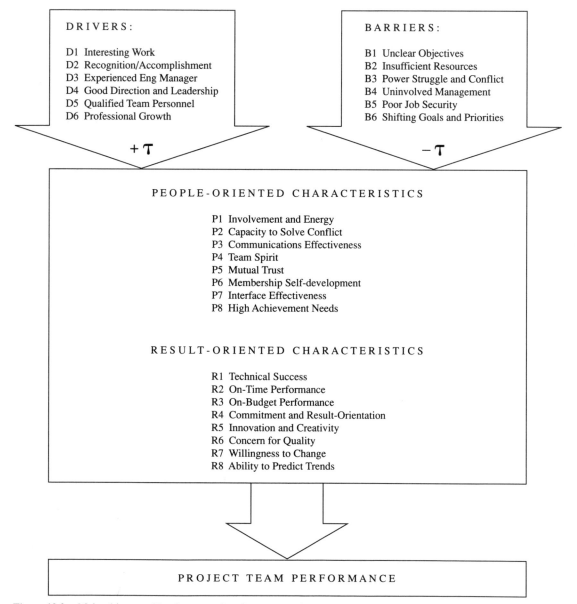

Figure 12.3.   Major drivers and barriers toward project team performance.

- Professional growth potential

while the *strongest barriers to project team performance are:*

- Unclear project objectives and directions,
- Insufficient resources,
- Power struggle and conflict,
- Uninvolved, disinterested senior management,
- Poor job security,
- Shifting goals and priorities.

It is furthermore interesting to note that the six drivers not only correlated favorably to the direct measures of high project team performance, such as technical success and on-time/on-budget performance, but also were positively associated with the 13 indirect measures of team performance shown in Figure 12.2. The six barriers have exactly the opposite effect. These findings provide some quantitative support to previous exploratory field studies by the authors.[35, 37] What we find consistently is that successful organizations pay attention to the human side. They appear effective in fostering a work environment conducive to innovative work, where people find the assignments challenging, leading to recognition and professional growth. Such a professionally stimulating environment also seems to lower communication barriers and conflict, and enhances the desire of personnel to succeed. This seems to enhance organizational awareness as well as the ability to respond to the often changing project requirements.

In addition, a winning team appears to have good leadership. That is, management understands the factors crucial to success. They are action-oriented, provide the needed resources, properly direct the implementation of the project, plan, and help in the identification and resolution of problems in their early stages.

Taken together, the findings offer support for the propositions P advanced earlier and restated here somewhat modified and more specifically in two parts:

P1: The degree of project success seems primarily determined by the strength of six driving forces and six barriers which are related to: 1) leadership, 2) job content, 3) personal needs, and 4) the general work environment.

P2: A professionally stimulating team environment, characterized by 1) interesting challenging work, 2) visibility and recognition for achievements, 3) growth potential, and 4) good project leadership, is strongly correlated with project success. It also leads to low perceived conflict, high commitment, high involved personnel, good communications, change-orientation, innovation and on-time/on-budget performance.

Taken together, the findings show that to be effective in organizing and directing a project team, the leader must not only recognize the potential drivers and barriers but also know when in the life cycle of the project they are most likely to occur. The effective project leader takes preventive actions early in the project lifecycle and fosters a work environment that is conducive to team building as an ongoing process.

The effective team builder is usually a social architect who understands the interaction of organizational and behavioral variables and can foster a climate of active participation and minimal dysfunctional conflict. This requires carefully developed skills in leadership, administration, organization, and technical expertise. It further requires the project leader's ability to involve top management to assure organizational visibility, resource availability, and overall support for the new project throughout its life cycle.

It is this organizational culture which adds yet another challenge to project team building. The new team members are usually selected from functional resource departments led by strong individuals who often foster internal competition rather than cooperation. In fact, even at the individual contributor level, many of the highly innovative and creative people are high individualistically oriented and often admit their aversion to cooperation. The challenge to the project manager is to integrate these individuals into a team that can produce innovative results in a systematic, coordinated, and integrated effort to accomplish the overall project plan. Many of the problems that occur during the formation of the new project team or during its life-cycle are normal and often predictable. However, they present barriers to effective team performance. They must be quickly identified and dealt with. The following section offers specific suggestions.

RECOMMENDATIONS FOR ENGINEERING TEAM MANAGERS

A number of recommendations have been derived from the broader context of this study which can potentially increase the project manager's effectiveness in building high performing teams.

1. *Barriers:* Project managers must understand the various barriers to team development and build a work environment conducive to the team's motivational needs. Specifically, management should watch out for the following barriers: 1) unclear project objectives, 2) insufficient resources and unclear funding, 3) role conflict and power struggles, 4) uninvolved and unsupportive management, 5) poor job security, 6) shifting goals and priorities.

2. *The Project Objectives* and their importance to the organization needs to be clear to all personnel who get involved with the project. Senior management can help develop a "priority image" and communicate the basic project parameters and management guidelines.

3. *Management Commitment:* Project managers must continuously update and involve their managements to refuel their interest and commitment to the new project. Breaking the project into smaller phases and being able to produce short-range results frequently, can be important to this refueling process.

4. *Image Building:* Building a favorable image for the project, in terms of high priority, interesting work, importance to the organization, high visibility, and potential for professional rewards is crucial in attracting and holding high-quality people. It is also a pervasive process which fosters a climate of active participation at all levels; it helps

to unify the new project team and minimizes dysfunctional conflict.

5. *Leadership Positions* should be carefully defined and staffed at the beginning of a new program. Key project personnel selection is the joint responsibility of the project manager and functional management. The credibility of project leaders among team members, with senior management, and with the program sponsor is crucial to the leader's ability to manage the multi-disciplinary activities effectively across functional lines. One-on-one interviews are recommended for explaining the scope and project requirements, as well as the management philosophy, organizational structure, and rewards.

6. *Effective Planning* early in the project life cycle will have a favorable impact on the work environment and team effectiveness. Since project managers have to integrate various tasks across many functional lines. Proper planning requires the participation of the entire project team, including support departments, subcontractors, and management. These comprehensive activities, which can be performed in a special project phase such as Requirements Analysis, Product Feasibility Assessment, or Product/Project Definition, usually have a number of team building benefits.

7. *Involvement:* One of the side benefits of proper project planning is the involvement of personnel at all organizational levels. Project managers should drive such an involvement, at least with their key personnel, especially during the project definition phases. This involvement will lead to a better understanding of the task requirements, stimulate interest, help unify the team, and ultimately lead to commitment to the project plan regarding technical performance, timing, and budgets.

8. *Project Staffing:* All project assignments should be negotiated individually with each prospective team member. Each task leader should be responsible for staffing his or her own task team. Where dual-reporting relationships are involved, staffing should be conducted jointly by the two managers. The assignment interview should include a clear discussion of the specific task, the outcome, timing, responsibilities, reporting relation, potential rewards, and importance of the project to the company. Task assignments should be made only if the candidate's ability is a reasonable match to the position requirements and the candidate shows a healthy degree of interest in the project.

9. Team Structure: Management needs to define the basic team structure and operating concepts early during the project formation phase. The project plan, task matrix, project charter, and policy are the principal tools. It is the responsibility of the project manager to communicate the organizational design and to assure that all parties understand the overall and interdisciplinary project objectives. Clear and frequent communication with senior management and the new project sponsor becomes critically important. Status review meetings can be used for feedback.

10. Team Building Sessions should be conducted by the project manager throughout the project lifecycle. An especially intense effort might be needed during the team formation stage. The team is being brought together in a relaxed atmosphere to discuss such questions as:

- How are we operating as a team? What is our strength? Where can we improve? What steps are needed to initiate the desired change?

- What problems and issues are we likely to face in the future? Which of these can be avoided by taking appropriate action now? How can we "danger-proof" the team?

11. Team Commitment: Project managers should determine lack of team member commitment early in the life of the project and attempt to change possible negative views toward the project. Since insecurity is often a major reason for lacking commitment, managers should try to determine why insecurity exists, then work on reducing the team members' fears. Conflict with other team members may be another reason for lack of commitment. It is important for the project leader to intervene and mediate the conflict quickly. Finally, if a team member's professional interests may lie elsewhere, the project leader should examine ways to

satisfy part of the team member's interests by bringing personal and project goals into perspective.

12. Senior Management Support: It is critically important for senior management to provide the proper environment for the project team to function effectively. Here the project leader needs to tell management at the onset of the program what resources are needed. The project manager's relationship with senior management and ability to develop senior management support is critically affected by his or her credibility, visibility, and priority image of the project.

13. Organization Development Specialists: Project leaders should watch for changes in performance on an ongoing basis. If performance problems are observed, they should be dealt with quickly. If the project manager has access to internal or external organization development specialists, they can help diagnose team problems and assist the team in dealing with the identified problems. These specialists can also bring fresh ideas and perspectives to difficult, and sometimes emotionally complex situations.

14. Problem Avoidance: Project leaders should focus their efforts on problem avoidance. That is, the project leader, through experience, should recognize potential problems and conflicts at their onset and deal with them before they become big and their resolutions consume a large amount of time and effort.

A FINAL NOTE

In summary, effective team building can be a critical determinant of project success. Building the engineering team for a new technical project is one of the prime responsibilities of the program leader. Team building involves a whole spectrum of management skills to identify, commit, and integrate the various personnel from different functional organizations into a single task group. In many project-oriented engineering organizations, team building is a shared responsibility between the functional engineering managers and the project manager, who often reports to a different organization with a different superior.

To be effective, the project manager must provide an atmosphere conducive to teamwork. Four major considerations are involved in the integration of people from many disciplines into an effective team: 1) creating a professionally stimulating work environment, 2) good program leadership, 3) providing qualified personnel, and 4) providing a technically and organizationally stable environment. The project leader must foster an environment where the new product team members are professionally satisfied, involved, and have mutual trust. The more effectively project leaders develop team membership, the higher is the quality of information exchanged, including the candor of sharing ideas and approaches. It is this professionally stimulating involvement that also has a pervasive effect on the team's ability to cope with change and conflict, and leads to innovative performance. By contrast, when a member does not feel part of the team and does not trust others, information will not be shared willingly or openly. One project leader emphasized this point: "There's nothing worse than being on a team when no one trusts anyone else. . . . Such situations lead to gamesmanship and a lot of watching what you say because you don't want your own words to bounce back in your face. . . . "

Furthermore, the greater the team spirit, trust, and quality of information exchange among team members, the more likely the team will be able to develop effective decision-making processes, make individual and group commitment, focus on problem solving, and develop self-forcing self-correcting project controls. These are the characteristics of an effective and productive project team.

Over the next decade we anticipate important developments in team building which will lead to higher performance levels, increased morale, and a pervasive commitment to final results. Areas which should be further investigated include 1) applicability of our findings to engineering teamwork in general, 2) the differences and similarities to nonengineering teams, 3) additional studies into team performance and their correlates, and 4) studies of team performance at various project life cycle stages. These are just a few of the areas that deserve future study, and we hope that this paper will stimulate additional thoughts and research activity.

This paper summarizes several important aspects of team building in an engineering environment. It should help both the professional in the field of engineering management as well as the scholar who studies contemporary organizational concepts to understand the intricate relationships between organizational and behavioral elements. It also provides a conceptional framework for specific research and situational analysis of engineering teambuilding practices.

APPENDIX: STATISTICAL MEASURES AND RANK-ORDER CORRELATION

Association between Team Characteristics and Team Performance

The association was measured by utilizing Kendall's Tau Rank-Order Correlation and Partial Rank-Order Correlation. First, projects were rank-ordered by managers according to their performance. Then the various factors describing the team characteristics were each rank-ordered by both managers and team members according to their strength. Finally, the Tau Coefficients and their significances were calculated for each association.[40] The Kruskal-Wallis Test was used to verify that both managers and project team members believe in essentially the same qualities that should be present within an effective, high performing project team.

Correlation of Drivers and Barriers to Team Performance

Project team members were asked to rate each of the influence factors, shown as Drivers and Barriers in Figure 12.3. The rating measured the presence of each of these factors in the team environment, using a five-point scale ranging from "strongly agree" to "strongly disagree." The team rankings based on these scores were then correlated against the team rankings based on performance (P and R scores) as perceived by senior managers (R-scores) and project managers (P-scores). While the correlation factors in Table 12.1 are based on the perception of managers and team members as indicated respectively, all factors were measured as

TABLE 12.1
Drivers and Barriers toward Technical Team Performance

	People-oriented characteristics								Result-oriented characteristics								Avge
	P1	P2	P3	P4	P5	P6	P7	P8	R1	R2	R3	R4	R5	R6	R7	R8	PR
Drivers (+ τ):																	
D1 Interesting Work	+.45	.55	.35	.40	.30	.10	.20	.55	.30	.30	.20	.50	.25	.25	.25	.10	.32
D2 Recognition/ Accomplishment	+.40	.35	.20	.25	.30	.30	.15	.60	.25	.25	.15	.35	.15	.40	.10	.15	.27
D3 Experienced Eng Manager	+.20	.10	.25	.20	.20	.25	.30	.25	.35	.30	.30	.30	.25	.30	.30	.35	.26
D4 Proper Direction & Leadership	+.10	.12	.35	.20	.05	.10	.20	.30	.55	.35	.30	.30	.25	.30	.25	.30	.25
D5 Qualified Team Personnel	+.12	.20	.30	.25	.10	.30	.20	.25	.25	.35	.30	.10	.35	.45	.10	.30	.24
D6 Professional Growth Potential	+.15	.10	.10	.15	.10	.10	.05	.25	.10	.15	.10	.25	.10	.30	.10	.20	.14
BARRIERS (− τ):																	
B1 Unclear Objectives	−.45	.45	.20	.35	.40	.20	.35	.15	−.40	.20	.20	.55	.25	.15	.30	.35	.31
B2 Insufficient Resources	−.30	.35	.05	.35	.25	.05	.10	.20	−.35	.40	.55	.40	.00	.35	.10	.35	.26
B3 Power Struggle & Conflict	−.25	.60	.10	.40	.45	.30	.25	.15	−.20	.15	.20	.35	.20	.30	.20	.10	.26
B4 Uninvolved Management	−.35	.25	.25	.45	.30	.05	.10	.05	−.35	.10	.15	.35	.20	.30	.15	.35	.23
B5 Poor Job Security	−.10	.30	.20	.40	.40	.10	.15	.10	−.30	.20	.15	.35	.15	.35	.20	.30	.23
B6 Shifting Goals & Priorities	−.30	.25	.15	.20	.15	.05	.25	.15	−.20	.35	.35	.15	.15	.40	.25	.10	.22

Significance Levels:
For τ ≥ .25; p ≤ .05
For τ ≥ .35; p ≤ .01

P1: Involvement and Energy
P2: Capacity to Solve Conflict
P3: Communications Effectiveness
P4: Team Spirit
P5: Mutual Trust
P6: Membership Self-development
P7: Interface Effectiveness
P8: High Achievement Needs

R1: Technical Success
R2: On-Time Performance
R3: On-Budget Performance
R4: Commitment & Result Orientation
R5: Innovation & Creativity
R6: Concern for Quality
R&: Willingness to Change
R8: Ability to Predict Trends

Kandell Tau Correlation of Team Characteristics and Team Performance a perception of both, in fact showing a reasonably high statistical concurrence. Finally, those influences which correlated predominately positive were characterized as drivers, those that correlated predominately negatively were characterized as barriers. The labeling of the variables in Table 12.1 is according to Figure 12.3, the statistical significance is indicated as follows: $\tau \geq 0.25$ indicates a 95-percent confidence level ($p \leq 0.05$), and $\tau \geq 0.35$ indicates a 99-percent confidence level ($p \leq 0.01$).

REFERENCES

1. J. R. Adams and N. S. Kirchof, "A training technique for developing project managers," *Project Manag. Quart.,* Mar. 1983.
2. J. J. Aquilino, "Multi-skilled work teams: Productivity benefits," *California Manag. Rev.,* Summer 1977.
3. J. D. Aram and C. P. Morgan, "Role of project team collaboration in R&D performance," *Manag. Sci.,* June 1976.
4. S. Atkins and A. Katcher, "Getting your team in tune," *Nation's Bus.,* Mar. 1975.
5. K. H. Baler, "The hows and whys of teambuilding," *Eng. Manag. Rev.,* Dec. 1985.
6. L. Benningson, "The team approach to project management," *Manag. Rev.,* vol. 61 pp. 48–52, Jan. 1972.
7. R. Carzo, Jr., "Some effects of organization structure on group effectiveness," *Admin. Sci. Quart.,* Mar. 1963.
8. W. J. Conover, *Practical Nonparametric Statistics.* New York: Wiley, 1971.
9. B. A. Diliddo, P. C. James, and H. J. Dietrich, "Managing R&D creatively: B. F. Goodrich's approach," *Manag. Rev.,* July 1981.
10. D. D. Ely, "Team building for creativity," *Personnel J.,* Apr. 1975.
11. R. N. Foster, "A call for vision in managing technology," *McKinsy Quart.,* Summer 1982.
12. P. R. Harris, "Building a high-performance team," *Training Dev. J.,* Apr. 1986.
13. J. L. Hayes, "Teamwork," *Manag. Rev.,* Sept. 1975.
14. D. S. Hopkins, "Roles of project teams and venture groups in new product development," *Res. Manag.,* Jan. 1975.
15. R. J. Howe, "Building teams for increased productivity," *Personnel J.,* Jan. 1977.
16. S. A. Huesing, "Team approach and computer development," *J. Syst. Manag.,* Sept. 1977.
17. J. Jewkes, D. Sawers, and R. Stillerman, *The Sources of Innovation.* New York: Macmillan, 1962.
18. F. E. Katz,"Explaining informal work groups in complex organizations," *Admin. Sci. Quart.,* no. 10, 1965.
19. J. T. Kidder, *The Soul of a New Machine.* New York: Avon, 1982.
20. R. Likert, "Improving cost-performance with cross-functional teams," *Manag. Rev.,* Mar. 1976.
21. D. H. Maister, "The one-firm: What makes it successful," *Sloan Manag. Rev.,* Fall 1985.
22. C. Pincus, "An approach to plan development and team formation," *Project Manag. Quart.,* Dec. 1982.
23. J. B. Quinn, "Technological innovation, entrepreneurship, and strategy," *Sloan Manag. Rev.,* Spring 1979.
24. R. M. Rantfl, "R&D Productivity," Tech. Rep., Hughes Aircraft Co., 1978.
25. E. Raudsepp, "Motivating engineers," *Eng. Manag. Rev.,* Mar. 1986.
26. W. J. Reddin, "Making the team work," *Bus. Manag.* (London), Feb. 1969.
27. L. A. Rogers, "Guidelines for project management teams," *Ind. Eng.,* Dec. 1974.
28. B. A. Salomon, "A plant that proves that team management works," *Personnel,* June 1985.
29. H. J. Thamhain, "Managing engineers effectively," *IEEE Trans. on Eng. Manag.,* Aug. 1983.
30. H. Thamhain and D. Wilemon, "Skill requirements of engineering program manager," in *Proc. 26th Eng. Manag. Conf.,* 1978.
31. H. J. Thamhain and D. L. Wilemon, "Anatomy of a high performing new product team," in *Conv. Rec. 16th Ann. Symp. Project Manag. Inst.*
32. H. J. Thamhain and G. R. Gemmill, "Influence styles of project managers: Some project performance correlates," *Acad. Manag. J.,* June 1974.
33. J. J. Thamhain, "Building a high-performance technical marketing team," in *Proc. Amer. Marketing Assoc. Conf.,* (Chicago, IL), Aug. 1986.
34. D. J. H. Watson, "Structure of project teams facing differentiated environments: An exploratory study in public accounting firms," *Accounting Rev.,* Apr. 1975.
35. D. L. Wilemon and H. J. Thamhain, "Team building in project management," *Project Manag. Quart.,* July 1983.
36. D. L. Wilemon, *et al.,* "Managing conflict on project teams," *Manag. J.,* 1974.
37. D. L. Wilemon and H. J. Thamhain, "A model for developing high-performance teams," in *Proc. Ann. Symp. Project Management Inst.* (Houston, TX), 1983.
38. J. H. Zenger and D. E. Miller, "Building effective teams," *Personnel,* Mar. 1974.
39. R. C. Ziller, "Newcomer's acceptance in open and closed groups," *Personnel Admin.,* Sept. 1962.
40. S. Seigel, *Nonparametric Statistics.* New York: McGraw-Hill, 1956.

13

How a Team at Digital Equipment Designed the 'Alpha' Chip

RALPH KATZ

If you had attended the 1992 International Solid-State Circuit Conference in San Francisco, you would have known that something special had happened. Dan Dobberpuhl, the technical leader of Digital Equipment's Alpha Chip design team, was simply being mobbed after his presentation. To quote a German reporter, "Dan was under siege!" Technologists from many of the world's most respected organizations, including Intel, Sun, HP, IBM, Hitachi, Motorola, Siemens, and Apple, were pressed around him, anxious to catch his responses to their follow-up questions. As one of the chip's lead designers described the scene to his colleagues back at Digital, "You'd have thought they'd found Elvis!" Clearly, the ALPHA chip was being hailed as one of the more significant technical developments in the microprocessor industry in recent years.[1]

How did this team of designers accomplish such a noteworthy advancement? Why were they successful? Clearly, there were many other excellent microprocessor design teams throughout the world; there were even other chip design teams within Digital. What were the organizational and managerial levers that permitted this group of designers to make this technological advancement and get it embedded into commercialized products? Was this technical and product development achievement a deliberately planned, well-managed, well-organized team effort; or was it more accidental, mostly a matter of luck in that the right people happened to come together at the right time to work on the right project?

Over the past years, a plethora of articles and books have surfaced emphasizing the virtues of teams and teamwork within organizations. The empowered, self-directed team is being hailed as the principal means by which organizations can revitalize their overall technological and market competitiveness. Some of the most dramatic stories in the popular press have attributed success to the effective use of crossfunctional or multidiscipline team efforts. The ability of people to commit to work together to achieve a common purpose has become one of the cornerstone ingredients of extraordinary achievement within organizations. Indeed, high performance teams have become the exemplary model for higher productivity, innovation, and breakthrough accomplishments, surpassing even the status of yesterday's entrepreneurial hero.

Given such testimonials, one might think that it would be somewhat straightforward to establish and lead a team-based work environment. More often than not, however, we are frustrated by our group, team, or task force experiences rather than energized by them. Even though we readily acknowledge the potential advantages of team-based interaction, it is not always easy to get engineers and scientists to function and behave as an effective team. It is often said that trying to manage R&D professionals is very much like "herding cats," that is, they tend to behave rather independently and are not especially responsive to or tolerant of their organization's formal rules, procedures, and bureaucratic demands. Nevertheless, to be both timely and effective in today's competitive global environment, technologists have to function collaboratively. They have to be able to integrate their insights, creativity, and accomplishments not only with each other but also with the demands and

Reprinted with permission from the author.

Ralph Katz is Professor of Management at Northeastern University's College of Business and Research Associate at MIT's Sloan School of Management.

activities of the functioning organization and business.

One could easily argue that the ALPHA team was successful simply because it possessed all the elements typically associated with high performing teams. After all, the ALPHA team members did have a clear performance goal with a shared sense of purpose, specifically, to design a RISC chip that would be twice as fast as any comparable commercially available chip. The team leadership was strongly committed, highly respected, and very credible both technically and organizationally. The team members were also extremely motivated, dedicated, technically talented, and tenaciously committed to solving tough problems. Furthermore, the individuals functioned as a cohesive unit, characterized by a collaborative climate of mutual support and trust, team spirit, and strong feelings of involvement and freedom of expression. They had a strong *esprit de corps*, communicating effectively with one another, working hard together, and valuing each other's ideas and contributions.

While it is certainly useful to generate such a descriptive list of high-performing team characteristics, the more critical questions surround the creation and management of these attributes. How, in fact, does one establish and manage these characteristics over time? How did the ALPHA team initially achieve and ultimately maintain its strong, unified sense of purpose and commitment to such difficult and risky technical objectives? Why were these very creative engineers able to work, trust, and communicate with each other so effectively?

In addition to this focus on internal team dynamics, it may also be important to learn how the ALPHA team interfaced with other business areas within Digital. Except perhaps in the case of start-ups, the activities and outcomes of most teams do not take place in organizational vacuums, and many technical teams that have enjoyed these same high performing characteristics have ended up unsuccessful in transferring their advances into commercialized products. For example, although the ALPHA design team was strongly committed to delivering its technical advances within an extremely tight and aggressive development schedule, the team did not have the strong unqualified support of senior management within the business systems and software groups, many of whom were very skeptical about what the ALPHA team was trying to do. Furthermore, although semiconductor management was supportive, outside Digital management could not assign the team any additional outside resource support from other technical or system development groups. For the most part, the team was not viewed by systems management or by many other groups within Digital as a well-disciplined, high-performing team. On the contrary, these individuals were often perceived as a somewhat arrogant, albeit respected, 'band of high-powered technical renegades'. The ALPHA team members may have trusted each other—they did not, however, trust management outside the semiconductor area. Yet, despite these apparent obstacles, the team was incredibly successful. How come?

PRISM: THE PREDECESSOR OF ALPHA

To fully appreciate the success of the ALPHA design team, it is necessary to understand more completely the historical context in which this technical effort took place. Many key members of the ALPHA team had originally worked together for several years under the leadership of Dan Dobberpuhl and Rich Witek, the chip's chief designer and chief architect, respectively, to design a new RISC/UNIX architecture that would be the fastest in the industry. They had hoped that the design of this new microprocessor would provide Digital the basis for developing and commercializing a new, more powerful, and less expensive line of computer products. Having been the major technical designer behind the first PDP-11 and the first VAX on a single chip, two of Digital's most successful product platforms, Dobberpuhl was able to attract some of the best technical minds to work with him and Witek on the design of this new RISC chip, including Jim Montanaro, one of the chip's lead designers. Given Dobberpuhl's history of successful accomplishment within Digital, he was extremely credible within both the technical and managerial communities. His informal, sensitive, but pacesetting technical leadership also made working for him very appealing to other highly competent technologists.

This developmental effort had not been the only attempt at getting Digital into RISC technology. There were, in fact, at least three other major efforts, the most critical being led in Seattle, Washington by David Cutler. After several years of ongoing internal competitive activity, corporate research management finally decided to merge these separate efforts into a single program architecture, code-named PRISM. On the west coast, Cutler assumed responsibility for the overall PRISM program architecture and became the technical leader behind the development of a new operating system. On the east coast, Dobberpuhl and his team assumed responsibility for the design and development of PRISM's new RISC chip. Unfortunately, this convergence around PRISM, did not end the program's or the chip design team's difficulties. Since Digital's existing VAX technology was still selling incredibly well, the company's need for this new RISC technology was not very great. As long as Digital's computer systems were 'flying high', that is, selling well enough to meet or exceed projected revenues, the case for developing a whole new RISC-based line of computers to complement Digital's already successful VAX-based machines could not be made convincingly to Digital's senior executives. Furthermore, one of the major assumptions within systems management was that CISC (Complex Instruction Set Computer) technology would always be better and therefore more preferred by users over RISC technology. As a result, it was hard to marshal much outside managerial interest in or support for PRISM, especially since the management of the systems groups kept changing. The design team felt that it was consistently being 'battered around', having been stopped and redirected many times over the course of several years.

By late 1987, however, as RISC technology became more proven and accepted within the marketplace, especially in workstations, Digital's management became increasingly interested in having its own RISC machines. Senior managers were also being heavily lobbied by representatives from MIPS Computer Systems, Inc. to license its existing and future family of RISC chips. Although PRISM was a cleaner, better-engineered design that had significantly higher performance potential than the MIPS chip, the Digital team had not completely finished its design work, nor had the chip been fabricated. More importantly, the associated computer and operating systems software were still in the early stages of development. MIPS, on the other hand, was much further along both in terms of hardware and software. Digital's senior executive committee decided it was more important for them to get a quick foothold in the open systems market than to wait for PRISM's more elegant but late design. Based on this rationale, Digital's senior leadership agreed to adopt the RISC architecture from MIPS—at the same time, however, they also decided to cancel PRISM.

ALPHA—THE OFFSPRING OF PRISM

The decision to cancel PRISM shocked everyone on the program, especially Cutler, Dobberpuhl, and Witek, none of whom had been asked to attend the MIPS presentation or had even been involved in the committee's subsequent deliberations. As a result, they all refused to accept the committee's explanation and became somewhat hostile towards them. After several years of hard work and effort, the team simply felt betrayed by senior management outside the semiconductor area. To give up their own technology and architecture and rely completely on a small outside company made no sense to them whatsoever. In the words of one designer, 'MIPS must have sold management a real "bill of goods"—it was all politics!'

This reaction is understandable in the light of what we know about such kinds of win/lose situations. Given the strong feelings and commitments that are reinforced within a team as its work progresses, the so-called 'losing team' refuses to believe that it really lost at least legitimately. Instead, it searches for outside explanations, excuses, and scapegoats upon which to blame the decision. Interestingly enough, however, if the losing group remains intact and is given a new opportunity to 'win', the team will often become even more motivated, ready to work harder to succeed in this next round. In such a situation, the losing group tends to learn more about itself and is likely to become even more cohesive and effective as the loss is put to rest and the members begin to plan and organize for their next attempt. They can even become more savvy about what it takes to succeed if they work together to identify previous obstacles and mistakes that they either have to overcome or don't want to see recur.

This scenario is very similar to what seems to have happened—at least to the PRISM chip design team. Because of his high credibility and history of success, Dobberpuhl was able to negotiate an agreement with his management to move his hardware team to the Advanced Development area where they could conduct advanced 'clocking' studies but where they could also discreetly finish the RISC design and test it even though the project had been officially cancelled. Within a few months, an initial design was completed and a fabricated PRISM chip was produced. It worked even better than the PRISM team had expected, almost three times faster than the comparable MIPS chip being licensed by Digital. Armed with this new evidence, Dobberpuhl circulated throughout Digital a scathing memo claiming that management had just decided to throw away an in-house technology that was two to three times better than what they were purchasing from MIPS. He had hoped to start a dialogue that might get management in the systems areas to reconsider their cancellation decision but this did not occur. Although a great many engineers responded positively to his memo, management was not impressed, most likely seeing it as 'sour grapes'.

Dobberpuhl's memo did succeed, however, in arousing the interest of Nancy Kronenberg, a senior VMS expert (VMS is the software operating system for Digital's VAX machines). Kronenberg called Dobberpuhl to discuss the status of PRISM which was working but had no computer operating system that could utilize it.[2] She suggested that if PRISM's RISC architecture could be modified to 'port' (i.e., 'work with') VMS, then systems management might be convinced to use the new RISC chip as the basis for developing new machines. The limits of VAX technology were being reached faster than expected and new products would be needed as quickly as possible to increase sales revenue. Kronenberg was part of a high-level committee that had recently been chartered to examine alternative strategies for prolonging or rejuvenating Digital's VAX technology. The possibility of using a modified RISC chip that was VMS compatible was not one of the committee's current considerations, especially since Dobberpuhl and Witek were sufficiently upset with the sudden cancellation of PRISM that they had declined to be members of this task force.

The more Dobberpuhl thought about Kronenberg's option, the more appealing it became. He convinced Witek that they could bring RISC speed to the VAX customer base and once they were back in business, they might even be able to supplant the MIPS deal. After several weeks of discussion, Dobberpuhl, Witek, and Kronenberg were sufficiently excited that they were ready to present a proposal to the VAX strategy task force. Dick Sites, one of the key task force members, was very skeptical about the feasibility of the proposed option. He just didn't think it could work—it would be much too difficult to get all of the existing customer software applications to run on this RISC architecture. When challenged, however, Sites could not clearly demonstrate why it wouldn't work, and after several weeks of working on the problem, he slowly realized that it really was feasible. Sites had become a 'convert'.

With this new basis of support, the VAX task force was now more inclined to endorse the proposal to design a new RISC chip that could port all current VMS customer applications. This new RISC architecture could then be used to extend the life of VAX technology; hence, the original code name for the ALPHA chip was EVAX (i.e., Extended VAX). In 1988, the Budgeting Review Committee formally approved a proposal to 'flesh out' an overall technical and business program but left the objectives and specific details to the vice presidents and the program's leadership. In addition, since Sites' own project on cooled chips had recently been cancelled, he and his small design group were very anxious to join the Dobberpuhl and Witek team to design the new RISC chip that would be the foundation for some of Digital's new computer systems. As a result, the ALPHA team was essentially formed through the merging of two small groups of extremely talented individuals whose projects had been recently cancelled and who were determined not to get cancelled again.

STRATEGIZING FOR SUCCESS

Even though they had been blessed by senior management, the ALPHA team remained skeptical. From their prior experiences with PRISM, however, Dobberpuhl and the team had learned some very valuable lessons. Technical advances and achievements *per se* would not be sufficiently convincing to shift Digital's base architecture from VAX to RISC. The ALPHA team would need a real demonstration vehicle to truly win support for their architecture. As pointed out by Montanaro, 'You could talk technical, but you needed to put on a true test.' Management in the systems areas had never seen PRISM 'boot' (i.e., 'bring to life') a real computer system.

The team also realized they could not rely on the official systems groups within Digital to build a test computer for the chip within the project's tight schedule. These groups were just too busy working to meet their own currently scheduled product development targets and commitments. The ALPHA project was a relatively small semiconductor effort that did not as yet have sufficient clout or sponsorship to capture the immediate attention or interest of these large system-development groups. Historically, the semiconductor area within Digital had been a component organization that had not played a strong leadership role in leading the corporation's computer systems strategy. Although they were an extremely critical compo-

nent, Digital's semiconductors had not been a driving, influential force. As a consequence, the design team realized that it would have to learn how to control and shape its own destiny.

To accomplish this, Dobberpuhl and Witek agreed that they would have to build their own computer system, that is, their own test vehicle. Using their informal networks of technical contacts, they successfully enrolled three very gifted technologists, namely, Dave Conroy, Chuck Thacker, and Larry Stewert, to develop on their own an ALPHA Development Unit (ADU) that would be based on the new RISC architecture. Since no computer system had ever been designed to the kind of speeds projected for ALPHA, management was incredulous as to whether a computer system could be built easily and inexpensively that could keep up with such a fast processor. The real challenge to the ADU group, therefore, was to build such a computer system using only off-the-shelf components.

The ALPHA team also learned that it would be very risky to go too long without showing management tangible results. As indicated by one designer, 'You had to show them something exciting—something that would capture their imagination'. As a result, the team would need to develop as quickly as possible a prototype version of the chip that could be demonstrated on the ADU test vehicle. This led to a two-tier approach in which the team would first design and fabricate an early version, that is, EVAX-3, that would not include ALPHA's full functionality but that could be convincingly validated. A fully functioning ALPHA chip, EVAX-4, would then be designed and fabricated using Digital's more advanced CMOS-4 process technology.

Organizing for Success

In addition to paying close attention to these outside management and organizational issues, the ALPHA team members functioned extremely effectively as a unit. The design group was comprised of individuals whose values, motivations, and work interests were of a very similar nature. Because the specific requirements of the ALPHA chip were left somewhat ambiguous by senior management, it was up to the design team to decide just how ambitious they were going to be. Extrapolating from the significant technical advances they had made in designing the PRISM chip to run at 75 MHz, the team was confident that they could 'push the technology' way beyond what others in the industry were expecting. They had learned enough from PRISM to know that a 200 MHz chip was feasible even though they really didn't know how they would accomplish it. Nonetheless, they were driven to build a chip that would be at least twice as fast as anything that might be available within the industry by the end of the project's 3-year development schedule.

They were also individuals who did not complain about hard work, long hours, or midnight E-mail as long as they were doing 'neat things'. No one had been assigned; they had all voluntarily agreed to work on ALPHA because they'd be 'testing the fringes' and 'pushing frontiers', which were fun and neat things to do! The ALPHA design team, as was customary within Digital, recruited and interviewed its own members as they scaled up in size or replaced individuals who had to leave. In the words of Conroy, 'We looked for people with fire in the belly, people who did not try to "snow" you but who knew what they were talking about, and people who would not panic or get discouraged when they found themselves in over their heads'.

Members of ALPHA were experienced individuals who could function independently and who did not need a lot of direction, hand-holding, or cheerleading. They were not preoccupied with their individual careers; they were more interested in having their peers within the engineering community see them as being one of the world's best design teams. Ambition, promotion, and monetary rewards were not the principal driving forces. Recognition and acceptance of their accomplishments by their technical peers and by society was, for them, the true test of their creative abilities.

Although team members had very different backgrounds, experiences, and technical strengths, they were stimulated and motivated by common criteria. In the words of one ALPHA member, 'We

see eye-to-eye on so many things'. This diversity of talent but singular mindset materialized within ALPHA not through any formalized staffing process but as a consequence of Digital's fluid boundaries and self-selection to projects. It is an organic process that may look messy and may lead to many unproductive outcomes; but it can also result in synergistic groups where the individual talents become greatly amplified through mutual stimulation and challenge.

'We'll Show Them!'

The intensity of the ALPHA team's motivation not only stemmed from its desire to do 'firsts', that is, to make the world's fastest chip, but also from fear that management could cancel them at any time, as they had done with PRISM. They stuck to aggressive goals and schedules not only because it was the right thing to do but also because they perceived the possibility of cancellation as real. This 'creative tension' between the team and senior management kept the group working 'on the edge', making them even more close-knit with a 'we'll show them attitude'. The group became resentful of management *per se* and normal management practices, stereotyping them and seeing them all as one big bureaucratic obstacle. No one on the team claimed to be a manager or wanted to be one. The group even kidded among themselves that 'Dobberpuhl is a great manager to have as long as you don't need one'. Just as the team members had a kindred spirit about technical work, they developed a uniform perspective about managerial practices and philosophies. This 'antimanagement' viewpoint allowed the ALPHA group to rely less on formal management structures and procedures for carrying out their task activities, and concentrate more on creating the team environment in which self-directed professionals could interact and problem solve together quickly and effectively.

Without the normal managerial roles, plans and reviews, the ALPHA team knew its success depended greatly on its ability to communicate openly and honestly among themselves. Because the team was relatively small and physically co-located, there was constant passing of information and decisions in the hallways. People didn't 'squirrel' away; instead, each member was cognizant of what the other team members were doing. Since the team also had to discover new circuit techniques, all kinds of wild and creative ideas had to be tried. To aid in this effort, the group instituted a series of weekly 'circuit chats'. In these hour long meetings, an individual would be given 10 minutes of preparation to present his or her work in progress. This was not meant to be a formal status report or rehearsed presentation with slides, rather it was an opportunity to see each others' problems, solution approaches, and mistakes. As explained by Montanaro, 'The intent was to establish an atmosphere where half-baked options could be freely presented and critiqued in a friendly manner and allow all team members to steal clever ideas from each other'.

The ALPHA team also realized that to get the performance speed they had targeted, the circuit design would have to be optimized across levels and boundaries rather than the suboptimizations that typically characterized previous designs. From their experience in designing PRISM, the team already knew where a lot of compromises had been made that may not have been necessary. Members would have to understand more fully the consequences of their individual design efforts on each other's work to overcome such compromises. The initial ALPHA documentation, therefore, was not so much one of detailed descriptions, specifications, and design rules, but one of intentions, guidelines, and assumptions. By knowing more about the intentions and what was trying to be accomplished, it was hoped that designers would have a broader exposure to both the microarchitecture of the chip and the circuit implementation from which the best tradeoffs could then be made. In the absence of formal management, members would have to be trusted to resolve their design conflicts by themselves. On the chance that it might be needed, a 'Critical Path Appeals Board' was created within the team to resolve intractable conflicts. The ALPHA team even discussed the advantages of holding 'Circuit Design Confessionals' during which members could admit to some error or design compromise and then solicit clever suggestions for fixing or repairing the problem.

No Room for Status Seekers

The team's effectiveness was also facilitated by certain normative and egalitarian behaviors. The group was conscious not to allow status or hierarchical differences to interfere with their joint problem solving activities. Even though there were some very high-powered senior people on the team, they were all senior people involved in technical work. They did not just tell people what to do, they were also doing it, from designing fancy circuitry to performing power and resistance calculations, to simple layout design. When team members had to stay late during particular crunch times, it was the custom that good dinners (not pizza) be brought in and served to them by the senior people. This degree of involvement and support helped solidify the group's confidence and trust in each other and prevented technical intimidation or status from becoming a problem.

A number of important behavioral norms were also established and reinforced by the ALPHA team. It was expected, for example, that one would inform other members as soon as one realized that one could not make a given deadline or milestone. It was okay to be in trouble; it was not okay to surprise people. Individuals were not expected to 'grind away' but to go for help. There was zero tolerance for trying to 'bull' your way through a problem or discussion. It was important to be tenacious and not to give up easily, but it was also essential to realize when you were no longer being productive. Pushing and working hard were okay, but it was also important to have fun. Humor and good-natured teasing were commonplace occurrences.

Dobberpuhl was also instrumental in keeping the group strongly committed to its aggressive goals. Generally speaking, when a group gets in trouble, there is a tendency for the members to want to change the nature of their commitments either by extending the schedule, enlarging the team, reducing the specified functionality, reducing features, accepting higher costs, etc. People would prefer to play it safe by saying 'I'll do my best' or 'I'll try harder' rather than voluntarily recommitting to achieve the difficult result. By not allowing these kinds of slack alternatives, Dobberpuhl challenged the team to search for creative solutions to very difficult problems. When management suddenly discovered, for example, that the ALPHA chip and its associated new products would be needed as much as a year earlier than originally scheduled, Dobberpuhl knew that by simply working harder, the team could not possibly reduce its schedule by that much. He also realized that if ALPHA was going to remain a viable option in Digital's strategic plans for filling this 'revenue gap', then the schedule would have to be speeded up; otherwise, their efforts would once again run the risk of being cancelled in favor of some other alternative product strategy. By committing to the speeded up schedule, the team was forced to find and incorporate what turned out to be some very creative breakthrough modifications in the design of the microprocessor and in the way it was being developed. This steadfast commitment not only ensured that the project would not be cancelled; it energized the technologists to stretch their creative abilities for extraordinary results. This supports Scherr's (1989) contention that breakthrough advances are achieved only when members commit unequivocally to overcome apparent obstacles or 'breakdowns'. Scherr, an IBM Fellow who studied several high performing breakthrough teams at IBM, argues that extraordinary results cannot be attained if the organization and its teams continue to play it safe by building in lots of comfortable slack and contingency strategies.

Other Groups Were Supportive

Finally, it is important to realize that a design project like ALPHA must have considerable support from other groups if it is to be successfully completed in such an aggressive timeframe. Following the persistent lead of Montanaro, the team found ways to work around the management bureaucracy to get the help it needed from other areas. The computer-aided design (CAD) groups were especially critical for providing very advanced design and verification tools that were not generally available.

They were also willing to modify and extend the software to the requirements of the new circuit design. The CAD people were responsive because they assumed that the ALPHA team was probably working on something very important and because they were an interesting and unusual group of 'techies' who delivered on their promises.

There were also a number of other design groups within Digital with good-natured rivalries taking place among them. Montanaro was able to build enough contacts within these groups that he could temporarily borrow (not raid or steal) additional personnel, resources, and even design documents to help the ALPHA team complete its design.

Even though it was customary within Digital to beg, borrow, and scrounge for resources, Montanaro soon realized that it was important for him and the team to find a way to say 'thank you'. Using adult-type toys he purchased from a mail-order catalogue, Montanaro started to give people phosphorescent insects and fishes, or floating eyeballs, and so forth, as a means of thanking them for their assistance. For example, if someone found a bug in the design, Montanaro would give them a phosphorescent roach or fish; if they found a bigger bug, then he would give them a bigger bug or fish, a phosphorescent squid for example. For the ALPHA team, these toys became a fantastic way for getting round the 'us vs. them' turf problem or stepping on people's toes. They became a great ice-breaking vehicle and as people collected them, they took on strong symbolic value. So many of these phosphorescent fishes were distributed that when the facility had a sudden blackout, many of the employees discovered that they did not have to leave the darkened building as they could easily continue their work by the glows of light from their fish toys!

CONCLUDING OBSERVATIONS

Digital Equipment is banking very heavily on ALPHA technology to help lead its resurgence in the industry. Not only is Digital designing and marketing its own line of ALPHA computers, it is also working with other vendors to use ALPHA in their product offerings. Microsoft, for example, is using ALPHA machines to demonstrate and market the capabilities of its new Windows operating system called Windows NT. Cray Computer's next generation of massive parallel processing supercomputers are designed to use large arrays of ALPHA chips. And Mitsubishi has become a second manufacturing source, adding substantial credibility to the ALPHA product's viability. Digital is even hoping that ALPHA can eventually be used and adopted as an open market PC standard.

What, then, enabled the success of the ALPHA chip development effort? Clearly, the fact that a very high-powered group of individual technologists had come together through self-selection to work towards a single-minded objective is a strong contributing factor. *These were not team-playing individuals—they were a collection of talented individual contributors willing to play together as a team!* For previously explained reasons, they were all eager to commit to a very aggressive set of goals and very willing to accept the risks that such a commitment entailed. There were no artificial barriers in the design process and the creative juices that flowed from the group's communication and problem solving interactions were exceedingly critical. At times they worked like maniacs, totally immersed in their project activities and buffered successfully from the normal managerial and bureaucratic demands and disruptions by Dobberpuhl. Because of their singular purpose and common motivational interests around technology, there was little of the in-fighting and turf-related issues that often characterize other teams. There was a genuine and unified team feeling of ownership in having contributed to the technical achievements as can be seen by the large number of names that have appeared on the technical publications and patent applications. Managers need to recognize that there is a world of difference between having team-playing people and having people playing together as a team.

All of the afore-mentioned characteristics focus primarily on the group's internal dynamics and were probably very instrumental in allowing the group to achieve its strong 'technical' success. It is less likely, however, that these dynamics con-

tributed to the 'organizational' success of the product. PRISM was also a major technical achievement and the PRISM team was very similar to ALPHA in terms of group membership and process. Yet, the ALPHA chip and not the PRISM chip is being commercialized.

Only when the ALPHA team shifted its emphasis from concentrating on its internal group process to worrying about how it should relate to other critical areas within the company did the seeds for organizational success get planted. Only when the team learned to integrate their technical goals with the company's strategic business interests were they successful at shifting senior management's attention from relying on the company's 'core' technology to relying on promised, but unproven, advancements in a much less familiar technology.

Unlike the PRISM episode, ALPHA was able to gain and strengthen over time its sponsorship within the organization. By sending out an irate memo, Dobberpuhl had taken a risk, albeit he had a strong basis from which to take this risk, but he managed to capture the attention of a few senior sponsors who helped link his technical interests to the strategic interests of the company. By making sure they had an ADU machine ready to demonstrate the new RISC architecture, the ALPHA team was able to increase its sponsorship even further. Neither Ken Olsen, Digital's CEO at that time, nor his senior staff had seen PRISM in action. They did, however, see a true demonstration of the EVAX-3 version of ALPHA and became so excited that they soon wanted ALPHA to become an open systems platform product that could run both VMS and UNIX operating systems. The demonstration had been a galvanizing moment for the project, shifting senior management's language and dialogue from 'Will we be doing this?' to 'Of course we're going to do all this!' Dobberpuhl, Witek, and the ALPHA team had learned not only the importance of developing new technology but the importance of protecting and marketing it within a large organization so that the technology becomes effectively coupled with the strategic interests and decisions of the established businesses.

For R&D groups to be successful, especially

under conditions of uncertainty, the teams must learn how to become politically effective within their organizational contexts. Either they can work in isolation and behave as spectators watching organizational events unfold; or they can actively insert themselves into the organization's decision-making and problem-solving processes. Either they can build and shape the networks, relationships, and strategies that 'make things happen' or, as in the case of PRISM, they can wake up one morning and say 'What the Hell happened'? As further evidence, Kelley and Caplan (1993) recently reported from their research on R&D productivity at Bell Labs that the true 'star performers' were not necessarily brighter than their technical colleagues, they were in fact more adept at nine particular work strategies. Interestingly enough, many of these work strategies were political in nature such as networking, navigating among competing organizational interests, promoting new ideas, coordinating efforts, taking initiative, and so on. Even in the more team-based cultures like Japan, it is readily acknowledged that important decisions are shaped and influenced through a political process, called *nemawashi*. Creating excellent intragroup processes are not enough. Technical teams have to learn to strengthen constructively their organizational sponsorship by becoming more effective players in the political processes that surround the making of key strategic decisions.

But what exactly crystalized the political energies and teamwork behaviors of the ALPHA team? Clearly, it was the unfathomable cancellation of PRISM that sparked the motivational responses and behaviors of the design team. *Without PRISM there would have been no ALPHA!* The cancellation of PRISM is what I call a 'marshaling' event, that is, an event that significantly arouses people so that they are finally willing to do something to redirect their efforts and attention.

If one examines many of the purported high performing team situations, one often finds that marshaling events have similarly influenced the motivational behaviors. Furthermore, it is not the collection of data or the presentation of analyses, logical arguments, or forecasts *per se* that typically stirs people to action. It is, instead, the emotional repercussions of seeing or feeling the reality of the data, information, or situation that awakens or persuades them. Collecting one's own disturbing benchmark data or experiencing first-hand the embarrassment of one's own product offering at an industry show relative to the products of what one had previously regarded as mediocre competitors can powerfully affect the efforts and motivations of product development teams when they return to work.

It is said, for example, that IBM's Thomas Watson Jr kept hundreds of transistorized radios on his shelf in his office. And whenever engineers came in to complain about the risks associated with designing IBM's first completely transistorized computer, called the '360', Watson simply turned on all the radios interjecting that only when the radios failed, would he be willing to listen to their arguments. It is also alleged that Estridge, the project manager for the original IBM PC, incited the members of his core design team by buying Apple II computers and placing them on the members' desks with a note essentially affirming that this was the product they'd be going after.[3] Toshi Doi, the product development manager of Sony's most successful computer product called News, sent his senior manager a 'rotting fish' to illustrate somewhat vividly what would happen to his product development effort if certain resources and decisions were not forthcoming. Even the project to land a person on the moon by the end of the 1960s, perhaps the most quoted example of a vision, fails to recognize the motivational importance of Sputnik. Had the Russians not embarrassed and scared Americans with the surprise launching of Sputnik, and later with the first person in space, there would have been no NASA and no lunar mission in the 1960s. Like Watson's transistorized radios, Estridge's Apple II computers, and Doi's rotting fish, Sputnik was the marshaling event that enabled Kennedy's man-on-the-moon speech to be so captivating. It is not only the marshaling event *per se* that is important; just as important is the focused leadership that arises to take advantage of the event. The combination is critical. For as in the case of ALPHA, it is the cancellation of PRISM coupled with the proactive leadership of Dobberpuhl and others that eventually gets all the design individuals to strategize, organize, and work together as a team so effectively.

SOME ADDITIONAL LESSONS

What additional managerial lessons might one deduce from R&D episodes such as ALPHA? First, projects like ALPHA do not seem to originate in a 'top-down' fashion; instead, they appear to evolve as pockets of individuals are able to come together and excite each other about relevant technological developments, problems, and possibilities. Every professional I interviewed indicated that senior management is just too caught up in the pressures of their present businesses to be receptive to the many uncertainties and risks associated with 'leapfrog-type' efforts. After all, did Intel's senior management really want to get out of the DRAM business and into microprocessors; did Hewlett-Packard executives really anticipate the strength of their laser and inkjet printer lines; did Motorola's sector managers really predict the growth of their current paging and cellular businesses; did Microsoft's Bill Gates really know how successful DOS and WINDOWS would be; and did Apple's corporate leaders really plan their transition to the MacIntosh product line? These and many similar examples from every industry suggest that if management truly wants to foster these kinds of accomplishments, then it must do more than simply encourage all technologists 'to take risks' and 'not fear failure'. It must provide the active sponsorship through which key talented technologists can come together to work on those 'far out' ideas and problems in which they have become strong believers. In some sense, the trick is to be more like the successful venture capitalist firms who realize that when they are dealing with a great deal of uncertainty, they are primarily justifying their investment in the track records, energies, and talents of the individuals behind the idea rather than in the idea itself.

In thinking about the ALPHA team's experiences, there are several important areas in which the team could have profited from stronger man-agement sponsorship. To speed up the commercialization of technical advances from projects like ALPHA, it is essential that management be ready to strengthen and push the downstream integration of these projects. There is no question in the minds of those with whom I talked that ALPHA could have benefitted greatly from the earlier involvements of key business functions, particularly marketing and advertising. Given the strong footholds that the Pentium and Power PC chips would probably have in the marketplace, the faster ALPHA could be commercialized ahead of them, the greater its chances would be of becoming a market success.

Business managers often strategize by projecting changes in their business environments and then planning only for those technical projects that are needed to meet these expected changes. It is just as important that management strategize by working jointly with the technical part of the organization to plan and sponsor those project developments that could help create or shape environmental changes. This kind of sponsorship is not achieved by simply giving or 'empowering' technical teams with freedom and autonomy. On the contrary, it is achieved by strengthening the linkages between technical development activities and business strategies. And as in the case of ALPHA, such connections are often established as the technical leadership discovers how to present their 'neat ideas', not in technical terms *per se*, but in terms that are meaningful to those who are managing and running the businesses.

Over time, a strong partnership feeling must develop between the technical and management parts of the business; otherwise, the organization runs the risk of amplifying their differences rather than being able to ameliorate them. Even if a project becomes a success, if the rifts and lack of supportive trust between the two camps are allowed to endure, then the images of 'good guys' versus 'bad guys'—'us versus them'—become the stories that key players remember and reinforce. Such negative dispositions are often exacerbated when the technical people feel that they have not been equitably recognized and rewarded, as has happened in so many of these cases. What typically happens is that the technical people see the noncontributing managers, that is, the 'bad guys' ending up with more exciting work and challenging positions as a result of the project's success while they, that is, the 'good guys' receive relatively little for their persevering efforts. Having focused all of their attention on completing the current project, the team members soon realize that there is also no new exciting assignment or project to capture their time and energies. What unfortunately happens is that neither the team nor the organization's management has planned the members' next projects or career assignments. Not only is this misplanning not a reward, but it can be rather demoralizing after having worked so hard. Under such conditions, the long-term continuity of technical developments can be seriously impaired through decreased morale and increased levels of turnover, particularly among the key technical contributors. An organization must not only sponsor the research projects and high performing teams that *get* it into the game; it must also learn to build the bridges and longer-term relationships, career plans and assignments, and reward alternatives that *keep* it in the game.

NOTES

The material for this study was derived by interviewing representative ALPHA team members and Digital managers and engineering staff. With the cooperation of Digital, in-depth interviews were conducted individually at DEC during normal work hours. An early version of this article was read by those interviewed to ensure the accuracy of the information and the flow of events.

1. As Digital Equipment's first announced microprocessor in RISC (Reduced Instruction Set Computer) technology, the ALPHA chip runs at more than two to three times the speed of its nearest competition. As of 1993, it had been included in the Guiness Book of World Records as the world's fastest chip with a clock speed of more than 200 MHz (megahertz).

2. When PRISM was cancelled, the software group working to develop the new advanced operating system that could be used by this chip also became upset. As David Cutler, the software development leader, told his team, "We really got screwed—years of development work just went down the drain." As they were located in Seattle, Cutler and many of the software team soon left Digital to work for Microsoft, where they used their ideas to produce the new operating system known as Windows NT.

3. The norm at IBM at this time was not to buy competitive products.

REFERENCES

Kelley, R. and Caplan, J. (1993) How Bell Labs Creates Star Performers. *Harvard Business Review,* **89,** 128–139.

Scherr, A.L. (1989) Managing for Breakthroughs in Productivity. *Human Resource Management,* **28,** 403–424.

14

Hot Groups

HAROLD J. LEAVITT AND JEAN LIPMAN-BLUMEN

A hot group is just what the name implies: a lively, high-achieving, dedicated group, usually small, whose members are turned on to an exciting and challenging task. Hot groups, while they last, completely captivate their members, occupying their hearts and minds to the exclusion of almost everything else. They do great things fast.

At one time or another, every successful executive has seen or been part of a group that was really hot. Whether it was called a team, a committee, or even a task force, its characteristics were the same: vital, absorbing, full of debate, laughter, and very hard work.

Although hot groups are almost never consciously planned, they can turn up in just about any setting: social, organizational, academic, or political. When the conditions are right, hot groups happen, inspired by the dedication of their members to solve an impossible problem or beat an unbeatable foe. When hot groups are allowed to grow unfettered by the usual organizational constraints, their inventiveness and energy can benefit organizations enormously.

Consider predivestiture Bell Telephone Laboratories. A mature company with more than 20,000 employees located in tradition-bound suburban New Jersey, Bell Labs was a tightly controlled, conservative organization. One senior manager often stationed himself at the entrance to the main lab in the morning, noting which employees arrived late. Back then, we counted nine levels in the organizational hierarchy. No place for hot groups, one would think. Yet this was the same company that invented modern communication theory, the

transistor, and a host of other advances thanks in large part to its hot groups.

In the case of Bell Labs, we believe that hot groups thrived for two primary reasons: a strong commitment to scientific values and an equally strong commitment to maintaining independence from AT&T. First, the core scientific values underlay everything at Bell Labs and were ingrained in everyone who worked there. The highest status in the organization went to the people in basic research, the ones doing the most far out and, in the short run, the most impractical work. In many other companies, those people would have been pilloried as nerds and longhairs, irrelevant to the real power structure of the organization. At Bell Labs, they were highly valued and encouraged to pursue whatever they believed to be the most interesting avenues of scientific inquiry.

Second, Bell Labs had been designed from the start to be independent from the rest of AT&T. While AT&T paid its bills, Bell Labs was sheltered from the usual business pressures. It was given an extended period of time before being required to demonstrate practical results. Not surprisingly, Bell Labs' senior managers were not managers in the traditional sense: They were outstanding engineers and scientists who demanded discipline and responsibility on the one hand, while encouraging creativity and communication on the other.

Is something like the Bell Labs experience with hot groups possible in other organizations? Unquestionably. Must the organization be unencumbered by a need to make money, fueled only by a thirst for scientific knowledge? Not at all. To

Reprinted by permission of *Harvard Business Review*. From "Hot Groups" by Harold J. Leavitt and Jean Lipman-Blumen, Vol. 73, 1995, pp. 109–116. Copyright © 1995 by the President and Fellows of Harvard College, all rights reserved.
Harold J. Leavitt is Professor Emeritus at Stanford University's Graduate School of Management. *Jean Lipman-Blumen* is Professor of Organizational Behavior at the Peter F. Drucker Management Center at the Claremont Graduate School in California.

compete successfully, most companies today are striving to develop breakthrough products and services. To do this, managers must understand that encouraging some behaviors at the edge of accepted organizational propriety can help their companies become hot.

No one really knows enough about hot groups to draw a blueprint for building them. After years of observing and participating in hot groups, however, we can describe the conditions under which such groups flourish, the behaviors they exhibit, the types of leadership they require, and the benefits they bring. To the question, How does one build hot groups? the answer is clear. One doesn't. Like plants, they grow naturally. We can instead tackle different—but equally important—questions: Under what environmental conditions are these groups most likely to flourish? How much moisture and light do they need?

GETTING TO KNOW HOT GROUPS

Hot groups labor intensely at their task—living, eating, and sleeping their work. Members believe that their group is on to something significant, something full of meaning. As individuals, they may feel that they have been more creative, capable, and productive while in their hot group than at most other times in their lives.

For many people, membership in such a group is a peak experience, something to be remembered wistfully and in considerable detail. Despite the intensity of the experience, members usually find it impossible to specify exactly what made it so hot. They are likely to feel that their group was unique, the product of a rare conjunction of the planets, impossible to reproduce.

The excitement, chaos, and joy generated in hot groups make all the participants feel young and optimistic regardless of their chronological age. In hot groups, the usual intellectual and social inhibitions are relaxed. These qualities almost re-create the sense of exuberant confidence people feel as children. In fact, people are more likely to participate in hot groups when they are young than when

they are old because the young feel omnipotent and immortal. They are eager to take on the exciting challenges that characterize hot groups. As people age, those challenges are usually redefined as dangerous risks.

Many people may have felt the excitement of a hot group when they were at school, putting together a show or a school magazine. It may have been in the military in a squad fighting its way up an impossible hill. Perhaps it was in a research group on the trail of an elusive gene or in a cross-functional new product team building the next generation of pasta makers. We have even received unsubstantiated reports of hot groups taking root in board rooms. Overall, however, hot groups are rare, especially within traditional organizations.

Total Preoccupation

The most distinguishing characteristic of any hot group is its total preoccupation with its task. Hot group members think about their task constantly. They talk about it anywhere, anytime. It is their top priority to the exclusion of almost everything else. Closing time often slips by without anyone noticing. Sometimes, hot group members bring cots to the office so that they can work most of the night. The more challenging, unusual, or "impossible" the task, the more dedicated they are to it.

Participants in hot groups achieve this level of preoccupation because they always feel that their task is immensely significant both in terms of the challenges it represents and in terms of its intrinsic meaning. The challenge may be one of design or of implementation. From a design perspective, the task must be a puzzle, a conundrum that is difficult to solve. In terms of implementation, it must be a feat that tests the group's mettle.

Above all, the task must be uplifting, one that is worth doing because it will make some kind of positive difference. Hot groups almost always believe that they are embarking on a journey that will make the world a better place. Sometimes the goal has broad societal impact: A group has the mission of developing a vaccine for AIDS or isolating the gene for Alzheimer's disease. Sometimes the goal is more pragmatic and local but absolutely central to members nonetheless: A group has the task of instituting 24-hour customer service for a department store. Whether or not outsiders see it that way, hot groups feel that what they are doing is relevant and important.

Not surprisingly, a hot group's preoccupation with its task is accompanied by extremely high performance standards. Without exception, hot groups shoot for the stars. Their members feel that they are stretching themselves, surpassing themselves, moving beyond their own prior performance limits. Hot group members are seldom motivated by the promise of bonuses or of other material rewards. The challenge of the task is its own pot of gold.

Intellectual Intensity, Integrity, and Exchange

All members of hot groups use their heads, intensely and continuously. This intellectual energy stems partly from the absence of inhibition that we discussed earlier. Members pump out ideas and possibilities at an astonishing rate. From the outside, many of their ideas may look wildly absurd and impossible to achieve. Although hot groups indeed push the limits, many of their extreme ideas are ultimately refined into practical actions.

Members often debate loudly and passionately about issues. They are not given to easy consensus. Because they are turned on by one another's ideas, and because their primary concern is finding the best possible solution, numerous noisy and seemingly disorganized discussions are more the rule than the exception.

Emotional Intensity

Hot group members behave like people in love. They are infatuated with the challenge of their task and often with the talent around them. They frequently sacrifice themselves, including their own resources and their outside relationships, to the cause. In contrast to traditional committees and task forces whose members may try hard to avoid extra duties, hot group members tend to volunteer for extra work and even to create it for themselves.

When hot group members bring the fruits of their solo efforts back to the group and its leader, they treat it as a gift, an offering of sorts. "I was thinking about that problem in bed last night, and I had an idea. So I got up and tried a few things on my PC, and here's what I got. What do you all think?" At first glance, one might think that such a desire to please could lead to "groupthink," but that is hardly a real danger. Hot groups are too dynamic, too open, too full of debate, challenge, and creativity for unquestioning conformity to set in.

Members of hot groups know they're hot, and they show it. They feel that their team and each individual member is something special. Even in hot groups composed of very dissimilar personalities, members respect and trust one another because they see themselves as highly capable people dedicated to an important task. Communication is typically wide open-up, down, and across the group. Members treat one another with casual respect and focus on colleagues' contributions to the task at hand, not on title, rank, or status. One aerospace executive, recounting his stint in an advanced design group, put it this way: "We even walked differently than anybody else. We felt we were way out there, ahead of the whole world. And," he added, "everybody else in the company knew it."

The emotional intensity that binds the members of a hot group together may come at a cost. First, it may isolate members from the rest of the organization. Hot groups are not pleased when their concentration is disturbed, and they dislike interruptions from outside. They do not readily welcome newcomers who might disrupt the dynamics of the group. And they certainly do not appreciate bureaucratic distractions, such as expense forms and formal progress reports. Their attitude and their freedom from organizational restrictions are apparent to outsiders who frequently resent them as both exclusive and arrogant. This resentment may ultimately harm the hot group and its mission, when the surrounding organization later fails to support its initiatives.

Second, the emotional intensity of hot groups may occasionally lead to burnout. Both leaders and members of hot groups must support one another, buoy up those who falter, and take breaks for short periods of relaxation and recharging. Although leaders need to stay alert to these critical human issues, they must also be careful not to overplan and overprogram. Hot groups usually handle these issues quite well on their own. The emotional needs of the group become especially important as the task nears completion. The sense of camaraderie is apt to dissipate as the group approaches its end, and members begin to feel a sense of sadness and loss. They begin to think again about their individual needs and interests as they prepare to re-enter the organization.

Fluid Structure/Small Size

It is difficult to define a hot group's structure. Roles and duties can change swiftly and subtly as the requirements of the task change. As priorities are identified, dealt with, and reordered, leadership may also shift from one member to another as the situation dictates. In sum, a hot group will organize as it sees fits. That said, however, we can generalize about two common structural characteristics.

First, hot groups are almost always small enough to permit close interpersonal relationships among their members. Thus they usually range in size from around 3 to perhaps 30 members, although groups as large as 30 are rare. Size varies with the organizational context, as well as the complexity and time frame of the task.

Occasionally, a large group of hundreds or even thousands of people may look hot for a period. More aptly classified as networks of small hot groups, these large hot organizations are usually held together by a small central core. Some are hot small companies, which seem to maintain their heat even as they grow. Others are protected organizations such as the National Institutes of Health (NIH) in its early days. Congress insulated the NIH, granting it freedom from oversight for several years. During that period, the NIH grew into a hot organization, innovative, risk-taking, exciting, and productive. The same was true of Bell Labs in its scientific glory years, when it was similarly insulated from the day-to-day pressures experienced by other units of the Bell System. Even as it grew in size, Bell Labs maintained its heat for a long time.

The second characteristic of hot groups is that they are almost always temporary and relatively short-lived. They share the happy attribute of dissolving when they finish their work. Unlike so many units in traditional organizations, hot groups do not try to guarantee their longevity. They are dedicated to excellence, speed, and flexibility; and when hot groups end, they end. On rare occasions, a few members remain bonded together, teaming up on other projects, like some pairs from the original Macintosh design team.

WHERE DO HOT GROUPS GROW?

One reason that hot groups are rare is because they grow only under the most special conditions. The environment inside the parent corporation must be hospitable, and the external environment must be challenging.

Internal Conditions

Like truffles, hot groups are not easily domesticated. Neatly organized institutions usually stifle them, whereas companies of the sort that Professor James March of Stanford University once called "organized anarchies" seem to provide quite fertile soil for growth. Hot groups need to feel that they can somehow be on their own, not fitting too neatly within the pre-ordained objectives of an organization.

Openness and Flexibility. While an intriguing task can be the magnet that pulls people together into a potentially hot group, often small sets of people with overlapping interests and shared values generate their own tasks and develop into hot groups. This, of course, requires easy, informal access across hierarchical levels and across departmental, divisional, and organizational boundaries. Indeed, we believe that such spontaneous conception is a very common form of genesis for hot groups. They frequently pop up in new, still-pliable start-up organizations and disappear as those organizations grow and calcify.

Consider, for example, the adolescent years of Apple Computer. In the early 1970s, Apple people, from top to bottom, averaged 20-something years old. Apple's early culture was exciting, urgent, flamboyant, defiant, ready to take on Big Blue (IBM) and anyone else in its path. Moreover, Apple's open culture was consistent with that of its Northern California location.

It is not surprising, therefore, that Apple's flagship product, the Macintosh, was developed by a small hot group consisting of people from all over the company. Led primarily by the aggressive, charismatic, fast-talking Steve Jobs, the group was spurred on by the ennobling challenge of building small computers for the masses. IBM, in contrast, made monstrously huge machines for the corporate few. Apple would occupy the moral mountain top, promising an agile little computer in every pot. Like many other hot groups, that dedicated hot Macintosh group devised and used its own emotional symbols: Members flew a skull and crossbones from a flagpole, with an Apple logo covering one eye socket. What could better express their youthful, free-spirited defiance of the stodgy, old establishment?

Independence and Autonomy. The Macintosh success story illustrates something repeatedly seen in organizations that successfully grow hot groups: To help keep them hot, it is wise to leave them alone for reasonable periods of time. Giving hot groups elbow room is difficult for many managers who understandably want to stay in close touch with what goes on in their organizations. Keeping hands off may also be bureaucratically difficult: Controllers and administrators exist to make sure that everyone in the organization abides by the rules. Nevertheless, as we have already seen, to help keep hot groups hot, senior managers must allow them substantial chunks of time before payoffs are demanded.

People First. The notion that hot people create hot groups has an organization corollary: People-first organizations of the type we saw in the Bell Labs example develop task-obsessed hot groups. Paradoxical though it seems, organizations that place more emphasis on people than on tasks spawn hot groups that focus tirelessly on tasks.

Why? The answer is straightforward: Organi-

zations that first devote a lot of effort to selecting their people and then allow them plenty of elbow room and opportunities to interact are likely to generate groups that will build challenging tasks for themselves. The logic of traditional organizational design is quite the opposite: First, define the task with great care; then, break it down into individual sized pieces; and, finally, select people with skills and aptitudes appropriate for each piece. Such organizations constrain and place limits on their people's behavior and activities. Hot groups do not prosper in such settings.

Great universities remain largely people-first organizations. They select their faculties very carefully and then grant them enormous freedom to interact informally. Good schools usually search for the best candidates in each broad field instead of seeking people to fill narrowly defined niches. Despite all the internal politics that plague many universities, the relative openness of debate within their cultures has always provided a rich seedbed for both hot individuals and hot groups.

Consider also that segment of the business world in which temporary organizations are the rule rather than the exception. Independent-film production companies are an example. For any project, producers must assemble a collection of writers, directors, actors, camera people, financial backers, and more. Most often, those temporary groupings do not become hot groups. They are simply a collection of specialists doing their own things. But, if the producer selects the very best people and leads the project with belief and passion, and if the project itself takes on great significance for the team, then there is a reasonable chance that such a diverse assemblage can become a hot group.

The Search for Truth. Hot groups seem to prosper in organizations that are deeply dedicated to seeking truth. Many research organizations in industry and government are quite traditional and hierarchical in their management styles, so at first glance they would seem unlikely places to look for hot groups. Yet at most of these institutions, like at Bell Labs, hot groups exist because the traditions and mores of science, which place a high value on the search for the truth, prevail. Those traditional scientific values, coupled with the realization that frequent failures are an inescapable feature of the research process, combine to make even rather authoritarian research institutions quite supportive of both hot groups and hot individuals.

External Conditions

Two of the most powerful and fast-acting sources of group heat have always been crises and competitors. Under the novel conditions and tight deadlines that major crises generate, the pressing task at hand overwhelms "normal" concerns about power and control. Formal hierarchies and status systems are often suspended in the desperate search for anything that might restore equilibrium. During crises, new voices may be heard and previously ignored alternatives may be considered. Consider the events during World War II. An obscure lieutenant colonel, Dwight D. Eisenhower, was promoted to a position of enormous power; women were welcomed into jobs previously reserved for men; and hot groups of scientists were funded to conduct their atomic witchcraft under the stands of the stadium at the University of Chicago.

Or consider the Tylenol crisis of over a decade ago, when cyanide was injected into a number of bottles of Tylenol capsules, which led to the death of seven people. In that case, all of Johnson & Johnson seemed to get hot. A top management committee debated options for long hours. Almost overnight, the company's PR people produced videos for network television use. The engineering and design people quickly repackaged the product to make it more tamper proof. Thousands of employees made over a million personal visits to physicians, hospitals, and pharmacists around the nation to restore confidence in the Tylenol brand name.

Crises, of course, do not always spawn hot groups. Some organizations revert to extreme authoritarianism in crises: Leaders (or would-be leaders) take command and bark out orders. Readers may recall that when President Ronald Reagan was shot and Vice President George Bush was out of town, Secretary of State Alexander Haig got himself into trouble with his career-limiting statement, "I am in control." The usual explanation for such behavior is that, in crises, time is of the essence, and people think, We don't have time for damn fool meetings. In many crises, that's true. In many others, however, that claim is invoked to justify precipitous action by panicky or egocentric leaders.

Competition, like crises, may generate high energy and dedication. But, while strong and visible competitors can indeed turn up group heat, it is dangerous to count too heavily on competition as a long-term motivator. For example, while high school or college teams can find the challenge of competition enormously motivating, professional teams show just a bit less of that competitive heat. Pro players, after all, are seasoned veterans. The enthusiasm of their younger days has been sandpapered away by injuries, salary disputes, and the other elements of the big business of professional sports. The same is true of mature companies. They may have been competitively hot a decade or two ago, but over the years they get a touch of arthritis. Good competitors are great for helping hot groups get started, but they're not to be depended on over the long haul.

Emerging Conditions

Modern information technology and the proliferation of alliances among organizations may facilitate the self-generating process that launches many hot groups. A critical mass of people who share interests, values, and thinking styles may be hard to find within a single organization. In our new, soft-boundaried world of networks and instantaneous communication, the birthrate of cross-organizational and even cross-national hot groups should rise. We suspect that the Internet will spawn a large number of hot groups.

WHO STARTS HOT GROUPS? AND WHO KEEPS THEM GOING?

Hot groups are always formed and carried by individuals, and mostly be individualists who by their very nature love to pursue markedly independent routes in life. A subset of the population of people who start most things, these are people with an intrinsic love of challenge. It is not ambition that drives them so much as a spirit of inquiry. They also like to prove that they can do what others insist cannot be done.

Still, individualism alone is far from sufficient. Certainly, many entrepreneurs are individualists, and, certainly, hot groups often take root in entrepreneurial soil. Yet, in our experience, most individualistic entrepreneurs are *not* great cultivators of hot groups. They prefer to run their own shows. They haven't the patience to share their goals and visions with others—nor do they feel the need. Only a subset of those strong, intrinsically driven individualists has both the interest and the ability to grow hot groups. That subset, which we call *connective individualists,* is worth a closer look.

Connective individualists are team players with strong egos; they are confident and stable enough to feel comfortable bringing other people into the act. They willingly share plans, goals, and glory, incorporating multiple approaches and multiple ideas. Unlike many other entrepreneurial individualists, connective types don't have to do it all by themselves. Much as parents can vicariously identify with their children's accomplishments, connective individualists can identify with the accomplishments of their groups, whether as leaders, members, or coaches.

Connective individualists can in turn be divided into three subgroups: *conductors,* who lead the orchestra, *patrons,* who support it, and *keepers of the flame,* who sustain it through time. When conductors find themselves challenged by an idea, they are likely to begin putting a group together immediately and to act as the group's inspirational leader. The charismatic power of conductors is contagious, attracting others to join in, help out, and identify with the group. That charismatic power may emanate from the flamboyance of many conductors, but it also flows from their extraordinary ability, which attracts the best and brightest young minds to their projects.

Conductors do best in face-to-face settings, where their personal styles inspire their people. Often, they show up as leaders of small, innovative companies or of autonomous units within large companies. They are also to be found building volunteer organizations, leading special service units in the military, or initiating all sorts of student activities in colleges. Conductors loom large in organizations. Their strong voices, although not always loved, are always heard. They become prominent figures, much talked and gossiped about. Everybody knows their names.

Patrons behave quite differently. They are catalysts in the formation of hot groups without themselves becoming active members: the high school teacher who inspires a group of students to take on difficult and exciting challenges, the soft-spoken boss who somehow always seems to get an important group going. Patrons protect and nourish their groups. They usually operate unobtrusively, often almost invisibly—coaching, listening, offering suggestions. In large organizations, many people don't even know their names, but those who do appreciate them. Patrons are particularly valuable to organizations. While the personal energy of conductors may spark successful small outfits that last for one generation, patrons are more likely to build enduring cultures that routinely support the growth of new hot groups.

Keepers of the flame, dedicated to solving a certain basic problem, nourish hot groups sequentially throughout their careers. In the pursuit of the solution to that problem, they realize that one hot group's completion of a task usually generates new, intriguing possibilities. Keepers of the flame end up nourishing new ideas, new solutions, and new partners in a long chain of hot groups.

One critical role of leaders, whatever the type, is to provide route markers for the hot group. These indicators of progress are usually of two kinds: hard markers, indicating real, measurable movement toward completing the task; and soft markers, in the form of approval and encouragement from the leader and from one another.

Hard markers are visible to all: "We have now finished segment four of our project. We have six more to go." Or, "Once we get this problem solved, we'll have a clear road ahead." Such markers recharge batteries, signaling that the group is on a positive, progressive path; however, they are often difficult to create. In many of the trailblazing tasks typically undertaken by hot groups, hard markers simply don't exist. There are no road signs in unexplored wilderness. Soft markers then become critical in keeping a hot group's heart pumping. These markers, however, require the management of meaning. Soft markers are voices of reassurance, encouragement, and support from people whose competence and good sense are trusted by the group: "Great idea! Let's keep pushing it." Or, "OK. So those two alternatives didn't work. Let's try the third alternative."

GROWING HOT GROUPS

Twenty-first century organizations will require the capacity to keep up with an intense pace of change as well as the capacity to reshape themselves continually. No longer can we build our organizational houses on the obsolete assumption that they will last for 100 years. Rigid, old corporate styles, like the inflexible steel and stone headquarters that symbolized them, are fast becoming quaint vestiges of things past.

A hot group is one form of small group that can be especially effective at performing relatively short, intensive bursts of highly innovative work. If we wish to reap the benefits of hot groups, however, we need to recognize and accept some of their potential costs. Like any other powerful tool, hot groups can be dangerous if mishandled. Hot groups work unconventionally—a fact that is often disturbing to the larger organization. In their wholehearted dedication to a task, hot groups may ignore

or challenge many conventional rules, making waves in other parts of the organization. Isolated in a hot group, members become temporarily unavailable to other parts of the organization. They may become blind to their own shortcomings and impervious to criticism. They may appear arrogant and contemptuous to employees from other parts of the organization. They may burn out and refuse to enlist in the next hot group.

Some senior managers are likely to interpret such organizational turbulence as disruptive to smooth and orderly operation. As a result, they will often try to eliminate the hot groups that cause it. But other, more connective managers will perceive that same turbulence as a stimulant to their organization, speeding up its metabolism and helping to inculcate a sense of urgency.

For those executives who feel that more hot groups might help stir the hearts and minds of their people, there remains the question of how to make them happen. There are a few suggestions managers can follow to create an environment fertile enough for hot groups to grow: Make room for spontaneity; encourage intellectual intensity, integrity, and exchange; value truth and the speaking of it; help break down barriers; select talented people and respect their self-motivation and ability; and use information technology to help build relationships, not just manage information.

At some point in the future, we may understand hot groups well enough to be able to manufacture them, but, until that time, an agricultural metaphor is more appropriate than a manufacturing one. For the time being, hot groups must be allowed to grow; they must be nurtured rather than engineered. Like plants, they are best raised from carefully selected seed, cultivated, and given plenty of room to mature.

The Management of Crossfunctional Groups and Project Teams

15

The Discipline of Teams

JON R. KATZENBACH AND DOUGLAS K. SMITH

Early in the 1980s, Bill Greenwood and a small band of rebel railroaders took on most of the top management of Burlington Northern and created a multibillion-dollar business in "piggybacking" rail services despite widespread resistance, even resentment, within the company. The Medical Products Group at Hewlett-Packard owes most of its leading performance to the remarkable efforts of Dean Morton, Lew Platt, Ben Holmes, Dick Alberting, and a handful of their colleagues who revitalized a health care business that most others had

written off. At Knight-Ridder, Jim Batten's "customer obsession" vision took root at the *Tallahassee Democrat* when 14 frontline enthusiasts turned a charter to eliminate errors into a mission of major change and took the entire paper along with them.

Such are the stories and the work of teams—real teams that perform, not amorphous groups that we call teams because we think that the label is motivating and energizing. The difference between teams that perform and other groups that don't is

Reprinted by permission of *Harvard Business Review*. From "The Discipline of Teams" by Jon R. Katzenbach and Douglas K. Smith, Vol. 17, 1993, pp. 111–120. Copyright © 1993 by the President and Fellows of Harvard College, all rights reserved.
Jon R. Katzenbach and Douglas K. Smith are partners at the management consulting firm of McKinsey.

a subject to which most of us pay far too little attention. Part of the problem is that *team* is a word and concept so familiar to everyone.

Or at least that's what we thought when we set out to do research for our book *The Wisdom of Teams*. We wanted to discover what differentiates various levels of team performance, where and how teams work best, and what top management can do to enhance their effectiveness. We talked with hundreds of people on more than 50 different teams in 30 companies and beyond, from Motorola and Hewlett-Packard to Operation Desert Storm and the Girl Scouts.

We found that there is a basic discipline that makes teams work. We also found that teams and good performance are inseparable; you cannot have one without the other. But people use the word *team* so loosely that it gets in the way of learning and applying the discipline that leads to good performance. For managers to make better decisions about whether, when, or how to encourage and use teams, it is important to be more precise about what a team is and what it isn't.

Most executives advocate teamwork. And they should. Teamwork represents a set of values that encourage listening and responding constructively to views expressed by others, giving others the benefit of the doubt, providing support, and recognizing the interests and achievements of others. Such values help teams perform, and they also promote individual performance as well as the performance of an entire organization. But teamwork values by themselves are not exclusive to teams, nor are they enough to ensure team performance.

Nor is a team just any group working together. Committees, councils, and task forces are not necessarily teams. Groups do not become teams simply because that is what someone calls them. The entire work force of any large and complex organization is *never* a team, but think about how often that platitude is offered up.

To understand how teams deliver extra performance, we must distinguish between teams and other forms of working groups. That distinction turns on performance results. A working group's performance is a function of what its members do as individuals. A team's performance includes both individual results and what we call "collective work-products." A collective work-product is what two or more members must work on together, such as interviews, surveys, or experiments. Whatever it is, a collective work-product reflects the joint, real contribution of team members.

Working groups are both prevalent and effective in large organizations where individual accountability is most important. The best working groups come together to share information, perspectives, and insights; to make decisions that help each person do his or her job better; and to reinforce individual performance standards. But the focus is always on individual goals and accountabilities. Working group members don't take responsibility for results other than their own. Nor do they try to develop incremental performance contributions requiring the combined work of two or more members.

Teams differ fundamentally from working groups because they require both individual and mutual accountability. Teams rely on more than group discussion, debate, and decision; on more than sharing information and best practice performance standards. Teams produce discrete work-products through the joint contributions of their members. This is what makes possible performance levels greater than the sum of all the individual bests of team members. Simply stated, a team is more than the sum of its parts.

The first step in developing a disciplined approach to team management is to think about teams as discrete units of performance and not just as positive sets of values. Having observed and worked with scores of teams in action, both successes and failures, we offer the following. Think of it as a working definition or, better still, an essential discipline that real teams share.

> A team is a small number of people with complementary skills who are committed to a common purpose, set of performance goals, and approach for which they hold themselves mutually accountable.

The essence of a team is common commitment. Without it, groups perform as individuals; with it, they become a powerful unit of collective performance. This kind of commitment requires a purpose in which team members can believe. Whether the purpose is to "transform the contributions of suppliers into the satisfaction of customers," to "make our company one we can be proud of again," or to "prove that all children can learn," credible team purposes have an element related to winning, being first, revolutionizing, or being on the cutting edge.

Teams develop direction, momentum, and commitment by working to shape a meaningful purpose. Building ownership and commitment to team purpose, however, is not incompatible with taking initial direction from outside the team. The often-asserted assumption that a team cannot "own" its purpose unless management leaves it alone actually confuses more potential teams than it helps. In fact, it is the exceptional case—for example, entrepreneurial situations—when a team creates a purpose entirely on its own.

Most successful teams shape their purposes in response to a demand or opportunity put in their path, usually by higher management. This helps teams get started by broadly framing the company's performance expectation. Management is responsible for clarifying the charter, rationale, and performance challenge for the team, but management must also leave enough flexibility for the team to develop commitment around its own spin on that purpose, set of specific goals, timing, and approach.

The best teams invest a tremendous amount of time and effort exploring, shaping, and agreeing on a purpose that belongs to them both collectively and individually. This "purposing" activity continues throughout the life of the team. In contrast, failed teams rarely develop a common purpose. For whatever reason—an insufficient focus on performance, lack of effort, poor leadership—they do not coalesce around a challenging aspiration.

The best teams also translate their common purpose into specific performance goals, such as reducing the reject rate from suppliers by 50% or increasing the math scores of graduates from 40% to 95%. Indeed, if a team fails to establish specific performance goals or if those goals do not relate directly to the team's overall purpose, team members become confused, pull apart, and revert to mediocre performance. By contrast, when purposes and goals build on one another and are combined with team commitment, they become a powerful engine of performance.

Transforming broad directives into specific and measurable performance goals is the surest first step for a team trying to shape a purpose meaningful to its members. Specific goals, such as get-

---

Not All Groups Are Teams: How to Tell the Difference

Working Group	Team
• Strong, clearly focused leader	• Shared leadership roles
• Individual accountability	• Individual and mutual accountability
• The group's purpose is the same as the broader organizational mission	• Specific team purpose that the team itself delivers
• Individual work-products	• Collective work-products
• Runs efficient meetings	• Encourages open-ended discussion and active problem-solving meetings
• Measures its effectiveness indirectly by its influence on others (e.g., financial performance of the business)	• Measures performance directly by assessing collective work-products
• Discusses, decides, and delegates	• Discusses, decides, and does real work together

ting a new product to market in less than half the normal time, responding to all customers within 24 hours, or achieving a zero-defect rate while simultaneously cutting costs by 40%, all provide firm footholds for teams. There are several reasons:

Specific team performance goals help to define a set of work-products that are different both from an organizationwide mission and from individual job objectives. As a result, such work-products require the collective effort of team members to make something specific happen that, in and of itself, adds real value to results. By contrast, simply gathering from time to time to make decisions will not sustain team performance.

The specificity of performance objectives facilitates clear communication and constructive conflict within the team. When a plant-level team, for example, sets a goal of reducing average machine changeover time to two hours, the clarity of the goal forces the team to concentrate on what it would take either to achieve or to reconsider the goal. When such goals are clear, discussions can focus on how to pursue them or whether to change them; when goals are ambiguous or nonexistent, such discussions are much less productive.

The attainability of specific goals helps teams maintain their focus on getting results. A product development team at Eli Lilly's Peripheral Systems Division set definite yardsticks for the market introduction of an ultrasonic probe to help doctors locate deep veins and arteries. The probe had to have an audible signal through a specified depth of tissue, be capable of being manufactured at a rate of 100 per day, and have a unit cost less than a preestablished amount. Because the team could measure its progress against each of these specific objectives, the team knew throughout the development process where it stood. Either it had achieved its goals or not.

As Outward Bound and other team-building programs illustrate, specific objectives have a leveling effect conducive to team behavior. When a small group of people challenge themselves to get over a wall or to reduce cycle time by 50%, their respective titles, perks, and other stripes fade into the background. The teams that succeed evaluate what and how each individual can best contribute to the team's goal and, more important, do so in terms of the performance objective itself rather than a person's status or personality.

Specific goals allow a team to achieve small wins as it pursues its broader purpose. These small wins are invaluable to building commitment and overcoming the inevitable obstacles that get in the way of a long-term purpose. For example, the Knight-Ridder team mentioned at the outset turned a narrow goal to eliminate errors into a compelling customer-service purpose.

Performance goals are compelling. They are symbols of accomplishment that motivate and energize. They challenge the people on a team to commit themselves, as a team, to make a difference. Drama, urgency, and a healthy fear of failure combine to drive teams who have their collective eye on an attainable, but challenging, goal. Nobody but the team can make it happen. It is their challenge.

The combination of purpose and specific goals is essential to performance. Each depends on the other to remain relevant and vital. Clear performance goals help a team keep track of progress and hold itself accountable; the broader, even nobler, aspirations in a team's purpose supply both meaning and emotional energy.

Virtually all effective teams we have met, read or heard about, or been members of have ranged between 2 and 25 people. For example, the Burlington Northern "piggybacking" team had 7 members, the Knight-Ridder newspaper team, 14. The majority of them have numbered less than 10. Small size is admittedly more of a pragmatic guide than an absolute necessity for success. A large number of people, say 50 or more, can theoretically become a team. But groups of such size are more likely to break into subteams rather than function as a single unit.

Why? Large numbers of people have trouble interacting constructively as a group, much less doing real work together. Ten people are far more likely than fifty are to work through their individual, functional, and hierarchical differences toward a common plan and to hold themselves jointly accountable for the results.

Large groups also face logistical issues, such as finding enough physical space and time to meet. And they confront more complex constraints, like crowd or herd behaviors, which prevent the intense sharing of viewpoints needed to build a team. As a result, when they try to develop a common purpose, they usually produce only superficial "missions" and well-meaning intentions that cannot be translated into concrete objectives. They tend fairly quickly to reach a point when meetings become a chore, a clear sign that most of the people in the group are uncertain why they have gathered, beyond some notion of getting along better. Anyone who has been through one of these exercises knows how frustrating it can be. This kind of failure tends to foster cynicism, which gets in the way of future team efforts.

In addition to finding the right size, teams must develop the right mix of skills, that is, each of the complementary skills necessary to do the team's job. As obvious as it sounds, it is a common failing in potential teams. Skill requirements fall into three fairly self-evident categories:

Technical or Functional Expertise. It would make little sense for a group of doctors to litigate an employment discrimination case in a court of law. Yet teams of doctors and lawyers often try medical malpractice or personal injury cases. Similarly, product-development groups that include only marketers or engineers are less likely to succeed than those with the complementary skills of both.

Problem-solving and Decision-making Skills. Teams must be able to identify the problems and opportunities they face, evaluate the options they have for moving forward, and then make necessary trade-offs and decisions about how to proceed. Most teams need some members with these skills to begin with, although many will develop them best on the job.

Interpersonal skills. Common understanding and purpose cannot arise without effective communication and constructive conflict, which in turn depend on interpersonal skills. These include risk taking, helpful criticism, objectivity, active listening, giving the benefit of the doubt, and recognizing the interests and achievements of others.

Obviously, a team cannot get started without some minimum complement of skills, especially technical and functional ones. Still, think about how often you've been part of a team whose members were chosen primarily on the basis of personal compatibility or formal position in the organization, and in which the skill mix of its members wasn't given much thought.

It is equally common to overemphasize skills in team selection. Yet in all the successful teams we've encountered, not one had all the needed skills at the outset. The Burlington Northern team, for example, initially had no members who were skilled marketers despite the fact that their performance challenge was a marketing one. In fact, we discovered that teams are powerful vehicles for developing the skills needed to meet the team's performance challenge. Accordingly, the team member selection ought to ride as much on skill potential as on skills already proven.

Effective teams develop strong commitment to a common approach, that is, to how they will work together to accomplish their purpose. Team members must agree on who will do particular jobs, how schedules will be set and adhered to, what skills need to be developed, how continuing membership in the team is to be earned, and how the group will make and modify decisions. This element of commitment is as important to team performance as is the team's commitment to its purpose and goals.

Agreeing on the specifics of work and how they fit together to integrate individual skills and advance team performance lies at the heart of shaping a common approach. It is perhaps self-evident that an approach that delegates all the real work to a few members (or staff outsiders), and thus relies on reviews and meetings for its only "work together" aspects, cannot sustain a real team. Every member of a successful team does equivalent amounts of real work; all members, including the team leader, contribute in concrete ways to the team's work-product. This is a very important element of the emotional logic that drives team performance.

When individuals approach a team situation, especially in a business setting, each has preexisting job assignments as well as strengths and weaknesses reflecting a variety of backgrounds, talents, personalities, and prejudices. Only through the mutual discovery and understanding of how to apply all its human resources to a common purpose can a team develop and agree on the best approach to achieve its goals. At the heart of such long and, at times, difficult interactions lies a commitment-building process in which the team candidly explores who is best suited to each task as well as how individual roles will come together. In effect, the team establishes a social contract among members that relates to their purpose and guides and obligates how they must work together.

No group ever becomes a team until it can hold itself accountable as a team. Like common purpose and approach, mutual accountability is a stiff test. Think, for example, about the subtle but critical difference between "the boss holds me accountable" and "we hold ourselves accountable." The first case can lead to the second; but without the second, there can be no team.

Companies like Hewlett-Packard and Motorola have an ingrained performance ethic that enables teams to form "organically" whenever there is a clear performance challenge requiring collective rather than individual effort. In these companies, the factor of mutual accountability is commonplace. "Being in the boat together" is how their performance game is played.

At its core, team accountability is about the sincere promises we make to ourselves and others, promises that underpin two critical aspects of effective teams: commitment and trust. Most of us enter a potential team situation cautiously because ingrained individualism and experience discourage us from putting our fates in the hands of others or accepting responsibility for others. Teams do not succeed by ignoring or wishing away such behavior.

Mutual accountability cannot be coerced any more than people can be made to trust one another.

But when a team shares a common purpose, goals, and approach, mutual accountability grows as a natural counterpart. Accountability arises from and reinforces the time, energy, and action invested in figuring out what the team is trying to accomplish and how best to get it done.

When people work together toward a common objective, trust and commitment follow. Consequently, teams enjoying a strong common purpose and approach inevitably hold themselves responsible, both as individuals and as a team, for the team's performance. This sense of mutual accountability also produces the rich rewards of mutual achievement in which all members share. What we heard over and over from members of effective teams is that they found the experience energizing and motivating in ways that their "normal" jobs never could match.

On the other hand, groups established primarily for the sake of becoming a team or for job enhancement, communication, organizational effectiveness, or excellence rarely become effective teams, as demonstrated by the bad feelings left in many companies after experimenting with quality circles that never translated "quality" into specific goals. Only when appropriate performance goals are set does the process of discussing the goals and the approaches to them give team members a clearer and clearer choice: they can disagree with a goal and the path that the team selects and, in effect, opt out, or they can pitch in and become accountable with and to their teammates.

The discipline of teams we've outlined is critical to the success of all teams. Yet it is also useful to go one step further. Most teams can be classified in one of three ways: teams that recommend things, teams that make or do things, and teams that run things. In our experience, each type faces a characteristic set of challenges.

Teams That Recommend Things. These teams include task forces, project groups, and audit, quality, or safety groups asked to study and solve particular problems. Teams that recommend things almost always have predetermined completion dates. Two critical issues are unique to such teams: getting off to a fast and constructive start and dealing with the ultimate handoff required to get recommendations implemented.

The key to the first issue lies in the clarity of the team's charter and the composition of its membership. In addition to wanting to know why and how their efforts are important, task forces need a clear definition of whom management expects to participate and the time commitment required. Management can help by ensuring that the team includes people with the skills and influence necessary for crafting practical recommendations that will carry weight throughout the organization. Moreover, management can help the team get the necessary cooperation by opening doors and dealing with political obstacles.

Missing the handoff is almost always the problem that stymies teams that recommend things. To avoid this, the transfer of responsibility for recommendations to those who must implement them demands top management's time and attention. The more top managers assume that recommendations will "just happen," the less likely it is that they will. The more involvement task force members have in implementing their recommendations, the more likely they are to get implemented.

To the extent that people outside the task force will have to carry the ball, it is critical to involve them in the process early and often, certainly well before recommendations are finalized. Such involvement may take many forms, including participating in interviews, helping with analyses, contributing and critiquing ideas, and conducting experiments and trials. At a minimum, anyone responsible for implementation should receive a briefing on the task force's purpose, approach, and objectives at the beginning of the effort as well as regular reviews of progress.

Teams That Make or Do Things. These teams include people at or near the front lines who are responsible for doing the basic manufacturing, development, operations, marketing, sales, service, and other value-adding activities of a business. With some exceptions, like new-product development or process design teams, teams that make or do things tend to have no set completion dates because their activities are ongoing.

In deciding where team performance might have the greatest impact, top management should concentrate on what we call the company's "critical delivery points," that is, places in the organization where the cost and value of the company's products and services are most directly determined. Such critical delivery points might include where accounts get managed, customer service performed, products designed, and productivity determined. If performance at critical delivery points depends on combining multiple skills, perspectives, and judgments in real time, then the team option is the smartest one.

When an organization does require a significant number of teams at these points, the sheer challenge of maximizing the performance of so many groups will demand a carefully constructed and performance-focused set of management processes. The issue here for top management is how to build the necessary systems and process supports without falling into the trap of appearing to promote teams for their own sake.

The imperative here, returning to our earlier discussion of the basic discipline of teams, is a relentless focus on performance. If management fails to pay persistent attention to the link between teams and performance, the organization becomes convinced that "this year we are doing 'teams.' " Top management can help by instituting processes like pay schemes and training for teams responsive to their real time needs, but more than anything else, top management must make clear and compelling demands on the teams themselves and then pay constant attention to their progress with respect to both team basics and performance results. This means focusing on specific teams and specific performance challenges. Otherwise "performance," like "team" will become a cliché.

Teams that Run Things. Despite the fact that many leaders refer to the group reporting to them as a team, few groups really are. And groups that become real teams seldom think of themselves as a team because they are so focused on performance results. Yet the opportunity for such teams includes groups from the top of the enterprise down through the divisional or functional level. Whether it is in charge of thousands of people or a handful, as long as the group oversees some business, on-going program, or significant functional activity, it is a team that runs things.

The main issue these teams face is determin-ing whether a real team approach is the right one. Many groups that run things can be more effective as working groups than as teams. The key judg-ment is whether the sum of individual bests will suffice for the performance challenge at hand or whether the group must deliver substantial incre-mental performance requiring real, joint work-products. Although the team option promises greater performance, it also brings more risk, and managers must be brutally honest in assessing the trade-offs.

Members may have to overcome a natural re-luctance to trust their fate to others. The price of faking the team approach is high: at best, members get diverted from their individual goals, costs out-weigh benefits, and people resent the imposition on their time and priorities; at worst, serious animosi-ties develop that undercut even the potential per-sonal bests of the working-group approach.

Working groups present fewer risks. Effective working groups need little time to shape their pur-pose since the leader usually establishes it. Meet-ings are run against well-prioritized agendas. And decisions are implemented through specific indi-vidual assignments and accountabilities. Most of the time, therefore, if performance aspirations can be met through individuals doing their respective jobs well, the working-group approach is more comfortable, less risky, and less disruptive than trying for more elusive team performance levels. Indeed, if there is no performance need for the team approach, efforts spent to improve the effec-tiveness of the working group make much more sense than floundering around trying to become a team.

Having said that, we believe the extra level of performance teams can achieve is becoming criti-cal for a growing number of companies, especially as they move through major changes during which

company performance depends on broad-based be-havioral change. When top management uses teams to run things, it should make sure the team suc-ceeds in identifying specific purposes and goals.

This is a second major issue for teams that run things. Too often, such teams confuse the broad mission of the total organization with the specific purpose of their small group at the top. The disci-pline of teams tells us that for a real team to form there must be a *team* purpose that is distinctive and specific to the small group and that requires its members to roll up their sleeves and accomplish something beyond individual end-products. If a group of managers looks only at the economic per-formance of the part of the organization it runs to assess overall effectiveness, the group will not have any team performance goals of its own.

While the basic discipline of teams does not differ for them, teams at the top are certainly the most difficult. The complexities of long-term chal-lenges, heavy demands on executive time, and the deep-seated individualism of senior people con-spire against teams at the top. At the same time, teams at the top are the most powerful. At first we thought such teams were nearly impossible. That is because we were looking at the teams as defined by the formal organizational structure, that is, the leader and all his or her direct reports equals the team. Then we discovered that real teams at the top were often smaller and less formalized—White-head and Weinberg at Goldman, Sachs; Hewlett and Packard at HP; Krasnoff, Pall, and Hardy at Pall Corp; Kendall, Pearson, and Calloway at Pepsi; Haas and Haas at Levi Strauss; Batten and Ridder at Knight-Ridder. They were mostly twos and threes, with an occasional fourth.

Nonetheless, real teams at the top of large, complex organizations are still few and far be-tween. Far too many groups at the top of large cor-porations needlessly constrain themselves from achieving real team levels of performance because they assume that all direct reports must be on the team; that team goals must be identical to corpo-rate goals; that the team members' positions rather than skills determine their respective roles; that a team must be a team all the time; and that the team leader is above doing real work.

Building Team Performance

Although there is no guaranteed how-to recipe for building team performance, we observed a number of approaches shared by many successful teams.

Establish urgency, demanding performance standards, and direction. All team members need to believe the team has urgent and worthwhile purposes, and they want to know what the expectations are. Indeed, the more urgent and meaningful the rationale, the more likely it is that the team will live up to its performance potential, as was the case for a customer-service team that was told that further growth for the entire company would be impossible without major improvements in that area. Teams work best in a compelling context. That is why companies with strong performance ethics usually form teams readily.

Select members for skill and skill potential, not personality. No team succeeds without all the skills needed to meet its purpose and performance goals. Yet most teams figure out the skills they will need after they are formed. The wise manager will choose people both for their existing skills and their potential to improve existing skills and learn new ones.

Pay particular attention to first meetings and actions. Initial impressions always mean a great deal. When potential teams first gather, everyone monitors the signals given by others to confirm, suspend, or dispel assumptions and concerns. They pay particular attention to those in authority: the team leader and any executives who set up, oversee, or otherwise influence the team. And, as always, what such leaders do is more important than what they say. If a senior executive leaves the team kickoff to take a phone call ten minutes after the session has begun and he never returns, people get the message.

Set some clear rules of behavior. All effective teams develop rules of conduct at the outset to help them achieve their purpose and performance goals. The most critical initial rules pertain to attendance (for example, "no interruptions to take phone calls"), discussion ("no sacred cows"), confidentiality ("the only things to leave this room are what we agree on"), analytic approach ("facts are friendly"), end-product orientation" everyone gets assignments and does them"), constructive confrontation ("no finger pointing"), and, often the most important, contributions ("everyone does real work").

Set and seize upon a few immediate perfor- mance-oriented tasks and goals. Most effective teams trace their advancement to key performance-oriented events. Such events can be set in motion by immediately establishing a few challenging goals that can be reached early on. There is no such thing as a real team without performance results, so the sooner such results occur, the sooner the team congeals.

Challenge the group regularly with fresh facts and information. New information causes a team to redefine and enrich its understanding of the performance challenge, thereby helping the team shape a common purpose, set clearer goals, and improve its common approach. A plant quality improvement team knew the cost of poor quality was high, but it wasn't until they researched the different types of defects and put a price tag on each one that they knew where to go next. Conversely, teams err when they assume that all the information needed exists in the collective experience and knowledge of their members.

Spend lots of time together. Common sense tells us that team members must spend a lot of time together, scheduled and unscheduled, especially in the beginning. Indeed, creative insights as well as personal bonding require impromptu and casual interactions just as much as analyzing spreadsheets and interviewing customers. Busy executives and managers too often intentionally minimize the time they spend together. The successful teams we've observed all gave themselves the time to learn to be a team. This time need not always be spent together physically; electronic, fax, and phone time can also count as time spent together.

Exploit the power of positive feedback, recognition, and reward. Positive reinforcement works as well in a team context as elsewhere. "Giving out gold stars" helps to shape new behaviors critical to team performance. If people in the group, for example, are alert to a shy person's initial efforts to speak up and contribute, they can give the honest positive reinforcement that encourages continued contributions. There are many ways to recognize and reward team performance beyond direct compensation, from having a senior executive speak directly to the team about the urgency of its mission to using awards to recognize contributions. Ultimately, however, the satisfaction shared by a team in its own performance becomes the most cherished reward.

As understandable as these assumptions may be, most of them are unwarranted. They do not apply to the teams at the top we have observed, and when replaced with more realistic and flexible assumptions that permit the team discipline to be applied, real team performance at the top can and does occur. Moreover, as more and more companies are confronted with the need to manage major change across their organizations, we will see more real teams at the top.

We believe that teams will become the primary unit of performance in high-performance organizations. But that does not mean that teams will crowd out individual opportunity or formal hierarchy and process. Rather, teams will enhance existing structures without replacing them. A team opportunity exists anywhere hierarchy or organizational boundaries inhibit the skills and perspectives needed for optimal results. Thus, new-product innovation requires preserving functional excellence through structure while eradicating functional bias through teams. And frontline productivity requires preserving direction and guidance through hierarchy while drawing on energy and flexibility through self-managing teams.

We are convinced that every company faces specific performance challenges for which teams are the most practical and powerful vehicle at top management's disposal. The critical role for senior managers, therefore, is to worry about company performance and the kinds of teams that can deliver it. This means that top management must recognize a team's unique potential to deliver results, deploy teams strategically when they are the best tool for the job, and foster the basic discipline of teams that will make them effective. By doing so, top management creates the kind of environment that enables team as well as individual and organizational performance.

16

From Experience:

Action Teams That Work

ROBERT J. HERSHOCK, CHARLES D. COWMAN, AND DOUGLAS PETERS

A growing awareness of workplace hazards and identification of airborne contaminants, coupled with a changing safety and health regulatory environment, created an unexpected demand for new and innovative respirators in the early 1980s. 3M's Occupational Health and Environmental Safety Division broke new ground by taking the team concept further than ever before in the company. The division's Action Teams successfully designed, built and introduced products in less than half the time it would have taken previously. The authors describe how 3M learned important lessons about team selection, training, performance and motivation, the importance of project sponsors, and the role of middle management.

INTRODUCTION

The 1980s was a decade of rapidly changing priorities in the nation's safety and health regulation agencies. In addition, the 3M Occupational Health and Environmental Safety Division's successful line needed new products and technologies. The marketplace was no longer as lenient as it had been in the past in terms of product development time. To maintain market leadership, the division had to broaden its technological base—and do it quickly.

It also had to speed up the rate at which new technology translated to products.

Fundamental changes in systems and procedures were called for, changes that would let us keep pace with the time compression demanded. Yet, no one was comfortable with the thought of making across-the-board changes to the entire divisional organization. Upper management and functional managers alike agreed that we could not upset the checks and balances carefully built into the system. As a manufacturer of respiratory devices that protect peoples' health, these checks and balances are critical to our operations. Work must be reexamined at every step in the process. The division also must document everything it does, including R&D efforts, purchasing decisions, manufacturing techniques, and quality control procedures. The changes we contemplated could not in any way endanger our ultimate product quality or our mechanisms for compliance with government regulations.

At first, our goals appeared to be mutually exclusive—to keep the *efficiency* of a tightly run organization, yet become more *effective* by loosening up the process. Compromise somewhere in the middle was out—there we would be neither efficient nor effective. Our goal was a healthy dose of both efficiency and effectiveness. That's when we came up with the Action Team concept.

Cross-functional teams had been used before in the company, so it seemed only logical that we should use them for this critical project. But we

Reprinted by permission of the publisher from "From Experience: Action Teams That Work," by Robert J. Hershock, Charles D. Cowman, and Douglas Peters, *The Journal of Product Innovation Management*, Vol. 11, pp. 95–104, Copyright 1994 by Elsevier Science, Inc.

Robert J. Hershock is Vice President, Marketing, for 3M. **Charles D. Cowman** is Technical Director of the 3M Specialty Chemicals Division. **Douglas Peters** is President of Douglas Peters & Associates, a management consulting firm.

wanted to take teams a step further than any previous attempts at 3M. These would be "Green Beret" teams that could cut through functional boundaries when necessary, yet work within them. With that kind of team effort, the division could maintain the advantages of functional specialization and add an important plus: the effectiveness and swiftness of an entrepreneurial organization.

A COLLABORATIVE APPROACH

When we first contemplated this approach, we were fully aware that our organizational policies and our management styles weren't set up to handle the special needs of teams. Our division was used to operating in a traditional top-down management style, with a tight organizational structure and highly structured job descriptions. Action Teams would require a new environment, one flexible enough to allow the teams to shape their own work assignments. The new environment would have to encourage collaboration because the Action Team concept required team members to familiarize themselves with other members' specialties. Learning those different perspectives would broaden everyone's job description and consolidate agendas. In effect, we were asking functional specialists to take a more "generalist" approach while on the teams. Yet the members still had to follow the rules and guidelines of their own functional specialty. To deal with the dichotomies of a "generalist vs. specialist" and "innovative vs. rule-bound" environment, we wrote a plan for Action Teams, one that dealt with five crucial variables. We cross-linked these variables with the most favorable characteristics of both the "efficient" and "effective" management styles. The result was a collaborative approach that spelled out our objectives in advance. It was the first step in the formation of our Action Teams.

THE FIVE VARIABLES

Goals

The entire organization had to share a common mission, in this case, translating technology into new products. With everyone supporting that goal, the teams would have an easier time focusing their efforts.

People

In an Action Team, members had to wear two hats—functional specialists and organizational generalists. Team members could formulate their ideas according to their specific functional specialty, but they were expected to contribute those ideas in the context of the bigger picture. Every team member had to develop a macro view. That meant sharing information and putting individual concerns on the table early in the process. Team members also had to evaluate whether their functionally specialized viewpoints would help the team meet its more general goals.

Process

The environment had to be one where participants felt unconstrained by the way things were done in the past. In this new environment, we would ask teams to take a responsible approach to policies and procedures while unleashing their creative energies. Ensuring strict adherence to both 3M and government policies and procedures had to be a high priority. However, within those guidelines, team members would be expected to break new ground in creative thinking. What we needed was entirely new ideas, not revisions of old themes.

Structure

Organizing Principle. The Action Team approach would require quick shifts in both human and financial resources. For example, Marketing played an important role by providing initial input into the product's design. Once the design was established however, Marketing had considerably less to do until a prototype was available. So there was an ebb and flow as to the amount of work needed from any given function at any given time. The organization had to see the team's needs as a priority and to respond quickly to facilitate these shifts. This represented a major policy change for management. Now, instead of the team serving the needs of management, the organization would serve its new internal customer—the team.

Chain of Command. Division managers and directors had to change their roles. Formerly they had acted in the traditional roles of controllers and delegators. Now they had to become enablers, going out of their way to help the Action Teams accomplish their goals.

Increase the Championing Spirit. In a marketplace where there was no time to be content with yesterday's advances, we wanted to create a lasting culture that encouraged creative thought and action. Inaction meant market-driven consequences.

Results

We wanted to avoid a situation where people came together, did whatever wouldn't rock the boat, and called that success. No team would be rewarded for just going through the motions while following 3M and government policies and procedures. Team participants had to understand that some of their discoveries were more important to us than others, and that there was a direct correlation between their efforts and the division's overall success in the marketplace. So rewards would be based, not only on the degree of success of the team's individual project, but also on the project's overall importance to the division. We wrote a list of eight critical success factors, similar to the IBM concept of process quality management (PQM) [2, p. 112]. The Action Teams had to:

- Increase our base of technology by a quantum leap
- Cut new product development time in half
- Develop products that resulted in new businesses
- Create a new atmosphere of entrepreneurship
- Push decision making down to the lowest possible level
- Build a management style that encouraged leadership throughout the division
- Eliminate barriers to innovation within the organization
- Take a strong stand on quality right from the start

GETTING SUPPORT FROM THE TOP

Goals in hand, we met with the other operating committee members in the OH&ES Division to win their support for our Action Team proposal. There were a number of concerns. Would teams divert staff resources and inhibit Marketing's ability to support existing products? Would teams disrupt the manufacturing process? What about the recognition process at 3M—would the team concept dilute that?

On the other hand, Marketing was excited about the possibility of new products. Manufacturing welcomed the opportunity to be involved in product design at a much earlier stage, and the Laboratory liked the thought of unleashing its creative energies. With advantages outweighing disadvantages, the concept won support.

PICKING TEAMS

Ideally, we believed that team leaders should volunteer for the assignment. But, because Action Teams were a new concept for us, we had to pick leaders. Obviously, the first thing we looked for was leadership ability. Second, we looked for somebody who was intimately involved in some way with the product we were focusing on. Third, we looked for someone with a good understanding of human relationships. These teams had a tough mission ahead of them and had to be united, making relationship awareness a critical factor.

When it came to staffing the teams, we avoided the temptation to pick one process engineer, one chemist, and one cost accountant, hand them over to the team leader, and walk away. We left the functional mix up to the teams themselves and give them the flexibility to make changes in the membership. We said up front, "If you don't think this is the right mix of people, fine. Just tell us and you can change it."

IS THIS FOR REAL?

The shift from our past mode of operation to teams that determined their own timelines and strategies was such a major change that team members reacted by wondering "How much of this can we take at face value?"

We realized that every member of division top management would have to take the first risk and trust the teams, so they, in turn, could trust us. We could help to build that trust by making resources available to the teams and supporting their efforts. But when the time came to deliver on commitments of support and cooperation, it didn't always happen. We didn't have total buy-in from all the division operating committee members. Even those who wanted to offer support and cooperation weren't quite sure how to go about it without feeling as though they had given up complete control. They were viewing it (incorrectly) as an all-or-nothing proposition. A team-building and training process was in order for both team members and the operating committee.

These sessions demonstrated the real risks involved in taking a new approach. After the training, one manager decided to leave the division. He understood what we were trying to accomplish and even agreed that it was the right approach. However, he personally didn't think he could act in the role of an enabler, rather than a controller. In the training process, people were able to select themselves either in or out. One result was the manager who elected to leave. Another was that we saw a very high level of commitment to the concept from those who stayed.

TRAINING THE TEAMS

In addition to control issues, the team members and operating committee members needed to learn how to successfully handle a situation in which functional specialists, with differing viewpoints and personalities, are charged with bringing out new products in a shortened timeframe. Training helped tremendously here.

The training program helped team members understand what kind of environment they worked in, who had the power to get things done, and how to get cooperation from others. The division already had a high degree of efficiency, so the training concentrated on building the effectiveness of members within the team and the effectiveness of the team within the organization. Training covered four areas:

1. (A) Understanding the dynamics of the five variables.

   (B) Learning why each team needed both generalist and functional roles.

   (C) Understanding management's vision of the future.

2. (A) Learning who has the power to get things done.

   (B) Learning how to influence.

   (C) Learning how to champion, how to empower, and how to build a working relationship in a large division.

3. Helping members understand that teams had to be self-directed in inventing new approaches and breaking new ground.

4. Teaching teams how to use their mandate from upper management to get things done within the mainstream of the organization.

The purpose of understanding the individual functional specialties was to break down the expectations of stereotypical behavior and role-playing by the team members. To facilitate that process, we used learning instruments including the Meyers-Briggs Type Indicator on Personality, the Personal Profile System, Fundamental Interpersonal Relationship Orientation Behavior (FIRO-B), Thomas Kilman Conflict Mode and the Creatrix (Creative and Risk Taking.)

In the first session, information from the learning instruments helped point out how barriers are created when people play functionally specialized roles in a group. Each team member had already been scored on his or her creativity and risk taking style, conflict style, behavioral style, influence style, personality style, and interpersonal relationship style. They then were asked to predict the style characteristics of each job function. They predicted that Laboratory people would be introverted and creative, but low risk-takers, whereas Marketing people would be high-energy, extroverted, high risk-takers. Together, we compared the actual scores to the predictions.

The team members were shocked at the results, because there were no patterns. Some of the most creative people were in Marketing, and some of the most extroverted were in the Laboratory. At one point in the exercise, a puzzled team member turned to another person and asked, "Then why do you act like a Laboratory person?" The second person replied, "Hey, that's my role. That's the way you have to act." After a while the role barriers came crashing down.

The team members got the message that they weren't there to play their functional roles and that the team couldn't accomplish its goals if its members spent all their time playing roles. They were there as professional people to solve important problems. The self-disclosures helped team members get to know—and for the first time really understand—their fellow workers, people they had worked with for years.

INCREASING THE LEVEL OF RISK AMONG PEERS

We showed team members a visual model comparing decision making processes in organizations. The team members saw that, in traditional, functional organizations, the goal is managing and controlling. People are specialists, institutional rules make up the process, the structure is tight, and the results efficient. This kind of organization had served the division well in the past. But our new goals called for change and Action Teams could foster it. In crossfunctional, integrated teams, the goal is leadership and empowerment. People act as generalists. Broad, general guidelines are the process; the structure is loose and the results effective.

Team members also learned that when tight organizational rules (*not* the safety rules, those were not negotiable) are eliminated, people invent new ones. In the process of inventing, the organi-

zation gets innovations. However, if people take the invention process too far, they get chaos—the kind of chaos that rules were meant to prevent in the first place.

Once again we used the information from the testing devices, this time to demonstrate how individuals who placed a high value on efficiency might be at odds with those who instead valued effectiveness. When a team member felt another member was being controlling, he or she was noting a value conflict, rather than a basic human flaw. The team members started to see that these differing visions of goals can lead to turf wars. That helped them complete the training with a more common corporate vision.

The very nature of such teams is that they are not always harmonious, because not everyone shares the same level or even the same definition of acceptable personal risk. The built-in paradox in group innovation is that, although the group initially welcomes each individual's creative contribution, additional creative suggestions disturb whatever status quo existed up to that point. It's an evolving process, and that's upsetting to people who seek consistency or control within the team. We had to teach team members how to cope with that lack of consistency and control, and how to turn it into a positive, rather than allowing it to result in gridlock.

Being open and honest with fellow workers requires personal risk, as well as willingness to confront. If our team members couldn't take the risk of being open and honest in their team's internal communications, we couldn't expect the teams to make the right decisions. So training placed a strong emphasis on interpersonal communications and the related issues of risk taking.

We started teams off making relatively minor decisions, such as to whom they wanted to report. Then they were given free rein to establish rules of operation within their team, provided, of course, that they fell within company and government rules for new product development. Next they moved on to set up their mission statements, establish criteria for success, form agendas, establish cost estimates, set meeting schedules, and so on.

Early in the process one participant approached us with a problem. He said, "I don't think the guys on this team are committed. I don't think this team's going to succeed—it's going to fail. And that's not going to be very good for my career." We agreed with him. Then he added, "On the other hand, I was assigned to this team by my boss. If I go back and say that I don't want to be part of this team, that looks like I'm a non-team player." Again we agreed with him. He was at a point where he had to either take a personal risk or pay a price for not risking. His choices were to be open and honest with his boss, explaining why this was a losing proposition, or take the risk with his fellow team members. He opted to take the risk with the team, confronting them on their commitment levels, forcing them off dead center. The situation illustrated how openness and honesty must extend to all levels of team participation, including disagreements over the team's direction or approach to a particular problem.

We always believed in our people. We never questioned either their capabilities or their professionalism. Our only purpose in using team-building training was to equip our teams with more management tools to ensure their success. An article in *Industry Week* confirmed our experience and our belief in team-building training. It quoted a Frito-Lay worker describing similar training: "Because of that training, 'we attack problems, not people,' one worker says. 'So, we decide *what's* right, not *who's* right'". With that kind of philosophy, the teams were ready to go to work.

THE ROLE OF THE SPONSOR

Our experience has shown that sponsors are crucial to the success of Action Teams. In the past, division-operating committee members had acted more as planners who charted courses and controlled their respective functions. Now they had to play a completely new role—that of enablers, reviewing, approving, and allocating resources.

The sponsors had their work cut out for them, not only in obtaining financial resources, but also in convincing middle managers to treat the Action Teams as internal customers. Without that latter directive, the Action Teams would have floundered without any clear-cut organizational support because they were not functional specialties.

One team member had this to say about his team's sponsor: "He's been the one who was more instrumental in making things happen and doing amazing things I never thought were possible. I always had the feeling he could bash through brick walls. The guy is totally amazing. I don't think we could have done it without him." That was exactly the role we expected sponsors to perform. They were miracle workers who pulled strings and called in favors within the organization.

By providing support, the sponsors were, in effect, plugged into the teams. Their presence reinforced the division's common vision, which was important if we were to succeed in breaking down barriers. Sponsors demonstrated management's continuing support of the teams. The upper management visibility also empowered the teams to work harder and to be more effective. Team participants knew that at least one member of the operating committee really knew what they personally did to get the product off the ground.

At times, the role of the sponsor changed. Sometimes the sponsor had to back away, switch to a teaching role, and act as the team's Dutch uncle, offering some of the wisdom he or she had gained from many years experience in the company.

One member of the operating committee who served as a team sponsor found that the nature of the requests from the team changed as it approached different stages. He recounts his sponsorship experience this way: "Early in the process I was asked fairly regularly to change the membership on the teams. So I helped them make changes. Then, as the teams started to do their job, I heard concerns that some team members were using the team as a training experience, rather than participating and making things happen." Something was getting in the way of full participation by all team members. So we investigated and uncovered some resistance by middle managers.

DEALING WITH RESISTANT MIDDLE MANAGERS

That eventually became a problem in all teams. When it really came down to it, a middle manager might see a team's work as having less priority than a department's. The sponsor would then have to meet with the manager in an attempt to elicit more support.

The root of the problem was that for each team member, being on an Action Team was an additional job, over and above the member's regular job description. Team members had to deal with the conflicts of where their time should be spent. Were they going to take direction from the Action Team, or were they going to take direction from their boss? In one case, a team member came back from his team meeting telling his manager what team projects he planned to work on over the next week. "No—tomorrow you're going to Abilene to solve this other problem," the middle manager responded. These types of conflicts were common enough to become a major hindrance.

We realized that we had given everyone in the division a new role to play—except for the middle managers. That proved to be a big mistake. Middle managers were still operating in their traditional roles as functional managers, still accountable for their departments' productivity, despite the fact that they had lost some resources. The middle managers also were concerned about maintaining their level of control—the same issue that had originally plagued the operating committee.

We told the middle managers that, if a product came out that was in their area of responsibility, they would get credit for it. We let them know that we were not going to judge them by whether they actually had rolled up their sleeves and gotten involved in every minute detail, but instead by how much support they provided to the teams. And we told them what we had already told the teams— that we were prepared to accept the failure that sometimes went hand-in-hand with new product development. But the middle managers weren't buying it.

When we realized that, we decided to go back into training—this time for middle managers. What we finally had found out—and what other companies can learn from our experience—is that you can't train just the Action Teams and then walk away. You have to train upper management and middle management too.

In isolated cases, even training didn't help, but after we had more experience, we found an extremely effective way of dealing with resistant middle managers. We would simply make the middle manager a team leader. Then, we saw a complete turnaround in attitude. It was a strong incentive to see the bigger picture.

ACTION TEAMS HIT THE GROUND

Two central theories describe how teams progress through the innovation process. One is Tuckman's forming, storming, norming, and performing model, which talks about a predictable movement of the team's behavior from one stage to another. The other is called punctuated equilibrium, put forth by Eldredge and Gould. This model says that the team makes progress until precisely halfway between the team's first meeting and the official deadline, at which point the team almost blows up. It goes through revolutionary change, changing leadership roles and power relationships, and finally arrives at a different approach to the problem than was originally put forth.

Our experience shows that neither theory dominated. In some cases our teams exhibited characteristics of the Tuckman theory, whereas others demonstrated punctuated equilibrium. A woman who is now a pilot plant manager headed the first Action Team. The team's job was to add more features to a dust/mist respirator. At the halfway point, this team had to stop and rethink its approach, as the Eldredge and Gould theory predicted. The halt was due to some incorrect criteria at the outset of the project, again in accordance with theory. Yet, unlike the rest of the Eldredge and Gould theory, the process was not revolutionary. Roles stayed pretty much the same and the same team leader remained in charge. Her account of the incident is almost matter-of-fact: "We scratched our heads and cried a little and then said, 'OK, let's get back to work.' In a week we had a new product designed. The new design was better than our first approach." That assessment of the final product was right. The new respirator proved itself in the marketplace. Development time from inception to introduction was ten months.

Two senior research specialists formed a team to begin work on a brand new high-efficiency particulate respirator. One, as team leader, pulled together a cross-functional team consisting of marketing, division engineering, quality assurance, technical service, laboratory, cost accounting, manufacturing, and packaging people. The second had strong feelings about making the team work, especially because it was dealing with his invention. "You really don't get credit for patents at 3M unless they become products. So I was enthusiastic about being on the team, but only if the team itself could assume the responsibility for its own destiny. In retrospect, I can say that it did that, and that it had clear support all the way to the top," he said later.

The leader's no-nonsense management style got the team off to a running start. Once-a-month meetings were short and to the point. Each team member had a copy of the agenda in advance. The team leader acted as facilitator by delegating assignments to members of the team, hearing progress reports, and keeping track of timelines. His recollection of the experience: "It was easy, natural. It was a team program all the way through. We needed everyone, and everyone who had a specific job did that job."

When the team ran into a problem with a raw material vendor, the leader picked up the phone and called the Purchasing Department directly. He received new samples in the plant within a few days. Manufacturing immediately ran tests on the material, and the project was back on track. This team built a new respirator from scratch in just thirteen months, including the time it took to get government regulatory approval.

Yet another team developed a revolutionary new design for a respirator, one that has already received four patents and has several more pending.

This team made steady progress. However, not every team experience was as smooth.

One technical supervisor and chemical engineer, who had previously been an Action Team leader, was assigned to be a team member on a new project. After only a few meetings, she became convinced that the solutions on which the team was focusing were short-term, and therefore did not meet the goals of the mission statement. Not getting much support from the team, she took her concerns directly to its sponsor. The sponsor met with the team to help them reformulate their criteria for success. Tuckman's model makes provisions for that kind of re-storming—the kind that enables the team to get back on track. Thus, the Action Team concept not only allowed members to go over the leader's head without fear of retribution, but also allowed the team to stop and regroup.

Most teams' work on respirators was made easier by the fact that they knew the technology and had written critical path methods (CPM) and program evaluation and review techniques (PERT) for other respirator products. However, one team, working with an entirely new technology, had no such advantage. In spite of that, this Action Team built an entirely new product, one that became the foundation of a new business.

The product concept originated in our Central Research Laboratory, then was assigned to the division to develop. It didn't yet exist; it was just a concept. Nobody was sure if it could be made at all, let alone manufactured on a large scale. A Ph.D. chemist who worked on this Action Team describes the experience as "like jumping out of an airplane. All I can tell you is that we got down to the ground and we're still alive."

This Action Team's membership was more diverse than other teams because it made use of several different manufacturing technologies. That required greater-than-usual coordination of functions within the organization. The team constantly ran into roadblocks, the kind that only a sponsor could surmount. Yet, once again, with the support of a sponsor, this Action Team got the product to market, shaving years off the usual development time for previous products of this complexity.

Some of the initial confusion this team experienced was due to working with an unfamiliar technology and wondering about the criteria for success from the viewpoint of the end user. 3M had never marketed such a product, so the team had no idea as to consumer preferences.

But the majority of the problems had to do with getting the tangent functional specialties to take broader responsibility. The team eventually brought together functional representatives from several plants and had them sit down and follow the process from start to finish. Representatives from a coating facility even traveled to a laminating facility to get a better understanding of one problem. That kind of information exchange, a team member noted, "helped an awful lot."

LOSING CONTROL OF THE BUDGET

When we talk about budget, remember that the entire division was challenged with transferring technology out of the laboratory and into the marketplace in a compressed timeframe. That kind of progress costs money, and it necessitated the setting of a long-term strategic priority for the division. We had to weigh short-term loss of control in our budgetary process against the potential success of the teams' efforts. The decision was to forego some of the budget controls in order to move the program ahead faster. We were prepared to lose control of budgets.

That's one of the challenges of an Action Team approach. Once management starts up teams, it can't put handcuffs on them by restricting their flow of money, especially when the priority is to bring out new products quickly.

Certain budgets did get out of hand, especially the Laboratory budgets. But overall, most teams did a very good job of managing their money. The entire Action Team program cost us only slightly more than the traditional product development process. We just spent it all in a shorter period of time. The division was able to bring new products to market three to four years sooner than in the past and that did a lot for our competitive position. It

also meant revenue streams that started three to four years earlier. Results demonstrated that Action Teams were well worth our investment.

WHAT WE HAVE LEARNED

The success of teams is built on more than formulas and theories; it requires the genuine commitment of top management and the dedication and professionalism of team leaders and members. We in management had to have enough faith in Action Teams to back off a little on our control mechanisms. We had to accept the risks and differences of outlook that came with this new operating mode.

The most important lesson we learned is how vital it is to train the entire organization. Training brought about upper management buy-in. Many of our problems with middle managers disappeared after they received training. In training, team members learned how to capitalize on the strengths of their fellow members and how to minimize their weaknesses; that knowledge helped them to unify their efforts.

Many of the techniques team members learned in training had great carry-over benefits for the rest of the division. People learned greater appreciation for what other functions do. Marketing people understood better how a new product is built. They knew why "simple" design changes could take longer than they had expected. Laboratory and Manufacturing people had a better understanding of just how hard it is for Marketing to come up with "firm forecasts"—they had learned there's more to it than simple formula manipulations. Everyone gained a larger perspective.

The question of who should direct team members is one that never went away. Managers and sponsors continued to bargain between themselves for human resources. We came to accept that as a "given" when using Action Teams.

We learned that sponsorship was crucial to the success of Action Teams and we strongly recommend the concept. We wouldn't consider starting a team without a sponsor.

Finally, we learned that successful Action

Teams may overload the existing infrastructure of the rest of the organization. With many new designs coming on line, the traditional functions become stretched to the limit. In those instances, the organization faces a scheduling conflict of significant importance, because no team wants to wait in a functional queue.

YOU'VE DONE A GREAT JOB . . .

No discussion about Action Teams would be complete without a reference to rewards. We found this an extremely touchy subject because there is no perfect way to handle it. At certain phases in a team's life, the membership changes drastically. For example, as the team nears scale-up for production, Laboratory people leave the team and more Manufacturing people enter. At what point do you reward? When one phase ends and the next begins? Or, should you wait until the final product introduction? And exactly what reward is appropriate?

We asked each team to come to us with a formal proposal for a reward program—one that would satisfy its members. We weighed their proposals against criteria that accounted for the level of risk demonstrated by the team, the length of time required to complete the project, the difficulty of the project, and finally, the financial impact the project would have on the division. Then we decided whether their proposal was in line with company reward policies. In most cases it was. Some teams asked only for a dinner; some asked for much more. Other teams refused any type of reward, insisting that their work was just part of their job.

AN OVERALL SUCCESS

The use of Action Teams was the key to achieving the goals we had set. The division succeeded in increasing its product offerings. New product development time was cut in half. An atmosphere of en-

trepreneurship with increased personal risk taking was created. The team concept expanded into manufacturing with the formation of manufacturing strategic impact teams (MSIT) to assist in manufacturing cost reduction. Teams were accepted throughout the division.

We were successful in developing a totally new product that gave rise to a new business. Quality in the division reached a new high. We significantly reduced internal barriers to innovation within the organization and pushed decisionmaking down to include more levels than ever before. And, we can honestly say that we built a management style that could serve well into the future. We met every single one of our objectives.

However, the biggest payoff came when we realized that the process perpetuates itself. With each new Action Team we got a little more efficiency, a little more speed, and a little more buy-in. Some team leaders relished the thought of getting another Action Team assignment, while others said they valued the experience at a million dollars, but wouldn't do it again for two. After we started Action Teams, business in the division doubled, and the percentage of new products in our line grew to exceed the corporate goal.

Suddenly, many former nonbelievers were volunteering for teams. That was the greatest achievement of all.

REFERENCES

1. Diamond, M.A. and Allcorn, S. The psychodynamics of regression in work groups. *Human Relations* 40(8):534 (1987).
2. Hardaker, M. and Ward, B. K. How to make a team work. *Harvard Business Review* 87(6):112 (November–December 1987).
3. Gersick, C. J. G. Time and transition in work teams: Toward a new model of group development. *Academy of Management Journal* 31(1):9–41 (March 1988).
4. Rohan, T. M. Bosses—who needs 'em? *Industry Week* 15 (February 23, 1987).
5. Smith, K. K. and Berg, D. N. A paradoxical conception of group dynamics. *Human Relations* 40(10):633, 648, 654 (1987).

17

Managing Creative Performance in R&D Teams

RALPH KATZ

The general neglect of a temporal perspective—the fact that group activities and reactions can change significantly over the course of a long project—has been one of the major problems in the study of project groups and teams. Yet until it is addressed, questions about how well a group is doing will receive answers that are, at best, incomplete. Engineers and scientists have long recognized the problems facing a technical group should its membership remain constant too long. As individuals are born, grow up, and grow older—first feeling their way uncertainly, then seeking out new challenges and experiences as they gain confidence, and finally, becoming a bit self-satisfied about their own knowledge and achievements—so the same process seems to occur within groups whose members have worked together for a long time. Research and Development groups seem to have performance curves analogous to the human life cycle—tentative youth, productive energy, and decline with maturity.

The analogy is a convenient one, though subject in both cases to variation: age *need not* mean stagnation in either an individual or a group. Still, a field study of research and development project teams, which Professor Tom Allen and I have been engaged in for some years, does tend to support a general finding of less intense involvement in job demands and challenges with increasing stability in project membership.

It is, of course, natural for both individuals and groups to attempt to structure their work activities to reduce stress and ensure a level of certainty. People do not deal well with uncertainty; they like to know, as much as possible, what will happen next,

how they will be affected, etc. Given this, group members interacting over a long time are likely to develop standard work patterns that are both familiar and comfortable, patterns in which routine and precedent play a relatively large part—perhaps at the expense of unbiased thought and new ideas. On the other hand, an environment devoid of structure and definition, one wholly unfamiliar and enigmatic, is equally undesirable. Without some sort of established pattern or perspective to serve as a basis for action, nothing at all would be accomplished. The task of management, then, is to create and maintain an atmosphere in which employees are both familiar with their job requirements and challenged by them.

THE REQUISITE FAMILIARITY

How long it takes to acquire the requisite familiarity with one's job to function efficiently depends on the length of time it takes an employee to feel accepted and competent in his or her new environment. This feeling is influenced both by the nature of the individual and the socialization process that unfolds for that person. In general, the time varies according to the level of complexity involved in the job requirements, ranging from as little as a few months to as much as a year or more in nonroutine kinds of professions such as R&D.

In engineering, for example, strategies and solutions are usually peculiar to specific settings. Research and development teams in different organizations may face similar problems, yet approach their solutions with widely divergent methods.

Reprinted with permission from the author.

Ralph Katz is Professor of Management at Northeastern University's College of Business and Research Associate at MIT's Sloan School of Management.

Thus, even though one may have received an excellent education in, say, mechanical engineering principles, one must still figure out how to be an effective mechanical engineer at Westinghouse, Alcoa, or General Electric.

In the course of long-term job tenure, an individual may be said to pass through three broad stages: *socialization, innovation,* and *stabilization.* A graphic representation of the model is shown in Figure 17.1.

During the *socialization* period, employees are primarily concerned with understanding and coming to terms with their new and unknown social and task environments. Newcomers must learn

the customary norms of behavior within their groups, how reward systems operate, the expectations of supervisors, and a host of other considerations that are necessary for them to function meaningfully. These considerations may vary to a surprisingly large extent even within a single organization. This is important for, while the necessity of such a "breaking-in" period has long been recognized in the case of recently hired members of an organization, it should also be understood that veteran employees assigned to new groups must also "resocialize" themselves since they, too, must now deal with unfamiliar tasks and colleagues. It is in this period that employees learn not only the

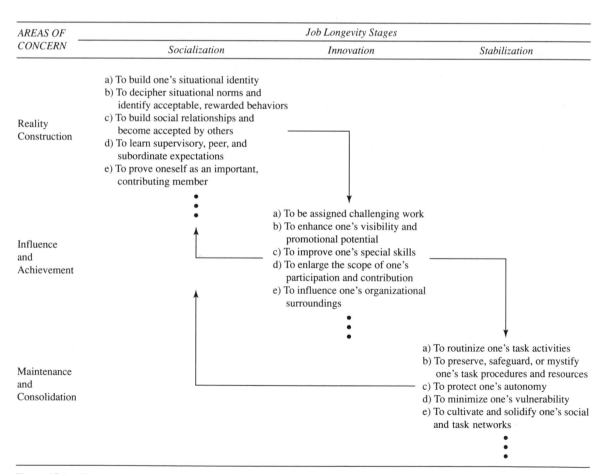

Figure 17.1.   Examples of special issues during each stage of job longevity.

technical requirements of their new job assignments, but also the behaviors and attitudes that are acceptable and necessary for becoming a true contributing member of the group.

As individuals gain familiarity with their work settings, they are freer to devote their energies and concerns less toward socialization and more toward performance and accomplishment. In the *innovation* stage of a job, employees become capable, to a greater extent, of acting in a responsive and undistracted manner. The movement from socialization to innovation implies that employees no longer require much assistance in deciphering their new job and organizational surroundings. Instead, they can divert their attention from an initial emphasis on psychological "safety and acceptance" to concerns for achievement and influence. Opportunities to change the status quo and to respond to new challenging demands within job settings become progressively more pertinent to employees in this stage. As the length of time spent in the same job environment stretches out, however, employees may gradually enter the *stabilization* phase, in which there is a slow shift away from a high level of involvement and receptivity to the challenges in their jobs and toward a greater degree of unresponsiveness to these challenges.

In time, even the most engaging job assignments and responsibilities can appear less exciting, little more than habit, to people who have successfully mastered and become accustomed to their everyday task requirements. It makes sense, then, that with prolonged job stability, employees' perceptions of their conditions at present and possibilities for the future will become increasingly impoverished. If employees cannot maintain, redefine, or expand their jobs for continued change and growth, then their work enthusiasm will deteriorate. If possibilities for development *are* continued, however, then the stabilization period may be held off indefinitely.

The irony of the situation is that employees with the greatest initial responsiveness to job challenges seem to retain that responsiveness for a *shorter* length of time than those expressing less of a need for high job challenge. The greater initial enthusiasm of high-need employees appears to drive them more swiftly through their socialization and innovation periods and into stabilization. They become bored more quickly with tasks that are now too familiar and routine to their growth-oriented natures.

Of course, job longevity does not exist in a vacuum. Many other factors may influence the level of job interest. New technological developments, rapid growth and expansion, or strong competitive pressures, or new excited co-workers could all help sustain or even enhance one's involvement in his or her job-related activities. On the other hand, working closely with a group of unresponsive peers in a relatively unchanging situation might shorten an individual's responsive period on that particular job rather dramatically.

Despite these other influences, though, the general trend does hold. In moving from innovation to stabilization, employees who continue to work in the same overall job situation for long periods gradually adapt to such steadfast employment by becoming increasingly indifferent to the challenging aspects of their assignments. And as employees come to care less about the intrinsic nature of the work they do, their absorption in contextual features such as salary, benefits, vacations, friendly co-workers, and compatible superiors tends to increase.

Interestingly, entry into the stabilization period does not necessarily imply a reduced level of job satisfaction. On the contrary, in fact. As employees enter the stabilization stage, they have typically adapted by becoming very satisfied with the comfortableness and predictability of their work environments; for when the chances of future growth and change become limited, existing situations become accepted as the desired. Only when a reasonable gap remains between what individuals desire and what they are presently able to achieve will there be energy for change and accomplishment.

With stability comes a greater loyalty to precedent, to the established patterns of behavior. In adapting to high job longevity, employees become increasingly content with customary ways of doing things, comfortable routines, and familiar sets of task demands that promote a feeling of security and confidence while requiring little exceptional effort or vigilance. The preservation of such patterns is likely to be a prime consideration, with the result that contact with information and ideas that threaten change may be curtailed. Moreover, strong biases may develop in the selection and interpretation of information, in abilities to generate new options and strategies creatively, and in the level of willingness to innovate or implement alternative courses of action. In a sense, the differences between the innovation and stabilization stages are indicative of the distinctions between creative performance and routine performance; between job excitement and work satisfaction. What they are asked to do, they do well—but that spark is missing. The willingness to go beyond what is requested, to experiment, to try something new, or to seek out new responsibilities is not there.

What is also important to note from the model portrayed in Figure 17.1 is that individuals can easily cycle between socialization and innovation (with on-going job changes and promotions) or they can slowly proceed from innovation to stabilization over time. Direct movement from stabilization back to innovation, however, is very unlikely without the individual first going through a new socialization (or resocialization) experience in order to unfreeze previously defined and reinforced habits and perspectives. Thus, rotation per se is not the solution to rejuvenation; instead, it is rotation coupled with a new socialization experience that provides the individual with a new opportunity to regain responsiveness to new task challenges and environmental demands. The intensity of the resocialization experience, moreover, must match the strength of the prior stabilization period. Organizations often spend much time and effort planning the movements and rotations of personnel. They often, however, spend very little time managing the socialization process that occurs *after* rotation. This is unfortunate, for it is the experiences and interactions that take place after rotation that are so important for influencing and framing an individual's attitudes and eventual responsiveness.

So far, we have described what happens to individual professionals as if they work independently and autonomously. Most of the time, technical professionals function interdependently either as members of specific project teams or specific technology-based groups. It may be more important, therefore, to know not only what happens to an individual over time but also what happens to the performances of teams or groups of individuals who have been working together over time. In any group, there is a changing mix of individuals, some of whom may be in socialization, some in the innovation stage, and still others in stabilization. It is not how this particular mix of individuals act that is important, but how they interact both amongst themselves and outside their group. Successful innovation, after all, is not a function of how well individuals act, but how they interact. While "invention" can result from individualistic actions, effective "innovation" is a function of collective activities and teamwork.

To investigate these issues, Professor Tom Allen and I conducted a study to examine how group longevity affects project performance and communication behavior, where group longevity (i.e., group age) measures the average length of time that project members have worked and shared experiences with one another. Group longevity or group age was determined simply by averaging the individual project tenures of all group members. The measure, therefore, is *not* the length of time the project has been in existence. Rather it represents the length of time group members have been working together in a particular project or technical area.

Data collection for the study took place at the R&D facility of a large American chemical company, employing 345 engineering and scientific professionals in 61 distinct project groups or work areas. Project groups were organized around specific, long-term kinds of problem areas such as fiber-forming development and urethane development, and ranged across three broad categories of R&D activity: (1) applied research, (2) product & process development, and (3) technical service and support.

The purpose of the study was twofold. First, to examine the level of communication activity by project groups at various stages in the group's "life" (that is, its group longevity) and, second, to discover any possible correspondence between a lessening of communication and a possible drop in performance. The focus was on interpersonal communication, which, as many previous studies have demonstrated, is the primary means by which engineering and scientific professionals transfer and process technical ideas and information.

To measure communication activity, participants kept track of all other professionals with whom they had work-related interaction on a randomly chosen day each week for fifteen weeks. Contacts both inside and outside the R&D facility were measured. Based on this frequency data, three independent measures of communication were calculated for each project to each of three separate areas of important information:

1. Intraproject Communication: The amount of communication reported among all project members.

2. Organizational Communication: The level or amount of contact reported by project members with individuals outside the R&D facility but within other corporate divisions, principally marketing and manufacturing.

3. Professional Communication: The amount of communication reported by project members with professionals outside the parent organization, including professionals in universities, consulting firms, and professional societies.

For all three areas or sources of information, project groups whose longevity index was greater than four years reported much lower levels of actual contact than project groups whose longevity index fell between one and a half and four years. Intraproject, organizational, and outside professional interaction were considerably lower for the longer-tenured groups. Members of these groups, therefore, were significantly more isolated from external sources of new ideas and technological advances and from information within other organizational divisions, especially marketing and manufacturing. Project members in these long-tenured groups even communicated less often amongst themselves about technically related matters.

In addition to these measures of actual communication behavior, a direct evaluation of the current technical performance of the project groups was obtained. All department managers and laboratory directors assessed the overall performance of all projects with which they were technically familiar, based on their knowledge of and experience with the various projects. The managers, in making their evaluations, considered such elements as schedule and cost performance; innovativeness; adaptability; and the ability to coordinate with other parts of the organization. Each project was independently rated by an average of five higher-level managers; consensus among the ratings was extremely high.

On average, the association between project performance and group longevity closely paralleled the association of longevity and communication trends. This is to say that for these 61 project teams, there was a strong curvilinear relationship between group age and project performance—the best performing groups being those with longevities between one and a half and four years. Performance was significantly lower for the relatively new teams and for teams that had been together for more than four years. In fact, *none* of the ten project groups with the highest levels of group age (i.e., five or more years) were among the facility's higher performing project teams, all being rated by the facility's management as either average or below average. It is also interesting to note that none of the managerial evaluators knew which project teams were the long-term ones or whether their organization even had any, since rotations and movements were always ongoing. In reality, over 20 percent of the R&D effort within this organization was being conducted by these ten lower-performing, long-term technical teams.

Almost by definition, projects with higher mean group tenure were staffed by older engineers. This raises the possibility that performance may be lower as a result of the increasing obsolescence of individuals' skills as they aged, rather than because of anything to do with the group's tenure composition. The data, however, do not bear this out. For both the communication and the performance data, it was found that group longevity and not the chronological age of individuals was more likely to have influenced the results.

Another possibility is that long-tenured project teams had simply come to be staffed by less technically competent or perhaps less motivated engineers and scientists. Follow-up visits to this facility over the next five years, however, reveal that about the same proportion of professionals from both the long- and medium-tenured teams were awarded promotions to higher level managerial positions above the project leadership level. Over this five-year period, 15 percent of the engineers who had worked in the medium-tenured groups attained managerial positions of either laboratory supervisor or laboratory manager, while the comparable proportion from the longer-tenured groups was 13 percent. In addition, the percentage of technical professionals promoted to the "technical" side of the facility's dual ladder promotional system was slightly greater for members in the longer-tenured project groups than the medium-tenured ones, 19 percent compared to 12 percent. This seems to indicate a relative parity in the area of individual competence and capability between the respective group memberships of the medium and long-term categories of group longevity.

Despite the parallel declines in both project communication and performance with increasingly high levels of group longevity, one must be careful not to jump to the conclusion that decays in all areas of communication contributed equally to the lower levels of project performance. Different categories of project tasks require different patterns of communication for more effective performance. Research project groups, for example, have been found to be higher performing when project members maintain high levels of technical communication with outside professionals. Performance in development projects, on the other hand, is related more to contact within the organization, primarily with divisions such as marketing and manufactur-

ing. Finally, for technical-service projects, communication within the team appears most crucial.

Significantly, for each project type, the deterioration in interaction was particularly strong in the area *most* important for high technical performance. This suggests that it is not a reduction in project communication per se that leads to less effective project performance; but rather it is an isolation from sources that can provide the most critical kinds of evaluation, information, and new ideas. Thus, overall effectiveness suffers when research project members fail to pay attention to events and information within the larger technical community outside the organization; or when development project members lose contact with client groups from marketing and manufacturing; or when technical-service project members do not interact among themselves.

Clearly—at least in the case of the groups studied here—there are strong relationships between longevity within a group and decreased levels of communication activity and project performance. In order to develop strategies that circumvent these unfortunate outcomes, the processes through which they occur must be understood in greater detail. What happens in long-term groups that leads to their being relatively cut off from sources of new ideas and information?

Essentially, project newcomers in the midst of socialization are trying to navigate their way through new and unfamiliar territories without the aid of adequate or even accurate perceptual maps. During this initial period, they are relatively more malleable and more susceptible to change, dependent as they are on other project members to help them define and interpret the numerous activities taking place around them. As they become more familiar with their project settings, however, they also become more capable of relying on their own perceptions and knowledge for interpreting events and executing their everyday project requirements. Having established their own social and task supports, their own outlooks and work identities, they become less easily changed and influenced.

If this process is allowed to continue among project members, healthy levels of self-reliance can easily degenerate into problematic levels of closed-mindedness. Rigidity in problem-solving activities—a kind of functional fixedness—may result from this, reducing the group's ability to react flexibly to changing conditions. Novel situations are either ignored or forced into established categories; new or changing circumstances either trigger old responses or none at all. New ideas, opportunities, or creative suggestions are greeted with resistance and easily disposed of with remarks like "it won't work," "it's infeasible," "it's too difficult," "we've never done that before," or "that's not our business."

Furthermore, the longer group members are called upon to follow and justify their problem-solving strategies and decisions, the more ingrained these approaches are likely to become. As as result, alternative ideas that were probably considered and discarded during previous discussions may never be reconsidered even though they may have become more appropriate or feasible. In fact, members may end up devoting much of their efforts to the preservation of their particular approaches against the encroachment of competing methods and negative evaluations. Essentially, they become overly committed to the continuation of their existing ideas and solutions, often without sufficient regard to their "true" applicability.

With this perspective, as one might suspect, the extent to which group members are willing or even feel the need to expose themselves to alternative ideas, solution strategies, or constructive criticism is likely to be diminished. A pattern of *increasing isolation* from external changes and new technological developments, coupled with a growing complacence about work-related challenges may be the result. Project groups with high levels of group longevity, then, appear to behave as if they possess so much expertise in their specialized technical areas that it is unlikely that outsiders might be producing important new ideas or information relevant to the performance of their project tasks. Rather than face the anxiety and discomfort inherent in learning or change, they tacitly assume that their abilities and experienced know-how are far better than those ideas or suggestions coming from

outside their group. They become increasingly reliant on their own technology and knowledge base, creating an appearance to the outside world of decreased relevance, which leads to a decrease in the team's motivation to communicate with and respond to the outside. It is this isolation and more narrow focus which in turn leads to poorer performance.

Another explanation contributing to the reduced levels of project member interaction is the principle of *selective exposure,* the tendency for group members to communicate only with those whose ideas and outlooks are in accord with their own current interests, needs, and existing attitudes. And group members tend to become more alike over time. Just as it is sometimes said that close friends or husbands and wives seem to grow closer in appearance, so groups may take on a kind of collective viewpoint after interacting for an extended period. As members stabilize their work settings and patterns of communication, a greater degree of similarity is likely to emerge. This, in turn, leads to further stability in communication, and, therefore, even greater isolation from different-thinking others.

There is at least one advantage to this. People who think alike are able to communicate more effectively and economically. This advantage is more than outweighed, however, by the fact that such communication is likely to yield less creative and innovative outcomes than communications containing a variety of differing perspectives.

It should also be recognized that under these kinds of circumstances even the outside information that is processed by long-tenured groups may not be viewed in the most open or unbiased fashion. Many kinds of cognitive defenses and distortions are commonly used by members in *selectively perceiving* outside information in order to support and maintain their decisional policies and strategies. Such defenses can easily be used to argue against any disquieting information and evidence in order to maintain their present courses of action. Such selectivity can also result in a more restricted perspective of one's situation, which can be very detrimental to the group's overall effectiveness, for it often screens out vitally important information cues.

These trends of *increasing isolation, selective exposure,* and *selective perception* can all feed off each other in a kind of vicious circle, leaving group members in a state of greater and greater distance from new advances and ideas, and greater and greater reliance on an increasingly narrow and homogeneous set of alternatives. The prior curvilinear relationship between group age and project performance, therefore, can really be thought of as the composite result of two component forces, as shown in Figure 17.2. One component term rises rapidly as group age begins to increase, showing the positive effects of "team-building." Group members develop a common language and frame of reference. They have more concrete understandings of each others' capabilities, contributions, and working styles. And such improvements in communication and working relationships translate into higher levels of group performance.

At the same time, however, a decay component term sets in, resulting in part from the previously described problem-solving, communication,

and cognitive processes that become more established, reinforced, and habitual as group members reduce uncertainty together within their group setting. This decay component, as shown in Figure 17.2, describes processes underneath the well-recognized "Not-Invented Here" or "NIH" syndrome in which groups gradually define themselves into a narrow field of specialization and convince themselves that they have a monopoly on knowledge and capability in their area of specialty. Between these two component curves lies the area for potentially influencing a project's innovative performance.

MANAGING FOR INNOVATION

Are these processes inevitable? Or can management alter the composition of current R&D groupings in order to minimize the effects of extended group longevity on project performance and still ensure an adequate level of stability for relatively smooth operation? What follows are a few suggestions toward the goal of managing for a continuously high level of innovation.

Employee perspectives and behaviors, and their subsequent effects on performance, can be significantly affected through the systematic and creative use of staffing and career decisions. For example, regular placement of new members into project groups may perform an energizing and destabilizing function—keeping the group longevity index from rising, thereby preventing the group from developing some of the tendencies described here (particularly isolation from critical information areas). New members have the advantage of fresh ideas and approaches, and of a fresh eye for old ones. With their active participation, established members might be kept responsive to the generation of new methods and behaviors as well as the reconsideration of alternatives that might otherwise be ignored. In short, project newcomers create a novelty-enhancing situation, challenging and improving the scope of existing methods and accumulated knowledge, provided of course that the newcomer(s) socialization process is appropriately

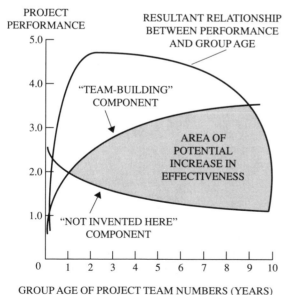

Figure 17.2. Relationship between group age and project performance analyzed by component forces.

managed (see Section 4 in this volume, entitled "Organizational Socialization and the Reduction of Uncertainty").

Clearly, the longevity framework suggests that periodic additions or rotations can help *prevent* the onset of the stabilization processes associated with high longevity. Provided the socialization period is not overly conforming, project groups can simply remain in an innovation cycle. While prevention is clearly easier, it is also suggested that the replacement or reassignment of certain long-tenured professionals to different project groups may be necessary for improving the performance of high longevity teams as well as for keeping such groups stimulated, flexible, and vigilant with respect to their project environments. Continued growth and development comes from adaptations to new challenges, often requiring the abandonment of familiar and stable work patterns in favor of new ones.

Interestingly, managers are usually not aware of the tenure demographics of their project groups. In our studies, managers are usually unable to identify which of their projects have high levels of group longevity. Many are even surprised that any of their project teams have a mean group age of five or more years. Once the behavioral patterns characterizing the NIH decay component are described to them, however, they can easily spot the appropriate groups.

Of course, rotations and promotions are not always possible, especially when there is little organizational growth. As important as job mobility is, it is no doubt equally crucial to determine whether project groups can circumvent the effects of high longevity without new assignments or rejuvenation from new project members. To do this, we must learn considerably more about the effects of increasing job and group longevities. For example, in the study presented here, none of the long-tenured project groups was above average in project performance. Yet different trends might have emerged with different kinds of organizational climates, different personnel and promotional policies, different economic and marketing conditions, or even different types of organizational structures.

Can project groups keep *themselves* energized and innovative over long periods, or are certain kinds of structures and managerial practices needed to maintain effectiveness and high performance as a team ages? Just how deterministic are these curves and relationships?

In more recent and extensive project data collected from twelve different technology-based organizations involving more than 300 R&D project groups, of which approximately fifty have group longevity scores of five or more years, it turns out that a large number of these long-tenured groups were judged to have a high level of performance. The data are still being processed, but preliminary analyses seem to indicate that the nature of the project's supervision may be the most important factor differentiating the more effective long-tenured teams from those less effective. In particular, engineers belonging to the high-performing, long-tenured groups perceived their project supervisors to be superior in dealing with conflicts between groups and individuals, in obtaining necessary resources for project members, in setting project goals, and in monitoring the activities and progress of project members toward these goals. Furthermore, in performing these supervisory functions, project managers of the more effective long-tenured groups were *not* very participative in their approaches, instead, they were extremely demanding of their teams, challenging them to perform in new ways and directions. In fact, the most participative managers (as viewed by project members) were significantly less effective in managing teams with high group longevity. Our study also revealed that not all managers may be able to gain the creative performances out of long-term technical groups. Typically, the managers of the higher performing long-term groups had been with their teams less than 3 years and had come to this assignment with a strong history of prior managerial success. It was not their first managerial experience! To the contrary, most were well-respected technical managers who had "made things happen" and who had developed strong power bases and strong levels of senior managerial support within their R&D units or divisions. It was this combination of technical credibility and managerial respect and power that enabled these managers to be effective with their long-term stabilized R&D project teams.

These and other preliminary findings suggest the following strategies for managing project groups with high levels of long-term stability and group age:

1. More emphasis should be placed on the particular skills and abilities of the project manager. Members of long-tenured groups are more responsive to the nature of their supervision than to the intrinsic nature of their work content.

2. In terms of managerial styles, project managers should place less emphasis on participative management and more emphasis on direction and control. As long as members of long-tenured groups are unresponsive to the challenges in their tasks, participative management will only be related to job satisfaction—not project performance.

3. Project managers, on the other hand, should be very responsive to the challenging nature of their project's work. Consequently, they should

be given considerable authority and freedom to execute their project responsibilities, but they, in turn, should be "tight-fisted" with respect to their subordinates.

In a sense, then, traditional managers may be effective for managing high group longevity teams. In a broader context, however, we need to learn how to manage workers, professionals, and project teams as they proceed through different stages of longevity. Clearly; different kinds of managerial styles and practices may be more appropriate at different stages of the process. Delegative or participative management, for example, may be very effective when individuals are highly responsive to their work, but much less successful when employees are not, as in the stabilization phase. As perspectives and responsiveness shift over time, the actions required of managers will vary as well. Managers may be effective to the extent that they can recognize and react to such developments. As in so many areas, it is the ability to manage change that seems most important in providing careers that keep employees responsive and organizations effective.

6

Managing Project Groups in a Matrix Structure

18

How Project Performance is Influenced by the Locus of Power in the R&D Matrix

RALPH KATZ AND THOMAS J. ALLEN

Abstract. This study examines the relation-ship between project performance and the relative influence of project and functional managers in 86 R&D teams in nine technol-ogy-based organizations. Analyses show higher project performance when influence over salaries and promotions is perceived as balanced between project and functional managers. Performance reaches its highest level, however, when organizational influ-ence is centered in the project manager and influence over technical details of the work is centered in the functional manager.

The matrix structure was first developed in research and development organizations in an attempt to

Reprinted with permission from the authors. An earlier version of this paper was published in 1985 titled Project Performance and the Locus of Influence in the R&D Matrix. *Academy of Management Journal*, 28(1):67–87.

Ralph Katz is Professor of Management at Northeastern University's College of Business and Research Associate at MIT's Sloan School of Management ***Thomas J. Allen*** is Senior Associate Dean and Professor of Management at MIT's Sloan School of Man-agement capture the benefits and minimize the liabilities of two earlier forms of organization, the functional structure and the project form of organization (Crawford, 1986; Allen, 1986).

The functional alternative, in which departments are organized around disciplines or technologies, enables engineers to stay in touch more easily with new developments in those disciplines or technologies than does the project form. It has, however, the disadvantage of creating separations between technologies, thereby making interdisciplinary projects more difficult to coordinate. The functional approach is generally considered incapable of dealing with the added complexity and information requirements associated with a critical program or project-development effort whose tasks are significantly interdependent. Organizing activities primarily around functional expertise contributes to miscommunications and bottlenecks not only because there is no formal coordination mechanism but also because functional specialists tend to adopt a more restricted and parochial view of the overall project.

The project form of organization overcomes the coordination problem by grouping engineers together on the basis of the project or program on which they are working, regardless of their disciplines. Speed and more focused alignment around common project objectives tend to be the attributes of project teams, fostering a greater sense of collective identity, commitment, and ownership. Although it eases the integration of multidisciplinary efforts, the project structure does not allow as much sharing of resources across projects and it removes technical specialists from their disciplinary departments. This resulting detachment makes it more difficult for professionals to keep pace with the most recent developments in their areas of expertise. This can be very detrimental in long-term programs, especially if there is a fast rate of change in the underlying technologies. It can also be problematic for individual members' careers once the program is over if they have become so wrapped up and specialized in their project's activities and demands that they are now viewed or have become somewhat obsolete in their basic disciplines.

FORCES INHERENT IN THE MATRIX

The matrix, by creating an integrating force in a program or project office, attempts to overcome the divisions that are inherent in the basic functional structure. In the matrix, project or program managers and their staffs are charged with the responsibility of integrating the efforts of engineers who draw upon a variety of different disciplines and technical specialities in the development of new products or processes. The managers of functional departments, on the other hand, are responsible for making sure that the organization is aware of the most recent developments in its relevant technologies, thereby insuring the technical integrity of products and processes that the program or project office is attempting to develop. As emphasized by Larson and Gobeli (1988), the project manager is responsible for defining what needs to be done, while the functional managers are concerned with how it will be accomplished.

While both parties are supposed to work closely together and jointly communicate and approve work-flow decisions, these disparate responsibilities often lead to conflict between the two arms of the matrix. Project managers are often forced by market needs and schedule pressures to assume a shorter range view of the research and development activities than functional managers need to have. Since they are responsible for developing a product that can be successfully produced and marketed, project managers take on a perspective that is sometimes more closely aligned to that of persons in marketing or manufacturing than to the perspective held in the research and development organization. Functional department heads, with their closer attachment to underlying technologies, are inclined to take a longer term view and consequently may be more concerned with the organization's capability to deliver the highest quality solution with the most relevant up-to-date technologies than with meeting immediate customer needs.

Both of these perspectives are necessary to the survival of the organization. Someone has to be concerned with getting new products out into the market, and someone has to be concerned with maintaining the organization's long-term capability to develop and incorporate technical advancements into future products. Research and development organizations, no matter how they are organized, always have both of these concerns. The matrix structure merely makes them explicit by vesting the two sets of concerns in separate managers.

In formalizing these two distinct lines of managerial influence, the R&D organization is generating "deliberate conflict" between two essential managerial perspectives as a means of balancing these two organizational needs (Cleland, 1968). Project managers whose prime directive is to get the product "out the door" are matched against functional managers who tend to hold back because they can always make the product "a little bit better", given more time and effort (Allen, 1984). When these two opposing forces are properly balanced, the organization should achieve a more nearly optimum balance, both in terms of product completion and technical excellence. Unfortunately, a balanced situation is not easy to achieve. Often one or the other arm of the matrix will dominate, and then, what appears to be a matrix on paper becomes either a project or a functional organization in operation.

These two conflicting forces of a matrix affect R&D project performance principally through their respective influences on the behaviors and attitudes of individual engineers. It is the engineers who perform the actual problem-solving activities that result in new products or processes. How they view the relative power of project and functional managers over their work lives will strongly influence how they respond to the different sets of pressures and priorities confronting them in the performance of their everyday tasks.

In any matrix organization, there are at least three broad areas of decision making in which both project and functional managers are supposed to be involved: (1) technical decisions regarding project work activities and solution strategies; (2) determination of salaries and promotional opportunities; and (3) staffing and organizational assignments of engineers to particular project activities. These are critical areas in which project and functional managers contend for influence, for it is through these supervisory activities that each side of the matrix attempts to motivate and direct each engineer's efforts and performance (Kingdon, 1973). The degree to which each side of the matrix is successful in building its power and influence within the R&D organization will have a strong bearing on the outcomes that emerge from the many interdependent engineering activities (Wilemon & Gemmill, 1971).

Although a great deal has been written about matrix organizations, there is very little empirical evidence about the effectiveness of these structures. What are the relationships between project performance and the distribution of power and influence within the organization? Will a balance in power between project and functionally oriented forces result in higher project performance? To answer such questions, the present study examines the relationships between project performance and the relative dominance of project and functional managers for 86 matrix project teams from nine technology-based organizations.

HYPOTHESES

Details of Project Work

This is the arena in which project and functional interests are most likely to come into direct conflict. The project manager has ultimate responsibility for bringing the new product into being and is, therefore, intimately concerned with the technical approaches used in accomplishing that outcome. However, if the project side of the matrix is allowed to dominate development work, two quite different problems can develop. At one extreme, there is the possibility that sacrifices in technical quality and long-term reliability will be made in order to meet budget, schedule, and immediate market demands (Knight, 1977). At the other extreme, the potential of products is often oversold by making claims that are beyond the organization's current technological capability to deliver.

To guard against these shortcomings, functional managers can be held accountable for the overall integrity of the product's technical content.

If the functional side of the matrix becomes overly dominant, however, the danger is that the product will include not only more sophisticated, but also perhaps less proven and riskier technology. The functional manager's desire to be technologically aggressive—to develop and use the most attractive, most advanced technology—must be countered by forces that are more sensitive to the operational environment and more concerned with moving developmental efforts into final physical reality (Mansfield & Wagner, 1975; Utterback, 1974).

To balance the influence of both project and functional managers over technical details is often a difficult task. While an engineer may report to both managers in a formal sense, the degree to which these managers both actively influence the direction or clarification of technical details and solution strategies will vary considerably from project to project, depending on the ability and willingness of the two managers to understand and become involved in the relevant technology and its applications. Nonetheless, project performance should be higher when team members can take both perspectives into account. Accordingly, the following is proposed:

Hypothesis 1: Project performance will be higher in a matrix structure when both project and functional managers are seen to exert equal influence over the detailed technical work of engineers.

Salaries and Promotions

Advocates of matrix organizations (e.g., Davis & Lawrence, 1977) have long agreed on the importance of achieving balanced influence over salary and promotion decisions. Both Roberts (1988) and Pinto, Pinto, and Prescott (1993) emphasize that matrix organizations require matching control systems to support their multidimensional structures; otherwise, they would be undermined by reward systems that are based on assumptions of unitary authority. The underlying argument is that when engineers view either their project or their functional managers as having more control over chances for salary increases and promotions, the engineers' behaviors and priorities are more likely to be influenced and directed solely by the side with that control.

This is one of the key issues in what are often described as "paper matrix" situations: management assumes that by drawing overlapping structures and by prescribing areas of mutual responsibility, balance will be achieved among appropriate supporting management systems. In practice, however, one of the two components of the matrix comes to dominate or appears to dominate in key areas such as determination of salaries or of promotions. It is important to stress here that it is the engineer's perception that counts. Unless engineers see both managers as affecting their progress in terms of income and status, there will be a natural tendency for them, particularly in conflict situations, to heed the desires of one manager to the neglect of the other. The matrix then ceases to function, resulting in a structure that is more likely to resemble either the pure project or the pure functional form of organization despite any "paper" claims to the contrary. We therefore expect that:

Hypothesis 2: Project performance will be higher in a matrix structure when both project and functional managers are seen to exert equal influence over the promotions and rewards of engineers than it will be when one or the other manager is seen as dominating.

Personnel Assignments

Personnel assignments often provide the focus for the priority battles that frequently afflict matrix organizations. With the pressure on them from both management and customers to produce, project managers often find themselves in tight competition for the resources necessary to provide results. One of the most critical of these resources is technical talent. Each functional department employs engineers of varying technical backgrounds, experiences, and capabilities. Every project manager learns quickly which engineers are the top performers and naturally wants them assigned to his project. As a result, an intense rivalry develops among project managers, with each attempting to secure the most appropriate and most talented engineers for his project (Cleland & King, 1968). Functional managers, on the other hand, have a different motivation. They have no difficulty finding resources to support their top performers, but they also have to keep the rest of their engineering staff employed. They must therefore allocate or market the services of their less talented engineers to all project groupings.

At this point we must make a distinction between performance at the project level and performance at the level of the entire R&D organization. Organizational performance might be higher when project and functional managers have equal influence over personnel assignments. The performance of a single project, however, will probably be higher when that project's manager has greater influence over personnel assignments, since presumably that project will then obtain the best talent. Since our study is at the project level, and although we realize that high individual project performance may be suboptimal for the entire R&D organization, we expect that:

Hypothesis 3: Project performance will, on the average, be higher when project managers are seen to exert greater influence over personnel assignments to their projects than functional managers.

Organizational Influence

We must consider more than the bases of supervisory influence that exist within a project group. Considerable research has shown that managers of high performing projects are also influential outside their project teams (e.g., Pfeffer, 1993; Katz et al. 1995). According to such studies, managers affect the behaviors and motivations of subordinates not only through leadership directed *within* the project group but also through their organizational influence *outside* the project. The critical importance of organizational influence on project outcomes has also been confirmed by many studies of technological innovation (e.g., Ancona & Caldwell, 1990; Howell & Higgins, 1990). In almost every instance, successful innovation required the strong support and sponsorship of organizationally powerful managers who could provide essential resources, mediate intergroup conflicts, and were positioned to protect the developmental effort from outside sources of interference.

Based on these findings, if engineers see either arm of the matrix as having greater power in the organization at large, their behavior should be affected, particularly in situations of conflict. Engineers want to be on the "winning team" (Kidder, 1981). Perceptions of organizational influence, therefore, will be an important determinant of what actually occurs in a project, for an imbalance would probably result in engineers' paying greater attention and attributing greater importance to the more powerful side of the matrix.

This does not mean that the locus of organizational influence necessarily determines the loci of influence over work, rewards, and assignments. There may be, for example, many instances in which the less organizationally powerful manager exerts greater influence over one of the other dimensions. Such incongruences place engineers in uncomfortable positions, particularly if there is strong disagreement between their two managers. Discomfort over technical direction can often lead to the postponement of critical technical decisions and the failure to narrow the scope of technical alternatives, resulting in lower project performance. From an exploratory standpoint, our research examines two important questions involving organizational and project influence. First, is there a strong association between perceived organizational influence and the relative dominance of project and functional managers over the rewards, personnel assignments, and technical work of project engineers? And second, to what extent do these dimensions of organizational and internal dominance interact to affect project performance? Do they independently relate to project performance or do they interact in determining performance?

The basic model (Figure 18.1) underlying our

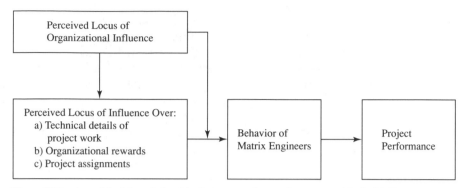

Figure 18.1   A model of the relationships between project performance and loci of influence.

study, then, is that the loci of power between project and functional managers relate to project performance through their respective effects on the behaviors and efforts of engineers in matrix situations. More specifically, how professionals perceive the distribution of influence between their functional and project managers over the technical details of their project work, over their chances for organizational rewards, and over their assignments to particular project activities will significantly affect their performances on their project teams, as hypothesized. These perceived loci of influence, moreover, may be strongly related to how engineers in a matrix organization see the relative power of the two managers within the larger organization.

On the other hand, the locus of organizational influence may not be associated with any of these three measures of internal influence; instead, it may be an additional factor that interacts with these measures to affect project performance. Most likely, the locus of organizational influence will interact with a particular measure of internal project influence only when the two influence measures are not strongly interconnected; otherwise, it is more likely that they will covary with project performance.

RESEARCH METHODS

Setting

The data presented in this paper derive from a study of R&D project teams in nine major U.S. organi-

zations. Although the selection of participating organizations could not be made random, they were chosen to represent several distinct work sectors and markets. Two of the sites are government laboratories; three are not-for-profit firms receiving most of their funding from government agencies. The four remaining companies are in private industry, two in aerospace, one in electronics, and one in consumer goods and products.

In each organization, we met with senior managers and administrators to ascertain the project assignments and reporting relationships of all R&D staff professionals. The questionnaires were then tailored to the specific membership and reporting structure of each project group using the appropriate terminology of that project. To ensure higher-quality data responses through voluntary participation, individuals were asked to complete their questionnaires on their own time and to mail them back to us directly using pre-stamped, return envelopes. Questionnaires were distributed through a number of brief explanatory meetings followed up by several reminder notes and "thank you" letters that were mailed over the course of the next few weeks. Response rates across the organizations were extremely high, ranging from as low as 82 percent in one organization to a high of 96 percent in another.

Although these procedures yielded over 2,000 respondents from 201 project teams, only 86 projects involved engineers and scientists in matrix dual-reporting relationships. A total of 486 engineers worked in matrix relationships in the 86 projects, an average of almost 6 engineers per project. Responses of these engineers, averaged to provide project measures, are the basic data analyzed. The proportion of the project team working in dual-reporting relationships varied from 20 percent (1 project) to 100 percent (18 projects); 19 projects had 70–99 percent, 21 projects had 60–69 percent, 20 projects had 50–59 percent, and 7 projects had 21–49 percent in matrix dual-reporting relationships. Results reported here are based only upon responses of engineers in matrix dual-reporting structures. Since the percentage of matrix engineers within projects varies considerably across the sample, significant findings will be reexamined as a function of these variations.

Matrix Relationships

We asked respondents in matrix structures to indicate on 7-point Likert-type scales the degree to which their project and functional managers influenced: (1) the technical details of their project work; (2) their salary increases and promotions; (3) their having been selected to work on the project; and (4) the overall conduct of the organization. For each of these dimensions of influence, scale responses ranged from 1 for "my project manager dominates" to 7 for "my functional manager dominates"; the middle point, 4, indicated that influence was balanced between the two. For each question, we averaged individual member responses to calculate overall project scores for the four influence areas.

For each of the four influence measures, appropriate statistical tests (cf. Katz and Tushman, 1979) were used to make sure it was permissible to combine individual perceptions to derive aggregated project scores. Except for a few isolated cases, there was sufficient consensus and reliability of individual responses within projects for each measure of influence. All of our analyses, therefore, are conducted at the project level; responses of individual engineers are averaged to provide project measures. Also, the influence scores for each project are based *only* on the aggregated perceptual responses of those engineers or scientists who were

actually in matrix-reporting relationships. For each dimension of influence, lower scores indicate project manager dominance, while higher scores represent functional manager dominance. Because some questions were not included in the initial stages of the research (it took 21 months to conduct the study across all nine organizations), the number of project teams from which complete data are obtained ranges from 63 to 86.

Project Performance

Since measures of objective performance that are comparable across different technologies have yet to be developed, we used a subjective measure similar to that of many previous studies. In each organization, we measured project performance by interviewing managers who were at least one hierarchical level above the project and functional managers, asking them to indicate on a 5-point Likert-type scale whether a project team was performing above, below, or at the level expected of them, given the particular technical activities on which they were working. Managers evaluated only those projects that they were personally familiar with and knowledgeable about. Evaluations were made independently and submitted confidentially to the investigators. On the average, between four and five managers evaluated each project. The evaluations showed very strong internal consensus within each organization (Spearman-Brown reliabilities range from a low of .74 to a high of .93). It was therefore safe to average the ratings of individual managers to yield reliable project performance scores. However, performance data were missing from two projects. Right after we collected our data, an expert panel of independent, outside R&D professionals exhaustively evaluated a small subset of our project base ($N = 8$). The ordering of their project performance evaluations agreed perfectly with the ordering of our own aggregated measures of performance. Such agreement between two separate sources provides considerable support for the validity of our project performance measures. Finally, our measures of relative project performance were not significantly related to the overall number of project members, to the number of matrix project members, or to the proportion of project members in matrix reporting relationships. To clarify the distinction between high and low project performance, performance measures were converted to normalized scores, with a mean of 0 (the original sample mean was 3.32).

RESULTS

As previously explained, we averaged responses to classify projects according to the degree to which project or functional managers exerted influence over each of four activity areas. Project scores of 1 through 3 were coded as signifying dominant influence by the project manager, while scores of 5 through 7 were taken to indicate functional manager dominance. Intermediate values, greater than 3 and less than 5, were considered as signifying balanced influence.

The locus of influence, as shown in Table 18.1, varies considerably both among projects and across dimensions of influence. Influence over technical details of work and over personnel assignments is balanced in the majority of cases. On the other hand, over half of the functional managers are seen as having greater influence over salaries and promotions: functional managers are viewed as controlling these rewards in almost 60 percent of the projects, project managers in only 7 percent. It is important to remember that it is the perceptions of engineers in matrix-reporting relationships that was measured, for it is perceived reality—not the

reality itself—that influences engineers' behavior. Project managers may in fact have equal influence over salaries and promotions, but unless this equality is clearly apparent to engineers, it cannot affect their behavior.

Organizational influence, in contrast, is almost equally distributed across the three influence categories, with 30 percent of the projects having a more dominant functional side, 31 percent a more dominant project side, and 38 percent a reasonably balanced situation.

Because the projects under investigation come from government, not-for-profit, and industrial organizations, it is also important to see if there are major differences among these sectors. Generally speaking, there are no significant differences in the distributions of managerial influence for the dimensions of technical content and personnel assignments. In each sector, the distributions are consistent with the percentages reported in Table 18.1. For the other two loci of influence, however, there are significant variations from the distributions of Table 18.1 by the type of organization. In the not-for-profit sector, functional managers are seen as having considerably more influence within their organizations than their project management counterparts and are perceived as dominating rewards in over 80 percent of the projects. In sharp contrast, project managers are viewed as having stronger organizational influence than functional managers in over half of the projects in the industrial and government sectors. These differences are not surprising, since not-for-profit organizations are some-

TABLE 18.1
Distribution of Managerial Influence by Area as Perceived by Project Members

Area of influence	Locus of influence			
	Functional manager	Balanced	Project manager	N^a
Influence within the project				
Technical content of project work	14.0%	50.0%	36.1%	86
Salaries and promotions	58.1	34.9	7.0	86
Personnel assignments	28.6	54.0	17.5	63
Influence within the organization	30.2	38.3	31.4	86

[a]As previously explained, N varies by area of influence.

what more oriented to academic research and probably place greater emphasis on the disciplines than either industry or government organizations; industry and government organizations, in turn, probably put more emphasis on project management and the clear-cut product or system that must be brought into being. We present these descriptive distributions not to test any specific hypothesis, but simply to give the reader a better view of our data base, especially since we could not undertake randomized sampling of organizations.

Project Performance

As the above distributions show, it is very clear that the degree to which project or functional managers exert influence over dual-reporting engineers differs considerably among projects. The locus of influence also differs for each dimension of influence. The next step, therefore, is to test our hypotheses by seeing how project performance varies with these loci of influence. To examine the proposed relationships, we performed an analysis of variance on each dimension of internal project influence. In each analysis, project performance was the dependent variable, and the three categories of managerial dominance and balance represent the comparative levels within the independent variable.

Technical Details of Project Work. Table 18.2 presents results on the relationship between project performance and the locus of influence over the technical details of project work. Performance does not vary significantly with the locus of influ-

TABLE 18.2
Project Performance as a Function of the Locus of Influence over Technical Content of Project Work

Locus of influence	Number of projects	Project performance[a]
Project manager	31	0.07
Balanced	42	−0.08
Functional manager	11	0.10

[a]Normalized means; a one-way analysis of variance indicated that mean performance did not differ significantly ($F = 1.43$)

TABLE 18.3
Project Perfomance as a Function of the Locus of Influence over Salaries and Promotions

Locus of influence	Number of projects	Project performance[a]
Project manager	6	0.40
Balanced	29	0.37
Functional manager	49	−0.27

[a]Normalized means; one-way analysis of variance indicated that mean performance differed significantly at the .02 level ($F = 4.69$).

ence over technical content. Although there is a slight tendency toward higher performance when the project manager is perceived to have moderately high influence or the functional manager to have strong influence, neither of these tendencies is significant. Also, the latter result stems from only 11 development projects. In any event, balanced involvement in technical matters of both sides of the matrix is not related to higher project performance; the data do not support hypothesis 1.

Salaries and Promotions. In the area of salaries and promotions, the ANOVA results of Table 18.3 show that project performance varies significantly across the loci of managerial influence. The mean performance levels in Table 18.3 indicate that project performance is highest when influence is either balanced or when project managers are viewed as controlling organizational rewards, although there are only six project cases in this latter category. Nevertheless, mean performance is significantly lower when functional managers are seen by project members as having more influence over their salaries and promotion opportunities.

Because the distribution of projects along the influence continuum is so extremely skewed towards functional control, we used Tukey's (1977) smoothing procedures as most appropriate for obtaining a more complete descriptive picture of the association between project performance and the locus of managerial influence over salaries and promotions. An examination of the resulting plot of smoothed performances (Figure 18.2) reveals a

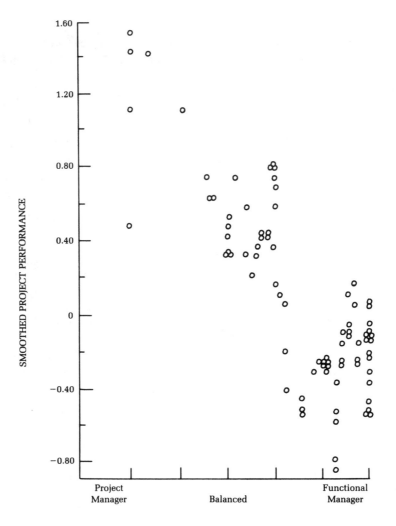

Figure 18.2 Smoothed project performance as a function of the locus of influence over salaries and promotions.

fairly regular pattern of decreasing performance with increasing functional control over monetary and career rewards. Although Tukey's smoothing procedures do not yield specific statistical tests, the pattern that emerges from Figure 18.2, together with the results from Table 18.3, support the hypothesis that project performance is directly associated with the degree to which project managers are seen as influential over the salaries and promotions of their subordinates.

Personnel Assignments. Project performance does not vary significantly with the locus of influence over personnel assignments (Table 18.4). Although we hypothesized that project performance would be higher when the project manager was seen to have greater influence than the functional manager over the staffing of project work, this does not turn out to be the case—at least not to the extent that its effects are evident in the different project groupings. It is interesting to note,

TABLE 18.4

Project Performance as a Function of the Locus of Influence over Personnel Assignments

Locus of influence	Number of projects	Project performance[a]
Project manager	10	0.04
Balanced	33	0.08
Functional manager	18	−0.41

[a]Normalized means; one-way analysis of variance indicated that mean performance did not differ significantly ($F = 1.07$).

TABLE 18.5

Correlation of Locus of Organizational Influence and Loci of Internal Influence

Internal influence over:	r
Technical content of work	−.02
Salaries and promotions	.65*
Personnel assignments	.49*

*$p < 0.001$

however, that the lowest-performing set of projects are those in which the functional managers are seen as controlling the allocation of project personnel.

Organizational Influence. To what extent is organizational influence associated with the three measures of internal influence within the project? The correlations in Table 18.5 show that the locus of organizational influence is closely related to the locus of influence over salaries and promotions and to the locus of influence over personnel assignments. The way in which engineers in a matrix structure view the relative power of project and functional managers within the organization is not independent of how they view their managers' relative power over organizational rewards and staffing decisions. The locus of organizational influence is, however, independent of how they see their project and functional managers' influencing the detailed technical content of their work. The correlation between these two areas of influence is close to zero.

Since there is not a strong connection between organizational influence and influence over technical content of the work, the final question is whether the loci of influence in these two areas operate separately on performance or whether they interact to affect project performance. A two-way analysis of variance (Table 18.6) reveals once again that influence over the technical details of project work is not related, at least as a main effect, to project performance. The locus of organizational influence, on the other hand, is significantly associated with project performance in that projects with

TABLE 18.6

Project Performance[a] as a Function of the Loci of Influence over Technical Content of Project Work and Influence in the Organization

Locus of influence within the organization	Locus of influence over technical content	
	Project manager	Functional manager
Project Manager	0.10 ($N = 30$)	0.80 ($N = 12$)
Functional manager	−0.05 ($N = 30$)	−0.59 ($N = 12$)
Sources of Variation for Two-Way ANOVA:	df	F	p
Influence over technical content	1	0.36	N.S.[b]
Influence in organization	1	4.88	.03
Interaction	1	6.45	.01

[a]Normalized means
[b]N.S. = not significant

relatively more powerful project managers are somewhat higher performing than are other projects.

More important, however, the ANOVA results also reveal an interaction effect on project performance between these two modes of influence. As shown by the performance means at the top of Table 18.6, project performance is higher when project managers are seen as having relatively more influence within the organization and functional managers are seen as having relatively more influence over the technical content of what goes into the project. Performance is lowest when functional managers are seen as dominant in both of these areas. Additional analyses did not uncover any interference with these findings by project size or organization sector; nor did they uncover any other significant interaction effects on project performance among the other influence combinations.

As previously discussed, it is important to investigate the robustness of the results from Table 18.6 since projects varied widely in their percentages of matrix engineers. It is possible, for example, that the relationships between project perform-ance and the distributions of power will be significantly different for projects with high proportions of matrix engineers than for projects with relatively low proportions of matrix engineers. To test for this possibility, the 86 projects were split into high and low subsamples based on the proportion of matrix engineers, and separate 2-way ANOVA tests were run on the split samples. In each case, the pattern of performance means strongly paralleled the results of Table 18.6. Project performance, for both subsamples, was highest when project managers were perceived as having relatively more organizational influence and functional managers were perceived as having relatively more influence over the technical details of the project work; in both instances, project performance was lowest when functional managers were seen as dominant along both of these influence dimensions.

DISCUSSION

Our findings suggest an appropriate separation of roles between the managers of R&D professionals in matrix structures. The project manager should be concerned with external relations and activities. He or she should have sufficient power within the organization to gain the backing and continued support of higher management, to obtain critical resources, and to coordinate and couple project efforts with marketing and manufacturing. The concern of functional managers, on the other hand, should be more inward-directed, focusing chiefly on the technology that goes into the project. They are usually more closely associated with the necessary technologies, and consequently, should be better able than project managers to make informed decisions concerning technical content.

But these roles can never be completely separate since, for example, relations with marketing and manufacturing have critical implications for technical content, and vice-versa. A strong working relationship must therefore exist between project and functional managers. However, the results of this study suggest that clearer distinction of managerial roles leads to more effective project performance than does managers' sharing responsibilities and involvement. Performance appears to be highest when project managers focus principally on external relations and the output side of the project work, leaving the technological input side to be managed primarily by the functional side of the matrix. These results are also very consistent with the recent study of Larson and Gobeli (1988). In their mail survey of some 500 managers, they reported that the most successful projects were organized as a project matrix in which project managers had primary authority and responsibility for overseeing and completing the project, while functional managers had primary authority and responsibility for providing the requisite technical expertise. This was also the most preferred structure, even among the subsample of functional managers.

Despite these findings, most of the projects in our sample do not have this role separation pattern, at least as judged by the project members themselves. In more than half of our project groups, for example, members report their project managers have substantially more influence over the technical content of project work than their functional counterparts. Perhaps this is not too surprising since it is the project manager who manages the output and who is ultimately responsible for the project's success. It is, moreover, the project manager's reputation and career that are most intimately tied to project outcomes. Nevertheless, according to our study, overall performance might be improved if functional managers, who know more than project managers about the technologies involved, had greater influence over the technical activities of personnel assigned to project managers.

An enhanced role for the functional manager might also provide some additional benefit in mitigating one of the problems characteristic of matrix organizations. Functional managers have often felt threatened by the introduction of the matrix. Where they formerly had power and visibility in their functional structures, they see, under the matrix, a drift of all of this "glamour" to the project side of the organization. As a result, the matrix has often been undermined by recalcitrant or rebellious department heads, who saw the technical content of their responsibilities diminishing, and their careers sinking into an abyss of personnel decisions and human relations concerns. A clearer delineation of technical responsibilities and an explicitly defined contributive role for functional managers in the technical content of project work may well alleviate this problem.

Over the years, there has been considerable discussion concerning the need to maintain a balance of power in matrix organizations. Very little has been done, however, to investigate the elements or components of power and influence that should be balanced. Using project performance as our criterion, the present study's results provide very little support for the theories of balanced responsibility. Except for joint influence over the areas of salary and promotion, higher project performance is not associated with a balanced state of influence within any of the other three areas of supervisory activity.

Where does this leave all of the theories and propositions regarding matrix balance? Our findings imply that it is *not* through mutual balance or joint responsibilities along single dimensions of influence that the matrix should be made to work, but rather that the matrix should be designed and organized around more explicit role differentiation among dimensions of influence. The project manager's role is distinctly different from that of a functional manager. The two have very different concerns and should relate to both project team members and the larger organization in distinctly different ways. It therefore makes sense that the influence which each should exert over the behaviors of matrix project members to bring about effective project performance will be along different dimensions.

Project performance appears to be higher when project managers are seen as having greater organizational influence. They have an outward orientation. As a result, they should be concerned with gaining resources and recognition for the project and with linking it to other parts of the business to insure that the project's direction fits the overall business plan of the organization. Functional managers, on the other hand, should be concerned with technical excellence and integrity, seeing that the project's inputs include reliable state-of-the-art technology. Their orientation is inward, focusing on the technical content of the project. Detailed technical decisions should be made by those who are closest to the technology. The localization of technical decision-making in functional departments, however, implies an important integrating role for project managers, who are responsible for making sure that the technical decisions overseen by several different functional managers all fit together to yield the best possible end result. Clearly, the greater project managers' organizational influence, the easier it will be for them to integrate and negotiate with functional managers whose technical goals are often in conflict.

Balanced authority need not exist along each dimension of managerial influence. Instead, the distribution of influence seems better accomplished through differentiation of input- and output-oriented roles to functional and project managers, respectively; although the joint involvement of both managers in the area of organizational rewards is important for fostering higher project performance. Since the data reported in this study are cross-sectional, it is important to realize that we cannot really be sure of what happens to a project team as its members continue to interact throughout the different innovative phases of a project (Roberts & Fusfeld, 1988). For example, the locus of influence that is most effective in the "upstream" or early phases of an innovation process may be very different from what is required as R&D efforts move further "downstream" into the engineering and manufacturing stages. Furthermore, while our discussion has emphasized the direct role that project and functional managers can play in influencing the overall performance of matrix project groups, the reverse situation is just as possible. With higher project performance, for example, project managers may come to be seen as more powerful and influential within an organization. Clearly, it remains for future research to look even more closely at these kinds of relationships so that we can learn how to alleviate the conflicts and frustrations that have become so pervasive as organization's try to structure and manage their portfolio of research and development projects.

REFERENCES

Allen, T. J. 1984. *Managing the Flow of Technology.* Cambridge, MA: MIT Press.

Allen, T. J. 1986. Organizational structure, information, technology, and R&D productivity. *IEEE Transactions on Engineering Management,* 33 (4): 212–17.

Ancona, D., & Caldwell, D. 1990. Improving the performance of new product development teams. *Research-Technology Management,* 33 (2): 25–29.

Cleland, D. I. 1968. The deliberte conflict. *Business Horizons,* 11 (1): 78–80.

Cleland, D. I., & King, W. R. 1968. *Systems Analysis and Project Management.* New York: McGraw-Hill.

Crawford, C. M. 1986. *New Products Management.* New York: Irwin.

Davis, S., & Lawrence, P. 1977. *Matrix.* Reading, MA: Addison-Wesley.

Howell, J. M., & Higgins, C. A. 1990. Champions of technological innovation. *Administrative Science Quarterly,* 35 (2): 317–41.

Katz, R., & Allen, T. J. 1982. Investigating the "not invented here" syndrome. *R&D Management,* 12 (1): 7–19.

Katz, R., & Allen, T. J. 1985. Project performance and the locus of influence in the R&D matrix. *Academy of Management Journal,* 28 (1): 67–87.

Katz, R., & Tushman, M. 1979. Communication patterns, project performance, and task characteristics: An empirical investigation in an R&D setting. *Organizational Behavior and Human Performance,* 23: 139–62.

Katz, R., Tushman, M., & Allen, T. J. 1995. The influence of supervisory promotion and network location on subordinate careers in a dual ladder RD&E setting. *Management Science,* 41 (5): 848–63.

Kidder, T. 1981. *The Soul of a New Machine.* New York: Little Brown.

Kingdon, O.R. 1973. *Matrix Organization: Managing Information Technologies.* London: Tavistock.

Knight, K. 1977. *Matrix Management.* London: Gower.

Larson, E. W., & Gobeli, D. H. 1988. Organizing for product development projects. *Journal of Product Innovation Management,* 5: 180–90.

Mansfield, E., & Wagner, S. 1975. Organizational and strategic factors associated with probability of success in industrial research. *Journal of Business,* 48: 179–98.

Pfeffer, J. 1993. *Managing with Power.* Cambridge, MA: Harvard Business School Press.

Pinto, M. B., Pinto, J. K., & Prescott, J. E. 1993. Antecedents and consequences of project team cross-functional cooperation. *Management Science,* 39 (10): 1281–90.

Roberts, E. 1988. Managing invention and innovation: What we've learned. *Research-Technology Management,* 31 (1): 11–29.

Roberts, E. B., & Fusfeld, A. R. 1988. Critical functions: Needed roles in the innovation process. In R. Katz (Ed.) *Managing Professionals in Innovative Organizations: A Collection of Readings:* 101–20, New York: Harper Business.

Tukey, J. 1977. *Exploratory Data Analysis.* Reading, MA: Addison-Wesley.

Utterback, J. M. 1974. Innovation in industry and the diffusion of technology. *Science,* 183: 620–26.

Wilemon, D. L., & Gemmill, G. R. 1971. Interpersonal power in temporary management systems. *Journal of Management Studies,* 8: 315–28.

19

Organizing and Leading "Heavyweight" Development Teams

KIM B. CLARK
STEVEN C. WHEELWRIGHT

Effective product and process development requires the integration of specialized capabilities. Integrating is difficult in most circumstances, but is particularly challenging in large, mature firms with strong functional groups, extensive specialization, large numbers of people, and multiple, ongoing operating pressures. In such firms, development projects are the exception rather than the primary focus of attention. Even for people working on development projects, years of experience and the established systems—covering everything from career paths to performance evaluation, and from reporting relationships to breadth of job definitions—create both physical and organizational distance from other people in the organization. The functions themselves are organized in a way that creates further complications: the marketing organization is based on product families and market segments; engineering around functional disciplines and technical focus; and manufacturing on a mix between functional and product market structures. The result is that in large, mature firms, organizing and leading an effective development effort is a major undertaking. This is especially true for organizations whose traditionally stable markets and competitive environments are threatened by new entrants, new technologies, and rapidly changing customer demands.

This article zeros in on one type of team structure—"heavyweight" project teams—that seems particularly promising in today's fast-paced world yet is strikingly absent in many mature companies. Our research shows that when managed effectively, heavyweight teams offer improved communication, stronger identification with and commitment to a project, and a focus on cross-functional problem solving. Our research also reveals, however, that these teams are not so easily managed and contain unique issues and challenges.

Heavyweight project teams are one of four types of team structures. We begin by describing each of them briefly. We then explore heavyweight teams in detail, compare them with the alternative forms, and point out specific challenges and their solutions in managing the heavyweight team organization. We conclude with an example of the changes necessary in individual behavior for heavyweight teams to be effective. Although heavyweight teams are a different way of organizing, they are more than a new structure; they represent a fundamentally different way of working. To the extent that both the team members and the surrounding organization recognize that phenomenon, the heavyweight team begins to realize its full potential.

TYPES OF DEVELOPMENT PROJECT TEAMS

Figure 19.1 illustrates the four dominant team structures we have observed in our studies of development projects: functional, lightweight, heavyweight, and autonomous (or tiger). These forms are described below, along with their associated project leadership roles, strengths, and weaknesses. Heavyweight teams are examined in detail in the subsequent section.

Copyright © 1992 by The Regents of the University of California. Reprinted from the *California Management Review,* Vol. 34, No. 3. By permission of The Regents.

Kim Clark is Dean of the Harvard Business School and Professor of Business Administration. **Steven Wheelwright** is Professor of Business Administration at the Harvard Business School.

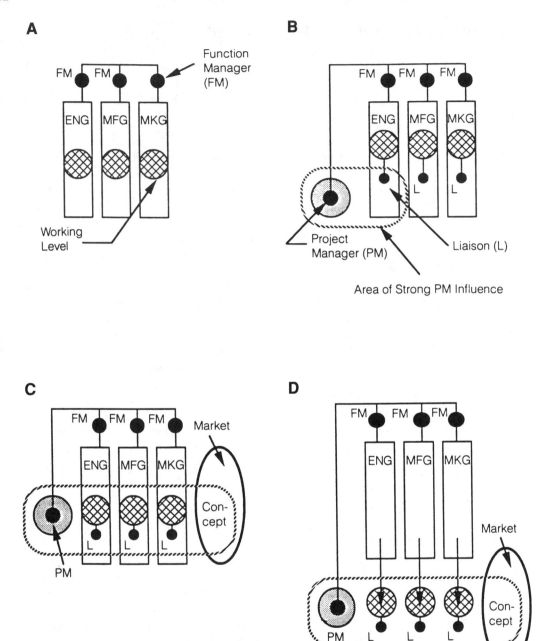

Figure 19.1 Types of development teams (a) Functional, (b) Lightweight, (c) Heavyweight, and (d) Autonomous.

Functional Team Structure

In the traditional functional organization found in larger, more mature firms, people are grouped principally by discipline, each working under the direction of a specialized subfunction manager and a senior functional manager. The different subfunctions and functions coordinate ideas through detailed specifications all parties agree to at the outset, and through occasional meetings where issues that cut across groups are discussed. Over time, primary responsibility for the project passes sequentially—although often not smoothly—from one function to the next, a transfer frequently termed "throwing it over the wall."

The functional team structure has several advantages, and associated disadvantages. One strength is that those managers who control the project's resources also control task performance in their functional area; thus, responsibility and authority are usually aligned. However, tasks must be subdivided at the project's outset, i.e., the entire development process is decomposed into separable, somewhat independent activities. But on most development efforts, not all required tasks are known at the outset, nor can they all be easily and realistically subdivided. Coordination and integration can suffer as a result.

Another major strength of this approach is that, because most career paths are functional in nature until a general management level is reached, the work done on a project is judged, evaluated, and rewarded by the same subfunction and functional managers who make the decisions about career paths. The associated disadvantage is that individual contributions to a development project tend to be judged largely independently of overall project success. The traditional tenet cited is that individuals cannot be evaluated fairly on outcomes over which they have little or no control. But as a practical matter, that often means that no one directly involved in the details of the project is responsible for the results finally achieved.

Finally, the functional project organization brings specialized expertise to bear on the key technical issues. The same person or small group of people may be responsible for the design of a particular component or subsystem over a wide range of development efforts. Thus the functions and subfunctions capture the benefits of prior experience and become the keepers of the organization's depth of knowledge while ensuring that it is systematically applied over time and across projects. The disadvantage is that every development project differs in its objectives and performance requirements, and it is unlikely that specialists developing a single component will do so very differently on one project than on another. The "best" component or subsystem is defined by technical parameters in the areas of their expertise rather than by overall system characteristics or specific customer requirements dictated by the unique market the development effort aims for.

Lightweight Team Structure

Like the functional structure, those assigned to the lightweight team reside physically in their functional areas, but each functional organization designates a liaison person to "represent" it on a project coordinating committee. These liaison representatives work with a "lightweight project manager," usually a design engineer or product marketing manager, who coordinates different functions' activities. This approach usually figures as an add-on to a traditional functional organization, with the functional liaison person having that role added to his or her other duties. The overall coordination assignment of lightweight project manager, however, tends not to be present in the traditional functional team structure.

The project manager is a "lightweight" in two important respects. First, he or she is generally a middle- or junior-level person who, despite considerable expertise, usually has little status or influence in the organization. Such people have spent a handful of years in a function, and this assignment is seen as a "broadening experience," a chance for them to move out of that function. Second, although they are responsible for informing and coordinating the activities of the functional organizations, the key resources (including engineers on the project) remain under the control of their respective functional managers. The lightweight project manager does not have power to reassign people or reallocate resources, and instead confirms schedules, updates time lines, and expedites across groups. Typically, such project leaders spend no more than 25% of their time on a single project.

The primary strengths and weaknesses of the lightweight project team are those of the functional project structure. But now at least one person over the course of the project looks across functions and seeks to ensure that individual tasks—especially those on the critical path—get done in a timely fashion, and that everyone is kept aware of potential cross-functional issues and what is going on elsewhere on this particular project.

Thus, improved communication and coordination are what an organization expects when moving from a functional to a lightweight team structure. Yet, because power still resides with the subfunction and functional managers, hopes for improved efficiency, speed, and project quality are seldom realized. Moreover, lightweight project leaders find themselves tolerated at best, and often ignored and even preempted. This can easily become a "no-win" situation for the individual thus assigned.

Heavyweight Team Structure

In contrast to the lightweight set-up, the heavyweight project manager has direct access to and responsibility for the work of all those involved in the project. Such leaders are "heavyweights" in two respects. First, they are senior managers within the organization; they may even outrank the functional managers. Hence, in addition to having expertise and experience, they also wield significant organizational clout. Second, heavyweight leaders have primary influence over the people working on the development effort and supervise their work directly through key functional people on the core teams. Often, the core group of people are dedicated and physically co-located with the heavyweight project leader. However, the longer-term career development of individual contributors continues to rest not with the project leader—although that heavyweight leader makes significant input to individual performance evaluations—but

with the functional manager, because members are not assigned to a project team on a permanent basis.

The heavyweight team structure has a number of advantages and strengths, along with associated weaknesses. Because this team structure is observed much less frequently in practice and yet seems to have tremendous potential for a wide range of organizations, it will be discussed in detail in the next section.

Autonomous Team Structure

With the autonomous team structure, often called the "tiger team," individuals from the different functional areas are formally assigned, dedicated, and co-located to the project team. The project leader, a "heavyweight" in the organization, is given full control over the resources contributed by the different functional groups. Furthermore, that project leader becomes the sole evaluator of the contribution made by individual team members.

In essence, the autonomous team is given a "clean sheet of paper"; it is not required to follow existing organizational practices and procedures, but allowed to create its own. This includes establishing incentives and rewards as well as norms for behavior. However, the team will be held fully accountable for the final results of the project: success or failure is its responsibility and no one else's.

The fundamental strength of the autonomous team structure is focus. Everything the individual team members and the team leader do is concentrated on making the project successful. Thus, tiger teams can excel at rapid, efficient new product and new process development. They handle cross-functional integration in a particularly effective manner, possibly because they attract and select team participants much more freely than the other project structures.

Tiger teams, however, take little or nothing as "given"; they are likely to expand the bounds of their project definition and tackle redesign of the entire product, its components, and subassemblies, rather than looking for opportunities to utilize existing materials, designs, and organizational relationships. Their solution may be unique, making it more difficult to fold the resulting product and process—and, in many cases, the team members themselves—back into the traditional organization upon project completion. As a consequence, tiger teams often become the birthplace of new business units or they experience unusually high turnover following project completion.

Senior managers often become nervous at the prospects of a tiger team because they are asked to delegate much more responsibility and control to the team and its project leader than under any of the other organization structures. Unless clear guidelines have been established in advance, it is extremely difficult during the project for senior managers to make midcourse corrections or exercise substantial influence without destroying the team. More than one team has "gotten away" from senior management and created major problems.

THE HEAVYWEIGHT TEAM STRUCTURE

The best way to begin understanding the potential of heavyweight teams is to consider an example of their success, in this case, Motorola's experience in developing its Bandit line of pagers.

The Bandit Pager Heavyweight Team

This development team within the Motorola Communications Sector was given a project charter to develop an automated, on-shore, profitable production operation for its high-volume Bravo pager line. (This is the belt-worn pager that Motorola sold from the mid-1980s into the early 1990s.) The core team consisted of a heavyweight project leader and a handful of dedicated and co-located individuals, who represented industrial engineering, robotics, process engineering, procurement, and product design/CIM. The need for these functions was dictated by the Bandit platform automation project and its focus on manufacturing technology with a minimal change in product technology. In addition, human resource and accounting/finance representatives were part of the core team. The human resource person was particularly active early on as subteam positions were defined and jobs posted

throughout Motorola's Communications Sector, and played an important subsequent role in training and development of operating support people. The accounting/finance person was invaluable in "costing out" different options and performing detailed analyses of options and choices identified during the course of the project.

An eighth member of the core team was a Hewlett Packard employee. Hewlett Packard was chosen as the vendor for the "software backplane," providing an HP 3000 computer and the integrated software communication network that linked individual automated workstations, downloaded controls and instructions during production operations, and captured quality and other operating performance data. Because HP support was vital to the project's success, it was felt essential they be represented on the core team.

The core team was housed in a corner of the Motorola Telecommunications engineering/manufacturing facility. The team chose to enclose in glass the area where the automated production line was to be set up so that others in the factory could track the progress, offer suggestions, and adopt the lessons learned from it in their own production and engineering environments. The team called their project Bandit to indicate a willingness to "take" ideas from literally anywhere.

The heavyweight project leader, Scott Shamlin, who was described by team members as "a crusader," "a renegade," and "a workaholic," became the champion for the Bandit effort. A hands-on manager who played a major role in stimulating and facilitating communication across functions, he helped to articulate a vision of the Bandit line, and to infuse it into the detailed work of the project team. His goal was to make sure the new manufacturing process worked for the pager line, but would provide real insight for many other production lines in Motorola's Communications Sector.

The Bandit core team started by creating a contract book that established the blueprint and work plan for the team's efforts and its performance expectations; all core team members and senior management signed on to this document. Initially, the team's executive sponsor—although not formally identified as such—was George Fisher, the Sector Executive. He made the original investment proposal to the Board of Directors and was an early champion and supporter, as well as direct supervisor in selecting the project leader and helping get the team underway. Subsequently, the vice president and general manager of the Paging Products division filled the role of executive sponsor.

Throughout the project, the heavyweight team took responsibility for the substance of its work, the means by which it was accomplished, and its results. The project was completed in 18 months as per the contract book, which represented about half the time of a normal project of such magnitude. Further, the automated production operation was up and running with process tolerances of five sigma (i.e., the degree of precision achieved by the manufacturing processes) at the end of 18 months. Ongoing production verified that the cost objectives (substantially reduced direct costs and improved profit margins) had indeed been met, and product reliability was even higher than the standards already achieved on the off-shore versions of the Bravo product. Finally, a variety of lessons were successfully transferred to other parts of the Sector's operations, and additional heavyweight teams have proven the viability and robustness of the approach in Motorola's business and further refined its effectiveness throughout the corporation.

The Challenge of Heavyweight Teams

Motorola's experience underscores heavyweight teams' potential power, but it also makes clear that creating an effective heavyweight team capability is more than merely selecting a leader and forming a team. By their very nature—being product (or process) focused, and needing strong, independent leadership, broad skills and cross-functional perspective, and clear missions—heavyweight teams may conflict with the functional organization and raise questions about senior management's influence and control. And even the advantages of the team approach bring with them potential disadvantages that may hurt development performance if not recognized and averted.

Take, for example, the advantages of owner-

ship and commitment, one of the most striking advantages of the heavyweight team. Identifying with the product and creating a sense of esprit de corps motivate core team members to extend themselves and do what needs to be done to help the team succeed. But such teams sometimes expand the definition of their role and the scope of the project, and they get carried away with themselves and their abilities. We have seen heavyweight teams turn into autonomous tiger teams and go off on a tangent because senior executives gave insufficient direction and the bounds of the team were only vaguely specified at the outset. And even if the team stays focused, the rest of the organization may see themselves as "second class." Although the core team may not make that distinction explicit, it happens because the team has responsibilities and authority beyond those commonly given to functional team members. Thus, such projects inadvertently can become the "haves" and other, smaller projects the "have-nots" with regard to key resources and management attention.

Support activities are particularly vulnerable to an excess of ownership and commitment. Often the heavyweight team will want the same control over secondary support activities as it has over the primary tasks performed by dedicated team members. When waiting for prototypes to be constructed, analytical tests to be performed, or quality assurance procedures to be conducted, the team's natural response is to "demand" top priority from the support organization or to be allowed to go outside and subcontract to independent groups. While these may sometimes be the appropriate choices, senior management should establish make-buy guidelines and clear priorities applicable to all projects—perhaps changing service levels provided by support groups (rather than maintaining the traditional emphasis on resource utilization)—or have support groups provide capacity and advisory technical services but let team members do more of the actual task work in those support areas. Whatever actions the organization takes, the challenge is to achieve a balance between the needs of the individual project and the needs of the broader organization.

Another advantage the heavyweight team brings is the integration and integrity it provides through a system solution to a set of customer needs. Getting all of the components and subsystems to complement one another and to address effectively the fundamental requirements of the core customer segment can result in a winning platform product and/or process. The team achieves an effective system design by using generalist skills applied by broadly trained team members, with fewer specialists and, on occasion, less depth in individual component solutions and technical problem solving.

The extent of these implications is aptly illustrated by the nature of the teams Clark and Fujimoto studied in the auto industry.[1] They found that for U.S. auto firms in the mid-1980s, typical platform projects—organized under a traditional functional or lightweight team structure—entailed full-time work for several months by approximately 1500 engineers. In contrast, a handful of Japanese platform projects—carried out by heavyweight teams—utilized only 250 engineers working full-time for several months. The implications of 250 versus 1500 full-time equivalents (FTEs) with regard to breadth of tasks, degree of specialization, and need for coordination are significant and help explain the differences in project results as measured by product integrity, development cycle time, and engineering resource utilization.

But that lack of depth may disclose a disadvantage. Some individual components or subassemblies may not attain the same level of technical excellence they would under a more traditional functional team structure. For instance, generalists may develop a windshield wiper system that is complementary with and integrated into the total car system and its core concept. But they also may embed in their design some potential weaknesses or flaws that might have been caught by a functional team of specialists who had designed a long series of windshield wipers. To counter this potential disadvantage, many organizations order more testing of completed units to discover such possible flaws and have components and subassemblies reviewed by expert specialists. In some cases, the quality assurance function has expanded its role to make sure sufficient technical specialists review designs at appropriate points so that such weaknesses can be minimized.

Managing the Challenges of Heavyweight Teams

Problems with depth in technical solutions and allocations of support resources suggest the tension that exists between heavyweight teams and the functional groups where much of the work gets done. The problem with the teams exceeding their bounds reflects in part how teams manage themselves, in part, how boundaries are set, and in part the ongoing relationship between the team and senior management. Dealing with these issues requires mechanisms and practices that reinforce the team's basic thrust—ownership, focus, system architecture, integrity—and yet improve its ability to take advantage of the strengths of the supporting functional organization—technical depth, consistency across projects, senior management direction. We have grouped the mechanisms and problems into six categories of management action: the project charter, the contract, staffing, leadership, team responsibility, and the executive sponsor.

The Project Charter A heavyweight project team needs a clear mission. A way to capture that mission concisely is in an explicit, measurable project charter that sets broad performance objectives and usually is articulated even before the core team is selected. Thus, joining the core team includes accepting the charter established by senior management. A typical charter for a heavyweight project would be the following:

> The resulting product will be selected and ramped by Company X during Quarter 4 of calendar year 1991, at a minimum of a 20% gross margin.

This charter is representative of an industrial products firm whose product goes into a system sold by its customers. Company X is the leading customer for a certain family of products, and this project is dedicated to developing the next generation platform offering in that family. If the heavyweight program results in that platform product being chosen by the leading customer in the segment by a certain date and at a certain gross margin, it will have demonstrated that the next generation platform is not only viable, but likely to be very successful over the next three to five years. Industries and settings where such a charter might be found would include a microprocessor being developed for a new computer system, a diesel engine for the heavy equipment industry, or a certain type of slitting and folding piece of equipment for the newspaper printing press industry. Even in a medical diagnostics business with hundreds of customers, a goal of "capturing 30% of market purchases in the second 12 months during which the product is offered" sets a clear charter for the team.

The Contract Book   Whereas a charter lays out the mission in broad terms, the contract book defines, in detail, the basic plan to achieve the stated goal. A contract book is created as soon as the core team and heavyweight project leader have been designated and given the charter by senior management. Basically, the team develops its own detailed work plan for conducting the project, estimates the resources required, and outlines the results to be achieved and against which it is willing to be evaluated. (The table of contents of a typical heavyweight team contract book are shown in Heavyweight Team, Contract Book—Major Sections.) Such documents range from 25 to 100 pages, depending on the complexity of the project and level of detail desired by the team and senior management before proceeding. A common practice following negotiation and acceptance of this contract is for the individuals from the team and senior management to sign the contract book as an indication of their commitment to honor the plan and achieve those results.

The core team may take anywhere from a long week to a few months to create and complete the contract book; Motorola, for example, after several years of experience, has decided that a maximum of seven days should be allowed for this activity. Having watched other heavyweight teams—partic-

---

Heavyweight Team, Contract Book— Major Sections

- Executive Summary
- Business Plan and Purposes
- Development Plan
    - —Schedule
    - —Materials
    - —Resources
- Product Design Plan
- Quality Plan
- Manufacturing Plan
- Project Deliverables
- Performance Measurement and Incentives

---

ularly in organizations with no prior experience in using such a structure—take up to several months, we can appreciate why Motorola has nicknamed this the "blitz phase" and decided that the time allowed should be kept to a minimum.

Staffing.   As suggested in Figure 19.1, a heavyweight team includes a group of core cross-functional team members who are dedicated (and usually physically co-located) for the duration of the development effort. Typically there is one core team member from each primary function of the organization; for instance, in several electronics firms we have observed core teams consisting of six functional participants—design engineering, marketing, quality assurance, manufacturing, finance, and human resources. (Occasionally, design will be represented by two core team members, one each for hardware and software engineering.) Individually, core team members represent their functions and provide leadership for their function's inputs to the project. Collectively, they constitute a management team that works under the direction of the heavyweight project manager and takes responsibility for managing the overall development effort.

While other participants—especially from design engineering early on and manufacturing later on—may frequently be dedicated to a heavyweight team for several months, they usually are not made part of the core team though they may well be co-located and, over time, develop the same level of ownership and commitment to the project as core team members. The primary difference is that the core team manages the total project and the coordination and integration of individual functional efforts, whereas other dedicated team members work primarily within a single function or subfunction.

Whether these temporarily dedicated team members are actually part of the core team is an issue firms handle in different ways, but those with considerable experience tend to distinguish between core and other dedicated (and often co-located) team members. The difference is one of management responsibility for the core group that is not shared equally by the others. Also, it is primarily the half a dozen members of the core group who will be dedicated throughout the project, with other contributors having a portion of their time reassigned before this heavyweight project is completed.

Whether physical colocation is essential is likewise questioned in such teams. We have seen it work both ways. Given the complexity of development projects, and especially the uncertainty and ambiguity often associated with those assigned to heavyweight teams, physical colocation is preferable to even the best of on-line communication approaches. Problems that arise in real time are much more likely to be addressed effectively with all of the functions represented and present than when they are separate and must either wait for a periodic meeting or use remote communication links to open up cross-functional discussions.

A final issue is whether an individual can be a core team member on more than one heavyweight team simultaneously. If the rule for a core team member is that 70% or more of their time must be spent on the heavyweight project, then the answer to this question is no. Frequently, however, a choice must be made between someone being on two core teams—for example, from the finance or human resource function—or putting a different individual on one of those teams who has neither the experi-

ence nor stature to be a full peer with the other core team members. Most experienced organizations we have seen opt to put the same person on two teams to ensure the peer relationship and level of contribution required, even though it means having one person on two teams and with two desks. They then work diligently to develop other people in the function so that multiple team assignments will not be necessary in the future.

Sometimes multiple assignments will also be justified on the basis that a function such as finance does not need a full-time person on a project. In most instances, however, a variety of potential value-adding tasks exist that are broader than finance's traditional contribution. A person largely dedicated to the core team will search for those opportunities and the project will be better because of it. The risk of allowing core team members to be assigned to multiple projects is that they are neither available when their inputs are most needed nor as committed to project success as their peers. They become secondary core team members, and the full potential of the heavyweight team structure fails to be realized.

Project Leadership. Heavyweight teams require a distinctive style of leadership. A number of differences between lightweight and heavyweight project managers are highlighted in Project Manager Profile. Three of those are particularly distinctive. First, a heavyweight leader manages, leads, and evaluates other members of the core team, and is also the person to whom the core team reports throughout the project's duration. Another characteristic is that rather than being either neutral or a facilitator with regard to problem solving and conflict resolution, these leaders see themselves as championing the basic concept around which the platform product and/or process is being shaped. They make sure that those who work on subtasks of the project understand that concept. Thus they play a central role in ensuring the system integrity of the final product and/or process.

Finally, the heavyweight project manager carries out his or her role in a very different fashion than the lightweight project manager. Most light-

Project Manager Profile

	Lightweight (limited)	Heavyweight (extensive)
Span of coordination responsibilities	├─────────────────────────────────┤	
Duration of Responsibilities	├─────────────────────────────────┤	
Responsible for specs, cost, layout, components	├─────────────────────────────────┤	
Working level contact with engineers	├─────────────────────────────────┤	
Direct contact with customers	├─────────────────────────────────┤	
Multilingual/multi-disciplined skills	├─────────────────────────────────┤	
Role in conflict resolution	├─────────────────────────────────┤	
Marketing imagination/concept champion	├─────────────────────────────────┤	
Influence in: engineering	├─────────────────────────────────┤	
marketing	├─────────────────────────────────┤	
manufacturing	├─────────────────────────────────┤	

weights spend the bulk of their time working at a desk, with paper. They revise schedules, get frequent updates, and encourage people to meet previously agreed upon deadlines. The heavyweight project manager spends little time at a desk, is out talking to project contributors, and makes sure that decisions are made and implemented whenever and wherever needed. Some of the ways in which the heavyweight project manager achieves project results are highlighted by the five roles illustrated in a Heavyweight Project Manager on a platform development project in the auto industry.

The Heavyweight Project Manager

Role	Description
Direct Market Interpreter	First hand information, dealer visits, auto shows, has own marketing budget, market study team, direct contact and discussions with customers
Multilingual Translator	Fluency in language of customers, engineers, marketers, stylists; translator between customer experience/requirements and engineering specifications
"Direct" Engineering Manager	Direct contact, orchestra conductor, evangelist of conceptual integrity and coordinator of component development; direct eye-to-eye discussions with working level engineers; shows up in drafting room, looks over engineers' shoulders
Program Manager "in motion"	Out of the office, not too many meetings, not too much paperwork, face-to-face communication, conflict resolution manager
Concept Infuser	Concept guardian, confronts conflicts, not only reacts but implements own philosophy, ultimate decision maker, coordination of details and creation of harmony

The *first role* of the heavyweight project manager is to provide for the team a direct interpretation of the market and customer needs. This involves gathering market data directly from customers, dealers, and industry shows, as well as through systematic study and contact with the firm's marketing organization. A *second role* is to become a multilingual translator, not just taking marketing information to the various functions involved in the project, but being fluent in the language of each of those functions and making sure the translation and communication going on among the functions—particularly between customer needs and product specifications—are done effectively.

A *third role* is the direct engineering manager, orchestrating, directing, and coordinating the various engineering subfunctions. Given the size of many development programs and the number of types of engineering disciplines involved, the project manager must be able to work directly with each engineering subfunction on a day-to-day basis and ensure that their work will indeed integrate and support that of others, so the chosen product concept can be effectively executed.

A *fourth role* is best described as staying in motion: out of the office conducting face-to-face sessions, and highlighting and resolving potential conflicts as soon as possible. Part of this role entails energizing and pacing the overall effort and its key subparts. A *final role* is that of concept champion. Here the heavyweight project manager becomes the guardian of the concept and not only reacts and responds to the interests of others, but also sees that the choices made are consistent and in harmony with the basic concept. This requires a careful blend of communication and teaching skills so that individual contributors and their groups understand the core concept, and sufficient conflict resolution skills to ensure that any tough issues are addressed in a timely fashion.

It should be apparent from this description that heavyweight project managers earn the respect and right to carry out these roles based on prior experience, carefully developed skills, and status earned over time, rather than simply being designated "leader" by senior management. A qualified heavy-weight project manager is a prerequisite to an effective heavyweight team structure.

Team Member Responsibilities. Heavyweight team members have responsibilities beyond their usual functional assignment. As illustrated in Responsibilities of Heavyweight Core Team Members, these are of two primary types. Functional hat responsibilities are those accepted by the individual core team member as a representative of his or her function. For example, the core team member from marketing is responsible for ensuring that appropriate marketing expertise is brought to the project, that a marketing perspective is provided on all key issues, that project sub-objectives dependent on the marketing function are met in a timely fashion, and that marketing issues that impact other functions are raised proactively within the team.

But each core team member also wears a team hat. In addition to representing a function, each member shares responsibility with the heavyweight project manager for the procedures followed by the team, and for the overall results that those procedures deliver. The core team is accountable for the success of the project, and it can blame no one but itself if it fails to manage the project, execute the tasks, and deliver the performance agreed upon at the outset.

Finally, beyond being accountable for tasks in their own function, core team members are responsible for how those tasks are subdivided, organized, and accomplished. Unlike the traditional functional development structure, which takes as given the subdivision of tasks and the means by which those tasks will be conducted and completed, the core heavyweight team is given the power and responsibility to change the substance of those tasks to improve the performance of the project. Since this is a role that core team members do not lay under a lightweight or functional team structure, it is often the most difficult for them to accept fully and learn to apply. It is essential, however, if the heavyweight team is to realize its full potential.

The Executive Sponsor. With so much more accountability delegated to the project team,

Responsibilities of Heavyweight Core Team Members

Functional Hat Accountabilities

- Ensuring functional expertise on the project
- Representing the functional perspective on the project
- Ensuring that subobjectives are met that depend on their function
- Ensuring that functional issues impacting the team are raised pro-actively within the team

Team Hat Accountabilities

- Sharing responsibility for team results
- Reconstituting tasks and content
- Establishing reporting and other organizational relationships
- Participating in monitoring and improving team performance
- Sharing responsibility for ensuring effective team processes
- Examining issues from an executive point of view (Answering the question, "Is this the appropriate business response for the company?")
- Understanding, recognizing, and responsibly challenging the boundaries of the project and team process

heads—have concerns or inputs to voice, or need current information on project status, these are communicated through the executive sponsor. This reduces the number of mixed signals received by the team and clarifies for the organization the reporting and evaluation relationship between the team and senior management. It also encourages the executive sponsor to set appropriate limits and bounds on the team so that organizational surprises are avoided.

Often the executive sponsor and core team identify those areas where the team clearly has decision-making power and control, and they distinguish them from areas requiring review. An electronics firm that has used heavyweight teams for some time dedicates one meeting early on between the executive sponsor and the core team to generating a list of areas where the executive sponsor expects to provide oversight and be consulted; these areas are of great concern to the entire executive staff and team actions may well raise policy issues for the larger organization. In this firm, the executive staff wants to maintain some control over:

- resource commitment—head count, fixed costs, and major expenses outside the approved contract book plan;
- pricing for major customers and major accounts;
- potential slips in major milestone dates (the executive sponsor wants early warning and recovery plans);
- plans for transitioning from development project to operating status,
- thorough reviews at major milestones or every three months, whichever occurs sooner;
- review of incentive rewards that have company-wide implications for consistency and equity; and
- cross-project issues such as resource optimization, prioritization, and balance.

Identifying such areas at the outset can help the executive sponsor and the core team better carry out their assigned responsibilities. It also helps other executives feel more comfortable working

establishing effective relationships with senior management requires special mechanisms. Senior management needs to retain the ability to guide the project and its leader while empowering the team to lead and act, a responsibility usually taken by an executive sponsor—typically the vice president of engineering, marketing, or manufacturing for the business unit. This sponsor becomes the coach and mentor for the heavyweight project leader and core team, and seeks to maintain close, ongoing contact with the team's efforts. In addition, the executive sponsor serves as a liaison. If other members of senior management—including the functional through the executive sponsor, since they know these "boundary issues" have been articulated and are jointly understood.

THE NECESSITY OF FUNDAMENTAL CHANGE

Compared to a traditional functional organization, creating a team that is "heavy"—one with effective leadership, strong problem-solving skills and the ability to integrate across functions—requires basic changes in the way development works. But it also requires change in the fundamental behavior of engineers, designers, manufacturers, and marketers in their day-to-day work. An episode in a computer company with no previous experience with heavyweight teams illustrates the depth of change required to realize fully these teams' power.[2]

Two teams, A and B, were charged with development of a small computer system and had market introduction targets within the next twelve months. While each core team was co-located and held regular meetings, there was one overlapping core team member (from finance/accounting). Each team was charged with developing a new computer system for their individual target markets but by chance, both products were to use an identical, custom-designed microprocessor chip in addition to other unique and standard chips.

The challenge of changing behavior in creating an effective heavyweight team structure was highlighted when each team sent this identical, custom-designed chip—the "supercontroller"—to the vendor for pilot production. The vendor quoted a 20-week turnaround to both teams. At that time, the supercontroller chip was already on the critical path for Team B, with a planned turnaround of 11 weeks. Thus, every week saved on that chip would save one week in the overall project schedule, and Team B already suspected that it would be late in meeting its initial market introduction target date. When the 20-week vendor lead time issue first came up in a Team B meeting, Jim, the core team member from engineering, responded very much as

he had on prior, functionally structured development efforts: because initial prototypes were engineering's responsibility, he reported that they were working on accelerating the delivery date, but that the vendor was a large company, with whom the computer manufacturer did substantial business, and known for its slowness. Suggestions from other core team members on how to accelerate the delivery were politely rebuffed, including one to have a senior executive contact their counterpart at the vendor. Jim knew the traditional approach to such issues and did not perceive a need, responsibility, or authority to alter it significantly.

For Team A, the original quote of 20-week turnaround still left a little slack, and thus initially the supercontroller chip was not on the critical path. Within a couple of weeks, however, it was, given other changes in the activities and schedule, and the issue was immediately raised at the team's weekly meeting. Fred, the core team member from manufacturing (who historically would not have been involved in an early engineering prototype), stated that he thought the turnaround time quoted was too long and that he would try to reduce it. At the next meeting, Fred brought some good news: through discussions with the vendor, he had been able to get a commitment that pulled in the delivery of the supercontroller chip by 11 weeks! Furthermore, Fred thought that the quote might be reduced even further by a phone call from one of the computer manufacturer's senior executives to a contact of his at the vendor.

Two days later, at a regular Team B meeting, the supercontroller chip again came up during the status review, and no change from the original schedule was identified. Since the finance person, Ann, served on both teams and had been present at Team A's meeting, she described Team A's success in reducing the cycle time. Jim responded that he was aware that Team A had made such efforts, but that the information was not correct, and the original 20-week delivery date still held. Furthermore, Jim indicated that Fred's efforts (from Team A) had caused some uncertainty and disruption internally, and in the future it was important that Team A not take such initiatives before coordinating with Team B. Jim stated that this was particularly true when an outside vendor was involved, and he closed the topic by saying that a meeting to clear up the situation would be held that afternoon with Fred from Team A and Team B's engineering and purchasing people.

The next afternoon, at his Team A meeting, Fred confirmed the accelerated delivery schedule for the supercontroller chip. Eleven weeks had indeed been clipped out of the schedule to the benefit of both Teams A and B. Subsequently, Jim confirmed the revised schedule would apply to his team as well, although he was displeased that Fred had abrogated "standard operating procedure" to achieve it. Curious about the differences in perspective, Ann decided to learn more about why Team A had identified an obstacle and removed it from its path, yet Team B had identified an identical obstacle and failed to move it at all.

As Fred pointed out, Jim was the engineering manager responsible for development of the supercontroller chip; he knew the chip's technical requirements, but had little experience dealing with chip vendors and their production processes. (He had long been a specialist.) Without that experience, he had a hard time pushing back against the vendor's "standard line." But Fred's manufacturing experience with several chip vendors enabled him to calibrate the vendor's dates against his best-case experience and understand what the vendor needed to do to meet a substantially earlier commitment.

Moreover, because Fred had bought into a clear team charter, whose path the delayed chip would block, and because he had relevant experience, it did not make sense to live with the vendor's initial commitment, and thus he sought to change it. In contrast, Jim—who had worked in the traditional functional organization for many years—saw vendor relations on a pilot build as part of his functional job, but did not believe that contravening standard practices to get the vendor to shorten the cycle time was his responsibility, within the range of his authority, or even in the best long-term interest of his function. He was more concerned with avoiding conflict and not roiling the water than with achieving the overarching goal of the team.

It is interesting to note that in Team B, engineering raised the issue, and, while unwilling to take aggressive steps to resolve it, also blocked others' attempts. In Team A, however, while the issue came up initially through engineering, Fred in manufacturing proactively went after it. In the case of Team B, getting a prototype chip returned from a vendor was still being treated as an "engineering responsibility," whereas in the case of Team A, it was treated as a "team responsibility." Since Fred was the person best qualified to attack that issue, he did so.

Both Team A and Team B had a charter, a contract, a co-located core team staffed with generalists, a project leader, articulated responsibilities, and an executive sponsor. Yet Jim's and Fred's understanding of what these things meant for them personally and for the team at the detailed, working level was quite different. While the teams had been through similar training and team startup processes, Jim apparently saw the new approach as a different organizational framework within which work would get done as before. In contrast, Fred seemed to see it as an opportunity to work in a different way—to take responsibility for reconfiguring tasks, drawing on new skills, and reallocating resources, where required, for getting the job done in the best way possible.

Although both teams were "heavyweight" in theory, Fred's team was much "heavier" in its operation and impact. Our research suggests that heaviness is not just a matter of structure and mechanism, but of attitudes and behavior. Firms that try to create heavyweight teams without making the deep changes needed to realize the power in the team's structure will find this team approach problematic. Those intent on using teams for platform projects and willing to make the basic changes we have discussed here, can enjoy substantial advantages of focus, integration, and effectiveness.

NOTES

1. See Kim B. Clark and Takahiro Fujimoto, *Product Development Performance* (Boston, MA: Harvard Business School Press, 1991).

2. Adapted from a description provided by Dr. Christopher Meyer, Strategic Alignment Group, Los Altos, CA.

20

Lessons for an Accidental Profession

JEFFREY K. PINTO AND OM P. KHARBANDA

Projects and project management are the wave of the future in global business. Increasingly technically complex products and processes, vastly shortened time-to-market windows, and the need for cross-functional expertise make project management an important and powerful tool in the hands of organizations that understand its use. But the expanded use of such techniques is not always being met by a concomitant increase in the pool of competent project managers. Unfortunately, and perhaps ironically, it is the very popularity of project management that presents many organizations with their most severe challenges. They often belatedly discover that they simply do not have sufficient numbers of the sorts of competent project managers who are often the key driving force behind successful product or service development. Senior managers in many companies readily acknowledge the ad hoc manner in which most project managers acquire their skills, but they are unsure how to better develop and provide for a supply of well-trained project leaders for the future.

In this article, we seek to offer a unique perspective on this neglected species. Though much has been written on how to improve the process of project management, less is known about the sorts of skills and challenges that specifically characterize project managers. What we do know tends to offer a portrait of successful project managers as strong leaders, possessing a variety of problem-solving, communication, motivational, visionary, and team-building skills. Authors such as Posner (1987), Einsiedel (1987), and Petterson (1991) are correct: Project managers are a special breed. Man-

aging projects is a unique challenge that requires a strategy and methodology all its own. Perhaps most important, it requires people willing to function as leaders in every sense of the term. They must not only chart the appropriate course, but provide the means, the support, and the confidence for their teams to attain these goals. Effective project managers often operate less as directive and autocratic decision makers than as facilitators, team members, and cheerleaders. In effect, the characteristics we look for in project managers are varied and difficult to pin down. Our goal is to offer some guidelines for an accidental profession, based on our own experiences and interviews with a number of senior project managers—most of whom had to learn their own lessons the hard way.

"Accidental" Project Managers

Project managers occupy a unique and often precarious position within many firms. Possessing little formal authority and forced to operate outside the traditional organizational hierarchy, they quickly and often belatedly learn the real limits of their power. It has been said that an effective project manager is the kingpin, but not the king. They are the bosses, it is true, but often in a loosely defined way. Indeed, in most firms they may lack the authority to conduct performance appraisals and offer incentives and rewards to their subordinates. As a result, their management styles must be those of persuasion and influence, rather than coercion and command.

Because of these and other limitations on the flexibility and power of project managers, project

Reprinted from *Business Horizons,* March-April, 1995, pp. 41–50. Copyright 1995 by the Foundation for the School of Business at Indiana University. Used with permission.

Jeffrey Pinto is Professor of Management at Penn State University in Erie, PA.   ***Om Kharbanda*** is an independent management consultant in Bombay, India.

management has rightly been termed the "accidental profession" by more than one writer. There are two primary reasons for this sobriquet. First, few formal or systematic programs exist for selecting and training project managers, even within firms that specialize in project management work. This results at best in ad hoc training that may or may not teach these people the skills they need to succeed. Most project managers fall into their responsibilities by happenstance rather than by calculation. Second, as Frame (1987) cogently observed, few individuals grow up with the dream of one day becoming a project manager. It is neither a well-defined nor a well-understood career path within most modern organizations. Generally, the role is thrust upon people, rather than being sought.

Consider the typical experiences of project managers within many corporations. Novice managers, new to the company and its culture, are given a project to complete with the directive to operate within a set of narrowly defined constraints. These constraints most commonly include a specified time frame for completion, a budget, and a set of performance characteristics. Those who are able to quickly master the nature of their myriad duties succeed; those who do not generally fail. This "fly or die" mentality goes far toward creating an attitude of fear among potential project managers. Generation after generation of them learn their duties the hard way, often after having either failed completely or stumbled along from one crisis to another. The predictable result is wasteful: failed projects; managers battling entrenched bureaucracy and powerful factions; money, market opportunities, and other resources irretrievably lost to the company.

The amazing part of this scenario is that it is repeated again and again in company after company. Rather than treating project management as the unique and valuable discipline it is, necessitating formal training and selection policies, many companies continue to repeat their past mistakes. This almost leads one to believe they implicitly view experience and failure as the best teacher.

We need to shed light on the wide range of demands, opportunities, travails, challenges, and vexations that are part of becoming a better project manager. Many of the problems these individuals struggle with every day are far more managerial or behavioral in nature than technical. Such behavioral challenges are frequently vexing, and though they can sometimes seem inconsequential, they have a tremendous impact on the successful implementation of projects. For example, it does not take long for many project managers to discover exactly how far their personal power and status will take them in interacting with the rest of the organization. Hence, an understanding of influence tactics and political behavior is absolutely essential. Unfortunately, notice project managers are rarely clued into this important bit of information until it is too late—until, perhaps, they have appealed through formal channels for extra resources and been denied.

Consider the following examples:

• A long-distance telephone company whose CEO became so enamored of the concept of high-profile project teams—or "skunkworks," as they have come to be called—that he assigned that title to the few most highly visible, strategically important projects. Quickly, both senior and middle managers in departments across the organization came to realize that the only way to get their pet projects the resources necessary to succeed was to redesignate all new projects as "skunkworks." At last report, there were more than 75 high-profile skunkworks projects whose managers report directly to the CEO. The company now has severe difficulties in making research allocation decisions among its projects and routinely underfunds some vital projects while overfunding other, less important ones.

• A large computer hardware manufacturer has been dominated by the members of the hardware engineering department to such an extent that practically all new product ideas originate internally, within the department. By the time marketing personnel (sneeringly called "order takers" by the engineering department) are brought on board, they are presented with a fait accompli: a finished product they are instructed to sell. Marketing managers are now so cynical about new projects that they usually do not even bother sending a representative to new product development team meetings.

• A medium-sized manufacturing firm made it a policy to reward and punish project managers on the basis of their ability to bring projects in on time and under budget. These project managers were never held to any requirement that the project be accepted by its clients or become commercially successful. They quickly learned that their rewards were simply tied to satisfying the cost accountants, so they began to cut corners and make decisions that seriously undermined product quality.

• Projects in one division of a large, multinational corporation are routinely assigned to new managers who often have less than one year of experience with the company. Given a project scheduling software package and the telephone number of a senior project manager to be used "only in emergencies," they are instructed to form their project teams and begin the development process without any formal training or channels of communication to important clients and functional groups. Not surprisingly, senior managers at this company estimate that fewer than 30 percent of new product development efforts are profitable. Most take so long to develop, or incur such high cost overruns, that they are either abandoned before scheduled introduction or never live up to their potential in the marketplace.

This ad hoc approach to project management—coupled, as it frequently is, with an on-the-job training philosophy—is pervasive. It is also pernicious. Under the best of circumstances, project managers are called upon to lead, coordinate, plan, and control a diverse and complex set of processes and people in the pursuit of achieving project objectives. To hamper them with inadequate training and unrealistic expectations is to unnecessarily penalize them before they can begin to operate with any degree of confidence or effectiveness. The successful management of projects is simultaneously a human and technical challenge, requiring a farsighted strategic outlook coupled with the flexibility to react to conflicts and trouble areas as they arise on a daily basis. The project managers who are ultimately successful at their profession must learn to deal with and anticipate the constraints on their project team and personal freedom of action while consistently keeping their eyes on the ultimate prize.

From Whence Comes the Challenge?

One of the most intriguing and challenging aspects of project management lies in the relationship of project teams to the rest of the parent organization. With the exception of companies that are set up with matrix or project structures, most firms using project management techniques employ some form of standard functional structure. When project teams are added to an organization, the structural rules change dramatically. The vast majority of personnel who serve on project teams do so while maintaining links back to their functional departments. In fact, they typically split their time between the project and their functional duties.

The temporary nature of projects, combined with the very real limitations on power and discretion most project managers face, constitutes the core challenge of managing projects effectively. Clearly the very issues that characterize projects as distinct from functional work also illustrate the added complexity and difficulties they create for project managers. For example, within a functional department it is common to find people with more homogenous backgrounds. This means that the finance department is staffed with finance people, the marketing department is made up of marketers, and so on. On the other hand, most projects are constructed from special, cross-functional teams composed of representatives from each of the relevant functional departments, who bring their own attitudes, time frames, learning, past experiences, and biases to the team. Creating a cohesive and potent team out of this level of heterogeneity presents a challenge for even the most seasoned and skilled of project managers.

But what is the ultimate objective? What determines a successful project and how does it differ from projects we may rightfully consider to have failed? Any seasoned project manager will usually tell you that a successful project is one that has come in on time, has remained under budget, and performs as expected (that is, it conforms to specifications). Recently, though, there has been a reassessment of this traditional model for project success. The old triple constraint is rapidly being replaced by a new model, invoking a fourth hurdle for project success: client satisfaction. This means that a project is only successful if it satisfies the needs of its intended user. As a result, client satisfaction places a new and important constraint on project managers. No wonder, then, that there is a growing interest in the project manager's role within the corporation.

THE VITAL DOZEN FOR PROJECT MANAGERS

Over the last several years, we have conducted interviews with dozens of senior project managers in which we asked them a simple question: "What information were you never given as a novice project manager that, in retrospect, could have made your job easier?" From the data gathered in these interviews, we have synthesized some of the more salient issues, outlined in Twelve Points to Remember and detailed below, that managers need to keep in mind when undertaking a project implementation effort. While not intended to appear in any particular order, these 12 rules offer a useful way to understand the challenge project managers face and some ways to address these concerns.

1. Understand the Context of Project Management.
Much of the difficulty in becoming an effective project manager lies in understanding the particular challenges project management presents in most corporations. Projects are a unique form of organizational work, playing an important role within many public and private organizations today. They act as mechanisms for the effective introduction of new products and services. They offer a level of intraorganizational efficiency that all companies

---

> **Twelve Points to Remember**
>
> **1. Understand** the context of project management.
> **2. Recognize** project team conflict as progress.
> **3. Understand** who the stakeholders are and what they want.
> **4. Accept** and use the political nature of organizations.
> **5. Lead** from the front.
> **6. Understand** what "success" means.
> **7. Build** and maintain a cohesive team.
> **8. Enthusiasm** and despair are both infectious.
> **9. One look** forward is worth two looks back.
> **10. Remember** what you are trying to do.
> **11. Use time** carefully or it will use you.
> **12. Above** all, plan, plan, plan.

---

seek but few find. But they also force managers to operate in a temporary environment outside the traditional functional lines of authority, relying upon influence and other informal methods of power. In essence, it is not simply the management of a project per se that presents such a unique challenge; it is also the atmosphere within which the manager operates that adds an extra dimension of difficulty. Projects exist outside the established hierarchy. They threaten, rather than support, the status quo because they represent change. So it is important for project managers to walk into their assigned role with their eyes wide open to the monumental nature of the tasks they are likely to face.

2. Recognize Project Team Conflict as Progress.
One of the common responses of project managers to team conflict is panic. This reaction is understandable in that project managers perceive—usually correctly—that their reputation and careers are on the line if the project fails. Consequently, any evidence they interpret as damaging to the prospects of project success, such as team conflict,

represents a very real source of anxiety. In reality, however, these interpersonal tensions are a natural result of putting individuals from diverse backgrounds together and requiring them to coordinate their activities. Conflict, as evidenced by the stages of group development, is more often a sign of healthy maturation in the group.

The result of differentiation among functional departments demonstrates that conflict under these circumstances is not only possible but unavoidable. One of the worst mistakes a project manager can make when conflicts emerge is to immediately force them below the surface without first analyzing the nature of the conflict. Although many interpersonal conflicts are based on personality differences, others are of a professional nature and should be addressed head-on.

Once a project manager has analyzed the nature of the conflict among team members, a variety of conflict handling approaches may be warranted, including avoidance, defusion, or problem-solving. On the other hand, whatever approach is selected should not be the result of a knee-jerk reaction to suppress conflict. In our experience, we have found many examples that show that even though a conflict is pushed below the surface, it will continue to fester if left unaddressed. The resulting eruption, which will inevitably occur later in the project development cycle, will have a far stronger effect than would the original conflict if it had been handled initially.

3. Understand Who the Stakeholders are and What They Want.

Project management is a balancing act. It requires managers to juggle the various and often conflicting demands of a number of powerful project stakeholders. One of the best tools a project manager can use is to develop a realistic assessment early in the project identifying the principal stakeholders and their agendas. In some projects, particularly those with important external clients or constituent groups, the number of stakeholders may be quite large, particularly when "intervenor" groups are included. Intervenors, according to Cleland (1983), may include any external group that can drastically affect the potential for project success, such as environmental activists in a nuclear plant construction project. Project managers who acknowledge the impact of stakeholders and work to minimize their effect by fostering good relations with them are often more successful than those who operate in a reactive mode, continually surprised by unexpected demands from groups that were not initially considered.

As a final point about stakeholders, it is important for a project manager's morale to remember that it is essentially impossible to please all the stakeholders all the time. The conflicting nature of their demands suggests that when one group is happy, another is probably upset. Project managers need to forget the idea of maximizing everyone's happiness and concentrate instead on maintaining satisfactory relations that allow them to do their job with a minimum of external interference.

4. Accept the Political Nature of Organizations and Use it to Your Advantage.

Like it or not, we exist in a politicized world. Unfortunately, our corporations are no different. Important decisions involving resources are made through bargaining and deal-making. So project managers who wish to succeed must learn to use the political system to their advantage. This involves becoming adept at negotiation as well as using influence tactics to further the goals of the project.

At the same time, it is important to remember that any project representing possible organizational change is threatening, often because of its potential to reshuffle the power relationships among the key units and actors. Playing the political system simply acknowledges this reality. Successful project managers are those who can use their personal reputations, power, and influence to ensure cordial relations with important stakeholders and secure the resources necessary to smooth the client's adoption of the project.

Pursuing a middle ground of political sensibility is the key to project implementation success. There are two alternative and equally inappropriate approaches to navigating a firm's political waters: becoming overly political and predatory—we call these people "sharks"—and refusing to engage in politics to any degree—the politically "naive." Political sharks and the politically naive are at equal disadvantage in managing their projects: sharks because they pursue predatory and self-interested tactics that arouse distrust, and the naive because they insist on remaining above the fray, even at the cost of failing to attain and keep necessary resources for their projects.

Table 20.1 illustrates some of the philosophical differences among the three types of political actors. The process of developing and applying appropriate political tactics means using politics as it can most effectively be used: as a basis for negotiation and bargaining. "Politically sensible" implies being politically sensitive to the concerns (real or imagined) of powerful stakeholder groups. Legitimate or not, their concerns over a new project are real and must be addressed. Politically sensible managers understand that initiating any sort of organizational disruption or change by developing a new project is bound to reshuffle the distribution of power within the firm. That effect is likely to make many departments and managers very nervous as they begin to wonder how the future power relationships will be rearranged.

Appropriate political tactics and behavior include making alliances with powerful members of other stakeholder departments, networking, nego-

tiating mutually acceptable solutions to seemingly insoluble problems, and recognizing that most organizational activities are predicated on the give-and-take of negotiation and compromise. It is through these uses of political behavior that managers of project implementation efforts put themselves in the position to most effectively influence the successful introduction of their systems.

5. Lead from the Front; the View is Better.

One message that comes through loud and clear is that project management is a "leader intensive" undertaking. Strong, effective leaders can go a long way toward helping a project succeed even in the face of a number of external or unforeseen problems. Conversely, a poor, inflexible leader can often ruin the chances of many important projects ever succeeding. Leaders are the focal point of their projects. They serve as a rallying point for the team and are usually the major source of information and communication for external stakeholders. Because their role is so central and so vital, it is important to recognize and cultivate the attributes project "leaders" must work to develop.

The essence of leadership lies in our ability to use it flexibly. This means that not all subordinates or situations merit the same response. Under some circumstances an autocratic approach is appropriate; other situations will be far better served by adopting a consensual style. Effective project lead-

TABLE 20.1
Characteristics of Policical Behaviors

Characteristics	Naive	Sensible	Sharks
Underlying Attitude	Politics is unpleasant	Politics is necessary	Politics is an opportunity
Intent	Avoid at all costs	Further departmental goals	Self-serving and predatory
Techniques	Tell it like it is	Network; expand connections; use system to give and receive favors	Manipulate; use fraud and deceit when necessary
Favorite Tactics	None—the truth will win out	Negotiate, bargain	Bully; misuse information; cultivate and use "friends" and other contacts

ers seem to understand this idea intuitively. Their approach must be tailored to the situation; it is self-defeating to attempt to tailor the situation to a preferred approach. The worst leaders are those who are unaware of or indifferent to the freedom they have to vary their leadership styles. And they see any situation in which they must involve subordinates as inherently threatening to their authority. As a result, they usually operate under what is called the "Mushroom Principle of Management." That is, they treat their subordinates the same way they would raise a crop of mushrooms—by keeping them in the dark and feeding them a steady diet of manure.

Flexible leadership behavior consists of a realistic assessment of personal strengths and weaknesses. It goes without saying that no one person, including the project manager, possesses all necessary information, knowledge, or expertise to perform the project tasks on his own. Rather, successful project managers usually acknowledge their limitations and work through subordinates' strengths. In serving as a facilitator, one of the essential abilities of an exceptional project manager is knowing where to go to seek the right help and how to ask the right questions. Obviously, the act of effective questioning is easier said than done. However, bear in mind that questioning is not interrogation. Good questions challenge subordinates without putting them on the spot; they encourage definite answers rather than vague responses, and they discourage guessing. The leader's job is to probe, to require subordinates to consider all angles and options, and to support them in making reasoned decisions. Direct involvement is a key component of a leader's ability to perform these tasks.

6. Understand What "Success" Means.

Successful project implementation is no longer subject to the traditional "triple constraint." That is, the days when projects were evaluated solely on adherence to budget, schedule, and performance criteria are past. In modern business, with its increased emphasis on customer satisfaction, we have to retrain project managers to expand their criteria for project success to include a fourth item: client use and satisfaction. What this suggests is that project "success" is a far more comprehensive word than some managers may have initially thought. The implication for rewards is also important. Within some organizations that regularly implement projects, it is common practice to reward the implementation manager when, in reality, only half the job has been accomplished. In other words, giving managers promotions and commendations before the project has been successfully transferred to clients, is being used, and is affecting organizational effectiveness is seriously jumping the gun.

Any project is only as good as it is used. In the final analysis, nothing else matters if a system is not productively employed. Consequently, every effort must be bent toward ensuring that the system fits in with client needs, that their concerns and opinions are solicited and listened to, and that they have final sign-off approval on the transferred project. In other words, the intended user of the project is the major determinant of its success. Traditionally, the bulk of the team's efforts are centered internally, mainly on their own concerns: budgets, timetables, and so forth. Certainly, these aspects of the project implementation process are necessary, but they should not be confused with the ultimate determinant of success: the client.

7. Build and Maintain a Cohesive Team.

Many projects are implemented through the use of cross-functional teams. Developing and maintaining cordial team relations and fostering a healthy intergroup atmosphere often seems like a full-time job for most project managers. However, the resultant payoff from a cohesive project team cannot be overestimated. When a team is charged to work toward project development and implementation, the healthier the atmosphere within that team, the greater the likelihood the team will perform effectively. The project manager's job is to do whatever is necessary to build and maintain the health (cohesion) of the team. Sometimes that support can be accomplished by periodically checking with team members to determine their attitudes and satisfaction with the process. Other times the project manager may have to resort to less conventional methods, such as throwing parties or organizing field trips. To effectively intervene and support a team, project managers play a variety of roles—movitator, coach, cheerleader, peacemaker, conflict resolver. All these duties are appropriate for creating and maintaining an effective team.

8. Enthusiasm and Despair are Both Infectious.

One of the more interesting aspects of project leaders is that they often function like miniaturized billboards, projecting an image and attitude that signals the current status of the project and its likelihood for success. The team takes its cue from the attitudes and emotions the manager exhibits. So one of the most important roles of the leader is that of motivator and encourager. The worst project managers are those who play their cards close to their chests, revealing little or nothing about the status of the project (again, the "Mushroom Manager"). Team members want and deserve to be kept abreast of what is happening. It is important to remember that the success or failure of the project affects the team as well as the manager. Rather than allowing the rumor mill to churn out disinformation, team leaders need to function as honest sources of information. When team members come to the project manager for advice or project updates, it is important to be honest. If the manager does not know the answer to their questions, he should tell them that. Truth in all forms is recognizable, and most project team members are much more appreciative of honesty than of eyewash.

9. One Look Forward is Worth Two Looks Back.

A recent series of commercials from a large computer manufacturer had as their slogan the dictum that the company never stop asking "What if?" Asking "What if?" questions is another way of saying we should never become comfortable with the status of the project under development. One large-scale study found that the leading determinant of project failure was the absence of any troubleshooting mechanisms—that is, no one was ask-ing the "What if?" questions. Projecting a skeptical eye toward the future may seem gloomy to some managers. But in our opinion, it makes good sense. We cannot control the future but we can actively control our response to it.

A good example of the failure to apply this philosophy is evidenced by the progress of the "Chunnel" intended to link Great Britain with France. Although now in full operation, it was not ready for substantial traffic until some 15 months later than originally scheduled. As a result, chunnel traffic missed the major summer vacation season with a concomitant loss in revenue. At the same time, the final cost (£15 billion) is likely to be six times the original estimate of £2.3 billion (O'Connor 1993). It is instructive to take note of a recent statement by one of the project's somewhat harassed directors who, when pressed to state when the Chunnel would be ready, replied, "Now it will be ready when it's ready and not before!" Clearly, the failure to apply adequate contingency planning has led to the predictable result: a belief that the project will simply end when it ends.

10. Remember What You Are Trying To Do.

Do not lose sight of the purpose behind the project. Sometimes it is easy to get bogged down in the minutiae of the development process, fighting fires on a daily basis and dealing with thousands of immediate concerns. The danger is that in doing so, project managers may fail to maintain a view of what the end product is supposed to be. This point reemphasizes the need to keep the mission in the forefront—and not just the project manager, but the team as well. The goal of the implementation serves as a large banner the leader can wave as needed to keep attitudes and motives focused in the right direction. Sometimes a superordinate goal can serve as a rallying point. Whatever technique project managers use, it is important that they understand the importance of keeping the mission in focus for all team members. A simple way to discover whether team members understand the project is to intermittently ask for their assessment of its status. They should know how their contributions fit into the overall installation plan. Are they aware of the specific contributions of other team members? If no, more attention needs to be paid to reestablishing a community sense of mission.

11. Use Time Carefully Or It Will Use You.

Time is a precious commodity. Yet when we talk to project managers, it seems that no matter how hard they work to budget it, they never have enough. They need to make a realistic assessment of the "time killers" in their daily schedule: How are they spending their time and what are they doing profitably or unprofitably? We have found that the simple practice of keeping a daily time log for a short time can be an eye-opening experience. Many project managers discover that they spend far too much of their time in unproductive ways: project team meetings without agendas that grind on and on, unexpected telephone calls in the middle of planning sessions, quick "chats" with other managers that end up taking hours, and so forth. Efficient time management—one of the keys to successful project development—starts with project managers. When they actively plan their days and stick to a time budget, they usually find they are operating efficiently. On the other hand, when they take each problem as it comes and function in an ad hoc, reactive mode, they are likely to remain prisoners of their own schedules.

A sure recipe for finding the time and resources needed to get everything done without spending an inordinate amount of time on the job or construction site is provided by Gosselin (1993). The author lists six practical suggestions to help project managers control their tasks and projects without feeling constantly behind schedule:

- Create a realistic time estimate without overextending yourself.
- Be absolutely clear about what the boss or client requires.
- Provide for contingencies (schedule slippage, loss of key team member).
- Revise the original time estimate and provide a set of options as required.

- Be clear about factors that are fixed (specifications, resources, and so on).
- Learn to say "Yes, and . . ." rather than "No, but. . . ." Negotiation is the key.

12. Above All, Plan, Plan, Plan.

The essence of efficient project management is to take the time to get it as right as possible the first time. "It" includes the schedule, the team composition, the project specifications, and the budget. There is a truism that those who fail to plan are planning to fail. One of the practical difficulties with planning is that so many of us distinguish it from other aspects of the project development, such as doing the work. Top managers are often particularly guilty of this offense as they wait impatiently for the project manager to begin doing the work.

Of course, too much planning is guaranteed to elicit repeated and pointed questions from top management and other stakeholders as they seek to discover the reason why "nothing is being done." Experienced project managers, though, know that it is vital not to rush this stage by reacting too quickly to top management inquiries. The planning stage must be managed carefully to allow the project manager and team the time necessary to formulate appropriate and workable plans that will form the basis for the development process. Dividing up the tasks and starting the "work" of the project too quickly is often ultimately wasteful. Steps that were poorly done are often steps that must be redone.

A complete and full investigation of any proposed project does take significant time and effort. However, bear in mind that overly elaborate or intricate planning can be detrimental to a project; by the time an opportunity is fully investigated, it may no longer exist. Time and again we have emphasized the importance of planning, but it is also apparent that there comes a limit, both to the extent and the time frame of the planning cycle. A survey among entrepreneurs, for example, revealed that only 28 percent of them drew up a full-scale plan (Sweet 1994). A lesson here for project managers is that, like entrepreneurs, they must plan, but they must also be smart enough to recognize mistakes and change their strategy accordingly. As is noted in an old military slogan, "No plan ever survives its first contact with the enemy."

PROJECT MANAGERS IN THE TWENTY-FIRST CENTURY

In our research and consulting experiences, we constantly interact with project managers, some with many years of experience, who express their frustration with their organizations because of the lack of detailed explication of their assigned tasks and responsibilities. Year after year, manager after manager, companies continue to make the same mistakes in "training" their project managers, usually through an almost ritualized baptism of fire. Project managers deserve better. According to Rodney Turner (1993), editor of the *International Journal of Project Management:*

> Through the 90's and into the 21st century, project-based management will sweep aside traditional functional line management and (almost) all organizations will adopt flat, flexible organizational structures in place of the old bureaucratic hierarchies. . . . [N]ew organizational structures are replacing the old. . . . [M]anagers will use project-based management as a vehicle for introducing strategic planning and for winning and maintaining competitive advantage.

Turner presents quite a rosy future, one that is predicated on organizations recognizing the changes they are currently undergoing and are likely to continue to see in the years ahead. In this challenging environment, project management is emerging as a technique that can provide the competitive edge necessary to succeed, given the right manager.

At the same time, there seems to have been a sea of change in recent years regarding the image of project managers. The old view of the project manager as essentially that of a decision maker, expert, boss, and director seems to be giving way to a newer ideal: that of a leader, coach, and facilitator. Lest the reader assume these duties are any easier, we would assert that anyone who has attempted to perform these roles knows from personal experience just how difficult they can be. As part of this metamorphosis, says Clarke (1993), the new breed of project manager must be a natural salesperson who can establish harmonious customer (client) relations and develop trusting relationships with stakeholders. In addition to some of the obvious keys to project managers' success—personal commitment, energy, and enthusiasm—it appears that, most of all, successful project managers must manifest an obvious desire to see others succeed.

For successful project managers, there will always be a dynamic tension between the twin demands of technical training and an understanding of human resource needs. It must be clearly understood, however, that in assessing the relative importance of each challenge, the focus must clearly be on managing the human side of the process. As research and practice consistently demonstrate, project management is primarily a challenge in managing people. This point was recently brought to light in an excellent review of a book on managing the "human side" of projects (Horner 1993):

> There must be many project managers like me who come from a technological background, and who suffered an education which left them singularly ill-prepared to manage people.

Leading researchers and scholars perceive the twenty-first century as the upcoming age of project management. The globalization of markets, the merging of many European economies, the enhanced expenditures of money on capital improvement both in the United States and abroad, the rapidly opening borders of Eastern European and Pacific Rim countries, with their goals of rapid infrastructure expansion—all of this offers an eloquent argument for the enhanced popularity of project management as a technique for improving the efficiency and effectiveness of organizational operations. With so much at stake, it is vital that we immediately begin to address some of the deficiencies in our project management theory and practice.

Project management techniques are well known. But until we are able to take further steps toward formalizing training by teaching the necessary skill set, the problems with efficiently developing, implementing, and gaining client acceptance for these projects are likely to continue growing. There is currently a true window of opportunity in the field of project management. Too often in the past, project managers have been forced to learn their skills the hard way, through practical experience coupled with all the problems of trial and error. Certainly, experience is a valuable component of learning to become an effective project manager, but it is by no means the best.

What conclusions are to be drawn here? If nothing else, it is certain that we have painted a portrait of project management as a complex, time-consuming, often exasperating process. At the same time, it is equally clear that successful project managers are a breed apart. To answer the various calls they continually receive, balance the conflicting demands of a diverse set of stakeholders, navigate tricky corporate political waters, understand the fundamental process of subordinate motivation, develop and constantly refine their leadership skills, and engage in the thousands of pieces of detailed minutiae while keeping their eyes fixed firmly on project goals requires individuals with special skills and personalities. Given the nature of their duties, is it any wonder successful project managers are in such short supply and, once identified, so valued by their organizations?

There is good news, however. Many of these skills, though difficult to master, can be learned. Project management is a challenge, not a mystery. Indeed, it is our special purpose to demystify much of the human side of project management, starting with the role played by the linchpin in the process: the project manager. The problem in the past has been too few sources for either seasoned or novice project managers to turn to in attempting to better understand the nature of their unique challenge and methods for performing more effectively. Too many organizations pay far too little attention to the process of selecting, training, and encouraging those people charged to run project teams. The predictable result is to continually compound the mistake of creating wave after wave of accidental project managers, forcing them to learn through trial and error with minimal guidance in how to perform their roles.

Managing projects is a challenge that requires a strategy and methodology all its own. Perhaps most important, it requires a project manager willing to function as a leader in every sense of the term. We have addressed a wide range of challenges, both contextual and personal, that form the basis under which projects are managed in today's organizations. It is hoped that readers will find something of themselves as well as something of use contained in these pages.

REFERENCES

B.N. Baker, P.C. Murphy, and D. Fisher, "Factors Affecting Project Success," in D.I. Cleland and W.R. King, eds., *Project Management Handbook* (New York: Van Nostrand Reinhold, 1983): 778–801.

K. Clarke, "Survival Skills for a New Breed," *Management Today,* December 1993, p. 5.

D.I. Cleland, "Project Stakeholder Management," in D.I. Cleland and W.R. King, eds., *Project Management Handbook* (New York: Van Nostrand Reinhold, 1983): 275–301.

J.C. Davis, "The Accidental Profession," *Project Management Journal, 15,* 3 (1984): 6.

A.A. Einsiedel, "Profile of Effective Project Managers," *Project Management Journal, !8,* 5 (1987): 51–56.

J. Davidson Frame, *Managing Projects in Organizations* (San Francisco: Jossey-Bass, 1987).

T. Gosselin, "What to Do With Last-Minute Jobs," *World Executive Digest,* December 1993, p. 70.

R.J. Graham, "A Survival Guide for the Accidental Project Manager," *Proceedings of the Annual Project Management Institute Symposium* (Drexel Hill, PA: Project Management Institute, 1992), pp. 355–361.

M. Horner, "Review of 'Managing People for Project Success,'" *International Journal of Project Management, 11* (1993): 125–126.

P.R. Lawrence and J.W. Lorsch, "Differentiation and Integration in Complex Organizations," *Administrative Science Quarterly, 11,* (1967): 1–47.

M. Nichols, "Does New Age Business Have a Message for Managers?" *Harvard Business Review,* March-April 1994, pp. 52–60.

L. O'Connor, "Tunneling Under the Channel," *Mechanical Engineering,* December 1993, pp. 60–66.

N. Pettersen, "What Do We Know About the Effective Project Manager?" *International Journal of Project Management, 9* (1991): 99–104.

J.K. Pinto and O.P. Kharbanda, *Successful Project Managers: Leading Your Team to Success* (New York: Van Nostrand Reinhold, 1995).

J.K. Pinto and D.P. Slevin, "Critical Factors in Successful Project Implementation," *IEEE Transactions on Engineering Management,* EM-34, 1987, p. 22–27.

B.Z. Posner, "What it Takes to be a Good Project Manager," *Project Management Journal, 18,* 1 (1987): 51–54.

W.A. Randolph and B.Z. Posner, "What Every Manager Needs to Know About Project Management," *Sloan Management Review, 29,* 4 (1988): 65–73.

P. Sweet, "A Planner's Best Friend," *Accountancy, 113* (1994): 56–58.

H.J. Thamhain, "Developing Project Management Skills," *Project Management Journal, 22,* 3 (1991): 39–53.

R. Turner, "Editorial," *International Journal of Project Management, 11* (1993): 195.

THE MANAGEMENT AND LEADERSHIP
OF TECHNICAL PROFESSIONALS

7

The Role of the Technical Manager

21

Why Managers Fail

MICHAEL K. BADAWY

Generally ill-equipped for a management career, engineers and scientists will fail as managers unless they understand the reasons for such failure and take steps to prevent it.

Many engineers and scientists have made, or will make, the transition to management smoothly and successfully. However, the record is less than promising. While there is no law of nature that says good technical practitioners cannot be good managers, it is unlikely that they will be. Although they are well qualified for management by virtue of their analytical skills and backgrounds, many technologists switch to management for the wrong reasons and to satisfy the wrong needs. Hence, they do not make competent managers. There is substantial evidence derived from my own research studies and those of others that the transition to management has been troublesome for many technologists, and that many of them have failed because they were generally ill-equipped for such a career.

From Michael K. Badawy, *Developing Managerial Skills in Engineers and Scientists: Succeeding as a Technical Manager,* copyright © 1982 by Van Nostrand Reinhold Co., Inc. Reprinted with permission.
Michael Badawy is Professor of Management at Virginia Polytechnic Institute and State University.

In order to understand why managers fail, one must first recognize that managerial competency has three interrelated components; knowledge, skills and attitudes. Although sophisticated knowledge in the principles and elements of administration is a prerequisite for managerial success, such knowledge by itself is not enough for managerial competency. While management theory is a science, management practice is an art. Therefore, to be effective, the manager must develop a set of professional skills. These skills are:

• *Technical:* Technical skills include the ability of the manager to develop and apply certain methods and techniques related to his tasks. The manager's technical skills also encompass a general familiarity with, and understanding of, the technical activities undertaken in his department and their relation to other company divisions. The manager's technical specialization, formal education, experience, and background form a strong foundation for the development of technical skills.

• *Administrative:* Administrative skills relate primarily to the manager's ability to manage. Effective management, of course, reflects the ability to organize, plan, direct, and control. It is the capacity to build a workable group or unit, to plan, to make decisions, to control and evaluate performance, and finally to direct subordinates by motivating, communicating, and leading them into a certain direction that would help the organization achieve its objectives most effectively. The core elements of administrative skills are the ability to search out concepts and catalog events; the capacity to collect, evaluate, and process pertinent information; the ability to distinguish alternatives and make a decision; and resourcefulness in directing others and communicating to them the reasons behind the decisions and actions. Superior administrative skill is, of course, related to and based on other skills such as cognitive and conceptual skills.

• *Interpersonal:* Interpersonal skills are probably the most important of all. Since managing is a group effort, managerial competency requires a superior ability to work with people. The manager, to be effective, must interact with, motivate, influence, and communicate with people. People make

an organization, and through their activities, organizations either prosper or fail. Managing people effectively is the most critical and most intricate problem for the manager of today.

ATTITUDES AND MANAGERIAL COMPETENCY

Attitudes, the third ingredient of managerial competency, are essentially the manager's value system and beliefs toward self, task, and others in the organization. Attitudes include those patterns of thought that enable one to characterize the manager and predict how well he will handle a problem. Attitudes are partly emotional in origin, but they are necessary because they determine two things. First, the acquisition of knowledge and skills is, in part, a function of attitudes, and second, attitudes determine how the manager applies her knowledge and techniques.

Attitudes are also important in determining managerial competency for another reason: They tell us what needs are dominant in an individual at a certain time, and thus we can predict and identify the individual's managerial potential. This identification is crucial for enhancing future managerial effectiveness.

Modern psychological research tells us that effective managers share at least three major attitudinal characteristics: a high need to manage, a high need for power, and a high capacity for empathy.

The need or will to manage has to do with the fact that no individual is likely to learn how to manage unless he really wants to take responsibility for the productivity of others, and enjoys stimulating them to achieve better results. The "way to manage" can usually be found if there is the "will to manage." Many individuals who aspire to high-level managerial positions—including engineers and scientists—are not motivated to manage. They are motivated to earn high salaries and to attain high status, but they are not motivated to get effective results through others. Thus, they will not make competent managers.

The need to manage is a crucial factor, therefore, in determining whether a person will learn and apply what is necessary to get effective results on the job. They key point here is that an outstanding record as an individual performer does not indicate the ability or willingness to get other people to excel at the same tasks. This partly explains, for example, why outstanding scholars often make poor teachers, excellent engineers are often unable to supervise the work of other engineers, and successful salesmen are often ineffective sales managers.

Second, effective managers are characterized by a strong need for the power derived from such sources as job titles, status symbols, and high income. The point is that power seekers can be counted on to strive to reach positions where they can exercise authority over large numbers of people. Modern behavioral science research suggests that individuals who lack this drive are not likely to act in ways that will enable them to advance far up the managerial ladder.[1] Instead, they usually scorn company politics and devote their energies to other types of activities that are more satisfying to them. For many engineers and scientists, power emanates from "professional" sources other than sources of managerial power. While managerial power is based on politics, titles, and organizational status, professional power is based on knowledge and excellence in one's discipline and profession. In short, the power game is part of management, and it is played best by those who enjoy it most.

The third characteristic of effective managers is the capacity for empathy—being able to cope with the emotional reactions that inevitably occur when people work together in an organization. Effective managers cannot be mired in the code of rationality, which explains, in part, the troublesome transition of some engineers and scientists to management. Individuals who are reluctant to accept emotions as part of being human will not make "human" managers, and, in turn, they will not be managerially competent.

THE MANAGERIAL SKILL MIX

The technical, administrative, and interpersonal skills are all closely interrelated and can be significant in determining your success in management. However, experience shows that the relative importance of these skills varies with the management level you are on and the type of responsibility you have.

As shown in Figure 21.1, technical skills are inversely related to your management level. They are most important at lower management levels but that importance tends to decrease as you advance to higher levels in the organization.

Managerial success on upper management levels is determined by your vision and ability to understand how the entire system works (the conceptual skill), as well as your capacity for organization and coordination between various divisions (the administrative skill). How much you know about the technical details of the operation becomes considerably less important. In fact, beyond middle management, "special knowledge" can actually be a detriment to the individual.

Handling people effectively is the most important skill at all levels of management. Knowing how to handle people effectively, I believe, is the art of the arts. If a manager has considerable technical and administrative skills, but his interpersonal skills are wanting, he is a likely candidate for managerial failure. Conversely, problems that occur because technical or administrative skills are not up to par will be more easily surmounted.

It is important to remember that success in management is largely determined by the manager's ability to understand, interact with, communicate with, coach, and direct subordinates. This statement should not be taken to undermine the importance of technical and administrative skills in

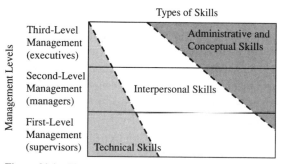

Figure 21.1 The managerial skill mix.

managerial effectiveness, but rather to underscore the ability to get along with people as a prerequisite for success in management.

While interpersonal skills are presumably important at all levels of management, they are perhaps most important at the lower and middle levels, where managers interact with subordinates, supervisors, and associates. At upper management levels, where the frequency of these interactions tends to decrease, the importance of interpersonal skills decreases as conceptual and administrative skills become more important. It is also possible that with the increased degree of power and influence upper-level managers typically have, they can afford to pay less attention to interpersonal relations, and hence they become less sensitive to human needs and individual satisfaction.

Some technical managers and supervisors find it difficult to get away from "the bench" and do what they are paid for—namely managing. But everything in life has a price. Perhaps this is one of the prices managers must pay—the price of management! I have seen quite a few technologists in management who were not willing to pay this price, so they tried to do technical and managerial tasks simultaneously—with the incompatible requirements of two different roles. I have seen others enter management without realizing what they were getting into. The paths taken by both groups turned out to be very costly—they failed! The lesson is quite clear: The "right" mix of the three skill types at different management levels must be properly maintained.

MANAGERIAL FAILURE

Organizations fail because managers fail. Managers fail because they perform poorly. Performance is one of the prime criteria that an organization uses in evaluating employee contributions. While many managers deny it in public, performance is hardly the sole basis for appraising employees. Managerial jobs are no exception. Given the difficulty of measuring managerial performance accurately and objectively, organizations consider the manager's

contributions to the accomplishment of the company's goal to be the most concrete basis for distributing rewards and making salary adjustments and promotion decisions. Thus, managerial failure can be defined as the inability of the manager to meet certain performance standards imposed by his superiors. It can also be defined in terms of organizational policies. A manager has failed if his performance is considered unsatisfactory or unacceptable by virtue of some preestablished criteria. Managerial success, on the other hand, is reflected in added responsibility, promotion, title change, and increased salary. Managerial "failure" is not intended to imply that the manager is demoted because he totally failed to get the job done but rather that he failed to accomplish results that he is capable of achieving.

Why do managers fail? Causes of managerial failure can be numerous. Since managerial performance is a product of the interaction of many factors inside the individual and in the surrounding environment, managerial success or failure will be determined by factors in both areas. Bear in mind that failures in management are rarely due to a single cause. Typically, aspects of the individual interact with aspects of the environment to create the problem.

Research has shown as many as 35 types of factors as potential causes of unsatisfactory managerial performance.[2] Any one of these factors can contribute to the failure of a manager. Some of these factors are more likely to operate than others because of the nature of managerial work. As shown in Table 21.1, there are three groups of factors containing nine categories representing possible causes of performance failures. The first four categories refer to aspects of the individual. The remaining five categories refer to different aspects of the environment: categories five to eight refer to the various groups of which the individual is a member, while the ninth category is contextual, referring to nonhuman aspects of the environment and the work itself which may be strategic to performance failure.

Note the relative importance of the different factors. As shown in the table, the most dominant

TABLE 21.1
Causes of Managerial Failure

Category	High	Low	Rare
A. Individual Factors			
I. *Problems of Intelligence and Job Knowledge*	X		
1. Insufficient verbal ability			
2. Insufficient special ability			
3. Insufficient job knowledge			
4. Defect judgment or memory			
II. *Emotional Problems*		X	
5. Frequent disruptive emotion (anxiety, depression, guilt, etc.)			
6. Neurosis (anger, jealousy, and so on, predominating)			
7. Psychosis			
8. Alcohol and drug problems			
III. *Motivational Problems*			
9. Strong motives frustrated at work (fear of failure, dominance, need for attention, and so on)	X		
10. Unintegrated means used to satisfy strong motives	X		
11. Excessively low personal work standards			X
12. Generalized low work motivation			X
IV. *Physical Problems*		X	
13. Physical illness or handicap including brain disorders			
14. Physical disorders of emotional origin			
15. Inappropriate physical characteristics			
16. Insufficient muscular or sensory ability or skill			
B. Group Factors			
V. *Family-Related Factors*	X		
17. Family crises			
18. Separation from the family and isolation			
19. Predominance of family considerations over work demands			
VI. *Problems Caused in the Work Group*	X		
20. Negative consequences associated with group cohesion			
21. Ineffective management			
22. Inappropriate managerial standards or criteria			
VII. *Problems Originating in Company Policies*	X		
23. Insufficient organizational action			
24. Placement error			
25. Organizational overpermissiveness			
26. Excessive spans of control			
27. Inappropriate organizational standards and criteria			
VIII. *Problems Stemming from Society and Its Values*			X
28. Application of legal sanctions			
29. Enforcement of societal values by means other than the law			
30. Conflict between job demands and cultural values (equity, freedom, religious values, and so on)			
IX. *Contextual Factors*			
C. Factors in the Work Context and the Job Itself			
31. Negative consequences of economic forces	X		
32. Negative consequences of geographic location	X		
33. Detrimental conditions in the work setting			
34. Excessive danger			
35. Problems in the work itself			

From Miner, John B., "The Challenge of Managing." Philadelphia: Saunders, 1975, pp. 330–331.

causes of performance failure are deficiencies of an intellectual nature, frustrated motivations, membership in and relations with different groups, and economic and geographic factors.

Discussing all possible causes of managerial failure in detail would be impractical. Thus, for our purposes here, I shall focus on the forces relating to the individual manager or to his or her job.

The development of management skills and the ability to convert them into effective actions are crucial to managerial competency. The lack of ingredients necessary for effective managerial performance will lead to poor results. Lack of knowledge of management principles and concepts, for example, will hamper a manager's performance. In addition, developing managerial skills is difficult when management knowledge is insufficient or lacking.

Many technical managers get fired, not because they lack technical competence, but because they lack managerial competence (another common practice, sadly, is to transfer incompetent managers back into a heavy technical role!). Managerial failure can thus result from inadequate management and administrative skills. Establishing a well-functioning unit or division with a sound structure and clear authority and responsibility relationships is crucial for achieving divisional objectives. In addition, developing policies and procedures consistent with objectives and goals, allocating resources, and monitoring progress toward goal achievement are key managerial tasks. These activities call for considerable administrative skill on the manager's part.

The major cause of managerial failure among engineers and scientists is poor interpersonal skills. Many technologists are more comfortable dealing with matters in the laboratory than they are dealing with people. Because many of them are loners, they are used to doing things for themselves. Once promoted to management, however, they have to delegate responsibility to others. They often find this extremely difficult, especially if they have less than complete confidence in their subordinates' abilities. As a result, many technologists find that their advancement—and their managerial careers—are limited more by human factors than by technical ability.

Managerial failure also occurs when an individual becomes a manager for the wrong reasons. This happens when a person seeks the attractive rewards (e.g., economic) associated with a managerial position, yet has no strong will to manage. Such managers do so poorly that they become "retired on the job."

JOB-RELATED FACTORS

A brief account of some of the job-related factors causing managerial failure follows.

Some managers, especially new managers, are unwilling to pay the price of being a manager, i.e., loneliness. They seem to be unaware that the higher one climbs on the managerial ladder, the more lonesome it becomes, the fewer peers one has to talk to, and the more restraint one must exercise over what one says. As a result, while they may enjoy the new challenges and the greater opportunity to make unilateral decisions, they find themselves nostalgic for the "good old days" when it was not so lonely. They therefore try to act like "one of the boys."[3] In doing so, they often lose the respect of the people they manage. Employees want to look up to the boss. They want to feel that they can turn to him or her for necessary decisions. The genesis of this managerial failure is the desire to be liked rather than respected! It is interesting that managers who are found to be most effective are usually categorized by their subordinates as "fair but firm."

In addition, new managers sometimes fail to adjust to the demands of their role. Managerial positions are usually characterized by a high degree of power over other people, some standards for controlling human behavior in work settings, large amounts of visibility and influence, and a keen understanding of how corporate power and politics work. These characteristics require that managers play multiple roles. If managers are uncomfortable with these factors, they could develop a strong fear of failure. This situation might very well lead to a poor managerial performance.

Other causes of managerial failure include the following:

Bias toward Objective Measurement. Having been trained in "hard" sciences, where exact measurement is one of the natural beauties of the scientific method, engineers and scientists are more comfortable working with things that they can objectively control and measure. Managers, on the other hand, must rely on intuition and judgment in dealing with attitudes, biases, perceptions, emotions and feelings. The fact that these intangible variables are hardly measurable—let alone controllable—makes the technical manager's job thoroughly frustrating. To be sure, one of the things that technologists must learn in order to succeed in management is to stop insisting on using a yardstick to measure everything. The nature of management—contrary to engineering and science—defies objective and tangible measurement.

Paralysis by Analysis. Engineers and scientists, more than others, suffer from this disease: the tendency to wait for all information to be in before they make a decision. I can think of no worse cause of managerial failure—it is a clear case of how the professional's technical training can hamper rather than enhance one's chances for success. In management, you will never have all the facts, nor will there ever be riskless decisions. All decision-making involves risk taking. An adaptation of Pareto's principle would be that 20 percent of the facts are critical to 80 percent of the outcome. Being slow to decide, waiting for more facts, is known as "paralysis by analysis."

The inability of engineering or R&D supervisors to adjust to making managerial decisions on the basis of incomplete data and in areas where they lack first-hand experience (since the information is usually provided by other people and divisions) results in managerial anxiety.[4] The fact that they must function within a highly ambiguous and unpredictable environment makes them unsure about the data available, thereby reinforcing a neurotic demand for more data in an attempt to make riskless decisions. If this cycle is not somehow broken and appropriate adjustments made, it can be a deadly time waster and a complicating factor in the transition to management.

Fear of Loss of Intimate Contact with Their Fields. Effective managers always focus on what needs to be done, when it should be done, and how much it should cost, rather than on how to do it. Since managers must get things done through other people, the question of "how" should always be left to them. Technologists usually find this difficult to understand, and in their zeal to stay professionally competent, they try to keep intimate contact with their specialties. As a result, they fail to delegate and they tend to handle the technical details as well—they try to do two jobs in the time of one! The manager, to be sure, is paid to get things done—not to do them himself; this is the job of his subordinates. Sacrificing some of their technical competence—in a relative sense—is the price technical managers must pay for staying managerially competent.

Technologists as Introverts. Many engineers and scientists are "introverts" rather than "extroverts." Research shows that introversion is usually associated with creativity. The problem is that while creating is an individual (introvert) activity, managing is a team (extrovert) activity. The ability to work with others and to be a good team player is one of the distinctive skills of successful and competent managers. The "lone wolf" nature of many technologists could, therefore, make it doubly difficult for them to function effectively as technical managers.

Poor Delegators. One of the most valuable skills a manager can possess is the ability to delegate. You should never undertake what you can delegate. You cannot grow as a technical manager unless you delegate, and your subordinates expect you to. However, technical managers have been found to be very poor in learning to achieve things through others. They are poor delegators. Technologists are doers rather than delegators because they believe, rightly or wrongly, that they perform a task better than anyone on their staff can. Developing the will to delegate requires a change in the technologist's attitudes, behavior, and assumptions about people working for him. She might even have to force herself to delegate tasks to her subordinates. At any rate, whatever it takes, delegation is one of the prime skills technical supervisors must acquire to enhance their managerial competence.

Farming out Responsibilities. Some managers do not recognize their responsibility for on-the-job training and coaching. They are all too eager to send their subordinates to courses conducted by staff agencies and outside trainers and consultants. While there are many occasions when it is wise to use these outside resources, the manager must make certain that such training is utilized by the subordinates when they return to the job. Without a standing policy of what training should cover and who should be trained and by whom, the manager runs the risk of abdicating coaching and training responsibilities. Poor development of subordinates hinders their professional growth, and the manager becomes indispensable. When a manager's responsibilities and salary remain the same over a long period of time, this stagnation is sometimes an indication of managerial failure. Upward movement on the managerial ladder, if based on one's managerial capability, is the ultimate reward of success.

In the absence of concrete figures on managerial "malpractice," it is difficult to estimate the number of ineffective or unsuccessful managers in organizations. However, experience shows that there are a lot of incompetent managers around. The best way to deal with performance failure, I believe, is to prevent it. Unfortunately, managers are willing enough to put out the fires but they take little interest in fire prevention. Dealing with ineffective performance requires diagnosing the causes and then coming up with appropriate remedies. The possible causes of managerial failure have been analyzed in this article. However, the scrutiny of your own performance and the development of a personal plan of action must remain your responsibility.

NOTES

1. McClelland, David C., and Burnham, David H. "Power-Driven Managers: Good Guys Make Bum Bosses." *Psychology Today* (December, 1975): pp. 69–70.

2. Miner, John. "The Challenge of Managing." Philadelphia: Saunders, 1975, pp. 215–216.

3. This discussion is partly based on McCarthy, John F. "Why Managers Fail." Second Edition. New York: McGraw-Hill, 1978, pp. 3–34.

4. For more on this point see Steele, Lowell W. "Innovation in Big Business." New York: Elsevier, 1975, p. 186; and Thompson, Paul and Dalton, Gene. "Are R&D Organizations Obsolete?" *Harvard Business Review* (November–December 1976).

22

The Hidden Side of Leadership in Technical Team Management

GARY GEMMILL AND DAVID WILEMON

Experienced managers know that simply labeling a group of individuals a "team" does not mean that they necessarily possess the skills to perform effectively as a team. Moreover, emphasis on the "leader as hero" has resulted in a lack of "team role" models for effective teamwork, especially at the top of organizations (1).

More often than not, senior management "teams" are made up of individuals promoted on the basis of their individual performance in functional areas, rather than on the basis of an ability to work imaginatively and constructively as team members within and across organizations. Few organizations have developed performance appraisal systems that accurately assess how well individuals function as team members or how well teams perform at a total system level (2). As a result, many managers have limited exposure to effective teamwork.

Surprisingly, in terms of the many important issues surrounding teamwork, there has been minimal theoretical or empirical research directed toward understanding the interpersonal concerns of team leaders. Our purpose in this article is twofold: First, to report an exploratory field study where team leaders identified and described their actual experiences in managing their teams; and second, to interpret the managerial and organization implications of our findings. Our research results are derived from interviews with 100 project team leaders, all of whom had at least five years of organizational experience. One-third of the team leaders had full-time team members while two-thirds of the leaders operated in a matrix, relying on functional personnel, most of whom were also supporting other projects and functional assignments.

MAJOR SOURCES OF FRUSTRATION

Table 22.1 summarizes the major frustrations team leaders experienced in leading their teams. Sixty-six of the leaders found apathy and lack of commitment among their team members a serious source of frustration, which they felt undermined their team's effectiveness.

The emotions associated with the issue of apathy are highlighted by the comments of one R&D team leader as he lamented:

> I can handle almost any kind of problem that occurs in a team: conflicts over technology options, a stubborn client, or even power struggles. What frustrates me the most is dealing with the uninvolved, the uncommitted, and the 'I don't cares.'

We found that project leaders often feel helpless and powerless when they encounter uncommitted and uninvolved team members. Rather than seeing the issue as frequently a team-produced or "systems" (organizational) issue (3), many of the leaders interviewed blamed themselves. They wondered if they had done something wrong or if they had not done enough to deal with their apathetic team members.

Reprinted with permission from *Research-Technology Management*, November-December, 1994.
Gary Gemmill is Professor of Organizational Behavior at Syracuse University's School of Management. **David Wilemon** is Professor of Marketing at Syracuse University's School of Management.

TABLE 22.1
Major Frustrations Team Leaders Experienced in Leading Project Teams

	Number of leaders mentioning (n = 100)
Lack of team member involvement reflected in apathy, lack of commitment and low energy.	66
Wasting time in covering the same ground and being unable to arrive at a consensus.	63
Feeling powerless in influencing team members.	61
Lack of openness in confronting "real issues."	58
Feeling powerless in influencing the larger organization in which the team is embedded.	46
Other: Unclear objectives, "hidden agendas," low trust, power struggles, "rubber stamping" mentality, personality conflicts, poor follow-through on commitments.	21

Note: Respondents frequently gave multiple responses to this question.

The common experience of "wheel spinning" was reported by 63 team leaders, who were frustrated by a seemingly unproductive use of time. One leader, managing an electronic hardware project, reported his frustration this way:

> If you've managed R&D personnel before, you know that there's much wasted time. Some of the people I work with are smart, aggressive, and they have strong ideas about how things should go. When you get seven or eight of them together, you'll spend lots of time airing views and trying to get consensus on direction. I remember one incident where we spent nearly four hours deciding what our PERT chart would look like and who ought to get copies. I initially thought we could make that decision in five or ten minutes.

Two types of powerlessness were revealed in the leaders' responses: (1) powerlessness over team member involvement and commitment (61 leaders), and (2) powerlessness over external resources, information, and cooperation (46 leaders) (5). Examples of what team leaders felt they needed from their organizations included resources, personnel, information, decisions, and facilities (6). One leader described his experiences with the larger organization this way:

> No team is self-sufficient. You never have enough of the right stuff to do it on your own—so you have to have help, support, and the approval of others. We did our homework and asked manufacturing to approve our design. That was 60 days ago and we're still waiting for a response.

This team leader remarked that "my team has a quick-shift mentality but the rest of the organization never seems to get out of first gear."

Fifty-eight of the team leaders were frustrated by the difficulties team members had in dealing openly with "real," but seemingly "undiscussable," issues. One leader noted the following incident:

> We were in a meeting discussing a critical design issue and my manufacturing guy would not agree on the new design that had been proposed for the product. Later, I found out it wasn't really the design that was the real issue; it was that the manufacturing coordinator strongly disliked the head of the design group. Unfortunately, it took me several meetings to discover what was going on.

As several of the project leaders noted, struggling with issues of trust, openness and assertiveness in teams is not "easy." They mentioned that learning to penetrate the "defensive routines" that team members rely on in order to make "undiscussable" topics into "discussable" ones is complex and requires a high level of interpersonal competence (4).

DIFFICULT TEAM ISSUES

While our first research question asked about the *major frustrations* team leaders encounter, our second question focused on the *most difficult issues* they face in leading their teams. We were interested in determining whether the most frustrating and the most difficult issues would be similar or very different.

Team leader perceptions regarding the most difficult issues they experienced in managing teams and how they coped with them are presented in Table 22.2.

Sixty-seven team leaders reported major difficulty dealing with apathetic team members. One leader, heading a manufacturing modernization project, described his experience with "team apathy" this way:

> Most people around here have had both good and bad experiences on teams. And they sure don't want a repeat of the bad times. So, what team members bring to the team is an attitude that says: "Show me what this is all about and show me that it (the project) is real and, if I agree with you, I'll probably help." In a nutshell, they are suspicious

and reluctant to dive in or grab an oar until they know the project and the team leader have substance. You have to be able to get them where they live.

Uninvolved team members were clearly a major source of difficulty and irritation for team leaders.

To cope with team apathy, team leaders told us that they typically confronted members about their level of commitment. These project leaders also reported that they were aware of the risks involved in such confrontation. At one time or another, many had experienced a situation where a confrontation resulted in team member withdrawal or teamwork sabotage.

The second most difficult issue reported by the team leaders concerned challenges to their leadership by team members. These challenges included open disagreement over the leader's initiatives and directions; criticism of the leader's abilities; and formation of covert alliances to re-

TABLE 22.2
Team Leaders' Perceptions of Difficult Team Issues and How They Deal with Them

Number of leaders reporting (n = 100)	When faced with	Most felt	Most responded by	Risk they perceived in responding
67	Team apathy.	Frustrated	Confronting the issue with team members.	Being met with denial, losing respect of members and being met with more apathy.
31	Challenges to the team leader's authority and competence	Angry	Doing nothing.	Shutting off dissent and being seen as a closed-minded leader.
27	Conflict and competitive power struggle among team members.	Helpless	Building a coalition.	Splintering and polarizing the group into working factions.
21	Overly dependent team member.	Annoyed	Expressing anger and frustration.	Being seen as an insensitive leader unwilling to help team members.

Note: The difficult team issues presented here were the most frequently mentioned team concerns of our team leaders. Due to space limitations, only the most important issues are mentioned. Our content analysis identified how those who mentioned a predominant issue felt about it; how they responded when the issue arose; and the risk they perceived in acting on the issue. Respondent frequently gave multiple responses to this question.

duce or derail the leader's power, authority and momentum.

Team leaders noted that they often became angry when challenged, but generally did not express it openly. They also feared that they would be seen as shutting off dissent and being viewed as authoritarian, closed-minded—or as "someone who couldn't take it." A leader of a medical instrumentation project team responsible for new product development shared the following incident about how challenges to his competence affected him:

> Sometimes I felt that I was being personally attacked. The words and the negativity are directed toward you because the leader is often the lightning rod for what people feel. Most of the time they are not really attacking me; what they are hostile about is the system (the organization) and the circumstances.

Additionally, 27 leaders reported that conflicts and power struggles among team members constitute another difficult team issue. Many of the team leaders reported frustration in such situations. They responded by smoothing over issues or by building alliances outside scheduled team meetings. Nevertheless, many were concerned that forming alliances or negotiating "outside" their groups could split or polarize their groups into "warring" factions (7).

Twenty-one leaders reported that having to deal with overly dependent team members was a difficult task. Often these leaders felt annoyed because these dependent members needed considerable direction and follow-up and they lacked initiative in responding to important tasks.

When asked about their response to dependent members, many noted that they became irritated and sometimes responded by expressing anger and impatience. Yet, they were concerned that in expressing their irritation they could be viewed as insensitive to the needs of the team members. Several of the leaders also feared that some of the dependent members might withdraw from the team if they became angry or if they "pushed" these team members too hard. A project leader in an advanced technology development group made this comment about overly dependent team members:

You get to work with two kinds of people on project teams. The first type is the person who wants to make something happen. They want freedom and some loose reins. They want to work with you. The second type is someone who always wants direction. So, you spend a lot of time telling them what's now and what's next. They are different from the first type—they want to work for you. I've seen absolutely no correlation between the two types of team members and intelligence or experience. The cost to the team leader is time and the neglect of other things that need to be done.

ASSESSING TEAM ISSUES

Tables 22.3 and 22.4 report how team leaders misread events within their teams and how they perceive difficult team issues. Table 22.3 indicates how team leaders perceive themselves *misreading* events within the team. The data in this Table underscore the importance of being aware of hidden

TABLE 22.3
How Team Leaders Misread Events within Project Teams

	Number of leaders mentioning (n = 100)
Unaware of interpersonal conflict between members of team.	41
Unaware of hidden agendas on part of team members.	33
Not understanding the motivations and needs of team members.	32
Unaware of expectations of team members.	31
Not listening carefully enough to team discussion.	28
Misreading lack of argument as agreement.	19
Interpreting conflict as unhealthy when it was actually constructive.	13
Misreading team members' ability to work together as a team.	6

Note: Respondents frequently gave multiple responses to this question.

TABLE 22.4
Team Leaders' Sources of Data for Identifying Emerging Team Issues

	Number of leaders mentioning (n = 100)
Focusing on non-verbal communications (facial expressions, body posture, note taking, etc.) of team members.	83
Listening with a "third ear" for hidden meanings, themes and patterns, what is not being said explicitly be team members.	76
Sensing energy level of team members.	73
Observing influence patterns and flow of communications (who talks to whom) between team members.	66
Having one-on-one discussions with team members outside of scheduled team meetings.	65

Note: Respondents frequently gave multiple response to this question.

interpersonal team dynamics. As one team manager commented:

> When you are appointed the project leader of a group and are given a team, sometimes you can have a terrible time sorting out what people are telling you. What is the underlying truth that they are telling you? When a team member says something, is that his real voice you hear or is he functioning as a spokesman or emissary for the R&D director? Some people join teams and serve as conduits for their home organization. There's good in that, and, of course, there's some bad to it, too, in terms of communication distortion.

This team leader's experience reflects some of the specific ways leaders report misreading their teams: Not being aware of interpersonal conflicts among members; hidden agendas among members; and what members expect from a team. The lack of effective interpersonal skills in managing teams is often highlighted by: (1) not recognizing conflict between team members (41 leaders), (2) not being aware of hidden agendas, (3) not understanding

team member motivations, (4) lack of awareness about team member expectations, and (5) not listening accurately enough to team discussions (8).

As indicated in Table 22.4, team leaders report using multiple sources of data to *identify* emerging team issues; e.g., attention to non-verbal communications, listening with a "third ear," sensing energy levels within the team, observing influence patterns, and having one-on-one discussions outside team meetings. One leader of an electronics project captured this behavior well when he said:

> It's amazing what you can see just by observing what goes on in status review meetings. I can usually tell when I'm stepping on someone's sensitive parts or when I've lost someone. You're talking and you're listening to what's going on, but probably more important, you're observing and reading the signals that are being emitted. Unless you can read a group, you'll miss what they are really trying to tell you.

FEARS AND APPREHENSIONS

The fears and apprehensions team leaders had about being a team leader are reported in Table 22.5 (9). The three most important fears reported were (1) dominating the team (67 leaders), (2) making a mistake or appearing incompetent, and (3) losing control of the team.

When we asked for elaboration about their fears of dominating their teams, the majority of team leaders were concerned that they might overpower their less-assertive team members and not realize the full benefits that can derive from a climate of openness, exchange, confrontation, and healthy dialogue. Some of the leaders noted and expressed concern that they frequently had informational advantages over team members and could use it to influence their teams in various directions. The sources of this advantage were knowledge related to their specific managerial responsibilities; e.g., schedules, costs, client or customer needs, and senior management's objectives for the project. Seldom did the team leaders report that they had

TABLE 22.5
Fears and Apprehensions about Being a Team Leader

	Number of leaders mentioning (n = 100)
Dominating the team.	67
Making a mistake or appearing incompetent.	60
Losing control of the team.	58
Rejecting member ideas, resulting in their withdrawal and lack of commitment.	35
Having an apathetic group with low commitment and minimal participation.	25
Other: Being saddled with a low-priority project; being caught in a power struggle, being given a hopeless project.	15

Note: Respondents frequently gave multiple responses to this question.

an informational advantage based on their knowledge about technological issues.

Many leaders were concerned about making a mistake or appearing incompetent. When we asked them to discuss the basis of these fears, they often noted that they were afraid that they might not regain their credibility if they erred, or that a mistake would seriously impact them and set their teams back. In terms of concerns over failing, one team leader managing a state-of-the-art project told us:

> Sure, I have fears. A big concern always is that nothing will really happen and I won't be able to move the project forward. I also don't want to look like I don't fully know or understand some of the technology and market entry choices we have to make. So the fear that you may not know enough is always present.

As a consequence of their fear of failing, many of the leaders noted that they were sometimes too cautious in making decisions and taking action. Several noted that how the organization dealt with failure shaped their willingness to take risks.

Finally, and paradoxically, many were concerned about "losing control." Losing control implied being impotent in leading, directing or influencing their teams. Some noted that such concerns prompted them to strengthen their own power by gaining the support of their management; by dealing directly with the more influential team members and key functional departments; and by carefully planning critical choices and strategic directions facing the team.

"SO WHAT"?

Much contemporary writing on team leadership has focused on prescriptions that leaders can follow in order to develop highly effective teams. For example, a comprehensive study by Kouzes and Pozner (10) concludes that high-performing leaders should engage in such behaviors as:

1. *Challenging the Process.*—Leaders search for new opportunities and experiment with new ideas and directions.

2. *Inspiring a Shared Vision.*—Leaders have the capacity to envision and shape the future. They are able to enlist the support of others in pursuing a shared vision.

3. *Enabling Others To Act.*—Leaders involve others in decisions; they give support and build confidence in their team members.

4. *Modeling the Way.*—Leaders are clear about their values and they live them by setting an example for others. They focus on key priorities and they celebrate small wins.

5. *Encouraging the Heart.*—Leaders create an environment conducive to strong motivation levels. This happens by recognizing the contributions of team members, by nurturing team spirit, and by celebrating accomplishments.

While such descriptions of desirable leader behavior can be helpful, they present an incomplete picture of the challenges team leaders face (11). We are surprised that inquiry into the interpersonal concerns of team leaders has been so limited.

Our study found that one of the most serious concerns faced by the team leaders is a lack of team member involvement and apathy toward team projects. Several leaders reported their teams wasted considerable time trying to gain agreement and consensus on issues. Many team leaders also felt powerless and frustrated when they attempted to influence their team members and the larger organization. Root causes of many of these frustrations can be found in unclear organizational priorities, conflicting goals, and a lack of coherent team or organizational vision.

Team leaders also stated that they experienced considerable risk when dealing with such issues as team apathy, detrimental power struggles, and overly dependent team members (Table 22.2). Much of the perceived risk centered on fears of exacerbating the situation or apprehensions about being too controlling as a leader.

It can be highly beneficial for team leaders to know that what they emotionally experience at a "gut level" is often shared by other leaders. Team leaders often feel they have "special" problems with their groups—that they are atypical. Our exploratory findings suggest just the opposite. Although in most organizations discussion of personal apprehensions and concerns is not encouraged, most team leaders clearly experience them. Many managers believe that by admitting their fears and concerns they will be perceived as weak.

Numerous examples were cited by team leaders where they "misread" important team issues (Table 22.3). Why do team leaders fail to diagnose team issues correctly? Many noted that they: 1) were unaware of conflicts between team members; 2) were unaware of hidden agendas; and 3) did not understand the full context of what was said. Team leaders noted that they were more likely to misread the "messages" of team members who came from functional areas different from their own.

Several approaches (Table 22.4) can be used to help team leaders accurately "read" and understand what is occurring in their teams (12). One approach is training to understand the likely meaning of various types of non-verbal behavior. Another is developing skills so that team leaders can "check

out" what they see and hear. Appropriate "checking out" behavior sends a signal that the leader is interested and wants to understand. This, in turn, engenders trust in the leader and helps create openness within the team. And far from least is the neglected art of simply asking questions. A leader's willingness and skill in posing questions can be a powerful way to open up the team's communication channels and processes.

We find an interesting paradox in our inquiries about the fears and apprehensions team leaders face. The most frequently mentioned fear was "dominating the team" (Table 22.5). When we asked for elaboration, some of the team leaders stated that their leadership position gave them too much power. Consequently, they were apprehensive about overpowering their team members. Yet, leaders were also fearful of losing control of their teams, which is opposite from "dominating" the team. Team leaders need to be clearly aware of the processes available for balancing situations of too little or too much control (13,14).

The fears and apprehensions team leaders experience in managing their teams also can erect significant interpersonal barriers within the team if leaders become paralyzed, defensive, or if they deny their underlying fears and concerns. Acknowledging to one's self the presence of fears and apprehensions is necessary to prevent them from becoming an interpersonal barrier to effective teamwork. Thus, the extent a team leader feels blocked and unable to develop, express and implement creative and innovative thoughts will be mirrored in the behavior of the team members. Recognizing fears about failure and not allowing them to paralyze one's actions constitutes a significant step in developing a team culture that encourages openness, creativity and innovative problem-solving.

At the team or project level, one powerful way for teams to deal with issues is to develop norms that encourage group discussion of individual concerns (15). Such norms can support the discovery and treatment of apathy, frustration and abuse of power. Certainly, team leaders need to demonstrate that these concerns are discussable. What restrains many team leaders from exploring such issues in team environments are common myths that surround team leadership issues. These myths include:

- "It's dangerous to talk openly about one's emotional experiences."

- "Interpersonal conflicts should be avoided."

- "When someone wins an argument, then someone else automatically loses."

- "If people feel powerless and frustrated in a team situation, they should remain silent, because discussing it can be detrimental to them and the group."

Our experiences with groups suggest that the above are largely just that—myths, scenarios of "emotional truths" requiring resolution. There are risks in initiating communication about emotionally charged topics. But a far greater risk resides in repressing or ignoring them. These issues are not only discussable but necessary for uncovering and unblocking whatever is impeding teamwork performance and team member satisfaction (16).

THE FUTURE OF TEAMWORK

There are many indicators that effective teamwork will be highly important in the global economy of the 1990s. Increasingly, teams are indeed becoming the basic "building blocks" of high-performing organizations (17). The results of our study suggest a great need for training in teamwork and in team leader skills. Too often managers learn these leadership skills by trial and error. Such an approach is costly, frustrating and inefficient. With increased skill and knowledge about teamwork, the transition to project leader can be far smoother (18).

Additionally, an organization's senior managers need to model effective teamwork within their organizations. Such modeling teaches by example. When senior managers work effectively and imaginatively as a team, this sends a powerful message throughout the organization about the importance of teamwork (19).

Senior management teamwork is a process

that far exceeds, both in contributions and results, the one-on-one mentoring approach often used to groom, coach and prepare individual team leaders. Modeling also reinforces the value of an organization's training and educational programs in teamwork.

Lastly, it is important for team leaders to consciously develop norms within their teams on the acceptability and desirability of discussing difficult and sensitive team issues (20,21). Developing such norms creates a team culture based on openness and a willingness to explore important human concerns (22). The result can be team performance levels that are indeed noteworthy.

REFERENCES

1. Bennis, Warren. *Why Leaders Can't Lead: The Unconscious Conspiracy Continues.* San Francisco: Jossey-Bass, Inc., 1989.
2. Mower, Judith and Wilemon, David. "Rewarding Technical Teamwork." *Research • Technology Management*, September-October 1989.
3. Kraus, George and Gemmill, Gary. "The Dynamics of Covert Role Analysis in Small Groups." *Small Group Behavior* 19 (August 1988): 299–311.
4. Argyris, Chris. *Strategy, Change, and Defensive Routines.* Boston: Pittman, 1985.
5. Brown, L. *Managing Conflict at Organizational Interfaces.* Reading, Mass.: Addison-Wesley, 1983.
6. Schein, E.H. "Intergroup Problems in Organizations." *Organizational Psychology*, Englewood Cliffs, N.J.: Prentice-Hall, 1980, pp. 172–181.
7. Neuhauser, P.C. *Tribal Warfare in Organizations.* Cambridge, Mass.: Ballinger, 1988.
8. Ross, R. *Small Groups in Organizational Settings.* Englewood Cliffs, N.J.: Prentice-Hall, 1989, pp. 221–233.
9. Gibb, J.R. "Fear and Facade: Defensive Management." In *Science and Human Affairs*, edited by R.E. Farson. Palo Alto, Cal.: Science and Behavior Books, 1965.
10. Pozner, B.Z. and Kouzes, J.M. *The Leadership Challenge.* San Francisco: Jossey-Bass, 1987.
11. Maccoby, M. *The Leader: A New Face for American Management.* New York: Ballantine Books, 1981.
12. Hackman, R. (Editor). *Groups that Work (and Those that Don't): Creating Conditions for Effective Teamwork.* San Francisco: Jossey-Bass, 1989.
13. Humphrey, Watts S. *Managing for Innovation:*

Leading Technical People. Englewood Cliffs, N.J.: Prentice-Hall, 1987.

14. Lawler, E. *High-Involvement Management: Participative Strategies for Improving Organizational Performance*. San Francisco: Jossey-Bass, 1986.

15. de la Porte, André, "Group Norms: Key to Building a Winning Team." *Personnel*, September-October 1974, pp. 60–67.

16. Gemmill, Gary. "The Mythology of the Leader Role in Small Groups." *Small Group Behavior* 44, 1 (1986).

17. Hanna, D. *Designing Organizations for High Performance*. Reading, Mass.: Addison-Wesley, 1988, p. 3.

18. Egan, G. *Interpersonal Living*. Monterey, Cal.: Brooks/Cole, 1976.

19. Chance, Paul. "Great Experiments in Team Chemistry." *Across the Board*, May 1989, p. 25.

20. Schein, E.H. *Organizational Culture and Leadership*. San Francisco: Jossey-Bass, 1985.

21. Roth, T. and Buchholz, S. *Creating the High Performance Team*. New York: John Wiley, 1987, pp. 29–32.

22. Argyris, Chris. "Teaching Smart People How To Learn." *Harvard Business Review* 69, 3, (May-June 1991): 99–109.

23. Weber, R.P. *Basic Content Analysis*. Beverly Hills, Cal.: Sage Publications, 1985.

8

The Role of the Technical Leader

23

The Middle Manager as Innovator

ROSABETH MOSS KANTER

When Steve Talbot, an operations manager, began a staff job reporting to the general manager of a product group, he had no line responsibility, no subordinates or budget of his own, and only a vague mandate to "explore options to improve performance."

To do this, Talbot set about collecting resources by bargaining with product-line managers and sales managers. By promising the product-line managers that he would save them having to negotiate with sales to get top priority for their prod-

ucts, he got a budget from them. Then, because he had the money in hand, Talbot got the sales managers to agree to hire one salesperson per product line, with Talbot permitted to do the hiring.

The next area he tackled was field services. Because the people in this area were conservative and tightfisted, Talbot went to his boss to get support for his recommendations about this area.

With the sales and service functions increasing their market share, it was easy for Talbot to get the product-line managers' backing when he

Reprinted by permission of *Harvard Business Review*. From "The Middle Manager as Innovator" by Rosabeth Moss Kanter, July–August 1982. Copyright © 1995 by the President and Fellows of Harvard College, all rights reserved.

Rosabeth Moss Kanter is Professor of Business Administration at the Harvard Business School.

pushed for selling a major new product that he had devised. And, to keep his action team functioning and behind him, Talbot made sure that "everyone became a hero" when the senior vice president of engineering asked him to explain his success to corporate officers.

Arthur Drumm, a technical department head of two sections, wanted to develop a new measuring instrument that could dramatically improve the company's product quality. But only Drumm thought this approach would work; those around him were not convinced it was needed or would pay off. After spending months developing data to show that the company needed the instrument, Drumm convinced several of his bosses two levels up to contribute $300,000 to its development. He put together a task force made up of representatives from all the manufacturing sites to advise on the development process and to ensure that the instrument would fit in with operations.

When, early on, one high-level manager opposed the project, Drumm coached two others in preparation for an officer-level meeting at which they were going to present this proposal. And when executives argued about which budget line the money would come from, R&D or engineering, Drumm tried to ease the tension. His persistence netted the company an extremely valuable new technique.

When Doris Randall became the head of a backwater purchasing department, one of three departments in her area, she expected the assignment to advance her career. Understandably, she was disappointed at the poor state of the function she had inherited and looked around for ways to make improvements. She first sought information from users of the department's services and, with this information, got her boss to agree to a first wave of changes. No one in her position had ever had such close contacts with users before, and Randall employed her knowledge to reorganize the unit into a cluster of user-oriented specialties (with each staff member concentrating on a particular need).

Once she had the reorganization in place and her function acknowledged as the best purchasing department in the region, Randall wanted to reorganize the other two purchasing departments. Her boss, perhaps out of concern that he would lose his position to Randall if the proposed changes took place, discouraged her. But her credibility was so strong that her boss's boss—who viewed her changes as a model for improvements in other areas—gave Randall the go-ahead to merge the three purchasing departments into one. Greater efficiency, cost savings, and increased user satisfaction resulted.

These three managers are enterprising, innovative, and entrepreneurial middle managers who are part of a group that can play a key role in the United States' return to economic leadership.

If that seems like an overly grand statement, consider the basis for U.S. companies' success in the past: innovation in products and advances in management techniques. Then consider the pivotal contribution middle managers make to innovation and change in large organizations. Top leaders' general directives to open a new market, improve quality, or cut costs mean nothing without efficient middle managers just below officer level able to design the systems, carry them out, and redirect their staffs' activities accordingly. Furthermore, because middle managers have their fingers on the pulse of operations, they can also conceive, suggest, and set in motion new ideas that top managers may not have thought of.

The middle managers described here are not extraordinary individuals. They do, however, share a number of characteristics:

- **Comfort with change.** They are confident that uncertainties will be clarified. They also have foresight and see unmet needs as opportunities.

- **Clarity of direction.** They select projects carefully and, with their long time horizons, view setbacks as temporary blips in an otherwise straight path to a goal.

- **Thoroughness.** They prepare well for meetings and are professional in making their presentations. They have insight into organizational politics and a sense of whose support can help them at various junctures.

- **Participative management style**. They encourage subordinates to put in maximum effort and to be part of the team, promise them a share of the rewards, and deliver on their promises.
- **Persuasiveness, persistence, and discretion**. They understand that they cannot achieve their ends overnight, so they persevere—using tact—until they do.

What makes it possible for managers to use such skills for the company's benefit? They work in organizations where the culture fosters collaboration and teamwork and where structures encourage people to "do what needs to be done." Moreover, they usually work under top managers who consciously incorporate conditions facilitating innovation and achievement into their companies' structures and operations.

These conclusions come from a study of the major accomplishments of 165 effective middle managers in five leading American corporations. I undertook this study to determine managers' contributions to a company's overall success as well as the conditions that simulate innovation and thus push a business beyond a short-term emphasis and allow it to secure a successful future.

Each of the 165 managers studied—all of whom were deemed "effective" by their companies—told the research team about a particular accomplishment; these covered a wide range. Some of the successes, though impressive, clearly were achieved within the boundaries of established company practice. Others, however, involved innovation: introduction of new methods, structures, or products that increased the company's capacity. All in all, 99 of the 165 accomplishments fall within the definition of an innovative effort.

Basic accomplishments differ from innovative ones not only in scope and long-run impact but also in what it takes to achieve them. They are part of the assigned job and require only routine and readily available means to carry them out. Managers reporting this kind of accomplishment said they were just doing their jobs. Little was problematic—they had an assignment to tackle; they were told, or they already knew, how to go about it; they used existing budget or staff; they didn't need to gather or share much information outside of their units; and they encountered little or no opposition. Managers performing such activities don't generate innovations for their companies; they merely accomplish things faster or better than they already know how to do.

In contrast, innovative accomplishments are strikingly entrepreneurial. Moreover, they are sometimes highly problematic and generally involve acquiring and using power and influence. Innovative accomplishments included establishing a new policy or changing direction; developing new product or market opportunities; introducing new methods, processes, or technologies; and designing new structures or major reorganizations.

In this article, I first explore how managers influence their organizations to achieve goals throughout the various stages of a project's life. Next I discuss the managerial styles of the persons studied and the kinds of innovation they brought about. I look finally at the types of companies these entrepreneurial managers worked in and explore what top officers can do to foster a creative environment.

THE ROLE OF POWER IN ENTERPRISE

Because most innovative achievements cut across organizational lines and threaten to disrupt existing arrangements, enterprising managers need tools beyond those that come with the job. Innovations have implications for other functions and areas, and they require data, agreements, and resources of wider scope than routine operations demand. Even R&D managers, who are expected to produce innovations, need more information, support, and resources for major projects than those built into regular R&D functions. They too may need additional data, more money, or agreement from extrafunctional officials that the project is necessary. Only hindsight shows that an innovative project was bound to be successful.

Because of the extra resources they require, entrepreneurial managers need to go beyond the limits of their formal positions. For this, they need power. In large organizations at least, I have observed that powerlessness "corrupts."[1] That is, lack of power (the capacity to mobilize resources and people to get things done) tends to create managers who are more concerned about guarding their territories than about collaborating with others to benefit the organization. At the same time, when managers hoard potential power and don't invest it in productive action, it atrophies and eventually blocks achievements.

Furthermore, when some people have too much unused power and others too little, problems occur. To produce results, power—like money—needs to circulate. To come up with innovations, managers have to be in areas where power circulates, where it can be grabbed and invested. In this sense, organizational power is transactional: it exists as potential until someone makes a bid for it, invests it, and produces results with it.

The overarching condition required for managers to produce innovative achievements is this: they must envision an accomplishment beyond the scope of the job. They cannot alone possess the power to carry their idea out but they must be able to acquire the power they need easily. Thus, creative managers are not empowered simply by a boss or their job; on their own they seek and find the additional strength it takes to carry out major new initiatives. They are the corporate entrepreneurs.

Three commodities are necessary for accumulating productive power—information, resources, and support. Managers might find a portion of these within their purview and pour them into a project; managers with something they believe in will eagerly leverage their own staff and budget and even bootleg resources from their subordinates' budgets. But innovations usually require a manager to search for additional supplies elsewhere in the organization. Depending on how easy the organization makes it to tap sources of power and on how technical the project is, acquiring power can be the most time-consuming and difficult part of the process.

Phases of the Accomplishment

A prototypical innovation goes through three phases: project definition (acquisition and application of information to shape a manageable, salable project), coalition building (development of a network of backers who agree to provide resources and support), and action (application of the resources, information, and support to the project and mobilization of an action team). Let us examine each of these steps in more detail.

Defining the Project. Before defining a project, managers need to identify the problem. People in an organization may hold many conflicting views about the best method of reaching a goal, and discovering the basis of these conflicting perspectives (while gathering hard data) is critical to a manager's success.

In one case, information circulating freely about the original design of a part was inaccurate. The manager needed to acquire new data to prove that the problem he was about to tackle was not a manufacturing shortcoming but a design flaw. But, as often happens, some people had a stake in the popular view. Even hard-nosed engineers in our study acknowledged that, in the early stages of an entrepreneurial project, managers need political information as much as they do technical data. Without political savvy, say these engineers, no one can get a project beyond the proposal stage.

The culmination of the project definition phase comes when managers sift through the fragments of information from each source and focus on a particular target. Then, despite the fact that managers may initially have been handed a certain area as an assignment, they still have to "sell" the project that evolves. In the innovative efforts I observed, the managers' assignments involved no promises of resources or support required to do anything more than routine activities.

Furthermore, to implement the innovation, a manager has to call on the cooperation of many others besides the boss who assigned the task. Many of these others may be independent actors who are not compelled to cooperate simply because the manager has carved a project out of a general assignment. Even subordinates may not be automatically on board. If they are professionals or managers, they have a number of other tasks and the right to set some of their own priorities; and if they are in a matrix, they may be responsible to other bosses as well.

For example, in her new job as head of a manufacturing planning unit, Heidi Wilson's assignment was to improve the cost efficiency of operations and thereby boost the company's price competitiveness. Her boss told her she could spend six months "saying nothing and just observing, getting to know what's really going on." One of the first things she noticed was that the flow of goods through the company was organized in an overly complicated, time-consuming, and expensive fashion.

The assignment gave Wilson the mandate to seek information but not to carry out any particular activities. Wilson set about to gather organizational, technical, and political information in order to translate her ambiguous task into a concrete project. She followed goods through the company to determine what the process was and how it could be changed. She sought ideas and impressions from manufacturing line managers, at the same time learning the location of vested interests and where other patches of organizational quicksand lurked. She compiled data, refined her approach, and packaged and repackaged her ideas until she believed she could "prove to people that I knew more about the company than they did."

Wilson's next step was "to do a number of punchy presentations with pictures and graphs and charts." At the presentations, she got two kinds of response: "Gee, we thought there was a problem but we never saw it outlined like this before" and "Aren't there better things to worry about?" To handle the critics, she "simply came back over and over again with information, more information than anyone else had." When she had gathered the data and received the feedback, Wilson was ready to formulate a project and sell it to her boss. Ultimately, her project was approved, and it netted impressive cost savings.

Thus, although innovation may begin with an assignment, it is usually one—like Wilson's—that is couched in general statements of results with the means largely unspecified. Occasionally, managers

initiate projects themselves; however, initiation seldom occurs in a vacuum. Creative managers listen to a stream of information from superiors and peers and then identify a perceived need. In the early stages of defining a project, managers may spend more time talking with people outside their own functions than with subordinates or bosses inside.

One R&D manager said he had "hung out" with product designers while trying to get a handle on the best way to formulate a new process-development project. Another R&D manager in our survey got the idea for a new production method from a conversation about problems he had with the head of production. He then convinced his boss to let him determine whether a corrective project could be developed.

Building a Coalition.   Next, entrepreneurial managers need to pull in the resources and support to make the project work. For creative accomplishments, these power-related tools do not come through the vertical chain of command but rather from many areas of the organization.

George Putnam's innovation is typical. Putnam was an assistant department manager for product testing in a company that was about to demonstrate a product at a site that attracted a large number of potential buyers. Putnam heard through the grapevine that a decision was imminent about which model to display. The product managers were each lobbying for their own, and the marketing people also had a favorite. Putnam, who was close to the products, thought that the first-choice model had grave defects and so decided to demonstrate to the marketing staff both what the problems with the first one were and the superiority of another model.

Building on a long-term relationship with the people in corporate quality control and a good alliance with his boss, Putnam sought the tools he needed: the blessing of the vice president of engineering (his boss's boss), special materials for testing from the materials division, a budget from corporate quality control, and staff from his own units to carry out the tests. As Putnam put it, this was all done through one-on-one "horse trading"—showing each manager how much the others were chipping in. Then Putnam met informally with the key marketing staffer to learn what it would take to convince him.

As the test results emerged, Putnam took them to his peers in marketing, engineering, and quality control so they could feed them to their superiors. The accumulated support persuaded the decision makers to adopt Putnam's choice of a model; it later became a strong money-maker. In sum, Putnam had completely stepped out of his usual role to build a consensus that shaped a major policy decision.

Thus, the most successful innovations derive from situations where a number of people from a number of areas make contributions. They provide a kind of checks-and-balances system to an activity that is otherwise nonroutine and, therefore, is not subject to the usual controls. By building a coalition before extensive project activity gets under way, the manager also ensures the availability of enough support to keep momentum going and to guarantee implementation.

In one company, the process of lining up peers and stakeholders as early supporters is called "making cheerleaders"; in another, "pre-selling." Sometimes managers ask peers for "pledges" of money or staff to be collected later if higher management approves the project and provides overall resources.

After garnering peer support, usually managers next seek support at much higher levels. While we found surprisingly few instances of top management directly sponsoring or championing a project, we did find that a general blessing from the top is clearly necessary to convert potential supporters into a solid team. In one case, top officers simply showed up at a meeting where the proposal was being discussed; their presence ensured that other people couldn't use the "pocket veto" power of headquarters as an excuse to table the issue. Also, the very presence of a key executive at such a meeting is often a signal of the proposal's importance to the rest of the organization.

Enterprising managers learn who at the top-executive level has the power to affect their projects (including material resources or vital initial approval power). Then they negotiate for these executives' support, using polished formal presentations. Whereas managers can often sell the project to peers and stakeholders by appealing to these people's self-interests and assuring them they know what they're talking about, managers need to offer top executives more guarantees about both the technical and the political adequacies of projects.

Key executives tend to evaluate a proposal in terms of its salability to *their* constituencies. Sometimes entrepreneurial managers arm top executives with materials or rehearse them for their own presentations to other people (such as members of an executive committee or the board) who have to approve the project.

Most often, since many of the projects that originate at the middle of a company can be supported at that level and will not tap corporate funds, those at high levels in the organization simply provide a general expression of support. However, the attention top management confers on this activity, many of our interviewees told us, makes it possible to sell their own staffs as well as others.

But once in a while, a presentation to top-level officers results in help in obtaining supplies. Sometimes enterprising managers walk away with the promise of a large capital expenditure or assistance getting staff or space. Sometimes a promise of resources is contingent on getting others on board. "If you can raise the money, go ahead with this," is a frequent directive to an enterprising manager.

In one situation, a service manager approached his boss and his boss's boss for a budget for a college recruitment and training program that he had been supporting on his own with funds bootlegged from his staff. The top executives told him they would grant a large budget if he could get his four peers to support the project. Somewhat to their surprise, he came back with this support. He had taken his peers away from the office for three days for a round of negotiation and planning. In cases like this, top management is not so much hedging its bets as using its ability to secure peer support for what might otherwise be risky projects.

With promises of resources and support in hand, enterprising managers can go back to the immediate boss or bosses to make plans for moving ahead. Usually the bosses are simply waiting for this tangible sign of power to continue authorizing the project. But in other cases, the bosses are not fully involved and won't be sold until the manager has higher level support.

Of course, during the coalition-building phase, the network of supporters does not play a passive role; their comments, criticisms, and objectives help shape the project into one that is more likely to succeed. Another result of the coalition-building phase is, then, a set of reality checks that ensures that projects unlikely to succeed will go no farther.

Moving into Action.   The innovating manager's next step is to mobilize key players to carry out the project. Whether the players are nominal subordinates or a special project group such as a task force, managers forge them into a team. Enterprising managers bring the people involved in the project together, give them briefings and assignments, pump them up for the extra effort needed, seek their ideas and suggestions (both as a way to involve them and to further refine the project), and promise them a share of the rewards. As one manager put it, "It takes more selling than telling." In most of the innovations we observed, the manager couldn't just order subordinates to get involved. Doing something beyond routine work that involves creativity and cooperation requires the full commitment of subordinates; otherwise the project will not succeed.

During the action phase, managers have four central organizational tasks. The technical details of the project and the actual work directed toward project goals are now in the hands of the action team. Managers may contribute ideas or even get involved in hands-on experimentation, but their primary functions are still largely external and organizational, centered around maintaining the boundaries and integrity of the project.

The manager's first task is to **handle interference** or opposition that may jeopardize the project. Entrepreneurial managers encounter strikingly little overt opposition—perhaps because their success at coalition-building determines whether a project gets

started in the first place. Resistance takes a more passive form: criticism of the plan's details, foot-dragging, late responses to requests, or arguments over allocation of time and resources among projects.

Managers are sometimes surprised that critics keep so quiet up to this point. One manufacturing manager who was gearing up for production of a new item had approached many executives in other areas while making cost estimates, and these executives had appeared positive about his efforts. But later, when he began organizing the manufacturing process itself, he heard objections from these very people.

During this phase, therefore, innovative managers may have to spend as much time in meetings, both formal and one-to-one, as they did to get the project launched. Managers need to prepare thoroughly for these meetings so they can counter skepticism and objections with clear facts, persuasion, and reminders of the benefits that can accrue to managers meeting the project's objectives. In most cases, a clear presentation of facts is enough. But not always: one of our respondents, a high-level champion, had to tell an opponent to back down, that the project was going ahead anyway, and that his carping was annoying.

Whereas managers need to directly counter open challenges and criticism that might result in the flow of power or supplies being cut off, they simply keep other interference outside the boundaries of the project. In effect, the manager defines a protected area for the group's work. He or she goes outside this area to head off critics and to keep people or rules imposed by higher management from disrupting project tasks.

While the team itself is sometimes unaware of the manager's contribution, the manager—like Tom West (head of the now-famous computer-design group at Data General)—patrols the boundaries.[2] Acting as interference filters, managers in my study protected innovative projects by bending rules, transferring funds "illicitly" from one budget line to another, developing special reward or incentive systems that offered bonuses above company pay rates, and ensuring that superiors stayed away unless needed.

The second action-phase task is **maintaining momentum** and continuity. Here interference comes from internal rather than external sources. Foot-dragging or inactivity is a constant danger, especially if the creative effort adds to work loads. In our study, enterprising managers as well as team members complained continually about the tendency for routine activities to take precedence over special projects and to consume limited time.

In addition, it is easier for managers to whip up excitement over a vision at start-up than to keep the goal in people's minds when they face the tedium of the work. Thus, managers' team-building skills are essential. So the project doesn't lose momentum, managers must sustain the enthusiasm of all—from supporters to suppliers—by being persistent and keeping the team aware of supportive authorities who are clearly waiting for results.

One manager, who was involved in a full-time project to develop new and more efficient methods of producing a certain ingredient, maintained momentum by holding daily meetings with the core team, getting together often with operations managers and members of a task force he had formed, putting on weekly status reports, and making frequent presentations to top management. When foot-dragging occurs, many entrepreneurial managers pull in high-level supporters—without compromising the autonomy of the project—to get the team back on board. A letter or a visit from the big boss can remind everyone just how important the project is.

A third task of middle managers in the action phase is to engage in whatever **secondary redesign**—other changes made to support the key change—is necessary to keep the project going. For example, a manager whose team was setting up a computerized information bank held weekly team meetings to define tactics. A fallout of these meetings was a set of new awards and a fresh performance appraisal system for team members and their subordinates.

As necessary, managers introduce new arrangements to conjoin with the core tasks. When it seems that a project is bogging down—that is, when everything possible has been done and no more results are on the horizon—managers often change the structure or approach. Such alterations can cause a redoubling of effort and a renewed attack on the problem. They can also bring the company additional unplanned innovations as a side benefit from the main project.

The fourth task of the action phase, **external communication**, brings the accomplishment full circle. The project begins with gathering information; now it is important to send information out. It is vital to (as several managers put it) "manage the press" so that peers and key supporters have an up-to-date impression of the project and its success. Delivering on promises is also important. As much as possible, innovative managers meet deadlines, deliver early benefits to others, and keep supporters supplied with information. Doing so establishes the credibility of both the project and the manager, even before concrete results can be shown.

Information must be shared with the team and the coalition as well. Good managers periodically remind the team of what they stand to gain from the accomplishment, hold meetings to give feedback and to stimulate pride in the project, and make a point of congratulating each staff member individually. After all, as Steve Talbot (of my first example) said, many people gave this middle manager power because of a promise that everyone would be a hero.

A MANAGEMENT STYLE FOR INNOVATION . . .

Clearly there is a strong association between carrying out an innovative accomplishment and employing a participative-collaborative management style. The managers observed reached success by:

> Persuading more than ordering, though managers sometimes use pressure as a last resort.
>
> Building a team, which entails among other things frequent staff meetings and considerable sharing of information.
>
> Seeking inputs from others—that is, asking for ideas about users' needs, soliciting suggestions

from subordinates, welcoming peer review, and so forth.

Acknowledging others' stake or potential stake in the project—in other words, being politically sensitive.

Sharing rewards and recognition willingly.

A collaborative style is also useful when carrying out basic accomplishments; however, in such endeavors it is not required. Managers can bring off many basic accomplishments using a traditional, more autocratic style. Because they're doing what is assigned, they don't need external support; because they have all the tools to do it, they don't need to get anyone else involved (they simply direct subordinates to do what is required). But for innovative accomplishments—seeking funds, staff, or information (political as well as technical) from outside the work unit; attending long meetings and presentations; and requiring "above and beyond" effort from staff—a style that revolves around participation, collaboration, and persuasion is essential.

The participative-collaborative style also helps creative managers reduce risk because it encourages completion of the assignment. Furthermore, others' involvement serves as a check-and-balance on the project, reshaping it to make it more of a sure thing and putting pressure on people to follow through. The few projects in my study that disintegrated did so because the manager failed to build a coalition of supporters and collaborators.

... AND CORPORATE CONDITIONS THAT ENCOURAGE ENTERPRISE

Just as the manager's strategies to develop and implement innovations followed many different patterns, so also the level of enterprise managers achieved varied strongly across the five companies we studied (see Table 23.1). Managers in newer, high-technology companies have a much higher proportion of innovative accomplishments than managers in other industries. At "CHIPCO," a computer parts manufacturer, 71 percent of all the

things effective managers did were innovative; for "UTICO," a communications utility, the number is 33 percent; for "FINCO," an insurance company, it is 47 percent.

This difference in levels of innovative achievement correlates with the extent to which these companies' structures and cultures support middle managers' creativity. Companies producing the most entrepreneurs have cultures that encourage collaboration and teamwork. Moreover, they have complex structures that link people in multiple ways and help them go beyond the confines of their defined jobs to do "what needs to be done."

CHIPCO, which showed the most entrepreneurial activity of any company in our study, is a rapidly growing electronics company with abundant resources. That its culture favors independent action and team effort is communicated quickly and clearly to the newcomer. Sources of support and money are constantly shifting and, as growth occurs, managers rapidly move on to other positions. But even though people frequently express frustration about the shifting approval process, slippage of schedules, and continual entry of new players into the stage, they don't complain about lost opportunities. For one thing, because coalitions support the various projects, new project managers feel bound to honor their predecessors' financial commitments.

CHIPCO managers have broad job charters to "do the right thing" in a manner of their own choosing. Lateral relationships are more important than vertical ones. Most functions are in a matrix, and some managers have up to four "bosses." Top management expects ideas to bubble up from lower levels. Senior executives then select solutions rather than issue confining directives. In fact, people generally rely on informal face-to-face communication across units to build a consensus. Managers spend a lot of time in meetings; information flows freely, and reputation among peers—instead of formal authority or title—conveys credibility and garners support. Career mobility at CHIPCO is rapid, and people have pride in the company's success.

RADCO, the company with the strongest R&D orientation in the study, has many of

TABLE 23.1

Characteristics of the Five Companies in Order of Most to Least "Entrepreneurial"

	CHIPCO	RADCO	MEDCO	FINCO	UTICO
Percent of effective managers with entrepreneurial accomplishments	71%	69%	67%	47%	33%
Current economic trend	Steadily up	Trend up but currently down	Up	Mixed	Down
Current "change issues"	Change "normal"; constant change in product generations; proliferating staff and units.	Change "normal" in products, technologies; recent changeover to second management generation with new focus.	Reorganized about 3-4 years ago to install matrix, "normal" product technology changes.	Change a "shock"; new top management group from outside reorganizing and trying to add competitive market posture.	Change a "shock"; undergoing reorganization to install matrix and add competitive market posture while reducing staff.
Organization structure	Matrix	Matrix in some areas; product lines act as quasi-divisions.	Matrix in some areas.	Divisional; unitary hierarchy within divisions, some central services.	Functional organization; currently overlaying a matrix of regions and markets.
Decision-Making	Decentralized	Mixed	Mixed	Centralized	Centralized
Information flow	Free	Free	Moderately free	Constricted	Constricted
Communication emphasis	Horizontal	Horizontal	Horizontal	Vertical	Vertical
Culture	Clear, consistent; favors individual initiative.	Clear, though in transition from emphasis on invention to emphasis on routinization and systems.	Clear; pride in company, belief that talent will be rewarded.	Idiosyncratic; depends on boss and area.	Clear but top management would like to change it; favors security, maintanance protection.
Current "emotional" climate	Pride in company, team feeling, some "burn-out."	Uncertainty about changes.	Pride in company, team feeling.	Low trust, high uncertainty.	High certainty, confusion.
Rewards	Abundant. Include visibility, chance to do more challenging work and get bigger budget for projects.	Abundant. Include visibility, chance to do more challenging work and get bigger budget for projects.	Moderately abundant. Conventional.	Scarce. Primarily monetary.	Scarce. Promotion, salary freeze; recognition by peer grudging.

CHIPCO's qualities but bears the burden of recent changes. RADCO's once-strong culture and its image as a research institute are in flux and may be eroding. A new top management with new ways of thinking is shifting the orientation of the company, and some people express concern about the lack of clear direction and long-range planning. People's faith in RADCO's strategy of technical superiority has weakened and its traditional orientation toward innovation is giving way to a concern for routinization and production efficiency. This shift is resulting in conflict and uncertainty. Where once access to the top was easy, now the decentralized matrix structure—with fewer central services—makes it difficult.

As at CHIPCO, lateral relationships are important, though top management's presence is felt more. In the partial matrix, some managers have as many as four "bosses." A middle manager's boss or someone in higher management is likely to give general support to projects as long as peers within and across functions get on board. And peers often work decisions up the organization through their own hierarchies.

Procedures at RADCO are both informal and formal: much happens at meetings and presentations and through persuasion, plus the company's long-term employment and well-established working relationships encourage lateral communication. But managers also use task forces and steering committees. Projects often last for years, sustained by the company's image as a leader in treating employees well.

MEDCO manufactures and sells advanced medical equipment, often applying ideas developed elsewhere. Although MEDCO produces a high proportion of innovative accomplishments, it has a greater degree of central planning and routinization than either CHIPCO or RADCO. Despite headquarters' strong role, heads of functions and product managers can vary their approaches. Employers believe that MEDCO's complex matrix system allows autonomy and creates opportunities but is also time wasting because clear accountability is lacking.

Teamwork and competition coexist at MEDCO. Although top management officially encourages teamwork and the matrix produces a tendency for trades and selling to go on within the organization, interdepartmental and inter-product rivalries sometimes get in the way. Rewards, especially promotions, are available, but they often come late and even then are not always clear or consistent. Because many employees have been with MEDCO for a long time, both job mobility and job security are high. Finally, managers see the company as a leader in its approach to management and as a technological follower in all areas but one.

The last two companies in the study, FINCO (insurance) and UTICO (communications), show the lowest proportion of innovative achievements. Many of the completed projects seemed to be successful *despite* the system.

Currently FINCO has an idiosyncratic and inconsistent culture: employees don't have a clear image of the company, its style, or its direction. How managers are treated depends very much on one's boss—one-to-one relationships and private deals carry a great deal of weight. Though the atmosphere of uncertainty creates opportunities for a few, it generally limits risk taking. Moreover, reorganizations, a top-management shake-up, and shuffling of personnel have fostered insecurity and suspicion. It is difficult for managers to get commitment from their subordinates because they question the manager's tenure. Managers spend much

time and energy coping with change, reassuring subordinates, and orienting new staff instead of developing future-oriented projects. Still, because the uncertainty creates a vacuum, a few managers in powerful positions (many of whom were brought into initiate change) do benefit.

Unlike the innovation-producing companies, FINCO features vertical relationships. With little encouragement to collaborate, managers seldom make contact across functions or work in teams. Managers often see formal structures and systems as constraints rather than as supports. Rewards are scarce, and occasionally a manager will break a promise about them. Seeing the company as a follower, not a leader, the managers at FINCO sometimes make unfavorable comparisons between it and other companies in the industry. Furthermore, they resent the fact that FINCO's top management brings in so many executives from outside; they see it as an insult.

UTICO is a very good company in many ways; it is well regarded by its employees and is considered progressive for its industry. However, despite the strong need for UTICO to be more creative and thus more competitive and despite movement toward a matrix structure, UTICO's middle ranks aren't very innovative. UTICO's culture is changing—from being based on security and maintenance to being based on flexibility and competition—and the atmosphere of uncertainty frustrates achievers. Moreover, UTICO remains very centralized. Top management largely directs searches for new systems and methods through formal mechanisms whose ponderousness sometimes discourages innovation. Tight budgetary constraints make it difficult for middle managers to tap funds; carefully measured duties discourage risk takers; and a lockstep chain of command makes it dangerous for managers to by-pass their bosses.

Information flows vertically and sluggishly. Because of limited cooperation among work units, even technical data can be hard to get. Weak-spot management means that problems, not successes, get attention. Jealousy and competition over turf kill praise from peers and sometimes from bosses. Managers' image of the company is mixed: they see it as leading its type of business but behind more modern companies in rate of change.

ORGANIZATIONAL SUPPORTS FOR CREATIVITY

Examination of the differences in organization, culture, and practices in these five companies makes clear the circumstances under which enterprise can flourish. To tackle and solve tricky problems, people need both the opportunities and the incentives to reach beyond their formal jobs and combine organizational resources in new ways.[3] The following create these opportunities:

- Multiple reporting relationships and overlapping territories. These force middle managers to carve out their own ideas about appropriate action and to sell peers in neighboring areas or more than one boss.

- A free and somewhat random flow of information. Data flow of this kind prods executives to find ideas in unexpected places and pushes them to combine fragments of information.

- Many centers of power with some budgetary flexibility. If such centers are easily accessible to middle managers, they will be encouraged to make proposals and acquire resources.

- A high proportion of managers in loosely defined positions or with ambiguous assignments. Those without subordinates or line responsibilities who are told to "solve problems" must argue for a budget or develop their own constituency.

- Frequent and smooth cross-functional contact, a tradition of working in teams and sharing credit widely, and emphasis on lateral rather than vertical relationships as a source of resources, information, and support. These circumstances require managers to get peer support for their projects before top officers approve.

- A reward system that emphasizes investment in people and projects rather than payment for past services. Such a system encourages executives to move into challenging jobs, gives them budgets to tackle projects, and rewards them after their accomplishments with the chance to take on even bigger projects in the future.

Some of these conditions seem to go hand in hand with new companies in not-yet-mature markets. But top decision makers in older, traditional companies can design these conditions into their organizations. They would be wise to do so because, if empowered, innovative middle managers can be one of America's most potent weapons in its battle against foreign competition.

NOTES

1. See my book *Men and Women of the Corporation* (New York: Basic Books, 1977); also see my article, "Power Failure in Management Circuits," *Harvard Business Review*, July–August 1979, p. 65.

2. Tracy Kidder, *The Soul of a New Machine* (Boston: Little, Brown, 1981).

3. My findings about conditions stimulating managerial innovations are generally consistent with those on technical (R&D) innovation. See James Utterback, "Innovation in Industry," *Science*, February 1974, pp. 620–26; John Kimberly, "Managerial Innovation," *Handbook of Organizational Design*, ed. W.H. Starbuck (New York: Oxford, 1981); and Goodmeasure, Inc., "99 Propositions on Innovation from the Research Literature," *Stimulating Innovation in Middle Management* (Cambridge, Mass., 1982).

24

Beyond the Charismatic Leader: *Leadership and Organizational Change*

DAVID A. NADLER AND MICHAEL L. TUSHMAN

Like never before, discontinuous organization change is an important determinant of organization adaptation. Responding to regulatory, economic, competitive and/or technological shifts through more efficiently pushing the same organization systems and processes just does not work.[1] Rather, organizations may need to manage through periods of both incremental as well as revolutionary change.[2] Further, given the intensity of global competition in more and more industries, these organizational transformations need to be initiated and implemented rapidly. Speed seems to count.[3] These trends put a premium on executive leadership and the management of system-wide organization change.

There is a growing knowledge base about large-scale organization change.[4] This literature is quite consistent on at least one aspect of effective system-wide change—namely, executive leadership matters. The executive is a critical actor in the drama of organization change.[5] Consider the following examples:

• At Fuji-Xerox, Yotaro Kobayashi's response to declining market share, lack of new products, and increasing customer complaints was to initiate widespread organization change. Most fundamentally, Kobayashi's vision was to change the way Fuji-Xerox conducted its business. Kobayashi and his team initiated the "New Xerox Movement" through Total Quality Control. The core values of quality, problem solving, teamwork, and customer emphasis were espoused and acted upon by Kobayashi and his team. Further, the executive team at Fuji instituted a dense infrastructure of objectives, measures, rewards, tools, education and slogans all in service of TQC and the "New Xerox." New heroes were created. Individuals and teams were publicly celebrated to reinforce to the system those behaviors that reflected the best of the new Fuji-Xerox. Kobayashi continually reinforced, celebrated, and communicated his TQC vision. Between 1976–1980, Fuji-Xerox gained back its market share, developed an impressive set of new products, and won the Demming prize.[6]

• Much of this Fuji-Xerox learning was transferred to corporate Xerox and further enhanced by Dave Kearns and his executive team. Beginning in 1983, Kearns clearly expressed his "Leadership Through Quality" vision for the corporation. Kearns established a Quality Task Force and Quality Office with respected Xerox executives. This broad executive base developed the architecture of Leadership Through Quality. This effort included quality principles, tools, education, required leadership actions, rewards, and feedback mechanisms. This attempt to transform the entire corporation was initiated at the top and diffused throughout the firm through overlapping teams. These teams were pushed by Kearns and his team to achieve extraordinary gains. While not completed, this transformation has helped Xerox regain lost market share and improve product development efforts.[7]

Copyright © 1990 by The Regents of the University of California. Reprinted from the *California Management Review*, Vol. 32, No. 2. By permission of The Regents.

David Nadler is President and Founder of the Delta Consulting Group, Inc. ***Michael Tushman*** is Professor of Management and Organizations at Columbia University's Graduate School of Business.

• At General Electric, Jack Welch's vision of a lean, aggressive organization with all the benefits of size but the agility of small firms is being driven by a set of interrelated actions. For example, the "work-out" effort is a corporate-wide endeavor, spearheaded by Welch, to get the bureaucracy out of a large-old organization and, in turn, to liberate GE employees to be their best. This effort is more than Welch. Welch's vision is being implemented by a senior task force which has initiated workout efforts in Welch's own top team as well as in each GE business area. These efforts consist of training, problem solving, measures, rewards, feedback procedures, and outside expertise. Similarly, sweeping changes at SAS under Carlzon, at ICI under Harvey-Jones, by Anderson at NCR, and at Honda each emphasize the importance of visionary leadership along with executive teams, systems, structures and processes to transfer an individual's vision of the future into organizational reality.[8]

On the other hand, there are many examples of visionary executives who are unable to translate their vision into organization action. For example, Don Burr's vision at People Express not only to "make a better world" but also to grow rapidly and expand to capture the business traveller was not coupled with requisite changes in organization infrastructure, procedures, and/or roles. Further, Burr was unable to build a cohesive senior team to help execute his compelling vision. This switch in vision, without a committed senior team and associated structure and systems, led to the rapid demise of People Express.

Vision and/or charisma is not enough to sustain large-system change. While a necessary condition in the management of discontinuous change, we must build a model of leadership that goes beyond the inspired individual; a model that takes into account the complexities of system-wide change in large, diverse, geographically complex organizations. We attempt to develop a framework for the extension of charismatic leadership by building on the growing leadership literature,[9] the literature on organization evolution,[10] and our intensive consulting work with executives attempting major organization change.[11]

ORGANIZATIONAL CHANGE AND RE-ORGANIZATION

Organizations go through change all the time. However, the nature, scope, and intensity of organizational changes vary considerably. Different kinds of organizational changes will require very different kinds of leadership behavior in initiating, energizing, and implementing the change. Organization changes vary along the following dimensions:

• *Strategic and Incremental Changes.* Some changes in organizations, while significant, only affect selected components of the organization. The fundamental aim of such change is to enhance the effectiveness of the organization, but within the general framework of the strategy, mode of organizing, and values that already are in place. Such changes are called *incremental changes*. Incremental changes happen all the time in organizations, and they need not be small. Such things as changes in organization structure, the introduction of new technology, and significant modifications of personnel practices are all large and significant changes, but ones which usually occur within the existing definition and frame of reference of the organization. Other changes have an impact on the whole system of the organization and fundamentally redefine what the organization is or change its basic framework, including strategy, structure, people, processes, and (in some cases) core values. These changes are called *strategic organizational changes*. The Fuji-Xerox, People Express, ICI, and SAS cases are examples of system-wide organization change.

• *Reactive and Anticipatory Changes.* Many organizational changes are made in direct response to some external event. These changes, which are forced upon the organization, are called *reactive*. The Xerox, SAS and ICI transformations were all initiated in response to organization performance crisis. At other times, strategic organizational change is initiated not because of the need to respond to a contemporaneous event, but rather because senior management believes that change in anticipation of events still to come will provide competitive advantage. These changes are called *anticipatory*. The GE and People Express cases as well as more recent system-wide changes at ALCOA and Cray Research are examples of system-wide change initiated in anticipation of environmental change.

If these two dimensions are combined, a basic typology of different changes can be described (see Figure 24.1).

Change which is incremental and anticipatory is called *tuning*. These changes are not system-wide redefinitions, but rather modifications of specific components, and they are initiated in anticipation of future events. Incremental change which is initiated reactively is called *adaptation*. Strategic change initiated in anticipation of future events is called *reorientation*, and change which is prompted by immediate demands is called *re-creation*.[12]

Research on patterns of organizational life and death across several industries has provided insight into the patterns of strategic organizational change.[13] Some of the key findings are as follows:

• *Strategic organization changes are necessary*. These changes appear to be environmentally driven. Various factors—be they competitive, technological, or regulatory—drive the organization (either reactively or in anticipation) to make system-wide changes. While strategic organization change does not guarantee success, those organizations that fail to change, generally fail to survive.

Discontinuous environmental change seems to require discontinuous organization change.

• *Re-creations are riskier*. Re-creations are riskier endeavors than reorientations if only because they are initiated under crisis conditions and under sharp time constraints. Further, re-creations almost always involve a change in core values. As core values are most resistant to change, re-creations always trigger substantial individual resistance to change and heightened political behavior. Re-creations that do succeed usually involve changes in the senior leadership of the firm, frequently involving replacement from the outside. For example, the reactive system-wide changes at U.S. Steel, Chrysler, and Singer were all initiated by new senior teams.

• *Re-orientations are associated more with success*. Re-orientations have the luxury of time to shape the change, build coalitions, and empower individuals to be effective in the new organization. Further, re-orientations give senior managers time to prune and shape core values in service of the revised strategy, structure, and processes. For example, the proactive strategic changes at Cray Research, ALCOA, and GE each involved system-wide change as well as the shaping of core values ahead of the competition and from a position of strength.

Re-orientations are, however, risky. When sweeping changes are initiated in advance of precipitating external events, success is contingent on making appropriate strategic bets. As re-orientations are initiated ahead of the competition and in advance of environmental shifts, they require visionary executives. Unfortunately, in real time, it is unclear who will be known as visionary executives (e.g., Welch, Iacocca, Rollwagen at Cray Research) and who will be known as failures (e.g., Don Burr at People Express, or Larry Goshorn at General Automation). In turbulent environments, not to make strategic bets is associated with failure. Not all bets will pay off, however. The advantages of re-orientations derive from the extra implementation time and from the opportunity to learn from and adapt to mistakes.[14]

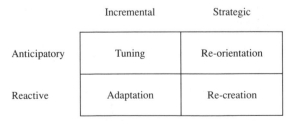

	Incremental	Strategic
Anticipatory	Tuning	Re-orientation
Reactive	Adaptation	Re-creation

Figure 24.1 Types of organizational changes.

As with re-creations, executive leadership is crucial in initiating and implementing strategic re-orientations. The majority of successful re-orientations involve change in the CEO and substantial executive team change. Those most successful firms, however, have executive teams that are relatively stable yet are still capable of initiating several re-orientations (e.g., Ken Olsen at DEC and An Wang at Wang).

There are, then, quite fundamentally different kinds of organizational changes. The role of executive leadership varies considerably for these different types of organization changes. Incremental change typically can be managed by the existing management structures and processes of the organization, sometimes in conjunction with special transition structures.[15] In these situations, a variety of leadership styles may be appropriate, depending upon how the organization is normally managed and led. In strategic changes, however, the management process and structure itself is the subject of change; therefore, it cannot be relied upon to manage the change. In addition, the organization's definition of effective leadership may also be changing as a consequence of the re-orientation or re-creation. In these situations, leadership becomes a very critical element of change management.

This article focuses on the role of executive leadership in strategic organization change, and in particular, the role of leadership in re-orientations. Given organization and individual inertia, re-orientations can not be initiated or implemented without sustained action by the organization's leadership. Indeed, re-orientations are frequently driven by new leadership, often brought in from outside the organization.[16] A key challenge for executives facing turbulent environments, then, is to learn how to effectively initiate, lead, and manage re-orientations. Leadership of strategic re-orientations requires not only charisma, but also substantial instrumental skills in building executive teams, roles, and systems in support of the change, as well as institutional skills in diffusing leadership throughout the organization.

THE CHARISMATIC LEADER

While the subject of leadership has received much attention over the years, the more specific issue of leadership during periods of change has only recently attracted serious attention.[17] What emerges from various discussions of leadership and organizational change is a picture of the special kind of leadership that appears to be critical during times of strategic organizational change. While various words have been used to portray this type of leadership, we prefer the label "charismatic" leader. It refers to a special quality that enables the leader to mobilize and sustain activity within an organization through specific personal actions combined with perceived personal characteristics.

The concept of the charismatic leader is not the popular version of the great speech maker or television personality. Rather, a model has emerged from recent work aimed at identifying the nature and determinants of a particular type of leadership that successfully brings about changes in an individual's values, goals, needs, or aspirations. Research on charismatic leadership has identified this type of leadership as observable, definable, and having clear behavioral characteristics.[18] We have attempted to develop a first cut description of the leader in terms of patterns of behavior that he/she seems to exhibit. The resulting approach is outlined in Figure 24.2, which lists three major types of behavior that characterize these leaders and some illustrative kinds of actions.

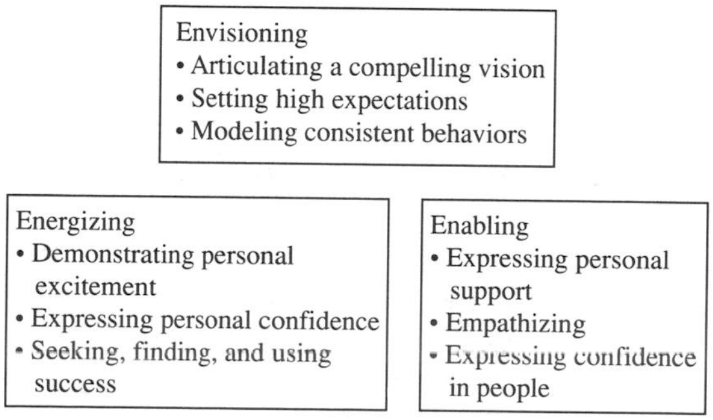

Envisioning
• Articulating a compelling vision
• Setting high expectations
• Modeling consistent behaviors

Energizing
• Demonstrating personal excitement
• Expressing personal confidence
• Seeking, finding, and using success

Enabling
• Expressing personal support
• Empathizing
• Expressing confidence in people

Figure 24.2 The charismatic leader.

The first component of charismatic leadership is *envisioning*. This involves the creation of a picture of the future, or of a desired future state with which people can identify and which can generate excitement. By creating vision, the leader provides a vehicle for people to develop commitment, a common goal around which people can rally, and a way for people to feel successful. Envisioning is accomplished through a range of different actions. Clearly, the simplest form is through articulation of a compelling vision in clear and dramatic terms. The vision needs to be challenging, meaningful, and worthy of pursuit, but it also needs to be credible. People must believe that it is possible to succeed in the pursuit of the vision. Vision is also communicated in other ways, such as through expectations that the leader expresses and through the leader personally demonstrating behaviors and activities that symbolize and further that vision.

The second component is *energizing*. Here the role of the leader is the direct generation of energy—motivation to act—among members of the organization. How is this done? Different leaders engage in energizing in different ways, but some of the most common include demonstration of their own personal excitement and energy, combined with leveraging that excitement through direct personal contact with large numbers of people in the organization. They express confidence in their own ability to succeed. They find, and use, successes to celebrate progress towards the vision.

The third component is *enabling*. The leader psychologically helps people act or perform in the face of challenging goals. Assuming that individuals are directed through a vision and motivated by the creation of energy, they then may need emotional assistance in accomplishing their tasks. This enabling is achieved in several ways. Charismatic leaders demonstrate empathy—the ability to listen, understand, and share the feelings of those in the organization. They express support for individuals. Perhaps most importantly, the charismatic leader tends to express his/her confidence in people's ability to perform effectively and to meet challenges.

Yotaro Kobayashi at Fuji-Xerox and Paul O'Neil at ALCOA each exhibit the characteristics of charismatic leaders. In Kobayashi's transformation at Fuji, he was constantly espousing his New Xerox Movement vision for Fuji. Kobayashi set high standards for his firm (e.g., the 3500 model and the Demming Prize), for himself, and for his team. Beyond espousing this vision for Fuji, Kobayashi provided resources, training, and personal coaching to support his colleagues' efforts in the transformation at Fuji. Similarly, Paul O'Neil has espoused a clear vision for ALCOA anchored on quality, safety, and innovation. O'Neil has made his vision compelling and central to the firm, has set high expectations for this top team and for individuals throughout ALCOA and provides continuous support and energy for his vision through meetings, task forces, video tapes, and extensive personal contact.

Assuming that leaders act in these ways, what functions are they performing that help bring about change? First, they provide a psychological focal point for the energies, hopes, and aspirations of people in the organization. Second, they serve as powerful role models whose behaviors, actions and personal energy demonstrate the desired behaviors expected throughout the firm. The behaviors of charismatic leaders provide a standard to which others can aspire. Through their personal effectiveness and attractiveness they build a very personal and intimate bond between themselves and the organization. Thus, they can become a source of sustained energy; a figure whose high standards others can identify with and emulate.

Limitations of the Charismatic Leader

Even if one were able to do all of the things involved in being a charismatic leader, it might still not be enough. In fact, our observations suggest that there are a number of inherent limitations to the effectiveness of charismatic leaders, many stemming from risks associated with leadership which revolves around a single individual. Some of the key potential problems are:

• *Unrealistic Expectations*. In creating a vision and getting people energized, the leader may create expectations that are unrealistic or unattainable. These can backfire if the leader cannot live up to the expectations that are created.

• *Dependency and Counterdependency.* A strong, visible, and energetic leader may spur different psychological response. Some individuals may become overly dependent upon the leader, and in some cases whole organizations become dependent. Everyone else stops initiating actions and waits for the leader to provide direction; individuals may become passive or reactive. On the other extreme, others may be uncomfortable with strong personal presence and spend time and energy demonstrating how the leader is wrong—how the emperor has no clothes.

• *Reluctance to Disagree with the Leader.* The charismatic leader's approval or disapproval becomes an important commodity. In the presence of a strong leader, people may become hesitant to disagree or come into conflict with the leader. This may, in turn, lead to stifling conformity.

• *Need for Continuing Magic.* The charismatic leader may become trapped by the expectation that the magic often associated with charisma will continue unabated. This may cause the leader to act in ways that are not functional, or (if the magic is not produced) it may cause a crisis of leadership credibility.

• *Potential Feelings of Betrayal.* When and if things do not work out as the leader has envisioned, the potential exists for individuals to feel betrayed by their leader. They may become frustrated and angry, with some of that anger directed at the individual who created the expectations that have been betrayed.

• *Disenfranchisement of Next Levels of Management.* A consequence of the strong charismatic leader is that the next levels of management can easily become disenfranchised. They lose their ability to lead because no direction, vision, exhortation, reward, or punishment is meaningful unless it comes directly from the leader. The charismatic leader thus may end up underleveraging his or her management and/or creating passive/dependent direct reports.

• *Limitations of Range of the Individual Leader.* When the leadership process is built around an individual, management's ability to deal with various issues is limited by the time, energy, expertise, and interest of that individual. This is particularly problematic during periods of change when different types of issues demand different types of competencies (e.g., markets, technologies, products, finance) which a single individual may not possess. Different types of strategic changes make different managerial demands and call for different personal characteristics. There may be limits to the number of strategic changes that one individual can lead over the life of an organization.

In light of these risks, it appears that the charismatic leader is a necessary component—but not a sufficient component—of the organizational leadership required for effective organizational reorganization. There is a need to move beyond the charismatic leader.

INSTRUMENTAL LEADERSHIP

Effective leaders of change need to be more than just charismatic. Effective re-orientations seem to be characterized by the presence of another type of leadership behavior which focuses not on the excitement of individuals and changing their goals, needs or aspirations, but on making sure that individuals in the senior team and throughout the organization behave in ways needed for change to occur. An important leadership role is to build competent teams, clarify required behaviors, built in measurement, and administer rewards and punishments so that individuals perceive that behavior consistent with the change is central for them in achieving their own goals.[19] We will call this type of leadership *instrumental leadership*, since it focuses on the management of teams, structures, and managerial processes to create individual instrumentalities. The basis of this approach is in expectancy theories of motivation, which propose that individuals will perform those behaviors that they perceive as instrumental for acquiring valued outcomes.[20] Leadership, in this context, involves managing environments to create conditions that motivate desired behavior.[21]

In practice, instrumental leadership of change involves three elements of behavior (see Figure 24.3). The first is *structuring*. The leader invests time in building teams that have the required competence to execute and implement the re-orientation[22] and in creating structures that make it clear what types of behavior are required throughout the organization. This may involve setting goals, establishing standards, and defining roles and responsibilities. Re-orientations seem to require detailed planning about what people will need to do and how they will be required to act during different phases of the change. The second element of instrumental leadership is *controlling*. This involves the creation of systems and processes to measure, monitor, and assess both behavior and results and to administer corrective action.[23] The third element is *rewarding*, which includes the administration of both rewards and punishments contingent upon the degree to which behavior is consistent with the requirements of the change.

Instrumental leadership focuses on the challenge of shaping consistent behaviors in support of the re-orientation. The charismatic leader excites individuals, shapes their aspirations, and directs their energy. In practice, however, this is not enough to sustain patterns of desired behavior. Subordinates and colleagues may be committed to the vision, but over time other forces may influence their behavior, particularly when they are not in direct personal contact with the leader. This is particularly relevant during periods of change when the formal organization and the informal social system may lag behind the leader and communicate outdated messages or reward traditional behavior. Instrumental leadership is needed to ensure compliance over time consistent with the commitment generated by charismatic leadership.

At Xerox, for example, David Kearns used instrumental leadership to further enliven his Leadership Through Quality efforts.[24] Beyond his own sustained behaviors in support of the Leadership Through Quality effort, Kearns and his Quality Office developed comprehensive set of roles, processes, teams, and feedback and audit mechanisms for getting customer input and continuous improvement into everyday problem solving throughout Xerox. Individuals and teams across the corporation were evaluated on their ability to continuously meet customer requirements. These data were used in making pay, promotion, and career decisions.

The Role of Mundane Behaviors

Typical descriptions of both charismatic and instrumental leaders tend to focus on significant events, critical incidents, and grand gestures. Our vision of the change manager is frequently exemplified by the key speech or public event that is a potential watershed event. While these are important arenas for leadership, leading large-system change also requires sustained attention to the myriad of details that make up organizational life. The accumulation of less dramatic, day-to-day activities and mundane behaviors serves as a powerful determinant of behavior.[25] Through relatively unobtrusive acts, through sustained attention to detail, managers can directly shape perceptions and culture in support of the change effort. Examples of mundane behavior that when taken together can have a great impact include:

- allocation of time; calendar management
- asking questions, following up
- shaping of physical settings
- public statements
- setting agendas of events or meetings
- use of events such as lunches, meetings, to push the change effort

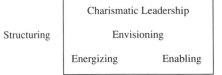

Instrumental Leadership

Structuring   Charismatic Leadership   Controlling
               Envisioning
               Energizing   Enabling

Rewarding

Figure 24.3   Instrumental leadership.

- summarization—post hoc interpretation of what occurred
- creating heroes
- use of humor, stories, and myths
- small symbolic actions, including rewards and punishments

In each of these ways, leaders can use daily activities to emphasize important issues, identify desirable behavior, and help create patterns and meaning out of the various transactions that make up organizational life.

The Complementarity of Leadership Approaches

It appears that effective organizational re-orientation requires both charismatic and instrumental leadership. Charismatic leadership is needed to generate energy, create commitment, and direct individuals towards new objectives, values or aspirations. Instrumental leadership is required to ensure that people really do act in a manner consistent with their new goals. Either one alone is insufficient for the achievement of change.

The complementarity of leadership approaches and the necessity for both creates a dilemma.[26] Success in implementing these dual approaches is associated with the personal style, characteristics, needs, and skills of the executive. An individual who is adept at one approach may have difficulty executing the other. For example, charismatic leaders may have problems with tasks involved in achieving control. Many charismatic leaders are motivated by a strong desire to receive positive feedback from those around them.[27] They may therefore have problems delivering unpleasant messages, dealing with performance problems, or creating situations that could attract negative feelings.[28]

Only exceptional individuals can handle the behavioral requirements of both charismatic and instrumental leadership styles. While such individuals exist, an alternative may be to involve others in leadership roles, thus complementing the strengths and weaknesses of one individual leader.[29] For example,

in the early days at Honda, it took the steadying, systems-oriented hand of Takeo Fujisawa to balance the fanatic, impatient, visionary energy of Soichiro Honda. Similarly, at Data General, it took Alsing and Rasala's social, team, and organization skills to balance and make more humane Tom West's vision and standards for the Eclipse team.[30] Without these complementary organization and systems skills, Don Burr was unable to execute his proactive system-wide changes at People Express.

The limitations of the individual leader pose a significant challenge. Charismatic leadership has a broad reach. It can influence many people, but is limited by the frequency and intensity of contact with the individual leader. Instrumental leadership is also limited by the degree to which the individual leader can structure, observe, measure and reward behavior. These limitations present significant problems for achieving re-orientations. One implication is that structural extensions of leadership should be created in the process of managing re-orientations.[31] A second implication is that human extensions of leadership need to be created to broaden the scope and impact of leader actions. This leads to a third aspect of leadership and change—the extension of leadership beyond the individual leader, or the creation of institutionalized leadership throughout the organization.

INSTITUTIONALIZING THE LEADERSHIP OF CHANGE

Given the limitations of the individual charismatic leader, the challenge is to broaden the range of individuals who can perform the critical leadership functions during periods of significant organizational change. There are three potential leverage points for the extension of leadership—the senior team, broader senior management, and the development of leadership throughout the organization (see Figure 24.4).

Leveraging the Senior Team
The group of individuals who report directly to the individual leader—the executive or senior team—

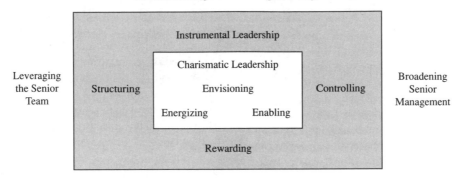

Figure 24.4 Institutionalized leadership.

is the first logical place to look for opportunities to extend and institutionalize leadership. Development of an effective, visible, and dynamic senior team can be a major step in getting around the problems and limitations of the individual leader.[32] Examples of such executive teams include the Management Committee established at Corning by Jamie Houghton or Bob Allen's Executive Committee at AT&T. Several actions appear to be important in enhancing the effectiveness of the senior team.

• *Visible Empowerment of the Team.* A first step is the visible empowerment of the team, or "anointing" the team as extensions of the individual leader. There are two different aspects to this empowerment: objective and symbolic. Objective empowerment involves providing team members with the autonomy and resources to serve effectively. Symbolic empowerment involves communicating messages (through information, symbols, and mundane behaviors) to show the organization that these individuals are indeed extensions of the leader, and ultimately key components of the leadership. Symbolic empowerment can be done through the use of titles, the designation of organizational structures, and the visible presence of individuals in ceremonial roles.

• *Individual Development of Team Members.* Empowerment will fail if the individuals on the team are not capable of executing their revised leadership roles. A major problem in re-orientations is that the members of the senior team frequently are the product of the very systems, structures, and values that the re-orientation seeks to change. Participating in the change, and more importantly, leading it, may require a significant switching of cognitive gears.[33] Re-orientations demand that senior team members think very differently about the business and about managing. This need for personal change at the most senior level has implications for the selection of senior team members (see below). It also may mean that part of the individual leader's role is to help coach, guide, and support individuals in developing their own leadership capabilities. Each individual need not (and should not) be a "clone" of the individual leader; but each should be able to initiate credible leadership actions in a manner consistent with their own personal styles. Ultimately, it also puts a demand on the leader to deal with those who will not or can not make the personal changes required for helping lead the re-orientation.

• *Composition of the Senior Team.* The need for the senior team to implement change may mean that the composition of that team may have to be altered. Different skills, capabilities, styles, and value orientations may be needed to both lead the changes as well as to manage in the reconfigured organization.[34] In fact, most successful re-orientations seem to involve some significant changes in the make-up of the senior team. This may require outplacement of people as well as importing new people, either from outside the organization, or from outside the coalition that has traditionally led the organization.[35]

• *The Inducement of Strategic Anticipation.* A critical issue in executing re-orientations is strategic anticipation. By definition, a re-orientation is a strategic organizational change that is initiated in anticipation of significant external events. Re-orientation occurs because the organization's leadership perceives competitive advantage from initiating change earlier rather than later. The question is, who is responsible for thinking about and anticipating external events, and ultimately deciding that re-orientation is necessary? In some cases, the individual leader does this, but the task is enormous. This is where the senior team can be helpful, because as a group it can scan a larger number of events and potentially be more creative in analyzing the environment and the process of anticipation.

Companies that are successful anticipators create conditions in which anticipation is more likely to occur. They invest in activities that foster anticipation, such as environmental scanning, experiments or probes inside the organization (frequently on the periphery), and frequent contacts with the outside. The senior team has a major role in initiating, sponsoring, and leveraging these activities.[36]

• *The Senior Team as a Learning System.* For a senior team to benefit from its involvement in leading change, it must become an effective system for learning about the business, the nature of change, and the task of managing change. The challenge is to both bond the team together, while avoiding insularity. One of the costs of such team structures is that they become isolated from the rest of the organization, they develop patterns of dysfunctional conformity, avoid conflict, and over time develop patterns of learned incompetence. These group processes diminish the team's capacity for effective strategic anticipation, and decreases the team's ability to provide effective leadership of the re-orientation.[37]

There are several ways to enhance a senior team's ability to learn over time. One approach is to work to keep the team an open system, receptive to outside ideas and information. This can be accomplished by creating a constant stream of events that expose people to new ideas and/or situations. For example, creating simulations, using critical incident techniques, creating near histories, are all ways of exposing senior teams to novel situations and sharpening problem-solving skills.[38] Similarly, senior teams can open themselves to new ideas via speakers or visitors brought in to meet with the team, visits by the team to other organizations, frequent contact with customers, and planned informal data collection through personal contact (breakfasts, focus groups, etc.) throughout the organization. A second approach involves the shaping and management of the internal group process of the team itself. This involves working on effective group leadership, building effective team member skills, creating meeting management discipline, acquiring group problem-solving and information-processing skills, and ultimately creating norms that promote effective learning, innovation, and problem solving.[39]

David Kearns at Xerox and Paul O'Neil at ALCOA made substantial use of senior teams in implementing their quality-oriented organization transformations. Both executives appointed senior quality task forces composed of highly respected senior executives. These task forces were charged with developing the corporate-wide architecture of the change effort. To sharpen their change and quality skills these executives made trips to Japan and to other experienced organizations, and were involved in extensive education and problem-solving efforts in their task forces and within their own divisions. These task forces put substance and enhanced energy into the CEO's broad vision. These executives were, in turn, role models and champions of the change efforts in their own sectors.

As a final note, it is important to remember that frequently there are significant obstacles in developing effective senior teams to lead re-orientations. The issues of skills and selection have been mentioned. Equally important is the question of power and succession. A team is most successful when there is a perception of common·fate. *Individuals have to believe that the success of the team will, in the long run, be more salient to them than their individual short-run success.* In many situations, this can be accomplished through appropriate structures, objectives, and incentives. But these actions may fail when there are pending (or anticipated) decisions to be made concerning senior management succession. In these situations, the quality of collaboration tends to deteriorate significantly, and effective team leadership of change becomes problematic. The individual leader must manage the timing and process of succession in relation to the requirements for team leadership, so that conflicting (and mutually exclusive) incentives are not created by the situation.[40]

Broadening Senior Management

A second step in moving beyond individual leadership of change is the further extension of the leadership beyond the executive or senior team to include a broader set of individuals who make up the senior management of the organization. This would include individuals one or two levels down from the executive team. At Corning, the establishment of two groups—the Corporate Policy Group (approximately the top 35) and the Corporate Management Group (about the top 120)—are examples of mechanisms used by Houghton to broaden the definition of senior management. This set of individuals is in fact the senior operating management of most sizeable organizations and is looked upon as senior management by the majority of employees. In many cases (and particularly during times of change) they do not feel like senior management, and thus they are not positioned to lead the change. They feel like participants (at best) and victims (at worst). This group can be particularly problematic since they may be more embedded in the current system of organizing and managing than some of the senior team. They may be less prepared to change, they frequently have molded themselves to fit the current organizational style, and they may feel disenfranchised by the very act of developing a strong executive team, particularly if that team has been assembled by bringing in people from outside of the organization.

The task is to make this group feel like senior management, to get them signed up for the change, and to motivate and enable them to work as an extension of the senior team. Many of the implications are similar to those mentioned above in relation to the top team; however, there are special problems of size and lack of proximity to the individual charismatic leader. Part of the answer is to get the senior team to take responsibility for developing their own teams as leaders of change. Other specific actions may include:

- *Rites of Passage.* Creating symbolic events that help these individuals to feel more a part of senior management.

- *Senior Groups.* Creating structures (councils, boards, committees, conferences) to maintain contact with this group and reinforce their sense of participation as members of senior management.

- *Participation in Planning Change.* Involving these people in the early diagnosing of the need to change and the planning of change strategies associated with the re-orientation. This is particularly useful in getting them to feel more like owners, rather than victims of the change.

- *Intensive Communication.* Maintaining a constant stream of open communication to and from this group. It is the lack of information and perspective that psychologically disenfranchises these individuals.

Developing Leadership in the Organization

A third arena for enhancing the leadership of re-organizations is through organizational structures, systems, and process for leadership development consistent with the re-orientation. Frequently leadership development efforts lag behind the re-orientation. The management development system of many organizations often works effectively to create managers who will fit well with the organizational environment that the leadership seeks to abandon. There needs to be a strategic and anticipatory thinking about the leadership development process, including the following:

• *Definition of Managerial Competence.* A first step is determining the skills, capabilities, and capacities needed to manage and lead effectively in the re-orientation and post re-orientation period. Factors that have contributed to managerial success in the past may be the seeds of failure in the future.

• *Sourcing Managerial Talent.* Re-orientations may require that the organization identify significantly different sources for acquiring leaders or potential leaders. Senior managers should be involved in recruiting the hiring. Because of the lead time involved, managerial sourcing has to be approached as a long-term (five to ten years) task.

• *Socialization.* As individuals move into the organization and into positions of leadership, deliberate actions must be taken to teach them how the organization's social system works. During periods of re-orientation, the socialization process ought to lead rather than lag behind the change.[41]

• *Management Education.* Re-orientation may require managers and leaders to use or develop new skills, competencies, or knowledge. This creates a demand for effective management education. Research indicates that the impact of passive internal management education on the development of effective leaders may be minimal when compared with more action-oriented educational experiences. The use of educational events to expose people to external settings or ideas (through out-of-company education) and to socialize individuals through action-oriented executive education may be more useful than attempts to teach people to be effective leaders and managers.[42]

• *Career Management.* Research and experience indicate that the most potent factor in the development of effective leaders is the nature of their job experiences.[43] The challenge is to ensure that middle and lower level managers get a wide range of experiences over time. Preparing people to lead re-orientations may require a greater emphasis on the development of generalists through cross-functional, divisional, and/or multinational career experiences.[44] Diverse career experiences help individuals develop a broad communication network and a range of experiences and competences all of which are vital in managing large-system change. This approach to careers implies the sharing of the burden of career management between both the organization and the employee as well as the deliberate strategy of balancing current contribution with investment for the future when placing people in job assignments.[45]

• *Seeding Talent.* Developing leadership for change may also require deliberate leveraging of available talent. This implies thoughtful placement of individuals leaders in different situations and parts of the organization, the use of transfers, and the strategic placement of high-potential leaders.[46]

Perhaps the most ambitious and most well-documented effort at developing leadership throughout the organization is Welch's actions at GE. Welch has used GE's Management Development Institute at Crotonville as an important lever in the transformation of GE. Based on Welch's vision of a lean, competitive, agile organization with businesses leading in their respective markets, Crotonville has been used as a staging area for the revolution at GE. With Welch's active involvement, Crotonville's curriculum has moved from a short-term cognitive orientation towards longer-term problem solving and organization change. The curriculum has been developed to shape experiences and sharpen skills over the course of an individual's career in service of developing leaders to fit into the new GE.[47]

SUMMARY

In a world characterized by global competition, deregulation, sharp technological change, and political turmoil, discontinuous organization change seems to be a determinant of organization adaptation. Those firms that can initiate and implement discontinuous organization change more rapidly and/or prior to the competition have a competitive advantage. While not all change will be successful, inertia or incremental change in the face of altered competitive arenas is a recipe for failure.

Executive leadership is the critical factor in the initiation and implementation of large-system organization change. This article has developed an approach to the leadership of discontinuous organization change with particular reference to re-orientations—discontinuous change initiated in advance of competitive threat and/or performance crisis. Where incremental change can be delegated, strategic change must be driven by senior management. Charismatic leadership is a vital aspect of managing large-system change. Charismatic leaders provide vision, direction, and energy. Thus the successes of O'Neil at ALCOA, Welch at GE, Kearns at Xerox, and Rollwagen and Cray are partly a function of committed, enthusiastic, and passionate individual executives.

Charisma is not, however, enough to effect large-system change. Charismatic leadership must be bolstered by instrumental leadership through attention to detail on roles, responsibilities, structures, and rewards. Further, as many organizations are too large and complex for any one executive and/or senior team to directly manage, responsibility for large-system change must be institutionalized throughout the management system. The leadership of strategic organization change must be pushed throughout the organization to maximize the probability that managers at all levels own and are involved in executing the change efforts and see the concrete benefits of making the change effort work. O'Neil, Welch, Kearns, and Rollwagen are important catalysts in their organizations. Their successes to date are, however, not based simply on strong personalities. Each of these executives has been able to build teams, systems, and managerial processes to leverage and add substance to his vision and energy. It is this interaction of charisma, attention to systems and processes, and widespread involvement at multiple levels that seems to drive large-system change.

Even with inspired leadership, though, no re-orientation can emerge fully developed and planned. Re-orientations take time to implement. During this transition period, mistakes are made, environments change and key people leave. Given the turbulence of competitive conditions, the complexity of large-system change and individual cognitive limitations, the executive team must develop its ability to adapt to new conditions and, as importantly, learn from both its successes and failures. As organizations can not remain stable in the face of environmental change, so too must the management of large-system change be flexible. This ability of executive teams to build-in learning and to build-in flexibility into the process of managing large-system organizational change is a touchstone for proactively managing re-orientations.

REFERENCES

1. R. Solow, M. Dertouzos, and R. Lester, *Made in America* (Cambridge, MA: MIT Press, 1989).
2. See M.L. Tushman, W. Newman, and E. Romanelli, "Convergence and Upheaval: Managing the Unsteady Pace of Organizational Evolution," *California Management Review*, 29/1 (Fall 1986):29–44.
3. E.g., K. Imai, I. Nonaka, and H. Takeuchi, "Managing the New Product Development Process: How Japanese Companies Learn and Unlearn," in K. Clark and R. Hayes, *The Uneasy Alliance* (Cambridge, MA: Harvard University Press, 1985).
4. E.g., A. Pettigrew, *The Awakening Giant: Continuity and Change at ICI* (London: Blackwell, 1985); J.R. Kimberly and R.E. Quinn, *New Futures: The Challenge of Managing Corporate Transitions* (Homewood, IL: Dow Jones-Irwin, 1984): Y. Allaire and M. Firsirotu, "How to Implement Radical Strategies in Large Organizations," *Sloan Management Review* (Winter 1985).
5. E.g., J. Gabbaro, *The Dynamics of Taking Charge* (Cambridge, MA: Harvard Business School Press, 1987); L. Greiner and A. Bhambri, "New CEO Intervention and Dynamics of Deliberate Strategic Change," *Strategic Management Journal*, 10 (1989):67–86; N.M. Tichy and M.A. Devanna, *The Transformational Leader* (New York, NY: John Wiley & Sons, 1986); D. Hambrick, "The Top Management Team: Key to Strategic Success," *California Management Review*, 30/1 (Fall 1987):88–108.
6. Y. Kobayashi, "Quality Control in Japan: The Case of Fuji Xerox," *Japanese Economic Studies* (Spring 1983).

7. G. Jacobson and J. Hillkirk, *Xerox: American Samurai* (New York, NY: Macmillan, 1986).

8. For SAS, see J. Carlzon, *Moments of Truth* (Cambridge, MA: Ballinger, 1987); for ICI, see Pettigrew, op. cit.; for NCR, see R. Rosenbloom, *From Gears to Chips: The Transformation of NCR in the Digital Era* (Cambridge, MA: Harvard University Press, 1988); for Honda, see I. Nonaka, "Creating Organizational Order Out of Chaos: Self-Renewal in Japanese Firms," *California Management Review*, 30/3 (Spring 1988):57–73.

9. Gabbaro, op. cit.; H. Levinson and S. Rosenthal, *CEO: Corporate Leadership in Action* (New York, NY: Basic Books, 1984); Greiner and Bhambri, op. cit.

10. Tushman et al., op. cit.; R. Greenwood and C. Hinings, "Organization Design Types, Tracks, and the Dynamics of Strategic Change," *Organization Studies*, 9/3 (1988):293–316; D. Miller and P. Friesen, *Organizations: A Quantum View* (Englewood Cliffs, NJ: Prentice-Hall, 1984).

11. D.A. Nadler and M.L. Tushman, "Organizational Framebending: Principles for Managing Re-orientation," *Academy of Management Executive*, 3 (1989):194–202.

12. For a more detailed discussion of this framework, see Nadler and Tushman, ibid.

13. Tushman et al., op. cit.; Greiner and Bhambri, op. cit.; Greenwood and Hinings, op. cit.; B. Virany and M.L. Tushman, "Changing Characteristics of Executive Teams in and Emerging Industry," *Journal of Business Venturing*, 1 (1986):261–274; M.L. Tushman and E. Romanelli, "Organizational Evolution: A Metamorphosis Model of Convergence and Reorientation," in B.M. Staw and L.L. Cummings, eds., *Research in Organizational Behavior*, 5 (Greenwich, CT: JAI Press, 1985), pp. 171–222.

14. J. March, L. Sproull, and M. Tamuz, "Learning from Fragments of Experience," *Organization Science* (in press).

15. R. Beckhard and R. Harris, *Organizational Transitions* (Reading, MA: Addison-Wesley, 1977).

16. See R. Vancil, *Passing the Baton* (Cambridge, MA: Harvard Business School Press, 1987).

17. J.M. Burns, *Leadership* (New York, NY: Harper & Row, 1978); W. Bennis and B. Nanus, *Leaders: The Strategies for Taking Charge* (New York, NY: Harper & Row, 1985); N.M. Tichy and D. Ulrich, "The Leadership Challenge: A Call for the Transformational Leader." *Sloan Management Review* (Fall 1984); Tichy and Devanna, op. cit.

18. D.E. Berlew, "Leadership and Organizational Excitement," in D.A. Kolb, I.M. Rubin, and J.M. McIntyre, eds., *Organizational Psychology* (Englewood Cliffs, NJ: Prentice-Hall, 1974); R.J. House, "A 1976 Theory of Charismatic Leadership," in J.G. Hunt and L.L. Larson, eds. *Leadership: The Cutting Edge* (Carbondale, IL: Southern Illinois University Press, 1977); Levinson and Rosenthal, op. cit.; B.M. Bass, *Performance Beyond Expectations* (New York, NY: Free Press, 1985); R. House et al., "Personality and Charisma in the U.S. Presidency," Wharton Working Paper, 1989.

19. Hambrick, op. cit.; D. Ancona and D. Nadler, "Teamwork at the Top: Creating High Performing Executive Teams," *Sloan Management Review* (in press).

20. V.H. Vroom, *Work and Motivation* (New York, NY: John Wiley & Sons, 1964); J.P. Campbell, M.D. Dunnette, E.E. Lawler, and K. Weick, *Managerial Behavior, Performances, and Effectiveness* (New York, NY: McGraw-Hill, 1970).

21. R.J. House, "Path-Goal Theory of Leader Effectiveness," *Administrative Science Quarterly*, 16 (1971):321–338; G.R. Oldham, "The Motivational Strategies Used by Supervisors: Relationships to Effectiveness Indicators," *Organizational Behavior and Human Performance*, 15 (1976):66–86.

22. See Hambrick, op. cit.

23. E.E. Lawler, and J.G. Rhode, *Information and Control in Organizations* (Pacific Palisades, CA: Goodyear, 1976).

24. Jacobson and Hillkirk, op. cit.

25. Gabbaro, op. cit.; T.J. Peters, "Symbols, Patterns, and Settings: An Optimistic Case for Getting Things Done," *Organizational Dynamics* (Autumn 1978).

26. R.J. House, "Exchange and Charismatic Theories of Leadership," in G. Reber, ed., *Encyclopedia of Leadership* (Stuttgart: C.E. Poeschel-Verlag, 1987).

27. M. Kets de Vries and D. Miller, "Neurotic Style and Organization Pathology," *Strategic Management Journal* (1984).

28. Levinson and Rosenthal, op. cit.

29. Hambrick, op. cit.

30. T. Kidder, *Soul of the New Machine* (Boston, MA: Little, Brown, 1981).

31. These are discussed in Nadler and Tushman, op. cit.

32. Hambrick, op. cit.

33. M. Louis and R. Sutton, *Switching Cognitive Gears* (Stanford, CA: Stanford University Press, 1987).

34. C. O'Reilly, D. Caldwell, and W. Barnett, "Work Group Demography, Social Integration, and Turnover," *Administrative Science Quarterly*, 34 (1989):21–37.

35. Hambrick, op. cit.; Virany and Tushman, op. cit.

36. See D. Ancona, "Top Management Teams: Preparing for the Revolution," in J. Carroll, ed., *Social Psychology in Business Organizations* (New York, NY: Erlbaum Associates, in press).

37. Louis and Sutton, op. cit.

38. March et al., op. cit.

39. See also C. Gersick, "Time and Transition in Work Teams," *Academy of Management Journal*, 31 (1988):9–41; Ancona and Nadler, op. cit.

40. See Vancil, op. cit.

41. R. Katz, "Organizational Socialization and the Reduction of Uncertainty," in R. Katz, *The Human Side of Managing Technological Innovation* (New York, NY: Oxford University Press, 1997, Chapter 4).

42. N. Tichy, "GE's Crotonville: A Staging Ground for Corporate Revolution," *Academy of Management Executive*, 3 (1989):99–106.

43. E.g., Gabbaro, op. cit.; V. Pucik, "International Management of Human Resources," in C. Fombrun et al., *Strategic Human Resource Management* (New York, NY: John Wiley & Sons, 1984).

44. Pucik, op. cit.

45. M. Devanna, C. Fombrun, and N. Tichy, "A Framework for Strategic Human Resource Management," in C. Fombrun et al., *Strategic Human Resource Management* (New York, NY: John Wiley & Sons, 1984).

46. Hambrick, op. cit.

47. Tichy, op. cit.

9

Informal Leadership Roles in the Innovation Process

25

Critical Functions:

Needed Roles in the Innovation Process

EDWARD B. ROBERTS AND ALAN R. FUSFELD

This article examines the main elements of the technology-based innovation process in terms of certain usually informal but critical "people" functions that can be the key to an effective organizational base for innovation. This approach to the innovation process is similar to that taken by early industrial theorists who focused on the production process. Led by such individuals as Frederick W.

Taylor, their efforts resulted in basic principles for increasing the efficiency of producing goods and services. These principles of specialization, chain of command, division of labor, and span of control continue to govern the operation of the modern organization (despite their shift from popularity in many modern business schools). Hence, routine tasks in most organizations are arranged to facili-

From E. Roberts and A. Fusfeld, "Critical Functions: Needed Roles in the Innovation Process," in *Career Issues in Human Resource Management*, R. Katz (ed.), © 1982, pp. 182–207. Reprinted by permission of Prentice-Hall, Inc., Englewood Cliffs, NJ.

Edward Roberts is Professor of Management at M.I.T.'s Sloan School of Management's Technology Group. **Alan Fusfeld** is President of The Fusfeld Group, a management of technology consulting firm.

tate work standardization with expectations that efficient production will result. However, examination of how industry has organized its innovation tasks—that is, those tasks needed for product/process development and for responses to nonroutine demands—indicates an absence of comparable theory. And many corporations' attempts to innovate consequently suffer from ineffective management and inadequately staffed organizations. Yet, through tens of studies about the innovation process, conducted largely in the last fifteen years, we now know much about the activities that are requisite to innovation as well as the characteristics of the people who perform these activities most effectively.

The following section characterizes the technology-based innovation process via a detailed description of a typical research and development project life cycle. The types of work activities arising in each project phase are enumerated. These lead in the third section to the identification of the five basic critical roles that are needed for effective execution of an innovative effort. Problems associated with gaps in the fulfillment of the needed roles are discussed. Detailed characteristics and specific activities that are associated with each role filler are elaborated upon in the fourth section. The multiple roles that are sometimes performed by certain individuals are observed, as are the dynamics of role changes that tend to take place over the life span of a productive career. The fifth section presents several areas of managerial implications of the critical functions concepts, beginning first with issues of manpower planning, then moving to considerations of job design and objective setting and to the determination of appropriate performance measures and rewards. How an organizational assessment can be carried out in terms of these critical functions dimensions is discussed in the last section.

THE INNOVATION PROCESS

The major steps involved in the technology-based process are shown in Figure 25.1. Although the project activities do not necessarily follow each other in a linear fashion, there is more or less clear demarcation between them. Moreover, each stage, and its activities, require a different mix of people skills and behaviors to be carried out effectively.

This figure portrays six stages as occurring in the typical technical innovation project, and sixteen representative activities that are associated with innovative efforts. The six stages are here identified as:

1. Pre-project
2. Project possibilities
3. Project initiation
4. Project execution
5. Project outcome evaluation
6. Project transfer

These stages often overlap and frequently recycle.[1] For example, problems or findings that are generated during project execution may cause a return to project initiation activities. Outcome evaluation can restart additional project execution efforts. And, of course, project cancellation can occur during any of these stages, redirecting technical endeavors back into the pre-project phase.

A variety of different activities are undertaken during each of the six stages. Some of the activities, such as generating new technical ideas, arise in all innovation project stages from pre-project to project transfer. But our research studies and consulting efforts in dozens of companies and government labs have shown other activities to be concentrated mainly in specific stages, as discussed below.

1. Pre-Project. Prior to formal project activities being undertaken in a technical organization, considerable technical work is done that provides a basis for later innovation efforts. Scientists, engineers, and marketing people find themselves involved in discussions internal and external to the organization. Ideas get discussed in rough-cut ways and broad parameters of innovative interests get established. Technical personnel work on problem-

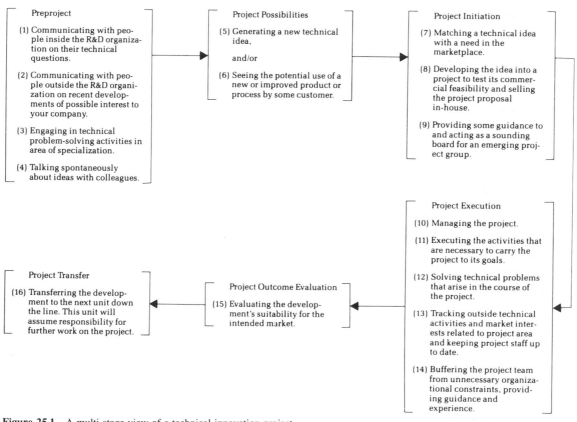

Preproject

(1) Communicating with people inside the R&D organization on their technical questions.

(2) Communicating with people outside the R&D organization on recent developments of possible interest to your company.

(3) Engaging in technical problem-solving activities in area of specialization.

(4) Talking spontaneously about ideas with colleagues.

Project Possibilities

(5) Generating a new technical idea,

and/or

(6) Seeing the potential use of a new or improved product or process by some customer.

Project Initiation

(7) Matching a technical idea with a need in the marketplace.

(8) Developing the idea into a project to test its commercial feasibility and selling the project proposal in-house.

(9) Providing some guidance to and acting as a sounding board for an emerging project group.

Project Execution

(10) Managing the project.

(11) Executing the activities that are necessary to carry the project to its goals.

(12) Solving technical problems that arise in the course of the project.

(13) Tracking outside technical activities and market interests related to project area and keeping project staff up to date.

(14) Buffering the project team from unnecessary organizational constraints, providing guidance and experience.

Project Transfer

(16) Transferring the development to the next unit down the line. This unit will assume responsibility for further work on the project.

Project Outcome Evaluation

(15) Evaluating the development's suitability for the intended market.

Figure 25.1   A multi-stage view of a technical innovation project.

solving efforts to advance their own areas of specialization. Discussions with numerous industrial firms in the United States and Europe suggest that from 30 to 60% of all technical effort is devoted to work outside of or prior to formal project initiation.

2. *Project Possibilities.* Arising from the preproject activities, specific ideas are generated for possible projects. They may be technical concepts for assumed-to-be-feasible developments. Or they may be perceptions of possible customer interest in product or process changes. Customer-oriented perspectives may be originated by technical or marketing or managerial personnel out of their imagination or from direct contact with customers or competitors. Recent evidence indicates that many of these ideas enter as "proven" possibilities, having already been developed by the customers themselves.[2]

3. *Project Initiation.* As ideas evolve and get massaged through technical and marketing discussions and exploratory technical efforts, the innovation process moves into a more formal project initiation stage. Activities occurring during this phase include attempts to match the directions of technical work with perceived customer needs. (Of course, such customer needs may exist either in the production organization or in the product's marketplace.) Inevitably, a specific project proposal has to be written up, proposed budgets and schedules have to get produced, and informal pushing as well as formal presentations have to be undertaken in order to sell the project. A key input during this stage is the counseling and encouragement that senior technical professionals or laboratory and marketing management may provide to the emerging project team.

4. *Project Execution.* With formal approval of a project aimed at an innovative output, activities increase in intensity and focus. In parallel, someone usually undertakes planning, leadership, and coordination efforts related to the many continuing technical idea-generating and problem-solving activities being done by the engineers and scientists assigned to the project. Technical people often make special attempts to monitor (and transfer in) what had been done previously as well as what is then going on outside the project that is relevant to the project's goals. Management or marketing people frequently take a closer look at competitors and customers to be sure the project is appropriately targeted.[3] Senior people try to protect the project from overly tight control or from getting cut off prematurely, and the project manager and other enthusiasts keep fighting to defend their project's virtues (and budget). Unless canceled, the project work continues toward completion of its objectives.

5. *Project Outcome Evaluation.* When the technical effort seems complete, most projects undergo another often intense evaluation to see how the results stack up against prior expectations and current market perceptions. If a successful innovation is to occur, some further implementation must take place, either by transfer of the interim results to manufacturing for embodiment in its process or for volume production activities, or by transfer to later stages of further development. All such later stages involve heavier expenditures and the post-project evaluation can be viewed as a pre-transfer screening activity.

6. *Project Transfer.* If the project results survive this evaluation, transfer efforts take place (e.g., from central research to product department R&D, or development to manufacturing engineering).[4] The project's details may require further technical documentation to facilitate the transfer. Key technical people may be shifted to the downstream unit to transfer their expertise and enthusiasm, since downstream staff members, technical or marketing, often need instruction to assure effective continuity. Within the downstream organizational unit, the cycle of stages may begin again, perhaps bypass-ing the earliest two stages and starting with project initiation or even project execution. This "pass-down" continues until successful innovation is achieved, unless project termination occurs first.

NEEDED ROLES

Assessment of activities involved in the several-stage innovation process, as just described, points out that the repeated direct inputs of five different work roles are critical to innovation. The five arise in differing degrees in each of the several steps. Furthermore, different innovation projects obviously call for variations in the required role mix at each stage. Nevertheless, all five work roles must be carried out by one or more individuals if the innovation is to pass effectively through all six steps.

The five critical work functions are:

- *Idea generating.* Analyzing and/or synthesizing (implicit and explicit) information (formal and informal) about markets, technologies, approaches, and procedures, from which an idea is generated for a new or improved product or service, a new technical approach or procedure, or a solution to a challenging technical problem.[5]

- *Entrepreneuring or championing.* Recognizing, proposing, pushing, and demonstrating a new (his or her own or someone else's) technical idea, approach or procedure for formal management approval.[6]

- *Project leading.* Planning and coordinating the diverse sets of activities and people involved in moving a demonstrated idea into practice.[7]

- *Gatekeeping.* Collecting and channeling information about important changes in the internal and external environments; information gatekeeping can be focused on developments in the market, in manufacturing, or in the world of technology.[8]

- *Sponsoring or coaching.* "Behind-the-scene" support-generating function of the protector and advocate, and sometimes of the "bootlegger" of funds; the guiding and developing of less-experienced personnel in their critical roles (a "Big Brother" role).[9]

Lest the reader confuse these roles as mapping one-for-one with different people, three points need emphasis: (1) some roles (e.g., idea generating) frequently need to be fulfilled by more than one person in a project team in order for the project to be successful; (2) some individuals occasionally fulfill more than one of the critical functions; and (3) the roles that people play periodically change over a person's career with an organization.

Critical Functions

These five critical functions represent the various roles in an organization that must be carried out for successful innovation to occur. They are critical from two points of view. First, each role is different or unique, demanding different skills. A deficiency in any one of the roles contributes to serious problems in the innovation effort, as we illustrate below. Second, each role tends to be carried out primarily by relatively few individuals, thereby making even more unique the critical role players. If any one critical function-filler leaves, the problem of recruiting a replacement is very difficult—the specifics of exactly who is needed is dependent on usually unstated role requirements.

We must add at this point that another role clearly exists in all innovative organizations, but it is not an *innovative* role! "Routine" technical problem-solving must be carried out in the process of advancing innovative efforts. Indeed the vast bulk of technical work is probably routine, requiring professional training and competence to be sure, but nonetheless routine in character for an appropriately prepared individual. A large number of people in innovative organizations do very little "critical functions" work; others who are important performers of the critical functions also spend a good part of their time in routine problem-solving activity. Our estimate, supported now by data from numerous organizations, is that 70 to 80% of technical effort falls into this routine problem-solving category. But the 20 to 30% that is unique and critical is the part we emphasize.

Generally, the critical functions are not specified within job descriptions since they tend to fit neither administrative nor technical hierarchies; but they do represent necessary activities for R&D, such as problem definition, idea nurturing, information transfer, information integration, and program pushing. Consequently, these role behaviors are the underlying informal functions that an organization carries out as part of the innovation process. Beyond the five above, different business environments may also demand that additional roles be performed to assure innovation.[10]

It is desirable for every organization to have a balanced set of abilities for carrying out these roles as needed, but unfortunately few organizations do. Some organizations overemphasize one role (e.g., idea generating) and underplay another role (e.g., entrepreneuring). Another organization might do just the reverse. Nonetheless, technical organizations tend to assume that the necessary set of activities will somehow be performed. As a consequence, R&D labs often lack sensitivity to the existence and importance of these roles, which, for the most part, are not defined within the formal job structure. How the critical functions are encouraged and made a conscious part of technology management is probably an organization's single most important area of leverage for maintaining and improving effective innovation. The managerial capabilities required for describing, planning, diagnosing problems, and developing the necessary teamwork in terms of the people functions demanded by an innovative program are almost entirely distinct from the skills needed for managing the technical requirements of the tasks.

Impact of Role Deficiencies

Such an analytic approach to developing an innovative team has been lacking in the past and, consequently, many organizations suffer because one or more of the critical functions is not being performed adequately. Certain characteristic signs can provide evidence that a critical function is missing.

Idea generating is deficient if the organization is not thinking of new and different ways of doing things. However, more often than not when a manager complains of insufficient ideas, we find the real deficiency to be that people are not aggressively entrepreneuring or championing ideas, either their own or others'. Evidences of entrepreneuring shortages are pools of unexploited ideas that seldom come to a manager's attention.[11]

Project leading is suspect if schedules are not met, activities fall through cracks (e.g., coordinating with a supplier), people do not have a sense for the overall goal of their work, or units that are needed to support the work back out of their commitments. This is the role most commonly recognized formally by the appointment of a project manager. In research, as distinct from development, the formal role is often omitted.

Gatekeeping is inadequate if news of changes in the market, technology, or government legislation comes without warning, or if people within the organization are not getting the information that they need because it has not been passed on to them. When, six months after the project is completed, you suddenly realize that you have just succeeded in reinventing a competitor's wheel, your organization is deficient in needed gatekeeping! Gatekeeping is further lacking when the wheel is invented just as a regulatory agency outlaws its use.

Inadequate or inappropriate sponsoring or coaching often explains projects that get pushed into application too soon, or project managers who have to spend too much time defending their work, or personnel who complain that they do not know how to "navigate the bureaucracy" of their organizations.

The importance of each critical function varies with the development stage of the project. Initially, idea generation is crucial; later, entrepreneurial skill and commitment are needed to develop the concept into a viable activity. Once the project is established, good project leading/managing is needed to guide its progress. Of course, the need for each critical function does not abruptly appear and disappear. Instead, the need grows and diminishes, being a focus at some point, but of lesser importance at others. Thus, the absence of a function when it is potentially very important is a serious weakness regardless of whether or not the role had

been filled at an earlier, less crucial time. As a corollary, assignment of an individual to a project, at a time when the critical role that he or she provides is not needed, leads to frustration for the individual and to a less effective project team.

Frequently, we have observed that personnel changes that occur because of career development programs often remove critical functions from a project at a crucial time. Since these roles are usually performed informally, job descriptions are made in terms of technical specialties, and personnel replacements are chosen to fill those job vacancies, rather than on their ability to fill the needs of the vacated critical roles. Consequently, the project team's innovative effectiveness is reduced, sometimes to the point of affecting the project's success. Awareness of which roles are likely to be required at what time will help to avoid this problem, as well as to allow people performing functions no longer needed to be moved to other projects where their talents can be better utilized.

CHARACTERISTICS OF THE ROLE PLAYERS

Compilation of several thousand individual profiles of staff in R&D and engineering organizations has demonstrated patterns in the characteristics of the people who perform each innovation function.[12] These patterns are shown in Table 25.1, indicating which persons are predisposed to be interested in one type of activity more than another and to perform certain types of activity well. For example, a person who is theoretically inclined and comfortable with abstractions feels better suited to the idea-generating function than does someone who is very practical and uncomfortable with seemingly discrepant data. In any unit of an organization, people with different characteristics can work to complement each other. Someone good at idea generating might be teamed with a colleague good at gatekeeping and another colleague good at entrepreneuring to provide necessary supporting roles. Of course, each person must understand his or her own expected role in a project and appreciate the roles of others for the teaming process to be

TABLE 25.1
Critical Functions in the Innovation Process

Personal characteristics	Organizational activities
Idea Generating	
Is expert in one or two fields	Generates new ideas and tests their feasibility
Enjoys conceptualization, comfortable with abstractions	Good at problem solving
	Sees new and different ways of viewing things
Enjoys doing innovative work	Searches for the break-throughs
Usually is an individual contributor, often will work alone	
Entrepreneuring or Championing	
Strong application interests	Sells new ideas to others in the organization
Possesses a wide range of interests	Gets resources
Less propensity to contribute to the basic knowledge of a field	Aggressive in championing his or her "cause"
Energetic and determined; puts himself or herself on the line	Takes risks
Project Leading	
Focus for the decision making, information, and questions	Provides the team leadership and motivation
	Plans and organizes the project
Sensitive to accommodating to the needs of others	Ensures that administrative requirements are met
Recognizes how to use the organizational structure to get things done	Provides necessary coordination among team members
Interested in a broad range of disciplines and how they fit together (e.g., marketing, finance)	Sees that the project moves forward effectively
	Balances the project goals with organizational needs
Gatekeeping[a]	
Possesses a high level of technical competence	Keeps informed of related developments that occur outside the organization through journals, conferences, colleagues, other companies
Is approachable and personable	
Enjoys the face-to-face contact of helping others	Passes information on to others; finds it easy to talk to colleagues
	Serves as an information resource for others in the organization (i.e., authority on whom to see and/or what has been done)
	Provides informal coordination among personnel
Sponsoring or Coaching	
Possesses experience in developing new ideas	Helps develop people's talents
Is a good listener and helper	Provides encouragement and guidance and acts as a sounding board to the project leader and others
Can be relatively more objective	
Often a more senior person who knows the organizational ropes	Provides access to a power base within the organization—a senior person
	Buffers the project team from unnecessary organizational constraints
	Helps the project team to get what it needs from the other parts of the organization
	Provides legitimacy and organizational confidence in the project

[a]Our empirical studies have pointed out three different types of gatekeepers: (1) technical, who relates well to advancing world of science and technology; (2) market, who senses and communicates information relating to customers, competitors, and environmental and regulatory changes affecting the marketplace; and (3) manufacturing, who bridges the technical work to the special needs and conditions of the production organization.

successful. Obviously, as will be discussed later, some people have sufficient breadth to perform well in multiple roles.

Table 25.1 underlies our conclusion that each of the several roles required for effective technical innovation presents unique challenges and must be filled with essentially different types of people, each type to be recruited, managed, and supported differently, offered different sets of incentives, and supervised with different types of measures and controls. Most technical organizations seem not to have grasped this concept, with the result that all technical people tend to be recruited, hired, supervised, monitored, evaluated, and encouraged as if their principal roles were those of creative scientists or, worse yet, routine technical problem-solvers. But only a few of these people in fact have the personal and technical qualifications for scientific inventiveness and prolific idea generating. A creative idea-generating scientist or engineer is a special kind of professional who needs to be singled out, cultivated, and managed in a special way. He or she is probably an innovative technically well-educated individual who enjoys working on advanced problems, often as a "loner."

The technical champion or entrepreneur is a special person, too—creative in his own way, but his is an aggressive form of creativity appropriate for selling an idea or product. The entrepreneur's drives may be less rational, more emotional than those of the creative scientist; he is committed to achieve, and less concerned about how to do so. He is as likely to pick up and successfully champion someone else's original idea as to push something of his own creation. Such an entrepreneur may well have a broad range of interests and activities; and he must be recruited, hired, managed, and stimulated very differently from the way an idea-generating scientist is treated in the organization.

The person who effectively performs project leading or project managing activities is a still different kind of person—an organized individual, sensitive to the needs of the several different people she is trying to coordinate, and an effective planner; the latter is especially important if long lead time, expensive materials, and major support are involved in the development of the ideas that she is moving forward in the organization.

The information gatekeeper is the communicative individual who in fact, is the exception to the truism that engineers do not read—especially that they do not read technical journals. Gatekeep-ers link to the sources of flow of technical information into and within a research and development organization that might enhance new product development or process improvement. But those who do research and development need market information as well as technical information. What do customers seem to want? What are competitors providing? How might regulatory shifts affect the firm's present or contemplated products or processes? For answers to questions such as these, research and development organizations need people we call the "market gatekeepers"—engineers or scientists, or possibly marketing people with technical background, who focus on market-related information sources and communicate effectively with their technical colleagues. Such a person reads journals, talks to vendors, goes to trade shows, and is sensitive to competitive information. Without him, many research and development projects and laboratories become misdirected with respect to market trends and needs.

Finally, the sponsor or coach may in fact be a more experienced, older project leader or former entrepreneur who now has matured to have a softer touch than when he was first in the organization. As a senior person, she can coach and help subordinates in the organization and speak on their behalf to top management, enabling ideas or programs to move forward in an effective, organized fashion. Many organizations totally ignore the sponsor role, yet our studies of industrial research and development suggest that many projects would not have been successful were it not for the subtle and often unrecognized assistance of such senior people acting in the role of sponsors. Indeed, organizations are more successful when chief engineers or laboratory directors naturally behave in a manner consistent with this sponsor role.

The significant point here is that the staffing needed to cause effective innovation in a technical organization is far broader than the typical research and development director has usually assumed. Our studies indicate that many ineffective technical organizations have failed to be innovative solely because one or more of these five quite different critical functions has been absent.

Multiple Roles

As indicated earlier, some individuals have the skills, breadth, inclination, and job opportunity to fulfill more than one critical function in an organization. Our data collection efforts with R&D staffs show that a few clusters explain most of these cases of multiple role-playing. One common combination of roles is the pairing of gatekeeping and idea generating. Idea-generating activity correlates in general with the frequency of person-to-person communication, especially external to the organization.[13] The gatekeeper, moreover, in contact with many sources of information, can often synergistically connect these bits into a new idea. This seems especially true of market gatekeepers, who can relate market relevance to technical opportunities.

Another role couplet is between entrepreneuring and idea generating. In studies of formation of new technical companies the entrepreneur who pushed company formation and growth was found in half the cases also to have been the source of the new technical idea underlying the company.[14] Furthermore, in studies of M.I.T. faculty, 38% of those who had ideas they perceived to have commercial value also took strong entrepreneurial steps to exploit their ideas.[15] The idea-generating entrepreneuring pair accounts for less than one half of the entrepreneurs, but not the other half.

Entrepreneuring individuals often become project leaders, usually in what is thought to be a logical organizational extension of the effective selling of the idea for the project. And some people strong at entrepreneuring indeed also have the interpersonal and plan-oriented qualities needed for project leading. But on numerous occasions the responsibility for managing a project is mistakenly seen as a necessary reward for successful idea championing. This arises from lack of focus upon the functional differences. What evidence indicates that a good salesperson is going to be a good manager? If an entrepreneur can be rewarded appropriately and more directly for his or her own function, many project failures caused by ineffective project managers might be avoided. Perhaps giving the entrepreneur a prominent project role, together with a clearly designated but different project manager, might be an acceptable compromise.

Finally, sponsoring, although it should be a unique role, occasionally gives way to a takeover of any or all of the other roles. Senior coaching can degenerate into idea domination, project ownership, and direction from the top. This confusion of roles can become extremely harmful to the entire organization. Who will bring another idea to the boss, once he steals some junior's earlier concept? Even worse, who can intervene to stop the project once the boss is running amok with his new pet?

All of the critical innovative roles, whether played singly or in multiples, can be fulfilled by people from multiple disciplines and departments. Obviously, technical people—scientists and engineers—might carry out any of the roles. But marketing people also generate ideas for new and improved products, "gatekeep" information of key importance to a project—especially about use, competition and regulatory activities—champion the idea, sometimes sponsor projects, and in some organizations even manage innovation projects. Manufacturing people periodically fill similar critical roles, as do general management personnel.

The fact of multiple role filling can affect the minimum-size group needed for attaining "critical mass" in an innovative effort. To achieve continuity of a project, from initial idea all the way through to successful commercialization, a project group must have all five critical roles effectively filled while satisfying the specific technical skills required for project problem-solving. In a new high-technology company this critical mass may sometimes be ensured by as few as one or two co-founders. Similarly, an "elite" team, such as Cray's famed Control Data computer design group, or Kelly Johnson's "Skunk Works" at Lockheed, or McLean's Sidewinder missile organization in the Navy's China Lake R&D center, may concentrate in a small number of select multiple-role players the staff needed to accomplish major objectives. But the more typical medium-to-large company organization had better not plan on finding "Renaissance persons" or superstars to fill its job requirements. Staffing assumptions should more likely rest on estimates that 70% of scientists and engineers will turn out to be routine problem-solvers only, and that most critical role-players will be single dimensional in their unique contributions.

Career-Spanning Role Changes

We showed above how some individuals fulfill multiple critical roles concurrently or in different stages of the same project. But even more people are likely to contribute critically but differently at different stages of their careers. This does not reflect change of personality, although such changes do seem partly due to the dynamics of personal growth and development. But the phenomenon also clearly reflects individual responses to differing organizational needs, constraints, and incentives.

For example, let us consider the hypothetical case of a bright, aggressive, potentially multiple-role contributor, newly joining a company fresh from engineering school. What roles can he play? Certainly, he can quickly become an effective routine technical problem-solver and, hopefully, a productive novel idea generator. But even though he may know many university contacts and also be familiar with the outside literature, he cannot be an effective information gatekeeper, for he does not yet know the people inside the company with whom he might communicate. He also cannot lead project activities. No one would trust him in that role. He cannot effectively act as an entrepreneur, as he has no credibility as champion for change. And, of course, sponsoring is out of the question. During this stage of his career, the limited legitimate role options may channel the young engineer's productive energies and reinforce his tendencies toward creative idea output. Alternatively, wanting to offer more and do more than the organization will "allow," this high-potential young performer may feel rebuffed and frustrated. His perception of what he can expect from the job and, perhaps more important, what the job will expect from him, may become set in these first few months on the job. Some disappointeds may remain in the company, but "turn off" their previously enthusiastic desire for multidimensional contributions. More likely, the frustrated high-potential will "spin-off" and leave the company in search of a more rewarding job, perhaps destined to find continuing frustration in his next one or two encounters. For many young professionals the job environment moves too slowly from encouraging idea generating to even permitting entrepreneurial activities.

With two or three years on the job, however, the engineer's role options may broaden. Of course, routine problem solving and idea generating are still appropriate. But some information gatekeeping may now also be possible, as communication ties increase within the organization. Project leading may start to be seen as legitimate behavior, particularly on small efforts.[16] And the young engineer's work behavior may begin to reflect these new possibilities. But perhaps his attempts at entrepreneurial behavior would still be seen as premature. And sponsoring is not yet a relevant consideration.

With another few years at work, the role options are still wider. Routine problem-solving, continued idea generating, broad-based gatekeeping (even bridging to the market or to manufacturing), responsible project managing, as well as project championing may become reasonable alternatives. Even coaching a new employee becomes a possibility. The next several years can strengthen all these role options, a given individual tending usually to focus on one of these roles (or on a specific multiple-role combination) for this midcareer period.

Getting out of touch with a rapidly changing technology may later narrow the role alternatives available as the person continues to age on the job. Technical problem-solving effectiveness may diminish in some cases, idea generating may slow down or stop, technical information gatekeeping may be reduced. But market and/or manufacturing gatekeeping may continue to improve with increased experience and outside contacts, project managing capabilities may continue to grow as more past projects are tucked under the belt, entrepreneuring may be more important and for higher stakes, and sponsoring of juniors in the company may be more generally sought and practiced. This career phase is too often seen as characterized by the problem of technical obsolescence, especially if the organization has a fixation on assessing engineer performance in terms of the narrow but traditional stereotypes of technical problem solving and idea generating. "Retooling" the engineer for an earlier role, usually of little current interest and satisfaction to the more mature, broader, and differently directed person, becomes a source of mutual grief and anxiety to the organization and the individual. An aware organization, thinking in terms of critical role differences, can instead recognize the self-selected branching in career paths that has occurred for the individual. Productive technically trained people can be carrying out critical functions for their employers up to retirement, if employers encourage the full diversity of vital roles.

At each stage of his evolving career, an individual can encounter severe conflicts between his organization's expectations and his personal work preferences. This is especially true if the organization is inflexible in its perception of appropriate technical roles. In contrast, with both organizational and individual adaptability in seeking mutually satisfying job roles, the scientist or engineer can contribute continuously and importantly to accomplishing innovation. As suggested in this illustrative case, during his productive career in industry the technical professional may begin as a technical problem solver, spend several years primarily as a creative idea generator, add technical gatekeeping to his performance while maintaining his earlier roles, shift toward entrepreneuring projects and leading them forward, gradually grow in his market-linking and project managing behavior, and eventually accrue a senior sponsoring role while maintaining senior project-program-organizational leadership until retirement. But this productive full life is not possible if the engineer is pushed to the side early as a technically obsolete contributor. The perspective taken here can lead to a very different approach to career development for professionals than is usually taken by industry or government.

MANAGING THE CRITICAL FUNCTIONS FOR ENHANCED INNOVATION

To increase organizational innovation, a number of steps can be taken that will facilitate implementa-

tion of a balance among the critical functions. These steps must be addressed explicitly or organizational focus will remain on the traditionally visible functions that produce primarily near-term incremental results, such as problem solving. Indeed, the "results-oriented" reward systems of most organizations reinforce this short-run focus, causing other activities to go unrecognized and unrewarded.

We are not suggesting that employees should ignore the problem-solving function for the sake of the other functions. Rather, we are emphasizing the need for a balance of time and energy distributed among all functions. As indicated earlier, our impressions and data suggest that 70 to 80% of the work of most organizations is routine problem-solving. However, the other 20 to 30% and the degree of teamwork among the critical functions make the difference between an innovative and a noninnovative organization.

Implementing of the results, language, and concepts of a critical functions perspective is described below for the selected organizational tasks of manpower planning, job design, measurement, and rewards. If critical functions awareness dominated managerial thinking, other tasks, not dealt with here, would also be done differently, including R&D strategy, organizational development, and program management.

Manpower Planning

The critical functions concept can be applied usefully to the recruiting, job assignment, and development or training activities within an organization. In recruiting, an organization needs to identify not only the specific technical or managerial requirements of a job, but also the critical function activities that the job requires. That is, does the job require consulting with colleagues as an important part of facilitating teamwork? Or does it require the coaching and development of less experienced personnel to ensure the longer-run productivity of that area? To match a candidate with the job, recruiting should also include identification of the innovation skills of the applicant. If the job requires championing, the applicant who is more aggressive and has shown evidence of championing new ideas in the past should be preferred over the less-aggressive applicant who has shown much more technically oriented interests in the past.

As indicated above, there is room for growth from one function to another, as people are exposed to different managers, different environments, and jobs that require different activities. Although this growth occurs naturally in most organizations, it can be explicitly planned and managed. In this way, the individual has the opportunity to influence his growth along the lines that are of most interest to him, and the organization has the opportunity to oversee the development of personnel and to ensure that effective people are performing the essential critical functions.

Industry has at best taken a narrow view of manpower development alternatives for technical professionals. The "dual ladder" concept envisions an individual as rising along either "scientific" or "managerial" steps. Attempted by many but with only limited success ever attained, the dual ladder reflects an oversimplification and distortion of the key roles needed in an R&D organization.[17] As a minimum, the critical function concept presents "multiladders" of possible organizational contribution; individuals can grow in any and all of the critical roles while benefiting the organization. And depending on an organization's strategy and manpower needs, manpower development along each of the paths can and should be encouraged. Most

job descriptions and statements of objectives emphasize problem-solving, and sometimes project leading. Rarely do job descriptions and objectives take into account the dimensions of a job that are essential for the performance of the other critical functions. Yet availability of unstructured time in a job can influence the performance of several of the innovation functions. For example, to stimulate idea generating, some slack time is necessary so that employees can pursue their own ideas and explore new and interesting ways of doing things. For gatekeeping to occur, slack time also needs to be available for employees to communicate with colleagues and pass along information learned, both internal to and external to the organization. The coaching role also requires slack time, during which the "coach" can guide less experienced personnel. Table 25.2 elaborates our views on the different emphasis on deadlines (i.e., the alternative to slack time) for each of the critical functions and the degree of specificity of task assignments (i.e., another alternative to slack) for each function.

These essential activities also need to be included explicitly in the objective of a job. A gatekeeper would, for example, see his or her goals as including provision of useful information to colleagues. A person who has the attitudes and skill to be an effective champion or entrepreneur could also be made responsible for recognizing good new

TABLE 25.2
Job Design Dimensions

Dimension of job	Critical function				
	Idea generating	Entrepreneuring or championing	Project leading	Gatekeeping	Sponsoring or coaching
Emphasis on deadlines	Little emphasis; exploring encouraged	Jointly set deadlines emphasized by management	Management identifies; needs strong emphasis	Set by the job (i.e., the person needing the information)	Little emphasis
Emphasis on specifically assigned tasks	Low; freedom to pursue new ideas	High; assignments mutually planned and agreed by management and champion	High with respect to overall project goals	Medium; freedom to consult with others	Low

TABLE 25.3
Measuring and Rewarding Critical Function Performance

Dimension of management	Critical function				
	Idea generating	Entrepreneuring or championing	Project leading	Gatekeeping	Sponsoring or coaching
Primary contribution of each function for appraisal of performance	Quantity and quality of ideas generated	Ideas picked up; percent carried through	Project technical milestones accomplished; cost/ schedule constraints met	People helped; degree of help	Staff developed; extent of assistance provided
Rewards appropriate	Opportunities to publish; recognition from professional peers through symposia, etc.	Visibility; publicity; further resources for project	Bigger projects; material signs of organizational status	Travel budget; key "assists" acknowledged; increased freedom and use for advice	Increased freedom; discretionary resources for support of others-

ideas. This person might have the charter to roam around the organization, talk with people about their ideas, encourage their pursuit, or pursue the ideas himself.

This raises a very sticky question in most organizations: Who gets the credit? If the champion gets the credit for recognizing the idea, not very many idea generators will be eager to let the champion carry out his job. This brings us to the next item, measures and rewards.

Performance Measures and Rewards

We all tend to do those activities that get rewarded. If personnel perceive that idea generating does not get recognized but that idea exploitation does, they may not pass their ideas on to somebody who can exploit them. They may try to exploit them themselves, no matter how unequipped or uninterested they are in carrying out the exploitation activity.

For this reason, it is important to recognize the distinct contributions of each of the separate critical functions. Table 25.3 identifies some measures relevant to each function. Each measure has both a quantity and quality dimension. For example, the objective for a person who has the skills and information to be effective at gatekeeping could be to help a number of people during the next twelve

months. At the end of that time, his manager could survey the people whom the gatekeeper feels he helped to assess the gatekeeper's effectiveness in communicating key information. In each organization specific measures chosen will necessarily be different.

Rewarding an individual for the performance of a critical function makes the function both more discussable and manageable. However, what is seen as rewarding for one function may be seen as less rewarding, neutral, or even negative for another function because of the different personalities and needs of the role fillers. Table 25.3 presents some rewards seen as appropriate for each function. Again, organizational and individual differences will generate variations in rewards selected. Of course, the informal positive feedback of managers to their day-to-day contacts is a major source of motivation and recognition for any individual performing a critical innovation function, or any job for that matter.

Salary and bonus compensation are not included here, but not because they are unimportant to any of these people. Of course, financial rewards should also be employed as appropriate, but they do not seem to be explicitly linked to any one innovative function more than another. Table 25.3 identifies the rewards that are related to critical roles.

The preceding sections demonstrate that the critical functions concept provides an important way of describing an organization's or a project team's resources for effective innovation activity. One technical organization, for example, in seeing the contributions of all five critical roles, made several important changes in their recruiting and staffing procedures. To begin with, the characteristic strengths behind each critical function were explicitly employed for identifying the skills necessary to do a particular job. This led to a framework useful for interviewing and evaluating candidates to determine how they might contribute over time to projects or organizational efforts. Upper management also became conscious of the unintended bias in their recruiting and staffing activities, as much of their focus had been on creative idea-generation needs and capabilities. As a result, upper management was more careful to have the mix of critical functions represented within the interviewing and staffing considerations.

Other values resulted from the analyses which were less tangible than those listed above but equally important. Jobs were no longer defined solely in technical terms (i.e., the educational background and/or work experience necessary). For example, whether or not a job involved idea generation or exploitation was defined, and these typical activities were included in the description of the job and the skills needed to perform it well. The objectives of the job, in the company's management-by-objectives (MBO) procedure, were then expanded to include the critical functions. However, since all five functions are essential to innovation and it is the very rare person who can do all five equally well, the clear need for a new kind of teamwork was also developed. Finally, the critical functions concept provided the framework for the selection of people and the division of labor on the "innovation team" that became the nucleus for all new R&D programs. In summary, to the extent that innovative outcomes, rather than routine production, are the outputs sought, we have confidence that the critical functions approach will afford use-ful insights for organizational analyses and management.

NOTES

1. For a different and more intensive quantitative view of project life cycles, see Edward B. Roberts, *The Dynamics of Research and Development* (New York: Harper & Row, 1964).

2. Eric von Hippel, "Users as Innovators," *Technology Review, 80,* No. 3 (January 1978), 30–39.

3. See Alan R. Fusfeld, "How to Put Technology into Corporate Planning," *Technology Review, 80,* No. 6, for issues that need to be highlighted in a comparative technical review.

4. For further perspectives on project transfer, see Edward B. Roberts, "Stimulating Technological Innovation: Organizational Approaches," *Research Management, 22,* No. 6 (November 1979), 26–30.

5. D.C. Pelz and F.M. Andrews, *Scientists in Organizations* (New York: Wiley, 1966).

6. E.B. Roberts, "Entrepreneurship and Technology," *Research Management, 11,* No. 4 (July 1968), 249–66.

7. D.G. Marquis and I.M. Rubin, "Management Factors in Project Performance," M.I.T. Sloan School of Management, Working Paper, Cambridge, Mass., 1966.

8. T.J. Allen, *Managing the Flow of Technology* (Cambridge, Mass.: MIT Press, 1977); and R.G. Rhoades, et al., "A Correlation of R&D Laboratory Performance with Critical Functions Analysis," *R&D Management, 9,* No. 1 (October 1978), 13–17.

9. Roberts, "Entrepreneurship and Technology," p. 252.

10. One role we have frequently observed is the "quality controller," who stresses high work standards in projects. Other critical roles relate more to organizational growth than to innovation. The "effective trainer" who could absorb new engineers productively into the company was seen as critical to one firm that was growing 30% per year. The "technical statesman" was a role label developed by an electronic components manufacturer which valued the ability of some engineers to generate a leadership technical reputation through authorship and presentation of advanced concepts.

11. One study that demonstrated this phenomenon is N.R. Baker, et al., "The Effects of Perceived Needs and Means on the Generation of Ideas for Industrial Research and Development Projects," *IEEE Transactions on Engineering Management, EM-14* (1967), 156–65.

12. For their research and consulting activities, the authors have developed a questionnaire methodology for collecting these kind of data.

13. Allen, *Managing the Flow of Technology.*

14. Roberts, "Entrepreneurship and Technology."

15. E.B. Roberts and D.H. Peters, "Commercial Innovations from University Faculty," *Research Policy, 10,* No. 2 (April 1981), 108–26.

16. One study showed that engineers who eventually became managers of large projects began supervisory experiences within an average of 4.5 years after receiving their B.S. degrees. I.M. Rubin and W. Seelig, "Experience as a Factor in the Selection and Performance of Project Managers," *IEEE Transactions on Engineering Management, EM-14,* No. 3 (September 1967), 131–35.

17. For a variety of industrial approaches to the dual ladder, see the special July 1977 issue of *Research Management* or, more recently, *Research Management,* November 1979, 8–11.

26

Innovation through Intrapreneuring

GIFFORD PINCHOT III

In-house entrepreneurs—those "dreamers who do"—can increase the speed and cost-effectiveness of technology transfer from R&D to the marketplace.

The economy of the United States is on an innovation treadmill. Our competitors enjoy cheaper labor, cheaper capital, and more government support than we. To maintain our competitive position, we need superior technology, more proprietary products and services, and better processes. As our competitors become more scientifically and managerially sophisticated, it takes them less and less time to understand and copy our innovations. We have to increase our speed and cost-effectiveness of innovation in our country to match our competitors' increasing sophistication in copying and capitalizing on our technology.

Most large companies operate stable businesses well. However, they are not as adept at starting new ones. Most are good at developing a new business from the idea stage on through research and prototype development. But they falter at the start-up stage—the stage of commercialization. Inefficient commercialization by big business has created opportunity for venture capitalists. The venture capital industry is producing 35 percent return on investment by taking frustrated R&D people and their rejected ideas out of large companies, and financing the commercialization of those ideas. That the venture capital community can make 35 percent ROI on rejected ideas and people should be a constant rebuke to everyone in the R&D community. Venture capitalists have found a different

way of managing innovation that gets returns which few of us can equal inside large organizations.

A MISSING FACTOR IN CORPORATE INNOVATION

The primary secret of the venture capitalists' success is revealed in the way they select ventures for investment. They say: "I would rather have a class A entrepreneur with a class B idea than a class A idea with a class B entrepreneur." They put their faith in choosing the right people and then sticking with them, while many corporate managers would feel uncomfortable with a strategy dependent on trusting the talent, experience, and commitment of those implementing it. I believe the primary cause for the lower returns of corporate managers of innovation is their failure to understand the importance of backing the right people—this is their failure to identify, support, and exploit the "intrapreneurs" who drive innovation to successful conclusions.

Imagine the organization as a cell, with R&D producing new genes. In the cell, there are also the productive capacity of the ribosomes, which are like factories ready to use the information in those new genes to produce new products. What's missing in most large organizations is linkage from idea to operation—by analogy the RNA. In most large organizations there are exciting new genes—new technologies but no broadly effective system of technology transfer. What is absent are large numbers of intrapreneurs devoted to turning new technologies into profitable new businesses, cost re-

Reprinted with permission from *Research-Technology Management,* Vol. 30, March-April, 1987.
Gifford Pinchot III is the founding Chairman of the consulting firm Pinchot & Company.

ductions, new features, and competitive advantages. Because we have tended to have scientific standards of excellence in R&D, we have tended to honor the inventor more than the implementor, more than the intrapreneur. The result is that we not only reward inventing more than intrapreneuring, but our management systems are far more supportive of invention than of commercialization.

The future role of R&D, the size of its budgets and its degree of autonomy all depend on efficient technology transfer. Older "hand-off systems" of development which ignore the role of the intrapreneur don't work, or at best are so slow and expensive they make R&D appear ineffective. Cost-effective innovation happens when someone becomes the passionate champion of a new idea and acts with great courage to push it through the system despite the "Not Invented Here" syndrome, and all the other forms of resistance which large organizations supply. It is therefore important for R&D managers to understand and recognize intrapreneurs who can, when properly managed, greatly increase the speed and cost effectiveness of technology transfer.

DREAMERS WHO DO

Intrapreneurs are the "dreamers who do." In most organizations people are thought to be either dreamers or doers. Both talents are not generally required in one job. But the trouble with telling the doers not to bother about their dreams is that they dream anyway. When they are blocked from implementing dreams of how to help your company, they're dreaming dreams of revenge. A mind is meant to imagine and then act. It is a terrible thing to split apart the dreamer and the doer.

What we need, then, is to restore the place for vision in everyone's job. One of my favorite stories is the story of Nikola Tesla who invented the three-phase electric motor and a host of other things. It is said that he would build a model in his mind of a machine, such as a new generator, and then push it into the background of his consciousness, set it running, and leave it going for weeks

while he went about his other business. At the end of that time he'd pull it back into the foreground of his mind, tear it down and check the bearings for wear. With such detailed imagination, what need is there for computer-aided design and finite element analysis?

While few of us can match Tesla's talent, imagination is the most concrete mental skill that people have. It is more concrete than all the tools we have for analyzing businesses and all the formulas we have for analyzing stresses. Imagination is simply the ability to see something that doesn't yet exist as it might be. Unless we have Tesla's clarity of imagination, what we see may not be as precise as the results we can reach from doing calculations, but our vision is more concrete and more whole than any formula describing some aspect of a new design. And without this concrete skill, we do not have innovation.

An intrapreneur's imagination is very different from an inventor's. Inventors look five or ten years ahead and say, "wouldn't it be wonderful if such and such." They imagine how a customer would respond to their new product, what the technology would be, how the technology could produce desired features, and all those sorts of things. Good inventors have the customer in mind, but their vision is usually incomplete unless they are also intrapreneurs. They don't imagine in detail how to get from the here and now to that desired future. An intrapreneur, on the other hand, having seen the Promised Land, moves back to the present and takes on the rather mundane and practical task of turning the prototype into a marketplace success. This too requires enormous imagination.

Intrapreneurs ask questions such as, "Who would I need to help me with this? How much would it cost? What things have to happen first?" and so forth. They may ask, "Could we release this technology onto the marketplace in product form aimed at such-and-such a customer need? No. If we did that it would immediately bite into a very important market of one of our competitors who has the ability to respond, and before we produced our second generation products there would be a tremendous competitive response. Let's back up a little bit. What if we put it out in this way instead? Well it wouldn't do quite as well on the first round, but I begin to see it would give us a little more time to develop unbeatable second generation products."

Intrapreneurs have to constantly juggle potential implementation plans. They do this in their imaginations initially. Of course, intrapreneurs also juggle implementation plans on paper as business plans and drawings, but much of the initial work is done in the shower, or when driving the car, or any situation in which one neither feels guilty about not doing something useful nor can one get to pencil and paper. At such times, we are forced to use our imaginations, and thus often do our most creative work.

DISTINGUISH INTRAPRENEURS FROM PROMOTERS

One of the keys to managing innovation cost-effectively is to choose the right people to trust. Too often when managers look for intrapreneurs they choose promoters instead. Promoters are very good at convincing people to back their ideas, but they lack the ability to follow through. Thus, one of the keys to managing innovation is to be able to distinguish between intrapreneurs and promoters.

One of the best ways to separate the intrapreneurs from the promoters is to see how they handle, and even how they think about, barriers to their ideas. When analyzing a potential intrapreneur, think of some of the ways their project might go wrong. Ask them how they might handle such a problem. Real intrapreneurs will have explored these problems in their imagination. They will have considered them while driving to work or taking a shower. The real intrapreneur has thought of three, five, or even ten possible solutions. They may pause for a moment trying to figure out which of those answers would appeal most to you because intrapreneurs do have a certain ability to sell, but they are not hearing the question for the first time. It will be very hard for you to think of a problem which they haven't considered.

Promoters, on the other hand, respond by saying the problem you bring up will never occur. They remind you again of how wonderful things will be ten years from now, of the hundreds of millions of dollars their product will be making. They will not even talk about the problem because they have no interest in the barriers along the way to implementation. They are counting on you to solve all problems by giving them enough funding. They just want to tell you why their idea is so much better than anyone else's. They are, in fact, so focused on getting approvals and funding, that they haven't planned how to get the job done. If you give them money in the name of intrapreneurship, you will not only give intrapreneurship a bad name, but you will waste everything you invested. The most important thing a manager can do when managing innovation is to separate out the promoters, and invest only in intrapreneurs.

Many people doubt that they want entrepreneurial people in their organizations. Entrepreneurs, they believe, are driven by greed. They are high risk-takers, they shoot from the hip, and furthermore, they are dishonest. Fortunately every one of these myths is false. In fact, entrepreneurs seem to be driven by a vision which they believe is so important that they are willing to dedicate their lives to it even when it starts to have trouble. Every new idea runs into terrible obstacles. People who are driven only by a desire for money, or promotion, or status, simply do not have the persistence to move a new idea forward. It is the person with the commitment to carry through who will move an idea into a practical reality.

Intrapreneurs and entrepreneurs are not high risk-takers, as many studies have shown. They like a 50-50 set of odds—not too easy, not too hard. Having chosen a challenging objective, they do everything they can to reduce the risk.

Intrapreneurs seem to be equally right brain and left brain, equally intuitive and analytic. They make decisions based on intuition when data or time don't permit analytical solutions. When analysis will work, they use it.

Intrapreneurs may operate a little differently than other people. They often have personalities which make them difficult to live with, but their difficulties stem less from dishonesty than excessive directness. They often get themselves in trouble by saying exactly what they think because they don't seem to be good at compromising—strong politics are inherent in the cultures of very large organizations.

A NEW MONITOR FOR THE FAA

Vision and imagination make up half of "the dreamers that do." Action is the other half.

Intrapreneurs are often in trouble because they act when they are supposed to wait. They tend to act beyond the territory of their own job description and function. This boundary crossing is important. Charles House at Hewlett-Packard is a perfect example. House developed a new monitor for the Federal Aviation Administration that turned out to not quite meet the specs. (Failure is a typical way for stories of innovation to begin.) He responded to the disappointment by observing that despite not meeting the spot size criteria for this particular application, the fact that he had a monitor which was half as heavy, used half the power, and cost half as much meant he should find out what else it could be used for. He took the idea to the marketing people who asked the division's traditional customers if they would like a monitor that was cheaper, but which had a slightly blurry display.

Nobody seemed to want it. Being an intrapreneur, as opposed to just a researcher, House wasn't satisfied with talk. He took out the front seat of his Volkswagen Bug, put the monitor in its place, and visited 40 customers in three weeks. At each stop he moved the monitor into the prospective customer's shop, hooked it up to their equipment, and asked whether this thing would do anything that's useful. By the end of the trip, he had found several new markets. House succeeded because he took the actions which were necessary for his prototype to go from technology to business reality.

There are two important points in this story. One is that intrapreneurs perform their own market research. If your scientists and engineers are not allowed to do their own market research, then you have a major barrier to innovation.

The second point is that generally a new idea is so ugly only its mother could love it. Consequently, it is unrealistic to think that people in mar-

keting will understand a research idea in its early stages well enough to do valid marketing research. In general, they ask the wrong questions. They are trying to find out if it is a good idea, which in the early stages is the wrong question. The right question is: "I know this is a good idea; how am I going to present it in a way that some class of customers will agree? What are the ways in which this is a good idea? Who really needs it? How do I have to say this so that they will understand?"

The early stage of market research is searching for the market, not testing whether or not it is there. It is only after we have found a group of customers and learned how to talk to them, redesigned the product to meet their needs, and figured out how to position the product, that we can do the traditional form of market research which asks, "Will they buy it—is this a good idea?"

The idea of technically-driven research is drifting into disrepute. We are told that we must first carefully identify market needs and then invent what customers already know they want. This is rarely the way fundamental innovation works because we are not smart enough to invent to order. We are lucky to invent anything with fundamentally new and protectable properties, and when we do so, we must then hunt for the most applicable markets.

To be sure, researchers do pursue what they perceive to be marketplace needs, but the final applications often turn out to be in some entirely different market. Scotch Tape was invented to better insulate refrigerated railroad cars. Radio was invented for point-to-point communication—missing the broadcast market entirely. Riston circuit board systems began with a failure to produce a new photopolymer-based photographic film.

It is important for researchers to know about the marketplace, but important also to realize that for all of the thousands of unfilled or poorly filled marketplace needs each of us wishes to invent a proprietary solution for, we have the ability to invent a few. We know an anti-gravity device would be useful and probably well received by customers. We don't work on it because we don't know how to begin.

We know that television sets with better reception are desirable. Most of us don't work on them because we believe others have a competitive advantage in making them inexpensively.

We left Hewlett-Packard's Charles House doing his own market research and thus doing somebody else's job, as intrapreneurs often do. He came home enthusiastic and his boss's boss, Dar Howard, believed in him and told him to go ahead for another year. Unfortunately, a few months later the chairman visited the laboratory in Colorado. David Packard listened to the marketing people say that the idea was no good, even after House's research. He also heard a negative vote from the corporate chief of technology, who was backing a different technology.

At the time, Tektronix was giving Hewlett-Packard a hard time in the division's core business, and Packard said that when he came back to this laboratory next year, he did not want to see this product in the lab. Dar Howard went back to House and told him he just didn't know what excuse he could give for going on now. With that remark he left the door open just wide enough for Chuck to get his foot in. He showed that he felt for Chuck, but . . .

House said, "What exactly did Packard say?" "When I come back to this laboratory next year, I don't want to see this product in the lab." "Good," said Chuck, "we'll have it out of the lab and into manufacturing." And so it was. The monitor was used in the first manned moon landing and turned out to be a great success.

A few years later, Packard awarded House the Hewlett-Packard Award for Meritorious Defiance. "For contempt and defiance above and beyond the call of engineering duty," the certificate read. He made it clear that at Hewlett-Packard, courage counts more than obedience. Innovation requires this attitude.

SUCCEEDING AT INTRAPRENEURSHIP

Every new idea will have more than its share of detractors. There is no doubt that being an intrapreneur is difficult, even in the most tolerant of companies. So how can people succeed at it?

1. *Do anything needed to move your idea forward.* If you're supposed to be in research but the problem is in a manufacturing process, sneak into the pilot plant and build a new process. If it is a marketing problem, do your own marketing research. If it means sweeping the floor, sweep the floor. Do whatever has to be done to move the idea forward. Needless to say, this isn't always appreciated, and so you have to remember that:

2. *It is easier to ask for forgiveness than for permission.* If you go around asking, you are going to get answers you don't want, so just do the things that need to be done and ask later. Managers have to encourage their people to do this. It may be necessary to remove some layers of management that complicate and slow down the approval process.

3. *Come to work each day willing to be fired.* I began to understand this more from talking to an old sergeant who had seen a lot of battle duty. He said, "You know, there is a simple secret to surviving in battle; you have to go into battle each day knowing you're already dead. If you are already dead, then you can think clearly and you have a good chance of surviving the battle."

Intrapreneurs, like soldiers, have to have the courage to do what's right instead of doing what they know will please the myriad of people in the hierarchy who are trying to stop them. If they are too cautious, they are lost. If they are fearful, the smell of fear is a chemical signal to the corporate immune system, which will move in quickly to smother the "different" idea.

I find that necessary courage comes from a sure knowledge that intrapreneurs have—that if their employer were ever foolish enough to fire them, they could rapidly get a better job. There is no way to have innovation without courage, and no real courage without self-esteem.

4. *Work underground as long as you can.* Every organization has a corporate immune system. As soon as a new idea comes up the white blood cells come in to smother it. I'm not blaming the organization for this. If it did not have an immune system it would die. But we have to find ways to hide the right new ideas in order to keep them alive. It is part of every manager's job to recognize which new ideas should be hidden and which new ideas should be exposed to the corporate immune system and allowed to die a natural death. Too often it is the best ideas that are prematurely exposed.

THE INTRAPRENEURIAL SHORTAGE

I've made an interesting discovery since I wrote *Intrapreneuring*. I used to think potential intrapreneurs were commonplace, that they were hard to find because they were in hiding. But I have found they are more rare in most large organizations than the 10 percent who are entrepreneurial in the population at large. There is a scarcity of people who are brave enough to take on the intrapreneurial role; therefore, we have to lower the barriers and increase the rewards.

If there are not enough intrapreneurs in your company, you can hire more. There are two ways to go about it: raiding successful intrapreneurs from other companies, and hiring more intrapreneurial people in entry positions.

Were I running an R&D organization, I would even take ads saying, "Wanted: Intrapreneurs." One could capitalize on widespread intrapreneurial frustration and selectively hire a fair number of courageous people who would move innovation forward. Second, I would focus on hiring potential intrapreneurs out of school. Here are two hints: One is that candidates' transcripts should contain both A's and D's. When intrapreneurial people are interested they get A's. When they are not interested, they don't pretend. They are self-driven.

The second hint is that any history of self-employment predicts intrapreneurial success. The strongest demographic predictor of intrapreneurial success is having one or more self-employed parents. It is more important than birth order or any of the other commonly cited predictors. I guess it is a matter of having an entrepreneurial role model.

It is a particularly good idea to hire farm kids. They seem to make good intrapreneurs. I guess farm kids grow up with a kind of a can-do attitude and it never occurs to them that there is anything they aren't supposed to do. If the hay is on the ground, the bailer is broken and it is going to rain

in six hours, you don't worry that you don't have a degree in bailer mechanics. Somehow farmers learn to get the job done.

TRAINING INTRAPRENEURS

Training your people in acquiring intrapreneuring skills is as important as knowing whom to hire. Though most people imagine that intrapreneurs are born and not made, we have had good results training intrapreneurs. In our Intrapreneur Schools we ask for volunteers. This way we are training a select group of people who are courageous enough to volunteer for an intrapreneurial role. Training succeeds partly because it gives people permission to use a part of themselves that their supervisors have been trying to beat out of them for quite some time. They look around the room and say, "My goodness, there are other people like me in this world and it seems that the corporation is really serious now about wanting this aspect of me employed." They get a tremendous rejuvenation and rebirth of vision and drive.

In addition, most intrapreneurs are missing skills for which training can help. They have some functional abilities which are often technical, and they've been convinced that they really cannot understand some things like accounting or marketing. They believe that those blind spots keep them from being the general manager of a new idea. They do not have to become excellent at all functions; they just have to understand enough to work easily with others in those fields. In fact, if the idea is good, success does not require great sophistication in many disciplines, just a journeyman-like job that doesn't overlook the obvious. Training should be structured to build teams and so the whole team should work together while training.

MANAGING INTRAPRENEURS

Managers must choose intrapreneurs who are persistent, impatient, who laugh, and who face the barriers. Then they have to be willing to trust that the intrapreneurs know how to do their jobs and must give them what they are asking for—resources and people to help carry forward their ideas. Since resources are not infinite, they may have to take these things away from other people who are not intrapreneurs.

I know we are living in an age of head-count restrictions. Too often this means that everything stays the same. Whoever has three people gets three people next year. Anything new and growing will have too few people resources, and any thing old and over the hill is going to have too many. We have to be courageous in sweeping out the old and giving the right people the resources they need to get the job done. The most effective use of a manager's time is in choosing whom to trust.

One very effective approach is to create heroes so intrapreneurs have role models within the company. Select a few of the most courageous intrapreneurs and publish their stories for every one in the company to read. These stories should be written honestly, so that all the difficulties and problems faced by the intrapreneurs are presented so that people can see how barriers were overcome.

KEEP R&D CLOSE TO THE ACTION

It is important to bring your researchers close to model shops and pilot plants that allow dirty-finger research. R&D people need to be able to test

---

Rewards are the Litmus Test

For many intrapreneurs who have given up and are hiding in the woodwork, rewards for innovation are the litmus test of a company's sincerity. If a company isn't willing to reward intrapreneurship, it does not really want it. I underestimated the importance of rewards when I wrote *Intrapreneuring* four years ago. It requires care since you can make a lot of mistakes designing a reward system. If you reward just the leader and not the whole team, for instance, you will have a disaster on your hands. But if you don't reward, then people will say you don't really want innovation.

Several kinds of rewards are useful. First is recognition programs which, though obvious, are generally underused. We advise our clients to create many award programs—awards for process innovation and various awards for different kinds of new product innovation. Each recipient will be one of a few who received that award even though in total large numbers are recognized. But recognition, no matter how well done, is not enough.

Financial rewards are also important and must be arranged so as not to arouse excessive jealousy in the managers of stable and mature businesses. One technique that works well in designing predetermined (prospective) rewards is to ask those who are signing up for a program that promises unusual rewards in the event of success to take personal risk. We often advise putting 10-20 percent of salary at risk or freezing salary until the rewards are due.

Compensation alone or even combined with recognition still does not make an adequate reward. In fact, if it is not combined with increasing freedom to try new things, bonuses may simply provide seed money for successful intrapreneurs to start their own businesses. The essential reward is freedom.

Entrepreneurs, in fact, find freedom to try their new ideas their most important reward. Their wealth is not mainly used for personal consumption: the bulk is used to find the next idea. The most tangible form of freedom in a large organization is a budget. We have developed a reward system called intracapital—a one-time earned discretionary budget to be used on behalf of the corporation to try out new ideas.

We know we must give intrapreneurs, inventors, and their collaborators an unusual degree of freedom. We all do this instinctively. As organizations grow and develop levels of bureaucracy, we must do it systematically.

their ideas themselves—if they can't, they will fall back on more intellectual forms of research. Obviously, we'll hear more about discretionary time, the so-called 15 percent rules that many companies have. Other useful reward tools are seed money programs, the creation of crossfunctional teams, and other ways to reduce the bureaucracy.

In conclusion, I issue a challenge to get your people to display courage, to display integrity and honesty, to have a sense of proprietorship—as if the business belonged to them. Help them to make the kind of decisions that would have to be made if that were true, rather than the kinds they have to make in order to negotiate the turfs of a hostile bureaucracy. Encourage them to go into action and not wait for permission. Talking about these ideas is not enough. Between the words of top management and the intrapreneurs who can carry them out there are layers of management which punish independent thought, courage, impatience, and blunt honesty. This is not something that you can devote a few hours to and fix. It is probably the most important aspect of your job, more important than getting the strategy right, because enough attention is being paid to strategy already.

You cannot have cost-effective innovation unless you hire, train and encourage intrapreneurs. The future legitimacy of R&D, the success of America's companies and of her economy depends on you, the R&D community, to do it right.

27

Cultural Differences in the Championing of Global Innovation

SCOTT SHANE

Managers in different countries clearly prefer different approaches to championing; a study offers guidelines for making the choice.

Two fundamental forces have altered the way multinational firms do business in the 1990s: 1) The rapid pace of technological and organizational change has made the ability to innovate quickly and successfully a virtual requirement for multinational firms; and, 2) The globalization of business has made essential the ability to direct, control and motivate a culturally diverse work force around the globe.

The need to keep up with change has left senior managers of multinational corporations asking, "How can I teach my people to promote innovation successfully in the different cultures in which our firm operates?"

Research on the innovation process has shown that it rarely occurs without the impetus of a "champion"—an advocate whose goal is to promote the innovation. The champion garners resources and support for the innovative idea. Specifically, he or she prevents the idea from being snuffed out by members of the organization who do not want to upset the existing balance of power in the organization, who are too busy with day-to-day operations to devote time or money to new things, or who simply are afraid to change.

The champion's goal is to convince people to support the innovation. To achieve this goal, he or she can use a multitude of approaches. In some in-

stances, the champion will use autonomy from the authority structure to get money or people for an innovative project outside the organization's normal budgetary procedures. In one electronics company that I studied, the champion behind the development of a new portable telephone was put in charge of a new venture unit that reported directly to the company president. His funding came directly from the president, and he did not have to request funds to develop the telephones through the normal channels.

In other instances, the champion might use his or her relationship with senior managers to change the strategic direction of the organization to incorporate a new project. In one chemical company, the champion was able to assemble a team to work on a new fertilizer by convincing the company's key strategic planner that the company's growth rate would be improved if it developed more agrichemicals.

Sometimes the champion will create a groundswell of support for the innovation among the firm's employees. In one financial services firm with a philosophy that stressed teamwork, a champion was able to convince senior management of the need for a new back office computer system by demonstrating to them the support of back office personnel for such a system. Other times, the champion will seek support only of senior management.

Champions may choose to break the organization's rules overtly by such actions as "bootlegging" resources, or they may decide to adhere to standard operating procedures in putting the inno-

An early version of this article was published in 1994 titled "Championing change in the global corporation." Research-Technology Management, 37(5): 29–35.

Scott Shane is Professor of Strategic Management at M.I.T.'s Sloan School of Management.

vation together. In the electronics company that I studied, champions often hid their new product ideas from senior management until they had evidence that the products would work. To get funding for these "hidden" projects, the engineers charged the costs to other budget items. By contrast, champions in the chemical company strictly adhered to its rules and procedures; they did not bootleg resources, nor did they violate any of the rules for getting resources allocated to a project.

The champion's personality is one of the many influences on how the champion seeks resources and support for innovation. Some champions are comfortable aggressively confronting their superiors; others are not. The industry in which a firm operates also affects championing style. In highly regulated industries, championing styles like the bootlegging of resources may run afoul of laws, so champions in these industries adhere to standard operating procedures. Corporate culture is another determinant of the approach a champion will take. In companies where hierarchy is deemphasized, champions may find it easier to appeal directly to senior managers for support than they would in more hierarchical companies.

In the global corporation, there is another, more fundamental, determinant of championing style. That factor is *national culture*. Over the past 40 years, an enormous amount of research has shown that managers in different countries make different strategic decisions and prefer different types of organizational structures because they hold different fundamental values about people and the way they should behave in organizations. These cultural differences influence the approaches to championing that managers believe are appropriate in their society.

The reason is simple. We know that innovation is difficult to accomplish unless its proponents can convince others to support their activities. We also know that it is easier to get people's support for something when one acts in a way that is appealing to them. Therefore, in multicultural environments, getting support for innovation is most effective when managers use culturally appropriate championing styles.

FOUR QUESTIONS ABOUT INNOVATION

Unfortunately for managers, while the importance of using culturally appropriate approaches has been identified, until now no one had documented the appropriate styles in different cultures. That is what I sought to accomplish in a recent study in which I surveyed some 4000 managers in 8 organizations in 32 countries to determine which approaches to championing they felt were most appropriate in their culture. The survey targeted organizations in financial services, electronics, consumer products, chemicals, and insurance, in the U.S. and other countries listed in Table 27.1

The survey queried managers about four aspects of championing innovation, summarized as follows:

1. Is it better for the champion to work within or outside the rules, procedures, norms, and hierarchy of the organization?
This question explored whether or not the champion should make it possible for the people working on an innovation to bypass standard operating, budgetary, and personnel procedures in order to get people and resources committed to an innovation. I also asked whether champions should create support among employees for an innovation before senior managers approved it formally, by making decisions without referring them to higher officials or outside the traditional hierarchy.

2. How should champions get others in the organization to support the innovation? Should they, for example, convince people in other departments that an innovation deserves their support by demonstrating how it will benefit them as individuals? Or should they convince them of the innovation's benefits to the organization as a whole?

3. How should champions monitor the innovation process? Should they closely supervise the people working on an innovation and allow them to get a budget and authority to undertake only one stage of the innovation at a time? Or should the champion allow the innovation team to get the budget and authority to undertake multiple stages of the innovation at a time? Also, should the cham-

TABLE 27.1
Championing Preference Scale

Country	Work outside the rules	Appeal to the organization as a whole	Closely monitor the innovation process	Treat all members of the innovation team as equals
Argentina	Low	High	Low	Low
Belgium	Med	Med	Med	Med
Brazil	Med	Med	Low	Med
Canada	High	Med	Med	Med
Chile	Low	High	Low	Low
Denmark	Med	Med	Low	Med
Finland	High	Low	Low	Med
France	High	Med	High	Med
Germany	Med	Low	Low	High
Hong Kong	Med	Med	Low	Low
India	Med	High	Low	Med
Ireland	High	High	Low	Low
Italy	Med	Low	Low	Med
Jamaica	Low	Low	Med	Med
Japan	Low	Low	Low	Low
Kenya	High	High	Med	Med
Malaysia	Med	High	Low	Med
Mauritius	Med	High	Med	Med
Mexico	Low	Med	Low	Med
New Zealand	High	High	Low	Med
Norway	Med	Low	Med	Med
Philippines	High	High	Low	Med
Portugal	Low	High	High	Med
South Africa	Med	High	Low	Med
Spain	Low	Med	Low	Med
Switzerland	High	High	Low	Med
Taiwan	Low	Med	Med	Med
Turkey	High	High	Low	Med
United Kingdom	High	High	Low	Med
United Stages	High	Med	Low	Med
Uruguay	Low	High	Low	Low
Zimbabwe	High	High	Med	Med

pion make it possible for people working on an innovation to take the initiative in acting on their own ideas without formal approval? Or should the champion require the innovation team to seek approval for their ideas before acting on them?

4. What should be the composition of the innovation team? Should the champion include all the people working on an innovation in the planning and decision-making process, and allow them to participate equally, regardless of their position in the organization? Or should the champion limit planning and decision-making to high-ranking members of the organization?

PREFERENCE FOR DIFFERENT APPROACHES

My study showed that managers in different countries clearly prefer different approaches to championing. Using a scale of high, medium, and low, I mapped out the preference for the four aspects of championing across the 32 countries. This championing preference scale (Table 27.1) identifies the most acceptable ways to promote innovation in different countries. The higher the score a country receives on a given championing dimension, the more receptive managers in that country are to that championing style.

For example, a strong contrast is evident between the United States and Japan on whether champions should work within organizational rules, procedures and hierarchy. While American managers felt that a champion should make it possible for the people working on an innovation to bypass standard operating, budgetary and personnel procedures to get people and resources committed to an innovation, Japanese managers disagreed. They felt that champions should not create support for an innovation among employees *before* formal approval of the innovation by senior managers. In contrast, American managers felt that the champion should make it possible for the innovators to make decisions without referring them to higher officials or outside the organization's traditional hierarchy. American managers also felt that the champion should make it possible for the people working on an innovation to avoid having to justify it financially at every stage of the development process—people ought to make decisions based on their intuition.

Another contrast is apparent in the way that Argentineans and Chileans on the one hand, and Italians on the other, felt the champion should convince others to support an innovation. The Italians said the champion should demonstrate the benefits of the innovation to them as individuals. Chileans and Argentineans said that the champion should demonstrate the benefit of the innovation to the organization as a whole. In contrast to the Italians, the Chileans and Argentineans felt that the champion should trust the decisions of people working on an innovation. They also said that the champion should always include the person who developed the idea for an innovation, regardless of his or her status in the organization.

There are also national differences in the preference for monitoring, in the innovation process. By monitoring, I mean the observation and evaluation of efforts by the members of the innovation team. Monitoring includes such things as comparison against written plans or results from the previous stage of the innovation effort, before authority and resources are allocated to proceed to the next stage. The opposite of monitoring is a "license

to innovate," in which the innovation team members are given the resources and authority to innovate and not evaluated on their efforts until they have completed their task.

In contrast to American and German managers, French managers said that the champion should monitor the innovation process. Unlike the American and German managers, the French managers felt that the champion should help the people working on an innovation to get a budget and authority to undertake only one stage of the innovation at a time. They also said that the champion should not make it possible for the innovators to take initiative on their ideas without getting formal approval.

National differences in the composition of innovation teams also existed, as can be seen from the contrast between Japan and Germany. In contrast to German managers, Japanese managers said that the champion should include all the people working on an innovation in the decision-making process. They also felt that the champion should make it possible for everybody working on an innovation to participate equally in the planning process regardless of their position in the organization.

STYLES TO AVOID

If American managers are to understand appropriate championing styles in the countries in which they manage innovation, they must also know which championing styles are not acceptable in different countries. Table 27.2 outlines the championing styles I believe managers should avoid in some of the more important countries in which Americans do business.

CULTURAL VALUES MATTER

I also asked managers about their cultural values (using a questionnaire devised by Geert Hofstede, formerly of IBM) and compared cultural values to preferred championing styles at the national level.

TABLE 27.2
Culturally Inappropriate Championing Styles

When doing business in Canada . . .

Don't expect champions to adhere to standard operating procedures, budgets, or personnel systems; don't expect decisions to be made through the hierarchy or by high-level managers; don't seek formal approval of the innovation without creating support for the innovation among employees; don't excpect people working on the innovation to justify the innovation financially at every stage; don't block champions, from making decisions based on their intuition.

In Chile . . .

Don't expect champions to violate standard operating procedures, budgets, or personnel systems; don't expect decisions to be made outside the hierarchy or by high-level managers; don't seek support for the innovation among employees without first getting formal approval of the innovation by senior managers; don't permit people working on the innovation to work without justifying the innovation financially at every stage; don't allow champions to make decisions based on their intuition; don't exclude the person who developed the idea for the innovation from the innovation development process; don't focus on benefits to individuals to get people in other departments to commit resources to the innovation; don't expect people working on the innovation to get a budget or authority to undertake only one stage of the innovation at a time; don't include all people working on an innovation in its decision-making process; don't treat all people working on an innovation as equals in the innovation-planning process.

In France . . .

Don't expect champions to adhere to standard operating procedures, budgets, or personnel systems; don't expect decisions to be made through the hierarchy or by high-level managers; don't seek formal approval of the innovation without creating support for the innovation among employees; don't expect people working on the innovation to justify the innovation financially at every stage; don't block champions from making decisions based on their intuition; don't help people working on the innovation to get a budget or authority to undertake multiple stages of the innovation at a time.

In Germany . . .

Don't focus on benefits to the organization as a whole to get people in other departments to commit resources to the innovaton; don't fail to test the decisons of people working on an innovation; don't expect people working on the innovation to get a budget or authority to undertake only one stage of the innovation at a time; do not expect people working on an innovation to get formal approval for ideas before undertaking them; don't exclude anyone working on an innovation from its decision-making process; don't treat some people working on an innovation as less important than others in the innovation-planning process.

In India . . .

Don't distrust the decisions of people working on an innovation; don't exclude the people who developed the idea for the innovation even if they are of low status in the organization; don't focus on benefits to individuals to get people in other departments to commit resources to the innovation; don't expect people working on the innovation to get a budget or authority to undertake only one stage of the innovation at a time; do not expect people working on an innovation to get formal approval for ideas before undertaking them.

In Japan . . .

Don't expect champions to violate standard operating procedures, budgets, personnel systems; don't expect decisions to be made outside the hierarchy or by high-level managers; don't seek support for the innovation among employees without first getting formal approval of the innovation by senior managers; don't permit people working on the innovation to work without justifying the innovation financially at every stage; don't allow champions to make decisions based on their intuition; don't include the people who developed the idea for the innovation in decision-making if they are of low status in the organization; don't fail to test the decisions of people working on an innovation; don't expect people working on the innovation to get a budget or authority to undertake only one stage of the innovation at a time; don't treat all people working on an innovation as equals in the innovation-planning process.

In Malaysia . . .

Don't distrust the decisions of people working on an innovation; don't exclude the people who developed the idea for the innovation even if they are of low status in the organization; don't focus on benefits to individuals to get people in other departments to commit resources to the innovation; don't expect people working on the innovation to get a budget or authority to undertake only one stage of the innovation at a time; do not expect people working on an innovation to get formal approval for ideas before undertaking them.

In Mexico . . .

Don't expect champions to violate standard operating procedures, budgets, personnel systems; don't expect decisions to be made outside the hierarchy or by high-level managers; don't seek support for the innovation among employees without first getting formal approval of the innovation by senior managers; don't permit people working on the innovation to work without justifying the innovation financially at every stage; don't allow champions to make decisions based on their intuition; don't expect people working on the innovation to get a budget or authority to undertake only one stage of the innovation at a time.

In The Philippines . . .

Don't expect champions to adhere to standard operating procedures, budgets, personnel systems; don't expect decisions to be made through the hierarchy or by high-level managers; don't seek formal approval of the innovation without creating support for the innovation among employees; don't expect people working on the innovation to justify the innovation financially at every stage; don't block champions from making decisions based on their intuition; don't distrust the decisions of people working on an innovation; don't exclude the people who developed the idea for the innovation even if they are of low status in the organization;

TABLE 27.2—*Continued*

don't focus on benefits to individuals to get people in other departments to commit resources to the innovation; don't expect people working on the innovation to get a budget or authority to undertake only one stage of the innovation at a time; do not expect people working on an innovation to get formal approval for ideas before undertaking them.

In Taiwan . . .

Don't expect champions to violate standard operating procedures, budgets, personnel systems; don't expect decisions to be made outside the hierarchy or by high-level managers; don't seek support for the innovation among employees without first getting formal approval of the innovation by senior managers; don't permit people working on the innovation to work without justifying the innovation financially at every stage; don't allow champions to make decisions based on their intuition; don't expect people working on the innovation to get a budget or authority to undertake only one stage of the innovation at a time.

In the United Kingdom . . .

Don't expect champions to adhere to standard operating procedures, budgets, personnel systems; don't expect decisions to be made through the hierarchy or by high-level managers; don't seek normal approval of the innovation without creating support for the innovation among employees; don't expect people working on the innovation to justify the innovation financially at every stage; don't block champions from making decisions based on their intuition; don't distrust the decisions of people working on an innovation; don't exclude the people who developed the idea for the innovation even if they are of low status in the organization; don't focus on benefits to individuals to get people in other departments to commit resources to the innovation; don't expect people working on the innovation to get a budget or authority to undertake only one stage of the innovation at a time; do not expect people working on an innovation to get formal approval for ideas before undertaking them.

The portions of the cultural values questionnaire I used explored individualism, power distance and uncertainty avoidance. As Hofstede has explained (1):

- *Individualism* is the belief that people should act in the interest of themselves and their immediate families, in contrast to collectivism in which people act in the interest of a wider group like a community or organization.

- *Power distance* is the tolerance for social inequality.

- *Uncertainty avoidance* is the degree of discomfort with uncertain, unclear or unstructured situations.

Table 27.3 shows the cultural values scores for different countries calculated from my survey. Like the championing scores, they are scored as high, medium, and low.

I found that the reason some championing styles are more appropriate in some countries than others is that people's cultural values influence their preferences for different approaches to championing. In my study, I found that national culture was far more important than corporate culture, industry, gender, level of education, functional area, age, length of work experience, or even champi-

oning experience in explaining preferences for different approaches to championing.

As I have described in other publications (4), the survey showed that cultural values are significantly associated with three of the dimensions of championing. In societies in which individualism is valued, like France or Switzerland, managers prefer that champions articulate individual rewards to specific people to get them to support innovation efforts rather than appeal to a sense of duty to the group. In societies in which people are power-distant, like Malaysia or Japan, managers prefer that champions closely monitor the innovation effort rather than giving managers a "license to innovate." And in societies in which people tend to avoid uncertainty, like Chile, managers prefer champions to work within rules, hierarchy and standard operating procedures to promote innovation rather than to go outside of these organizational systems.

These overarching cultural values, present to greater and lesser extent in different countries, determine the appropriateness of different championing styles. Managers, therefore, can use Tables 27.1 and 27.3 to identify championing styles to use in different countries. Where individualism is low, champions should appeal to the organization as a whole. Where power distance is high, champions

TABLE 27.3
Cultural Values Measures

Country	Power distance	Individ-ualism	Uncertainty avoidance
Argentina	High	Med	Med
Belgium	High	High	Low
Brazil	Med	Med	Med
Canada	Med	High	Med
Chile	Low	Low	High
Denmark	Low	High	Med
Finland	Med	High	Low
France	High	High	Med
Germany	Med	High	High
Hong Kong	High	High	Low
India	Med	Med	Med
Ireland	Med	High	Low
Italy	Low	Med	Med
Jamaica	Med	Low	Med
Japan	High	Med	High
Kenya	Med	Med	Med
Malaysia	High	Med	Med
Mauritius	High	Low	Med
Mexico	Med	Med	Med
New Zealand	Med	High	Med
Norway	Low	High	Low
Philippines	High	Med	High
Portugal	Med	Low	Med
South Africa	Med	Med	High
Spain	Med	Med	Med
Switzerland	Med	High	Med
Taiwan	Med	Med	High
Turkey	Med	High	Med
United Kingdom	Med	High	Med
United States	Med	High	Low
Uruguay	Med	Low	High
Zimbabwe	High	Med	High

should closely monitor the innovation process. And where uncertainty avoidance is low, champions should work outside the formal system's rules.

Managers need to adapt their approaches to promoting innovation to different cultures to get their ideas accepted. This is true at the level of national culture, and probably holds for subcultures as well. Managers who seek to promote innovation in culturally diverse work forces within a single country are also better off promoting innovation in ways that conform to the preferences of the people they are trying to persuade.

This research raises the question of why some societies tend to be more innovative and inventive than others. In earlier research published in the *Journal of Business Venturing (2,3)*, I showed that societies that are more individualistic and less power-distant than others are also more inventive (with inventiveness measured as per capita number of patents produced annually). Societies that are less uncertainty-avoiding, less power-distant and more individualistic are more innovative (I measured innovativeness as per capita number of trademarks produced annually).

An interesting pattern emerges from putting the two sets of research together. The more individualistic, less power-distant and less uncertainty-avoiding societies are the ones in which freedom from monitoring, the provision of individual rewards and a tolerance for rule-breaking are the preferred norms for championing. These cultures are also the most innovative and inventive, by these measures. Research on American champions has traditionally shown that allowing freedom from monitoring, tolerance of rule-breaking and provision of individual rewards are important aspects of championing behavior. This suggests that successful innovation may require this type of championing behavior worldwide.

Since cultural norms influence the tolerance of managers for these types of behaviors, however, cultural values influence national rates of innovativeness and inventiveness by allowing or not allowing effective championing behavior.

RESOLVING A STRATEGIC DILEMMA

This situation creates a strategic dilemma in the management of innovation in global corporations. Managers cannot be ethnocentric and always apply American championing styles overseas, as these approaches are likely to be rejected where they are culturally inappropriate. However, managers also cannot be polycentric and always apply culturally appropriate championing styles overseas, as many of these championing styles are associated with low rates of innovation and invention.

The solution to this dilemma appears to be a choice between two alternatives. The first is to locate activities that require high levels of innovation in countries in which the culture is tolerant of the championing styles that encourage innovation and invention. The second is to encourage cultural change among their employees in the societies in which companies wish to enhance rates of innovation but the culture is uncomfortable with effective championing styles. This approach may be less difficult than it sounds. Cultures can change within and between generations. The globalization of the media has made culture transfer easier. So by hiring younger managers, who have been exposed to foreign culture through media or other means, firms can enhance this culture change within the organization.

While adhering to cultural preferences will not guarantee a successful innovation effort, particularly if the preferred championing style is one that is not effective in encouraging innovation, working against these preferences is likely to make the effort fail. When faced with the problem of championing in a culturally appropriate way or in a way that is more likely to enhance innovation, managers must make a strategic choice. The competitive global environment that most businesses find themselves in today makes it likely that more and more managers will need to make this choice.

REFERENCES

1. Hofstede, Geert. *Culture's Consequences: International Differences in Work-Related Values.* Beverly Hills: Sage, 1980.
2. Shane, Scott. "Why do some societies invent more than others?" *Journal of Business Venturing*, 7(1):29–46, 1992.
3. Shane, Scott. "Cultural influences on national rates of innovation." *Journal of Business Venturing*, 8(1):59–74, 1993.
4. Shane, Scott, Venkataroman, S., and MacMillan, I. "Cultural differences in innovation championing strategies." *Journal of Management*, 21(5):931–952, 1995.

4

THE MANAGEMENT OF PROFESSIONALS WITHIN INNOVATIVE ORGANIZATIONS

10

Managing Technical Communications and Technology Transfer

28

Distinguishing Science from Technology

THOMAS J. ALLEN

Technology is not science—engineers are not scientists. Few would contest these statements; and yet, the failure to recognize the distinction has created untold confusion in the literature. Despite the fact that they should be the last to commit such an egregious error, social scientists studying the behavior of scientists and engineers seldom distinguish properly between the two groups. The social science literature is replete with studies of "scientists," who upon closer examination turn out to be engineers. Worse still, in many studies the populations are mixed, and no attempt is made to distinguish between the two subsets.[1] Many social scientists still view the two groups as essentially the same and feel no need to distinguish between them. This sort of error has led to an unbelieveable amount of confusion over the nature of the populations that have been studied and over the applicability of research results to specific real-life situations. A common practice is to use the term *scientist* throughout a presentation, preceded by a disclaimer to the effect that "for ease of presentation, the term *scientist* will be assumed to include both engineers and scientists." This approach to-

Reprinted with permission from Allen, Thomas J.

Thomas J. Allen is Senior Associate Dean and Professor of Management at M.I.T's Sloan School of Management.

tally neglects the vast differences between the two professions. Managers are not immune from this problem either. Many managers of R&D fail to recognize the true differences and often assume differences that are really non-existent.

At this point, many readers will accuse the author of magnifying what they may consider a trivial issue. But it is just that failure to recognize the distinction that has resulted in so much misdirected policy. In the field of information science, it has often resulted in heavy investments in solutions to the wrong problem. Engineers differ from scientists in their professional activity, their attitudes, their orientations, and even in their typical family background. To interpret the results of research, it is essential to know whether those results were derived from the study of technical professionals working either as engineers or as scientists because the behavior of the two is so different.

One area in which distinctions are very marked is technical communication. Engineers and scientists communicate about their work in very different ways. The reasons for this are many. Not only are the two groups socialized into entirely different subcultures but their educational processes are vastly different, and there is a considerable amount of evidence to show that they differ in personality characteristics and family backgrounds as well. Krulee and Nadler (1960) contrast the values and career orientation of science and engineering undergraduates in the following ways:

> [Students] choosing science have additional objectives that distinguish them from those preparing for careers in engineering and management. The science students place a higher value on independence and on learning for its own sake, while, by way of contrast, more students in the other curricula are concerned with success and professional preparation. Many students in engineering and management expect their families to be more important than their careers as major sources of satisfactions, but the reverse pattern is more typical for science students. Moreover, there is a sense in which the science students tend to value education as an end in itself, while the others value it as a means to an end.

Note that Krulee and Nadler do not distinguish between engineering students and students in management. There is considerable evidence to show that many engineering students see the profession as a transitional phase in a career leading to higher levels of management. Krulee and Nadler go on to argue that engineering students are less concerned than those in science with what one does in one's specialty and are more concerned with the attainment of organizational rewards and promotions. They are more prepared than their fellow scientists to sacrifice some of their independence and opportunities for innovative work in order to take on particular organizational or managerial responsibilities.

In the same vein, Ritti (1971) finds a marked contrast between the work goals of scientists and engineers after graduation. Ritti found, for example, that over 60 percent of the engineers in his sample indicated that it was "very important" for them to know the company's management policies and practices and to help the company increase its profits. Less than 30 percent of the scientists indicated that these were very important work goals. On the other hand, more than 80 percent of the scientists said that it was very important for them to publish articles in technical journals and to establish a professional reputation outside the company—the corresponding percentages for engineers were less than 30 percent. From all the analyses of his data, Ritti draws the following general conclusions:

> First, the notion of a basic conflict in goals between management and the professional is misapplied to engineers. If the goals of the business require meeting schedules, developing products that will be successful in the marketplace, and helping the company expand its activities, then the goals of engineering specialists are very much in line with these ends.
>
> Second, engineers do not have the goals of scientists. And evidently they never had the goals of scientists. While publication of results and professional autonomy are clearly valued goals of Ph.D. scientists, they are just as clearly the least valued goals of the baccalaureate engineer. The

reasons for this difference can be found in the work functions of engineers as opposed to research scientists. Furthermore, both groups desire career development or advancement but for the engineer advancement is tied to activities within the company, while for the scientist advancement is dependent upon the reputation established outside the company.

The type of person who is attracted to a career in engineering is fundamentally quite different from the type who pursues a scientific career. On top of all of this lies the most important difference: level of education. Engineers are generally educated to the baccalaureate level; some go on to a Master of Science degree; some have no college degree at all. The scientist is almost always assumed to have a doctorate. The long, complex process of academic socialization that is involved in reaching this stage is bound to result in a person who differs considerably in his lifeview. These differences in values and attitudes toward work will almost certainly be reflected in the behavior of the individuals. To treat both professions as one and then to search for consistencies in behavior and outlook is almost certain to produce error and confusion of results.

THE NATURE OF TECHNOLOGY

The differences between science and technology lie not only in the kinds of people who are attracted to them; they are basic to the nature of the activities themselves. Both science and technology develop in a cumulative manner, with each new advance building on and being a product of vast quantities of work that have gone before. In science all of the work up to any point can be found permanently recorded in literature, which serves as a repository for all scientific knowledge. The cumulative nature of science can be demonstrated quite clearly (Price, 1965a, 1970) by the way in which citations among scientific journal articles cluster and form a regular pattern of development over time.

A journal system has been developed in most technologies that in many ways emulates the system originally developed by scientists; yet the literature published in the majority of these journals lacks, as Price (1965b, 1970) has shown, one of the fundamental characteristics of the scientific literature: it does not cumulate or build upon itself as does the scientific literature. Citations to previous papers or patents are fewer and are more often to the author's own work. Publication occupies a position of less importance than it does in science where it serves to document the end product and establish priority. Because published information is at best secondary to the actual utilization of the technical innovation, this archival function is not as essential to ensure the technologist that he is properly credited by future generations. The names of Wilbur and Orville Wright are not remembered because they published papers. The technologist's principal legacy to posterity is encoded in physical, not verbal, structure. Consequently, the technologist publishes less and devotes less time to reading than do scientists.

Information is transferred in technology primarily through personal contact. Even in this, however, the technologist differs markedly from the scientist. Scientists working at the frontier of a particular specialty know each other and associate together in what Derek Price has called "invisible colleges." They keep track of one another's work through visits, seminars, and small invitational conferences, supplemented by an informal exchange of written material long before it reaches archival publication. Technologists, on the other hand, keep abreast of their field by close association with co-workers in their own organization. They are limited in forming invisible colleges by the imposition of organizational barriers.

BUREAUCRATIC ORGANIZATION

Unlike scientists, the vast majority of technologists are employed by organizations with a well-defined mission (profit, national defense, space exploration, pollution abatement, and so forth). Mission-oriented organizations necessarily demand of their technologists a degree of identification unknown in most scientific circles. This organizational identification works in two ways to exclude the technologist from informal communication channels outside his or her organization. First, they are inhibited by the requirements that they work only on problems that are of interest to their employer, and second, they must refrain from early disclosure of the results of their research in order to maintain their employer's advantage over competitors. Both of these constraints violate the strong scientific norms that underlie and form the basis of the invisible college. The first of these norms demands that science be free to choose its own problems and that the community of colleagues be the only judges of the relative importance of possible areas of investigation, and the second is that the substantive findings of research are to be fully assigned and communicated to the entire research community. The industrial organization, by preventing its employers from adhering to these two norms, impedes the formation by technologists of anything resembling an invisible college.

Impact of "Localism" on Communication

What is the effect of this enforced "localism" on the communication patterns of engineers? Because proprietary information must be protected to preserve the firm's position in a highly competitive marketplace, free communication among engineers of different organizations is greatly inhibited. It is always amusing to observe engineers from different companies interacting in the hallways and cocktail lounges at conventions of professional engineering societies. Each one is trying to draw the maximum amount of information from his competitors while giving up as little as possible of his own information in return. Often the winner in this bargaining situation is the person with the strongest physical constitution.

Another result of the concern over divulging proprietary information will be observed in looking at an engineer's reading habits. A good proportion of the truly important information generated in an industrial laboratory cannot be published

in the open literature because it is considered proprietary and must be protected. It is, however, published within the organization, and, for this reason, the informal documentation system of his or her parent organization is an important source of information for the engineer.

THE EFFECT OF TURNOVER

It is this author's suspicion that much of the proprietary protectionism in industry is far overplayed. Despite all of the organizational efforts to prevent it, the state of the art in a technology propagates quite rapidly. Either there are too many martinis consumed at engineering conventions or some other mechanism is at work. This other mechanism may well be the itinerant engineer, who passes through quite a number of organizations over the course of a career. Whenever engineers leave an employer, voluntarily or otherwise, they carry some knowledge of the company's operations, experience, and current technology with them. We are gradually coming to realize that human beings are the most effective carriers of information and that the best way to transfer information between organizations or social systems is to physically transfer a human carrier. Roberts's studies (Roberts and Wainer, 1967) marshal impressive evidence for the effective transfer of space technology from quasi-academic institutions to the industrial sector and eventually to commercial application in those instances in which technologists left university laboratories to establish their own businesses. This finding is especially impressive in view of the general failure to find evidence of successful transfer of space technology by any other mechanism, despite the fact that many techniques have been tried and a substantial amount of money has been invested in promoting the transfer.

This certainly makes sense. Ideas have no real existence outside of the minds of people. Ideas can be represented in verbal or graphic form, but such representation is necessarily incomplete and cannot be easily structured to fit new situations. The human brain has a capacity for flexibly restructuring information in a manner that has never been approached by even the most sophisticated computer programs. For truly effective transfer of technical information, we must make use of this human ability to recode and restructure information so that it fits into new contexts and situations. Consequently, the best way to transfer technical information is to move a human carrier. The high turnover among engineers results in a heavy migration from organization to organization and is therefore a very effective mechanism for disseminating technology throughout an industry and often to other industries. Every time an engineer changes jobs he brings with him a record of his experiences on the former job and a great amount of what his former organization considers "proprietary" information. Now, of course, the information is usually quite perishable, and its value decays rapidly with time. But a continual flow of engineers among the firms of an industry ensures that no single firm is very far behind in knowledge of what its competitors are doing. So the mere existence of high turnover among R&D personnel vitiates much of the protectionism accorded proprietary information.

As for turnover itself, it is well known that most organizations attempt to minimize it. Actually, however, a certain amount of turnover may be not only desirable but absolutely essential to the survival of a technical organization, although just what the optimum turnover level is for an organization is a question that remains to be answered. It will vary from one situation to the next and is highly dependent upon the rate at which the organization's technical staff is growing. After all, it is the influx of new engineers that is most beneficial to the organization, not the exodus of old ones. When growth rate is high, turnover can be low. An organization that is not growing should welcome or encourage turnover, despite the costs of hiring and processing new personnel. Although it is impossible to place a price tag on the new state-of-the-art information that is brought in by new employees, it may very well more than counterbalance the costs of hiring. This would be true at least to the point where turnover becomes dis-

ruptive to the morale and functioning of the organization.

COMMUNICATION PATTERNS IN SCIENCE AND TECHNOLOGY

Scientists all share a common concern and responsibility for processing information, which is the essence of scientific activity. As physical systems consume and transform *energy*, so too does the system of science consume, transform, produce, and exchange *information*. Scientists talk to one another, they read each other's papers, and most important, they publish scientific papers, their principal tangible product. Both the input and output of this system we call science are in the form of information. Each of the components, whether individual investigations or projects, consume and produce information. Furthermore, whether written or oral, this information is always in the form of human language. Scientific information is, or can be, nearly always encoded in a verbal form.

Technology is also an ardent consumer of information. The engineer must first have information in order to understand and formulate the problem confronting him. Then she must have additional information from either external sources or memory in order to develop possible solutions to her problem. Just like his counterpart in science, the technologist requires verbal information in order to perform his work. At this level, there is a very strong similarity between the information input requirements of both scientists and technologists.

It is only when we turn to the nature of the outputs of scientific and technological activity that really striking differences appear. These, as will be seen, imply very real and important second-order differences in the nature of the information input requirements.

Technology consumes information, transforms it, and produces a product in a form that can still be regarded as information bearing. The information, however, is no longer in a verbal form. Whereas science both consumes and produces information in the form of human language, engineers transform information from this verbal format to a physically encoded form. They produce physical hardware in the form of products or processes.

The scientist's principal goal is a published paper. The technologist's goal is to produce some physical change in the world. This difference in orientation, and the subsequent difference in the nature of the products of the two, has profound implications for those concerned with supplying information to either of the two activities.

The information-processing system of science has an inherent compatibility between input and output. Both are in verbal form (Figure 28.1). The output of one stage, therefore, is in the form in which it will be required for the next stage. The problem of supplying information to the scientist thus becomes one of systematically collecting and organizing these outputs and making them accessible to other scientists to employ in their work.

In technology, on the other hand, there is a fundamental and inherent incompatibility between input and output. Because outputs are in form basically different from inputs, they usually cannot serve directly as inputs to the next stage. The physically encoded format of the output makes it very difficult to retrieve the information necessary for further developments. That is not to say that this is impossible: technologists frequently analyze a competitor's product in order to retrieve information; competing nations often attempt to capture one another's weapon systems in order to analyze them for their information content. This is a difficult and uncertain process, however. It would be much simpler if the information were directly available in verbal form. As a consequence, attempts are made to decode or understand physically encoded information only when one party to the exchange is unavailable or unwilling to cooperate. Then an attempt is made to understand how the problems were approached by analyzing the physical product. In cases where the technologists responsible for the product are available and cooperative, this strategy is seldom used. It is much more effective to communicate with them directly, thereby obtaining the necessary information in a verbal form.

A question that arises concerning the documentation produced in the course of most techno-

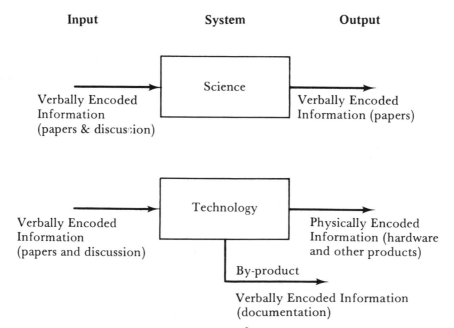

Figure 28.1 Information Processing in Science and Technology

TABLE 28.1
Sources of Messages Resulting in Technical Ideas Considered during the Course of Nineteen Projects*

Channel	Seventeen technological projects		Two scientific research projects	
	Number of messages produced	Percentage of total	Number of messages produced	Percentage of total
Literature	53	8	18	51
Vendors	101	14	0	0
Customer	132	19	0	0
Other sources external to the laboratory	67	9	5	14
Laboratory technical staff	44	6	1	3
Company research programs	37	5	1	3
Analysis and experimentation	216	31	3	9
Previous personal experience	56	8	7	20

*From Allen (1984).

logical projects is why it cannot serve to meet the information needs of subsequent stages in technological development. The answer is that it is not quite compatible with other input requirements although it meets the requirements of verbal structure. First, as seen in Figure 28.1, it is merely a by-product. The direct output is still physical, consequently it is incomplete. It generally assumes a considerable knowledge of what went into the physical product. Those unacquainted with the actual development therefore require some human intervention to supplement and interpret the information contained in this documentation. Thus, technological documentation is often most useful only when the author is directly available to explain and supplement its content.

Now if all of this is true, it leads to an interesting conclusion: whereas the provision of information in science involves the gathering, organizing, and distribution of publications, the situation in technology is very different. The technologist must obtain his information either through the very difficult task of decoding and translating physically encoded information or by relying upon direct personal contact and communication with other technologists. His reliance upon the written word will be much less than that of the scientist. Thus, there are very different solutions to the problems of improving the dissemination and availability of in-

formation in the two domains. If, for example, one were to develop an optimum system for communication in science, there is no reason to suspect that it would be at all appropriate for technology. It is essential that we bear these distinctions in mind while exploring the nature of the communication processes in technology. Much has been written about scientific information flow; we may even understand something about it. One must be extremely cautious, however, in extrapolating or attempting to apply this understanding of science to the situation in technology.

The difference between communication patterns in science and technology is amply illustrated by the data originally reported by Allen (1984). Among a sample of nineteen projects, seventeen were clearly developmental in their nature. The remaining two had clear-cut goals, but these were directed toward an increased understanding of a particular set of phenomena. While the information generated by these two teams would eventually be used to develop new hardware, this was not the immediate goal of the teams, who were far more interested in the phenomena than in the application. For this reason, their work can be considered to be much more scientific than technological in nature.

A comparison of the two scientific projects with the seventeen technological projects (Table 28.1) shows a marked disparity in the use of eight information channels. The scientists engaged in the phenomena-oriented project concentrated their attention heavily upon the literature and upon colleagues outside their laboratory organization. The engineers spread their attention more evenly over the channels and received ideas from two sources unused by the scientists. The customer (in this case, a government laboratory) suggested a substantial number of ideas, demonstrating the importance of the marketplace for technologists. Vendors are another important channel in technology because they are important potential suppliers of components or subsystems, and they provide information that they hope will stimulate future business. Involvement in the marketplace, either through the customer or potential vendors, exerts a significant influence upon the communication system, providing channels for the exchange of information in two directions and connecting buyers and sellers through both the procurement and marketing functions of the organization.

Scientists and engineers also differ in the way they allocate their time between oral and written channels of communication. From his studies of R&D projects, Allen (1984) shows that scientists spend substantially more of their time reading and communicating with each other about their disciplines' literatures than do engineers. In contrast, engineers spend more of their time in personal contact than in reading. The comparisons are quite revealing. Despite all the discussion of informal contact and invisible colleges among scientists (and scientists do make use of personal contacts), it is the engineer who is more dependent upon colleagues. The difference between communication behavior of scientists and engineers is not simply quantitative, however. The persons contacted by scientists are very different from those contacted by engineers, and the relationship between the engineer and those with whom she or he communicates is vastly different from the relationship that exists among scientists. In written channels, too, there are significant differences. The literature used by scientists differs qualitatively from that used by engineers. And engineers not only read different journals, but as discussed in Allen (1984), they use the literature for entirely different purposes.

THE RELATION BETWEEN SCIENCE AND TECHNOLOGY

Given the vast differences between science and technology, how do the two relate to each other? This is a question that has intrigued a number of researchers in recent years. It is generally assumed that the two are in some way related, and in fact national financing of scientific activity is normally justified on the basis of its eventual benefits to technology. Is there any basis for this, and what, if any, is the relation of science to technology? How are the results of scientific activity incorporated into technological developments? To what extent is technology dependent upon science? What are the time lags involved?

The Process of Normal Science

Kuhn (1962) describes three classes of problems that are normally undertaken in science:

1. The determination of significant facts that the research paradigm has shown to be particularly revealing of the nature of things.
2. The determination of facts, which (in contrast with problems of the first class) may, themselves, be of little interest, but which can be compared directly with predictions made by the research paradigm.
3. Empirical work undertaken to articulate the paradigm theory.

The first two of these—the precise determination and extension to other situations of facts and constants that the paradigm especially values (for example, stellar position and magnitude, specific gravities, wave lengths, boiling points) since they have been used in solving paradigmatic problems, and the test of hypotheses derived from the central body of theory—will not concern us here. These are the normally accepted concerns of science, but the third-listed function is probably the most important, and I shall address myself to this category of activity that comprises empirical work undertaken to extend and complete the central body of theory. It may, itself, be subdivided into three classes of activity (Kuhn, 1970):

1. The determination of physical constants (gravitational constants; Avogadro's Number; Joule's Coefficient; etc.).

2. The development of quantitative laws. (Boyle's, Coulomb's, and Ohm's Laws).

3. Experiments designed to choose among alternative ways to applying the paradigm to new areas of interest.

Within the third class lie problems that have resulted from difficulties encountered during the course of scientific research or during the process of technological advance. This, as we shall see, is a form of scientific activity of extreme interest and importance.

The Dependence of Technology on Science

Despite the long-held belief in a continuous progression from basic research through applied research to development, empirical investigation has found little support for such a situation. It is becoming generally accepted that technology builds upon itself and advances quite independently of any link with the scientific frontier, and often without any necessity for an understanding of the basic science which underlies it. Price (1965b), a strong advocate of this position, cites Toynbee's view that

> physical science and industrialism may be conceived as a pair of dancers, both of whom know their steps and have an ear for the rhythm of the music. If the partner who has been leading chooses to change parts and to follow instead, there is perhaps no reason to expect that he will dance less correctly than before.

Price goes on to marshal evidence refuting the idea of technology as something "growing out of" science and to make the claim that communication between the two is at best a "weak interaction." Communication between the two is restricted almost completely to that which takes place through the process of education.

Kuhn (1970) describes science as the activity or process of knowledge making. It is a stream of human activity devoted to building a store of knowledge and can be traced back to the beginning of recorded history. Science can thereby be represented as a stream of events over time cumulating in a body of knowledge. There are two other streams of human activity that operate parallel to science and that function both as contributors to scientific development and as beneficiaries of scientific accomplishment. First there is the activity we have labeled "technology." This is a stream of human activity oriented toward incorporating human knowledge into physical hardware, which will eventually meet with some human use. Then there is a much more general form of human activity in which the ideas of science and the hardware of technology are actually put to some use in the stream of human affairs. This last stream we will label *utilization* (Figure 28.2).

The activities of technology and of utilization in commerce, industry, welfare, and war, while at various times in close harness with science, have developed for the most part independently. Science builds on prior science; technology builds on prior technology; and utilization grows and spreads in response to needs and benefits.

The familiar notion of science providing the basis upon which technology is built to be later utilized in commerce or industry has been shown by the historians of science to have only a limited basis in historical fact. Civilizations have often emphasized activity in one or two of these areas to the exclusion of the others. The Greeks, for example, were very active in science, but they were relatively little concerned with the practical applications or implications of their discoveries. The Romans, in contrast, developed a highly practical civilization, which was greatly concerned with the building of artifices to aid in coping with the physical and social environment. They devoted much effort to the construction of roads and aqueducts and of improvement of armor and weapons without much concurrent increase in their understanding of the natural basis of their developments. History shows quite independent paths through the succeeding centuries to the present time. The three streams appear now in rapid parallel growth; an increased emphasis in one is usually accompanied by an increase

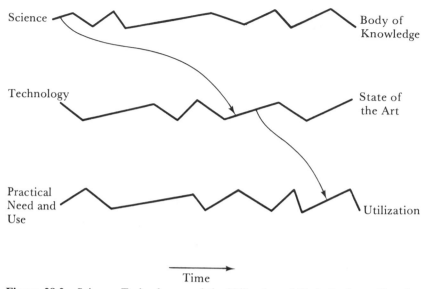

Figure 28.2   Science, Technology, and the Utilization of Their Products, Showing the Normal Progression from One to the Other

in the other two. It is probable that the streams are more closely coupled now than they have been historically, but the delays encountered in any of the communication paths between them remain substantial.

The Flow of Information between Science and Technology

Over the past ten years several studies have attempted to trace the flow of information from science to technology. In one of the earlier of these, Price (1965b), after investigating citation patterns in both scientific and technological journals, concluded that science and technology progress quite independently of one another. Technology, in this sense, builds upon its own prior developments and advances in a manner independent of any link with the current scientific frontier and often without any necessity for an understanding of the basic science underlying it.

Price's hypothesis certainly appears valid in light of more recent evidence. There is little support for direct communication between science and technology. The two do advance quite independently, and much of technology develops without

a complete understanding of the science upon which it is built.

Project Hindsight was the first of a series of attempts to trace technological advances back to their scientific origins. Within the twenty-year horizon of its backward search, Hindsight was able to find very little contribution from basic science (Sherwin and Isenson, 1967). In most cases, the trial ran cold before reaching any activity that could be considered basic research. In Isenson's words, "It would appear that most advances in the technological state of the art are based on no more recent advances than Ohm's Law or Maxwell's equations."

Project TRACES (IIT Research Institute, 1968), partially in response to the Hindsight results, succeeded in tracing the origins of six technological innovations back to the underlying basic sciences but only after extending the time horizon well beyond twenty years. In a follow-up, Battelle (1973) investigators found similar lags in five more innovations. In yet another study, Langrish found little support for a strong science-technology interaction. In tracing eighty-four award-winning innovations to their origins, he found that "the role of university as a source of ideas for [industrial] innovation is fairly small" and that "university science and industrial technology are two quite separate activities which occasionally come into contact with each other" (Langrish, 1971). He argued very strongly that most university basic research is totally irrelevant to societal needs and can be only partially justified for its contributions through training of students.

Gibbons and Johnston (1973) attempted to refute the Langrish hypothesis. They presented data from thirty relatively small-scale technological advances and found that approximately one-sixth of the information needed in problem solving came from scientific sources. Furthermore, they claimed greater currency in the scientific information that was used. The mean age of the scientific journals they cited was 12.2 years. This is not quite twenty, but with publication lags, it can safely be concluded that the work was fourteen or fifteen years old at the time of use. They showed considerable use of personal contact with university scientists, but nearly half of these were for the purpose of either referral to other sources of information or to determine the existence of specialized facilities or services. So, while Gibbons and Johnston may raise some doubt over the Price-Langrish hypothesis, the contrary evidence is hardly compelling.

The evidence, in fact, is very convincing that the normal path from science to technology is, at best, one that requires a great amount of time. There are certainly very long delays in the system, but it should not be assumed that the delays are always necessarily there. Occasionally, technology is forced to forfeit some of its independence. This happens when its advance is impeded by a lack of understanding of the scientific basis of the phenomena with which it is dealing. The call then goes out for help. Often a very interesting basic research problem can result, and scientists can be attracted to it. In this way, science often discovers voids in its knowledge of areas that have long since been bypassed by the research front. Science must, so to speak, backtrack a bit and increase its understanding of an area previously bypassed or neglected.

Morton (1965) described several examples in which technology has defined important problems for scientific investigation. For example, he pointed out that progress in electronic tube technology had advanced without a real understanding of the principles involved. It did this largely by "cut and dry" methods, manipulating the geometry of the elements and the composition of the cathode materials with little real understanding of the fundamental physics underlying the results. This block to the advance of a burgeoning technology forced a return to basic classical physics and a more detailed study of the interactions of free electrons and electromagnetic waves. The return allowed scientists to fill a gap in their understanding and subsequently permitted the development of such microwave amplifiers as the magnetron, klystron, and traveling wave tube. From such examples, it is important to note that there was first of all communication of a problem from technology to science, followed by a relatively easy transfer of scientific results back to the technologists. The two conditions are clearly related. When technology is the source of the problem, technologists are ready and capable of understanding the solution and putting it to work.

Additional support for this idea is provided by Project Hindsight (Sherwin and Isenson, 1967). While is most cases, Hindsight was unable to find any contribution to technology from basic science, it is the exception to this discontinuity between science and technology that chiefly concerns us at the present. Isenson reports[2] that he discovered exceptions to his general finding and that these exceptions are usually characterized by a situation in which, similar to Morton, technology has advanced to a limit at which an understanding is required of the basic physical science involved. Thus technology defines a problem for science. When this problem is attacked and resolved by scientists, its solution is passed immediately into technology. A close coupling thus exists for at least an isolated point in time, and the researchers of Project Hindsight were able to trace the record back from an improved system in what we have labeled the "utilization stream" through an advance in the technological state of the art to the closure of a gap in the body of scientific knowledge. To distinguish this latter form of research from "frontier science," I propose calling it "technology-pull" science.

Technology-pull science is by its nature directly responsive to technological need, and the advance of technology is often contingent upon the pursuit of such science. So when the connection between science and technology is of this form, little delay is encountered in the transfer of information (Figure 28.3). Communication is rapid and direct, and the long delays of the normal transfer process are circumvented. The transfer from technology-pull science can be further accelerated by including in the technological development team former scientists or individuals whose training was in science. The advantages of such a strategy were clearly demonstrated during World War II when many scientists became engineers, at least temporarily, and were very effective in implementing the results of fundamental research.

A similar phenomenon is occurring at the present time in genetic engineering. Molecular biologists have been attracted by the potential economic benefits into what is now becoming a new technology. These former basic research scientists both carry with them substantial scientific knowledge and retain information ties to the scientific community.

The point to be made is that at least a segment of basic science is not conducted at what is called the "frontier" of knowledge. Technology—and often investigation in a different scientific area—will raise problems that attract investigators to an area that has been worked on before. The investigation then proceeds, looking perhaps from a somewhat different vantage at items that had not previously been deemed important phenomena. That such investigations are searching in what had been considered secure territory makes them no less fundamental in their nature.

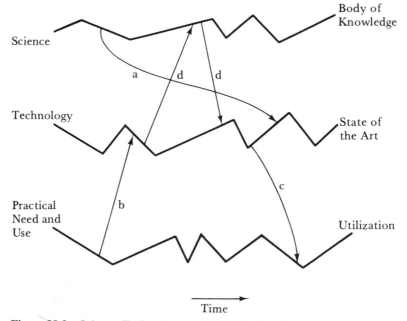

Figure 28.3 Science, Technology, and the Utilization of Their Products, Showing Communication Paths Among the Three Streams ([a] The normal process of assimilation of scientific results into technology. [b] Recognized need for a device, technique, or scientific understanding. [c] The normal process of adoption of technology for use. [d] Technological need for understanding of physical phenomena and its response [from Marquis and Allen, 1966])

While technology and science in general may progress quite independently of each other, there very probably are some technologies that are more closely connected with science than others. For example, electronics technology is more closely related to frontier work in physics than say, mechanical technology. Nuclear technology should be more closely coupled to the advance of physical knowledge than either of these two. And of course, genetic engineering still retains a very close association with its parent science. Citation studies of engineering and scientific journals, for example, have shown the ratio of technological to scientific citations to range from about six to one to less than one to one. The data clearly indicate that a wide variation exists in the degree to which technologies are coupled to their respective sciences.

NOTES

1. Even Pelz and Andrews (1966), who are careful to preserve the distinction throughout most of their book, a study of 1,300 engineers and scientists, chose *Scientists in Organizations* as its title, forgetting the majority of their sample.

2. Personal communication.

REFERENCES

Allen, T. J. 1984. *Managing the Flow of Technology*. Cambridge: MIT Press.

Battelle Memorial Institute. 1973. *Interactions of science and technology in the innovation process*: *Some case studies*. Final report to the National Science Foundation NSF-C667, Columbus, Ohio.

Gibbons, M., and Johnston, R. D. 1974. The roles of science in technological innovation. *Research Policy* 3:220–242.

IIT Research Institute. 1968. *Technology in retrospect and critical events in science*. Report to the National Science Foundation NSF C-235.

Krulee, G. K., and Nadler, E. B. 1960. Studies of education for science and engineering: Student values and curriculum choice. *IEEE Transactions on Engineering Management* 7:146–158.

Kuhn, T. B. 1970. *Structure of Scientific Revolutions*. Rev. ed. Chicago: University of Chicago Press.

Langrish, J. 1971. Technology transfer: Some British data. *R&D Management* 1:133–136.

Marquis, D. G., and Allen, T. J. 1966. Communication patterns in applied technologies. *American Psychologist* 21:1052–1060.

Morton, J. A. 1965. From physics to function. *IEEE Spectrum* 2:62–64.

Pelz, D. C., and Andrews, F. M. 1966. *Scientists in Organizations*. New York: Wiley.

Price, D. J. DeSolla. 1965a. Networks of scientific papers. *Science* 149:510–515.

—1965b. Is technology independent of science? *Technology and Culture* 6:553–568.

—1970. In D. K. Pollock and Nelson, C. E. (eds.) *Communication Among Scientists and Technologists*. Lexington, Mass.: Heath.

Ritti, R. R. 1971. *The Engineer in the Industrial Corporation*. New York: Columbia University Press.

Roberts, E. B., and Wainer, H. A. 1971. Some characteristics of technical entrepreneurs. *IEEE Transactions on Engineering Management*, EM-18, 3.

Sherwin, E. W., and Isenson, R. S. 1967. Project Hindsight. *Science* 156:1571–1577.

29

Communication Networks in R&D Laboratories

THOMAS J. ALLEN

Communication networks in R&D laboratories are shown to have structural characteristics, which when properly understood can be employed to more effectively keep the laboratories' personnel abreast of technological developments. Informal relations and physical location are shown to be important determinants of this structure.

INTRODUCTION

To date, attempts to automate the transmission of scientific and technological information have been most notable for their failure. The reason for this does not lie in any lack of attention or inadequate effort allocated to the problem, since very large sums of money have been expended on storage and retrieval systems for scientific and technological information. Rather, it is due to the nature and complexity of the information itself, and to the uncertainty and very personal nature of each user's needs.

For this reason, the human being is still the most effective source of information, communication with a technically competent colleague being conducted on a two-way basis, with the output of the source tracking and responding to the expressed needs of the user. In this manner, the ability of the source to adapt flexibly and respond rapidly to communicated needs enables it to cope effectively with the uncertain nature of those needs.

A large number of recent studies show that increased use of organizational colleagues for information is strongly related to scientific and technological performance. The relation to performance

is, perhaps, demonstrated most clearly in a recent study by a group at M.I.T. Some of the results of this study are presented in this paper as a basis for a discussion on strategies for properly structuring the flow of technical information in research and development organizations.

THE INTERNAL CONSULTING STUDY

Eight pairs of individuals in different organizations, but working on identical problems, were compared on the extent to which each of them consulted with organizational colleagues. Since there were always two individuals attempting to solve the same problem, their solutions could be compared for relative quality and the sample split between 'high' performers and 'low' performers. Performance evaluations were made by competent technical evaluators in the government laboratories that had sponsored the projects. Dividing the sample into high and low performers allowed a further comparison to be made, now on an aggregate basis, of behaviour leading to high or low performance.

When such a comparison was made with respect to the number of times organizational colleagues were consulted during the project, it showed that high performers made far greater use of this source of technical information (Figure 29.1). As a matter of fact, high performers not only reported a significantly greater frequency of consultation with organizational colleagues, they also spent significantly more time in their discussions with colleagues.

Furthermore, they relied on more people both

Reprinted with permission from T. J. Allen, "Communication Networks in R&D Labs," *R&D Management*, 1971, Vol. 1, 14–21.
Copyright © 1971 by Blackwell Publishers. All rights reserved.
Thomas J. Allen is Senior Associate Dean and Professor of Management at M.I.T's Sloan School of Management.

within their own technical speciality and on other specialties (Figures 29.2a and 29.2b). The high performer was in closer touch than the low performer with developments in his own field. Through his wide range of contact within his specialty he is less likely to miss an important development which might have some impact on the problem to which he is assigned. He also had wider contact with people in specialties other than his own. In fact, it was only the high performers who showed any real contact outside of their specialty (Figure 29.2b). The low performers seldom ventured outside of their field. These findings agree with those of Pelz & Andrews (1966) who noted that colleague contacts both within the immediate work group and with other groups in the organization were positively related to a person's performance and that the variety of contacts and their frequency each contributed independently to performance.

One cannot of course determine very easily whether communication causes high performance or whether high performers merely communicate more. Pelz & Andrews (1966), in their study, obtained data on which of the two parties initiated the contact. They then assumed that an individual's high performance would be more likely to attract contact from others than to induce him to initiate contacts himself. They then looked only at contacts initiated by the information user and found that the relation with performance remained strong. They concluded:

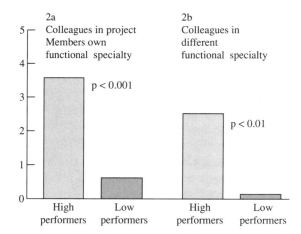

Figure 29.2 Number and Location of Organizational Colleagues with Whom Project Members Communicate

large amounts of colleague contact tended to go with high performance even when one looked only at scientists who themselves were the primary initiators of the contacts. Under these conditions it was difficult to believe that the contacts were primarily the *result* of previous high performance. Thus the hypothesis that contacts with colleagues stimulated performance seemed to be supported (p. 47).

SUPPORT FROM OUTSIDE THE PROJECT: A PARADOX

Given the benefits to be derived from internal consultation, one would expect project members to rely heavily upon their technical staff for information. In fact, this is not the case. During the nineteen projects studied by Allen (1966), project members actually obtained more of their ideas from outside of their firms than from their own technical staff—although in general a poor performance was shown by sources outside of the firm. In fact, when individuals inside and outside of the firm were compared as sources of ideas, there was an inverse relation between frequency of outside use and performance.

Those information sources that reward the user by contributing more to his performance are used less than those that do not. Such a situation

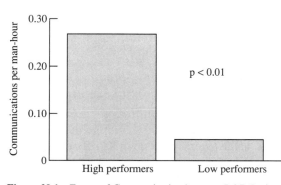

Figure 29.1 Extent of Communication between R&D Project Members and Organizational Colleagues Not Assigned to the Project

would seem to conflict with the principles of psychological learning theory. One might expect a person to return more frequently to those channels that reward him most consistently. The data show just the opposite to be true. The paradox can, however, be resolved with the introduction of an additional parameter. It can be safely predicted that an individual will repeat a behaviour that is rewarded more frequently than one that is unrewarded, only if the cost to him of the rewarded behaviour is less than or equal to the cost of the unrewarded behaviour. In other words, both cost and benefit may be taken into consideration when deciding upon a source of information.

Gerstberger and Allen (1968) actually studied this decision process in some detail. They found no relation at all between the engineers' perception of the benefits to be gained from an informal information channel and the extent to which the channel was used. However, a very strong relation existed between extent of use and the engineers' perception of the amount of effort that it took to use the channel. Cost in that case was the overriding determinant of the decision. Working back from this finding, one might speculate that the failure to consult with organizational colleagues is attributable to a high cost associated with such consultation. In fact, there is evidence to indicate that the organizational colleague is a high cost source of information for research and development project teams (Allen *et al.*, 1968). It can, for example, be very costly for a project member to admit to a colleague that he needs his help.

TECHNOLOGICAL 'GATEKEEPERS'

A number of recent studies have indicated that technologists do not read very much, and one might conclude that literature is not a very effective vehicle for bringing new information into the organization; and while it is found that outside personal contact is used very heavily by organizational technologists, further analysis suggests that this means of transfer is not much more instrumental than literature. The reason for this is that the average technologist cannot communicate effectively with outsiders. This is reflected in the results of several research studies which are consistent in their discovery of an inverse relation between outside personal contact and technical performance (Allen, 1964; Shilling & Bernard, 1964).

How then does information enter the organization? First of all, it is clear that entry does occur, because without it no R&D organization could long survive. No R&D organization, no matter how large, can be fully self-sustaining. In order for the organization to survive its members must maintain themselves abreast of current developments in those technologies which are central to the organization's mission. It must, in other words, constantly import technical information. Not only were the organizations under study surviving; they were, to all appearances, thriving. They were extremely successful, and highly regarded technically. They must, therefore have been successful, somehow, in acquiring information from outside, and disseminating it within their borders. The question remains, how?

The first important clue lies in the observation that, of all possible information sources, only one appears to satisfactorily meet the needs of R&D project members. That one source is the organizational colleague. This has been shown in the case of R&D proposal competitions (Allen, 1964) for preliminary design studies (Allen, 1966; Allen *et al.*, 1968); for 'idea generating groups' (Baker, *et al.*, 1967); for engineers and scientists in a wide variety of industrial, governmental and university settings (Pelz & Andrews, 1966); and for the members of 64 laboratories in the biological sciences (Allen, 1964).

Following this clue, Allen & Cohen (1969) discovered that the process by which organizations most effectively import information is an indirect one (Figure 29.3). There existed, in the organizations that they studied, a small number of key people upon whom others relied very heavily for information. These key people, or 'technological gatekeepers', differ from their colleagues in their orientation toward outside information sources. They read far more, particularly the 'harder' liter-

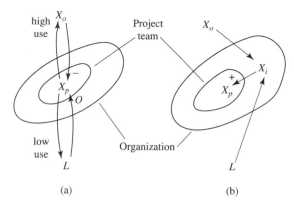

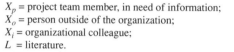

X_p = project team member, in need of information;
X_o = person outside of the organization;
X_i = organizational colleague;
L = literature.

Figure 29.3 The Dilemma of Importing Information into the Organization (Direct paths do not work (A), because literature is little used by the average technologist and because the direct contact with outside persons is ineffective. An indirect route, through the technological gatekeeper (B) has been shown to be more effective. Symbols next to incoming arrows indicate the polarity of the correlation with performance).

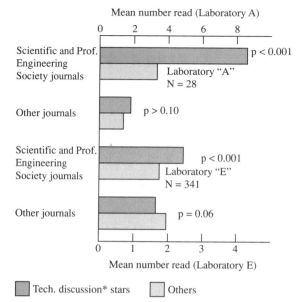

Figure 29.4 Journal Readership by Technical Discussion Stars (Laboratory 'A' is the original laboratory reported in Allen & Cohen [1969]. Laboratory 'E' is the advanced technology component of a large aerospace firm)

ature. Their readership of professional engineering and scientific journals is significantly greater than that of the average technologist (Figure 29.4). They also maintain broader-ranging and longer-term relationships with technologists outside of their organizations (Figure 29.5). The technological gatekeeper mediates between his organizational colleagues and the world outside, and he effectively couples the organizational to scientific and technological activity in the world at large.

NETWORKS OF GATEKEEPERS

Using the techniques of the earlier study (Allen & Cohen, 1969), the structure of the communication network in the research and advanced technology division of a large aerospace firm was measured. The laboratory under study was organized on a functional basis around five engineering specialties and three scientific disciplines.

The gatekeepers in each specialist department were identified, as well as the structure of the com-

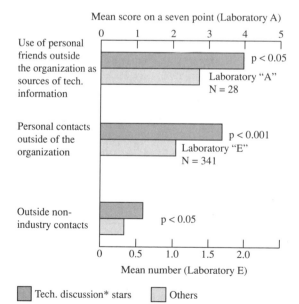

Figure 29.5 Personal Contact Outside of the Organization by Technical Discussion Stars (Laboratory 'A' is the original laboratory reported in Allen & Cohen [1969]. Laboratory 'E' is the advanced technology component of a large aerospace firm)

*Persons receiving one standard deviation or more above the overall mean number in their laboratory (Laboratory "A") or in their department (Laboratory "E").

munication network in that department. Because of the complexity of the networks in such a large organization (Figure 29.6), an attempt was made to simplify them through graph-theoretic reduction.

A communication network (or portions thereof) can be characterized according to the degree of interconnectedness that exists among its nodes. There are several degrees of interconnectedness or 'connectivity' that can exist in a network (Flament, 1963). In the present analysis, only that degree of connectivity which Flament has called 'strong' will be considered. A strongly connected component, or strong component in a network, is one in which all nodes are mutually reachable. In a communication network, a potential exists for the transmission of information between any two members of a strong component (Flament, 1963; Harary

et al., 1965). For this reason, the laboratory's communication network was reduced into its strong components and their membership was examined.

When the departmental networks of the organization are reduced in this manner, two things become apparent. First of all, the formation of strong components is not aligned with formal organizational groups, and second, while there were in each functional department anywhere from one to six non-trivial strong components, nearly all of the gatekeepers can be found together as members of the same strong component (see, for an example, Figure 29.7). On the average, 64% of all gatekeepers can be found in eight strong components, one for each of the five technological and three scientific specialties. In each technical specialty, there is one strongly connected network in which most

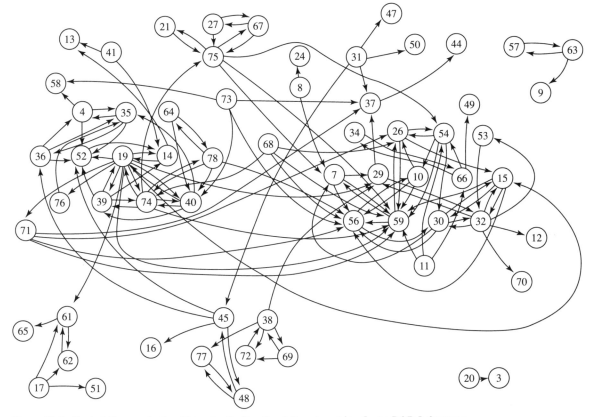

Figure 29.6 Typical Communication Network of a Functional Department in a Large R&D Laboratory

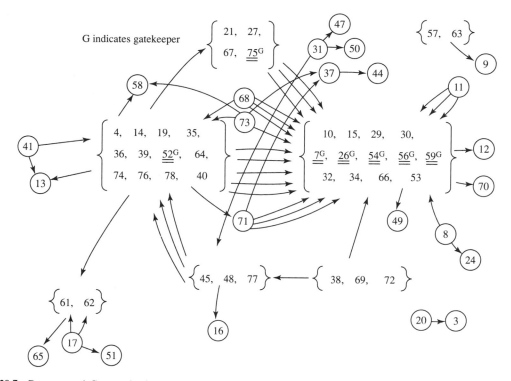

Figure 29.7 Departmental Communication Network After Reduction into Strong Components (Strong components are shown in brackets, and gatekeepers are shown by underlining with 'G' superscript)

of the gatekeepers are members. The gatekeepers, therefore, maintain close communication among themselves, thus increasing substantially their effectiveness in coupling the organization to the outside world.

In fact, if one were to sit down and attempt to design an optimal system for bringing in new technical information and disseminating it within the organization, it would be difficult to produce a better one than that which exists.

New information is brought into the organization through the gatekeeper. It can then be communicated quite readily to other gatekeepers through the gatekeeper network and disseminated outward from one or more points to other members of the organization (Figure 29.8). Perhaps the most interesting aspect of this functioning of the organizational communication network is that it has de-

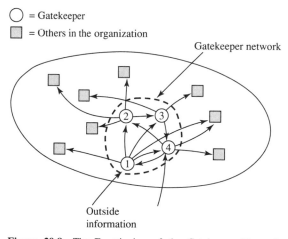

Figure 29.8 The Functioning of the Gatekeeper Network (New information is brought into the organization by 1. It can be transmitted to 2, 3, and 4 via the gatekeeper network. It reaches its eventual users [squares] through their contacts with gatekeepers)

veloped spontaneously, with no managerial intervention. In fact, there was scarcely a suspicion on the part of management that the network operated in this way.

THE INFLUENCE OF NONORGANIZATIONAL FACTORS ON THE STRUCTURE OF COMMUNICATION NETWORKS

An organization's formal structure (that which generally appears on an organizational chart) is, as one would expect, a very important determinant of communication patterns. It is not the sole determinant, however. In addition to formal organizational structure, there are available to management at least two other factors that can be used to promote (or discourage) communication. The first of these operates through the extension of informal friendship-type relations within the organization. Allen & Cohen (1969) have shown how informal relations influence the structure of communication networks, and Allen et al. (1968) explore in detail how this influence comes about. Simply stated, people are more willing to ask questions of others whom they know, than of strangers. The key lies in the expected damage sustained by the ego if one's question is met with a critical response. To be told that you have asked a dumb or foolish question is the ultimate in rebuffs. Few people are willing to entertain such a risk. Now, out of all the people in the world, there are hopefully only a small percentage who would meet even a truly stupid question with such a retort. Even given that this percentage is very small, however, many people will follow the strategy of minimum regret and assume that everyone belongs to this set unless proven otherwise. This results in a situation in which, of all people who are known, only a small percentage are unapproachable, but all unknowns are unapproachable. To increase the proportion of people in the organization, who can be approached for information, management would be well advised to increase the number of acquaintanceships among its technical personnel. This it can do very easily.

People will not become acquainted until they first meet. There are, however, a number of ways through which technical people can come to meet one another. Interdepartmental projects are one such device. People who come to know one another through service on projects or other inter-functional teams retain their effectiveness as channels between departments for some time even after the project or team had been disbanded. Interdepartmental teams can, and do, provide an indirect benefit, through the persistence of the relations that they establish, over and above their direct contributions to coordination. The same thing can be said for transfers within the organization. For a period of time following a transfer, the transferred individual will provide a communication path back to his old organization. His influence extends far beyond this direct link, though. Probably the most important contribution of the transferred person lies in his ability to make referrals. The number of communication paths that potentially become available when a man is transferred is the product of the number of acquaintanceships which he developed in the two parts of the organization. For some people this can be a very large number. So with only a very few transfers, a large number of communication paths can be created and coordination thereby improved.

Of course, the effect diminishes with time, since both people and activities will change in the old group, and the transferred person will gradually lose touch. Kanno (1968) has shown that following a transfer between divisions of a large chemical firm, the transferred persons provided an effective communication link back to their old divisions for $1^1/_2$ years. The duration over which communications remain effective following a transfer is determined by many factors; principal among these are the rate of change of activities and turnover of personnel in the old organization. If projects are of short duration, with many new ones constantly being initiated and the turnover of personnel is high, one would expect that the effect of a transfer in promoting communication would be short-lived. Where the activity is more stable and turnover low, the transfer can be effective over a longer period of time. With estimates of these parameters and of the number of people (and their work) with whom the average transfer is acquainted, a systematic program of intra-organizational transfer can be developed. Such a program would contribute directly to communication, coordination and empathy among the sub-elements of the organization.

THE EFFECTS OF GEOGRAPHICAL LOCATION

In addition to formal organizational and information relations there is a third very important factor that can be used to influence the structure of organizational communication networks, i.e. the physical configuration of the facilities in which that organization is placed.

The data on the effect of spatial separation to be presented now were obtained in three very different organizations. The first organization is a 48-man department in a medium-sized aero-space firm. The 48 people were all engineers and scientists, primarily in electrical and mechanical engineering and applied physics. The second organization that was studied is a 52-man section of a medical school laboratory. The third organization comprised 57 social psychologists, economists and applied mathematicians in a management school.

To determine the influence of physical separation on the probability of two people communicating, the distance between every possible pair of people was measured. Moving outward in 5-yard intervals from each person, a measurement was made of the proportion of people within each interval with whom the focal person communicated. The measurement of distance was the actual distance that the focal person would have to walk in order to reach another person's desk. All measurements were taken on a single floor.

The proportion of people with whom an individual communicates, or the 'probability of communication' as it is labelled in the figure, decays with the square of distance outward from the focal person (Figure 29.9). The fact that the probability

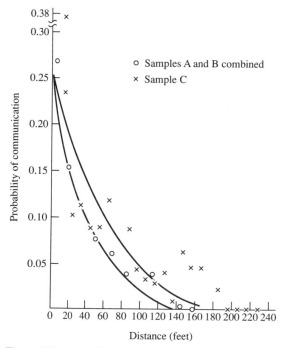

Figure 29.9 Probability of Communication as a Function of the Distance Separating Pairs of People

of communication decays with the distance separating people is not too surprising. Nor is the fact that it follows an inverse square law. What is surprising is the extreme sensitivity of probability to distance. The function, naturally, must become asymptotic beyond the minimum point of the parabola. The striking thing is that it reaches this asymptote within 25 yards. This was true in all three organizations. In fact, for the first two organizations, the curves fall so close together that the data are combined in Figure 29.9. The result, therefore, appears to be general and independent of the nature of the technical work being performed.

As though, by itself, physical separation were not serious enough, there appear to be circumstances which can exacerbate its effect. The amount of difficulty, by way of corners to be turned, indirect paths to be followed, etc., encountered in traversing a path intensifies the effect of separation on communication probability. One index of this difficulty, something which might be called a 'nuisance factor' is the difference between the straight line and actual travel distances (Figure 29.10) separating two people. When communication probability is plotted as a function of the magnitude of the 'nuisance factor' (Figure 29.10) the effect is quite startling. This effect holds true whether the nuisance factor is computed on an absolute basis or as a proportion of straight line separation distance.

ORGANIZATIONAL STRUCTURE

To encourage communication between project teams and the supporting technical staff, separation distances must be kept to a minimum. To locate a project in a separate facility is essentially to cut it off from support by the rest of the laboratory staff. There is a trade-off that must be made in locating project members. Effective coordination of all elements of project activity may require that all or most of the team members be located together in a specially assigned place. On the other hand, to maintain the specialists assigned to the project abreast of developments in their technical fields demands that they be kept in contact with the specialist colleagues. This, in turn, favours locating them with their specialist groups. Marquis (1969) has argued for the latter alternative on very large projects. All of the projects in Marquis's sample were of fairly long duration; several years. This may well hold the key to the trade-off. For long-term projects, technical personnel should remain in the same location with their specialist colleagues.

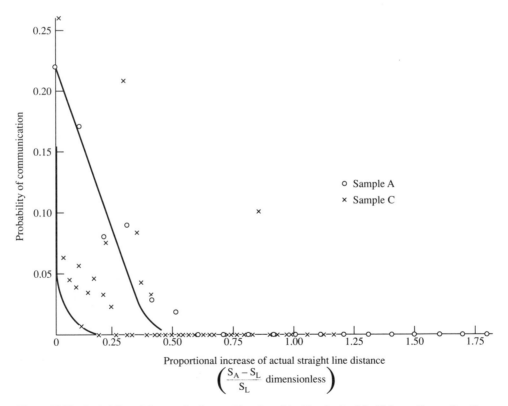

Figure 29.10 Probability of Communication as a Function of the Magnitude of the Nuisance Factor (0 = Sample A; X = Sample C)

Assignment to a project of long duration can force a person to lose touch with his field unless steps are taken to enable his free interaction with colleagues in the field. The result is technical obsolescence and difficulty for both the person and the organization in dealing with future assignments. In the case of a brief project, the length of separation will be too short to have these results, and the balance swings in favour of locating all project members together.

Long projects demand functional organization, while short-duration projects may be organized on a project basis with all team members located together.

Functional organization has the undesirable consequence of making intra-project coordination difficult. A possible solution to this problem lies in overlaying a coordinating team across the functional departments in what has come to be known as a matrix organization. This is not always as easy to accomplish as it first sounds, but when it functions properly it can achieve the desired goals of the functional organization without the loss in project coordination.

Project and matrix organization have the undesirable consequence of making communication between functional departments difficult. Transfers, where possible, and short-duration interdepartmental projects, assist in countering this problem. In addition, the overall configuration of the laboratory should be structured in such a way that inter-functional communication is eased. Where it is desirable to have communication between groups, they should be located near each other. Where this is impossible they can be made to share certain facilities that will force interaction. The nature of the facility is secondary. It may be as humble as a coffee pot or men's room or as grandiose as a computer or an expensive instrument. What matters is that it brings people into contact who would otherwise not meet. It is quite easy, in any organization, to think of a large number of such facilities for promoting interaction. Where possible they should be located where they will promote the desired patterns of group interaction. In those cases in which it is not feasible to manipulate the posi-

tion of the interaction facility, then desired patterns of interaction should be given serious consideration in allocating the use of the facility among groups and in positioning groups around it. In the latter situation it must be borne in mind that the extent to which a facility will be used is also an inverse function of distance. Frohman (1968), for example, found the principal determinant of use of a technical library in an industrial firm to be the distance separating users from it. Interaction facilities must be positioned in such a way that they promote interaction among groups that would not otherwise interact, while at the same time they are not so far removed from any of the groups that they lose their effectiveness.

SUMMARY AND CONCLUSIONS

The importance to research and development projects of technical staff support cannot be overstressed. Seldom, if ever, is management able satisfactorily to predict and obtain all of the talents that will be needed in a project and incorporate them in the project team. The project must, therefore, obtain much of its required information from sources beyond its own membership.

Research shows very clearly that the best source for this support lies in the technical staff of the laboratory itself. Attempts to bring information to the project directly from outside of the organization usually have been ineffective. The process by which an organization imports and disseminates outside information is more complex than people normally assume. The best way to maintain the project team abreast of outside developments lies in understanding and making proper use of existing information systems. This includes the use of technological gatekeepers for project support. Outside information can then be delivered to the project quite effectively, albeit by an indirect route. Research evidence indicates quite strongly that the indirect approach is far more effective than any direct approach to coupling project members to outside sources, whether personal or written.

There are available a wide variety of techniques for improving communication and coordination between projects and their supporting staff. A number of formal organizational mechanisms have been described in detail. In addition to these, use may also be made of the informal relationships that will develop when people come into contact with one another. A very effective means for increasing the level of acquaintanceships in an organization is the inter-group transfer. Physical location is also a very strong determinant of interaction patterns. People are more likely to communicate with those who are located nearest to them. Individuals and groups can therefore be positioned in ways that will either promote or inhibit communication. Architectural design thus becomes an important determinant of the structure that an organization's communication network will assume. Shared facilities or equipment can also be used to promote interaction between groups.

All of these factors must be taken into account and properly arranged in order to effectively couple the research and development project to its supporting information system.

REFERENCES

Allen, T. J. (1964) 'The Use of Information Channels in R&D Proposal Preparation', Cambridge, Mass.: M.I.T. Sloan School of Management, Working Paper No. 97–64.

Allen, T. J. (1966) 'Managing the Flow of Scientific and Technological Information, Ph.D. Dissertation, Cambridge, Mass.: M.I.T. Sloan School of Management.

Allen, T. J., Gerstenfeld, A. & Gerstberger, P. G. (1968) 'The Problem of Internal Consulting in the R&D Laboratory', Cambridge, Mass.: M.I.T. Sloan School of Management, Working Paper No. 319–68.

Allen, T. J. & Cohen, S. I. (1969) 'Information flow in two R&D laboratories', Administrative Science Quarterly, Vol. 14.

Baker, N. R., Siegmann, J. & Rubenstein, A. H. (1967) 'The effects of perceived needs and means on the generation of ideas for industrial research and development project', I.E.E.E. Transactions on Engineering Management, Vol. 14.

Flament, C. (1963) 'Applications of Graph Theory to Group Structure', New York: Prentice Hall.

Frohman, A. (1968) 'Communication problems in an industrial laboratory', Unpublished term paper, Cambridge, Mass.: M.I.T. Sloan School of Management.

Gerstberger, P. G. & Allen, T. J. (1968) 'Criteria used in the selection of information channels by R&D engineers', Journal of Applied Psychology, Vol. 52.

Harary, F., Norman, R. S & Cartwright, D (1965) 'Structural Models', New York: Wiley.

Kanno, M. (1968) 'Effect on Communication Between Labs and Plants of the Transfer of R&D Personnel', S.M. Thesis, Cambridge, Mass.: M.I.T. Sloan School of Management.

Marquis, D. G. (1969) 'Organizational factors in project performance', Program Management (ed. J. Galbraith), Cambridge, Mass.: M.I.T. Press.

Pelz, D. C. & Andres, F.M. (1966) 'Scientists in Organizations', New York: Wiley.

Shilling, C. W. & Bernard, C. W. (1964) 'Informal Communication Among Bio-Scientists', George Washington University Biological Sciences Communication Project, Report 16A–64.

30

A Study of the Influence of Technical Gatekeeping on Project Performance and Career Outcomes in an R&D Facility

RALPH KATZ AND MICHAEL L. TUSHMAN

This study investigated the role of gatekeepers in the transfer of information within a single R&D location by comparing directly the performance of project groups with and without gatekeepers. The results show that gatekeepers performed a linking role only for projects performing tasks that were 'locally-oriented' while 'universally-oriented' tasks were most effectively linked to external areas by direct project member communication. Gatekeepers also appear to facilitate the external communication of other technologists, in addition to influencing positively the career outcomes of young engineers.

R&D project teams must process information from outside sources in order to keep informed about relevant external developments and new technological innovations. Furthermore, empirical studies over the past 25 years have demonstrated that oral communications, rather than written technical reports or publications, are the primary means by which engineering professionals collect and disseminate important new ideas and information into their project groups (Allen, 1984). While such personal contacts may be essential, there are alternative communication structures by which R&D groups can effectively draw upon information outside their organizations (Katz & Tushman, 1979).

In particular, the research reported here focuses explicitly on the role played by gatekeepers in the effective transfer and utilization of external technology and information. (Gatekeepers are defined as those key individual technologists who are strongly connected to both internal colleagues and external sources of information (Allen & Cohen, 1969).) Since most gatekeepers are also project supervisors, this study also examines the broader leadership role of gatekeeping supervisors in influencing the subsequent rates of organizational turnover and promotion among technical subordinates.

COMMUNICATION AND PERFORMANCE

Generally speaking, previous research has shown that project performance is strongly associated with high levels of technical communication by all project members to information sources within the organization (i.e., high levels of internal communication). The positive findings of Allen (1984), Pelz & Andrews (1976), and others strongly argue that direct contacts between project members and other internal colleagues can enhance project effectiveness.

While direct communication by all project members may be effective for internal communications, the particular method for effectively keeping up-to-date with technical advances outside the organization are probably very different. Numerous

Earlier versions of this paper were published in Katz, R. & Tushman, M. (1981) "An investigation into the managerial roles and career paths of gatekeepers and project supervisors in a major R&D facility," *R&D Management*, Vol. 11, 103–10; and Katz, R. & Tushman, M. (1983) "A longitudinal study of the effects of boundary spanning supervision on turnover and promotion in research and development," *Academy of Management Journal*, Vol. 26, 437–56.

Ralph Katz is Professor of Management at Northeastern University's College of Business and Research Associate at M.I.T.'s Sloan School of Management. *Michael Tushman* is Professor of Management and Organizations at Columbia University's Graduate School of Business.

studies, for example, have shown that project performance is not positively associated with direct project member communication to external information areas. In fact, most studies have found them to be inversely related (e.g, Allen, 1984; Katz and Tushman, 1979). It seems that most engineers are simply unable to communicate effectively with extraorganizational information sources. Widespread direct contact by all engineering project members, then, is *not* an effective method for transferring technical information into a project from external sources.

One explanation for these significant differences stems from the idea that technological activities are strongly local in nature in that their problems, strategies, and solutions are defined and operationalized in terms of particular strengths and interests of the organizational subculture in which they are being addressed (Katz & Kahn, 1978; Allen, 1984). Such localized definitions and shared language schemes gradually unfold from the constant interactions among organizational members, the tasks' overall objectives and requirements, and the common social and task related experiences of organizational members. These idiosyncratic developments are a basic determinant of attitudes and behaviours in that they strongly influence the ways in which project members think about and define their various problems and solution strategies.

Such localized perspectives eventually become a double-edged sword. As long as individuals share the same common language and awareness, communication is rather easy and efficient. Conversely, when individuals do not share a common coding scheme and technical language, their work-related communications are less efficient, often resulting in severe misperceptions and misinterpretations. Thus, the evolution of more localized languages and technological approaches enables project members to deal effectively with their more local information processing activities within the organization; yet at the same time, it hinders the acquisition and interpretation of information from areas outside the organization. This lack of commonality across organizational boundaries serves as a strong communication impedance causing considerable difficulty in the communications of most engineers with external consultants and professionals.

Given this burden in communicating across differentiated organizational boundaries, how can project groups be effectively linked to external information areas? One way is through the role of project gatekeeper; that is, certain project members who are strongly connected to outside information domains but who are also capable of translating technical developments and ideas across contrasting coding schemes (Allen & Cohen, 1969). Through these key members, external information can be transferred effectively into project groups by means of a two-step communication process. First, gatekeepers gather and understand outside information, and subsequently they channel it in more meaningful and relevant terms to their locally constrained colleagues. Gatekeepers, as a result, perform an extremely valuable function, for they may be the principal means by which external ideas and information can be effectively transferred into R&D project groups.

While substantial literature applauds this gatekeeper concept, there is virtually no direct evidence that gatekeepers enhance project performance. Support has to be inferred indirectly either from the empirical findings of Katz & Tushman (1979) and Allen, Tushman & Lee (1979) or from the case studies in project SAPPHO (Achilladeles, Jervis & Robertson, 1971). Our initial research question, then, concerns the association between project gatekeepers and technical performance. Is this relationship positive across all forms of R&D activity or are some project areas more effectively linked to external technology through direct contact by all project members rather than through a gatekeeper? Moreover, if gatekeepers are necessary for effective technology transfer, must they then be the primary source for collecting outside information, or can they also serve to facilitate the external communication of their more locally constrained colleagues?

GATEKEEPERS, PERFORMANCE, AND THE NATURE OF THE TASK

The need for a two-step process of information flow depends on a strong communication impedance between the project group and its external information areas. To the extent that different technical languages and coding schemes exist between project members and their external technical environments, communication across organizational boundaries will be difficult and inefficient. Most technological activities (unlike the sciences) are strongly local in nature. The coupling of bureaucratic interests and demands with localized technical tasks and coding schemes produces a communication boundary that differentiates these project groups from their outside areas. Product development groups in different organizations, for example, may face similar problems yet may define their solution approaches and parameters very differently. As a result, it becomes increasingly difficult for most technologists to integrate external ideas, suggestions and solutions with internal technology that has become locally defined and constrained. It is hypothesized, therefore, that locally oriented projects (i.e., development and technical service projects) will require gatekeepers to provide the necessary linkages to external information areas—without gatekeepers, direct external contacts by members of local projects will be ineffective.

In contrast, if external information sources do not have different language and coding schemes from members of the project group, then a significant communication impedance will not exist. Work that is more universally defined (scientific or research work, for example) is probably less influenced and constrained by local organizational factors, resulting in less difficulty *vis-à-vis* external communications. Under these conditions, project members are more likely to share similar norms, values, and language schemes with outside professional colleagues, thereby, permitting effective communication across organizational and even national boundaries. They are simply more capable of understanding the nature of the problems and corresponding solution approaches employed by their relevant external colleagues. Hagstrom (1965), for instance, found a strong positive correlation between the productivity of scientists and their levels of contact with colleagues from other universities. For universally defined tasks, therefore, it is hypothesized that gatekeepers are not required to link projects with their relevant external

information areas; instead, direct outside interaction by all project members is more advantageous. The nature of a project's work, therefore, should be a critical factor affecting the development of localized languages and orientations and consequently will moderate significantly the relationship between project performance and the usefulness of gatekeepers.

ROLE OF GATEKEEPERS

If gatekeepers enhance the performance of project groups working on locally defined tasks, then what specific information processing activities of gatekeepers contribute to higher project performance? There are at least two alternatives. The more traditional explanation is that gatekeepers function as the primary link to external sources of information and technology—information flows through these key individuals to the more local members of the project team (Allen & Cohen, 1969). Relevant external information is transferred effectively into a project group because of the capable boundary spanning activities of the project's gatekeeper.

Another possibility is that gatekeepers also assume an active training, development, and socialization role within their work groups. From this perspective, gatekeepers not only gather, translate, and encode external information, but they also facilitate the external contacts of their project colleagues. By helping to direct, coach, and interpret the external communications of their fellow project members, gatekeepers act to reduce the communication boundary separating their projects from outside information areas.

If gatekeeping permits other project members to communicate effectively with external areas, then for localized projects with gatekeepers, there should be a positive association between a project's external communication and its performance. On the other hand, if gatekeepers do not play this more active role, then an inverse relation is more likely to exist between the external communications of locally oriented group members and project performance. Because they work and interact so closely with other project members about technically related problems, it is argued that gatekeepers fulfill this larger role of both gathering outside information and facilitating the external communications of their project colleagues. Since most technical gatekeepers are also first-level project supervisors, it is hypothesized that there will be a significant positive association between project performance and external interaction for projects *with* gatekeeping supervisors. On the other hand, for those projects *without* gatekeeping supervisors, that is, project groups led by non-gatekeeping supervisors, there will be an inverse relationship between project performance and external communication.

GATEKEEPERS AND CAREER OUTCOMES

Even though boundary spanning gatekeeping has been recognized as one of the more important elements of effective leadership in Research, Development, and Engineering (i.e., RD&E) settings, very little is known about how these communication and network activities affect other important managerial functions and organizational outcomes. If there is a significant distinction between the information processing contributions and capabilities of project supervisors who function as gatekeepers and those who do not, then to what extent will they also have different career paths within the technical organization? Are gatekeeping supervisors more likely to be promoted to particular laboratory positions than non-gatekeeping supervisors, for example?

In addition to examining the career outcomes of gatekeeping supervisors, it is also important to investigate how they affect the job experiences and work activities of their technical subordinates. If career decisions are strongly influenced by how well individuals are connected to their company's formal and informal networks, then engineers working for gatekeeping supervisors should have substantial career advantages over technologists assigned to non-gatekeeping supervisors. Through their more elaborate contacts, valuable technical insights, and close working relationships, gate-

keeping supervisors may directly impact the personal growth and development of their technical subordinates (Tushman and Katz, 1980). And to the extent that gatekeeping supervisors help project members participate more effectively within their work settings and gain clearer working relationships with and exposure to other corporate areas and higher-level managers, project members are not only less likely to leave the organization but also more likely to be recognized and subsequently promoted.

From an exploratory point of view, therefore, this research focuses on the formal and informal aspects of leadership by investigating (over a 5-year period) the influence of gatekeeping supervisors on the organizational turnover and promotional outcomes of project subordinates. Although career outcome effects will be generally explored, younger employees are more likely to benefit from the socialization and developmental role played by gatekeeping supervisors (Katz, 1980), especially since most turnover occurs within the first years of organizational employment (Schein, 1978) and because engineers usually expect to be promoted to a managerial position between the ages of 30 and 40 (Dalton et al, 1982). Finally, as previously discussed, boundary spanning gatekeeping is more critical in development work than in either research or technical service. As a result, the influence of gatekeeping supervisors on the career outcomes of engineering subordinates is most likely to be especially important in development project areas.

METHODOLOGY

This study was conducted among all project members working in a large corporate RD&E facility. At the start of the study, the facility's professionals ($N = 345$) were divided into seven separate functional departments, which in turn were subdivided into 61 projects organized around specific, long term types of discipline and product focused problems. Each professional was a member of only one project group.

Communication

To measure actual communication activity, project members reported (on specially provided lists) all those individuals with whom they had work-related oral communication on a randomly chosen day each week for 15 weeks. Professionals were asked to report all contacts both within and outside the laboratory, including how many times they may have talked to a given person that day. Social and written communications were not reported. An overall response rate of 93 percent was achieved over the 15 weeks and almost 70 percent of all pairwise communication episodes within the RD&E facility were reciprocally reported by both parties. Given these high rates of response and mutual agreement, these sociometric methods provide a rather clear and accurate picture of each project member's communication network.

For each project member, internal communications was measured by summing the number of work-related contacts reported over the 15 weeks between that member and all other professionals within the organization, including all project and departmental colleagues and supervisors. External or outside communication was measured by summing the member's reported communications to other professional individuals outside the organization, including R&D consultants, professors, vendors, customers, and the like. As discussed by Katz & Tushman (1979), these individual scores were also aggregated to obtain project measures of internal and external communication.

Conceptually, project gatekeepers are defined as those members who are high internal communicators and who also maintain a high degree of outside communication. In line with previous studies (see Allen, 1984), this study operationalized gatekeepers as those project members who were in the top fifth of both the internal and external communication distributions. Gatekeepers were identified in 20 project groups while 40 projects had no gatekeepers within their memberships.

Project Type

R&D tasks differ along several dimensions, including time span of feedback, specific vs. general problem-solving orientation, and the generation of new knowledge vs. utilization of existing knowledge and experience (Rosenbloom & Wolek, 1970). Based on these dimensions, distinct project categories were defined ranging from research to development to technical service. Such a categorization also forms a universal (research) to local (technical service) project continuum. As discussed by Katz & Tushman (1979), respondents were asked to use these specific project definitions and indicate how well each category represented the objectives of their task activities. A second question asked respondents to indicate what percentage of their project work fell into each of the project categories. A weighted average of these two answers was calculated for each respondent (Spearman-Brown reliability = 0.91).

To categorize projects, however, the homogeneity of members' perceptions of their task characteristics had to be examined to check for the appropriateness of pooling across individual project members (see Tushman, 1977 for details). As pooling was appropriate, individual responses were averaged to get final project scores, yielding 14 Research, 23 Development, and 23 Technical Service projects. Research projects carried out more universally oriented scientific work (discovering new knowledge in glass physics, for instance) while development and technical service projects were more locally oriented in that they worked on organizationally defined problems and products.

Project Performance

To get comparable measures of project performance across significantly different technologies, all departmental and laboratory managers ($N = 9$) were interviewed individually and asked to evaluate the overall technical performance of all projects with which they were sufficiently familiar. When they could not make an informed judgment, they did not rate that project. Each project was independently evaluated by an average of five managers using a 7-point Likert type scale ranging from (1) very low to (7) very high. Individual ratings were averaged to yield overall project performance scores (Spearman-Brown reliability = .81).

CAREER OUTCOMES

Almost five years after the collection of the preceding data, we returned to the RD&E facility to collect data on the organizational turnover and dual ladder promotions (i.e., managerial and technical) of all those project members in our original sample. Despite the facility's strong growth, 31 percent of the project members and 19 percent of the project supervisors had left the company over the course of this five year interval, and an additional 8 percent had retired. In this organization, the formal managerial and technical ladder positions and titles start within the departments above the project supervisory level.

RESULTS

Gatekeeper Presence and Project Performance

The performance means reported in the first row of Table 30.1 clearly indicate that, in general, the performances of projects with gatekeepers were not significantly different from the performances of projects without gatekeepers. As previously discussed, however, locally oriented projects (i.e., development and technical service) should display a positive association between gatekeeper presence and project performance. Universal-type or research projects, on the other hand, should show an inverse relation between gatekeeper presence and project performance.

The breakdown of performance means by project type strongly supports these differences in the appropriateness of the gatekeeping function. As shown by Table 30.1, research projects *without* gatekeepers were significantly higher performing than research projects *with* gatekeepers. It may be that research projects are more effectively linked to external information areas through direct member contacts.

In sharp contrast, development projects *with* gatekeepers were significantly more effective than development projects *without* gatekeepers. Unlike research groups, then, development projects are linked to outside information areas more effectively through the use of gatekeepers. No significant differences in project performance, however, were discovered between technical service groups with and without gatekeepers.

Role of Gatekeepers

It was suggested that on locally oriented tasks, gatekeepers may do much more than simply channel outside information into their project groups. They may also act to reduce communication impedance by facilitating the external communications of their

TABLE 30.1
Project Performance as a Function of Gatekeeper Presence and Project Type

Project type	Mean performance for projects:		
	With gatekeepers	Without gatekeepers	Mean difference in performance
All projects	4.70 (N = 20)	4.53 (N − 40)	0.17
Project type			
Research	4.22 (N = 5)	4.92 (N = 9)	−0.70**
Development	4.91 (N = 8)	4.15 (N = 15)	0.76***
Technical service	4.80 (N = 7)	4.67 (N = 16)	0.13

**p < 0.05 and ***p < 0.01 indicate significant mean differences in project performance.

TABLE 30.2

Correlations between Project Performance and External Communication by Project Type and Gatekeeper Presence

Measures of external communication for:	Correlation with performance for projects:	
	With gatekeeping leaders	Without gatekeeping leaders
Research projects:		
(a) All project members	0.53	0.46*
(b) All members excluding project leaders†	0.37	0.70**
(c) Project leaders	0.55	0.29
	($N = 5$)	($N = 9$)
Development projects:		
(a) All project members	0.31	−0.45**
(b) All members excluding project leaders	0.55*	−0.21
(c) Project leaders	0.37	−0.51**
	($N = 8$)	($N = 15$)
Technical service projects:		
(a) All project members	0.31	−0.19
(b) All members excluding project leaders	0.64*	−0.03
(c) Project leaders	0.77*	−0.34*
	($N = 7$)	($N = 16$)

†In the first column of correlations, project leader refers to the project's gatekeeper, 75% of whom were also project supervisors. In the second column, project leader simply refers to the project's supervisor.

*$p < 0.10$; **$p < 0.05$; pairwise correlations that are significantly different at the $p < 0.10$ level or less have been underlined.

fellow project colleagues. In contrast, locally oriented projects without gatekeepers will have no effective link to external areas. Results reported in Table 30.2 support this notion for projects within the development and technical service categories. For local projects without gatekeepers, there was a consistent inverse association between members' external communication and project performance. For projects with gatekeepers, however, a significantly different pattern emerged—external communication was positively associated with project performance. Furthermore, these correlation differences were strong even after the direct communication effects of gatekeepers were removed. For both development and technical service groups, gatekeepers *and* their project colleagues were able to communicate effectively with outside professionals.

The significant correlational differences between projects with and without gatekeepers strongly support the argument that gatekeepers influence the ability of local project members to communicate effectively with external sources of technical information. Members of research projects, on the other hand, do not seem to face a communication impedance when communicating externally, for Table 30.2 shows that the level of outside interaction by all research project members was positively associated with performance independent of a gatekeeper's presence within the group. Gatekeepers as a result, may not play an important information processing role in the more universally oriented research projects, but they appear to play a vital role in the more locally defined development and technical service projects.

Gatekeepers and Project Supervisors

Can project supervisors substitute for gatekeepers in linking their projects to external information areas? The correlations reported in Table 30.2 do not support this position. For development and technical service projects, the more non-gatekeeping project supervisors communicated with information sources outside the organization, the lower their project's performance (correlations of −.51 and −.34, respectively). On the other hand, the associations between outside contact and project performance were very positive for supervisors who were also gatekeepers (correlations of .37 and .77, respectively). Such significant correlational differences strongly imply that these two kinds of supervisors play a very different role and contribute very differently within their project groups.

In light of these differences, were gatekeeping and non-gatekeeping supervisors likely to receive the same kinds of promotions? Our results suggest they did not. The follow-up study of the facility some five years later revealed that almost all of the gatekeeping supervisors had been promoted up the management ladder. Of the 12 gatekeeping supervisors remaining with the company, 11, or 92 percent, were in higher-level managerial positions. The one remaining gatekeeping supervisor was on the technical side of the organization's dual-ladder reward system.

Although non-gatekeeping supervisors were almost as likely to be promoted, they were not as likely to receive managerial promotions. Only 46 percent of the 35 remaining non-gatekeeping supervisors were in higher-level managerial positions some five years later. Surprisingly enough, almost as many were promoted up the technical ladder, about 34 percent. In fact, of the thirteen project supervisors who were promoted to the technical ladder, only one had been functioning as a technical gatekeeper at the be-

ginning of our research study. (Actually, this one gatekeeper had initially been promoted up the managerial ladder but was switched to a technical ladder position when it became clear that he was not functioning effectively as a manager.)

While gatekeeping supervisors were essentially promoted up the managerial ladder, could one have differentiated between non-gatekeeping supervisors promoted managerially and those promoted technically? The means reported in Table 30.3 indicate that there were significant communication differences between these two promotional categories. Project supervisors promoted up the technical ladder had only half as many internal interactions as project supervisors selected for managerial positions. Interestingly enough, there were almost identical levels of internal communications for gatekeeping and nongatekeeping supervisors promoted to managerial positions. External communications did not differentiate between the promotional ladders of non-gatekeeping supervisors. Thus, the level of interpersonal activity and skills that one has demonstrated within the organization may have been a strong factor in shaping one's promotional ladder within this dual ladder system.

TURNOVER INFLUENCE

Our first analysis here concerned the influence of boundary spanning gatekeeping supervisors on the

TABLE 30.3
Comparisons of Mean Internal and External Communications of Project Supervisors Promoted over the Next 5 Years

Promotional positions above the project level	Mean internal communication (per person per week)	Mean external communication (per person per week)
(a) Gatekeeping supervisors promoted to managerial positions (N = 11)	74.3[a]	4.8[a]
(b) Non-gatekeeping supervisors promoted to managerial positions (N = 16)	70.6[a]	1.5[b]
(c) Supervisors promoted to technical positions† (N = 12)	39.7[b]	1.4[b]

†Of these project supervisors, only one had functioned as a project gatekeeper.
Note: In each column, means with superscript 'a' are significantly greater than means with superscript 'b' at the $p < 0.01$ level.

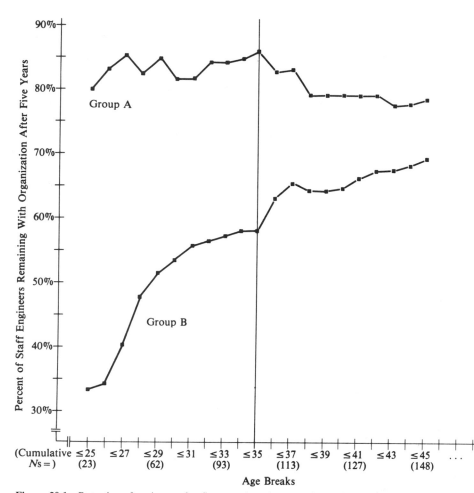

Figure 30.1 Retention of engineers after five years by prior type of reporting relationships at successive age breaks[a].

turnover rates of project engineers. For the sample as a whole, project members who had reported to gatekeeping supervisors had a significantly lower rate of organizational turnover (17 percent turnover over the five-year interval) than did engineers assigned to non-gatekeeping supervisors, (33 percent turnover for the same five years). It appears that working for supervisors who also function as gatekeepers has a strong positive effect on employee retention rates.

Because 70 percent of the turnover occurred for project members less than 36 years of age, additional comparisons were carried out for younger versus older age groupings. In fact, to pinpoint the influence of gatekeepers on subordinate turnover, Figure 30.1 plots as a function of age the cumulative retention rates of projection members reporting to gatekeeping supervisors (Group A), versus those members not reporting to gatekeeping supervisors (Group B).

Of those project subordinates who were age 25 or less, only 33 percent remained in the organization if they had *not* reported to a gatekeeping supervisor. The comparable percentage for project members assigned to a gatekeeping supervisor was almost 80 percent. Similarly, of those project subordinates who were 35 years old or less, only 57 percent remained with the organization if they had *not* been working with a gatekeeping supervisor. The comparable percentage in Group A was 84 percent. Although this difference is statistically significant, the figure clearly shows that most of the difference in retention rates between Groups A and B occurs among members less than 30 years of age. Almost 85 percent of these young engineers were still with the organization after five years if they had been assigned to a gatekeeping type supervisor, while only 51 percent of their counterparts who had not reported to gatekeeping supervisors were still employed.

Although gatekeeping supervisors may help reduce the turnover rates among young professionals, it was previously suggested that this influence might be especially strong for members of development and technical service projects. This possibility was examined. However, the turnover differences between project members with and without gatekeeping supervisors was consistently positive for all three types of project categories. In each case, over half the young project members not reporting to a gatekeeping supervisor had left the company within the five-year interval (despite substantial growth within the RD&E facility). In sharp contrast, none of the corresponding turnover rates for project members reporting to gatekeeping supervisors exceeded 25 percent.

Clearly gatekeeping supervisors had considerable influence over the turnover rates of young professionals within this facility. What is it about gatekeeping supervisors that brings about these lower levels of turnover? As previously discussed, turnover may be a function of how well young professionals get integrated into their organization's formal and informal networks. Because gatekeepers are key individuals in these networks, reporting to a gatekeeping supervisor may well facilitate the young professional's linkages to important information sources both within and outside the organization. An investigation was therefore made as to whether young project members reporting to gatekeeping supervisors had different interaction patterns than did project members reporting to non-

gatekeeping supervisors. The analyses did not reveal any significant differences in their comparative levels of collegial interaction. Young engineers who left had as much communication activity with internal colleagues as those young engineers who remained. What did differentiate young stayers from leavers was their much higher levels of contact not only with their gatekeeping supervisor but also, and perhaps more important, with their departmental manager. Thus, it may not be the assignment of young project members to gatekeeping supervisors per se that enhances long-term retention. What really makes the difference is the stronger degree of hierarchical interaction and integration—the kind of communication and connectedness that is so important and helpful for reducing stress and uncertainty during the socialization phase of any young professional's career (Katz, in Press).

Promotion Influence

During the five-year interval, 23 of the remaining project members had been promoted to managerial positions. As with turnover, project members who had reported to gatekeeping supervisors had a slightly higher rate of managerial promotion than did project members reporting to non-gatekeeping supervisors, 14.6 versus 11.2 percent, respectively. However, because almost 70 percent of the project members promoted to managerial positions were between the ages of 27 and 32 at the start of our study, the data within this more limited age range were reanalyzed for the whole subsample, as well as within each type of project category.

As shown in Table 30.4, the promotion rate for all project members reporting to gatekeeping supervisors within this restricted age subsample was 41.2 percent, whereas only 17.4 percent of the comparable engineers reporting to a non-gatekeeping supervisor were similarly promoted—a significant difference of 23.8 percent. Although proportionately more engineers who had reported to gatekeepers were promoted to management within this general subsample, Table 30.4 also reveals that most of this difference takes place in the area of product and process development. No significant

TABLE 30.4
Proportion of Engineers Promoted to High Level Managerial Positions over the Next Five Years by Prior Reporting Relationship and Project Task Areas[a]

| | Prior reporting relationship percent | | |
Prior project areas	Assigned to a gatekeeping supervisor (%)	Not assigned to a gatekeeping supervisor (%)	Proportional differences (%)
Across all areas	41.2	17.4	23.8*
	($n = 17$)	($n = 46$)	
By project area			
Applied research	33.3	20.0	13.3
	($n = 6$)	($n = 10$)	
Product/process development	66.7	18.5	48.2**
	($n = 6$)	($n = 27$)	
Technical service	20.0	11.1	8.9
	($n = 5$)	($n = 9$)	

[a]Table includes only those engineers in the age range (27 through 32) in which almost 70 percent of the promotions took place.
*$p < .10$
**$p < .05$.

advantage was uncovered in the promotion rates of project engineers reporting to gatekeepers in either research or technical service areas. On the other hand, two-thirds of the engineers reporting to gatekeepers in development projects received management promotions, in contrast to only 18.5 percent of the engineers reporting to non-gatekeeping supervisors. Even though the subsample sizes in Table 30.4 are rather small, development work is precisely the project area in which gatekeepers were hypothesized to have the strongest influence over career outcomes.

As in the turnover analyses, the communication patterns of project members within the 27–32 year old age range were examined to see if those promoted also had differential patterns of contacts and interactions within their work settings. None of the communication measures, however, was significantly related to managerial promotions for these individuals.

DISCUSSION

In engineering and scientific environments, there are at least two distinct methods by which R&D

project groups can keep abreast of technical ideas and developments outside their organizations: (1) by direct contact by all project members and (2) by contact mediated by project gatekeepers. Our findings suggest that the effectiveness of these two alternatives is strongly affected by the communication impedance separating project groups from their external information areas. Universally oriented research projects, for example, face little communication impedance when processing outside ideas and information since their work is less constrained by local organizational factors. Therefore, instead of relying on gatekeepers to keep informed about outside developments and advances, members of higher performing research groups were able to rely on their own external contacts. In fact, a significant inverse relationship between project performance and gatekeeper presence was uncovered among the facility's 14 research groups.

As project activities become more specialized and locally defined, however, language and cognitive differences between project members and external professionals increase, creating substantial communication impedance and more tendentious information flows. As a result, individual interaction across organizational boundaries becomes more difficult and ineffective. To wit, higher performing development and technical service groups had significantly less outside contact by all project members. Nevertheless, important technical information must be acquired from relevant outside sources. Gatekeeping, as a result, can be a necessary and effective process for transferring external technology into localized project groups. In particular, within our sample of development projects, those with gatekeepers were considerably more effective than those without gatekeepers. Thus, what are needed to introduce outside information effectively into development projects are specialized project individuals who keep current technically, are readily conversant across different technologies, and who are contributing to their project's work in direct and meaningful ways, i.e., technical gatekeepers.

Unlike development projects, the performances of technical service projects were not positively related to the presence of gatekeepers even though their project members could not communicate effectively with outside information areas (see Table 30.2). Perhaps the specialized gatekeeping role may not be as necessary in technical service projects because the work tends to deal with more mature technologies and existing knowledge and products than in development projects. The managerial hierarchy, instead, may be able to keep members sufficiently informed about external events and information through formal reporting channels and operating procedures.

Generally speaking, the particular method by which R&D projects can effectively connect with external technical information appears to differ significantly across the research, development, and technical service spectrum of R&D activities. The particular method is strongly contingent on both the nature of the project's work and the stability of the involved technologies. Thus, it seems that the combination of localized yet dynamic technologies necessitates the active presence and participation of gatekeepers within engineering project groups.

The Gatekeeping Role and Project Supervision

In linking local project groups to extra-organizational areas, our results indicate that gatekeepers not only bring in outside information, but just as important, they facilitate the external communication of their more locally oriented colleagues. As a result, localized engineering projects with gatekeepers are in a better position to take advantage of external technology since other members are now capable of communicating effectively across organizational boundaries. This additional capacity lessens the project's complete dependence on gatekeepers for gathering and disseminating all important outside information.

In research-type tasks, on the other hand, gatekeepers are not an effective method for obtaining external information; nor does it appear that they serve in any communication facilitating capacity. In higher performing research projects, members did not rely on gatekeepers for their external information; in a sense, they functioned as their own technical gatekeepers.

One should also note that many supervisors of locally-oriented projects could not adequately perform a gatekeeping role in linking their projects to outside technology. In contrast to gatekeeping supervisors, the external interactions of supervisors who were not gatekeepers were negatively associated with project performance. While these non-gatekeeping supervisors may have developed important internal linkages, they are unable to fulfill the same external function as their gatekeeping peers. Such findings suggest distinguishing between two types of project leaders: (1) locally oriented supervisors who may be appropriate for more administrative and technical support and development projects in which the rates of information and technology change are not high and (2) gatekeeping supervisors who may be more contributive on product- and process-development activities, especially if the rates of change in the underlying technologies are high.

These different capabilities also seem to have led to different kinds of career paths. All project gatekeepers remaining in the organization over a 5-year period were promoted along the managerial ladder. Almost all non-gatekeeping supervisors were also promoted during this interval. However, only about half were positioned on the managerial ladder—the other half being promoted along the technical ladder. While there were no strong differences between the technical performances of project groups which had supervisors promoted managerially versus those which had supervisors promoted technically, there had been very strong differences between their communication activities. Those selected for managerial positions had been high internal communicators; in fact, they were as high as project gatekeepers. In sharp contrast, supervisors promoted along the technical ladder had been extremely low internal communicators. Thus, what differentiated between these two alternative career paths for non-gatekeeping supervisors was not technical competence but interpersonal connectedness and competence. Thus, supervisors promoted along the technical ladder were probably not the most networked or influential individuals. And by promoting people to the technical ladder based on this differentiation, the organization over time runs the risk of reinforcing even more their feelings of isolation and lack of influence or power.

Perhaps it is these network and work experience differences that have caused so many companies to have substantial difficulty with the effective implementation of dual ladder reward systems (for a more recent discussion of the influence of gatekeepers on the dynamics of dual ladder promotions, see Katz, Tushman, & Allen, 1995). Supervisors who had behaviorally demonstrated their ability to interact effectively with other professionals within the organization were given higher-level managerial responsibilities and positions. Such findings clearly illustrate that technical skills were not considered sufficient for attaining these high-level managerial positions; rather, technical and interpersonal skills have to be combined. As expected, RD&E managers not only have to be technically competent, but they must also be able to communicate and interface effectively with other individuals, since most of their responsibilities have to be carried out and/or coordinated with these people. But this combination of skill requirements should not be so exclusively one-sided that it leads to perceptions that those promoted managerially are competent interpersonally while those promoted to the technical ladder are not. Under such conditions, the technical ladder will not be viewed as a reward but rather as a consolation prize for being regarded as *not* having the potential for being a "good manager."

SUBORDINATE CAREER OUTCOMES

Our research findings also support the idea that supervisory behavior has a critical influence on an engineer's organizational career. Not all supervisors, however, had comparable relationships with the career outcomes of their technical subordinates. Only boundary spanning gatekeeper supervisors were significantly associated with reduced turnover rates and higher rates of managerial promotion. These relationships, moreover, were particularly strong for young professionals; they disappeared for older, more experienced engineers.

Why were proportionately more of the young engineers who had gatekeeping supervisors still working and contributing to the organization after five years than those engineers whose supervisors were not functioning as gatekeepers? The strong communication differences that emerged suggest that gatekeepers lower turnover through the higher levels of interaction and activity that they foster for the young engineers, not only with themselves but also with more senior departmental managers. Thus, it may not be the gatekeeping role or supervisory status per se that influences turnover. What seems most beneficial are meaningful amounts of exposure and support coupled with work-related contact and involvement with relevant competent supervisors—interactions and work experiences that occur most frequently with gatekeeping supervisors.

In addition to these turnover relationships, gatekeeping supervisors were linked to the managerial promotions of project subordinates who were between the ages of 27 and 32 at the start of the study. Within this age range, project members working for gatekeeping supervisors attained a significantly higher rate of promotion to management than did project members working for nongatekeeping supervisors. Furthermore, the promotion rate for young project members reporting to gatekeepers in development areas was more than three times the promotion rate of development project members assigned to non-gatekeeping supervisors. In development work, gatekeepers are highly influential individuals who strongly enhance project performance by connecting engineers to more useful ideas and information outside the project. Having better access to critical information, along with working for influential supervisors, may be associated with greater work opportunities and organizational visibility which, in turn, lead to higher rates of management promotion.

From a broader perspective, the relationships between lower turnover and high interpersonal involvement with gatekeeping supervisors affirms the important role that project supervisors can and should play during the early socialization years of young professionals. As discussed by many researchers, young employees build perceptions of their work environment and establish their new organization identities through the plethora of interactions and interpersonal activities that take place during the early years of their laboratory integration. Young engineers, therefore, not only need to interact with their colleagues and peers, but they also require considerable interaction with and feedback from relevant supervisors to learn what is expected of them and to decipher how to be a high performing contributor.

Because they are well-connected professionally and organizationally, gatekeepers are particularly qualified to meet the breaking-in concerns of young professionals, directing and coupling the professional orientations of young engineers with a more appropriate organizational focus. Most likely, the high level of interpersonal contact between gatekeeping supervisors and young project engineers not only facilitates socialization but also results in more accurate expectations, perceptions, and understanding about one's role in the project and in the larger organization—all of which are important in decreasing the turnover and increasing the contribution of newcomers. Gatekeeping supervisors, therefore, fulfill an important leadership and training function for young engineers, operating effectively as important socializing agents as well as early sponsors of and network builders for these young technical professionals.

Organizations have to recognize that the problems and concerns of young engineers are real and must be dealt with before they become effective organizational members. Although specific training programs could be developed to teach project managers how to "break-in" the young engineer more effectively, the careful selection of supervisors for young professionals also would go a long way toward alleviating many of the problems that usually occur during this joining-up process. It is also important to note that gatekeeping supervisors were not related to the career outcomes of older, more established project members. The turnover and promotion rates of these more veteran technologists are probably influenced more by individual differences and by task and organizational factors than by the characteristics of their immediate supervisors.

Finally, one should realize that in a longitudinal field study of this sort, the random assignment of project members to gatekeeping and nongatekeeping supervisors was not possible. Although the thinking here emphasizes the direct role that gatekeepers might play in influencing project members' careers, it also is possible that gatekeepers either attracted or were assigned members who were more likely to stay or were of higher promotion potential. Furthermore, other uncontrolled organizational factors could have influenced the results. For example, data were not collected on how long project members worked for their respective supervisors. What is known is that project members who reported to gatekeeping supervisors early in their careers had more successful organizational outcomes. It remains for future research to look even more closely at these types of relationships.

CONCLUSIONS

In conclusion, gatekeepers perform a critical role within R&D settings that often goes unrecognized. By realizing the importance of the gatekeeping role within development tasks, R&D managers can link their product or process efforts to sources of external technology more effectively. A manager could examine, for example, the extent to which important technologies utilized within various development projects are actually 'covered' by a gatekeeping type person. However, the degree to which these communication activities can be managed may be limited. Gatekeeping is an informal role in that other project engineers must feel sufficiently secure and comfortable psychologically to approach gatekeepers with their technical problems, mistakes, and questions without fear of personal evaluation or other adverse considerations (Allen, 1984). Therefore, to the extent that the organization tries to formalize such a gatekeeping function, it runs the risk of inhibiting the very kinds of interaction it wishes to promote.

This is not meant to imply that gatekeeping cannot be managed or helped; on the contrary, it can. In fact, a number of R&D facilities have instituted formal gatekeeper programmes. What is important to recognize is that the interest and ability of individuals to link with external technology cannot be suddenly 'decreed' by management. Typically, such outside professional interests are a 'given' and are not easily influenced by the organization, although they can be made easier to pursue. What can be more easily influenced is the degree to which gatekeepers are actually present and participating in project tasks as well as their accessibility to other project members. Their work positions, for example, could be located close to other project engineers to foster easier and more frequent communication. However, the development of sufficient internal contacts and communications to be an effective gatekeeper takes time. In the present sample, for example, all of the gatekeepers had been working in their present project groups for a period of at least two years. In short, the external side of the gatekeeping role is usually being performed by the gatekeeper anyway. It is the internal side that can be facilitated and made more effective.

REFERENCES

Achilladeles, A., Jervis, P. & Robertson, A. (1971) *Success and Failure in Innovation.* Project Sappho, Sussex: University of Sussex Press.

Allen, T. J. (1977) *Managing the Flow of Technology.* Cambridge, MA: M.I.T. Press

Allen, T. J. & Cohen, S. (1969) "Information flow in R&D laboratories," *Administrative Science Quarterly,* Vol. 14, 12–19.

Allen, T. J., Tushman, M. & Lee, D. (1979) "technology transfer as a function of position on research, development, and technical service continuum," *Academy of Management Journal,* Vol. 22, 694–708.

Dalton, G., Thompson, P. & Price, R. (1982) "The four stages of professional careers; A new look at performance by professionals." In R. Katz (Ed.), *Career Issues in Human Resource Management,* Englewood Cliffs, NJ: Prentice-Hall, 129–53.

Hagstrom, W. (1965) *The Scientific Community.* New York: Basic Books.

Katz, D. & Kahn, R. (1966) *The Social Psychology of Organizations.* New York: Wiley Co.

Katz, R. (1980) "Time and work: Toward an integrative perspective." In B. Staw & L. L. Cummings (Eds.), *Research in Organizational Behavior* (Vol. 2), Greenwich, CT: JAI Press, 81–127.

Katz, R. (In press) "Organizational socialization and the reduction of uncertainty." In R. Katz (Ed.), *The Human Side of Managing Technological Innovation: A Collection of Readings,* New York: Oxford University Press.

Katz, R. & Tushman, M. (1979) "Communication patterns, project performance, and task characteristics," *Organizational Behavior and Human Performance,* Vol. 23, 139–62.

Katz, R., Tushman, M., & Allen, T. (1995) "The influence of supervisory promotion and network location on subordinate careers in a dual ladder RD&E setting," *Management Science,* Vol. 41, 848–63.

Pelz, D. & Andrews, F. M. (1966) *Scientists in Organizations.* New York: Wiley Co.

Rosenbloom, R. & Wolek, F. (1970) *Technology and Information Transfer.* Boston, MA: Harvard Business School.

Schein, E. H. (1978) *Career Dynamics.* Reading, MA: Addison-Wesley.

Tushman, M. (1977) "Technical communication in R&D laboratories: the impact of project work characteristics," *Academy of Management Journal,* Vol. 20, 624–45.

Tushman, M. & Katz, R. (1980) "External communication and project performance: An investigation into the role of gatekeepers," *Management Science,* Vol. 26, 1071–85.

11

Creating Innovative Climates

31

A Skunkworks Tale

THOMAS J. PETERS

Innovation is unpredictable. It thrives in the chaos of "skunkworks," where product champions go scrounging for success.

Yellow Post-it Note Pads have quickly become as commonplace in the American office as paper clips. The product is a $100 million winner for 3M. The idea behind it came from a 3M employee who sang in a choir. The slips of paper he used to mark the hymnals kept falling out, and it dawned on him that adhesive-backed pieces of paper might solve his problem.

The requisite technology existed, and a prototype was soon available. "Great story," you say—but wait, this tale's not quite over yet. Major office-supply distributors thought the idea was silly. Market surveys were negative. But 3M secretaries got hooked on the product once they actually used it. Post-it's breakthrough finally came when 3M mailed samples to the personal secretaries of Fortune 500 CEOs, using the letterhead of the 3M chairman's secretary.

The Post-it story would amount to nothing more than a charming tale were this development

Copyright © 1983 Tom Peters. All rights reserved. Reprinted with permission.
Tom Peters is founder and president of The Tom Peters Group.

process not repeatedly played out at companies across the U.S. The course of innovation (idea generation, prototype development, contact with an initial user, and breakthrough to the final market) is highly uncertain. Moreover, it will always be sloppy, disorganized, and unpredictable, and that is the important point. It's important because we must learn to design organizations that explicitly take into account the unavoidable sloppiness of the process and use it to their advantage rather than fight it.

From America's best-run companies come tales of incredible perseverance, countless experiments, perverse and unusual product-users, five-person "skunkworks" sequestered in dingy warehouses for 60 days, plans gone awry, inventions made in the wrong industry at the wrong time for the wrong reason, and specifications for complex systems scrawled across the backs of envelopes. Innovation just doesn't happen the way it's supposed to.

THE 10 MYTHS OF INNOVATION

The hyperorganized approach leads companies to fall prey to the 10 myths of innovation management, which have already hampered many a firm. These false beliefs must be put to rest, and the sloppy side of innovation must be exploited. The 10 myths are as follows:

1. Specs and a market plan are the first steps to success.

2. Detailed strategic and technological plans greatly increase the odds of a no-surprises outcome.

3. Only a big team can blitz a project, especially if it is a complex one.

4. Contemplation stimulates creativity.

5. Big projects are inherently different from small projects and must be managed differently.

6. An organization must have a rigid hierarchy if would-be innovators are to get a fair hearing.

7. Product compatibility is the key to economic success.

8. Customers will tell you only about yesterday's needs.

9. Technology push is the cornerstone of success.

10. Perfectionism pays off.

Some companies love to make plans more than they love to make profitable new products. In these bureaucratic behemoths, someone's bright idea is turned into a six-month, $2 million study—a paper study. A paper evaluation of the study by various interested parties takes another three months. Some sort of design go-ahead is given, and writing the technical specs, at a cost of $3 million, takes six more months. The specs are evaluated in the four months after that.

During this last stage, a prototype is finally built. It costs $5 million to $10 million and takes four to six months to complete. And guess what? It doesn't work. Throughout the history of successful corporation innovation—from the development of French-fries seasoning at McDonald's to faded jeans at Levi Strauss & Company to the System 360 computer at IBM—neither the first nor the second prototype has *ever* worked. The successful innovators just go back to the drawing board.

But now the people in charge of the project really begin to sweat. By this time, careers are on the line and a lot of time, money, and pride has been invested in the design. So now they enter the "ignore the misfit data and make the damn think work" stage. Meanwhile, the competitors have introduced three or four new products, each with several new features. As time goes by, the plodding planners fall further behind. So they recomplicate the product. "We're going to get it exactly right," they boast. But when they finally get it to the marketplace, it's adorned with so many bells and whistles that it doesn't work well.

This mentality is the antithesis of the Wee Willie Keeler approach. Wee Willie Keeler was a consummate opportunist who played baseball from 1892 to 1910. He once said, "Hit 'em where they ain't," and he proved that strategy's worth by making it into the Baseball Hall of Fame even though he stroked only 34 home runs in 19 seasons. His approach is imitated to a T by firms like Hewlett-

Packard, 3M, McDonald's, Wang Laboratories, PepsiCo, Citicorp, Johnson & Johnson, Digital Equipment, and others like them. This philosophy says, in effect: *Start out by spending $25,000, or even as much as a quarter of a million dollars. Build a prototype, or a big hunk of one, in the first 60 to 90 days. And then poke it to see if it moves.*

Whether projects like these involve aircraft, missiles, or French fries, the results achieved by scores of companies suggest that something can always be built in this length of time. The evaluation of the prototype should take another 60 days. (Even at such an early stage, firms following this approach may decide—explicitly or not—to start up second team doing roughly the same work as the first, just to get a different look.)

"We're already playing with something tangible," say project leaders at these companies. "Now we take the next little step. We build another new version in 90 days. It's a more developed prototype that will cost a little more, around $100,000 to $200,000. After it's built, we can probably get it, or part of it, into a user's hands—not an average user (that's still years away), but a lead user who's willing to experiment with us. Even an in-house lead user might do the trick." And on goes the process, always involving investments that increase little by little and time-frames that do the same.

At each step the innovators learn a little more, because they set up harsh reality tests with hard products and real users. If something doesn't work, they weed it out quickly before career lock-in and irreversible psychological addiction to hitting home runs take place.

In the aircraft manufacturing industry, one such harsh confrontation with reality is known as the chicken test. Aircraft engines have to be built to withstand possible ingestion of flocks of birds. To determine what would happen in that unlikely event, engineers buy 15 or 20 gross of chickens, stuff some into a cannon with a barrel four feet in diameter, and fire them at engines running full throttle. It's the ultimate pragmatic tests. Rolls-Royce spent several years and several hundred million dollars on a new graphite-material engine. After all that, it failed the chicken test.

What the Wee Willie Keeler, or experimental, approach boils down to is getting your inevitable chicken test out of the way early. Every new product fails a chicken test or two at some point. The burning issue is, when does it fail? At the end of four years, by which time the competitors have a new array of products on the market? Or at the end of 90 days?

BUREAUCRACY UNDER ATTACK

Strategic planning is being attacked on all fronts. Many claim that it is too rigid. Others say it's too bureaucratic. Some believe that corporations should at least decentralize such planning (General Electric and Westinghouse, who were early pioneers in strategic planning, are doing just that). A few even suggest that we get rid of it altogether.

But do we really want to do that? The new "in" terms are *technology* and *production*. "Technology planning" and "manufacturing planning" are the preferred substitutes for strategic planning. Before heading off down a new trail, though, let's look at the record of technology planning. It's hardly spotless.

Think of recent inventions that we're all familiar with. "We do not consider that the aeroplane will be of any use for war purposes," declared the British minister of war in 1910. In the late 1940s, market research predicted that the total sales of mainframe computers would be about a dozen. Even though the robotics industry is crowded with such competitors as United Technologies Corporation, General Electric, Westinghouse Electric, and IBM, the first "intelligent mobile robot" will come from a less-than household name—Denning Systems Inc. of Washington, D.C., a classic three-inventors-in-a-garage operation.

A highly systematic analysis of this phenomenon may be found in the book *The Sources of Invention* by John Jewkes, a professor of economic organization at Oxford University. After studying the development of 58 of this century's major inventions, Jewkes concluded that at least 46 of them occurred in "the wrong place." Note the unusual origins of the following inventions:

- Kodachrome film was invented by a couple of musicians.
- A watchmaker fooling around with brass castings came up with the process involved in the continuous casting of steel.
- The developers of the jet engine were told by reciprocating-aircraft-engine people that it was useless. (They finally peddled their invention not to engine-makers but to airframe-makers.)

According to Jewkes, there is no industry group in which much innovation has taken place as or when it was supposed to. On top of this, "the initial use and vision for a new product is virtually never the one that is ultimately of the greatest importance commercially," reports Jim Utterback, an MIT associate professor of engineering who for more than a decade has studied the development of inventions. He has concluded that users play a special role in this process. To support his point, he recounts the path to success of invention after invention.

His analysis of incandescent lighting is typical. Its first use was on ships, which in retrospect seems natural enough: it's dangerous to keep gas lamps on a seafaring vessel, whose rolling motion can upset them. Thus the incandescent light found its first home in a highly specialized market niche. Then, in a move that *every* marketresearch department could easily have predicted, incandescent lighting spread to—baseball parks! Night games have been with us ever since. From there the invention moved to neighborhoods, where it replaced gas streetlamps, and only 15 years later did incandescent lights begin to make it into homes. As a more recent example of this pattern, transistors were first used for missile guidance systems; their use by home consumers lagged 20 years behind.

The role of corporations in all this is truly frightening. Organizations have an apparently inherent tendency to make exactly the wrong moves in trying to stimulate innovation, according to Utterback, who states, "In 32 of 34 companies, the current product leaders reduced investment in the new technology in order to pour more money into the old."

Not only, then, does the leader *not* embrace the new, he actually reduces his investment in the new to hold on to the old. The problems involved in switching to a new technology are manifold. First, there's scientific hubris (the engineer knows best, he can predict the use of the product most accurately); then comes marketing hubris (how could all those tons of data on the Edsel be wrong?). Jewkes offers three rules of thumb regarding technological planning, all of which are well worth heeding:

- Peering into the future is a popular and agreeable pastime that, if not taken seriously, is also comparatively innocuous.
- There is a great virtue in picking and choosing from a variety of available options.
- The industrial laboratory does not appear to be a particularly favorable environment for the inducement of innovation.

Does this mean that corporations should do away with central planning? Should centralized R&D activity be abolished? The answer is no. First, one does need to make general bets on technological directions: it's important to know the difference between, say, north and northwest. That's fine. What isn't sensible is trying to prespecify the difference between a course of 43 degrees and a course of 46 degrees. As a former managing director at the consulting firm McKinsey & Company liked to argue, "About the best you can hope for is to get the herd heading roughly west." And this is a task that centralized research can do.

"As a regimen or discipline for a group of people, planning is very valuable," notes Fletcher Bryom, the iconoclastic former chairman of Koppers Company. "My position is, go ahead and plan, but once you've done your planning, put it on the shelf. Don't be bound by it. Don't use it as a major influence on the decision-making process. Use it mainly to recognize change as it takes place."

QUICK-AND-DIRTY SOLUTIONS

When the U-2 spy plane emerged as the country's most sophisticated airborne surveillance system 30 years ago, many experts said that it would never fly. It's still doing yeoman service. The developers were a retired aeronautical engineer named Kelly Johnson and a small band of Lockheed Corporation mavericks. They called their off-line group "the Skunk Work"—the original business use of an apt term that (as far as I can determine) may have been coined by Al Capp, who drew the comic strip *Li'l Abner.*

Lockheed is not unique. At GE the same activity is called "bootlegging"; at 3M they label it "scrounging." It would not be difficult to argue that 3M, Hewlett-Packard, Digital Equipment, and Johnson & Johnson are today nothing more than collections of skunkworks.

The finding stands out more and more clearly as the evidence rolls in: whenever a practical innovation has occurred, a skunkwork, usually with a nucleus of six to 25 people, has been at the heart of it. Most skunkworks seem to do things in an incredibly short period of time. While visiting a Westinghouse lab, General Curtis LeMay, then Chief of Staff of the Air Force, found a pencil sketch of what was at the time a beyond-the-state-of-the-art product: a side-mounted radar. He asked if he might have one within 90 days. The next day he sent Westinghouse an airplane to hang it on. He got his device less than 90 days later. In the recent book *The Soul of a New Machine* by Tracy Kidder, Data General's computer-project leader, Tom West, speculates that the company's crucial breakthrough in microcoding may have taken place in less than a week. [*Editor's note:* Microcoding builds into a computer the instructions that make it operate.]

But what happens with a quick-and-dirty skunkwork project? Is the quality as high? Does it ever fit into the rest of the product line? The record shows, delightfully, that the stuff that comes from skunkworks is often of high quality, even though it was invented in a fraction of the so-called normal time.

The creative impetus behind skunkworks boils down to ownership and commitment. In *The Soul of a New Machine,* West describes the phenomenon: "There are 30 guys out there who think they've invented it; I don't want that tampered with." Firms like 3M, Johnson & Johnson, and Hewlett-Packard all agree that in creating the sense of ownership, intense commitment, and unbounded energy that comes from turned-on teams, a surprisingly small group is optimal.

A struggle against others is also important. It, too, engenders feelings of ownership and commitment. Interestingly, its most important form is rivalry with others *inside* the company, not with an outside competitor. Few companies are really familiar with their competitors, but their divisions sure know one another. Constructive internal competition is difficult to manage. There are a great number of subtleties and traps. The net result, however, is almost always positive.

The skunkwork cannot do all things. On the other hand, the empirical indications seem to say, loud and clear, "Ignore this form of organization for innovation at your own peril." The alternative is *de novo* design of the tiniest parts, excessively long product-development cycles, large teams in which ownership and commitment are missing, do-everything-inside attitudes, overcomplexity, and situations in which competing central staffs make the decisions on technical issues or delay them endlessly on the basis of the most tenuous market or financial projections. The show just doesn't get on the road.

HELL-BENT ON SUCCESS

If big, well-orchestrated teams were at the heart of successful innovation, we would expect to find them populated with powerful thinkers who regularly ascended to their mountaintop retreats to look out over the pines. As a result of such reflection, they would accomplish the necessary breakthroughs, presumably on schedule. If, on the other hand, rough-and-tumble skunkworks, hell-bent on outproducing some formal group, were the norm, we would expect to find bleary-eyed folks staring at computer screens or test tubes in dirty, forgotten basement corners.

It does turn out that bleary eyes play quite a large role in innovations. When a year's worth of work is routinely accomplished in five weeks, someone called a "champion" will be found at the heart of the operation. Formal IBM in-house studies of research projects always unearth a champion. National Science Foundation studies suggest that the champion's role in pushing an idea to fruition is crucial. When the brand manager of a consumer-goods company, even in a highly structured system, becomes a determined champion, the odds of success go up tenfold. Looking back over his career in *Adventures of a Bystander,* Peter Drucker, the noted business expert, remarks, "Whenever *anything* is accomplished, it is being done, I have learned, by a monomaniac with a mission."

A crucial corollary is that the corporation that would nourish inventors must also tolerate, even praise, failure. Going through 3M's roster of senior officers with one of the company's executives a couple of years ago, I discovered that virtually every 3M officer had reached the top because he himself had introduced several important new products. Moreover, each story, as it was recounted in conventional form, focused on the rough places in the road: the 10 years of ups and downs when the product was too advanced for the marketplace, when it had to be reformulated, when the manufacturing scale-up didn't work. Setbacks are considered standard operating procedure. Above all else, the winners are those who persist.

SMALL WITHIN BIG

Massive projects like the manned space program or the development of the transistor at AT&T Bell Labs aren't that different from less complex undertakings; they're just bigger. They too can be treated, to a substantial degree, as collections of skunkworks. In an important sense, the principle "small within big" turns out to be essential to the success of big projects. Most of the breakthroughs

in these cases are the results of champions' operating off-line. Charles Brown, chairman of AT&T, said recently, "Today the long-distance network looks like one big, perfectly conceived solution. The reality that we often forget when we think about innovation planning is that the network is a collection of thousands of small breakthroughs that occurred here and there, and certainly not according to schedule or by courtesy of a flawless master plan."

The story of Boeing's recent development of the air-launched cruise missile is even more pertinent. The system is complex. Undoubtedly it should have been developed all at once, with the aid of a 100,000-bubble PERT chart (a "program evaluation and review technique" diagram that indicates the relationships among the phases of a project). The missile-development program was in fact broken down into seven major pieces. Modest-size teams were assembled to deal with the seven projects. Each task was then accomplished in a remarkably short period of time relative to the norm. Each had a champion. Each was in competition with all the others on several vital fronts.

Then what happened? You guessed it. Put the seven pieces together and they don't fit exactly right. So you have to spend some time, as much as a few months, getting the interfaces just right, despite the prior effort that went into interface specifications. (Twice-a-week meetings of a "tie-breaker" group sorted out many of the issues in question.) The final design isn't as technically beautiful as ideals of theoretical perfection suggest is possible. But multiple passes usually take less time and result in the development of simpler, more practical systems than a single everything-at-once pass. (Boeing's cruise missile was delivered more than a year ahead of schedule and well under budget.)

But back to the question of whether big differs from small. There is no question that it does. The Boeing 767 and the French-fries seasoning change at McDonald's are not the same. On the other hand, commitment, championing, small within big, piece-versus-piece competition, the overtight deadline, and the turned-on modest-size group are the keys to breaking down a big, forbidding task into smaller, more manageable ones.

CHARGED-UP TEAMS

The conventional wisdom holds that only a strong functional monolith will keep the engineers' (and innovators') viewpoints to the fore. It's a nice argument on paper, but it doesn't hold much water in practice. What actually happens is that engineers lose out to marketing and finance people in divisional organizations. The divisions are interested only in short-term profit.

By definition, the functional monolith is almost always bureaucratic; it's not oriented to commitment and small-team action. Too many firms force creative people to work on five or six projects that span three or four divisions. But my experience on this one is crystal-clear. No one with one-seventh of the responsibility for anything ever felt committed to it. Peter Drucker's "monomaniacs with missions" were not monomaniacs with *seven different* missions.

Under some forms of management, divisional organizations that grow too big become hopelessly bureaucratic. On the other hand, "the division is the solution" (and the strategy) for Hewlett-Packard, 3M, Johnson & Johnson, Emerson Electric, and the like. Johnson & Johnson constantly creates new divisions. Its corporate watchword is simple: "Growing big by staying small."

These companies carefully monitor the size of their divisions. At HP, divisions are kept to less than a thousand people so that, in president and CEO John Young's words, "the general manager will know all his people by their first names." Bill Gore, chairman of W.L. Gore & Associates, comments, "As the number of people in an organization approaches 200, the group somehow becomes a crowd in which individuals grow increasingly anonymous and significantly less cooperative." The low numbers, whether 200 or 1,000, are all aimed at enhancing ownership and commitment.

Another vital part of the small-team, small-division mentality is the ability to manage, with rel-atively little muss and fuss, the bureaucratic conflicts that fatally delay much development. As an old hand at skunkworking once said, "Let's be clear about the magnitude of the effects that small teams have. The charged-up team that contains 10 to 50 people isn't in the '10 percent productivity improvement' game. Its results are often 300, 400, even 700 percent beyond those achieved by larger groups."

GET IT OUT THE DOOR

Some firms don't believe in meeting product-release dates. First the date is pushed back three months; then it gets shoved back another 45 days. All the while the bosses are thinking, "We've got to make sure that the software is totally compatible with all the rest of the product family." So the logic goes.

Compatibility is important, particularly in the case of systems-related high-technology products. But sometimes the last 2 percent that's needed for 100 percent compatibility takes 12 months to achieve. Meanwhile, 10 competitors have found a solution to the problem and gotten their products to the marketplace. In such extremely fast-paced markets as data handling, computers, and telecommunications, though, there are literally thousands of entrepreneurs who will fill in the spaces and do the last 2 percent of the work for you.

Digital Equipment's products overlap; users occasionally found that some of its products are incompatible with products that they're supposed to be compatible with. HP's engineers, marketers, and salesmen also lament the incompatibility of some of their products. But companies that wait, trying to achieve the last percentage point of compatibility, may well go belly-up.

The same principle holds true in many other markets, although they show a little less intensity. That's the reason Proctor & Gamble, 3M, Mars, and Johnson & Johnson are so insistent about spurring competition among their own divisions and brand managers. Bloomingdale's does the same thing with buying and floor-space assignments in its stores, and Macy's has done extremely well emulating Bloomingdale's. In most markets, new things are happening all the time. The lion's share is often virtually invisible—that is, you frequently don't see it until it's too late. To keep up with the competition, you have to keep getting new items into the market.

Errors of premature release can be (and frequently are) disastrous. Often a product hits the marketplace before the bugs have been worked out. Its technical superiority is blunted by poor reliability or insufficient support. This type of nightmare must be avoided at all costs. But getting that last possible feature, that last degree of complexity (read "overcomplexity"), that last percentage of compatibility, may cost you more of the market than you would have gained by making a perfect product. Unfortunately, the perfectionists tend to get their way because they always use the argument "It'll only take us another 30 days." But we all know that those 30-day projects always seem to take 120 days—if you're lucky.

CUSTOMERS GENERATE IDEAS

The evidence is overwhelming: the great majority of ideas for new products come from the users. Eric von Hippel, a professor at MIT's Sloan School of Management, has studied scientific-instrument equipment manufacturers, and his results are revealing. He reviewed 160 inventions and found that more than 70 percent of the product ideas originated with users. And these weren't just bells-and-whistles ideas, either. Sixty percent of the minor modifications came from users, as did 75 percent of the major modifications. But astonishingly, *100 percent* of the so-called "first of type" ideas for sophisticated devices like the transmission electron microscope were user-generated. According to von Hippel's studies, users that got their ideas across to the producers did a lot more than whisper into their ears. The users came up with the ideas, they prototyped them, they debugged them, and they had them working. Only then did they tap the produc-

ers for their experience in reliable production of multiple copies.

Lead users don't have to be Ph.D.'s or work in germ-free labs. One classic lead user was a housewife whose husband worked at the Corning Glass labs. One day he took home a new glass container that he was going to store acid in. She accidentally used it to heat some food in the oven, and it didn't break. Such is the origin of Pyrex cookware!

Stay in touch with users. It's important in every industry from fast food to computers. Hewlett-Packard has coined the term MBWA— "Management by Wandering Around." Wandering around should mean listening to the user in a direct, not an abstract or shorthand, way. A general manager who designed a major new computer describes a neat trick he pulled off: "I bought my uncle a computer store. I spent nights and weekends working there. My objective was to stay close to the ultimate user, to observe his frustrations and needs firsthand and incognito." What he learned was reflected in the eventual computer design in a thousand little ways and several big ones.

SERVICE AND QUALITY COUNT

"More scientists in bigger labs" seems to be the conventional watchword, along with "Better planning, better tools." The heck with skunkworks. But it's more than skunkworks. It's more than listening to users, too. Service and quality hold as much value as gee-whiz technology—or more.

Recently I talked with the president of a technology company about commodities. He was disturbed by some people's unfortunate tendency to call high-technology products (chips, instruments, personal computers) "commodities." The problem with this is that if you label a specific product a commodity, you'll start to behave as if it is one, neglecting service and quality. For instance, let's take a mundane product: toilet paper. If you go to your local grocery store and purchase a four-roll, 220-square-foot package of one-ply generic-brand toilet paper, the price will be around 79 cents. But if you go to a Seven-Eleven-type grocery, a package of Procter & Gamble's Charmin will cost you $1.99. The difference in distribution channels (Seven-Eleven) and the quality difference (P&G) is obviously enough to add $1.20 to a 79-cent product—or, more accurately, to add $1.20 to a product that cost about a quarter to produce.

Technology push is crucial, but it is not the principal reason that America is undergoing so many industry setbacks. User-unfriendliness, the inability to realize that the customer perceives a product in his own terms, is at least as big a weakness. If you don't believe me, ask 'em in Detroit.

PERFECTIONISTS FINISH LAST

If it weren't for people, 10,000-person research groups would be the most efficient. If it weren't for people, execution via 100,000-bubble PERT charts would be the most efficient. If it weren't for people, huge amounts of money invested in technical forecasting would allow companies to anticipate competition, customer-related problems and technological surprises. If it weren't for users, in-house development of every part that went into every invention would be the best way to assure quality.

Optimization. What's optimal? It's hard to believe, but the "suboptimal" system is often the most truly optimal. Go back to the big-versus-small debate. As a way to do the job, skunkworking is faster, cheaper, and higher-quality than the optimization route. Getting 90 percent compatibility and letting the marketplace do the rest turns out to be optimal, not suboptimal. Getting the last 10 percent may cost you 60 percent of the market.

Tom West of Data General didn't care a whit about building a machine that the "technology bigots" would like. He was interested in people who "wanted to get a machine out the door with their name on it." The stories about the U-2, the missile-development program broken down into seven parts, and the Post-it pads seem to be the same. Committed people, people competing against the market and other corporations and other divisions, those are the people who get the job done. Hail to the skunkworks!

32

The One-Firm Firm:

What Makes It Successful

DAVID H. MAISTER

What do investment bankers Goldman Sachs, management consultants McKinsey, accountants Arthur Andersen, compensation and benefits consultants Hewitt Associates, and lawyers Latham & Watkins have in common? Besides being among the most profitable firms (if not *the* most profitable) in their respective professions? Besides being considered by their peers among the best *managed* firms in their respective professions? The answer? They all share, to a greater or lesser extent, a common approach to management that I term the "one-firm firm" system.

In contrast to many of their competitors, one-firm firms have a remarkable degree of institutional loyalty and group effort that is clearly a critical ingredient in their success. The commonality of this organizational orientation and management approach among each of these firms suggest that there is indeed a "model" whose basic elements are transferable to other professions. The purpose of this article is to identify the elements of this model of professional firm success, and to explore how these elements interact to form a successful management system.

METHODOLOGY

The information on specific firms contained in this article has been gleaned from a variety of "public domain" sources, as well as selected interviews (on and off the record) at a number of professional service firms, including but not restricted to those named herein. However, none of the information presented here represents "official" statements by the firms involved. As with most professional service organizations, the firms discussed here are private partnerships with no requirement, and with little incentive, to expose their inner workings. Consequently, public information on the management practices (and economic results) of such firms is difficult to obtain.

This situation is regrettable because the professional service firm represents the confluence of two major trends in the U.S. (and worldwide) economy: the growing importance of the service sector, and the increasing numbers of "knowledge workers." As a result, any lessons that can be learned about successful management of such enterprises could potentially be of importance not only to the professions but also to other service entities and organizations grappling with the problems of managing large numbers of highly educated employees.

In an attempt to discover the principles of "good management" of professional service firms, I have worked very closely with a broad array of service firms in a variety of capacities. My research has been driven by two propositions: first, that professional service firms are sufficiently different from industrial corporations to warrant special study; and second, that the management issues faced by professional service firms are remarkably similar, regardless of the specific profession under

Reprinted from "The One-Firm: What Makes it Successful" by David Maister, *Sloan Management Review,* Fall 1985, pp. 3–14 by permission of the publisher. Copyright © 1985 by the Sloan Management Review Association. All rights reserved.

David Maister is President of Maister Associates, a Boston-based consulting firm specializing in the management of professional service organizations.

consideration. I have chosen in this article to concentrate on the second proposition.

WHAT IS MEANT BY "WELL MANAGED?"

The firms chosen for discussion were identified in the following way. In the course of my research and consulting work, I have made it my practice to ask repeatedly the question, "Which do you consider the best managed firm in your profession?" The question is, of course, ambiguous. In any business context, "well managed" can be taken to refer, alternatively, to profitability, member satisfaction, size, growth, innovativeness, quality of products or services, or any of a number of other criteria. The difficulty in identifying "successful" firms is particularly acute in the professions because many of the conventional indicators of business success do not necessarily apply. For example, since there are few economies of scale in the professions,[1] neither size nor rate of growth can be taken as unequivocal measures of success: many firms have chosen to limit both. Even if "per-partner" profit figures were available (which they are not), they would also be unreliable measures, since many professional firms are prepared to sacrifice a degree of profit maximization in the name of other goals such as professional satisfaction and/or quality of worklife. Finally, since "quality" of either service or work product is notoriously difficult to assess in professional work,[2] few reliable indicators of this aspect of success are obtainable.

In spite of these difficulties, it has been remarkable how frequently the same names appear on the list of "well-managed" firms in the professions, as judged by their peers and competitors. The firms discussed here were on virtually everyone's list of admired firms, often together with the comment, "I wish we could do what they do." It should be noted that other firms, not discussed here, were also mentioned frequently. However, as expressed earlier, what makes Arthur Andersen, Goldman Sachs, Hewitt Associates, and Latham & Watkins worthy of some special attention is not only that they are successful and well respected, but that, in spite of being in different professions, they appear to share a common approach to management (the one-firm firm system) that is readily distinguishable from many of their competitors. This approach is clearly now the only way to run a professional service firm, but it is certainly *a* way that is worthy of special study.

THE "ONE-FIRM FIRM" SYSTEM

Loyalty

The characteristics of the one-firm firm system are institutional loyalty and group effort. In contrast to many of their (often successful) competitors who emphasize individual entrepreneurialism, autonomous profit centers, internal competition and/or highly decentralized, independent activities, one-firm firms place great emphasis on firmwide coordination of decision making, group identity, cooperative teamwork, and institutional commitment.

Hewitt Associates (described along with Goldman Sachs in a recent popular book as one of "The 100 Best Companies in America to Work For")[3] says that, in its recruiting, it looks for "SWANs": people who are Smart, Work hard, and Ambitious, and Nice. While emphasis on the first three attributes is common in all professional service firms, it is the emphasis on the last one that differentiates the one-firm firm from all the others. "If an individual has ego needs that are too high," notes Peter Friedes, Hewitt's managing partner, "they can be a very disruptive influence. Our work depends on internal cooperation and teamwork."

The same theme is sounded by Geoffrey Boisi, the partner in charge of mergers and acquisitions at Goldman Sachs: "You learn from day one around here that we gang-tackle problems. If your ego won't permit that, you won't be effective here."[4] By general route, Goldman has achieved its eminance with a minimum of the infighting that afflicts most Wall Street firms. In contrast to many (if not most) of its competitors on the street, Goldman frowns upon anything resembling a star system.

Downplaying Stardom

The same studied avoidance of the star mentality is evidenced at Latham & Watkins. As Clinton Stevenson, the firm's managing partner, points out: "We want to encourage clients to retain the firm of Latham and Watkins, not Clint Stevenson."[5] Partner Jack Walker reinforces this point: "I don't mean to sound sentimental, but there's a bonding here. People care about the work of the firm."[6] The team philosophy at McKinsey, one senior partner explained to me, is illustrated by its approach to project work: "As a young individual consultant, you learn that your job is to hold your own: you can rest assured that the team will win. All you've got to do is do your part."

Above all else, the leaders and, more important, all the other members of these firms view themselves as belonging to an *institution* that has an identity and existence of its own, above and beyond the individuals who happen currently to belong to it. The one-firm firm, relative to its competitors, places great emphasis on its institutional history, broadly held values, and a reputation that all actively work to preserve. Loyalty to, and pride in, the firm and its accomplishments approaches religious fervor at such firms.

Teamwork and Conformity

The emphasis on teamwork and "fitting in" creates an identity not only for the firm but also for the individual members of the firm. This identity, for better or worse, is readily identifiable to the outside world. Reference by others in the profession to members of one-firm firms are not always flattering. Members of other Big-8 firms, particularly those where individualism and individual contributions are highly valued, often make reference to "Arthur Androids." The term "A McKinsey-type" has substantive meaning in the consulting profession—sometimes even down to the style of dress. In the 1950s, I am told by a McKinsey-ite, a set of hats in the closet of a corporation's reception room was an unmistakable sign that the McKinsey consultants were in. The hats have disappeared, but the mentality has not. Goldman Sachs professionals are referred to by other investment bankers as the "IBM clones of Wall Street."

Long Hours and Hard Work

For all the emphasis on teamwork and interpersonal skills, one-firm firm members are no slouches. All of the firms discussed here have reputations for long hours and hard work, even above the norms for the all-absorbing professions in which they compete. Indeed, the way an individual illustrates his or her high involvement and commitment to the firm is through hard work and long hours. Latham & Watkins lawyers are reputed to bill an *average* of 2,200 hours apiece, with some heroic performers reaching the heights of 2,700 hours in some years: this contrasts with a professionwide average of approximately 1,750. At Goldman Sachs, sixteen-hour days are common. It has been said: "If you like the money game, here's [Goldman's] a good team to play on. If you like other games, you may not have time for them."[7] James Scott, a Columbia Business School professor, has commented: "At Goldman, the spirit is pervasive. They all work hard, have the same willingness to work all night to get the job done well, and yet remain in pretty good humor about it."[8] Similarly, McKinsey, Hewitt, and Arthur Andersen are all hard-working environments, above the norms for their respective professions.

Sense of Mission

In large part, the institutional commitment at one-firm firms is generated not only through a loyalty to the firm but also by the development of a sense of "mission," which is most frequently seen as client service. *All* professional service firms list in their mission statement what I call the "3 S's": the goals of (client) Service, (financial) Success, and (professional) Satisfaction. What is recognizable about one-firm firms is that, in their internal communications, there is a clear priority among these.

Within McKinsey, a new consultant learns within a very short period of time that the firm believes that the *client comes first*, the firm second, and the individual last. Goldman Sachs has a reputation for being "ready to sacrifice anything—including its relations with other Wall Street firms—to further the client's interests."[9] At Hewitt Associates, firm ideology is that the 3 S's must be carefully kept in balance at all times; however, client service is clearly number one. None of this is meant to suggest that one-firm firms necessarily render superior service to their clients compared with their competitors; nor that they always resolve inevitable day-to-day conflicts among the 3 S's in the same way. The point is that there *is* a firm ideology which everyone understands and which no one is allowed to take lightly.

Client Service

The emphasis at one-firm firms is clearly one of significant attention to managing client relations. In these firms, client service is defined more broadly than technical excellence: it is taken to mean a more far-ranging attentiveness to client needs and the quality of interaction between the firm and its clients. Goldman Sachs pioneered the concept on Wall Street of forming a marketing and new business development group whose primary responsibility is to manage the interface between the client and the various other parts of the firm that provide the technical and professional services. In most other Wall Street firms, client relations are the responsibility of the individual professionals who do the work, resulting in numerous (and potentially conflicting) contacts between a single client and the various other parts of the firm. Hewitt Associates, alone in its profession, has also pioneered such an "account management" group.[10] At McKinsey, in the words of one partner, "Here everyone realizes that the (client) *relationship* is paramount, not the specific project we happen to be working on at the moment."

The high-commitment, hard-working, mission-oriented, team-intensive characteristics of one-firm firms are reminiscent of another type of organization: the Marine Corps. Indeed, one-firm firms have an elite, Marine Corps attitude about themselves. An atmosphere of a special, private club prevails, where members feel that "we do things differently around here, and most of us couldn't consider working anywhere else." While all professional firms will assert that they have the best *professionals* in town, one-firm firms claim they have the best *firm* in town, a subtle but important difference.[11]

SUSTAINING THE ONE-FIRM FIRM CULTURE

Up to this point, we discussed a type of firm culture, a topic much discussed in recent management literature.[12] Our task now is to try and identify the management practices that have created and sustained this culture. Not surprisingly, since human assets constitute the vast majority of the productive resources of the professional service firm, most of these management practices involve human resource management.

A good overview of the mechanisms by which an "elite group" culture, with emphasis on the *group*, can be created is provided by Dr. Chip Bell,[13] a training consultant, who suggests that the elements of any high performance unit include the following:

- Entrance requirements into the group are extremely difficult.
- Acceptance into the group is followed by *intensive* job-related training, followed by team training.
- Challenging and high-risk team assignments are given early in the individual's career.
- Individuals are constantly tested to ensure that they measure up to the elite standards of the unit.
- Individuals and groups are given the autonomy to take risks normally not permissible at other firms.
- Training is viewed as continuous and related to assignments.
- Individual rewards are tied directly to collective results.

- Managers are seen as experts, pacesetters, and mentors (rather than as administrators).

As we shall see, all of these practices can be seen at work in the one-firm firms.

Recruiting

In contrast to many competing firms, one-firm firms invest a significant amount of *senior* professional time in their recruitment process, and they tend to be much more selective than their competition. At one-firm firms, recruiting is either heavily centralized or well coordinated centrally. At Hewitt Associates, over 1,000 students at sixty-five schools were interviewed in 1980. Of the seventy-two offers that were made, fifty accepted. Each of the 198 invited to the firm's offices spent a half-day with a psychologist (at a cost to the firm of $600 per person) for career counseling to find out if the person was suited for Hewitt's work and would fit within the firm's culture. At Goldman Sachs, 1,000 MBAs are interviewed each year; approximately thirty are chosen. Interviewing likely candidates is a major responsibility of the firm's seventy-three partners (the firm has over 1,600 professionals). Goldman partner James Gorter notes, "Recruiting responsibilities almost come before your business responsibilities."[14] At Latham & Watkins, all candidates get twenty-five to thirty interviews, compared to a norm in the legal profession of approximately five to ten interviews. As a McKinsey partner noted:

> In our business, the game is won or lost at the recruiting stage: we take it very seriously. And it's not a quantity game, it's a quality game. You've got to find the best people you can, and the trick is to understand what *best* means. It's not just brains, not just presentability: you have to try and detect the potentially fully developed professional in the person, and not just look at what they are *now*. Some firms hire in a superficial way, relying on the up-or-out system to screen out the losers. We do have an up-or-out system, but we don't use it as a substitute for good recruiting practices. To us, the costs of recruiting-mistake turnover are too high, in dollars, in morale, and in client service, to ignore.

Training

One-firm firms are notable for their investment in firmwide training, which serves both as a way to add to the substantive skills of juniors and as an important group socialization function.[15] The best examples of this practice are Arthur Andersen and McKinsey. The former is renowned among accounting students for its training center in St. Charles, Illinois (a fully equipped college campus that the firm acquired and converted to its own uses), to which young professionals are sent from around the world. In the words of one Andersen partner: "To this day, I have useful friendships, forged at St. Charles, with people across the firm in different offices and disciplines. If I need to get something done outside my own expertise, I have people I can call on who will do me a favor, even if it comes out of their own hide. They know I'll return it."

Similarly, McKinsey's two-week training program for new professionals is renowned among business school students. The program is run by one or more of the firm's senior professionals, who spend a significant amount of time inculcating the firm's values by telling Marvin Bower stories—Bower, who ran the firm for many years, is largely credited with making McKinsey what it is today. The training program is not always held in the U.S. but rotates between the countries where McKinsey has offices. This not only reinforces the one-firm image (as opposed to a headquarters with branch offices) but also has a dramatic effect on the young professionals' view of the firm. As one of my ex-students told me: "Being sent to Europe for a two-week training program during your first few months with the firm impresses the hell out of you. It makes you think: 'This is a class outfit.' It also both frightens you and gives you confidence. You say, 'Boy, they must think I'm good if they're prepared to spend all this money on me.' But then you worry about whether you can live up to it: it's very motivating." All young professionals are given a copy of Marvin Bower's history of the firm, *Perspectives on McKinsey*, which, unlike many professional firm histories, is as full of philosophy and advice as it is dry on historical facts.

"Growing Their Own" Professionals

Unlike many of their competitors, all of the one-firm firms tend to "grow their own" professionals, rather than to make significant use of lateral hiring of senior professionals. In other words, in the acquisition of human capital, they tend to "make" rather than "buy." This is not to say that no lateral hires are made—just that they are done infrequently, and with extreme caution. "I had to meet with the associates (i.e., not only the partners) before the firm [Latham & Watkins] took me on," Carla Hills [former Secretary of Housing and Urban Development] recalls. "Lateral entry is a big trauma for this place. But that's how it should be."[16]

Avoiding Mergers

A related practice of one-firm firms is the deliberate avoidance of growth by merger. Arthur Andersen, unlike most of the Big-8 firms, did not join in the merger and acquisition boom of the 1950s and early 1960s, in an attempt to become part of a nationwide accounting profession network. Instead, it grew its own regional (and international) offices. Similarly, the decade-long merger mania in investment banking has left Goldman Sachs, which opted out of this trend, as one of the few independent partnerships on the street. In contrast to many other consulting firms, McKinsey's overseas offices were all launched on a grow-your-own basis, initially staffed with U.S. personnel, rather than on an acquisition basis. With one recent exception, all of Latham & Watkins's branch offices were all grown internally.

It is clear that this avoidance of growth through laterals or mergers plays a critical role in both creating and preserving the sense of institutional identity, which is the cornerstone of the one-firm system.

Controlled Growth

As a high proportion of the professional staff shares an extensive, common work history with the one-firm firm, group loyalty is easier to foster. Of course, this staffing strategy has implications for the *rate* of growth pursued by the one-firm firm.

At such firms (in contrast to many competitors), high growth is not a declared goal. Rather, such firms aim for *controlled* growth. The approach is one of, "We'll grow as fast as we can train our people." As Ron Daniel of McKinsey phrases it: "We neither shun growth nor idolize it. We view it as a by-product of achieving our other goals." All of the one-firm firms assert that the major constraint on their growth is not client demand, but the supply of qualified people they can find and train to their way of practicing.

Selective Business Pursuits

Related to this issue is the fact that one-firm firms tend to be more selective than their competitors in the type of business they pursue. It has been reported that an essential element of the Goldman culture is its calculated choosiness about the clients it takes on. The firm has let it be known, both internally and externally, that it "adheres to certain standards—and that it won't compromise them for the sake of a quick buck."[17] At McKinsey, the firm's long-standing strategy is that it will only work for "the top guy" (i.e., the chief executive officer) and, as illustrated internally with countless Marvin Bower stories, will only do those projects where the potential value delivered is demonstrably far in excess of the firm's charges. Junior staff at McKinsey quickly hears stories of projects the firm has turned down because the partner did not believe the firm could add sufficient value to cover its fees. Similarly, while Andersen has been an aggressive marketer (a property common to all the one-firm firms), Andersen appears to have taken a more studied, less "opportunistic" approach to business development than have their competitors.

Consequently, one-firm firms tend to have a less varied practice-mix and a more homogeneous client base than do their more explicitly individualistic competitors. Unlike, say, Booz, Allen, McKinsey's practice is relatively focused on three main areas: organization work, strategy consulting, and operations studies. In the late 1970s, the heyday of "strategy boutiques," many outsiders commented on the firm's reluctance to chase after fast-growing new specialties.[18] But McKinsey, like all of the other one-firm firms, enters new areas "big, or not at all." Andersen's strategy in its consulting work (the fastest growing area for all of the Big-8) has been more clearly focused on computer-based systems design and installation than has the variegated practices of most of its competitors. Goldman has been notably selective in which segments of the investment market it has entered, and has become a dominant player in virtually every sector it has entered.

Outplacement

One of the fortunate consequences of the controlled growth strategy at one-firm firms and the avoidance of laterals and mergers is that these firms, in contrast to many competitors, rarely lose valued people to competitors. At each of the firms named above, I have heard the claim that, "Many of our people have been approached by competitors offering more money to help them launch or bolster a part of the practice. But our people prefer to stay." On Wall Street, raiding of competing firms' top professionals has reached epidemic proportions; yet, this does not include Goldman Sachs. It is said that one of the rarest beasts on Wall Street is an *ex*-Goldman professional: very few leave the firm.

Turnover at one-firm firms is clearly more carefully managed than it is among competitors. Those one-firm firms that do enforce an up-or-out system (McKinsey and Andersen) work actively to place their alumni/ae in good positions preferably with favored clients. McKinsey's regular alumni/ae reunions, a vivid demonstration of its success in breeding loyalty to the firm, are held two or three times a year. In part, due to the "caring" approach taken to junior staff, one-firm firms are able to achieve a very profitable high-leverage strategy (i.e., high ratio of junior to senior staff) without *excessive* pressures for growth to provide promotion opportunities.[19]

Compensation

Internal management procedures at one-firm firms constantly reinforce the team concept. Most important, compensation systems (particularly for partners) are designed to encourage intra-firm coopera-

tion. Whereas many other firms make heavy use of departmental or local-office profitability in setting compensation (i.e., take a *measurement*-oriented, profit-center approach), one-firm firms tend to set compensation (both for partners *and* juniors) through a *judgmental* process, assessing total contribution to the firm. Unique among the Big-8, Andersen has a single worldwide partnership cost-sharing pool (as opposed to separate country profit centers): individual partners share in the joint economics of the whole firm, not just their country (or local office). "The virtue of the 'one-pool' system, as opposed to heavy profit-centering, is that a superior individual in an otherwise poor-profit office can be rewarded appropriately," one Andersen partner pointed out. "Similarly, a weaker individual in a successful office does not get a windfall gain. Further, if you tie individual partner compensation too tightly to departmental or office profitability, it's hard to take into account the particular circumstances of that office. A guy that shows medium profitability in a tough market probably deserves more than one with higher profitability in an easy market where we already have a high market share."

Hewitt Associates sets its partner compensation levels only after all partners have been invited to comment on the contributions (qualitative *and* quantitative) made by other partners on "their" projects and other firmwide affairs. Vigorous efforts are made to assess contributions to the firm that do not show up in the measurable factors. Peter Friedes notes:

> We think that having no profit centers is a great advantage to us. Other organizations don't realize how much time they waste fighting over allocations of overhead, transfer charges, and other mechanisms caused by a profit-center mentality. Whenever there are profit centers, cooperation between groups suffers badly. Of course, we pay a price for not having them: specific accountability is hard to pin down. We often don't know precisely whose time we are writing off, or who precisely brought in that new account. But at least we don't fight over it: we get on with our work. Our people know that, over time, good performance will be recognized and rewarded.

Goldman Sachs also runs a judgment-based (rather than measurement-based) compensation system, including "a month-long evaluation process in which performance is reviewed not only by a person's superiors but by other partners as well, and finally by the management committee. During that review, 'how well you do when other parts of the firm ask for your help on some project' plays a big part."[20] At Latham & Watkins, "15 percent of the firm's income is set aside as a separate fund from which the executive committee, at its sole discretion, awards partners additional compensation based on their general contribution to the firm in terms of such factors as client relations, hours billed, and even the business office's 'scoring' of how promptly the partner has logged his or her own time, sent out and collected bills, and otherwise helped the place run well."[21]

Investments in Research and Development

In most professional service firms, particularly in those with a heavy emphasis on short-term results or year-by-year performance evaluations, any activity that takes an individual away from direct revenue-producing work is considered a detour off the professional success track within the firm and is therefore avoided. This is not the case with one-firm firms.

As the one-firm culture is based on a "team-player" judgment-system approach to evaluations and compensation (at both the partner and junior level), it is *relatively* easier (although it is never easy) for one-firm firms to get their best professionals to engage in nonbillable, stafflike activities such as research and development (R&D), market research, and other investments in the firm's future. For example, McKinsey is noted in the consulting profession for its internally funded R&D projects, of which the most famous example is the work that resulted in the best seller, *In Search of Excellence*. This book, however, was only one of a large number of staff projects continually under way in the firm. An ex-student of mine noted that "at McKinsey, to be selected to do something for the firm is an honor: it's a quick way to get famous in the firm if you succeed. And, of course, you're expected to succeed. Firm projects are treated as seriously as client work, and your performance is closely examined. However, my friends at other firms tell me that firm projects are a high-risk thing to do: they worry about whether their low chargeable hours will be held against them later on."

Andersen likewise invests heavily in firmwide activities. For instance, it conducts extensive cross-office and cross-functional industry programs, which attempt to coordinate all of the firm's activities with respect to specific industries. In fact, it is rumored, although no one has the statistics, that Andersen invests a higher proportion of its gross revenues in firmwide investment activities than does any other firm.

Goldman's commitment to investing in its own future is illustrated by the firm's policy of forcing partners to keep their capital in the firm rather than to take extraordinarily high incomes. Hewitt's commitment to R&D is built into its organizational structure. Rather than scatter its professional experts throughout its multiple office system (staffed predominantly with account managers), it chose to concentrate its professional groups in three locations in order to promote the rapid cross-fertilization of professional ideas. Significant investments of professional time are made in nonbillable research work under the guidance of professional group managers who establish budgets for such work in negotiation with the managing partner.

Communication

Communication at a one-firm firm is remarkably open and is clearly used as a bonding technique to hold the firm together. All the firms described above make *heavy* use of memorandums to keep everyone informed of what is happening in other parts of the firm, above and beyond the token efforts frequently made at other firms. Frequent firmwide meetings are held, with an emphasis on cross-boundary (i.e., interoffice and interdepartmental) gatherings. Such meetings are valued (and clearly designed) as much as for the social interaction as for whatever the agenda happens to be: people *go* to the meetings. (At numerous other firms I have observed, meetings are seen as distractions from the firm's, or the individual's, business, and people bow out whenever they can.)

At most one-firm firms, open communication extends to financial matters as well. At Hewitt, they believe that "anyone has a right to know anything about the firm except the personal affairs of another individual." At an annual meeting with all junior personnel (including secretaries and other support staff), the managing partner discloses the firm's economic results and answers any and all questions from the audience. At Latham & Watkins, junior associates are significantly involved in all major firm committees, including recruiting, choosing new partners, awarding associate bonuses, and so on. All significant matters about the firm are well known to the associates.

Absence of Status Symbols

Working hard to involve nonpartners in firm affairs and winning their commitment to the firm's success is a hallmark of the one-firm firm and is reinforced by a widely common practice of sharing firm profits more deeply within the organization than is common at other firms. (The ratio between the highest paid and lowest paid partner tends to be markedly less at one-firm firms than it is among their competitors.) There is also a suppression of status differentials between senior and junior members of the firm: an important activity if the firm is attempting to make everyone, junior and senior alike, feel a part of the team. At Hewitt Associates, deemphasizing status extends to the physical surroundings: everyone, from the newest hire to the oldest partner, has the same size office.

The absence of status conflicts in one-firm firms is also noticeable across departments. In today's world of professional megafirms composed of departments specializing in vastly different areas, one of the most significant dangers is that professionals in one area may come to view *their* area as somehow more elite, more exciting, more profitable, or more important to the firm than another area. Their loyalty is to their department, or their local office, and not to the firm. Yet the success of the firm clearly depends upon doing well in all ar-

eas. On Wall Street, different psychological profiles of, and an antipathy between, say, traders and investment bankers is notorious: many attribute the recent turmoil at Lehman Brothers (now Shearson Lehman) to this syndrome. In some law firms, corporate lawyers and litigators are often considered distinct breeds of people who view the world in different ways. In some accounting firms, mutual suspicion among audit, tax, and consulting partners is rampant. In consulting firms, frequently there are status conflicts between the "front-room" client handlers and the "back-room" technical experts.

What strikes any visitor to a one-firm firm is the deeply held mutual respect across departmental, geographic, and functional boundaries. Members of one-firm firms clearly *like* (and respect) their counterparts in other areas, which makes for the successful cross-boundary coordination that is increasingly essential in today's marketplace. Jonathan Cohen of Goldman Sachs notes that out-of-office socialization among Goldman professionals appears to take place more frequently than it does at other Wall Street firms. Retired Marvin Bower of McKinsey asserts that one of the elements in creating the one-firm culture is mutual trust, both horizontally and vertically. This atmosphere is created primarily by the behavior of the firm's leadership, who must set the style for the firm. Unlike many other firms, leaders of one-firm firms work hard not to be identified with or labeled as being closer to one group than another. Cross-boundary respect is also achieved at most one-firm firms by the common practice of rotating senior professionals among the various offices and departments of the firm.

Governance: Consensus-building Style

How are one-firm firms governed? Are they democracies or autocracies? Without exception, one-firm firms are led (*not* managed) in a consensus-building style.[22] All have (or have had) strong leaders who engage in extensive consultation before major decisions are taken. It is important to note that all of these firms do indeed have leaders: they are not anarchic democracies, nor are they dictatorships. Whether one is reading about Goldman's two Johns (Weinberg and Whitehead), McKinsey's (retired) Marvin Bower and Ron Daniels, Latham & Watkins's Clinton Stevenson, or Hewitt's Peter Friedes, it is clear that one is learning about expert communicators who see their role as preserver of the "true religion." Above all else, they are cheerleaders who suppress their own egos in the name of the institution they head. Such firms also have continuity in leadership: while many of them have electoral systems of governance, leaders tend to stay in place for long periods of time. What is more, the firm's culture outlasts the tenure of any given individual.

Of course, the success of the consensus-building approach to firm governance and the continuity of leadership at one-firm firms is not fortuitous. Since their whole philosophy (and, as I have tried to show, their substantive managerial practices) is built upon cooperative teamwork, consensus is more readily achieved here than it is at other firms. The willingness to allow leaders the freedom to make decisions on behalf of the firm (the absence of which has stymied many other "democratic" firms) was "prewired" into the system long ago, since everyone shares the same values. The one-firm system *is* a system.

CONCLUSION: POTENTIAL WEAKNESSES

Clearly, the one-firm firm system is powerful. What are its weaknesses? The dangers of this approach are reasonably obvious. Above all else, there is the danger of self-congratulatory complacency: a firm that has an integrated system that *works* may, if it is not careful, become insensitive to shifts in its environment that demand changes in the system. The very commitment to "our firm's way of doing things," which is the one-firm firm's strengths, can also be its greatest weakness. This is particularly true because of the chance of "inbreeding" that comes from "growing-your-own" professionals. To deal with this, there is a final ingredient required in the formula: self-criticism. At McKinsey, Andersen, Goldman, and Hewitt, partners have asserted to me that "we have no harsher

critics than ourselves: we're constantly looking for ways to improve what we do." However, it must be acknowledged that, without the diversity common at other professional service firms, one-firm firms with strong cultures run the danger of making even self-criticism a proforma exercise.

Another potential weakness of the one-firm firm culture is that it runs the danger of being insufficiently entrepreneurial, at least in the short run. Other more individualistic firms, which promote and reward opportunistic behavior by individuals and separate profit centers, may be better at reorganizing and capitalizing on emerging trends early in their development. Although contrary examples can be cited, one-firm firms are rarely "pioneers": they try to be (and usually are) good at entering emerging markets as a late second or third. And because of the firmwide concentrated attack they are able to effect, they are frequently successful at this. (The similarity to IBM in this regard, as is much of what has been discussed above, is readily noticeable.)

The one-firm approach is *not* the only way to run a professional service firm. However, it clearly is a very successful way to run a firm. The "team spirit" of the firms described here is broadly admired by their competitors and is not easily copied. As I have attempted to show, the one-firm firm system is *internally* consistent: all of its practices, from recruiting through compensation, performance appraisal, approaches to market, governance, control systems, and above all, culture and human resource strategy, make for a consistent whole.

REFERENCES

1. D. H. Maister, "Profitability: Beating the Downward Trend," *Journal of Management Consulting,* Fall 1984, pp. 39–44.
2. D. H. Maister, "Quality Work Doesn't Mean Quality Service," *American Lawyer,* April 1984.
3. R. Levering, M. Moskowitz, and M. Katz, *The 100 Best Companies to Work for in America* (Reading, MA: Addison-Wesley, 1984).
4. B. McGoldrick, "Inside the Goldman Sachs Culture," *Institutional Investor,* January 1984.
5. S. Brill, "Is Latham & Watkins America's Best Run Firm?" *American Lawyer,* August 1981, pp. 12–14.

6. Ibid.
7. Levering et al. (1984).
8. McGoldrick (January 1984).
9. Ibid.
10. D. H. Maister, *Hewitt Associates* (Boston, MA: Harvard University, Graduate School of Business, HBS Case Services).
11. D. H. Maister, "What Kind of Excellence?" *American Lawyer,* January–February 1985, p. 4–6.
12. See, for example, V. J. Sathe, *Culture and Related Corporate Realities* (Homewood, IL: Richard D. Irwin, Inc., 1985).
13. C. Bell, "How to Create a High Performance Training Unit," *Training*, October 1980, pp. 49–52.
14. McGoldrick (January 1984).
15. D. H. Maister, "How to Build Human Capital," *American Lawyer,* June 1984.
16. Brill (August 1981).
17. McGoldrick (January 1984).
18. See, for example, "The New Shape of Management Consulting," *Business Week*, 21 May 1979.
19. For a discussion of the role of turnover on professional service firm success, see D. H. Maister, "Balancing the Professional Service Firm," *Sloan Management Review,* Fall 1982, pp. 15–29.
20. McGoldrick (January 1984).
21. Brill (August 1981).
22. For a discussion of governance in professional firms, see D. H. Maister, "Partnership Politics," *American Lawyer,* October 1984.

33

3M's Post-it Notes: A Managed or Accidental Innovation?

P. RANGANATH NAYAK AND JOHN KETTERINGHAM

In late 1978, the bleak reports from the four-city market tests came back to the 3M Corporation. The analyses were showing that this "Post-it Note Pads" idea was a real stinker. Such news came as no surprise to a large number of 3M's most astute observers of new product ideas, for this one had smelled funny to them right from the beginning! From its earliest days, Post-it brand adhesive had to be one of the most neglected product notions in 3M history. The company had ignored it before it was a notepad, when the product-to-be was just an adhesive that didn't adhere very well. The first product to reach the marketplace was a sticky bulletin board whose sales were less than exciting to a company like 3M.

But why was this adhesive still around? For five years, beginning before 1970, this odd material kept coming around, always rattling in the pocket of Spencer Silver, the chemist who had mixed it up in the first place. Even after the adhesive had evolved into a stickum-covered bulletin board, and then into notepad glue, there was manufacturing saying that it couldn't mass-produce the pads and marketing claiming that such scratch pads would never sell. So by 1978, when the reports came in from the test markets, it seemed everyone who'd said disparaging things about the Post-it Note Pad was right after all. 3M was finally going to do the merciful thing and bury the remains. At that critical moment, it was only one last try by two highly placed executives, Geoffrey Nicholson and Joseph Ramey, that kept "those little yellow sticky pads" from going the way of the dinosaur.

To understand Silver's persistence with his innovative commercial challenge, it is necessary to go back to his moment of discovery. Silver's role in the development of Post-it Note Pads began in 1964 with a "Polymers for Adhesives' program in 3M's Central Research Laboratories. The company has always had a tradition of periodically reexamining its own products to look for ways to improve them. "Every so many years," said Silver, "3M would put together a bunch of people who looked like they might be productive in developing new types of adhesives." In the course of that "Polymers for Adhesives" research program, which went on for four years, Silver found out about a new family of monomers developed by Archer-Daniels Midland, Inc., which he thought contained potential as ingredients for polymer-based adhesives. He received a number of samples from ADM and began to work with them. This was an open-ended research effort, and Silver's acquisition of the new monomers was the sort of exploration the company encouraged. "As long as you were producing new things, everybody was happy," said Silver. "Of course, they had to be new molecules, patentable molecules. In the course of this exploration, I tried an experiment with one of the monomers to see what would happen if I put a lot of it into the reaction mixture. Before, we had used amounts that would correspond to conventional wisdom." Silver had no expectation whatsoever of what might occur if he did this. He just thought it might be interesting to find out.

In polymerization catalysis, scientists usually

This article is a modified, shortened version of a chapter from P. R. Nayak and J. M. Ketteringham's book *Breakthroughs,* an Arthur D. Little international study of 16 major innovations (Rawson Press, 1986). Published with permission of ADL with additions and modifications made by Professor Ralph Katz, based on his 1996 interviews with Art Fry of 3M.

P. R. Nayak and John Ketteringham are Management Consultants at Authur D. Little. Ralph Katz is Professor of Management at Northeastern University and Research Associate at MIT.

control the amounts of interacting ingredients to very tightly defined proportions, in accordance with prevailing theory and experience. Silver said with a certain measure of glee, "The key to the Post-it adhesive was doing the experiment. If I had sat down and factored it out beforehand, and thought about it, I wouldn't have done the experiment. If I had limited my thinking only to what the literature said, I would have stopped. The literature was full of examples that said you can't do this." Highly regarded publications and experts would have told Silver there was no point in doing what he did. But Silver understood that science is one part meticulous calculation and one part fooling around. "People like myself," said Silver, "get excited about looking for new properties in materials. I find that very satisfying, to perturb the structure slightly and just see what happens. I have a hard time talking people into doing that—people who are more highly trained. It's been my experience that people are reluctant just to try, to experiment—just to see what will happen!"

When Silver went ahead with the "wrong" proportions of the ADM monomers, just to see what would happen, he got a reaction that departed from the predictions of theory. It was what some call an "accident" and what Silver called a "Eureka moment." What Silver experienced was the appearance of what would become the Post-it adhesive polymer. It was the moment for which all scientists become scientists—the emergence of a unique, unexpected, previously unobserved and reliable scientific phenomenon. Each time Silver put those things together, they fell into the same pattern—every time. "It's one of those things you look at and you say, this has got to be useful! You're not forcing materials into a situation to make them work. It wanted to do this. It wanted to make Post-it adhesive," Silver said.

Technically the material was what the research program called for, a new polymer with adhesive properties. But in examining it, Silver noticed among its other curious properties that this material was not "aggressively" adhesive. It would create what scientists call "tack" between two surfaces, but it would not bond tightly to them. Also, and this was a problem not solved for years, this material was more "cohesive" than it was "adhesive." It clung to its own molecules better than it clung to any other molecules. So if you sprayed it on a surface (it was sprayable, another property that attracted Silver) and then slapped a piece of paper on the sprayed surface, you could remove all or none of the adhesive when you lifted the paper. It might "prefer" one surface to another, but not stick well to either. Someone would have to invent a new coating for paper if 3M were to use this as an adhesive for pieces of paper. But paper? Not very likely, thought Silver, and on this point, at least, everyone agreed with him.

What Silver had done was more than the usual 3M lab synthesis; it was a discovery—the sort of thing a scientist can put his or her name on. When he watched the reaction, Silver was achieving fatherhood, and he was falling in love. He knew he might never again be responsible for so pure and simple a phenomenon. Almost instantly, he personified this viscous goo, calling the stuff "my baby." It may not have been very sticky, but Spencer Silver got very attached to it. As he started to present this discovery to other 3Mers, however, he soon realized that few people shared his views about the beauty of this glue. Interested in practical applications, they had only a passing appreciation for the science embodied in Silver's adhesive. More significantly, they were "trapped by the metaphor" that insists that the ultimate adhesive is one that forms an unbreakable bond! The whole world in which they lived was looking for a better glue, not a worse glue. And like any other sensible adhesives manufacturer, 3M's sights had never wavered from a progressive course of developing stronger and stronger adhesives. Suddenly, here was Spencer Silver, touting the opposite of what was considered normal product virtue.

Although he couldn't say exactly what it was good for, "it had to be good for something," he would tell them. Aren't there times, Silver would ask people, when you want a glue to hold something for a while but not forever? Let's think about those situations. Let's see if we can turn this adhesive into a product that will hold tight as long as people need it to hold but then let go when people want it to let go. From 1968 through 1973, company support systematically slipped away from him. First, the Polymers for Adhesives Program disappeared. 3M had given its researchers a specified time and a limited budget to conduct that program. When the time and money were used up, the researchers were reassigned even though some, like Silver, were just starting to have fun.

"The adhesives program died a natural death," Silver recalled. "The company's business went off, and, in the usual cycle of things, the longer-range research programs were cut. So the emphasis was diminished and we still had invented some interesting materials that we wanted to push." The members of the Polymers for Adhesives group were assigned to new research projects. Left as a team, they might have fought together to keep alive a number of their odd little discoveries. But all those discoveries were shelved, with Silver's one glaring exception, and he got little assistance from his teammates in promoting the survival of his oddball adhesive. So he did what seems to happen frequently at 3M. He shrugged at the organization and he did it himself. He had to wage a battle to get the money just to patent his unique polymer. 3M eventually spent the minimum money possible. Post-it adhesive was patented *only* in the United States. "We really had to fight to get a patent," said Silver, "because there was no commercial product readily apparent. It's kind of a shame. I wish it would change. If 3M commits itself to millions of dollars for research, it ought to allow you to follow up with the money for a patent."

People at 3M, when they fight for something, seem to do it with an understated grace, a politeness that conceals their tenacity. This is true of Silver, who quietly began the arduous struggle to capture the imagination of his colleagues and superiors. Silver's only advantage was that he was, after all, in love. "I was just absolutely convinced that this had potential," Silver said. "There are some things that have a little spark to them—that are worth pursuing. You have to be almost a zealot at times in order to keep interest alive, otherwise it will die off. It seems like the pattern always goes like this: In the fat times, R&D groups appear and we do a lot of interesting research. And then the lean times come just about at the point when you've developed your first goody, your gizmo. And then you've got to go out and try to sell it. Well, everybody in the divisions is so busy that they don't want to touch it. They don't have time to look at new product ideas with no end product already in mind."

Silver went door-to-door to every division at 3M that might be able to think up an application for his adhesive. The organization never protested his search. When he sought slots of time at in-house technical seminars, he always got a segment to show off his now-it-works, now-it-doesn't adhesive. At every seminar, some people left, some people stayed. Most of them said, "What can you do with a glue that doesn't glue?" But *no one* said to Silver, "Don't try. Stop wasting our time." In fact, it would have violated some very deeply felt principles of the 3M Company to have killed Silver's pet project. Much is made of 3M's "environment for innovation," but 3M's environment is, more accurately, an environment of nonintervention, of expecting people to fulfill their day's responsibilities, every day, without discernible pressure from above. Silver, no matter how much time he spent fooling around with the Post-it adhesive, never failed in his other duties, and so, at 3M, there was no reason whatsoever to overtly discourage his extracurricular activities. The positive side of this corporate ethic is the feeling of independence each worker experiences in doing his job. The disadvantage is that, when you have a good idea that requires more than one person to share the work and get the credit, it can be hard to convince people to postpone their chores and help with yours.

As Silver pursued his lonely quest, his best inspiration for applying his adhesive was a sticky bulletin board, a product that wasn't especially stimulating even to its inventor. He got 3M to manufacture a number of them—through a fairly low-tech and inexpensive process—and they were sent out to the company's distribution and retail network. The outcome was predictable. 3M sold a few, but it was a slow-moving item in a sleepy market niche. Silver knew there had to be a better idea. "At times I was angry because this stuff is so obviously unique," said Silver. "I said to myself, 'Why can't you think of a product? It's your job!' "

Although Silver had overcome the metaphorical trap of always striving for stickier stickum, he, too, became trapped, albeit by a different metaphor. The bulletin board, the only product he could think of, was totally coated with adhesive—it was sticky everywhere. The metaphor said that something is either sticky or not sticky. Something *partly sticky* did not occur to him. More constraining was the fact that, until Silver's adhesive made it possible, there had been no such thing as a self-adhesive piece of note paper. Note paper was cheap and trivial, and the valuable elements used with these bits of paper were their durable fasteners of pins, tacks, tapes, and clips. So silver was immersed in an organization whose lifeblood was tape: Scotch brand tapes like magic tape, cellophane tape, duct tape, masking tape, electrical tape, caulking tape, diaper tape, and surgical tape, to name a few. In this atmosphere, imaging a piece of paper that eliminates the need for tape is almost unthinkable.

In the early 1970s, 3M transferred Silver to its System Research group within the Central Research labs. There he met Oliveira, a biochemist who shared Silver's fascination with things that did stuff you didn't think they could do. Silver and Oliveira kept each other from getting discouraged; they were a duo that eventually presented the adhesive technology to Geoff Nicholson, which in the course of the seemingly accidental nature of Post-it notes, may have been the biggest accident of all. Nicholson was, in 1973, appointed the leader of a new venture team in the Commercial Tape Division laboratory. Now venture teams were open-ended research and development groups formed, when funds are available, to explore new directions in one of 3M's many lines of business and technology. Nicholson had been given a fresh budget and a free hand to develop new products in the company's Commercial Tape Division, whose new product development had grown sluggish. It is a standing policy at 3M that each division must generate 25 percent of its annual revenue from products developed in the last five years, a tall order for any division, especially those in the old, established product lines, and one on which Commercial Tape consistently had been coming up short.

Silver had been to see the people in Com-mercial Tape at least twice before. Both times they had rejected his adhesive. Two days before Nicholson arrived in Commercial Tape, Silver and Oliveira had been around again, trying to sell the idea to the division's technical director, James Irwin. Irwin sidestepped them by saying there would be a new guy running research projects there in a couple of days. Two days later, Silver and Oliveira were almost the first people in Nicholson's new office. "Here I am, brand-new to the division, and I don't know a lot about adhesives. And here they were talking to me about adhesives," Nicholson recalled. "I'm ripe for something new, different, and exciting. Most anybody who had walked in the door, I would have put my arms around them."

Silver explained his adhesive discovery for the umpteenth time, and Nicholson, who didn't understand half of what he was saying, was intrigued. "It sure sounded different and unique to me," said Nicholson. "I was ripe for the plucking." Finally, Silver's unloved, uncommitted adhesive had a home. Nicholson went about recruiting people for the new venture team; Silver hoped that one of those people would arrive with a *problem* to match his five-year-old *solution*. The one who had the problem was a chemist, a choir director, and an amateur mechanic named Arthur Fry. It was Fry who eventually took the baton from Silver's weary grasp and carried it over a host of discouraging hurdles. Even before joining the new venture team in Commercial Tape, Fry had seen Silver show off his adhesive and had kept the idea turning slowly in the back of his mind. He agreed with Silver that this adhesive was special, although he too wondered what to do with it.

"Then one day in 1974, while I was singing in the choir of the North Presbyterian Church in north St. Paul, I had one of those creative moments," Fry explained. "To make it easier to find the songs we were going to sing at each Sunday's service, I used to mark the places with little slips of paper." Inevitably, when everyone in the church stood up, or when Fry had to communicate through gestures with other members of the choir, he would divert his attention from the placement of his array of bookmarks. One unguarded move, and they either fluttered to the floor or sank into the deep crack of the hymnal's binding. Suddenly, while Fry leafed frantically for his place in the book, he thought "Gee, if I had a little adhesive on these bookmarks, that would be just the ticket." Fry decided to check into that idea the next week at work. What he had in mind, of course, was Silver's adhesive.

What had happened in Fry's ever-searching curiosity was the creative association of two unrelated ideas. When Fry went to work on Monday, he ordered a sample of the adhesive, mixed different concentrations, and invented what he called "the better bookmark." Encouraged by Silver's enthusiasm and Nicholson's push for new products, Fry began to realize the magnitude of his creative activity. "I knew I had made a much bigger discovery," said Fry. "I soon came to realize that the primary application for Silver's adhesive was not to put it on a fixed surface, like the bulletin boards. That was a secondary application. The primary application concerned paper to paper." Fry had also coated only the edge of the paper so that the part protruding from the book wouldn't be sticky. In using these bookmarks for notes back and forth to his boss, Fry had come across the heart of the idea. It wasn't a bookmark at all, it was a note—a system of communication where the means of attachment and removal were built in and did not damage the original surface!

Over the years, Fry has been ordained as the Post-it notes champion, a title which, in ensuing years, has imposed some unusual burdens on him. Today, rather than working side-by-side in a lab with old friends like Silver and Oliveira, Art Fry is ensconced in his own laboratory. To a chemist, this is the equivalent of the corporate corner office—lofty among the echelons of the organization, but such loftiness often makes for a lonely job. On the other hand, Fry is often freed from the splendid isolation of his private lab to speak, as a company spokesman, to large groups of businessmen about the climate for creativity at 3M. He has been interviewed and quoted so often that business writers invariably peg him as the sole Post-it notes product champion. With Fry trapped by this role

and its demands, it's easy to see why Spence Silver seems relieved, perhaps even grateful at the comparatively short shrift given to his role in the Post-it story. Silver is still in 3M's basement, working out of a cramped, windowless office in a large, open, multihood laboratory, a place where experimental ferment still seems to take place. In Silver, the scientific playfulness that gave birth to the Post-it adhesive still seems intact. In fact, without much prompting, he will hold up a glass cylinder of the old Post-it polymer, showing its milky white color in its restful state. He then squeezes the polymer with a plunger and, under pressure, the contents magically become crystal clear. Silver releases the pressure and the adhesive becomes opaque again! Silver doesn't know why it does that. "Isn't that wonderful?" he says. "There must be some way you can *use* that!"

In 1974, after Silver had been making the same exclamation for many years, Fry had provided the first truly affirmative response. But with the "Eureka moment" at the North Presbyterian Church came many other problems. On the bulletin board, Silver's adhesive was attached to a favorable "substrate." It stuck to the bulletin board better than anything else. Move it to paper, however, and it peeled off onto everything it touched. If you couldn't change this property, you still couldn't make a future for Silver's Post-it adhesive. Says Fry, "You had to get the adhesive to stay in place on the note instead of transferring to other surfaces. I think some of the church hymnals have pages that are still sticking together." The two members who invented a paper coating that made the Post-it adhesive work were named Henry Courtney and Roger Merrill. Silver said, "Those guys actually made one of the most important contributions to the whole project, and they haven't received a lot of credit for it. The Post-it adhesive was always interesting to people, but if you put it down on something and pulled it apart, it could stay with either side. It had no memory of where it should be. It was difficult to figure out a way to prime the substrate, to get it to stick to the surface you originally put it on. Roger and Hank invented a way to stick the Post-it adhesive down. And they're the ones who really made the breakthrough discovery, because once you've learned that, you can apply it to all sorts of different structures."

Courtney and Merrill's contribution was the first in a series of actions that definitely were not accidents. Although there was still organizational resistance after Fry's choir book epiphany, every action thereafter, including Courtney and Merrill's research, was directed toward the development, production, and market success of the Post-it note. Fry was a tenacious advocate of the product through all phases from development to production scale-up. While Silver's task had been simply to convince his corporation that his glue was not just a footnote in the obscure history of adhesives, the job Fry assumed was to overcome the natural resistance of people to manufacturing a product differently from their normal experience base. The engineers in 3M's Commercial Tape Division were accustomed to tape, which is sticky all over on one side and then gets packaged into rolls. To apply glue selectively to one side of the paper, and to move the product from rolls to sheets, the engineers would have to invent at least two entirely unique machines. Furthermore, even though 3M is noted for its coating expertise, the company did not have the coating equipment capable of putting the necessary precision on an imprecise surface such as paper. Nor did they have a good way of measuring the coating's weight. Have you ever noticed, for example, that the pads are no thicker at the adhesive layer then at the rest of the pad?

In war and politics, the best strategy is to divide and conquer. In production engineering, the reverse seems to be true. Fry brought together the production people, designers, mechanical engineers, product foremen, and machine operators and let them describe the many reasons why something like that could not be done. He encouraged them to speculate on ways that they might accomplish the impossible. A lifelong gadgeteer, Fry found himself offering his own suggestions. Although the problems bothered the production people, they delighted Fry. "Problems are wonderful things to have if, in overcoming them, you've created a product that is easy for customers to use but difficult for competitors to make."

Inevitably, from these discussions people started thinking of places around 3M where they'd seen machines and parts they could use to piece together the impossible machines they needed to build. And they thought of people who could help. "In a small company, if you had an idea that would incorporate a variety of technologies and you had to go out and buy the equipment to put those together, you probably couldn't afford it, or you'd have to go as inexpensively or as small as possible," said Fry. "At a large company like 3M, we've got so many different types of technology operating and so many experts—guys that really know all about any subject you want—and so much equipment scattered here and there, that we can piece things together when we're starting off. It's the old 80:20 rule; that is, 80 percent of the equipment and materials needed can probably be found within the company and can be scrounged by an 'entrepreneuring' champion."

Then there was Art Fry's basement. He had had arguments with several mechanical engineers about a difficult phase of production, applying adhesive to paper in a continuous roll. He said it could be done; they said it couldn't. Fry assembled a small-scale basic machine in his basement, then adapted it until he'd solved the problem. The machine worked, and it would work even better once the mechanical engineers had a chance to refine it. But the next problem Fry had was worse: the new machine was too big to fit through his basement door. If he couldn't get it out of his cellar, he couldn't show it off to the engineers. Fry accepted the consequences of his genius and did what he had to do. He broke down an external wall in his ground-level basement and delivered his machine by caesarean section!

Within two years, Fry and 3M's mechanical engineers had tinkered their way to a series of machines that, among other things, coated the yellow paper with its "substrate," applied adhesive, and cut the sticky paper into little square and rectangular note pads. All of the machines are unique and proprietary to the company. They are the key to the Post-it Notes' marvelous high-quality consistency and dependability. The immense difficulty of duplicating 3M's machinery is part of the reason few competitors have made it to the market with Post-it note imitations. Fry and the engineers worked on their unique machines and mass-production methods in a pilot plant in the Commercial Tape lab. The project team mapped out every raw material, processing step, test procedure, and intermediate product needed to produce the final output (according to Fry, the quality is so good that there have been fewer than 75 complaints since Post-its were introduced nationwide in 1980). The pilot plant produced more than enough Post-it note prototypes to supply all the company's offices. All the sticky pads went to Nicholson's office. From there his secretary carried out a program of providing every office at 3M with Post-it Notes. Early in the program, secretaries on the fourteenth floor, where the senior managers work, all received Post-it Notes and became hooked. Jack Wilkins, the Commercial Tape Division's marketing director at the time, described the process of discovery that hit people the first time they encountered the Post-it Notes. "Once people started using them it was like handing them marijuana," said Wilkins. "Once you start using it you can't stop."

Strangely enough, the personal enthusiasm of secretaries and marketing people like Wilkins did not impress the people responsible for putting Post-it Notes onto the market. For the division's marketing organization, fear of the unfamiliar repeatedly raised its head and threatened to scuttle the program. The marketing department had got out of the habit of dealing directly with consumers. This is ironic, because that much-heralded 3M hero, William L. McKnight, had established a tradition of direct contact with consumers in 1914. That year, as the company's brand-new national sales manager, the first act performed by the young McKnight was to visit furniture factories in Rockford, Illinois, and find out from workers what was wrong with 3M's mediocre sandpaper, which was then the company's only product. That trip to Rockford was the first instance of an executive from 3M walking in the door, approaching a user, and saying, "Here! Try this! Tell me what you think!"

By 1978 the Commercial Tape Division's marketing department was involved in the introduction of half a dozen new products that met eas-

ily identified needs for clearly defined markets, products like book binding tape for libraries and PMA adhesives for the art market. The Post-it note was just another new product, and not a high-priority product at that. While the company's marketing people had become mesmerized by Post-it Notes in their own offices, they couldn't imagine that other people would feel the same way. They said you could only sell these things if you gave them away free, because who's going to pay a dollar for scratch paper? Although most of the marketing group had used Post-it Notes, when they created marketing materials to present the new product they included no samples. Instead they wrote brochures describing the note pads, they sent boxes of samples separately—which people would open only if they got excited by the brochures. The 3M marketing group was trapped by its own paradigm. It was their job, as marketing experts, to explain products, not to demonstrate them. And as explainers, they had no words to overcome the "scratch paper" metaphor. If they couldn't explain them, they couldn't sell them.

Nicholson, who had spread Post-it Notes like an infection within 3M, only had limited power to push them outside the company. When the four-city market test failed, he alone might not have had the influence to keep the produce alive. But by this time Nicholson had a heavyweight ally in his own boss Joe Ramey, a Division vice president and General Sales Manager of the Commercial Tape Division. Nicholson and Ramey were curious as to why a product that to them had obvious appeal had bombed so terribly. Had 3M's conventional marketing approach victimized an unconventional product? They were sufficiently curious about the trial to fly to one of the market-test cities—Richmond, Virginia. Ramey had been a marketing troubleshooter and he knew realistically that some market problems are just too far advanced to be saved. Nevertheless, he agreed to go to Richmond because he liked Nicholson, not because he liked Post-it Notes' chances of survival.

If Nicholson and Ramey hadn't gone to Richmond, 3M almost certainly would have ceased pilot production of Post-it Notes, retired the new machinery they'd designed for the job, and let the several hundred thousand note pads dwindle into dusty inventory. 3M had always been a company very skilled at developing new variations from old products and then expanding their range of activities as a result of such developments. But Post-it Note Pad was unique, a product entirely unrelated to anything that had ever been sold by 3M. The reason Nicholson made the extra effort to go to Richmond with Ramey to engineer a market reversal was that they had both used Post-it Notes. They knew how clever and irresistible they were. They also knew that their own marketing people had approached the market tests in the four cities of Tulsa, Denver, Richmond, and Tampa in a traditional style. These were tests that relied heavily on advertising to generate enthusiasm in distributors who did not themselves use Post-it Notes and who saw little sense in exerting sales efforts for a scratch pad that represented both an exorbitant price and a dubious profit margin. Nicholson and Ramey took to Richmond a bit of understanding that had eluded all the marketers and distributors: Post-it Notes were just something you had to *use* to appreciate.

Nicholson and Ramey took the next logical step: they stopped depending on the organization. They went out and did it themselves. To do this, they returned to the two things that had already "sold" Post-it Notes more than once. First, like Spencer Silver shuffling from one 3M division to another with his queer adhesive, Nicholson and Ramey went door-to-door. Second, they gave away the product, which is what they had been doing within 3M for more than a year. Throughout the banks and offices of Richmond's business district, Nicholson and Ramey introduced themselves and handed out little sticky pads of Post-it Notes, saying, "Here, try this." And they watched as all kinds of people, from secretaries to programmers to vice-presidents, did just that. They tested Post-it Notes in the flesh and saw firsthand the excitement and addiction of first-time users. In one day of personal contacts in Richmond, Nicholson and Ramey had obtained vivid assurance, not only that people liked these things, but that they were pleading for 3M to make more and that they were going to tell their friends about them. As was later demonstrated in a

massive marketing giveaway program in Idaho, now immortalized in 3M as the "Boise Blitz," people loved the Post-it Notes they got free at first, and if getting more meant they had to pay a dollar a pad, it was well worth the price. Post-it Notes seem to spoil office people forever, for they do something no product ever did before. They convey messages in the exact spot you want with no after marks, dents, or holes. They can be moved from place to place and they come in various sizes (and now in colors) for different kinds of messages. Once you've used them, it's hard to go back to staples and paper clips.

The Boise Blitz was unusual but not unique at 3M. The company had saturated test markets before with products and ads. In addition to spending a small fortune on advertising, promotions, and free Post-it Notes, 3M diverted most of its Office Supply Division sales force and a battalion of temporary employees to the city of Boise in Idaho. The blitz confirmed the appeal of Post-it Notes, revealing that sales inevitably follow the distribution of free samples. Reorders came in at a rate of 90 percent, which is double the rate of any other wildly successful office product. But Boise notwithstanding, the real key to the market breakthrough for Post-it Notes was the first effort in Richmond, when Nicholson and Ramey did what 3M sales representatives had been trained to do since the early days when sandpaper was their only product; they talked directly to the end-user and then they showed distributors and retailers the results.

Recalling the trip to Richmond, Nicholson called it an "accident" and "an act of desperation." Neither he nor Ramey were hopeful that they could rejuvenate a doomed product by an impulsive flight to Richmond to knock on strange doors. "What made me go out into the market was the enthusiasm of Nicholson and Fry," said Ramey. "I just figured for their morale I should get out and find out whether we ought to kill it once and for all. My reaction when I first went out into those markets was that we probably had a dead duck on our hands. Frankly, I thought it was a product that people just wouldn't buy." Nicholson described the Richmond revelation as the last in a series of accidents from the initial invention of the adhesive technology by Silver to the invention of the Post-it note itself. Fry was around the adhesive and he had a problem that he needed to solve. Had Fry not been in an environment where people were playing around with that adhesive, he never would not have come up with his contribution.

Retrospective writings about Post-it Notes refer effusively to the encouragement provided to creative people by champions and patrons in 3M management. Silver often wonders where all that management encouragement was during the first five years of his struggle to be heard. The 3M organization does not provide interesting soil for new ideas to grow, but until Nicholson listened to a presentation by Silver and his colleague Oliveira, 3M management had given no hint of support for what eventually became the Post-it Notes project. Until then, the flame was borne by researchers from below, acting largely in solitude and occasionally in defiance of the organization's implicit desires. Silver's adhesive (and the sticky bulletin board it spawned) lasted out a half decade of cold shoulders only because 3M has a tradition of "internal selling"; that is, anyone with a product idea can shop it around the company's many divisions for developmental support. This means that inventors never really get stopped at 3M—there isn't any central overseer saying, "Cut that out and get back to work!" Instead, inventors labor in their spare time, experiencing mounting rejections from managers, most of whom do not have the imagination, the patience, or the budget to take a serious look at their ideas. As in other companies, product ideas die at 3M, but their deaths are often more slow and lingering.

Silver and Oliveira were chemists, working at 3M's central R&D lab to develop variations in chemical products. Like other chemists, they worked within specific programs set out by 3M to attain certain results, but they also had encouragement to follow up on interesting, unexpected results—within reason, of course! According to 3M policy, scientists can use up to 15 percent of their time pursuing interests outside their primary assignments. But when asked who keeps track of 3M researchers' use of the 15 percent rule, and how this is done, the answer is that no one really keeps track. In fact, Fry points out that "No one really has extra time. The 15 percent is time that's put in after 5:00 or in weekends. (The 'bootleg' rule was instituted by McKnight after he had ordered Dick Drew back in 1923 to stop working on what turned out to be masking tape.) It gives us a chance to shape our own careers, for McKnight recognized that people give their best efforts to projects they're most interested in. The reward for the extra effort is that we are soon officially asked to do what we wanted to do all along." Fry goes on to emphasize that the beauty of bootleg projects is that they don't rely on top-down decision making. "If you are going after an established market with existing technology, then top-down decision making is fine, but new-to-the-world things generally require perspectives and information from people scattered within the organization. While innovation starts with the initial idea for a creative product, a lot more creativity and new ideas are needed to build the idea into a business." The creative climate allows one to keep a low profile during the time when the early, tough problems arise that require creative solutions. One of the things that Fry had going for him right away was the support from his immediate lab supervisor, Bob Molenda, to charge expenses to "miscellaneous accounts." This is another of the ways the corporation puts teeth into McKnight's policy of giving freedom to chase new ideas. The company had provided Fry with just enough time and money to get started. "Throwing a lot of money or people at the task not only won't speed it up," says Fry, "it will only cut down on management's ability to afford to be patient. Things can be easily killed before they get a real chance."

Silver also kept the Post-it adhesive alive for a remarkably, and perhaps unreasonably, long time because he also kept busy with other research tasks assigned by the company and didn't devote his entire energy to his funny discovery. He is also a cheerful man with an amazing tolerance for rejection. For more than five years, Silver's adhesive was a really oddball idea that make little sense either technically or commercially. It had no perceptible application; it was a solution looking for a problem. And of all the ways to devise new products, probably the most difficult and inefficient is to invent some substance with novel properties and then search for ways to use it, especially when the goal is to develop a product for which people will pay. Nevertheless, seeing face-to-face the reactions of people in Richmond "playing" with Post-it Notes was so dramatic to Ramey and Nicholson that they finally had all the evidence they need to orchestrate the Boise Blitz.

It's remarkable that Post-it Notes and sandpaper, two of the company's greatest breakthroughs, sixty-six years apart, grew out of a similar style and faith in the wisdom of sitting down with customers and asking questions, without any of the trappings of corporate protocol. It could be just a coincidence, but according to many analysts, Post-it Notes finally succeeded because 3M's corporate culture creates a positive environment for innovation. Although corporate culture is one of those ill-defined and overused business concepts, suffice it to say that there is something in 3M's style that tends to encourage a measure of individual ingenuity among its workers. Fry comments in his talks that "if managers aren't innovative, if they don't provide the climate for creativity, if they can't set aside their carefully laid plans to take advantage of a new opportunity, then intrapreneurs (entrepreneurs within a large established business) have little encouragement."

"3M operates on a simple principle," Forbes magazine once said, "that no market, no end product is so small as to be scorned; that with the proper organization, a myriad of small products can be as profitable, if not more so, than a few big ones." This tolerance of the small-scale certainly helped Spence Silver, and then Art Fry, to keep the company from stomping on the Post-it Notes project before the project had developed a life of its own. But there was also the benefit of bigness. Over the years, 3M has grown into a loosely integrated cluster of divisions, with senior management in the St. Paul corporate headquarters. One of the results of this corporate sprawl is that it permits the clever researcher to hide in the crevices and carry out his

own version of the "15 percent principle." Silver benefited more from this "neglect" than from anyone overtly encouraging him to innovate. Fry also enjoyed this dispensation from scrutiny as he fostered the Post-it project through the touchy and costly labor of product development. Although Fry started out as the team leader, the project's formal coordination passed back and forth between marketing and engineering. "Others were better suited to that function than I," says Fry, "and I needed to be free to focus on technical problems."

A more provocative issue, though, is why people at 3M enjoy such unchecked opportunity to "get away with things." A hasty judgment might be that the company's senior management is consciously fostering and rewarding innovative growth. But there is ample evidence to challenge this assertion. The company tends to recognize its most successful creative people by investing them into the company's Carlton Society or, as in the case of Fry, installing them in private laboratories. After each unexpected invention emerges at 3M, the company tends to follow up by creating new programs for innovation (the latest is called Genesis) and new honors to motivate inventors. 3M also gives "Golden Step Awards" for products that sell $2 million, at a profit, within the first two or three years of national introduction. When Post-it Notes won a Golden Step Award in 1981, 13 other products also won the award. In 1987, 3M had over 50 Golden Step Winners. Yet there seems to have been no desire for trophies, promotions, or rewards in any of the Post-it project principals nor in any of 3M's prior inventors. They were people obsessed with problems, not rewards, and they usually invented their own program in order to get a problem solved.

Extrinsic incentives simply don't explain why 3M gets creativity from its Silvers and Frys. There might be a more credible explanation in the company's origins. Since 1910, 3M has been inextricably linked with the city of St. Paul, and some 80 percent of its employees have historically come from the upper Midwest. One of the striking characteristics of community-linked Midwestern companies like 3M is that company and community have grown up together, and they like to think they know what to expect from each other. This bond among town, corporate management, and workers creates trust, and with trust comes an air of amiability. The ease and unpretentiousness of the highest officials at 3M is different from the formality and status sensitivity of managements in other regions, especially in the East. Nicholson and Ramey, for example, did not need to overcome a lot of deep-seated conditioning in order to go out on the streets and behave like peddlers. Fry himself sold pots and pans and luggage door-to-door while he was in college. At 3M, it is simply not good form for management to watch too closely over the shoulders of its veteran employees. It is equally bad form for employees to violate the trust placed in them by a less than vigilant management. There is an honor system, and it works.

The source of this heartland ethos may lie in the farms that surround St. Paul and the pioneering spirit from which they originated. A midwestern American farm is a place where—for generations— each worker has been expected to complete his daily chores before sitting down to supper. Nobody ever watches him do his chores; if he doesn't do them, the disastrous evidence will become apparent by the next day's dawn. Nobody ever asks him if he did his chores, because he wouldn't be eating if he hadn't. People carry on without permission at 3M because they're trustworthy. And they're trustworthy because trust is a part of the larger culture that has surrounded and affected 3M for eighty-five years. In fact, one thing 3M has shown is that when it gets too structured and self-conscious about managing its innovation, it doesn't innovate any better than any other company. As Nicholson said, Post-it Notes came from accidents, not calculations.

The Post-it note accidents were Spence Silver's polymer discovery, Arthur Fry's bookmark epiphany, and Geoff Nicholson's dragging Joe Ramey off to Richmond. Each accident occurred after one person took an entirely independent course of action from the one assigned by the corporation. Each time, the individual got frustrated by either the indifference or the resistance of the organization. Similar accidents had occurred in the past. In 1956 a researcher spilled a tube full of totally useless fluorocarbon compound on her shoes—and from that accident, chemists Patsy Sherman and Sam Smith created Scotchguard fabric protector. In 1950, after three polite 3M requests to stop wasting money, researcher Alvin W. Boese squeezed synthetic fibers mixed with wood pulp through a makeshift comb and created one of the most successful types of nonwoven decorative ribbon ever devised. Masking tape, cellophane tape, and many other big product successes can trace their origins to a similar sequence of "happy accidents."

These accidents happened because when the organization, or management, discouraged people from doing something, the cancellation order didn't carry much conviction. Ego is not popular at 3M, and it is clear that the people thinking up things often have more room to express their egos than the people who are supposed to be running things. If there is an organizational key to breakthrough at 3M, a significant element of corporate culture, it is the fact that people there don't believe in placing the values of the corporation above the values of the individual. People keep the organization vital by not taking the organization too seriously. As a result, when the creative people, Silver and Fry and Nicholson, inevitably ran into the resistance of the organization, they felt the freedom to say, "Well, okay. Never mind. I'll do it myself." The organization simply did not have an equal measure of persistence in response. 3M gives in to people who are sure of themselves. Just as important, everybody at 3M knows that, if someone's pet project blows up in his face, it isn't the end of the world. If Silver, Fry, or Nicholson had failed, they wouldn't have been dismissed or disgraced. As long as they had their chores done, they always had a place at the table.

12

Maintaining Innovative Climates

34

That's Easy for You to Say

LUCIEN RHODES

An obsession with "corporate culture" can be worse than no culture at all. Just ask the man who wrote the book on the subject.

It all began on Labor Day weekend in 1982. Allan A. Kennedy was sitting in a low beach chair on the shore in front of his cottage on Cape Cod. Next to him was his friend and fellow consultant Tony Merilo. As they relaxed there, watching the sailboats drift across the Cape Cod Bay, drinking beer, and listen-ing to a Red Sox game on the radio, Kennedy turned to Merilo and, with the majestic eloquence suited to great undertakings, said: "Gee, Tony, you know, we ought to start some kind of business together."

This identical thought has, of course, passed between countless friends ever since the discovery of profit margins. Coming from most people, it would have fallen into the general category of loose talk. But Kennedy was not most people. For one thing, he was a 13-year veteran of McKinsey & Co., the management consulting firm, and partner

Reprinted with permission, *Inc.* magazine, June 1986. Copyright © 1986 by Goldhirsh Group, Inc., 38 Commercial Wharf, Boston, MA 02110.

Lucien Rhodes is a freelance writer.

in charge of its Boston office. More to the point, he was the coauthor of a recently published book that offered a startling new perspective on corporate life—one that challenged the whole way people thought about business.

The book was entitled *Corporate Cultures,* a term that was itself new to the language, and it dealt with an aspect of business that, up to then, had been largely ignored. Broadly speaking, that aspect involved the role played by a company's values, symbols, rites, and rituals in determining its overall performance. Citing examples from some of the country's most dynamic companies, Kennedy and co-author Terrence E. Deal showed that these "cultural" factors had a major effect on the attitudes and behavior of a company's employees, and were thus of critical importance to its long-term success.

By any measure, the book was a groundbreaking work, challenging, as it did, the rational, quantitative models of corporate success that were so popular in the 1960s and '70s. But its impact had as much to do with its timing as its content. Published in June 1982, during a period of economic stagnation—with unemployment at 9.5%, the prime over 16%, and trade deficits soaring to record levels—*Corporate Cultures* offered a welcome antidote to the doom and gloom that was abroad in the land. Like *In Search of Excellence,* which appeared a few months later, it suggested that Japan was not the only nation capable of producing strong, highly motivated companies that could compete effectively in the international arena. America could produce—in fact, was already producing—its own.

What the book did not detail, however, was how corporate cultures were actually constructed. The authors could describe a particular culture and demonstrate its effects, but they offered few clues as to how a company might develop a culture in the first place. So the news that Allan Kennedy was going into business was greeted with more than passing interest among the followers of corporate culture. Here was an opportunity to find out how a living, breathing culture could be created, and the creator would be none other than the man who wrote the book.

After an extensive survey of business opportunities, Kennedy and Merilo decided to develop microcomputer software for sales and marketing management. They felt this was their most promising option, given the anticipated growth of the microcomputer market and their own experience as consultants. Acting on that assessment, they resigned from McKinsey and, in February 1983, formally launched Selkirk Associates Inc. with four of their friends.

Kennedy had lofty ambitions for Selkirk. More than a business, he saw it as a kind of laboratory for his theories. He wanted it to function as a society of professional colleagues committed to building a culture and a company that would stress collaboration, openness, decentralization, democratic decisions, respect, and trust. In this society, each individual would be encouraged to devise his or her own entrepreneurial response to the challenges of the business.

For Kennedy, this was not a long-term goal, something that would evolve naturally in the fullness of time. On the contrary, it was a pressing, immediate concern. Accordingly, he focused all his attention on creating such a culture from the start. "I spent lots of time," he says, "trying to think about what kind of values the company ought to stand for and therefore what kind of behavior I expected from people." These thoughts eventually went into a detailed statement of "core beliefs," which he reviewed and amplified with each new employee. In the same vein, Kennedy and his colleagues chose a "guiding principle" namely, a commitment to "making people more productive." They would pursue this ambition, everyone agreed, "through the products and services we offer" and "in the way we conduct our own affairs."

And, in the beginning at least, Selkirk seemed to be everything Kennedy had hoped for. The company set up shop in Boston, in an office that consisted of a large, rectangular room, with three smaller attachments. Each morning, staff members would pile into the main room and sort themselves out by function—programmers and systems engineers by the windows; administrations in the middle, sales and marketing folk at the other end. In keeping with Kennedy's cultural precepts, there were no private offices or, indeed, any physical demarcations between functions.

It was a familial enterprise, informed with the very qualities Kennedy had laid out in his statement of core beliefs. The work was absorbing, the comradeship inspiring. Most mornings, the staff feasted on doughnuts, which they took to calling "corporate carbos," as a wordplay on "corporate cultures." They began a scrapbook as an impromptu cultural archive. Included among the memorabilia was "The Ravin," an Edgar Allan Poe takeoff that commemorated Selkirk's first stirrings in earlier temporary headquarters:

Once upon an April morning,
    disregarding every warning,
In a Back Bay storefront,
    Selkirk software was begun:
True, it was without a toilet,
    but that didn't seem to spoil it.

To strengthen their bonds even further, the staff began to experiment with so-called rites, rituals, and ceremonies—all important elements of a corporate culture, according to Kennedy's book. Selkirk's office manager, Linda Sharkey, recalls a day, for example, when the whole company went out to Kennedy's place on Cape Cod to celebrate their common purpose with barbecues on the beach. "The sun was shining, and we were all there together," she says. "It was a beautiful day. That's the way it was. We didn't use the terms among ourselves that Allan uses in the book. With us, corporate cultures was more by seeing and doing." Sharkey remembers, too, Friday afternoon luncheons of pizza or Chinese food, at which everyone in the company had a chance to talk about his or her accomplishments or problems, or simply hang out.

Kennedy was pleased with all this, as well he might be. "We were," he says, "beginning to develop a real culture."

Then the walls went up.

The problem stemmed from the situation in the big room, where the technical people were la-

boring feverishly to develop Selkirk's first product, while the salespeople were busy preselling it. The former desperately needed peace and quiet to concentrate on their work; the latter were a boisterous lot, fond of crowing whenever a prospect looked encouraging. In fact, the salespeople crowed so often and so loudly that the technicians complained that they were being driven to distraction. Finally, they confronted Kennedy with the problem. Their solution, which Kennedy agreed to, was to erect five-foot-high movable partitions, separating each functional grouping from the others.

In the memory of Selkirk veterans, "the day the walls went up" lives on as a day of infamy. "It was terrible," says Sharkey. "I was embarrassed."

"It was clearly a symbol of divisiveness," says Kennedy.

"I don't know what would have been the right solution," says Reilly Hayes, Selkirk's 23-year-old technical wizard, "but the wall certainly wasn't. It blocked out the windows for the other end of the room. Someone [in marketing] drew a picture of a window and taped it to the wall. The whole thing created a lot of dissension."

Indeed, the erection of the walls touched off a feud between engineering and marketing that eventually grew into "open organizational warfare," according to Kennedy. "I let the wall stand, and a competitive attitude developed where engineering started sniping at marketing. We had two armed camps that didn't trust each other."

As if that weren't bad enough, other problems were beginning to surface. For one thing, the company was obviously overstaffed, having grown from 12 people in June 1983 to 25 in January 1984, without any product—or sales—to show for it. "That was a big mistake," says Kennedy. "We clearly ramped up the organization too fast, particularly given the fact that we were financing ourselves. I mean, for a while, we had a burn rate of around $100,000 per month."

Even more serious, however, was the problem that emerged following the release of the company's initial product, Correspondent, in February 1984. Not that there was anything wrong with the product. It was, in fact, a fine piece of software, and it premiered to glowing reviews. Designed as a selling tool, it combined database management, calendar management, word processing, and mail merge—functions that could help customers organize their accounts, track and schedule sales calls and followups, and generate correspondence. And it did all that splendidly.

The problem had to do with the price tag, a whopping $12,000 per unit. The Selkirk team members had come up with this rarefied figure, not out of greed, but out of a commitment to customer service—a goal to which they had pledged themselves as part of their cultural mission. In order to provide such service, they figured, a Selkirk representative might have to spend two or three weeks with each customer, helping to install and customize the product. Trouble was, customers weren't willing to *pay* for that service, not at $12,000 per unit anyway. After a brief flurry of interest, sales dropped off.

"We just blew it," says Kennedy. "We were arrogant about the market. We were trying to tell the market something it wasn't interested in hearing. We took an arbitrary cultural goal and tried to make it into a strategy, rather than saying we're a market-driven company and we've got to find out what the market wants and supply it." Unfortunately, six months went by before Kennedy and his colleagues figured all this out and began to reduce Correspondent's price accordingly.

By then, however, Selkirk's entire sales effort was in shambles, a victim of its commitment to employee autonomy. Sales targets were seldom realized. Indeed, they were scarcely even set. At weekly meetings, salespeople would do little more than review account activity. "If a salesman said each week for three weeks in a row that he expected to close a certain account, and it never happened," say Merlo, "well, we didn't do anything about it. In any other company, he would probably have been put on probation." As it was, each of the participants entered the results of the meeting in a red-and-black ledger book and struck out once again to wander haphazardly through uncharted territory. "The mistake we made," reflects Merlo, "was using real money in a real company to test hypotheses about what sales goals should be."

Finally, in June 1984, Kennedy took action, laying off 6 people. In July, Correspondent's price was dropped to $4,000 per unit, but sales remained sluggish. In September, Kennedy laid off 5 more people, bringing the size of the staff back to 12.

One of those laid off was the chief engineer, a close friend of Kennedy's, but a man whose departure brought an immediate ceasefire between the warring factions. That night, the remaining staff members took down the walls and stacked them neatly in the kitchenette, where they repose to this day. "We felt," says Sharkey, "like we had our little family back together again."

With morale finally rebounding, Selkirk again cut Correspondent's price in the early fall, to $1,500. This time, sales responded, and, in November, the company enjoyed its first month in the black.

But Selkirk was not yet out of the woods. What remained was for Kennedy to figure out the significance of what had happened, and to draw the appropriate conclusions. Clearly, his experiment had not turned out as he had planned. His insistence on a company without walls had led to organizational warfare. His goal of providing extraordinary service had led to a crucial pricing error. His ideal of employee autonomy had led to confusion in the sales force. In the end, he was forced to fire more than half of his staff, slash prices by 87%, and start over again. What did it all mean?

Merlo had one answer. "We're talking about an experiment in corporate culture failing because the business environment did not support it," he says. "The notion of corporate culture got in the way of tough-minded business decisions." He also faults the emphasis on autonomy. "I don't think we had the right to be organized the way we were. I think we should have had more discipline."

Kennedy himself soon came around to a similar view. "Look in [the statement of core beliefs] and tell me what you find about the importance of performance, about measuring performance or about the idea that people must be held accountable for their performance," he says. "That stuff should have been there. I'm not discounting the importance of corporate culture, but you have to worry about the business at the same time, or you simply won't have one. Then you obviously won't *need* a culture. Where the two come together, I think, is in the cultural norms for performance, what kind of performance is expected of people. And that's a linkage that wasn't explicit in my mind three years ago. But it is now." He adds that, if the manuscript of *Corporate Cultures* were before him today, he would include a section on performance standards, measurement systems, and accountability sanctions.

On that point, he might get an argument from his co-author, Terrence Deal, a professor at Vanderbilt University and a member of Selkirk's board of directors since its inception. Deal does not disagree about the importance of discipline and performance standards, but he questions the wisdom of trying to impose them from above. The most effective performance standards, he notes, are the ones that employees recognize and accept as the product of their own commitment, and these can merge only from the employees' experience. "One of the things that we know pretty handsomely," says Deal, "is that it's the informal performance standards that really drive a company."

In fact, Kennedy may have gotten into trouble not by doing too little, but by doing too much. Rather than letting Selkirk's culture evolve organically, he tried to impose a set of predetermined cultural values on the company, thereby retarding the growth of its own informal value system. He pursued culture as an end in itself, ignoring his own caveat, set down in his book, that "the business environment is the single greatest influence in shaping a corporate culture." Instead, he tried to shape the culture in a vacuum, without synchronizing it with the company's business goals.

In so doing, Kennedy reduced corporate culture to a formula, a collection of genetic "principles." It was a cardinal error, if not an uncommon one. "There are a lot of people," says Deal, "who take our book literally and try to design a culture much as if they're trying to design an organization chart. My experience across the board has been that, as soon as people make it into a formula, they start making mistakes." By following the "for-

mula," Kennedy wound up imposing his own set of rules on Selkirk—although not enough of them, and not the right kind, he now says. The irony is that a real corporate culture allows a company to manage itself *without* formal rules, and to manage itself better than a company that has them.

Deal makes another point. Kennedy, he observes, might be less concerned with performance today if he had not hired so many friends at the beginning. Friends are nice to have around, but it's often hard to discipline them, or subject them to a company's normal sanctions. Over the long run, Deal says, their presence at Selkirk probably undermined the development of informal performance standards.

Kennedy himself may have played a role in that, too. He estimates that, over the past year, he has spent only one day a week at Selkirk. The rest of the time he has been on the road as a consultant, using his fees to help finance the company. In all, he has sunk some $1 million of his own money into Selkirk, without which the company might not have survived. But it has come at a price. "Nobody had to pay attention to things like expenses, because there was a perception of an infinite sink of money," Kennedy says.

The danger of that perception finally came home to him last summer, when three of Selkirk's four salespeople elected to take vacations during the same month. The result was that sales for the month all but vanished. Kennedy had had enough. "I told the people here that either you sustain the company as a self-financing entity, or I will let it go under. I'm unwilling to put more money on the table."

And yet, in the end, it was hard to avoid the conclusion that a large part of Selkirk's continuing problem was Allan Kennedy himself—a thought that did not escape him. "I've got a lot to learn about running a business successfully," he says, "about doing it myself, I mean. I think I know everything about management except how to manage. I can give world-class advice on managing, but—when it comes right down to it—I take too long and fall into all the traps that I see with the managers I advise."

Whatever his shortcomings as a manger, there is one thing Kennedy can't be faulted for, and that is lack of courage. Having drawn the inevitable conclusion, he went out looking for someone who could help him do a better job of managing the company. For several months, he negotiated with the former president of a Boston-based high-tech firm, but the two of them were unable to come to terms. Instead, Kennedy has made changes at Selkirk, that he hopes will achieve the same effect. In the new structure, Merilo is taking charge of the microcomputer end of the business, while Betsy Meade—a former West Coast sales representative—has responsibility for a new minicomputer version of Correspondent, to be marketed in conjunction with Prime Computer Corp. As for Kennedy, he will concern himself with external company relations, product-development strategies, and, of course, corporate culture.

Kennedy is full of optimism these days. He points out that, despite its checkered history, Selkirk has emerged with a durable product and an installed base of about 1,000 units. In addition, the company will soon be bolstered with the proceeds from a $250,000 private placement. Meanwhile, he says, some of the company's previous problems have been dealt with, thanks to the introduction of a reliable order-fulfillment process, the decision to put sales reps on a straight commission payment schedule, and the establishment of specific sales targets for at least the next two quarters. "I think we have much more focused responsibility," he says, "and much more tangible measures of success for people in their jobs."

Overall, Kennedy looks on the past three years as a learning experience. "There are times when I think I should charge up most of the zigs and the zags to sheer rank incompetence," he admits. "But then there are other times when I look back and say, 'Nobody's that smart, and you can't do everything right.' In life, you have to be willing to try things. And if something doesn't work, you have to be willing to say, 'Well, that was a dumb idea,' and then try something else." Now, he believes, he has a chance to do just that.

In the meantime, he is in the process of writing another book. He already has a proposal circulating among publishers. In his idle moments, he occasionally amuses himself by inventing titles. One of those titles speaks volumes about where he has been: *Kicking Ass and Taking Names.*

35

Organizational Issues in the Introduction of New Technologies

RALPH KATZ AND THOMAS J. ALLEN

1. INTRODUCTION

More than ever before, organizations competing in today's world of high technology are faced with the challenges of "dualism," that is, functioning efficiently today while planning and innovating effectively for tomorrow. Not only must these organizations be concerned with the success and market penetration of their current product mix, but they must also be concerned with their long-run capability to develop and incorporate in a timely manner the most appropriate technical advancements into future product offerings. Research and development–based corporations, no matter how they are organized, must find ways to internalize both sets of concerns.

Now it would be nice if everyone in an organization agreed on how to carry out this dualism or even agreed on its relative merits. This is rarely the case, however, even though such decisions are critically important to a firm competing in markets strongly affected by changing technology (Allen, 1977; Roberts, 1974). Amidst the pressures of everyday requirements, decision makers representing different parts of the organization usually disagree on the relative wisdom of allocating resources or particular RD&E talents among the span of technical activities that might be of benefit to today's versus tomorrow's organization. Moreover, there are essentially no well-defined principles within management theory on how to structure organizations to accommodate these two sets of con-

flicting challenges. Classical management theory with its focus on scientific principles deals only with the efficient production and utilization of today's goods and services. The principles of high task specialization, unity of command and direction, high division of labor, and the equality of authority and responsibility all deal with the problems of structuring work and information flows in routine, predictable ways to facilitate production and control through formal lines of authority and job standardization. What is missing is some comparable theory that would also explain how to organize innovative activities within this operating environment such that creative, developmental efforts will not only take place but will also become more accepted and unbiasedly reviewed, especially as these new and different ideas begin to "disrupt" the smooth functioning organization. More specifically, how can one structure an organization to promote the introduction of new technologies and, in general, enhance its longer-term innovation process, yet at the same time, satisfy the plethora of technical demands and accomplishments needed to support and improve the efficiency and competitiveness of today's producing organization?

Implicit in this discussion, then, is the need for managers to learn how to build parallel structures and activities that would not only permit these two opposing forces to coexist but would also balance them in some integrative, meaningful way. Within the RD&E environment, the operating organization can best be described as an "output-ori-

Reprinted with permission of Plenum Press, "Organizational Issues in the Introduction of New Technologies" in *The Management of Productivity and Technology in Manufacturing*, P. R. Kleindorfer (ed.), © 1985, pp. 275–300.

Ralph Katz is Professor of Management at Northeastern University's College of Business and Research Associate at M.I.T.'s Sloan School of Management. **Tom Allen** is Senior Associate Dean and Professor of Management at M.I.T.'s Sloan School of Management.

ented" or "downstream" set of forces directed towards the technical support of the organization's current products and towards getting new products out of development and into manufacturing or into the marketplace. Typically, such pressures are controlled through formal structures and through formal job assignments to project managers who are then held accountable for the successful completion of product outputs within established schedules and budget constraints.

At the same time, there must be an "upstream" set of forces that are less concerned with the specific architectures and functionalities of today's products but are more concerned with the various core technologies that might underlie the industry or business environment not only today but also tomorrow. They are, essentially, responsible for the technical health and excellence of the corporation, keeping the company up-to-date and technically competitive in their future business areas.

In every technology-based organization, as discussed by Katz and Allen (1985), the forces that represent this dualism compete with one another for recognition and resources. The conflicts produced by this competition are not necessarily harmful; in fact, they can be very beneficial to the organization in sorting out project priorities and the particular technologies that need to be monitored and pursued, provided there are mechanisms in place to both support and balance these two forces.

If the product-output or downstream set of forces becomes dominant, then there is the likelihood that sacrifices in using the latest technical advancements may be made in order to meet budget, schedule, and immediate market demands. Given these pressures, there are strong tendencies to strip the organization of its research activities and to deemphasize longer-term, forward-looking technological efforts and investigations in order to meet current short-term goals which could, thereby, mortgage future technical capabilities. Under these conditions, requirements for the next generation of new product developments begin to exceed the organization's in-house expertise, and product potentials are then oversold beyond the organization's technical capability.

At the other extreme, if the research or upstream technology component of the organization is allowed to dominate development work within R&D, then the danger is that products may include not only more sophisticated but also perhaps less proven, more risky, or even less marketable technologies. This desire to be technologically aggressive—to develop and use the most attractive, most advanced technology—must be countered by forces that are more sensitive to the operational environments and more concerned with moving research efforts into some final physical reality. Technology is not an autonomous system that determines its own priorities and sets its own standards of performance. To the contrary, market, social, and economic considerations eventually determine priorities as well as the dimensions and levels of performance necessary for successful commercial application (Utterback, 1974).

To balance this dualism—to be able to introduce the new technologies needed for tomorrow's products while functioning efficiently under today's current technological base, is a very difficult task. Generally speaking, the more the organization tries to operate only through formal mechanisms of organizational procedures, structures, and controls, the more the organization will move towards a functioning organization that drives out its ability to experiment and work with new technological concepts and ideas. More informal organizational designs and processes are therefore needed to influence and support true innovative activity, countering the organization's natural movement towards more efficient production and bureaucratic control. These informal mechanisms are also needed to compensate for the many limitations inherent within formal organizational structures and formal task definitions. In the rest of this paper, we will describe three general areas of informal activity that need to take place within an RD&E environment (in parallel with the formal, functioning organization) in order to enhance the innovation process for the more timely introduction of new technologies into the corporation's product portfolio. The general proposition is that these areas of informal activity need to be managed within the

RD&E setting, strengthening and protecting them from the pressures of the "productive" organization in order to increase the organization's willingness and ability to deal with the many advancements that come along, especially with respect to new areas of technology.

2. PROBLEM SOLVING, COMMUNICATIONS, AND THE MOBILITY OF PEOPLE

To keep informed about relevant developments outside the organization as well as new requirements within the organization, R&D professionals must collect and process information from a large variety of outside sources. Project members rarely have all the requisite knowledge and expertise to complete successfully all of the tasks involved in new technical innovations; information and assistance must be drawn from many sources beyond the project both within and outside the organization. Furthermore, if one assumes that the world of technology outside the organization is larger than the world of technology inside the organization, then one should also expect a great deal of emphasis within R&D on keeping in touch with the many advancements in this larger external world. Allen's (1977) 20 years of research work on technical communications and information flows clearly demonstrates just how important this outside contact can be in generating many of the critical ideas and inputs for more successful research and development activity.

At the same time, the research findings of many studies, including Katz and Tushman (1981), Allen (1977), and Pelz and Andrews (1966), have consistently shown that the bulk of these critical outside contracts comes from face-to-face interactions among individuals. Interpersonal communications rather than the formal technical reports, publications, or other written documentation are the primary means by which engineering professionals collect and transfer important new ideas and information into their organizations and project groups. In his study of engineering project teams, for ex-

ample, Allen (1977) carefully demonstrated that only 11% of the sources of new ideas and information could be attributed to written media; the rest occurred through interpersonal communications. Many of these "creative" exchanges, moreover, were of a more spontaneous nature in that thy arose not so much out of formal project requirements and interdependencies but out of factors relating to past project experiences and working relationships, the geographical layouts of office locations and laboratory facilities, attendances at special organization events and social functions, chance conversations with external professionals and vendors at conferences and trade shows, and so on. Anything that can be done to stimulate informal contacts among the many parts of the organization and between the organization's R&D professionals and their outside technology and customer environments is likely to be helpful in terms of both technology development and technology transfer.

Since communication processes play such an important role in fostering the creative work activities of R&D members, it would be nice if each individual or project team were naturally willing or always motivated to expose themselves to fresh ideas and new points of view. Unfortunately, this is usually not the case as engineering individuals continue to work in a particular project area or in a given area of technology. In fact, one of the more important assumptions underlying human behavior within organizations is that people are strongly motivated to reduce uncertainty (Katz, 1982). As part of this process, individuals, groups, and even organizations strive to structure their work environments to reduce the amount of stress they must face by directing their activities and interactions toward a more predictable level of certainty and clarity. Over time, then, engineers and scientists are not only functioning to reduce technical uncertainty, they are also functioning to reduce their "personal and situational" uncertainty within the organization (Katz, 1980). In the process of gaining increasing control over their task activities and work demands, three broad areas of biases and behavioral responses begin to emerge. And the more these trends are allowed to take place and become reinforced, the more difficult it will be for the organization to consider seriously the potential, long-term advantages of the many new and different technologies that are slowly being developed and worked on by the larger outside R&D community.

2.1 Problem-Solving Processes

As R&D professionals work together in a given area for a long period of time and become increasingly familiar with their work surroundings, they become less receptive toward any change or innovation that threatens to disrupt significantly their comfortable and predictable work patterns of behavior. In the process of reducing more and more uncertainty, these individuals are likely to develop routine responses for dealing with their frequently encountered tasks in order to ensure predictability, coordination, and economical information processing. As a result, there develops over time increasing rigidity in their problem-solving activities—a kind of functional stability that reduces their capacity for flexibility and openness to change. Behavioral responses and technical decisions are made in fixed, normal patterns; and consequently, new or changing situations that may require technical strategies that do not fit prior problem-solving modes are either ignored or forced into these established molds. R&D professionals interacting over a long period, therefore, develop work patterns that are secure and comfortable, patterns in which routine and precedent play a relatively large part. They come, essentially, to rely more and more on their customary ways of doing things to complete project requirements. In their studies of problem-solving strategies, for example, Allen and Marquis (1963) show that within R&D there can be a very strong bias for choosing those technical strategies and approaches that have worked in the past and with which people have gained common experience, familiarity, and confidence; all of which inhibit the entry of competing tactics involving new technologies, new ideas, or new competencies.

What also seems to be true is that as engineers continue to work in their well-established areas of technology and develop particular problem-solving procedures, they become increasingly committed to these existing methods. Commitment is a function of time, and the longer individuals are asked to work on and extend the capabilities of certain technical approaches, the greater their commitment becomes toward these approaches. Furthermore, in accumulating experience and knowledge in these technical areas, R&D has often had to make clear presentations, showing progress and justifying the allocation of important organizational resources. As part of these review processes, alternative or competing ideas and approaches were probably considered and discarded, and with such public refutation, commitments to the selected courses of action become even stronger. Individuals become known for working and building capability in certain technical areas, both their personal and organizational identities become deeply ensconced in these efforts, and as a result, they may become overly preoccupied with the survival of their particular technical approaches, protecting them against new technical alternatives or negative evaluations. All of the studies that have retrospectively examined the impact of major new technologies on existing organizational decisions and commitments arrive at the same general conclusion: those working on and committed to the old, invaded technology fail to support the radical new technology; instead, they fight back vigorously to defend and improve the old technology (e.g., Cooper and Schendel, 1976; Schon, 1963). And yet, it is often these same experienced technologists who are primarily asked to evaluate the potential effects of these emerging new technologies on the future of the organization's businesses. It is no wonder, therefore, that in the majority of cases studied, the first commercial introduction of a radical new technology has come from outside the industry's traditional competitors.

2.2 Communication and Information Processing

One of the consequences of increased behavioral and technical stability is that R&D groups also become increasingly isolated from outside sources of relevant information and important new ideas. As engineers become more attached to their current work habits and areas of technical expertise, the extent to which they are willing or even feel they need to expose themselves to new ideas, approaches, or technologies becomes progressively less and less. Instead of being vigilant in seeking information from the outside world of technology or from the market place, they become increasingly complacent about external events and new technological developments. After studying the actual communication behaviors of some 350 engineering professionals in a major R&D facility, Katz and Allen (1982) found that as members of project teams worked together, gained experience with one another, and developed more stable role assignments and areas of individual contribution, the groups also communicated less frequently with key sources of outside information. Research groups, for example, failed to pay sufficient attention to events and information in their external R&D community while product development and technical support groups had reduced levels of communication with their internal engineering colleagues and with their downstream client groups from marketing and manufacturing. Such low levels of outside interaction also result in stronger group boundaries, creating tougher barriers to effective communication and more difficult information flows not only among R&D groups but also to other organizational divisions and to other areas outside the organization.

Another set of forces that affects the amount and variety of outside contact that R&D employees may have is the tendency for individuals to want to communicate only with those who are most like themselves, who are most likely to agree with them, or whose ideas and viewpoints are most likely to be in accord with their own interests and established perspectives. Over time, R&D project members learn to interact selectively to avoid messages and information that might be in conflict with their current dispositions toward particular technologies or technical approaches, thereby restricting their overall exposure to outside views and allowing themselves to bias the interpretation of their limited outside data to terms more favorable to their existing attitudes and beliefs. Thus, the organization ends up getting its critical and evaluative information and feedback not from those most likely to challenge or stretch their thinking but from those with whom they have developed comfortable and secure relationships, i.e., friends, peers, long-term suppliers and customers, etc. And it is precisely these latter kinds of relationships that are least likely to provide the inputs and thinking necessary to stimulate the organization's movement into new technical areas.

2.3 Cognitive Processes

One of the dilemmas of building in-house capability in particular areas of technology is that engineers responsible for the success of these technical areas become less willing to accept or seek the advice and ideas of other outside experts. Over time, these engineers may even begin to believe that they possess a monopoly on knowledge in their specialized areas of technology, seriously discounting the possibility that outsiders might be producing important new ideas or advances that might be of use to them. And if this kind of outlook becomes mutually reinforced within a given R&D area or project group, then these individuals often end up relying primarily on their own technical experiences and know-how, and consequently, are more apt to dismiss the critical importance of outside contacts and pay less attention to the many technical advances and achievements in the larger external world. It is precisely this attitude, coupled with the communication and problem-solving trends previously described, that helps explain why many of the most successful firms in a very new area of technology had never participated in the old or substituted area of technology.

This rather myopic outlook within R&D is also encouraged as technologists become increasingly specialized, that is, moving from broadly defined capabilities and solution approaches to more narrowly defined interests and specialties. Pelz and Andrews (1966) argue from their study of scientists and engineers that with increasing group stability, project member preferences for probing deeper and deeper into a particular technological area becomes greater and greater while their preferences for maintaining technical breadth and flexibility gradually decrease. Without new challenges and opportunities, the diversity of skills and of ideas generated are likely to become progressively more narrow. They are, essentially, learning more and more about less and less. And as engineers welcome information from fewer sources and are exposed to fewer alternative points of view, the more constricted their cognitive abilities become, resulting in a more restricted perspective of their situation and a more limited set of technological responses from which to cope. One of the many signs of obsolescence occurs when engineers retreat to their areas of specialization as they feel insecure addressing technologies and problems outside their direct fields of expertise and experience. They simply feel more comfortable and creative when they can see their organizational contributions in terms of their past performance standards rather than on the basis of future needs and requirements.

Finally, there is not only a strong tendency for technologists to communicate with those who are most like themselves, but it is just as likely that continued interaction among members of an R&D project team will lead to greater homogeneity in knowledge and problem-solving behaviors and perceptions. The well-known proverb "birds of a feather flock together" makes a great deal of sense, but it is just as accurate to say that "the longer birds flock together, the more of a feature they become." One can argue, therefore, that as R&D project members work together over a long period, they will reinforce their common views and commitments to their current technologies and problem-solving approaches. The group not only tries to hire or recruit new members like themselves, thereby exacerbating the trend towards greater homogeneity and consensus and less diversity. Such shared values and perceptions, created through group interactions, act as powerful constraints on individual attitudes and behaviors and provide group members with a strong sense of identity and a great deal of assurance and confidence in their traditional activities. At the same time, however, these shared systems of meaning and beliefs restrict individual creativity into new areas and isolate the group even further from important outside contacts and tech-

nical developments, thereby causing the old technologies to become even more deeply entrenched.

2.4 Mobility of People and the "Not Invented Here" Syndrome

What is implied by all of this discussion is that R&D managers need to learn to observe the strong biases that can naturally develop in the way engineers select and interpret information, in their willingness to innovate or implement radically new technological approaches, or in their cognitive abilities to generate or work with new technical options so that appropriate actions can be undertaken to encourage R&D to become more receptive and responsive to new ideas and emerging technological opportunities. The trends described here are observable; one can determine the extent to which project groups are communicating and interacting effectively with outside information sources, whether project groups are exposing themselves to new ideas and more critical kinds of reviews, or whether a project group is becoming too narrow and homogeneous through its hiring practices.

In the best-selling book, *In Search of Excellence,* organizations are encouraged by Peters and Waterman to practice the Hewlett Packard philosophy of MBWA (Management by Wandering Around). But managers have to know what to look for as they wander around. In particular, technical managers can try to detect the degree to which these different trends are materializing, for the way engineering groups come to view their work environments will be very critical to the organization's ability to introduce and work with new technologies. The more the perceptual outlook of an R&D area can be characterized by the problem-solving, informational, and cognitive trends previously described, the more likely it has internalized what has become known in the R&D community as the "Not Invented Here" (NIH) or the "Nothing New Here" (NNH) syndrome. According to this syndrome, project members are more likely to see only the virtue and superiority of their own ideas and technical activities while dismissing the potential contributions and benefits of new technologies and competitive ideas and accomplishments as inferior and weak.

It is also argued here that the most effective way to prevent R&D groups from developing behaviors and attitudes that coincide with this NIH syndrome is through the judicious movement of engineering personnel among project groups and organizational areas, keeping teams energized and destabilized. Based on the findings of Katz and Allen (1982), Smith (1970), and several other studies, new group members not only have a relative advantage in generating fresh ideas and approaches, but through their active participation, project veterans might consider more carefully ideas and technological alternatives they might otherwise have ignored. In short, project newcomers represent a novelty-enhancing condition, challenging and improving the scope of existing methods and accumulated knowledge.

The mobility of people within the organization is a most fruitful approach for keeping ideas fresh, building insights, and maintaining innovative flexibility. Japanese organizations, for example, assume that the best course of development for capable individuals is lateral rotation across major functional areas of the firm before upward advancement takes place. In a Japanese company, an engineer progressing well may move from R&D into marketing, then into manufacturing, and perhaps back into R&D at a higher level. This is seldom the kind of career track that American firms find appropriate; yet, we all know for sure the kinds of problems one is avoiding as well as the benefits that would accrue over the long run through the greater use of rotation programs even if rotation were limited to between research and development and engineering groups.

In an additional attempt to foster new thinking and to build stronger intraorganizational bridges and communication networks, some companies hold special meetings in which organizational areas report on what they have been doing and on the kind of capability they have. The 3M Corporation, for example, holds a proprietary company fair at which there are presentations of technical papers, exhibits, and demonstrations of projects and prototypes. The fair enables the rest of the people in the company to begin to learn about what is taking place in other divisions or laboratories. The Monsanto Company uses what it calls the Monsanto technical community to bring together technical people, trained in similar disciplines but employed in different divisions of the firm, and it convenes these people in different workshops and groups, encouraging them to exchange ideas and information. Many other companies, such as Procter and Gamble, Corning, and Motorola, have similar kinds of internal forums. These kinds of programs can be very helpful in fostering communication and in stimulating the identification of new technical capabilities as well as the identification of new market and technical needs throughout the firm.

3. ORGANIZATIONAL STRUCTURES

Unlike productivity, which is the efficient application of current solutions, innovation usually connotes the first utilization of a new or improved product, process, or practice. Innovation, as a result, requires both the generation or recognition of a new idea followed by the implementation or exploitation of that idea into a new or better solution. So far, we have discussed organizational processes to the extent that they primarily affect the idea-generation phase of the innovation process. It is just as important, of course, for an organization to plan for the idea-exploitation phase, where exploitation includes the appraisal, focusing, and transferring of research ideas and results for their eventual utilization and application. To say that one is managing or organizing for the introduction of new technologies within the innovation process implies that one is "pushing" the development and movement of new technical ideas and capabilities downstream through the organization from research to development to engineering and even into manufacturing and perhaps some phase of customer distribution.

Innovation, then, is a dynamic process involving the movement and transfer of technologies across internal organizational boundaries. Formal organizational design, on the other hand, is a static concept, describing how to organize collections of activities within well-defined units and reporting relationships, e.g., research, advanced development, product development, engineering, quality assurance, etc. Formal organizational structures tell us what to manage and with whom to interact within certain areas of interdependent activity; they tell us little about how to move information, ideas, and in particular technologies across different organizational areas, divisions, or formal lines of authority. In fact, formal structures tend to separate and differentiate the various organizational groupings, making the movement of ideas and technologies particularly difficult across these groupings, especially if there are no compensating integrating mechanisms in place. And it is in the movement of new technological concepts from research to advanced development to successful product development that we are particularly interested.

The effective organization, therefore, needs to cause the results of R&D to be appropriately transferred. Technically successful R&D, especially if it embraces new radical technologies, is very likely to pose major problems of linkages with the rest of the firm, particularly product development, engineering, manufacturing, marketing, sales, field service, and so on. A company can do a terrific job of R&D and a terrible job of managing the innovating process overall simply because the results of R&D have never been fully exploited and successfully moved downstream. Witness, for example, the problems of Xerox, where the R&D labs have generated and surfaced many major new advances and approaches only to discover that the company has failed to fully exploit and capture benefit from many of them. Other corporations, on the other hand, have benefited extremely well from Xerox's research activities—so many in fact that some have quipped that Xerox's research facilities should be declared a national resource instead of a resource for Xerox (see *Fortune* magazine, September, 1983).

Over the past decade or so, Roberts (1979) has been studying the problems of moving R&D results through the organization. From carrying out these studies, he has found that most large organizations have been dissatisfied with the degree of transfer of their own R&D results and feel very uncom-

fortable about how little of their good technical outcomes ever reach the marketplace and generate profitable pay-back for the firm. The R&D labs he studied seemed to have broad enough charters to do almost anything they chose, but ended up being quite narrow as to what they in fact implemented within their own organizations. To enhance the transfer of R&D results across the barriers of organizational structures, Roberts (1979) advocates the building of bridges; and in particular, he recommends three different groups of bridges: procedural, human, and organizational.

The procedural approaches, according to Roberts, try to tie together both the R&D unit and the appropriate receiving units by joint efforts. In the case of new technological concepts, the most immediate receiving unit is typically some advanced development group or some divisional product development organization that receives the output from a centralized research and development lab. The kinds of procedural bridges that have been suggested include joint planning of R&D programs and joint staffing of projects, especially immediately before and after transfer, for those are the most critical phases of the process in which key know-how and information can easily slip through the cracks.

Joint appraisal of results by research, development, and any other appropriate downstream unit or customer is also employed in some labs. From the viewpoint of generating useful information, the best time to carry out joint appraisal of results is when failure has occurred, for there is usually something objective to look at from which one might be able to learn and improve. At the same time, however, this exercise must be done carefully and sensitively to prevent this opportunity from becoming a situation of mutual fingerpointing, showing why the other group is really at fault and how those people caused the failure. In these joint appraisals, the attributions of failure should be centered around substantive issues that can be dealt with behaviorally, structurally, or procedurally; otherwise, intergroup conflicts and differences will be strengthened, which is likely to cause even greater difficulty in future technological handoffs.

Joint appraisal of successes should also not be overlooked, for they can be very helpful in generating the goodwill and trust necessary to strengthen organizational linkages, especially after a history of prior difficulty or failure.

The establishment of human bridges also helps to cope with transfer issues. Interpersonal alliances and informal contacts inevitably turn out to be the basis of integration and intraorganizational cooperation that really matter. The human approaches focus on the relationships that convey information between people, that convey the shift of responsibility from one person to another, and that convey enthusiasm for the project. Roberts argues strongly, in fact, that the building of human bridges is by far the best way to transfer this vital enthusiasm and commitment.

Technology moves through people, and the most effective of these human bridges is the actual movement of people in two directions. Upstream movement of development engineers to join the R&D effort well in advance of the intended transfer is a very important step. This transfers information from the product development areas into the research process, creates an advocate to bring the research results downstream, and builds interpersonal ties for the later assistance that will inevitably be needed as the technology encounters problems. Downstream movement of research individuals will also be helpful in providing the technical expertise necessary for development to build up its own understanding and capability.

In addition to the specific movement of people, human bridges are also built through the interpersonal communication systems that have developed over time through the history of working relationships, rotation programs, task force participation, and other organizational events and activities. Another important device to be considered is the joint problem-solving meeting in which development individuals are asked to sit down with research colleagues to let them explain their difficulties and initial problem-solving thinking. Such meetings are not only helpful in dealing with specific project problems, but will also be useful in building stronger human bridges between the related R&D areas and may even be helpful in solving additional related problems that were not initially put forth.

The final area for considering the movement of R&D results towards development and eventual commercialization consists of organizational changes and organizational bridges. According to Roberts, these are the toughest kinds to create and implement effectively in an organization. It is far easier to alter procedures or to try to build human bridges across groups than it is to change organizational arrangements and relationships. Nevertheless, several different structural approaches can be effective under different organizational conditions. Some organizations have developed specialized transfer groups, created solely for the purpose of transferring important technical advances or important new processes. Under this approach, the transfer group is like the licensor of a technology who is not just sending equipment and documentation but who is also responsible for training others to work with the technology, for installing the equipment, etc. If used, the specialized transfer group should consist of at least a few of the key technical players. Senior management should not be allowed to argue that they cannot spare the superstars of the research organization to support development or manufacturing engineering.

Another organizational approach is to employ integrators or integrating groups that are given responsibility for straddling the various parts of the RD&E organization. This is a very uncomfortable and a very difficult job to assume because it is extremely difficult to ask someone to take care of an integrating function across two separate suborganizations when he or she does not have responsibility for either the sending or the receiving organization. To perform this function successfully requires someone who can cope with the political sensitivies of multiple groups and who has built substantial informal influence and credibility within the organization.

Finally, a variety of corporate venture strategies can be considered by companies that are concerned with developing new technical approaches, new product lines, or want a stronger emphasis on technical entrepreneurship. Roberts (1980) suggests a large variety of possible venture strategies, ranging from the high corporate involvement of internal venturing to low corporate involvement through venture capital investments in outside firms for the purpose of gaining windows on technology and new market opportunities. Additional venture strategies are also described by Roberts, including the coupling of R&D efforts from both the large corporation and the small independent firm. In general, there is no single best way to organize for the effective introduction of new technologies; but the more informal mechanisms one puts in place to foster both the idea generation and the idea exploitation phases, the more one is likely to be successful at managing the innovation process.

4. ORGANIZATIONAL CONTROLS

All of these organizational attempts at stimulating new technological innovation will fall flat, of course, if organizational controls are not consistent with the innovation process. In looking at many case histories of successful versus unsuccessful innovations based on radical new technologies. Cohen *et al.* (1979) and several other studies have identified a number of factors as being critically important for trying to influence the generation and successful movement of new technologies through the organization.

4.1 Technical Understanding

One of the most important issues in working with new technologies is that the research function must fully understand the main technical issues of the technology before passing it on. Although this point seems obvious, it is often overlooked. The research function must focus not only on the benefit of the new technology in and of itself; it must also deal with the technology's limitations relative to conventional technologies and to other new technological approaches. In the early days of transistors, for example, one large electronics company spent a great deal of money and many years of research effort on understanding the materials and process-

ing problems of germanium for point contacts and junction transistors. Unfortunately, the research organization failed to compare the use of germanium to silicon, whose own development was continuing to make a great deal of progress. Only after many years did the organization finally realize the limitations in the advantages of germanium over silicon and these limitations had less to do with the devices themselves and more to do with device implementation in packaging and circuitry.

It is also important, therefore, to make sure that research understands where the new technology might fit in with respect to the product line or at least what requirements must be met to reach this fit. Research should not waste its time solving problems that do not exist or producing technologies that cannot be sold. Whirlpool, for example, invested substantial research resources in making appliance motors more energy efficient long before the oil crisis, but of course, the marketplace was not yet interested in these kinds of advances. Similarly, GE conducted a great deal of research in environmental concerns in the 1940s but at that time there was very little interest in improving the ecology of our environment. As a last example, DuPont developed Corfam as a synthetic substitute for leather, but unfortunately for DuPont, the public was perfectly satisfied with leather and saw no need for the manmade substitute.

Full understanding also means that research must begin to examine the means of manufacturing, the availability of key materials and technical talents, the ease of use, and so on. Air Products and Chemicals, for example, spent millions of dollars to develop a fluorination process so that textile manufacturers could make fabrics, especially polyesters, more resistant to oil and grease. Unfortunately, textile manufacturers did not want fluorine—a poisonous and corrosive gas—anywhere near their plants and refused to buy the system. Research should also be able to make, at the very least, preliminary cost estimates. One of the most basic elements of a technology is its cost. In fact, a study of technology programs at GE concluded that most of the barriers to the introduction of new technologies (even hardware and software) were cost constraints and not technical feasibility; it was getting the technology to perform capably at a marketable cost.

To help ensure these kinds of requirements, some labs have begun to hire full-time marketing representatives and cost estimators as a regular part of the R&D organization. Previously, corporate R&D organizations were completely dependent on product line divisions for both marketing and sales effort and for business and economic analysis as well. These dependencies, especially the latter, were harmful in getting research projects justified, supported, and accepted by the divisions who were supposed to be the eventual customer of the research results.

4.2 Technical Feasibility

All too often, a technology is transferred before there has been sufficient time within research to demonstrate true feasibility. Such pressures can come from the downstream organization or they can arise from the "unbridled enthusiasm" of the researchers themselves. In either case, it would be more beneficial to discuss what constitutes feasibility and for research to strive to achieve it.

Most new technical concepts do not succeed simply because they must run a gauntlet of barriers as they enter the main part of the functioning organization. In many cases, the new technology is embedded within a system of established technologies. The question then is whether the new technology will offer a sufficient competitive advantage to warrant its incorporation into this interdependent system, perhaps changing drastically the tooling and the overall manufacturing process. Experienced technologists will typically warn you that what you do not yet know about the workings of a new technical advance will probably come back to haunt you. What often appears to be a simple technical issue turns out to be more complicated than we realize. GE discovered a fiber, for example, that looked and behaved more like wool than any synthetic yet known. Unfortunately, the fiber disintegrates in today's cleaning solvents, and the problem has yet to be solved.

4.3 Research and Development Overlap

As previously discussed, it is very helpful to the movement of a new technology if development, or some other appropriate receiving organization, also has a group of technical people who have been getting up to speed on the technology before the actual transfer, e.g., the presence of "ad tech" groups. Such advanced technical activities within development can greatly aid the movement of technology and the smoothing of conflicts.

In a similar fashion, it is also important for research to maintain some activity to support and defend the new technology or to find new ways to extend the technology. Research must not be allowed to feel that it is "finished" at the time of transfer, for if this feeling is present, their willingness and enthusiasm to support the technology will be minimal. Most new technologies are relatively crude at first. Ball-point pens, for example, blotted, skipped, stopped writing all together, and even leaked in consumers' pockets when they first appeared on the market. The first transistors were expensive and had sharply limited frequencies, power capabilities, and temperature tolerances. Such experiences are very typical of new technologies, especially radical new technologies. And the more prepared research is to help "push" the technology, the less likely it will be for the new technology to be dismissed prematurely as a "fad" or as a technology with very limited application.

4.4 Growth Potential

As a related point, all too often a research program sells itself short by being too narrow and not showing a clear path towards technical growth and growth in product applicability. In almost every instance, when the new technology appears on the scene, the old technology is forced to "stretch" itself, often with major advances being achieved in the threatened technology. Under these circumstances, the new technology is in the position of trying to chase or catch a "changing target." Moreover, this new potential in the old technology often holds back the entry of the new technology. Advances in flashbulbs, for example, held off the widespread use of electronic flash for quite some time, while advances in magnetic tape audio and video recording have prevented the emergence of thermoplastic recording. In their well-known study of strategic responses to technological threats, Cooper and Schendel (1976) indicate that in the majority of cases, sales of the old technology did not decline after the introduction of a new technology. To the contrary, sales of the old technology expanded even further. It is for these reasons that the diffusion and substitution of a radical new technology must be viewed as a long-term process and research and development must carefully prepare to argue and demonstrate why the pressured organization should be patient during this time period.

4.5 Organizational Slack and Sponsorship

When an organization pushes too hard for productivity within the RD&E environment, trying to measure and control all aspects of the innovation process, there is little room or slack for experimenting or pursuing novel ideas and concepts. The environment is simply too tightly run and the climate becomes unfavorable for very new or long-term innovation. Engineers and scientists become anxious, restrict the depth of exploration along new paths, and center their attention upon issues closely related to the company's immediate output. Creative innovation, on the other hand, is harder to measure and takes a long period to assess. It requires speculative investments on the part of the firm that wants to nurture the ideas and the experimenting activities that will eventually be worth it.

Given all of the resistance and testing that a new technological idea will eventually encounter from the functioning organization and from operational review committees, strong corporate sponsorship is needed to protect new technological innovations. And the more radical the new technology, the stronger the corporate sponsorship has to be. One of the observations we have made from working and consulting with many technology companies is that most (and in some high technology companies, all) radical new technologies

have had to have well-identified sponsorship at the corporate level in order to succeed.

Another important finding from retrospective studies of radical innovation is that new technologies are not really new! By this, we mean that technological changes is a relatively continuous and incremental process which casts shadows far ahead. According to Utterback and Brown (1972), the information incorporated in successful new innovations has been around for roughly 5–30 years prior to its use. They further argue that there are many multiple signals within the external environment that can be used to predict the direction and impact of future technological changes and development. Von Hippel (1983), for example, argues that one can often anticipate future innovations by identifying what he calls "lead users," that is, users whose needs today foreshadow the needs of the general marketplace tomorrow. Nevertheless, even if particular areas of new technology were identified as extremely important, without strong sponsorship it is unlikely that sufficient resources would be diverted to it, that engineers would be isolated from other pressures or tasks to work on it, or that they would be given sufficient uninterrupted time to complete it. One of the reasons why so many new technologies are introduced through the emergence or spin-offs of new firms is that in these situations, the new technology does not encounter resistance from or have to fight against already existing businesses and entrenched technical approaches.

Another benefit of strong sponsorship is that it helps protect the individual risk taker who is willing to take on the entrepreneurial burden of moving the new technology through the organization. No matter how beneficial the new technology appears to be, someone must be willing to sell the effort and make it happen. Schon's (1963) analysis of successful radical innovation is quite clear. At the outset, the new technological concept encounters sharp resistance, which is usually overcome through vigorous promotions by one emerging champion. What is important to recognize here is that these champions are typically self-selected; it is extremely difficult to appoint someone to withstand all of the pressures, hassles, and risks associated with being an idea champion and then to expect him or her to do it excitedly for a long period.

Finally, we also know from research studies that the ultimate use of a new technology is often not known or may change dramatically as the technology becomes further developed. The new technology, moreover, often invades traditional industry by capturing a series of submarkets, many of which are insulated from competition for some extended period. The earliest application of the transistor, for example, was in hearing aids, but its use was not immediately transferred to the organization's defense divisions. Because of these more limited niche markets (and consequently, relatively low sales volume), R&D often concludes that it does not have to work closely with marketing; nor does it want to subject its technological concept to the typical market screens of revenue and volume. Such a conclusion, however, does not help to build the strong harmonious relationship between marketing and R&D that has been shown to be so important for successful commercialization of new innovations (e.g., Souder, 1978). The key to success in these kinds of situations may be to find a pioneering application where the advantages of the new capability are so high that it is worth the risks. This would require the coupling of technical perspective with creative marketing development to identify such pioneering applications. On this basis, early involvement of marketing could be very helpful in providing inputs and market perspective (but not market screens) to the new technological effort.

4.6 Organizational Rewards

Ultimately, we all know that those activities which are measured or get rewarded are those which get done. If the managerial and organizational recommendations and suggestions discussed in this chapter are to be effectively implemented, then the reward systems must be consistent and commensurate with the hoped-for behaviors. One of the most important of these is that research engineers and scientists must come to see that part of their reward system is not just the generation of publi-

cations of new technological concepts and advances, but that part of their responsibilities is also the successful transfer of their work. A few high-technology companies we know have been making such reward systems explicit within their corporate labs, and although it has taken some time to take hold, it has been quite effective in moving technology through the development cycle. It has also resulted in research seeking more joint sponsorship of its activities, especially with the development divisions—all of which has helped to strengthen the communications and bridging mechanisms within the corporation.

Finally, in most areas of day-to-day functioning, productivity rather than creativity is and should be the principal objective. Even where innovation and creativity are truly desired and encouraged, activities that are potentially more creative may be subordinated to those activities of higher organizational priority or more closely tied to identified organizational needs. Nevertheless, organizations exhibit simultaneous demands for routinization and for innovation. And it is in the balance of these countervailing pressures that one determines the organization's true climate for managing and encouraging the introduction of new technological opportunities.

REFERENCES

Allen, T. J., and Marquis, D. G. (1983). Positive and negative biasing sets. The effect of prior experience on research performance, *IEEE Trans Eng. Manag.* 11, 158–162.

Allen, T. J. (1977). *Managing the Flow of Technology,* MIT Press, Cambridge, Massachusetts.

Cooper, A. C., and Schendel, D. (1976). Strategic responses to technological threats, *Bus. Hor.* February, 61–69.

Cohen, H., Keller, S., and Streeter, D. (1979). The transfer of technology from research to development, *Res. Manag.* May, 11–17.

Katz, R. (1980). Time and work: Toward an integrative perspective, *Res. in Organ. Behav.* 2, 81–127.

Katz, R. (1982). The effects of group longevity on project communication and performance, *Admin. Sci. Q.* 27, 81–104.

Katz, R., and Allen, T. J. (1982). Investigating the not

invented here (NIH) syndrome, *Res. Dev. Manag.* 12, 7–19.

Katz, R., and Allen, T. J. (1985). Project performance and the locus of influence in the R&D matrix, *Acad. Manag. J.* 26, 67–87.

Katz, R., and Tushman, M. (1981). An investigation into the managerial role and career paths of gatekeepers and project supervisors in a major R&D facility, *Res. Dev. Manage.* 11, 103–110.

Pelz, D. C. and Andrews, F. M. (1966). *Scientists in Organizations,* Wiley, New York.

Roberts, E. B. (1974). A simple model of R&D project dynamics, *Rev. Dev. Manage.* 5, 1–15.

Roberts, E. B. (1979). Stimulating technological innovations: Organizational approaches, *Res. Manage.* 22, 26–30.

Roberts, E. B. (1980). New ventures for corporate growth, *Harv. Bus. Rev.* July–August, 58, 134–142.

Schon, D. D. (1963). Champions for radical new inventions, *Harv. Bus. Rev.* 41, 76–84.

Souder, W. E. (1976). Effectiveness of product development methods, *Ind. Market. Manage.* 7, 299–307.

Utterback, J. M. (1974). Innovation in industry and the diffusion of technology, *Science* 183, 620–626.

Utterback, J. M., and Brown, J. W. (1972). Monitoring for technological opportunities, *Bus. Hor.* 15, 5–15.

von Hippel, E. (1983). *Novel Product Concept from Lead Users: Segmenting users by Experience,* Massachusetts Institute of Technology Working Paper No. 1476–83.

36

Managing Improvement in Process Technology Through Episodic Windows of Opportunity

MARCIE TYRE AND WANDA ORLIKOWSKI

To sustain their competitive positions, companies must not only develop new technologies, but they must also apply and then adapt advanced technologies into their organizational and operating systems. Yet little is known about how organizations actually go about modifying new process technologies, or how they adapt their own practices in response to technological changes. By technological "adaptation" or modification, we refer to the many adjustments and changes following the installation and application of a new technology, including not only the physical aspects of the technology but also the users' procedures, knowledge, or relationships. The actual use of a new technology in a real functioning arena typically reveals problems and contingencies that were not previously apparent or expected (Leonard-Barton, 1988; Dutton and Thomas, 1985). And these unanticipated problems, in turn, require adaptation of the technologies already in use.

Most of the research on this topic has assumed that users and developers learn about and modify new technologies gradually. Thus, the familiar learning curve shows a regular accretion of improvements over time, and managers are exhorted to "allow plenty of time" to digest new process technologies and strive for "continuous improvement" (Imai, 1986; Abernathy and Utterback, 1978). But, at the level of a specific new technology in a single organizational setting, the process of learning about and modifying the new process may not be continuous at all. In fact, our research findings, as illustrated in Figure 36.1, suggest that the pattern of adaptation for an individual new technology is often "lumpy" or episodic. It appears that, in general, the introduction of a new technology into an operating environment triggers an initial burst of adaptive activity, as users explore the new technology and unexpected problems get resolved. However, this activity is often short-lived, with effort and attention declining dramatically after the first few months of use. In effect, the ways in which the technology functions and is used, including both strengths and weaknesses, quickly become acceptable modes of behavior and the basis of standard operating procedures. This initiates a period of stability in which users focus attention more on the pressures of regular production tasks than on further adaptation. Later on, users' attention is often rekindled by unresolved problems or new challenges, creating additional spurts of adaptive activity. In many cases, this episodic pattern continues over time, with brief periods of adaptation followed by longer periods of relatively stable use. This pattern is very consistent with much behavioral research showing that while organizational groups and individuals tend toward increasingly habitual modes of operation and problem-solving behavior over time, specific events or milestones can help to refocus attention on problems or needed improvements (e.g., Katz, 1994; Gersick, 1991). In this chapter, we summarize our previous evidence for this episodic pattern of adaptation and also discuss how such an episodic pattern, if it is understood and managed, can serve as an effective way to pursue ongoing improvement of new process technologies.

Marcie Tyre is Professor of Management of Technology and Innovation at M.I.T.'s Sloan School of Management. *Wanda Orlikowski* is Professor of Information Systems at M.I.T.'s Sloan School of Management.
Earlier versions of this study were published in Tyre, M. and W. Orlikowski (1993) "Exploiting Opportunities for Technological Improvement in Organizations," *Sloan Management Review*, 35, 13–26; and Tyre, M. and W. Orlikowski (1994) "Windows of Opportunity: Temporal Patterns of Technological Adaptation in Organizations," *Organization Science*, 5, 98–118.

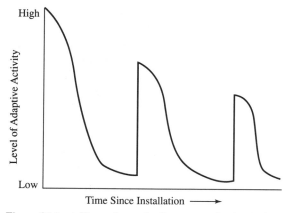

Figure 36.1 A "lumpy" or episodic pattern of technological adaptation.

EXPLICATING THE PATTERN OF ADAPTATION ACTIVITY OVER TIME

In our prior research (see Tyre and Orlikowski, 1994), we investigated how three manufacturing and service organizations in the United States and Europe adapted new process technologies. The first site was BBA (names have been disguised), a leading manufacturer of precision metal components, where we studied forty-one projects involving the introduction of new capital equipment in European and U.S. factories. The second site was SCC, a multinational software developer of custom-built computer applications, where we followed the introduction of computer-aided software engineering (CASE) tools in three U.S. offices. The third site was Tech, a research university in the United States, where we examined modifications made to user-customizable computer tools such as text editors and electronic mail utilities.

Our main findings are consistent with the pattern described in Figure 36.1. First, we found that the installation of a new process technology was followed by an immediate and relatively brief burst of adaptation efforts. Thereafter, such efforts fell off precipitously. Thus, experimentation was more likely to occur and significant changes more apt to be implemented *immediately* following introduction than at any later time. This rapid fall-off of adaptive activity was apparently not a simple

"learning curve" phenomenon, because it occurred even when outstanding problems had not been fully addressed.

However, the initial period was not the only time when important modifications were made. In each company, events sometimes triggered new episodes of intensive adaptation effort. These later episodes were also short-lived, but they were critical because they enabled users to tackle outstanding problems and to apply the additional insights gained through use over time. Thus, the cycle of intensive improvement followed by relatively stable operations tended to repeat itself.

The timing of adaptation at BBA illustrates this pattern. Although modifications were made for more than three years, we found that most of the adaptations made were accomplished within a very short time after implementation; on average, 54 percent of all adaptive activity was completed in the first three months. This pattern was remarkably consistent across all of the projects analyzed; the episode of adaptation that seemed to accompany initial implementation lasted about the same time (approximately three months) whether the project involved five people or fifty, and whether the technology was familiar or a departure from current procedures. Further, it was clear that adaptation efforts were not falling off simply because the users had resolved all problems within this period; on average, respondents reported five significant problems still outstanding at the time when initial adaptation efforts were curtailed. Indeed, most of the new technologies were not considered "production worthy" for many months.

Following the initial burst of activity, most of the technologies entered a phase of regular use as a part of the overall production process. On the other hand, participants did not completely ignore possible improvements to new technologies after the initial period of adaptation. In most projects, they regrouped and refocused attention on modifications some time later, again in a concentrated manner and for a short period (two to three months). Three-quarters of all projects at BBA showed a second spurt of adaptive activity. On average, this episode began about eleven months after the initial installation, and it accounted for an average of 23 percent of all reported adaptive activities. Further, in several of the projects, there was a third such spurt of adaptive activity about six to twelve months after the second episode.

Similar patterns emerged at the other two firms studied. At SCC, a large amount of adjustment and modification took place directly following initial installation of CASE tools into a new project site. In each project, the tools had to be fitted to the particular client organization. However, once application programmers (i.e., the users responsible for the actual production of new application software) began work on the project and started to use the CASE tools as process technology, further changes to the tools halted. These tool users required that their process technology be stable and reliable to facilitate production work. Thus, further refinement of the tools declined very sharply after the initial spurt of adaptive activity. As in the BBA projects, however, a significant surprise or breakdown later in a project could turn users' attention back to the need for ongoing improvements. At these times, technical support personnel were reassigned to undertake a new round of adaptations.

At Tech, too, users' adaptation of their computer tools fell off abruptly soon after initial implementation. In particular, exploring or experimenting to learn about the technology virtually ceased after the first few weeks of use. Instead, users quickly settled on a computing environment and then tried to maintain its stability. As one Tech employee explained, few people even thought about making changes once they had become comfortable with the software: "It's just the way I do it. . . . It's not that [further changes would be] hard, it's just that it's not worth the effort." Yet most users at Tech (forty-nine of fifty-one) noted that specific events did occasionally refocus their attention on the software and trigger further customizations; thus, further adaptations occurred, clustered in relatively brief spurts that were interspersed with periods of routine use of the technology.

In short, all three of these very different organizations displayed a distinctly discontinuous pattern in the way they adapted new process technologies. Significantly, this did not seem to be a conscious management policy in any of the companies. To the contrary, managers (and users) frequently stated that they recognized the need for continuous ongoing changes to new technologies, but that it was difficult to keep people focused on this sort of modification activity for more than a short time. Thus, once users became familiar with a new technology, it tended to become a "taken for granted" part of normal operations.

The forces for stability and routinization, however, were occasionally disrupted by events that forced—or allowed—technology users to ask new questions and to reexamine old problems. Typically, the events that created additional opportunities for adaptation were new developments that somehow interrupted routine operations. At BBA, for instance, the reported new episodes of adaptation were generally associated with events that placed new demands on existing operations and also created a pause in the normal production schedule. For example, when new machines were added to the production line where the technology was in use, they often created increased demands for high-precision or high-speed processing that had not yet been achieved. At the same time, the installation of the new machines imposed a temporary line shutdown. Users in our study often took advantage of this time to address old problems and to initiate new adaptations to their technology. Similarly, the introduction of new products or product requirements, the imposition of new production procedures, or occasional breakdowns of the new technology were also times when the need for improvement became apparent, while providing a brief and sanctioned stop in the action. At Tech, the release of new versions of computer software forced users to interrupt their normal routines; these events accounted for almost one-third of all later episodes of adaptation observed there. Users at Tech also reported that they occasionally returned their attention to making software modifications when existing procedures became too frustrating, or when they were exposed to new ideas for making routines more efficient.

ORGANIZATIONAL FORCES INFLUENCING TECHNOLOGICAL ADAPTATION

Why are the improvements episodic and not continuous, as conventional wisdom would have had us believe? Why is the initial burst of adaptation limited in duration, quickly giving way to a longer period of relative routine operation until some unusual or interrupting event triggers a new period of adaptive activity? In interviewing representative managers and project members in the three research sites, four organizational forces were consistently mentioned or observed as shaping this pattern of adaptation: (1) the pressure or production, (2) the constraining effect of habitual patterns of use, (3) the adjustment of expectations based on experience, and (4) the erosion of team membership and enthusiasm over time.

1. *Production Pressure Impedes Adaptation.* Data from all three sites suggest that one of the most powerful forces behind the failure of continuous modification was that, once technology was put into use, production activities quickly began to siphon off the time, energy, and resources that were needed to identify and solve new problems. Thus, even when users wanted to continue to improve the technology and its applications, they felt they could not, due to external pressures. Interviewees explained that success tends to be measured by production output, so that, once real output is being produced, engineering and/or developers can't get in to play—lots of experimentation and improvements may be possible, but it is too difficult to get in there to do them.

At SCC, for example, both programmers and technical developers were acutely aware that making changes to the tools or experimenting with different technology options meant time away from producing application software. Since software was produced on-site to tight client specifications and time frames, SCC could not afford to let schedules slip. As expressed by one developer:

> The project's budgetary and time restriction cause problems in scope. It forces a narrow view

on us. It's frustrating for us to see and know what should be done to improve, refine, or generalize the tool, but we can't do that as we are required to get the specific application system done.

Such problems are consistent with SCC's intensive focus on short-term productivity performance. More surprising is that similar patterns emerged at Tech. Despite users' stated preference for ongoing innovation and refinement, these same users were unlikely to adapt operational systems once they were in production mode unless forced to do so by external events. One user commented that making changes is something one does when one has "leisure time."

In part, such comments reflect the conflict between the certainty required by the production process, and the uncertainties involved in making changes to the technology. Users engaged in production perceived a significant risk that a seemingly straightforward adaptation would balloon into a major project. One user explained that due to work demands, "I can't afford to be a guinea pig."

Further, users recognized the potential to make a mistake that would cause greater problems than the one they were trying to fix. One Tech user commented on his prior experiences of adaptation that had resulted in major rework and, therefore, lost productivity. At BBA, an engineer at one of the German plants described the conflict between production and adaptation by explaining that "once we got the equipment into the factory, time to do important engineering work was squeezed out by everyday work to keep things running."

Some users expressed the conviction that, since near-term production requirements left them no time to pursue further changes, extending the time frame for implementation would provide more opportunities for adaptation. However, our data suggest that this was not the case. As we discuss below, we found that when users took a longer time to complete the introduction of the new technology, further barriers to adaptation often arose.

2. *Patterns of use Congeal and Become Constraining over Time.* Another barrier to ongoing change in all three operating settings was the fact that users quickly adapted *themselves* to their new process technologies. As users gained experience, they established stable routines, norms, and habits for using the technology which decreased the need for discussion, coordination or effortful decision making. This constrained further exploration and adaptation, apparently stunting the "learning" process that was expected by many managers.

The constraining effects of increased experience were pronounced at BBA. For instance, in the case of one novel grinding machine, productivity benefits were predicated on the integration of the new equipment into an existing automated processing line. However, initial integration problems forced project engineers to install a temporary manual "workaround." Although the manual workaround was inefficient, operators quickly learned to depend on it. Later, when the grinder was finally fully repaired, users clung to the system they had become accustomed to, and prevented engineers from dismantling the "temporary" workaround. Because of this, the new grinder's capabilities for efficient, high-precision machining were never fully developed and exploited.

The same tendencies surfaced among software users at Tech. Once functions became habitual or automatic, users resisted further change. To illustrate, when new software versions were installed, users often simply retrofitted the new versions to mimic functions of the familiar, original version. Users often hastened the process of making their use of the new technology habitual by "customizing themselves" to the software as they first received it. For, once a given approach or customized set of commands had been learned, users were very reluctant to change.

Where production pressures were especially intense, the tendency for patterns of use to congeal was exacerbated. In SCC, users chose tool repertoires that enabled them to meet production deadlines, and then quickly become dependent on those tools in their current form. They resisted ideas for improvements or adjustments that threatened to disrupt established ways of using the system. When such changes were occasionally introduced, users

often tried to ignore them by bypassing the new versions to work with the original technology. A project manager noted that:

> We [were frustrated] during the spec stage, as the technical developers wanted continual changes to the tools. . . . So we decided that we would just continue with [our version of the tools] so that we could get on with our schedules.

Even if the new tools were potentially superior, programmers admitted that "We often go around it [a new module of the tools]," because they were not willing to bear the cost of learning a new technique. The fact that new tools often contained system errors also induced users to stick with existing sets of CASE tools. A programmer explained:

> When things went wrong with the tools, we used to circumvent the tools left and right so that we could get on with our work.

3. *Expectations Adjust to Fit Experience.* In many of the projects studied, expectations regarding the performance capabilities of a new technology changed over time. Specifically, expectations were amended to fit actual achievement or capability. Therefore, as time went on, problems or opportunities often disappeared from view—not because the technology was improved, but because standards were lowered or interpretations amended.

For example, one project at BBA involved the introduction of an advanced precision grinding machine. The original objective of the project, according to both development engineers and original project documentation, was to develop the capability to machine all five "faces" of a particularly complex metal part. Indeed the plant manager had explained that "grinding all five faces was *the* key objective in this project," more important than the productivity improvements expected from the machine. Developers had demonstrated five-face grinding in the lab, but they had not been able to test whether the machine would hold required tolerances under actual plant conditions. Therefore, the project team agreed to continue development in the factory.

But as time wore on development was blocked by the very success of the project on other criteria. Within several months the new machine was operating at speeds up to six times those of the equipment it had replaced, even without the addition of five-face grinding. Production personnel found they had sufficient slack to run complex parts through additional grinding machines to complete all five faces. Users soon reconstructed the original project objectives to fit this new reality. In fact, several of those interviewed many months later denied that five-face grinding had ever seriously been considered as a key project objective, claiming that they were only trying five faces "as an experiment—a sort of add-on that didn't work."

Users at Tech also displayed a variety of ways in which experience with a new technology affected their perception of potential problems and opportunities. For example, one user explained that he had tried to use a special feature of the software called Zephyr when this system was new, and that he had failed to get the feature working satisfactorily in his first two days of trying. Months later, he explained that he had no interest in trying Zephyr again: "Once burned off, I don't come back. . . ." In another case, a manager noted that one of the software functions he used most had failed some time ago and was no longer available. In fact, the function had been repaired and was again available (other users were employing it at the time), but since this user's expectation had already adjusted, he had not thought to inquire whether the problem had been corrected.

4. *Erosion of Team Membership and Enthusiasm.* Another barrier to adaptation was that when projects bogged done, the relevant teams tended to dissolve and lose momentum. For instance, one project at BBA involved the introduction of a novel thermal-forming approach for producing complex metal parts. The lead project engineer explained that:

> Our approach was to create a team consisting of a manufacturing engineer, a service technician,

and a skilled operator to put the machine into production. But each time the machine went down, we had to disband and send the team members to other activities while we waited for new parts or tools. This really hampered our learning and you don't always get the same people back. Sometimes members get involved in other, more urgent projects that are not dragging on as much.

Another project manager stated that it was difficult to keep the team focused. He found that it was easy to get plant engineers to start working on large projects but extremely difficult to keep their attention focused on the details over time. "People drift away to other problems when the work is only half done," he commented. In another example, a BBA project participant noted:

> For the first three months, we had a really intensive effort—the engineers [assigned to the project] were 100% *on*. But after that, well . . .

Similarly at SCC, once projects reached a stage where the CASE technology had been installed and programmers began using the technology to do their production work, many of the technical developers requested assignment to other projects with "more interesting" work. And finally, technical developers were often reassigned to production tasks on the project once the process technology was sufficiently stable. Their new task assignment effectively precluded further work on the process technology.

EPISODIC TECHNOLOGICAL ADAPTATIONS

All of the previously described organizational forces block the implementation of detailed process technology changes after the initial period of installation and adjustment. Our findings suggest that adaptation becomes increasingly difficult as process technologies become more thoroughly embedded and routinized in the user environment. Yet, paradoxically, routine use is also necessary for ongoing adaptation. It provides the data and experi-

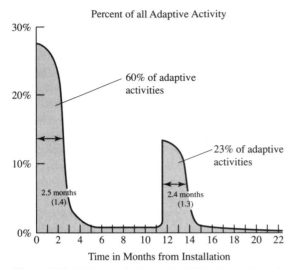

Percent of all Adaptive Activity

Figure 36.2   Episodes of adaption in BBA schematic graph showing timing of adaptive activity. $N = 41$ projects.

31 of the 41 projects studied demonstrated a later spurt of adaptive activity. In four of these cases more than one later spurt of activity was reported.

Later episodes of adaptive activity, like the initial episode, were of limited duration. At BBA these later spurts of activity lasted for an average of 2.4 months (similar to the initial period of 2.5 months, or 2.8 months for the 32 longer projects), and there was little variation across projects (there were only two instances where the episode lasted longer than three months.) Figure 36.2 show the general pattern of adaptation observed at BBA. As shown, the second spurt of activity began, on average, about 11 months after initial installation, and accounted for an average of 23% of all reported adaptive activities.

In almost every case, the existence of a later spurt of adaptive activity at BBA was associated with a specific, disruptive event in the project life cycle (see Table 36.1). Most often, respondents reported that attention was refocused on the technology and its mode of use by the addition of new machines or tools to the same cell or line. In other cases, new project requirements or changed factory procedures forced participants to revisit decisions made earlier and to improve technical capabilities or procedures. In a few cases, a new episode of

ences that can lead to improvements in the technology or in the way it's applied in the local context.

In each of the sites studied there was evidence that users did, at least occasionally, reexamine existing technology and make important modifications after gaining additional experience. At BBA,

TABLE 36.1
Subsequent Windows of Opportunity—Triggering Further Adaptation at BBA

# of instances	% of all instances[1]	Trigger
14	40%	New machines or tools added
6	17%	New product requirements
6	17%	New management action (intervention by new plant or senior management)
3	9%	New factory procedures
3	9%	New personnel or break in schedule create slack resources
2	6%	Machine breakdown
1	3%	Existing management request action

[1]Identification of triggers was based on interviews and users' designation of critical events. New episodes were defined as beginning when recorded adaptive activity increased by more than 100%, or began again after a period of no such reported activity. Episodes were defined as ending when the month-to-month change in the level of adaptive activity was negative and greater than 50%.

TABLE 36.2
Subsequent Windows of Opportunity—Triggering Further Adaptation at Tech

# times mentioned	% of all users mentioning this issue[1]	Trigger
34	68%	New system release or changes to existing systems
22	43%	Saw an opportunity to automate commonly used routines
21	41%	Existing system becomes too annoying or frustrating
20	39%	Exposure to other users ideas
15	29%	Problems with existing systems
11	22%	Thought of something new

[1]Identification of major triggers was based on users' responses to interview questons about what provokes adaptation activity, i.e., "what are the circumstances under which you choose to modify your work environment?" This column adds to more than 100% because users listed more than one trigger. Only triggers mentioned more than 10 times are listed.

adaptation was induced by an unusual but not disruptive event, as in two cases where the arrival of new, unassigned technical personnel provided extra resources for handling outstanding problems with the process technology. Management action also triggered some new adaptive activity. This was generally linked to the arrival of new managers at the company or local level. For example, one new machine was plagued with problems for more than two years because users were unable to reconfigure the technology on the shop floor. They were unable to accomplish much until a new group of divisional managers took over and focused attention on the troubled project. In only one case did existing managers explicitly instigate further adaptation efforts.

At Tech, users were generally reluctant to alter software systems once a serviceable configuration had been found. Yet most users (49 out of 51) did note that specific events could refocus their attention on the software and trigger further customizations. As at BBA, triggers were often disruptive or aberrant events, such as the release of a new system or the breakdown of an existing one (see Table 36.2). For example, in one case an experienced user was given a special assignment that required him to process greatly increased amounts of data in a very short time. To cope with the resulting crisis, he created a new set of program rules that automatically sorted, labeled, and routed his electronic messages. Once the special assignment was completed, he discovered that these new rules

significantly improved his effectiveness even under normal circumstances. In another instance, a user who normally did not travel went on an extended trip. Upon returning, he was overwhelmed with accumulated electronic mail messages, and he quickly developed new rules to deal with the situation. He soon discovered that these modifications proved useful additions to his regular work routine.

In other cases at Tech, opportunities for change were created when normal workflow and thought patterns were interrupted by outsiders. For example, when a visitor asked whether the electronic mail system routed messages reliably, some nontechnical users expressed surprise and concern that the technology might *not* work correctly. As a result of this interruption, they began to undertake new experiments with their technology. Sometimes the impetus for further adaptation effort was internal. A significant number of users modified their system when they thought of new ideas, or when old procedures simply became too frustrating.

Disruptive events or new ideas, however, did not always trigger changes that advanced the technology. As noted earlier, the most common form of adaptation at Tech following new system releases was a retrofit that enabled uses to continue to operate as if no change had occurred.

At SCC there was evidence of only one incident of technological adaptation during a later phase of a project. This is not surprising given that formal procedures explicitly dictated that the CASE tools be defined at the beginning of the project and then held stable. Even after projects were complete, there were few opportunities to revisit questions about the technology and its mode of use. A senior consultant commented that, once projects were finished, we were never asked to reflect on the problems we had. He further explained: "No one asks how are these tools used after their time so we can fine-tune the process or correct and eliminate the problems."

Yet even at SCC, a crisis could create an opportunity to rethink earlier choices. In the one project where users did seek to modify the process technology later in the project cycle, they did so because the existing CASE tools had ceased to produce useful output. Many production requirements had changed over time, and the CASE tools in use no longer reflected the current requirements. Eventually, project management recognized that the tools had become inadequate to the task, and technical personnel were called in to help modify the existing technology.

JAPANESE ADAPTATION ACTIVITY

It is important to note that our research was carried out exclusively in Western organizations, which may manage adaptation differently from other (e.g., Asian) organizations. In order to compare these results with those from other settings, we examined several detailed accounts of how some successful Japanese firms absorb and modify new technologies. We were particularly interested in Japanese firms that purportedly embrace "continuous improvement" in their overall operation. We asked whether the pattern of adaptations around a specific new technology in such firms is in fact gradual and continuous over time, or whether it reflects the episodic pattern that we observed in our data.

We discovered that the successful Japanese operations do not invite or expect continuous adaptations to specific new technologies. Instead, we found a discontinuous model of adaptation that basically resembled our findings. An important difference, however, was that these Japanese firms appeared to consciously and carefully manage the timing of adaptations. Managers in these organizations apparently create *and exploit* the very episodic pattern that we described. Specifically, the managers in these companies appear to do three things. First, they aggressively utilize the introduction period to adapt new technologies. That is, they identify and make the maximum number of modifications as early as possible. Then, following this period, they impose routine on the use of new technologies, *and* they exploit that routine for what it can teach them. Third, they consciously and periodically create new opportunities for further adaptations.

The Japanese operations we examined truly exploit the initial period of technology introduction. They do not build in a great deal of extra time for debugging a new technology before moving into full production schedules. Rather, they develop very demanding, early production commitments for new technologies—and then they take steps to ensure that the new process technology will be ready. The ability to do this stems partly from careful early design of new products and processes, as documented by Wheelwright and Clark (1992). What is less widely understood is that meeting tight production deadlines in Japanese operations also stems from "the intensity of revisions on the spot during start-up" (Hall, 1983:197). At Toyota, for instance, there is "a direct engineering assault to correct [problems] in the beginning, [which] prevents the need to dribble a constant stream of engineering changes through the formal system over a long period of time" (Hall, 1983:199).

This early spurt of activity is often not apparent to outsiders. U.S. observers, for example, who toured a successful Japanese electronics operation reported that "the Japanese can simply 'flick a switch' " to start up new process technologies at high yield. In reality, successful introduction required three months of intensive, exhausting effort by a team of engineers. These engineers knew that there would be problems, but they also knew that they had to resolve the problems during the brief ramp-up period. Production commitments were absolutely firm, and profitability depended on meeting them (Langowitz, 1986). In the automobile industry, Clark and Fujimoto (1991) describe the Japanese approach to managing initial ramp-up of new technologies as far more intense than normal problem-solving activities; in fact, they label it "the Japanese 'war time' approach." They find that, while U.S. and European automobile manufacturers typically allow close to one year after the start of production to meet their target quality levels on a new line, the Japanese allow only one to two months to work through the engineering changes necessary to get the new line to run smoothly. This strategy is backed up with significant resource commitments such that, in the Toyota example, design engineers, manufacturing engineers, production control personnel, quality managers, and anyone else who is necessary "live" on the production floor during start-up.

Imposing and Exploiting Routine. While many Japanese firms pursue continuous improvement, this does not mean that a newly implemented technology is subjected to a constant stream of changes. Instead, before any improvement is undertaken, "it is essential that the current standards be stabilized" and institutionalized (Imai, 1986:63). In the *kaizen* philosophy, there can be no improvement where there are no standards. This means that standards and measures must be imposed, "and it is management's job to see that everyone works in accordance with the established standards" (Imai, 1986:75). Once the initial episode of debugging and modifying the new process technology is completed, standard operating routines are developed and enforced. Managers do not expect or allow operators to introduce modifications on an informal, everyday basis.

This does not mean that technology users in such firms ·neglect ongoing improvements—only that the changes they actually implement are tightly controlled. Operators in these firms perform considerable off-line experimentation, but they do not make unauthorized changes to production technology (Schonberger, 1982). Except for urgent corrections, they are permitted to make adaptations to the technology or production practices only at designated times. This emphasis on routinization is

also echoed in nonmanufacturing operations. In Japan's new software factories, there is rigid adherence to existing standards and little allowance for individuals to make changes during the production of new software systems (Cusumano, 1991). Managers in Hitachi's software works, for example, realized that creating standardized procedures not only helped them to improve programming efficiency and productivity, but also "helped them identify best practices within the company and within the industry for dissemination to all projects and departments" (Cusumano, 1992:468).

Episodic Opportunities for Adaptation. Descriptions of technological adaptation in these Japanese firms reveal that, at the level of a given technology, continuous change really involves repeated cycles of change and stability. Imposing the discipline of routine procedures ensures that the timing of further changes is carefully managed. Whenever possible, modifications are batched together systematically and implemented in one intensive episode of adaptation. Very often these episodes are timed to coincide with other major changes, such as product-model changeovers, releases of new software versions, or yearly factory shutdowns. Hall (1983) explains that the most efficient manufacturing companies generally plan engineering changes one to two months ahead and then implement them at particular schedule-change times. Similarly, in Japanese software factories, development methods, tools, and products are generally held steady during a given project, but are periodically and systematically upgraded or revised. A review of Hitachi's software factory shows that Hitachi managers knew that the procedures they initially created would not be perfect; they "clearly recognized that these procedures and standards would have to evolve as personnel and technology changed, and they made provisions to revise performance standards annually" (Cusumano, 1992: 468).

In short, by creating distinct episodes of adaptation, managers provide the operation with both the benefits of routine and the vitality of ongoing change.

Why Episodic Adaptation Can Be Effective

One way of interpreting the evidence from our research and the Japanese studies is to suggest that effective companies take the naturally "lumpy" pattern of adaptation and exploit it. That is, managers in the firms cited achieve maximum benefit from their adaptation efforts by carefully managing both spurts of adaptation and periods of routine operation. Indeed, there is evidence that such a *dis*continuous pattern of modification can yield important benefits. First, there appears to be a natural surge of energy at the start of projects that smart managers exploit fully. Second, managers can enhance both learning and efficiency goals by imposing (and using) periods of routine operation in between periods of rapid change. And third, by revisiting the adaptation agenda at intervals, managers can make problems more tractable and can render change more attractive and more manageable.

The Importance of Beginnings. The period immediately following initial introduction of a new technology provides a special "window of opportunity" for adaptation. At the start of the project, the level of energy is high. The novelty of the situation helps people to focus on the new technology, and to see it as a distinct and malleable tool. In the three organizations we studied, the motivation to change and to achieve targets was clearly highest at the start of the introduction period. Beginnings are so important simply because challenging project objectives have a catalyzing effect at the start that typically fades quickly as a consequence of the four broad categories of organizational forces previously discussed. Identifying and resolving problems during the initial introduction period is easier because there are fewer competing demands on people's time. Later on, production pressures and measures tend to dominate priorities as the technology becomes increasingly integrated into production processes. Some project managers in our study hoped that they could continue to modify the technology gradually, "as they went along," but they soon found that production and adaptation did not mix well. Although there was often plenty of money, the time to search, examine, and test new ideas and solutions was the scarce resource.

Learning from Routine Use. Once an initial set of modifications has been identified and implemented, there are several reasons to hold the technology relatively constant for a period of time. First, there are obvious efficiency benefits to allowing the operation to run for some time in a stable fashion without imposing frequent, disruptive changes. Hayes and Clark (1985) have shown that plants that are not subject to high levels of "confusion" from frequent changes in their tasks and technology have superior growth in productivity relative to "higher-confusion" environments. Hall's (1983) argues that "dribbling a constant stream of changes" into the operating system can seriously compromise operating effectiveness.

Second, routine operations are an important test bed; if constant and uncontrolled changes are being made, it will be very difficult to assess the effectiveness of previous modifications (Imai, 1986). Especially in "noisy," complex environments, where signals can be misleading or difficult to interpret, problem solvers need to observe the system over relatively long periods of time before defining further adaptations (Levinthal and March, 1981). Finally, periods of routine operation allow users to explore a new technology, and to learn from their own reactions. Through extended use, they can identify features that are inconvenient, or that cannot meet the evolving daily demands of a particular operating environment (von Hippel and Tyre, 1995). As Imai (1986) nicely explains, progress can only occur when one "institutionalizes [a given] improvement as a new practice to improve on."

Windows of Opportunity for Episodic Adaptation. There are several reasons why it makes sense to return to the adaptation agenda in short but intensive spurts, rather than to try for a more gradual pattern of change. First, short but intensive episodes of adaptive activity exploit "economies of scale" in problem solving. Many of the problems that affect a new technology require diverse resources for resolution. Managers, engineers, and users must often create a cross-functional team, call in outside experts, set up experimental apparatus, develop prototypes, and so on. Frequently, regular operations must come to a halt. Gathering these resources only *once* to attack a number of issues is obviously more efficient than gathering them repeatedly as issues arise. Changes, as a result, are less disruptive to ongoing operations if they are bundled together than if they are trickled out piecemeal to operations. Furthermore, some problems simply cannot be solved—or cannot be solved effectively—unless they are examined as part of a complex set of interdependent issues. When problems are dealt with en mass, instead of one-by-one, these interdependencies can be identified and utilized.

There are also motivational economies of scale associated with brief, intensive spurts of adaptive activity. A team (or even an individual) may be more easily motivated to devote attention and energy when the goal is large and obviously significant (resolving many problems) than when it is small and apparently unimportant (solving just one issue). Similarly, the rewards and satisfaction that come from resolving a significant set of issues can motivate team and individual efforts. And finally, episodic cycling between short spurts of change and longer periods of regular use makes it possible to revisit problems or issues as knowledge is gained with experience. Multiple cycles make it possible to respond to changes in the operating environment that occur long after initial implementation of a new system, whether these are exogenous developments or shifts in uses' preferences and expectations (von Hippel and Tyre, 1995). When users move gradually into an adaptation mode, problems that eluded their understanding during one phase can be reframed and perhaps approached more successfully and energetically during another phase.

Managing Attention and Effort over Time

These arguments suggest that a lumpy pattern of adaptation around a specific new technology may not be ineffective. Instead, relatively long periods of routine use, coupled with occasional but intensive episodes of adaptation, may be a powerful combination. Reaping the joint benefits of short episodes of adaptation and longer periods of regular use, however, is not automatic. It requires explicit management of the attention and effort applied in both phases.

Managing cycles of change and routine use of technologies demands a way of thinking that is unfamiliar to many managers. Users in all three of our research sites noted that managers very seldom took explicit action to create episodes of adaptation. For example, managers seldom intervened in a specific project to raise performance expectations, nor did they require regular project audits that might have helped to focus attention on persistent performance shortfalls. Indeed, our interviews with managers showed that, while they were concerned with the way their organizations were introducing and using new process technologies, they were not sure how to manage the process. None of the people we interviewed seemed aware of the need to create or take advantage of discrete windows of opportunity for technological adaptation.

Our findings suggest that managers must consider how to create opportunities for adaptation, how to utilize those opportunities, and how to exploit periods of regular use of technologies for generating new insights and ideas. Although we cannot offer a recipe for doing this, we hope that our findings and discussion will be useful in helping managers move toward a more conscious management of their windows of opportunity for technological improvement. And we also hope that our study will help managers frame these issues so that they are in fact viewed as opportunities within the organization.

REFERENCES

Abernathy, W. J. and J. M. Utterback (1978) "Patterns of Industrial Innovation," *Technology Review,* 50, 25–36.

Clark, K. B. and T. Fujimoto (1991) *Product Development Performance.* Boston: Harvard Business School Press.

Cohen, W. M. and D. A. Levinthal (1990) "Absorptive

Capacity: A New Perspective on Learning and Innovation," *Administrative Science Quarterly, 35,* 128–52.

Cusumano, M. A. (1991) *Japan's Software Factories.* New York: Oxford University Press.

Cusumano, M. A. (1992) "Shifting Economies: From Craft Production to Flexible Systems and Software Factories," *Research Policy, 21,* 453–80.

Dutton, J. M. and A. Thomas (1985) "Relating Technological Change and Learning by Doing." In R. S. Rosenbloom (Ed.) *Research on Technological Innovation, Management and Policy, 2,* 235–47.

Gersick, C. J. (1991) "Revolutionary Change Theories: A Multilevel Explanation of the Punctuated Equilibrium Model," *Academy of Management Review,* 16, 1, 10–36.

Hayes, R. H. and K. B. Clark (1985) "Exploring the Sources of Productivity Differences at the Factory Level." In Clark et al. (Eds.) *The Uneasy Alliance.* Boston: Harvard University Press.

Imai, M. (1986) *Kaizen: The Key to Japan's Competitive Success.* New York: McGraw-Hill Publishing.

Katz, R. (1994) "Managing High Performance R&D Teams," *European Management Journal,* 12, 243–52.

Langowitz, N. S. (1986) "Plus Development Corp (A)", Harvard Business School case 9-687-001.

Leonard-Barton, D. A. (1988) "Implementation as Mutual Adaptation of Technology and Organization," *Research Policy, 17,* 251–67.

Levinthal, D. and J. March (1981) "A Model of Adaptive Organizational Search," *Journal of Economic Behavior and Organization 2,* 307–33.

Schonberger, R. J. (1982) *Japanese Manufacturing Practices.* New York: The Free Press.

von Hippel, E. and M. Tyre (1995) "How 'Learning by Doing' Is Done: Problem Identification in Novel Process Equipment," *Research Policy, 24,* 1–12.

Wheelwright, S. C. and K. B. Clark, (1992) *Revolutionizing Product Development: Quantum Leaps in Speed, Efficiency, and Quality.* New York: The Free Press.

5

THE MANAGEMENT OF ORGANIZATIONAL PROCESSES

13

Decision-making Processes

37

Managing Organizational Deliberations in Nonroutine Work

WILLIAM A. PASMORE

For a few organizations that exist in stable environments, inflexible thinking isn't a problem; but for most, the ability to change and adapt is critical to success.[1] Flexible thinking is especially important in R&D, marketing, and management. In fact, flexible thinking is a good thing in any part of an organization in which creating or applying knowledge is an important element in task completion. In these parts of the organization, work is nonroutine in nature. That is, tasks are frequently changing and rarely performed in exactly the same way

twice. Routine tasks are repetitive, requiring little learning or creativity once they have been mastered. Nonroutine tasks demand some degree of both creativity and expertise; people may be professionally prepared to undertake nonroutine tasks, but still find their completion challenging or impossible. Medical researchers may be trained to look for a cure for the AIDS virus, for example, but still experience difficulty in finding one.

The fact that nonroutine work involves human thinking rather than machine performance makes it

Reprinted with permission from Pasmore, William.

William Pasmore is Professor of Organizational Development at Case Western Reserve University's Weatherhead School of Management.

fascinatingly unpredictable and subject to all sorts of human foibles. In the wonderful and wacky world of nonroutine work, whether you like the person you are working with can make the difference between succeeding at a task or failing; doubling the number of people working on a project may just slow things down; and relying on what you think you know may only get in the way. It's as if nonroutine work takes place in some science fiction-inspired other dimension in which the laws of normal work don't hold. "Do it right the first time" and "zero defects" make no sense at all; goals can change in midstream; productivity is virtually immeasurable until the task is finished, and even then people argue about what has been accomplished. The history of product development is replete with examples of failures turned into successes and accidental inventions that appear brilliant only in retrospect. More than a few ulcers have resulted from people betting their careers on the outcomes of work that at its very core is inherently unpredictable and nonroutine.

R&D ORGANIZATIONS AS SOCIOTECHNICAL SYSTEMS

In traditional sociotechnical systems theory, it is held that organizations should be designed around their core production process; in R&D organizations, the core process is clearly that of producing ideas about products or processes. This work is knowledge-based; the availability and utilization of knowledge determine to a large extent the quality and viability of the ideas that are eventually conceived. Thus to improve R&D organizations we must understand the ways in which social and technical systems influence the development and utilization of knowledge. This emphasis on knowledge in R&D systems is made clearer when one contrasts the nature of work in routine (manufacturing) versus nonroutine (R&D) units. Table 37.1 shows some of the major differences between routine and nonroutine work.

Nonroutine work is, by definition, partially undefined at its commencement. How the work will be performed and even by whom the work will be carried out is determined along the way as new information influences thinking about the task. Given the lack of prior experience regarding the current task, many decisions are made intuitively rather than on the basis of complete data and logic. Moreover, many methods can be employed to work toward objectives, which themselves are often in conflict: Consumers desire products that are relatively inexpensive, but they demand high quality as well; trade-offs are made between such things as product durability and weight as different materials are considered; working toward a major breakthrough is played against utilizing familiar development techniques. Finding the correct solutions to such trade-offs is complicated by the fact that information regarding consumer tastes, competitors' plans, and many other crucial inputs may be lacking and difficult to obtain. Even if such information is available, forecasting how long it will take to complete the development task or how much the product will ultimately cost to manufacture is often more like reading entrails than running a railroad. Thus, in nonroutine environments like R&D, the inputs that would allow logic, data, and science to guide plans for the use of resources in task completion are often missing. In the absence of this information, choosing the right path to the desired outcome is necessarily an intuitive and political process.

Partly because of this uncertain information and partly because of the nature of R&D itself, success is defined differently in R&D than in traditional manufacturing operations. In manufacturing, repetitive performance of the same tasks allows micromeasurement of routinely observable manufacturing parameters. Often these measures are referred to as indicators of manufacturing "efficiencies." The emphasis in manufacturing is on doing the same thing better and faster with less waste and higher quality—efficiency. In R&D, managers are more concerned with results than in process measures. Achieving the goal is of paramount importance, not how efficiently material or labor is utilized. Productivity is difficult to measure in the R&D environment. How does one cal-

TABLE 37.1
Differences between Routine and Nonroutine Systems

	Routine	Nonroutine
Nature of work	• Defined • Repetitive • One right way • Clear, shared goals • Information readily available • Forecasting helpful	• Undefined • Nonrepetitive • Many right ways • Multiple, competing goals • Information hard to obtain • Forecasting difficult
Nature of success	• Efficiency • Technical perfection • Productivity measurable • Physical technology • Standard information	• Effectiveness • Human perfection • Productivity unmeasurable • Knowledge technology • Nonstandard information
Nature of decision making	• Rules applicable • Experience counts • Authority-based • Complete operational specs • Authority by position	• Rules inhibiting • Experience may be irrelevant • Consensus-based • Incomplete operational specs • Authority by virtue of expertise
Nature of context	• Short time horizon • Stable environment • Predefined outcomes	• Long time horizon • Unstable environment • Emergent outcomes
Nature of variances	• Obvious	• Hidden

culate the productivity of an engineer who makes only one major breakthrough in his career, but with it ensures the company's future?

Because of these difficulties in measuring R&D performance, surrogate measures are often applied. Project reports are written and submitted regularly as an indication that "we're working on it"; budgets are measured against what other companies are spending or what we spent last year; headcount is changed in the vain hope that the number of people in the lab somehow relates to the number of new ideas produced there. More appropriately, efforts are made to recruit and develop high-caliber people who have the right education or a good track record. In manufacturing, the emphasis is on finding the best machine for the job; in R&D, the focus is on getting the best people. It

follows that decisions about personnel are a key to the evolution of knowledge in R&D systems.

The way decisions are made in R&D organizations also differs from the approach in manufacturing organizations. In manufacturing, technical understanding of the process is nearly complete, leading to tight specifications that dictate how the system is to be operated. Past experience is directly applicable to future operations, so that those with experience are accorded greater authority in decision making. As these people rise in the system, the combination of their expertise and the tight operating specifications for the system lends strength to the hierarchy. Many decisions are made in a top down fashion; little input is required from those below in order to reach decisions of acceptable quality. In R&D organizations, expertise is widely distributed throughout the organization. Past experience may not be applicable to the development of new products and in fact may inhibit creative thinking. There are few rules to govern the creative process, yet the pieces of complex products must somehow fit together before they are handed to manufacturing. This leads to consensus-based decision making in R&D, as specialists who often understand more about their work than their supervisors meet together over coffee and doughnuts to work out the bugs in promising designs.

Time is measured differently, as well. In manufacturing, timeclocks are punched and minutes of downtime are recorded. In R&D, quarters or years are the appropriate unit of time for most discussions. R&D specialists can go for months without receiving feedback on their performance and even longer before they know whether the product they have designed is a success.

By the time products reach manufacturing and facilities have been constructed for their fabrication, someone has already determined that there is at least a semistable consumer demand for the product. This means that the environment of the manufacturing organization is relatively stable compared to that of the R&D Unit. In R&D, projects are started (and stopped) on the basis of incomplete information about consumer demand for the product, projections of manufacturing costs, evidence of unintended environmental impacts, the departure of key scientists, or the whims of the R&D manager. Hence R&D units tend to be more subject to their environments than are routine operations. They are also more sensitive to the loss of knowledge that accompanies the departure of even a few individuals, if those figures have played key roles in the development of important products.

Finally, there is an important difference between manufacturing and R&D operations regarding the variances or problems that affect the quality or quantity of outputs from the system. In manufacturing, variances tend to be visible and repetitive. With some detective work, they can be tracked down and identified. This in turn makes them relatively easy to control. In R&D, variances are often hidden and sometimes go undetected un-til the product is in manufacturing or even later. The variances are hidden because they tend to occur in people's heads when they are thinking about how to design the product. Incorrect assumptions, mistakes, guesses, misinformation, misunderstandings, and trade-offs are an integral part of virtually every complex product development process. Often it is difficult to trace these variances to their source or to catalogue them for future reference. It is even difficult to recognize variances after they have occurred, for they gradually become an accepted part of organizational life. Since delays, misunderstandings, and miscommunications are taken to be par for the course, they are consequently ignored when people discuss what can be done to improve the system. Understanding what variances look like in nonroutine environments and how they can be controlled requires new sociotechnical systems thinking.

TYPICAL VARIANCES IN R&D OPERATIONS

Since the core product of R&D organizations is knowledge, it follows that variances in R&D systems will be knowledge-related. Here are some quotes from a first-rate Research and Development organization in a very respected company that characterize the kinds of variances often encountered in R&D:

> Product development teams don't like to report bad news upward, sometimes they will even hide unfavorable data. When you raise issues, you get an arrow through the heart. Upper management doesn't want to hear the truth.

Does that affect the speed of product development when it happens? You bet!

> Managers are aligned with their *functional* accountabilities. They can go away from a meeting and have very different perspectives on what was agreed upon.

Does that affect cooperation among their people on projects later on? You bet!

"We need to find ways to pass on decisions and earlier work. Usually, when a new person representing a new function comes onto the team, they want to challenge the work done previously."

Does it slow things down when you hand off work between departments? You bet!

People we hire think that working in industry is going to be just like graduate school. It isn't. It takes us years to teach them to work in teams instead of as individuals and to learn to ask the right questions instead of just answering a question raised by the professor.

Does socializing and integrating professionals into an organization's technical culture take time. You bet!

There's a great deal of uncertainty associated with early test data. Market research often tries to make it look like science—almost to fool people.

Do departmental boundaries create mistrust? You bet!

Turning over our ideas to marketing is like giving the keys to a race car to a three-year-old.

Do departmental boundaries get in the way of communication and teamwork? You bet!

A problem in the organization is that everybody can say "no" and nobody can say "yes."

Does the hierarchy sometimes slow things down? You bet!

ORGANIZING FOR KNOWLEDGE WORK

It used to be that the way to manage knowledge work was a combination of brute force and wishful thinking. The best people were hired or recruited to a large team. They were given space, equipment and resources; told to go to work; and then flogged regularly for not producing results fast enough. The nature of knowledge work, being inherently nonroutine, made for lots of flogging. As Albert Einstein said, "Science is a wonderful thing as long as one doesn't have to make a living at it."

But what other choice did the manager of knowledge workers have? He or she could get involved directly, but since the subordinates know more than the manager, the result of direct involvement was a lot of time spent in educating the boss just enough to screw up the decision-making on the project. Leaving people alone didn't feel very comfortable either, particularly with someone higher up the chain of command breathing down the manager's neck. Something must be done, action must be taken, people need leadership! They need management! So lead! The manager would lead, if the or she could just figure out how, when neither he nor others know exactly what is supposed to be done or how to do it.

In knowledge work organizations especially, the brightest people often do get promoted. Even so, being prompted doesn't make them the brightest person in everything, in every specialty, in every situation. But the pressure is on to demonstrate leadership and that means making decisions. Or, more precisely, making certain the right decisions are made. Bradford and Cohen state that, in order to feel competent, managers often feel compelled to live up to the following myths:[2]

- A good manager knows at all times what is going on in the department.
- A good manager should have more technical expertise than any subordinate.
- A good manager should be able to solve any problem that comes up.
- A good manager should be the primary person responsible for how the department is working.

The answer, it turns out, is neither to jump in nor to stand back. It's to make certain that people and teams are adequately prepared for the tasks they have been given, that the problem has been framed properly, and to help people organize themselves to answer the critical questions they have identified. What does organizing for knowledge work entail?

It's here that Calvin Pava's breakthrough in perceiving knowledge work as a series of deliberations, rather than discrete decisions, provides important clues.[3] Pava's argument, essentially, is that by the time people are ready to decide something, the knowledge work is over. Therefore, all of the attention that has been placed on organizational decision-making is in fact *mis*placed. The real knowledge work goes on long before the meeting at which the decision is made; and it tends to be a very messy, disorganized process, open to the full negative force of all the human foibles and social dynamics described earlier. By the time the decision is framed, the battle is lost; it's classic garbage in–garbage out.

Instead, Pava suggests that we trace the process of developing knowledge concerning key decisions over time, in all the various forums in which learning and discussion take place. Some of this work is individual in nature, some of it is collective. Some work is open for all to see, other work goes on in the minds of one or two people or behind closed doors in private sessions. To understand how knowledge is invented, processed, and eventually made available for decisions, we need to trace the evolution of knowledge about a topic through what Pava labeled *deliberations* to distinguish them from what we typically think of as meetings or decisions. Deliberations are times when people think about a topic, when they learn what they think they know, when they share their learnings with others, and when, ultimately, sense is made of that knowledge and concretized into a decision. If the quality of decisions can't be affected much once the knowledge work that goes into the decision is over, it follows that the point of optimal intervention in knowledge work is *while the knowledge is still being developed*. Organizing for knowledge work and *managing knowledge workers* means making the process by which people in the organization learn and influence each other much more explicit, and then working to improve that process over time, as its mechanisms are better understood and experiments with new ways of approaching knowledge tasks are conducted.

Typically, deliberations are spontaneous, un-planned events that we regard as practically inconsequential, yet they are the essence of knowledge work. Deliberately planning and managing them allows us to enhance the quality of knowledge work; it's almost like putting a power tool in the hands of someone who has been doing a task manually. Since knowledge work is made up of a series of deliberations, if we improve individual deliberations, we eventually improve the overall knowledge output and application. The secret is in recognizing what knowledge work is, and how to improve it at the microlevel. What have we learned from past examples of effective and ineffective deliberations? Well, some characteristics of effective deliberations are listed in the box entitled Characteristics of Effective Deliberations.

The first characteristic, knowledge highly developed and available, is determined primarily by effective preparation. The next two, knowledge utilized fully and without bias and apolitical discussion, have more to do with the dynamics that occur during the deliberation process. Having the right people present is a matter of deliberation planning. Often, we forget to include people with knowledge relevant to a problem or, worse, actively exclude them because they are not from our department, not at the proper "level" to be part of the discussion, or have opinions contrary to our own. Disruptive people are those who use their position power to influence deliberation outcomes even when they know nothing about the content being discussed. Planning and holding discussions at key choice points eliminates some of the problems associated with people who want to work alone and commit others to their decisions without the others' input. The next four items have to do with preparation and opportunity framing: goals clear and shared, challenging but realistic time frames, decision-making procedures clear, and appropriate attention to the external environment. The last item is a reminder that the purpose of planning deliberations is not to add bureaucracy or to slow things down, but rather to try to make certain that knowledge work is performed as effectively as it possibly can be.

Ineffective deliberations, by contrast, proceed

> ## Characteristics of Effective Deliberations
> - Knowledge highly developed and available
> - Knowledge utilized fully and without bias
> - Apolitical discussion of facts and alternatives
> - People with most knowledge present
> - Disruptive/inappropriate people absent
> - Discussion held at key choice points
> - Goals clear and shared
> - Challenging but realistic time frames
> - Decision making procedures clear
> - Appropriate attention to external environment
> - Minimum bureaucracy

without highly developed knowledge, resulting in the wrong decisions being made or decisions constantly being postponed. Knowledge that is available may be set aside, as in the *Challenger* incident, for a variety of social or political reasons. Parties to ineffective deliberations may enter dialogue with one another from an adversarial or defensive posture, leading to incomplete or misleading information in key decisions. Disruptive parties can undo months of careful work as powerful individuals inject opinions or push personal agendas. The avoidance of deliberations at key decision points makes it impossible for people with relevant knowledge to influence the course of knowledge work in a timely fashion. Goals not clearly set forth cause knowledge workers to diverge their thinking and then to become set in the paths they have chosen. Unrealistic time frames cause people to forego adequate preparation, rush through deliberations, exclude important external parties, and settle for lower quality than desired. Unclear procedures for making decisions leave the door open for one-on-one lobbying, subgroup influence, majority voting, and a host of other threats to quality decision-making. Inadequate attention to the external environment, as in the case of Xerox, creates self-sealing

truths, and an insistence on internal decisions being the only logical way to look at the world. Too much structure constrains flexible thinking and causes people to avoid the deliberation process altogether. Based on my consulting and research experiences, here's a more detailed list of the kinds of ineffective deliberations that I have been able to observe:

Lack of Knowledge

Perhaps the most obvious variance consists of a lack of knowledge needed to complete a task appropriately. Typically the lack of relevant knowledge is demonstrated in wrong decisions or in decisions being delayed or avoided altogether. When R&D professionals lack relevant knowledge, they are usually quite aware of it—making this one of the simpler variances to detect in nonroutine systems. Controlling this variance, however, may be difficult or even impossible. Sometimes the knowledge is too costly to develop or simply beyond our capacity to create; under these circumstances, risks are assessed, guesses are made, and consequences are measured somewhere down the road. But often this variance can be corrected by exposing the area of relevant uncertainty and involving people with appropriate expertise to answer the questions being posed.

Failure to Use Knowledge

More difficult to detect is the failure to utilize knowledge that already exists within the system. In common parlance, we generally refer to the results of this variance as "mistakes." In contrast to the preceding variance—lack of knowledge, which is viewed as beyond a person's control—the failure to use existing knowledge to make a proper decision is clearly attributable to human error. People sometimes "forget" to check with the appropriate authority on an issue or forget what they themselves know. Alternatively, they may fail to communicate what they know to others who need it because they assume that the others either would not understand it or "wouldn't value their input." Detecting this variance usually requires an analysis of past project performance, including interviews to discover why existing knowledge was not utilized when it should have been.

Lack of Cooperation

When parties who possess knowledge relevant to the tasks of others deliberately withhold it, incorrect decisions often result. People may withhold knowledge if they view their relationships with others as fundamentally competitive rather than cooperative, if they feel wronged by the other party in the past, if they are working toward opposing objectives, if they stand to lose political power by making the other look good, or if they feel that their help is not desired. Lack of cooperation is also apparent when one group shows reluctance to adopt or evaluate fairly the ideas generated by another group. People tend to work on their own ideas and to resist input from others. This tendency is so common in R&D that it has become known as the "Not Invented Here Syndrome." Its occurrence frequently results in delays or even barriers to innovation.

Many organizations are designed in ways that heighten the chances that competition and politics will overshadow cooperation and mutual support. Raises and promotions are limited in number; tall pyramidal hierarchies and clear functional boundaries interfere with natural tendencies by those at lower levels to help others in need; those who play political games are often the most highly rewarded; cooperation is given little recognition. All too often, those who cooperate feel as if they do so at their own peril and almost in violation of the wishes of their superiors.

Missing Parties in Key Discussions

One of the beliefs underlying hierarchical forms of organization is that the most qualified decision makers rise to the top. When this belief is not challenged during key discussions, those in positions of authority may trust themselves to make the choices without soliciting the opinion of others. A notorious example of this type of variance occurred at Morton Thiokol, where lower-level engineers tried to stop the launch of the *Challenger* but were excluded from key discussions by their superiors. This variance also occurs when colleagues in other functions are excluded from discussions in which their ideas would be crucial. The old "toss it over the transom" relationship between R&D and production units is a classic expression of this variance. Production people are explicitly excluded from R&D discussions that will affect production because R&D people tend to view production people as inflexible, anti-innovation, and too narrowly focused on efficiencies rather than the "pull" of the product in the marketplace.

Wrong Parties in Key Discussions

This variance is the obverse of the previous one. Just as excluding certain people can bias decisions, so can including others. Some people are invited to important meetings because they always have been invited, not because they possess technical information or experience relevant to the choices at hand. Nevertheless, because of their status or verbal dexterity, they are allowed to influence decisions in disastrous ways. Many organizations will never know the missed potential of ideas shot down by those who did not know what they were talking about. Instead, we have only reminders of a persistent few who risked their careers to prove that what others thought was impossible was indeed feasible.

No Key Discussions at All

These days, everyone hates meetings. Scientists and engineers may hate them more than most people. Given the choice of attending a meeting to have her ideas ripped apart by others or trusting her own professional judgment, a scientist may not hesitate to press on alone. The same is true of managers; if there is a chance that an idea may be shot down, many would prefer to make the decision on their own and live with the consequences than to take the time to have it reviewed. There may at times be powerful reasons for avoiding discussions of one's work with others. But when discussions are not held, knowledge cannot be transferred or developed among decision makers.

Lack of Goal Clarity

Even in single projects, efforts often proceed in multiple directions because goals are unclear.

Should the product be elegant or cheap? Should it be developed quickly or incorporate all the latest discoveries? Should it be considered high priority or low priority? In many projects, the answers to such questions are unclear. Even when goals are clearly stated at the beginning of a project, they may change as the project proceeds. Add to this the fact that most R&D organizations need to juggle multiple projects simultaneously, and the goals of the individual engineer or scientist become even more confused. In the face of this confusion, knowledge crucial to the project's success may not be developed at all, while knowledge that is in reality much less important is developed fully.

Another variance in this genre is goal displacement. In the search for certainty in an uncertain world, some managers of R&D organizations place more emphasis on paperwork being completed properly than on actual project results. When secondary tasks occupy the time needed to work on knowledge development, knowledge output suffers.

Time Frame Too Short or Too Long

The most common form of this variance occurs when insufficient time is allotted to develop critical knowledge on a project. Under the pressure of arbitrary deadlines, knowledge development is sacrificed for the sake of expediency, thereby precluding the expected level of success. At times, however, time frames can be too long. When project deadlines are set too far into the future, they may be regarded as nonexistent. When those trying to develop knowledge for the project approach others for assistance, they may find that attention is riveted on projects with tighter deadlines. In a world where there is never enough time to do everything one would like, short deadlines are used to focus attention on certain projects and away from others.

Procedures Unclear or Nonexistent

When procedures are not clearly stated for such things as project review sessions, the allocation of resources, or project selection, the informal system is allowed to drive decision making. Often this works out well because the informal system may utilize knowledge more effectively than the formal system does. But the informal system also has a way of making decisions that optimize local benefits and short-term gains. Procedures help to specify who should be involved in making key decisions and what knowledge they should use. In the fight against all things bureaucratic, some R&D organizations neglect opportunities to ensure that sound decisions are made more consistently.

Inadequate Attention to External Environment

By now, the joke about what the customer requested versus what the engineer designed has become trite. Nevertheless, it remains true far too often. Contact with the customer, or with other relevant segments of the external environment, is frequently less than it should be. As a result, critical information never enters the design process or is overlooked once the process has begun.

Too Much Bureaucratic Structure

Earlier we noted that a lack of procedures may prevent the utilization of knowledge in allocating resources. At the same time, we recognize that adding too much structure to an R&D organization can kill it. Numerous levels of hierarchy, an overabundance of rules and regulations, a flood of trivial paperwork—such things sap energy that would otherwise be available for the creation and application of knowledge. Tom Peters has claimed repeatedly that "skunkworks" outperform major research labs, ostensibly because the research and organizational bureaucracies get in the way of people doing what they would naturally do.[4] But if one reads accounts of how highly successful skunk work groups actually function (such as the Data General Eagle computer group described by Kidder, 1981),[5] it becomes clear that a very definite structure is in place. The difference is that the structure is largely self-generated and appropriate to the challenge at hand. Structure is a liability when it interferes with knowledge generation and utilization. It adds little or no value to the outcome and serves mainly to calm the nerves of frightened administrators.

IMPROVING DELIBERATIONS

There are many ways to improve the quality of deliberations. Knowledge workers can form *learning action teams* which are the parallel of quality action teams in routine work settings. Learning action teams conduct regular brainstorming, analysis, and action planning about how to improve knowledge availability, knowledge utilization, and the flexibility of organizational thinking processes. Learning action teams can be formed within a single function, such as marketing, or across functions, such as marketing and R&D. Like quality action teams, learning action teams are authorized to try experiments to improve performance within limbs imposed by a steering committee. Proposals from learning action teams can range from simple changes in data gathering procedures to changes in organizational design.

Deliberation quality also can be improved by studying past deliberations and performing a critical review of what went well and what went poorly. Particularly if outsiders are invited to join in the discussion and ask innocent questions regarding the culture of deliberations, the learnings can be eye opening.

Alternately, deliberations can be improved by planning them in advance, making certain that the right people are involved, that they come prepared with the right knowledge, and that rules are agreed upon before interaction begins. Planning important deliberations in advance makes sense, particularly in these days of impossibly busy calendars and multiple responsibilities.

Ultimately, however, the most important intervention to improve deliberation quality is to redesign the organization so that effective deliberations take place naturally, rather than fighting against improper structural influences. The organization design for effective deliberating takes into account the need to constantly realign knowledge with authority, yet integrate the outcomes of separate deliberations. What kind of organization design allows both flexibility and integration? Clearly, the design can't be based upon hierarchy. Hierarchy is one means of achieving integration,

but it is not the only means and hierarchy destroys flexibility and almost guarantees that knowledge will not be aligned with authority. So the first principle is that the *design must be nonhierarchical.* The examples of ineffective deliberations illustrate a fundamental problem associated with knowledge work in hierarchical organizations: *The people with the most knowledge about something are often the least empowered to make decisions.* Even when they are invited to be part of the discussion, as in the case of Roger Boisjoly and the *Challenger* tragedy, their testimony is often discounted or their opinion isn't even asked. Why do we manage knowledge workers this way?

When I ask managers this question, their most frequent answer is, "There's too much at stake." But what's the logic here? That the more important the decision is, the less important it is to have knowledgeable people making it? When managers say, "There's too much at stake," what are they really saying? There's too much at stake for the company? Or there's too much at stake in their own careers? Or is it that they just don't trust others to make the same decisions they would make themselves? Don't knowledge workers also have a lot at stake? Don't their continued employment and well-being depend on the organization's finding the right answers to the tough questions?

The second principle is that people with knowledge must be capable of working with others who need that knowledge in order to complete their thinking about an interdependent task. Maximum freedom of movement is achieved by reducing role and boundary restrictions. So, the second principle is that *the organization should maximize freedom of movement.*

Third, because it is extremely important for everyone to know what knowledge exists in the system and how to access it, the organization must be holographic; that is, everyone needs to know a little about what is going on in the rest of the organization. So, the third principle is that *knowledge must be widely shared and easily accessible.*

Fourth, in order to provide integration and direction, there must be ways for people to agree on goals and strategies. Based on these goals and strategies, further choices regarding projects and teams can be made. Since it is important for people with knowledge to be involved in setting direction, the fourth principle is that *the organization must involve people with knowledge in goal setting and integration activities.*

Finally, because the development and utilization of knowledge requires the development of people who are knowledgeable and highly committed, *the organization must be designed to encourage, support, and reward learning.* Together, these five principles point toward a form of organization which is quite different from the norm in use today.

REFERENCES

1. Pasmore, W. *Creating Strategic Change: Designing the Flexible, High Performing Organization.* New York: Wiley & Sons, 1994.
2. Bradford, D. and Cohen, A. *Managing for Excellence.* New York: Wiley & Sons, 1984.
3. Pava, C. *Managing New Office Technology: An Organizational Strategy.* New York: The Free Press, 1983.
4. Peters, T. *Liberation Management: Necessary Disorganization for the Nanosecond Nineties.* New York: Alfred Knopf, 1992.
5. Kidder, T. *Soul of a New Machine.* Boston: Little Brown, 1981.

38

Speed and Strategic Choice:

How Managers Accelerate Decision Making

KATHLEEN M. EISENHARDT

Strategy making has changed. The carefully conducted industry analysis or the broad-ranging strategic plan is no longer a guarantee of success. The premium now is on moving fast and keeping pace. More than ever before, the best strategies are irrelevant if they take too long to formulate. Rather, especially where technical and competitive change are rapid, fast strategic decision making is essential.

But how do people make fast choices? Conventional wisdom suggests several strategies. One strategy is to skimp on analysis. That is, managers could look at limited information, consider only one or two alternatives, or gather data from only a few sources. Yes, this is fast. But the obvious problem is that such skimping seriously compromises the quality of the choice. A more subtle concern is whether decision makers will actually have enough confidence to make major choices with so little information and analysis to bolster their decisions.

Another strategy suggested by conventional wisdom is to limit conflict. Conflict drags out decision making, and the more powerful the combatants, the longer this conflict is likely to persist. So, minimizing conflict seems likely to accelerate choice. But, how can managers actually go about repressing real conflict among key executives? And if it can be suppressed, will managers support decisions if their opinions have been ignored? Most importantly, is it possible to make high-quality decisions without conflict? A wide spectrum of research indicates that high conflict yields more innovative, thorough decision making.

Conventional wisdom also suggests a third strategy to accelerate choices. Be an autocrat—make bold and rapid unilateral moves. While such a leader can move quickly, the era of swashbucklers is over. Such leaders often become isolated. This means poor information for making important choices, lack of support once those choices are made, and disabling anxiety which plagues people attempting to make major decisions alone.

Thus, at first glance, conventional wisdom offers strategies which appear to accelerate choices. More often, they are ineffective because they fail to deal with important realities. How can decision makers formulate high-quality choices when information and analysis are limited? How can they maintain a committed group if conflict and debate are suppressed? How can they avoid the natural tendency to procrastinate, especially when information is poor and stakes are high? The purpose of this article is to explore how managers actually do make fast, yet high-quality, strategic decisions.

RESEARCH BASE

The ideas described here partially rest on data which I collected with a colleague, Jay Bourgeois. Our motivation was to study how executives coped with strategic decision making in fast-moving,

Copyright © 1990 by The Regents of the University of California. Reprinted from the *California Management Review*, Vol. 32, No. 3. By permission of The Regents.

Kathleen Eisenhardt is professor of Industrial Engineering and Engineering Management at Stanford University.

high-technology environments. Past research on choice processes had neglected such environments in favor of studying large bureaucracies in stable settings. We tracked decision-making processes in 12 microcomputer firms. We relied on extensive interviews with each member of the top management team of every firm, plus questionnaires, observations of group meetings, and various secondary data. I then followed up the microcomputer study with contacts with numerous Silicon Valley firms and their key executives.

These field data suggest striking differences in the pace of strategic decision making across firms. Some decision makers are fast. They make decisions on critical issues such as product innovations, strategic alliances, and strategic redirection within several months. Others are slow. They spend 6 months, more often 12 to 18 months, on decisions that the fast decision makers can execute in 2 to 4 months.

The ideas in this article are bolstered by recent psychological research. Writings on artificial intelligence and problem solving under time pressure are useful for understanding how people accelerate cognitive processing by more efficient use of information.[1] Work on the effects of emotion on decision making is also germane. Particularly relevant are findings about how individuals cope with anxiety and stress when dealing with high uncertainty. Finally, the psychological literature provides insight into how groups build cohesive interactions and ensure perceptions of equity when resolving conflict situations.[3] Thus, the combination of field study plus related psychological research led to the portrait of fast, yet high-quality, decision making that follows.

Overall, fast decision makers use simple, yet powerful tactics to accelerate choices (see Table 38.1). They maintain constant watch over real time operating information and rely on fast, comparative analysis of multiple alternatives to speed cognitive processing. They favor approaches to conflict resolution which are quick and yet maintain a cohesive group process. Lastly, their use of advice and integration of decisions and tactics creates the self-confidence needed to make a fast

choice, even when information is limited and stakes are high.

At the other end of the spectrum, slow decision makers become bogged down by the fruitless search for information, excessive development of alternatives, and paralysis in the face of conflict and uncertainty.

TRACKING REAL TIME INFORMATION

One of the myths of fast strategic decision making is that limiting information saves time. That is, slashing the amount of information, the number of information sources, and the depth of analysis accelerates choice. But, is this what fast decision makers actually do? The answer is "no." They do just the opposite. They use as much, and sometimes more, information than do their slower counterparts.

However, there is a crucial difference in the kind of information. Slow decision makers rely on planning and futuristic information. They spend time tracking the likely path of technologies, markets, or competitor actions, and then develop plans. In contrast, the fast decision makers look to real time information—that is, information about current operations and current environment which is reported with little or no time lag.

Fast decision makers gather real time information in several ways. One critical source is operational measures of internal performance. Fast decision makers typically examine a wide variety of operating measures on a monthly, weekly, and even daily basis. They prefer indicators such as bookings, backlog, margins, engineering milestones, cash, scrap, and work-in-process to more refined, account-based indicators such as profitability. The key finance manager often has a critical role in the fast decision-making organization. This executive typically is charged with providing this "constant pulse" of what is happening. In comparison with the classic big-company view, fast decision makers keep the key financial manager close to operations, and not in a watch-dog, staff role.

For less quantitative data, fast decision mak-

TABLE 38.1
Fast versus Slow Strategic Decision Making

Fast	Implications
• Track real time information on firm operations and the competitive environment	• Acts as a warning system to spot problems and opportunities early on • Builds a deep, intuitive grasp of the business
• Build multiple, simultaneous alternatives	• Permits quick, comparative analysis • Bolsters confidence that the best alternatives have been considered • Adds a fallback position
• Seek the advice of experienced counselors	• Emphasizes advice from the most useful managers • Provides a safe forum to experiment with ideas and options • Boosts confidence in the choice
• Use "consensus with qualification" to resolve conflicts	• Offers proactive conflict resolution which recognizes its inevitability in many situations • Is a popular approach which balances managers' desires to be heard with the need to make a choice
• Integrate the decision with other decisions and tactics	• "Actively" copes with the stress of choice when information is poor and stakes are high • Signals possible mismatches with other decisions and tactics in the future

Slow	Implications
• Focus on planning and futuristic information, keeping a loose grip on current operations and environment	• Can be time-consuming to develop • Quick obsolete in fast changing situations
• Develop a single alternative, while moving to a second only if the first fails	• Obscures real preferences • Limits confidence that the best alternatives have been considered • Eliminates a fall back position
• Solicit advice haphazrdly or from less experienced counselors	• Fails to take best advantage of the experienced executives
• Use of consensus or deadlines to resolve conflicts	• Consensus is often wishful thinking in complex business decisions • Deadlines may not exist and so decisions can be postponed indefinitely
• Consider the decision as a single choice in isolation from other choices	• Increases stress by keeping the decision in the abstract • Risks the chance that the decision will conflict with other choices

ers emphasize frequent operational meetings—2 or 3 such meetings per week are not unusual. And, the intensity of such meetings is high, with each being a "must" on all calendars. Typically, these meet-ings cover "what's happening" with sales, engineering schedules, releases, or whatever comprises the critical operating information of the organization. But, these meetings are not limited to internal information. Fast decision makers also relay to each other external real time information such as new product introductions by competitors, competition at key accounts, and technical developments within the industry.

A good example is Zap Computers (a fictitious name for an actual firm). Zap's top management team is known for rapid decisions. Typically, they execute, in 2 or 3 months, decisions which elsewhere often drag on for a year or more. How do they do it? The popular press highlights their "laid back" and "fun-loving" California culture. A closer inspection reveals slavish dedication to real time information.

Zap executives claim to "over-MBA it," to "measure everything." They come close. Zap executives review bookings, scrap, inventory, cash flow, and engineering milestones on a weekly and sometimes daily basis. The monthly review is more comprehensive, emphasizing ratios such as revenue per employee and margins. Firm executives maintain fixed targets for margins and key expense categories. These targets themselves are not so unusual, but what is striking is the number of people who can recite them. Zap executives also attend three regularly scheduled operations meetings each week. One is a staff meeting for general topics while another is for products and the third is a review of engineering schedules. The tone is emotional, intense, and vocal.

The Zap top management team plays an important role in gathering real time data. The VP Finance, described as "having a good understanding of business" and years of experience, oversees more than just the usual treasury and accounting functions. He is responsible for the financial model of the firm which is run at least weekly. The model itself is simple, but it allows Zap executives to translate possible decisions into their impact on basic operating results. His group also provides updated operational data, usually available on a daily basis.

Other executives are also essential to the real time information network at Zap. For example, the VP Marketing is charged with tracking the moves of competitors as they occur. This means constant phone calls and frequent travel. The VP R&D also

works the phone to maintain a complex web of university and business contacts which keep him cognizant of the latest technical developments.

Zap executives also favor electronic mail or face-to-face meetings. As they described it, "We e-mail constantly." They are also frequently in and out of each other's offices. On the other hand, Zap executives avoid time delayed media such as memos. They are seen as too slow and too dated. Overall, dedication to real time information gives Zap executives an extraordinary grasp of the details of their business.

In contrast, slow decision makers have a much looser grip on current operations and the competitive environment. For example, decision makers in the slower firms track few operational measures and they review them less frequently than do their faster counterparts. Their emphasis is on future, not current, information.

The lack of real time information is also evident in the use of group meetings. In the microcomputer study, slow decision makers had few, if any, weekly operations meetings. Several firms did not have a VP Finance or else relied on a less experienced executive. For example, one used an ex-engineer, claimed by all to be "weak" in financial matters. At another firm, the VP Finance had left the firm and there were no current plans to replace him.

Instead of real time data, these executives prefer planning information. For example, executives at one corporation spent close to a year doing a technology study of various operating systems for microprocessors as a prelude to a new product decision. At another firm, executives responded to a performance decline by spending 6 months developing a technology forecast for the industry. The elapsed decision-making time in both firms was over a year.

Why does real time information speed decision making? An obvious reason is that the continual tracking allows managers to spot opportunities and problems sooner. Real time information acts as an early warning system so that managers can respond before situations become too problematic. When crises do arise, such managers can go right to the problem, rather than groping about for relevant information.

However, a more subtle explanation comes from artificial intelligence. Research on the development of intuition suggests that the basis of intuition is experience.[4] For example, chess players develop their inuition by playing chess over and over again. This repeated practice allows the chess player to play the game using what lay people term "intuition." In fact, intuitive chess players have actually learned to process information in patterns or blocks. Because they recognize and manipulate information in blocks, they can process information much faster than others who think only in single items of information.

Consistent with this view, managers who track real time information are actually developing their intuition. Aided by intuition, they can then react quickly and accurately to changing events. Indeed, in the microcomputer study, the executives who were most attuned to real time data were also those most described as intuitive. For example, one executive was described as a "numbers" person and claimed to "over-MBA it." Yet, he was also described by his colleagues as "intuitive," "a lateral thinker," and as having "the best sense of everything in the business." Another also claimed to be a "numbers guy." His VP Finance praised "the quality of his understanding" and frequent use of operating data. This executive was also described as having "an immense instinctive feel" and a superior "grasp of the business."

In contrast, slow strategic decision makers emphasize planning and forecasting information. They look to the future and attempt to predict it. Or, they hope that, by waiting, the future will become clear. Yet, their faster counterparts maintain that this is foolish. They claim that extensive planning wastes time. Why? It's difficult to predict what will happen and impossible to predict who will do it and when. As one fast-moving executive claimed, "No company can know how things will evolve. You can only monitor the outside world and direct the evolving strategy at what you see." Overall, it appears that real time information—which gives executives an intimate knowledge of their business—speeds choice, but planning information—which attempts to predict the future—does not.

BUILDING MULTIPLE, SIMULTANEOUS ALTERNATIVES

A second myth is that fast decision makers save time by focusing on only one or two alternatives. The underlying logic is that fewer alternatives are faster to analyze than more. But, in fact, fast decision makers do the reverse. They explicitly search for and debate multiple alternatives, often working several options at once. At the extreme, some fast decision makers will support alternatives that they oppose if doing so furthers debate, and they will even introduce alternatives which they do not actually support.

A good example of multiple alternatives occurred at one of the microcomputer firms. Here, a new CEO was faced with improving the lacklustre performance of the firm. New products were slow in coming out and there was pressure from investors to do something. This new CEO launched a fact-gathering exercise. Almost simultaneously firm executives began to develop a rough set of alternatives. As the fact-gathering continued, so did the shaping of alternatives. In less than 2 months, the executives had developed 4 options. They considered selling some of their technology—there were willing buyers, especially from overseas. They also considered a major strategic redirection of the firm which would involve using the base technology to enter a new market. A third option involved various tactical changes in the form of redeployment of some engineering resources and adjustments to the marketing approach. The final option was extreme—liquidation of the firm.

Executives at the firm admitted that this decision strategy was ambiguous and complicated. Why did they do it? As one executive claimed, they and the CEO, in particular, liked to have multiple options, "a larger set of options than most people do." There was a preference for "working a multiple array of possibilities instead of just a couple."

At another firm, the problem was cash flow. The business was prospering, but the cash flow was not keeping pace. These executives also developed multiple alternatives. One executive negotiated with banks to extend credit lines. Others developed several strategic alliance alternatives with both U.S. and foreign firms. A third set of executives planned a major equity financing. With rough details of each option in hand, firm executives chose the strategic alliance for flexibility and marketing reasons. When the first choice alliance partner backed out, firm executives quickly cut a deal with the second. The credit and equity plans were waiting on the shelf, if the alliance option had failed.

In contrast, surprisingly, slow decision makers work with fewer, not more, alternatives. They typically develop and analyze a single alternative, and only seriously consider other alternatives if the first becomes infeasible. Thus, slow decision makers favor a highly sequential approach to alternatives—and, one which emphasizes depth of analysis over breadth of options.

A new product decision at one of the microcomputer firms illustrates this process. These executives wanted to develop a new product which made greater use of VLSI technology. The rationale was that increased integration would lower product costs. Firm executives explored the possibility of in-house development for several months. When they concluded that the firm lacked sufficient expertise, they then migrated to a second alternative, a strategic alliance with a major U.S. firm. They spent about six months getting to know the personnel of their could-be partner and negotiating the terms of the deal. However, the deal fell through when the two parties could not reach a final agreement. At this point, firm executives then had to search several months for another partner. After further delay, they eventually closed the deal with this second firm.

This same pattern of single, sequential alternatives is characteristic of many slow decisions. At another firm, executives were also interested in developing a new product. They too explored the in-house route to a new product for several months. When they determined that in-house development would be too slow, they belatedly went outside for a product source. It took several more months to locate a suitable partner. At another firm, executives noted increasing competition in their market-place. They spent almost a year deciding whether they needed a new strategy. Only after they decided that the old strategy was no longer workable did they then seriously consider what that new strategy should be.

Why are multiple, simultaneous alternatives fast? One reason is that multiple alternatives (at least, in the range of 3 to 5) are faster to analyze than 1 or 2. Why? The reason is comparison. Comparative analysis sharpens preferences. For example, car buyers often find it difficult to understand their preferences in the abstract. Rather, actually driving cars and then comparing across cars helps prospective buyers to decide whether they prefer a leather or plush interior, a standard or rally suspension package, one make over another, and so forth. Comparative analysis is also fast because it allows decision makers to use rankings to assess alternatives. The superiority of an alternative is often apparent in comparison, even if its superiority cannot be readily quantified.

Multiple alternatives also speed decision making because they are confidence building. With multiple alternatives, decision makers are more likely to feel that they have not missed a superior alternative. Again, to use the car buying example, it is difficult to buy a car without seeing others because buyers often cannot overcome the feeling that they may be missing something better elsewhere.

Finally, multiple alternatives are fast because they provide a fall back position. When on option falls through, decision makers can quickly move on to a second. Although a first choice option sometimes prevails, situations can change rapidly and dramatically. So, the odds are good that adjustments will be needed. In the illustrations above, the firms which pursued multiple alternatives simultaneously had fall back positions when one or more options proved infeasible. In contrast, the firms pursuing sequential alternatives lost time because they waited until an option failed before looking for a new one.

Overall, there is a fundamental difference in how fast and slow decision makers treat alternatives. Fast decision makers develop multiple alternatives, but analyze them rapidly. They rely primarily on quick, comparative analysis, which reveals relative rankings and sharpens preferences. Theirs is a "breadth-not-depth" strategy. Recent laboratory research indicates that this is the efficient cognitive processing approach when the decision maker is under time pressure.[5]

In contrast, slow decision makers emphasize depth of analysis. They analyze few alternatives, but do so in greater depth. And so, they often conduct a similar amount of analysis, but without gaining the confidence in their choice that multiple alternatives bring and without gaining the advantage of fall back positions.

RELYING ON THE ADVICE OF COUNSELORS

A third critical aspect of fast strategic decision making is the judicious use of advice. Most fast decision makers rely on a two-tier advice process in which all executives offer some advice, but the key decision maker focuses on the advice provided by one or two of the most experienced executives in the group, who are termed "counselors." By contrast, slow decision makers typically have no one in this counselor role.

What do these counselors do? Typically, they work in the background advising the key decision maker about a wide range of issues. They also serve as an early and confidential sounding board for ideas. For example, at one firm, the counselor played an important role in a new product decision. The situation was triggered by an unexpected new product introduction by an important competitor. In private, the counselor alerted the CEO to the imminent introduction. The two then conferred, with the counselor helping the CEO to shape and test alternatives. Even after the CEO brought the issue to the attention of the entire top management team, the counselor continued to work behind the scenes with the CEO. As the CEO described, "Our interaction is more general than just sales . . . When I talk with Joe it's often about company issues."

A striking feature of the counselor role is the consistent demographic profile of these individuals. The counselor is typically an older and more experienced person, who is recognized as "savvy" or "street smart" by colleagues. For example, the counselors at one firm were 10 to 20 years older than the rest of the top management team. One of these executives had been a senior manager at a major, international firm. He was described as "the best manager" on the top management team. The other had been a senior executive at two important firms in the industry. He was credited with being the "most knowledgeable about the outside world." Counselors are also frequently on a career plateau, with their aspirations no longer centering on the fast-track to the top. Rather, they relish the personal challenge. As one counselor claimed, "It's fun to build an organization again."

What do fast decision makers do when they have no colleague who fits the counselor profile? In one such case, a consultant was hired to play the role. This consultant had extensive industry contacts, had been a senior executive at two other firms, and had known the CEO for many years. This executive was credited with an important advisory role to the CEO as well as to several other executives.

In contrast, slow strategic decision makers typically have no executive who acts as a counselor. These decision makers usually do not develop any kind of a close, advisory relationship with another colleague. Or, if they do, that colleague often is a poor choice. For example, the counselor to a CEO in a slow decision making firm was considered to be "bright," but "young." He was in his early 30s and had only functional staff experience. Given his modest background, his ability to be an effective counselor was limited.

Why do experienced counselors accelerate choices? Clearly, one reason is that these individuals can provide high-quality advice to decision makers more readily than less experienced colleagues. They have simply seen more and done more. Not surprisingly, they can usually assess situations more rapidly and offer better advice than less experienced people.

Second, they are excellent sounding boards. They combine strong experience with a trustworthiness that comes with limited personal ambition and often long acquaintance with the key decision maker. These are people who understand discretion and the subtle exercise of power.

Perhaps most importantly, counselors can boost the confidence of decision makers to decide. One of the highest barriers to fast decision making is anxiety. Big stakes decision making with high uncertainty is stressful, and so it is extraordinarily tempting simply to procrastinate. However, conversations with an experienced confidante can counteract this tendency to delay by bolstering decision makers' confidence to make difficult choices.

RESOLVING CONFLICT

Another myth of fast strategic decision making is that conflict slows down the pace of choice. Obviously, conflict can have this effect. But, fast decision makers know how to gain the advantages of conflict without extensive delays in their decision process. The key is conflict resolution.

Fast decision makers typically use a two step process, termed "consensus with qualification" by one executive, to resolve deadlocks among individuals. This process works as follows. First, executives talk over an issue and attempt to gain consensus. If consensus occurs, the choice is made. However, if consensus is not forthcoming, the key manager and most relevant functional head make the choice, guided by the input from the rest of the group. As one executive told us, "Most of the time we reach consensus, but if not Randy makes the choice."

A description of decision making at Forefront (a fictitious name for an actual firm) serves an an illustration. Forefront was faced with a major challenge in its principal market from an important competitor. This firm had unexpectedly announced a new machine which appeared to challenge Forefront's leadership in its primary area of business. Forefront executives confronted the problem, and substantial disagreement was apparent. Several executives wanted to shift R&D resources to counter

this competitive move. The price was diverting significant engineering talent from a more innovative product currently in design. Others argued that a simple extension of an existing product was appropriate. Under this plan, Forefront would simply repackage an existing product with a few new features from its stable of modest technical improvements. A third set of executives perceived that the threat was not all that important and that Forefront should continue with current plans, making no response.

The team held a series of meetings over several weeks. Consensus was not in the cards. Given the stalemate, the CEO and his marketing VP simply made the choice. Not all agreed with their selection, but everyone had a voice in the process. As the CEO claimed, "The functional heads do the talking . . . I pull the trigger."

The approach to conflict used by fast decision makers, such as the executives at Forefront, constrasts markedly with that used by the slow decision makers. Sometimes slow decision makers wait for consensus. They forage for an option which satisfies everyone. However, since conflict is common in decision making, the search for consensus often drags on for months. For example, the decision makers at one firm debated the specifications of a new product for about a year. Finally, consensus came—after several executives who opposed one of the options left the firm.

Sometimes slow decision makers wait for deadlines, which then energize them to make a choice. For example, the annual meeting triggered a decision at one firm. The CEO had worked for almost a year on a proposal to develop a new market. Others in the group felt that such a project would stretch sales and engineering resources too much. The CEO was unwilling to do nothing and yet also unwilling to decide. So, he continually refined his proposal in the hopes of gaining others' agreement. What was the result? Each refinement improved the proposal, but also stiffened the opposition. This pattern might have dragged on indefinitely except for the annual meeting. Frustrated by repeated rejections and facing the impending deadline, the CEO came up with a new alternative and as he claimed, "shoved it down their throats."

Why is consensus with qualification rapid? One reason is that it takes a realistic view of conflict. Conflict is seen as natural, valuable, and almost always inevitable. Therefore, fast decision makers recognize that choices must be made even if there is disagreement. The other reason that consensus with qualification is rapid is its popularity. Managers like it. Most people want a voice in the decision-making process, but are willing to accept that their opinions may not prevail. Consensus with qualification gives people this voice, and goes one better by giving them added influence when the choice particularly affects their part of the organization.

In contrast, slow decision makers are stymied by conflict. They delay in the hopes that uncertainty will magically become certain. Or, they look for consensus. But unfortunately, consensus is often wishful thinking in most complex business situations. People are likely to have differing opinions, expecially regarding big and important choices. Although consensus sometimes emerges, often it does not. Rather, as one executive described, "We found that operating by consensus essentially gave everyone veto power. There was no structure. Nothing accomplished." Overall, many managers dislike a strictly consensual approach to choice and prefer simply to "get on with it."

INTEGRATING DECISIONS AND TACTICS

The final key to fast decision making is the integration of the focal decision with other key choices and tactical plans. In effect, fast strategic decision makers fit any single decision into a web of interlocking choices. This decision integration does not imply any sort of elaborate planning. In fact, frequently there is no written plan. Rather, fast decision makers maintain a cognitive map which they can readily describe or sketch on a piece of paper. At most, fast decision makers stitch together a 5 to 10 page document describing the relationship among choices and tactics.

A good example of decision integration oc-curred at Triumph (a fictitious name for an actual firm). The decision began with the arrival of a new CEO. The firm was struggling in the wake of the highly mercurial, former CEO. The new CEO spent several weeks learning about people and products. He and other executives also began developing options for how to energize the firm. In the process of defining and refining these options, the executive group also decided on the specifications for a new product, scheduled three new product releases, reprioritized engineering assignments, and rebudgeted the firm for the year. All of this occurred in about 2 months.

These decisions contrast with a similar one executed by a slower team. These executives also faced deteriorating financial performance. However, their response was a technology forecasting project. This project was completed several months later. Firm executives then spent the next several months debating whether to change the firm strategy or to execute the existing approach more effectively. Key firm executives were seriously split on the issue. Finally, after several opponents left the firm and the financial situation had deteriorated to the point that the existing strategy could no longer by salvaged, the CEO chose to alter the strategy. Only then did the executives think about what the new strategy would be. Five more months passed before the new strategic direction was set. And, there were still tactical plans such as engineering assignments to be made.

The constrast with the Triumph case is striking. Triumph executives made a similar decision on strategic redirection—plus they chose a new product, scheduled 3 new product releases, reassigned engineering priorities and rebudgeted the firm—in less than 2 months, compared to the 18-month period of the second company.

Why does decision integration accelerate decision making? On the surface, it appears time-consuming to link together decisions and tactics. However, this surface view neglects the value of decision integration for building the confidence of decision makers. Anxiety is a major impediment to fast choice. Making choices, when information is poor and stakes are high, is paralyzing. The psychological literature indicates that a key to efficacy in such stressful situations is proactive and structuring behavior—that is, formulation of concrete action steps to structure one's unstable world.[6] Such "active coping" enhances feeling of competence and control which, in turn, boost the confidence to decide. Consistent with this view, managers who integrate decisions and tactics are actually engaging in active coping. Aided by enhanced feelings of competence and control, they can make choices more quickly and confidently in high stress and information poor situations.

Secondly, decision integrations does more than simply give a psychological illusion of control. The process also provides better understanding of alternatives and potential conflicts with other decisions. By linking together decisions and tactics at the outset, managers can avoid many of the delays that occur when executing one action has unanticipated consequences for other actions.

In contrast, slow decision makers treat each decision as a separate event, detached from other major choices and from tactics of implementation. In effect, they employ a linear view of decision making. Unfortunately, such an approach does nothing to diminish anxiety. Decisions remain in the abstract, unattached to other activities within the organization. Evidence from several firms confirms that anxiety looms large for slow decision makers. For example, one slow decision maker worried that "we don't know if we have the confidence to do it." A second executive lamented,"Maybe we saw too much mystery. Maybe we needed more gut." His conclusion was simple: "You don't know any more even though you wait." Overall, slow decision makers see decisions as very large, discrete, and anxiety-provoking events whereas fast decision makers see individual decisions as a smaller part of an overarching pattern of choices.

MANAGERIAL IMPLICATIONS

Strategy making is changing. Strategies that may have been viable in the past are no longer feasible if they take too long to formulate. The field data echo this point. For example, the microcomputer study revealed that fast strategic decision makers led either high performing organizations or organizations that achieved performance turnarounds.[7] These fast decision makers also explicity linked the speed of their strategic decision making to success. They claimed: "you have to keep up with the train," "you've got to catch the big opportunities," "simply do *something*," and so on.

In contrast, the slow strategic decision makers managed mediocre organizations, some of which have since failed. These decision makers usually recognized that speed was important, but they did not understand how to be fast. As a result, they missed opportunities and lost the learning that comes with making frequent choices. As one described, "The company wound up doing a random walk. Our products were too late and they were too expensive."

How do managers actually make fast, yet high-quality, strategic decisions? This article has identified five key tactics for accelerating decision making. They involve simple behaviors which decision makers in a variety of settings can use. To summarize:

- Before decisions arise, track real time information to develop a deep and intuitive grasp of the business. Focus on both operating parameters and critical environmental variables to hone your intuition.

- During the decision process, immediately begin to build multiple alternatives using your intuitive grasp of the business. Be certain to analyze the alternatives quickly and in comparison with one another. Possibly even begin execution of several before settling on a final choice.

- Ask everyone for advice, but depend on one or two counselors. Be selective in your choice of counselors. Look for savvy, trustworthy, and discreet colleagues.

- When it's time to decide, involve everyone. Try for consensus. But, if it doesn't emerge, don't delay. Make the choice yourself or better yet, with the others most affected by the decision. Delaying won't make you popular and won't make you fast.

- Ensure that you have integrated your choice with other decisions and tactical moves. You'll feel more confident and you will have avoided many of the headaches of mismatched decisions down the road.

CONCLUSION

Previous scholarly research on decision making has ignored speed in favor of topics such as the breakdown of rationality and the difficulty of identifying goals. It has also emphasized the study of large bureaucracies in stable settings, rather than the high velocity environments which many decision makers actually face.

However, most managers have recognized that speed matters. A slow strategy is as ineffective as the wrong strategy. So, fast strategic decision making has emerged as a crucial competitive weapon. But, knowing how to be fast is difficult. The process involves accelerating information processing, building up the confidence to decide, and

yet maintaining the cohesiveness of the decision-making group. Should managers learn how to be fast? One executive summarized the prevailing reality in many industries: "No advantage is long-term because our industry isn't static. The only competitve advantage is in moving quickly."

REFERENCES

1. J. Hayes, *The Complete Problem Solvers* (Philadelphia, PA: Franklin Press, 1981); H. Simon, *"Making Management Decisions," Academy of Management Executive* (1987); J. Payne, J. Bettman, and E. Johnson, "Adaptive Strategy Selection in Decision Making," *Journal of Experimental Psychology* (1988).
2. R. Gal and R. Lazarus, "The Role of Activity in Anticipating Stressful Situations," *Journal of Human Stress* (1975); E. Langer, "Illusion of Control," *Journal of Personality and Social Psychology* (1975).
3. P. C. Earley and E. A. Lind, "Procedural Justice and Participation in Task Selection: The Role of Control in Mediating Justice Judgments," *Journal of Personality and Social Psychology* (1987).
4. Simon, op. cit.
5. Payne et al., op. cit.
6. Gal and Lazarus, op. cit.
7. K. Eisenhardt, "Making Fast Strategic Decisions in High Velocity Environments," *Academy of Management Journal,* 28/3 (1989).

39

Managing Performance with The *Real* Numbers

TONY HOPE AND JEREMY HOPE

Recent studies have shown that most organisations generate huge amounts of work for which the consumer receives no benefit. Estimates have ranged from 20% to 50% of total costs depending on the type of business and the efficiency of the organisation. Jim Rigby, a divisional controller at Hewlett Packard's South Queensferry plant in Scotland has been one of the pioneers of activity based management in the UK. He said recently:

> researchers claim that most organisations have a minimum of 30% waste in their cost structure, yet typically accountants have not seen waste elimination as a major source of profit improvement. When you consider that HP in 1992 was a $16 billion company spending $8 billion in expenses, then if our wastage was 30% it represents a $2.4 billion opportunity for profit improvement. This dwarfs the impact of downsizing and the other techniques that finance directors and managements introduce.[1]

By eliminating non-value-adding work, managers would transform the profitability of their organisations overnight. So why hasn't such a transformation occurred? Why do so many companies repeat their annual cost reduction exercises? The reason is simple. The measurement systems used by managers do not produce the right numbers. Managers are using numbers designed for financial reporting and controlling budgets, purposes which have little to do with the real value-adding performance of the business.

Managers today need to look at more than just financial performance. They need, for example, to measure quality, innovation, and customer service, and ensure that profitable products and services are being sold to profitable customers. These are the *real numbers,* the critical gauges which tell them whether their organisations are successful. But these numbers do not flow up and down the traditional organisational hierarchy. Rather they flow *horizontally* across functional boundaries, following the chain of the organisation's value-adding processes. They emphasise improvement rather than control. At their heart lies the key issue—*the measurement of work*—and the key question—*does it add value to the customer?*

We believe that a *horizontal information system* can be designed to provide managers with the *real numbers.* We argue that better management information, more relevant performance measures, and more thoughtful reward systems can change management behaviour, support strategy and transform the bottom line. But for managers to complete this transformation process successfully—to move from a hierarchical organisation to one which emphasises teamwork, value creation, customer service and continuous improvement—they must tackle a number of deep rooted problems. They must, for example, change the orientation of their information systems to place strategy, innovation, and the customer, at their core.

RECENT DEVELOPMENTS

The recognition of these issues is not new—it is not some blinding flash of insight on our part. A

Reprinted with permission from the authors. For more discussion of the material in this article, see *Transforming the Bottom Line* by T. Hope and J. Hope, London: Nicholas Brealey Publishing, 1995. Also published by Harvard Business School Press in 1996.

Tony Hope is a chartered accountant and Visiting Professor at the University of Manchester Business School and INSEAD.
Jeremy Hope is a chartered accountant and consulting partner in Hope Associates.

brief survey of recent improvement initiatives shows how close many have come to finding the answers, only to find the way forward blocked by unforeseen barriers and bottlenecks. Accountants must shoulder much of the blame, for they have failed to understand the behavioural consequences of their systems and reports. Typically these have encouraged actions and decisions which have proved fatal to improvement initiatives.

In an attempt to focus performance more on the customer, many organisations have adopted *horizontal management structures*. Often driven by re-engineering projects, the horizontal model has demonstrated how both productivity and profitability can dramatically be improved, especially when responsibility and accountability are firmly established at the team-based level. But this transition is often undermined by the entrenched control philosophy of traditional accounting systems.

Re-engineering and total quality programmes have both been embraced by eager managers, often with evangelical zeal. And it is not hard to see why. They focus on the central issue—the total satisfaction of customer needs. And to achieve this objective they look to improve the quality and relevance of work. But, crucially, neither has succeeded in finding a way to measure these improvements. So how can managers tell if these initiatives are successful on a month by month basis? This weakness has invariably meant that existing budgets, performance measures, and reward systems gradually re-assert their authority. Consequently, much of the early progress is difficult to sustain, and when other issues capture the attention of managers, the momentum is often lost and the quality or re-engineering initiative is left to wither on the vine.

But the problem is not so much one of measures *per se,* it is the choice of the *right* measures which is crucial to success. Many companies have recognised that financial measures only tell part of the story. The ultimate objective is to *link performance measures to strategy,* but this is seldom straightforward. Attributes such as speed, flexibility, innovation, price, and the performance of value-adding work, all require multi-faceted mea-

sures, which cut across organisational boundaries. And care must be taken that the choice of measure, however appropriate it might seem in its own context, encourages the right sort of behaviour. But, more often than not, strategic targets and performance measures are at odds with each other. Kaplan and Norton's[2] work on the 'balanced scorecard'—which gives executives a view of performance from various internal and external perspectives including that of the customer—is important in this respect. But despite the progress made with customer-oriented and other nonfinancial performance measures, financial results continue to dominate where it matters—in the corporate boardroom.

THE HIDDEN BARRIERS

Despite the extensive use of the latest management techniques and a supporting army of willing consultants, the vast majority of business improvement initiatives fail to make any lasting impression. And because such initiatives stress the importance of leadership, vision, strategy, quality, culture, and management commitment, failure is invariably rationalised in these terms. But the real reasons often lie with the day to day forces that influence management behaviour rather than with the clarion calls for improvement. For no matter what executives might say about strategy, vision, and culture, their rhetoric often fails to penetrate the walls of budgeting systems, reward and recognition structures, and performance measures. These are the collision points where the forces of change meet the immovable objects of traditional systems. And the (sometimes unwitting) defenders of the traditional faith are accountants and IT managers.

Traditional management structures and, in particular the accounting systems which support them, emphasise control rather than improvement and focus on internal performance rather than customer value. Indeed one need look no further than the language of contemporary accounting—fixed and variable cost, break-even analysis, capacity planning, standard costing, absorption costing, marginal costing, budgetary control, variance analysis, cost centres, profit centres, and inventory valuation. It is hard to find a vocabulary which stresses strategy, customers, competition, value-added, efficiency, productivity, quality, innovation, and organisational learning.

Accounting systems have not been developed independently of the organisational structure they serve. Thus, in traditional organisations, the objectives of such systems are planning and control, and the keywords are consistency, standardisation, ease of audit, and speed of reporting. In essence they allow the bosses to 'command and control'. And nowhere is this control mentality more ingrained than in traditional budgeting systems. Jack Welch[3], CEO of GE, highlighted the extent of the budgeting problem when he was recently asked to comment on the difference between setting goals and achieving them. He replied:

> It takes an atmosphere where a goal doesn't become part of the old fashioned budget. The budget is the bane of corporate America. It never should have existed. A budget is this: if you make it, you generally get a pat on the back and a few bucks. If you miss it, you get a stick in the eye— or worse. . . . Making a budget is an exercise in minimalisation. You're always trying to get the lowest out of people, because everyone is negotiating to get the lowest number.

Budget meetings should be a time for learning and understanding, and applying the resources of the firm to maximise competitive advantage. But the opposite is more often the case. Management decisions based on reported costs alone (whether 'planned' or 'actual') can lead firms into dangerous waters with unexpected consequences for profitability and cash flow.

Suppose, for example, you have responsibility for approving the budget of an IT department for the following year. Cash is tight but new investment is needed and, according to the IT manager, an extra 12 programmers and 3 analysts are required. The actual expenditure for last year and the budget you have been asked to approve for the following year are presented to you as follows:

	Actual	Budget
Salaries and benefits (85 staff)	3,000,000	3,200,000
Extra staff costs (15 staff)	—	600,000
Travelling	400,000	450,000
Department expenses	1,150,000	1,250,000
Other costs	450,000	500,000
	£5,000,000	£6,000,000

The IT manager is quite persuasive and easily justifies his position. A small increase in basic salaries is in tune with the mood (and performance) of the firm. But, for the firm to improve, it needs better information systems and thus extra resources. Your inclination is to accept the budget without much argument, although you might question the levels of productivity within the department.

But imagine your reaction if last year's actual costs were presented in the following way:

	Actual	%
Planning new systems	900,000	18
Analysing and coding	1,200,000	24
Documenting and testing	900,000	18
Solving problems caused by downtime	600,000	12
Reworking and corrections	1,000,000	20
Meetings of no value	400,000	8
	£5,000,000	100%

In other words, value-adding costs (i.e. the first three headings totalling £3 million) amount to 60% of last year's costs, leaving 40% of costs representing waste. How would this alternative presentation change your view? It would be strange if you didn't react by demanding to know the detailed causes of these non-value-adding costs and how they could be eliminated. Nor is it likely that you would approve any further increase in overall costs—the extra resources being requested are already in place—the non-productive work merely needs removing. In fact the reality is that you would be demanding *cost reductions* and dramatic increases in productivity.

Because managers usually think in terms of reported costs and not the *causes of costs,* they fail to ask the right questions. But without this type of work-based analysis what happens in practice? Budgets are invariably approved on the basis of percentage adjustments to the previous year's figures, and thus all the non-value-adding costs hidden within accounting descriptions (such as salaries and travelling) are adjusted in the same way. *The result is usually an uplift in the budget for unnecessary and wasteful costs!* Budget holders who are rewarded on their ability to stay within the agreed budget have little incentive to ask searching questions concerning strategic and work-based issues that should underpin the whole process. The net result is a huge wasted opportunity.

Many companies have taken their first step down the transformation path by recognising the challenges confronting them. But neither flatter management structures, re-engineering, empowerment, nor quality initiatives can, on their own, bring them success. This was what a recent CAM-I report[4] on advanced management techniques had to say:

> Techniques like total quality, re-engineering, activity based costing, and empowerment are all useful tools, but each appears to address somewhat different goals and only limited aspects of performance. Ideas are colliding, not connecting. A comprehensive and unifying management approach is needed that responds to the new business environment.

A new approach is needed, and the action begins right at the heart of the organisation—with the management and measurement of *work.* Management structures and information systems must begin to look *horizontally towards the customer*—across functions and departments at the value-adding processes that define the core strength of any business—and reward systems should support the key performance objectives chosen, not undermine them.

THE CAUSES OF COSTS

The underlying assumption of most costing systems is that costs can be classified as either variable (they vary with output), or fixed (they don't vary with output). Pricing strategies, cost management, and performance measurement are all geared to recovering fixed costs as fast as possible leaving the way clear for profits to flow through to the bottom line. In the traditional model volume is the primary cause of costs and the 'recovery mentality' dictates that by increasing volume, unit costs are reduced. It is easy to see how such a simple argument feels intuitively right to managers and accountants. And in the production-led world from which most of them came, this was indeed valid. But this is no longer the case. In a world full of demanding customers and agile competitors, not only are many costs caused by factors other than volume, but many of them are also caused by work which should not be done at all.

Because accountants have focused on the allocation of costs to products rather than understanding their causes, they have failed to realise that many costs are increasingly driven not by volume, but by scope and diversity, caused by a wide variety of customer demands, such as product customisation, special packaging and delivery, and service arrangements. Moreover they have failed to see the speed and scale of the problem. The dramatic rise in the proportion of overheads to total costs has stretched the credibility of allocation methods to breaking point. This point was well put by one senior executive[5]:

> We've been brought up to manage in a world where burden rates (the ratio of overhead costs to labour costs) are 100% to 200% or so. But now some of our plants are running with burden rates of over 1000%. We don't even know what that means.

The recognition of these problems has led to the recent rise in popularity of *activity based costing (ABC)* which is now used by many firms to provide a better understanding of which products are profitable after charging all the resources they consume. ABC recognises that the driving forces of costs are the work that people do and that this work can be analysed into its component parts (activities), some of which add value and some of which don't. Although activity based costing is an important evolutionary step forward towards a better understanding of cost attribution, most practical applications of ABC have concentrated on the 'C' rather than the 'A'. But the real opportunity offered by the activity approach—*how to identify and, where appropriate, eliminate the causes of costs*—has not been taken by most accountants. They have persisted with finding better methods of attributing existing costs to products. Cooper and Kaplan[6], the pioneers of ABC, recently put this in context when they said, *"an improved costing system is a means to an end. The goal is to increase profits, not to obtain more accurate product costs"*.

Managers are also becoming more aware that there are many other important factors which cause costs to be higher or lower than they might otherwise be. For example, although most cost management efforts concentrate on the production process, far greater leverage can be gained in minimising costs throughout the lifecycle of products by improving their design and manufacturability and getting them to market quickly. Studies by McKinsey & Co[7] have shown that getting products to market on time but over the cost budget can have a far greater impact on profitability than being late to market but keeping within the cost budget. Clearly, encouraging engineers to spend more time on the right value-adding work, and less time on meetings, reports, and budgets, has important implications for profitability. But accounting systems don't recognise these crucial issues. They continue to tie key knowledge workers to mindless budgets, which has the effect (as one article recently put it) of *grinding genius into gruel"*.

The second issue concerns costs which add little or no value to customers. Activity audits have consistently shown the scale of these costs to be far greater than most managers realised. But how and why are these costs caused and, more importantly, how can they be identified and eliminated? The key question is which work adds value? Unless this question can be answered by everyone in the organisation, any system designed to deal with this issue will be severely handicapped.

Value-adding work is generally agreed to be work which the customer is willing to pay for. But who is the customer? This question is not always easy to answer. Of course the ready answer is that the customer is the immediate person or organisation who buys the product or service. But who is the customer of 'new product development' or the 'manufacturing' process? Is it the sales process (an 'internal' customer), or is it the (external) customer who actually pays for the product? In our view the focus of value-adding work should, as far as possible, be the final customer at the end of the external value chain. For example, a car parts supplier sells to a manufacturer but his ultimate customer is the purchaser of the car. Similarly, a car manufacturer sells to a dealer but his ultimate customer is still the final buyer.

Neither is value-adding work always easy to identify. Take for example work done at the testing stage during the production of the chassis of a car. This activity is necessary to the production process and is therefore an essential activity, but is it of value to the customer? Imagine displaying the following items on the price list in a dealer's showroom: Sun-Roof £900; Chassis Testing £90? Of course this would be laughable, so how can such testing add value, if the customer is not prepared to pay for it? The fact is that this cost is incurred because the quality of the chassis is not sufficiently stable. The answer is to improve quality, not to expect the customer to pay.

While the customer is recognised as the primary focus of value-adding work, there are many other worthwhile causes which must not be overlooked. For example, strategic objectives might include becoming more 'environmentally friendly' or improving the spread of knowledge throughout the organisation. Work done towards these worthy objectives does not *directly* benefit the customer (although it may well do so indirectly). Nor does the work of administrators and accountants fulfilling government regulations benefit the customer, but it must be done.

The causes of non-value-adding work are often complex, interrelated, and part of a 'chain reaction'. Some of the more common causes can be identified as follows:

• *Management structures.* Most large organisations, because of their fragmented departmental structures, employ many people whose work is irrelevant to the customer, and therefore adds little or no value. This work is more prevalent in such departments as audit, legal, and administration which support the internal machinery of the company. However, this work is difficult to remove without changing the organisational structure itself. There is much anecdotal evidence to show that flatter, team-based structures, will deliver more value to customers than hierarchical, functionally based structures. Similarly, small, highly focused business units, will deliver more value than large, centrally managed structures.

• *Production processes.* Miller and Vollmann[8] have suggested that there is an entire *'hidden factory'* within the more obvious physical production setting. This hidden factory, they argue, is made up of four types of transaction, none of which adds value to the product or customer. Thus firms incur *logistical costs* by employing 'indirect' workers to receive, expedite, ship, and account for the moving of materials between locations; they employ people to ensure that the supply and demand for materials, labour and capacity is in *balance*; they require people to ensure that transactions have taken place with the correctness or *quality* that should occur; and finally, and most critically in cost terms, they employ people in the 'hidden factory' to simply update their systems to account for *changes* in schedules, specifications of materials, and engineering designs.

• *Excessive customer demands.* For work to be value-adding, it must be converted into cash. However, many customer-driven costs are caused by a misguided perception of value (usually in the eyes of salespeople). The promise of a rosy future with a customer is often the trigger for a series of non-value-adding costs, including product variations, special packaging, free management services, and

a host of other benefits, which taken together, can have a material impact on overall costs and profitability.

• *Poor quality of work.* We all know of people who are 'not up to the job'. Either through lack of skills or training, or because they are just out of their depth, they cannot do the job properly the first time. However, the real extent of the non-value-adding costs incurred by poor work can be seen only when the whole chain of events (of which the poor work is a part) is threaded together. Shoddy work started in one part of the organisation often has a multiplier effect as the transaction progresses through the chain. For example, failure to complete a sales order correctly can cause extra work for production, order-processing, sales, shipment, accounting, and debt collection. Moreover, the self preservation attitude, and indeed functionally-based performance measures, guarantee that the problem is passed on to the next person in the chain.

Although most managers are aware that the costs of poor quality are high and that a great deal of work adds little value to customers, they would be shocked if they knew the extent of these costs (a recent survey[9] in the UK showed that for many companies the costs of poor quality alone were between 5% and 25% of sales). That these costs have remained invisible for so long only serves as a reminder that accountants have rarely been asked to report on what work people actually do, why they do it, how well it is done, and whether the customer values it. Where such requests have been made, the view has invariably been that the benefits of such detailed analysis would not justify its cost. Moreover, most accounting systems are already stretched in their attempts to produce regular and speedy financial information. The objective, and the time pressure often associated with its achievement, militates against questions of work measurement and performance.

The quality movement has pointed organisations in the right direction, and a number of them have recognised that the costs of quality have been a significant factor in their poor performance. Texas Instruments, for example, has instigated a number of quality measurement projects. According to Tom Haggar[10], Controller Metallurgical Metals Division at TI:

> The cost of quality shocked managers. We initially showed them figures of 10%: 10% of sales value, and an even greater percentage of profits, down the hole. . . . We now recognise that budgeting for bad quality production is ridiculous

An Arthur D. Little survey shows the extent of the non-value-adding work of a typical engineer in an American automotive company:

	Value-adding	Non-value-adding
Solo Work:		
Scrap or rework		10%
Valuable work	20%	
Make-work		10%
Meetings:		
Useful meetings	5%	
Useless meetings		10%
Management reviews		5%
Preparation for reviews		10%
Paperwork:		
Work documentation	5%	
Reporting for administrative control & other paperwork		10%
Communications:		
Team talk	5%	
Crisis management		5%
Miscellaneous:		5%
Totals	30%	70%

Johnson[11] has noted the shock that such a discovery can cause:

> Discovering a high percentage of nonvalue work is one shocking revelation of an activity audit. Greater shock hits when companies realise that years spent managing costs never prompted them to ask if the work causing these costs had any value for customers. It seems incredible that so much nonvalue work can occur in companies that have assiduously managed costs for long periods,

in some cases for decades. Most nonvalue work is caused by the way companies control unit costs of output in the many activities it takes to design, make and sell a product

The recognition that non-value-adding costs represent a huge opportunity for profit improvement is one thing, but measuring and eliminating these costs is proving to be a challenge too far for most companies. This is not to say that some haven't tried. Texas Instruments, for example, went some way down the measurement path with its quality improvement programme in the 1980's, and with some success. Between the formal inception of the cost of quality (COQ) system in 1982 and the end of 1987, COQ as a percentage of net sales billed had fallen from 10.7% to 7.8%. But Werner Schuele, VP, People and Asset Effectiveness at TI, felt strongly that the costs tracked by the system were only 50% of actual quality costs, resulting in inadequate attention being focused on major sources of quality costs:

> My major concern is that determining the real cost of "indirect scrap" is not precise and has no foundation in our accounting system. For example, nowhere is the cost of retyping a letter with a mis-spelled word tracked

Quality improvement programs, such as those at TI, often run out of steam due to the lack of an effective measurement system. Activity based approaches have been much more successful. Hewlett Packard is one company that has gone further than most with activity analysis and thus in exposing and eliminating non-value-adding costs. Its UK operations, in particular, have made significant progress in recent years. We will examine two of these projects, one in a sales region and one in a Scottish manufacturing plant.

In 1992, HP conducted a survey into the effectiveness of one of its UK sales regions. The identification and elimination of non-value-adding work was a primary objective. It was made clear at the outset that the purpose of the project was not one of cost cutting—it was to identify choke points or bottlenecks, which were causing problems for customers, and therefore potentially damaging sales. The company was enjoying a good year—sales were 20% up and costs were within budget. However, there was a feeling among the salespeople that they could do even better, and so, with the help of an external consultant, they began to examine their effectiveness.

Managers were asked to consider the necessity of the tasks they performed and the value that these tasks contributed to the overall selling process. Lack of hard data on the nature of work performed was a recurring problem throughout the study, and considerable reliance was placed on the detailed knowledge of employees. The results were surprising. The sales process was analysed into six major activity centres and the percentage of non-value-adding costs identified. The results are shown below in Figure 39.1.

The study produced a 'top-ten' hit list of non-value-adding costs to attack. This list (in order of total non-value-adding costs) shows the percentage of total cost in each activity which is wasted.

Activity	NVA%
Incorrect deliveries	76%
Ineffective negotiations	31%
Poor order processing	45%
Incorrect quotations	43%

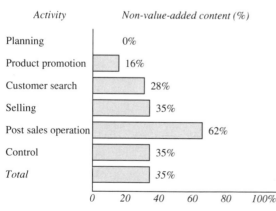

Figure 39.1   Percentage of non-value-added work across six activity centers.

Inconsequential demonstrations	66%
Incorrect configurations	53%
Ineffective relationship building	42%
Wasted time with partners	41%
Wasted travelling time	24%
Ineffective communications	39%

These figures demonstrated the extent of the problem. For the sales region as a whole, 35 pence in every pound was spent on wasted work, clearly a huge opportunity for profit improvement. Armed with this type of information, HP managers implemented measures to reduce these unnecessary costs. By March 1994 over half the non-value-adding costs had been 'recovered'. In particular, the non-value-adding costs associated with negotiations, communications, and dealing with partners had been eliminated altogether. Moreover, the sales team were far more conscious of which work added value to customers and which didn't.

These cost reductions made a significant contribution to profit improvements over the next few years. In fact, following a doubling of HP's worldwide profits in 1993 over those of the previous year (and with the UK operation being the star performer), the managing director of the UK subsidiary, John Golding[12], said on the announcement of the results, "the company's performance was the result of quality programmes, eliminating waste, consolidating operations, and keeping expenses under control".

At one of the Scottish manufacturing divisions, HP specialise in producing testing and measuring equipment for the worldwide telecommunications industry. Following an extensive review of performance, HP managers re-designed the business operations into six key processes. But when the accountants re-analysed the old functional costs—first into processes and secondly into their value-adding and non-value-adding components—some surprises came to light. Table 39.1 shows the results.

Not only did managers realise that out of total costs of £13.3 million, more than 15% of total costs was spent on controlling parts of the business

TABLE 39.1
Process Cost Analysis (£000's)

Process	MFG	R&D	MKTG	ADMIN	TOTAL	NVA%	NVA COSTS
Business-product strategy	20	500	320	100	940	30	282
Product generation	500	3,800	400	50	4,750	50	2,375
New product introduction	340	340	810	40	1,530	40	612
Order fulfilment	2,520	10	30	240	2,800	15	420
Sales development	100	50	1,100	70	1,320	50	660
Control	800	200	300	690	1,990	40	796
Total	4,280	4,900	2,960	1,190	13,330	40	5,145

and therefore added little or no value to customers, but also they also realised that 40% of all their total expenditure was adjudged to be of no value to customers. But HP managers would not have recognised this huge opportunity for improving profits without activity analysis. According to Jim Rigby:

> the results of the analysis helped to stimulate thoughts about restructuring the organisation— away from a functional focus into an empowered process team, cross functional so that process and performance improvements could be generated and implemented

But, as we noted earlier, activity based approaches are invariably project-driven and used primarily as a more accurate method of applying overheads to products and services. The greater opportunity of using activity analysis as a platform for understanding the root causes of costs—promoting those that create value and eliminating those that don't— has generally been missed. But to achieve long-term success such analysis must be systematic. it should be woven into the fabric of the management reporting system. But to achieve this, new systems must be designed and developed.

HORIZONTAL INFORMATION SYSTEMS

There is a growing acknowledgement in the managerial community that 'horizontal' information is now required, but such a description and the way to derive this information is not yet commonly recognised. We believe that with current information technology and no little effort of the part of accountants and systems designers, a horizontal information system can be developed and implemented alongside (and indeed integrated with) the financial system.

The objective of horizontal systems is to *systematically* report both on value-added performance and on the profitability of products, services, and customers. There are two distinct stages: the first involves the re-analysis of 'financial' data into 'activity' data which provides the platform for developing value-adding performance indices; and the second involves attributing activity data to reporting categories such as products and customers. Such analysis will be familiar to ABC practitioners.

We advocate a new measure of performance— an index of 'value-adding work'. Such an index must distinguish, at its core, between work which is irrelevant to the needs of the customer (the relevance criterion), and work which is performed badly and necessitates correction (the quality criterion). This distinction has not always been clearly accentuated in the literature, but is vital to a comprehension of performance.

But how does an organisation, or business unit, employing large numbers of people, begin to derive this sort of detail? Activity analysis points the way. Most firms find that they have between

200–300 activities, and that each employee is involved in one to four major ones. By borrowing a well worn management concept—*exception reporting*—information systems can be designed to record when a person spends time working on his or her non-core activities. In other words, *by recording what people are not supposed to be doing* (correcting work caused by others, revisiting, chasing, changing, and generally solving problems that would not have occurred if the job had been done correctly first time), a picture can be painted by the information system of those extra costs that add no value to the customer. Thus the real costs of poor quality can be derived.

HP managers at the Scottish plant defined these costs in terms of *waste, duplication, or the cost of inefficiency*. Examples included having to re-layout a printed circuit board design, re-write test procedures, or re-run a computer report. When reporting on their work, each department gave a fairly honest appraisal of their activities, and in many cases this was supported or contradicted by the evidence of the supplying and receiving departments.

Moreover, not all work—even work done correctly every time—adds value to customers (many activities are simply not relevant to customer needs). By assigning a 'relevance rating' to individual activities, systems can be designed to report on activity costs according to the value they provide to the customer. The HP experience was again illuminating. Here's Jim Rigby again:

in advance we asked each manager to think through, sometimes with key staff, the tasks and activities undertaken and the key processes that initiated or benefited from the work. . . . All along we accepted that 'near enough was good enough'—none of the typical accountant's fixation with fourth decimal place accuracy. . . . 'If that's what it costs, I don't need it', was a typical management reaction. Another benefit was to recognise the linkages between departments. Who was the customer and did it meet their needs? The exercise contributed significantly to the recognition that we had a top heavy organisation with too many departments

Horizontal information systems will enable managers to organise work is such a way that irrelevant activities are minimised, poor quality is identified and eliminated, and value creating activities encouraged, until eventually these account for most of the work performed. And an index of value-adding work will allow them to continuously improve the performance of their processes.

Suppose, for example, that HP managers had analysed their non-value-adding costs into those caused by poor quality work and those caused through their irrelevance to customer needs. And suppose further that their analysis led to the (hypothetical) results in Table 39.2.

The value of this type of analysis is to provide a platform for continuous improvement. By *systematically* measuring the costs of quality and the percentage of work which is relevant to customers, managers can set targets for improvement throughout the organisation. Moreover, such a system can

TABLE 39.2
Summary of Value-Adding Work

Processes	Total cost	NVA costs poor quality	NVA costs irrelevance	New value-adding work	Quality index	Relevance index	Value-adding work index
Business-product strategy	940	47	235	658	95.0%	75%	70.0%
Product generation	4,750	1,900	475	2,375	60.6%	90%	50.0%
New product introduction	1,530	612	0	918	60.0%	100%	60.0%
Order fulfilment	2,800	420	0	2,380	85.0%	100%	85.0%
Sales development	1,320	1232	528	660	90.0%	60%	50.0%
Control	1,990	0	796	1,194	100.0%	60%	60.0%
TOTALS	13,330	3,111	2,034	8,185	76.7%	84.7%	61.4%

measure the performance of knowledge and service workers. For example, by placing a premium rating on the time spent by knowledge workers disseminating their experience and know-how throughout the firm, managers can encourage organisational learning. Moreover, it is likely that such measures will go some way towards meeting one of Peter Drucker's primary concerns of recent years, encapsulated in this observation

> The productivity revolution is over because there are too few people employed in making and moving things for their productivity to be decisive. . . . The chief economic priority for developed countries, therefore, must be to raise the productivity of knowledge and service work. The country that does this first will dominate the twenty-first century economically.[13]

These work-based indices can be seen as new measures of productivity—but the factors in the traditional economic model are not 'people' and 'output' but *work* and *value added*. We believe that such indices can become the new driving force of continuous improvement in every type of organisation. They can also be applied to business units, processes, activities, and teams—in fact any segment of business activity. Managers can 'drill down' into the information system to locate the causes and thus be able to take remedial action. But care must be taken with the approach. The objective is to promote value-adding work not to impose further controls on people's time.

The second aspect of horizontal information systems concerns the profitability of products, services, customers, channels, and markets. The system design can take many forms and will depend on a number of factors such as the business structure, existing information systems, and reporting objectives. We suggest that a horizontal information system begins with the setting up of the *activity chart of accounts and the activity ledger,* a discipline which requires managers to decide which processes and activities to include in the new account structure. New software is needed to convert costs into activities. In other words, financial data entered into the general ledger will also be entered

into the activity ledger—but instead of being analysed by such headings as 'salaries' or 'telephone'—it will be analysed by activity accounts such as 'visiting customers' or 'processing orders'. Activity accounts can also have budgets and historic information, similar to those included in standard general ledger accounts. Actual cost can then be compared with budget, with the previous period, and with previous years.

Once costs have been analysed to processes and activities (i.e. into the activity ledgers), the final step is to attribute them to products or customers. In a horizontal reporting system the overall objective is to aim for as much 'direct linking' as possible. The problem of tracing overheads to products and customers is the downfall of most costing systems, but in a horizontal system new opportunities arise. For example, the computer itself can help by tracking data and the time it takes to carry out activities. Moreover, by following transactions across the internal value chain, horizontal systems have less problems dealing with linking problems than systems within traditional organisations.

But if a direct link cannot be made, cost drivers must be used. The most appropriate cost driver represents the primary cause of the activity cost, but sometimes they are difficult to select. For example, it is unlikely that functional costs (such as central IT resources) will be easily traceable to individual products and customers. The choice of reporting categories, whether they be customers, sales channels, retail outlets, territories, product groups, or any permutation of these, has a direct bearing on the way data is collected and analysed. Not only the software design is affected by these decisions. The system architecture and data collection systems must also be designed to process data in the best possible way.

The purposes of traditional systems and horizontal systems are quite different. Traditional systems emphasise control and have reporting structures designed for executives and shareholders, whereas horizontal systems emphasise improvement and report on the real value-adding performance to managers.

Traditional (Vertical) System	*Horizontal System*
Revenue	Revenue
↓	↓
Costs (e.g. wages, salaries, travel, facilities)	Value-adding costs by activity (e.g. selling, designing, producing)
↓	↓
Profit by business product, segment (e.g. cost centre)	'Real profit' by product, customer, channel, market
	↓
	Non-value-adding costs (poor quality) Non-value-adding costs (irrelevant to the customer)
	↓
	Net profit by product, customer, channel, and market

Managers need to see a moving picture of organisational performance. They need to be able to see how well product lines, markets, territories, business units, distribution channels are doing. They need to ensure that their strategic targets are being met. And they need to see if there is improvement in the value-adding performance of key processes. But traditional accounting systems don't produce these numbers—it's as though they exist in a different dimension. Horizontal information systems must be the way forward. But they also pose new questions for accountants.

For example, should non-value-adding costs be charged to products and customers thus significantly changing their reported profitability? This is a difficult issue and it depends on how these costs are caused. If they are caused by excessive customer demands then they should be charged against the customer, but if they are caused by poor quality work they should not be charged. We suggest that quality costs are charged separately to the profit and loss account in the same way that excess capacity costs might be shown. This highlights the costs of quality but doesn't give misleading information on the underlying profitability of products or customers.

Horizontal information systems present new challenges to software designers and accountants. Translating financial data to activity data, tracing costs from their source to products and customers, and most important of all, getting sensible information on non-value-adding time from all key employees, are not insignificant problems. But such systems will develop rapidly once software designers put their minds to the task. Modern computer systems now have the power and flexibility to cope with the challenge. It took many years and countless versions of hardware and software before existing general ledger analysis reached its current level of analytical detail. The same evolution can be expected with horizontal information systems, but compacted within a much shorter time frame. The development and integration of data collection devices such as radio controlled digital systems will be a significant factor in the improvement of horizontal information systems.

CUT THE WORKLOAD NOT THE WORKFORCE

The 'horizontal' approach to both the management and information systems can profoundly change the decision perspectives of managers. Take for example rationalisation or, to put it in its crudest form, cost-cutting. The solution adopted by most executive teams is to cut the work*force*, demand lower prices from suppliers, outsource non-core activities, and replace labour intensive activities with technology. Although some of these measures may well be necessary, we believe that most organisations can achieve dramatic performance improvements by considering an alternative approach—cutting the work*load*—which involves eliminating the huge amounts of unnecessary work which, we have argued, lie embedded within the cost structures of most firms.

We have also noted that traditional accounting systems, with their emphasis on control rather than improvement, have fooled managers into believing they can run their companies by manipulating costs, jobs, and capital. They have forgotten that underneath this pyramid of numbers lie real people whose work determines the quality of products and services and ultimately the success of the business itself. But accountants have not been interested in the measurement of work or quality—their attention has been focused on the measurement and control of unit costs and whether the actual costs of functions and departments are within budget.

But in the meantime, the real work that people do—that proportion of work which benefits the customer—is diminishing each year. Because accounting systems only see the cost of jobs, not the underlying work that people do, cost reduction efforts have focused on reducing the number of *jobs* rather than the reduction of unnecessary *work*. By reducing jobs, managers appear to create an instant boost in productivity and a fall in the unit cost of output, thus creating an improving (but often illusory) picture of competitiveness. But such a unit cost mentality has had a devastating effect on the business landscape. Many large organisations have butchered their workforces in the pursuit of higher productivity and lower unit costs. In 1993, for example, large American organisations laid off 600,000 employees, a 25% increase over the previous year. The recently privatised British utilities are another example. They have shed tens of thousands of jobs whilst at the same time increasing management rewards and shareholder dividends.

There is no doubt that cutting jobs, stretching targets, and increasing rewards can offer short term gains. But, more often than not, however many jobs are cut in divisions, departments, and factories, the work usually remains the same, thus throwing extra demands on fewer people and causing a downward spiral of morale and disaffection among managers and employees, which in turn leads to declining levels of customer service and ultimately lower profitability.

The alternative approach to cost reduction fo-cuses on the amount of work undertaken every year which adds little or no value to customers. By rooting out this work, large (and often permanent) cost savings can be made, leading to long-term improvements in profitability. Jeffrey Pfeffer[14] offers powerful evidence that those companies that have made long-term commitments to their workforce, and placed value-adding work at the centre of their competitive strategy, have been highly successful over the long-term. For example, he notes that this approach is the only common factor shared by the five top performing American companies by stock market growth over a 20 year period from 1972–1992. They are (in order): Southwest Airlines, Wal-Mart, Tyson Foods, Circuit City, and Plenum Publishing.

Another popular approach to reducing costs (and the workforce) is through outsourcing. Should work be performed inside the company or provided by an external supplier? In making this decision it is likely that most managers will look simply at the cost of the particular function or department under discussion, and accept the outsourcing tender if there is an evident cost advantage in favour of the external bid. However, there will often be hidden costs which the outsourcing contract might not cover. For example, the contract may not concern itself with the 'problem fixing activities' previously carried out by the staff of the newly outsourced department.

These problems, which may well have been caused elsewhere within the organisation, will, of course, still remain after the contract is signed. When this situation comes to light, the company must either incur further costs in solving the problems (its problem-fixers having departed), or the outsourcing company will demand more money to take them on. Because of such 'hidden traps', managers must be clear that the outsourcing contract covers the whole *process* and does not simply replace the functional, budgetary costs of the department. But all the available evidence suggests that managers do not understand this question. The issue once again is clear. Costs, or in this case cost savings, are not always what they appear to be. Unless managers understand the impact of their decisions on the amount of *work* caused or saved, then the quality of decision making will suffer.

By focusing on the real numbers, value creating activities will be clearly identified and expanded, profits will improve, and new investment proposals (with lower budgeted costs) will become more acceptable. A new virtuous circle would then be created—one which increases movement, improves profits, and expands the workforce.

A LONG-TERM SOLUTION

Organisations run on positive cash flows. The primary source of cash is satisfied customers. Satisfied customers are created by honest, hard working people who, through their creative skills and team efforts, provide customers with what they want. If people are properly recognised and rewarded for their efforts they will come back each day and do it all over again. Jack Welch, the CEO at GE, put it rather succinctly when he said, *"the three most important things you need to measure in a business are customer satisfaction, employee satisfaction, and cash flow"*.

The problem is that in almost every organisation—large and small—accounting systems do not measure and reward these efforts. They don't say anything about how work is done, and they don't identify which work adds any value to the customer. Moreover, most existing accounting measures don't help managers make important business decisions such as whether to expand or contract the business; how to select the least costly sales channels; how to cut costs without damaging the customer; or whether to outsource work. These are decisions that go to the heart of the company's operations.

Without good information systems, managers are groping in the dark. The result is often poor decision making which has a disastrous impact on long-term performance. Look at recent corporate history—at how once large and proud companies, and indeed whole industries, failed to respond to competitive threats which triggered a downward spiral of decline and, in some cases, self-destruction. How, for example did so many large organisations, including General Motors, IBM, Groupe-Bull, United Airlines, Air France, American Express, and British Coal, get it so wrong?

Most businesses today are failing their customers and employees by misreading cost and performance indicators. The opportunity to learn lessons from the catalogue of corporate failures has been missed. And, often through no fault of their own, managers repeatedly ask the wrong questions, arrive at the wrong conclusions, and take the wrong course of action. How can we improve profitability and cash flow? How can we maintain dividends and the share price? How can we improve sales per employee? These are the pressing questions in most companies today, but they have little to do with their fundamental problems.

However, there is light in the tunnel. There are a number of organisations that have recognised the importance of value-adding performance and have gone some way down the road of 'horizontal' measurement. *GE and Hewlett-Packard,* for example, have made great strides in understanding the causes of costs and have embraced horizontal structures, begun to eliminate non-value-adding work, and improve employee productivity. GE is now the number one company in the western world in terms of market capitalisation, and HP's recent profits growth has been both impressive and consistent in an intensely competitive market. Companies such as *Motorola and Xerox* have realised substantial benefits from adopting horizontal team-based structures involving the removal of multiple layers of management and resulting in both a reduction in costs and much improved service levels to the customer. Xerox has achieved a spectacular turnaround in performance and both companies have since risen high in the rankings of profits growth and have gained the respect and admiration of other companies. *British Airways and Southwest Airlines* have both focused on customer service and value-adding performance with spectacular results.

There are, however, many more who have missed the boat. The continuous cost cutters who have reduced jobs and closed companies, offices, and factories in every town and city throughout Europe and America have still not come to terms with their underlying problems. They need to be convinced that there is a better and more coherent way for changes to be made. Such a coherence is offered by horizontal information systems. Their impact—both direct and indirect—on long-term profitability is potentially huge. The following benefits await those willing to go down the horizontal road.

• *Costs are reduced.* Once non-value-adding costs (particularly the costs of poor quality) are made visible to managers, corrective action can be taken, and the root causes eradicated. This will take time, but the impact on long-term profitability is potentially immense. Available evidence suggests that an extra 10%–20% profit on turnover is not out of the question.

• *Productivity is improved.* A horizontal information system, and the measures which can be derived from it, addresses the key issues of productivity and value creation. By measuring and rewarding improvements in the *value of work to customers,* managers will focus their energies on the productivity of individuals, teams, processes, and business units. The implications of these changes on employment policies and management decision making will be far reaching. Productivity improvements of up to ten-fold have been suggested as the potential magnitude of change between team-based structures and traditional structures.

• *Organisational learning is promoted.* Horizontal information systems have the capability to plan, track, and reward individual pieces of work. Indeed, a premium can be placed on certain activities if they are thought to add more value than the rest. Such might be the case for those activities that involve the dissemination of knowledge throughout the organisation. By encouraging the spread of knowledge such systems would significantly add to the productivity momentum.

• *Management decisions are improved and the profit consequences made clear.* These proposals give managers the opportunity to derive net profitability by product, customer, channel, and business unit. Knowing which costs to cut, which prod-

ucts and services to expand and contract, and which sales channels to choose, will be easier to achieve if managers can distinguish between value-adding and non-value-adding costs. A clearer understanding of product and customer profitability can only help managers improve those decisions which have a major impact on profits.

• *More appropriate reward and recognition systems can be implemented.* A number of companies are now realising that the only effort really worth rewarding is that which adds a value for which the customer is prepared to pay. However, these reward systems cannot be invoked without the information to support them. Once horizontal information systems are in place, there is scope for implementing reward and incentive systems that drive the company towards its strategic targets. IBM and other computer companies have begun to reward sales people on the bases of measures of customer profitability and customer satisfaction.

• *Forward planning is improved.* By budgeting for work instead of costs managers must seek answers to a whole new (and more relevant) set of questions. And the right value-adding behaviour will be encouraged where it counts—before costs are committed.

• *Continuous improvement is encouraged.* Horizontal information will enable a range of more relevant performance measures to be monitored including those relating to strategy, value added, internal efficiency, quality, and innovation. In other words, both financial and non-financial measures. These measures give managers a complete picture of business progress.

We don't suggest that horizontal systems can, on their own, bring success, any more than re-engineering or quality initiatives. But they might just be the missing piece in the jigsaw—the piece that brings the whole improvement picture into focus. They also put managers back in charge. In fact, we would suggest that horizontal information systems put *the management back into management accounting.* They ensure that 'the numbers' are no longer the preserve of accountants and boards of directors, but represent valuable, practical information to be used by everyone to improve the organisation's performance. The challenges are daunting, but the prize for success is immense.

REFERENCES

1. Jim Rigby: *Activity Based Costing and Process Re-engineering at Hewlett Packard:* Successful Change Strategies: Bernard Taylor: Director Books, 1994.

2. Robert S. Kaplan and David P. Norton: *The Balanced Scorecard—Measures That Drive Performance* (Harvard Business Review: January–February, 1992) pp 71–79.

3. Article in Fortune Magazine, May 29, 1995.

4. *"A Journey to Advanced Management Systems: A Report on the Research and Findings of the CAM-I Advanced Budgeting Group"*, CAM-I Inc, September, 1994.

5. Jeffrey G. Miller and Thomas E. Vollmann: *The Hidden Factory* (Harvard Business Review, September–October, 1985) pp 142–151.

6. Robin Cooper and Robert S. Kaplan: *Activity-Based Systems: Measuring the Costs of Resource Usage* (Accounting Horizons September, 1992).

7. "A Smarter Way to Manufacture", *Business Week,* 30/4/90, pp 110–117.

8. Jeffrey G. Miller and Thomas E. Vollmann: *The Hidden Factory* (Harvard Business Review, September–October, 1985) pp 142–151.

9. JJ Plunkett, BG Dale, and RW Tyrell: *Quality Costs:* (London DTI 1985).

10. Robin Cooper and Robert S Kaplan: *The Design of Cost Management Systems—Text, Cases and Readings.* Prentice-Hall International, 1991.

11. H. Thomas Johnson: *Professors, Customers, and Value: Bringing a Global Perspective to Management Accounting Education:* Proceedings of 1989 Symposium.

12. Report in the Financial Times 11/1/94.

13. Peter F Drucker: *The New Productivity Challenge* (Harvard Business Review: November–December, 1991) pp 69–79.

14. Jeffrey Pfeffer: *Competitive Advantage through People:* Harvard Business School Press, 1994.

14

Organizational Practices and Policies

40

Managing a Diverse Work Force:
Women in Engineering

KATE KIRKHAM AND PAUL THOMPSON

In competing for quality engineers, it will pay to have your people develop the awareness and skills necessary to manage a diverse work force.

Prior to 1975, very few women obtained degrees in engineering in the United States. However, that situation began to change, and by 1980 over 10 per-cent of all bachelor degrees in engineering were awarded to women (a total of 5,948).(*1*) Women now make up 4.3 percent of total engineers with percentages as high as 11.3 percent in some fields.(*2*)

The major influx of women into engineering is an encouraging development when many people are forecasting a shortage of engineers in the United States in the next decade.(*3*) As more women seek employment in engineering organizations, man-

Reprinted by permission from *Research-Technology Management,* March–April, 1984, pp. 9–16.
Kate Kirkham is Associate Professor of Organizational Behavior at Brigham Young University. ***Paul Thompson*** is Professor of Organizational Behavior at Brigham Young University.

agers face a greater challenge to effectively manage an integrated work force which reflects a wider range of work styles and diversity of individuals not now found in many engineering organizations. Although qualifications of women are similar, often their values, experiences and professional expectations are different.

In an effort to find out how organizations were responding to the increasing number of women entering engineering, we interviewed men and women entering engineering, we interviewed men and women in eight engineering organizations. Our interest was in understanding the total impact of the increasing diversity in engineering, rather than in evaluating compliance with basic requirements of equal employment opportunity laws. We wanted to identify what helps or hinders working relationships, as well as expand our ways of thinking about this issue. The organizations sampled included companies in a variety of industries, including basic metals, defense, electronics, and energy.

The interviews included individual contributors and managers, as well as staff people in personnel or employee relations. The small sample of responses included in the box (next page) illustrates the wide range of opinions on how well women were being accepted. Most of the men we interviewed said there was no problem with women being accepted in their organizations. However, almost all of the women and a few of the men had quite a different view. They see a number of situations that make acceptance of women as peers and professionals quite difficult.

In one organization we saw a dramatic example of those different views. In that company we held individual interviews and group discussions with 44 engineers and managers, exploring several topics including the acceptance of women engineers. Thirty-nine of those interviewed said there was no problem—women were completely accepted and were treated just the same as men. Only five people said that women were not being treated equally. It was interesting that all three of the women in the sample indicated that women were not being treated equally. After gathering additional information about practices in the company,

it became clear that there were significant problems in the lack of opportunities for women engineers in terms of job assignments, travel, and promotions. The surprising finding was that only 2 out of 41 men were able to see (or perhaps were willing to admit) these problems.

As we analyzed all of the interviews, we realized that the words "acceptance" and "equal treatment" were being used quite differently by the respondents. Some people were thinking about men and women receiving equal pay and being called engineers; others were looking at job assignments and opportunities to travel to field sites or professional conferences; still others were concerned about informal relationships, including going to lunch together or being accepted as one of the "boys." A number of organizations did not grant us permission to interview because the topic itself was viewed as "too sensitive," either by the employee or the employer. In other cases, we were discouraged by personnel staff from talking about differences because of the legal implications. Apparently, some people were thinking about the issues of diversity only in terms of violations of EEO laws.

We concluded that there are significant challenges facing managers who want to be effective in managing women and men in engineering, and that there isn't just "one problem" that can be located at one level of the organization or can be attributed only to women or only to men. The important issue is understanding the total dynamics of the demographic changes in the engineering profession—what helps or hinders working relationships and how to think about these issues in order to better manage a diverse work force.

A FRAMEWORK FOR UNDERSTANDING

In our interviews we heard many managers express an interest in improving their effectiveness in managing a diverse work team of men and women. Unfortunately, many of them did not have useful ways to think about the issue. Some of the men were only dealing with very elementary questions related to their interactions with women, such as, "Should I open the door for them or not?"

We want to expand the thinking on these issues by considering three different perspectives: interpersonal, group and organizational. Each level of this framework has a primary expression of differences that can negatively affect the management of diversity:

1. *Interpersonal dynamics involve interactions between individuals who are different.* At the individual level, it is prejudice—the voiced attitudes or non-verbal behaviors that indicate personal bias.

2. *Group dynamics involve a group identity.* They may involve an individual interacting with a different group of others or an individual's stereotypes about a group of others. At the intergroup level, the collective appearance of prejudice is expressed as stereotyping or discrimination. Even individuals who would consider themselves nonprejudicial can unintentionally contribute to discrimination initiated by a larger group.

3. *Organizational dynamics involve the impact of a company's policies and practices—intended or not—on individuals who are different.* When we combine individual prejudicial attitudes with discriminatory acts, they can produce policies and practices at the organizational level that can alter the climate and "terms and conditions" of employment. This produces what is referred to as institutional patterns of sexism.

Learning to think critically about the dynamics at each level can aid a manager in *selecting* appropriate responses. Invariably, there are more alternatives than "is this legal to do or not to do?" For example, friction may be occurring between men and women on the same work team. Examination from the perspective of the three levels reveals that the problem is not originating from a biased supervisor, but from the supervisor's role in implementing a long-standing company practice about travel.

The framework not only introduces a broader perspective for thinking about and understanding the complexities of a diverse work force, but it also suggests the need for different management strategies on each level.

DYNAMICS BETWEEN INDIVIDUALS

This level of analysis focuses on the relationship between individual male and female employees, where personal prejudice is the main problem in managing diversity. Most men have not worked with women professionals before and, as a result, they are not sure how to relate to women engineers. Prejudice can be a product of just such a lack of experiences and hence unintentional, or it may be an expression of intended attitudes about another because of his/her gender. Let's examine some examples from our interviews.

The women that we interviewed said that many of their male colleagues had adjusted quite well to working with women, but that others were having problems. Unfortunately, a few men who have difficulty treating women as professionals can create significant problems for women entering engineering. The most obvious examples of inappropriate behavior toward a professional woman include:

- Calling female engineers "girls".
- Making frequent jokes about women not being as smart as men or that "they should be home having babies".
- Seeing a woman engineer primarily as someone to flirt with or tease.

We were surprised at the number of men who continue to refer to females with college degrees as "girls." Many of these "girls" are 30 or 40 years old. But for most women engineers, this is a minor issue compared to other things. One woman said, "I don't care what they call me as long as they give me a good job assignment." This view was somewhat typical of the response on that issue, but other women indicated that they are getting tired of not being treated as professionals. In some cases, the joking was seen as more serious. One woman said:

> My boss is very sexist. He makes a lot of jokes about women drivers, women staying at home, etc. When a mistake is made, he'll say, "Some dumb broad probably did it." I try to get him to stop by joking back, but he doesn't stop. His boss is aware of the problem, but he doesn't do anything about it.

It's obvious that this woman sees her boss's behavior as more than a minor irritation. She was quite unhappy about the treatment she was receiving and felt that it interfered with her work. Women are particularly concerned about these "minor" problems when they represent an attitude that women are not full-fledged professionals. Less obvious examples of prejudice occur as a form of "helping" or protecting. One woman described her concern about her boss's overconsideration of her dual role as engineer and wife:

> My manager tells me that I should go home every day before six o'clock so I can fix dinner for my husband. I know he means well, but it still upsets me because I don't want to get the reputation that I can't be relied on to stay and complete a project when we have a tight deadline.

Another example came from a helpful executive who hired a management consultant to conduct a teambuilding seminar with the people who reported directly to him. Of his 14 immediate subordinates, the one woman was not invited to attend the session. When the consultant discovered the situation and asked why she had not been invited, the executive replied, "I thought Ann would feel uncomfortable being the only woman in the session." The consultant replied, "How do you think she will feel when she finds out she was the only one of your subordinates who was not invited to the session?" She was included in the next session. The executive was "protecting" the woman from what he saw as an awkward situation for her based on his values of how men and women interact, without realizing that the work situation required a different attitude on his part.

Problems that arise in interpersonal relations are often difficult to handle because when women bring up the issue, they are often accused of being too sensitive. One woman commented:

> It bothers me when someone makes a negative comment about women. But I've been told that I'm too sensitive. I don't know if I'm too sensitive. There is quite a bit of stereotyping here. At school there was a more liberal atmosphere. But coming to work here was like stepping back ten years. Here men compare you to their wives, not to other engineers. It's a subtle influence, but it's there.

DYNAMICS INVOLVING GROUP IDENTITY

This level of analysis enables us to look at employee interactions that are a product of group dynamics. A great deal of the activity in organizations takes place in groups including both work groups and social groups. While some of the women we interviewed were quickly integrated into the on-going groups in their organizations, many women, unfortunately, did not find such a supportive environment. The quote in the box about "Sexism is rampant in my department . . ." illustrates this problem of a woman who feels excluded.

When we consider group behavior, several facets of male/female interactions are sharpened:

- Sometimes men are not able to clearly see the individual characteristics of a specific woman because they hold stereotypic views of women in general which block their perception.

- Women may experience a collective impact from the behavior of a group of men that individual men in that group are not aware of.

- A non-prejudiced man in a group of men may not be aware that he is part of the collective impact which restricts a woman's performance.

For example, in one organization a group of male professionals played basketball together during the lunch hour several days a week. In those sessions, a lot of information was shared about joint projects, developments in the group, etc. When two women were hired into the group, they were not involved in the basketball games and hence did not have access to the information exchanged in those informal sessions. Individually, the men expressed no intent to discriminate against the women, but their collective behavior had a negative impact on the women's ability to perform. Unfortunately, the manager didn't handle the situation very well. In trying to give the women access to the information, he caused the men to feel that they were being asked to give up their noon-time recreation to accommodate the women, or else invite them into the locker room. Few women are asking for that type of a response. However, they would like access to information that's important to their work.

Some people have not been too sympathetic when we've described this problem, because it doesn't seem to relate to work. They argue that the organization can't be responsible for regulating the social activity of its employees. But, as is evident, these group activities are not just social get-togethers. Many times important work takes place in social settings.

Another aspect of this problem concerns womens' participation in informal discussions in their own departments. One woman engineer reported that when she entered a room and a group of men were talking, the conversation often changed abruptly. Where the conversation had been focused on important business or technical problems, they would switch to lighter subjects which they assumed would be of interest to her.

These stereotyped assumptions about women which the men were imposing on her prevented her from having access to important information which affected her job. She added:

> When I first came to work here, I noticed that conversations with me were different than with the young men—not as open about how the organization works and how you get ahead. With men, they discuss the secrets of how the system works, but with women that was taboo. I felt that they didn't even take me seriously. They may not have meant to exclude me, but they didn't tell me how to publish or where to publish. I had to do it on my own. Once I had some articles published, then they began to respect me. Now I'm doing joint

research and publishing with men, but they wouldn't work with me until I had developed a reputation outside the lab.

It's not clear why some men will not take women engineers seriously, but that behavior puts the women at a disadvantage. And it often takes exceptional effort and ability to overcome that disadvantage, as these women discovered.

Another example of the tendency for men to rely on stereotypes about women as a group, rather than to look at *individual* qualifications, is in their assumptions about relationships among women in an organization. Many women are assigned "women's work" simply because superiors assume that all women have certain women's skills. One woman computer scientist was assigned by her boss to handle all communications with the women in the typing pool. The department was having some problems in its relationship with the typing pool and the boss assumed that a woman would be more effective in communicating with other women. The computer scientists resented this because it gave her less time in the area where she was trained.

But even for women who have succeeded in gaining acceptance from the men in their group as a professional engineering woman, there are still dilemmas which they must contend with on the job in order to *maintain* their group's acceptance. Many women are afraid to confront problems because they don't want to be seen as troublemakers or "women's libbers." One woman described her dilemma on this issue as follows:

> I work with a group of male engineers. One of them is quite obnoxious in the way he talks about women. I sit at the desk next to his and sometimes when a secretary walks by, he describes in great detail what he'd like to do sexually with her. I have to decide whether to speak up and lose my effectiveness with the group, or remain silent. I have to neuter myself to get along with the men in engineering.

This woman has decided that confronting male engineers about their language is too costly to her effectiveness in the group, so she says nothing. Eventually she may decide that silence is too high a cost to pay and she may leave the organization. Managers need to become aware of the impact of such situations. Male engineers need to be cognizant of how their behavior and attitude is affecting the lone woman in the group. Women in groups of men benefit from male "allies" who, by voicing their similar opinions, help change the tendency to stereotype.

Unfortunately, two traps operate at the group level to immobilize many men who could be effective in confronting stereotypes. First of all, many men rely on their personal experience as the only criteria for checking on the legitimacy of an issue. In effect, they are saying, "If I haven't observed that, it probably didn't happen." Secondly, they use the entire group as a reference to support their rationalizations. "Well, not everyone here, Jane, is like that."

While both of these statements contain some truth, they do not contribute to gaining insight into the experience of someone else, nor to effectively solving problems in organizations.

IMPACT OF ORGANIZATIONAL POLICIES AND PRACTICES

This level of analysis focuses on policies and practices that may impact men and women differently. Since women are newcomers to professional jobs in most organizations, managers may not have taken a careful look at policies which may have a negative impact on women. For example, a chief engineer in a large company in the defense industry reported that he was unsuccessful in getting his company to adapt its policies to accommodate women. He said they had hired "a very competent woman engineer" who after two years decided to have a baby and wanted to take a one-year maternity leave. "Our company policy wouldn't permit that, so I tried to get them to change it. The company had nothing to lose by approving a one-year leave. We wanted her back and we're having trouble finding engineers these days. It was a leave without pay, but they still wouldn't approve it. No

wonder we have difficulty attracting women to our organization."

At a time when engineers are in short supply, it seems logical that engineering firms could only help themselves by adapting their policies and practices to accommodate women.

A common attitude toward organizational level problem is, "We have an EEO office and they'll handle this issue." Unfortunately, the EEO office can't handle all of these problems alone. We are not opposed to an organization having a separate EEO office which can provide technical resources, but the existence of such an office should not be used as an excuse for managers and individual contributors to ignore their on-going responsibility for skill development in this important area, or delay action until the issues require attention by the EEO office. Too often, managers use organizational policy as an excuse not to take action.

When there is no specific organizational policy to direct managers as they make decisions about women, they tend to rely on assumptions. One supervisor decided that all the engineers on his project needed to travel to the plant to get a better understanding of production problems. His boss approved the trip, but said none of the women should go. The supervisor was very upset because the women had important assignments on the project.

Managers should take responsibility for their role in reviewing the impact of internal policies, or lack of policy, especially those which concern traveling and working in the field. Managers may be uneasy about women traveling alone (or traveling with a man, for that matter). One manager said:

> We have a dilemma about assigning women to some jobs—for example, jobs that require a lot of travel alone. Some of the projects are in areas where it's not very safe. Should we send women to work in areas where they might get attacked?

This last problem is a real dilemma and not all women want to travel alone or travel into unsafe areas. However, almost all women would like to be involved in the decision. They would like an opportunity to consider the assignment and decide for themselves whether they would like to accept it.

Official policies regarding work and travel are not the only problems women face: the organizational climate can often hinder women's informal support. Since there are few women in the top management of companies, most senior executives are not aware of the issues on other levels of the organization and do not have an effective way of understanding the situations which women encounter. One woman who tried to organize a women's support group within her company encountered unwarranted negative reactions from top management.

> A few weeks ago, three of us (all women) got together to discuss the problems women face here due to lack of awareness and support. Later, we met with the V.P. of Industrial Relations to talk about creating a women's support group. He went straight to the president. The president was very concerned and told the V.P. to stop it before it got started. He said if we get a women's support group, before long we'll have a Ku Klux Klan group, etc. It got blown all out of proportion. We just wanted a chance to discuss some issues. We weren't planning to picket the plant.

Attitudes of people in influential positions can have a major impact on the management of diversity in organizations. The organization can be blocked on these issues when those in key positions assume that no problem exists until it is objectively proven to them, or when they believe that the outcome of a policy will be experienced by everyone the way it was intended.

THE INTERLOCKING LEVELS

Our examples have been an effort to illustrate the three different levels of diversity and the traps that can block effective behaviors. It is important before we begin examining the implications for change to look at two issues that consistently surfaced during our study. These issues emphasize the importance of diagnosis, because they appear across all three levels. They are job assignment and availability of feedback.

Job assignment can be simultaneously influenced by personal bias, by stereotypic assumptions about women in general, and by organizational practices. Consider these examples:

- A woman chemical engineer was assigned to a supervisor who did not want a woman working for him. He assigned her to paint the floor in the department. The women got very upset and told her supervisor's boss. A review was conducted and the supervisor was fired.

- A manager of employee relations said some managers are reluctant to give a woman work that is challenging. They are afraid the woman will get pregnant or leave when her husband gets transferred. As a result, they give women routine jobs where they can be easily replaced, independent of their personal situation.

- Some organizations have unwritten policies that women will not be assigned to jobs that involve traveling to the field. As a result, they do not get field experience, which affects the kind of job assignments they get later in their careers.

Almost all of the women that we interviewed indicated that job assignment was very important to them. They were very concerned that organizations take whatever action was necessary to see that they were given equal access to challenging jobs. They did not want a biased manager, group dynamics, or organizational policies to stand in the way of their receiving meaningful work.

The second issue that surfaced across all levels was the availability of feedback. Many of the women we interviewed indicated that it was hard for them to get concrete feedback about their performance. They would like specific information about job expectations, an evaluation of their work on a specific project, etc. A variety of explanations were given for the apparent reluctance of male managers to give female engineers critical feedback. One woman suggested that men don't believe that women are generally willing to change in order to get ahead in the organization. She said:

Recently I was talking with a department manager about the development plans for one of his female subordinates. He reported that she is bright and articulate, but she would not become a supervisor because she isn't aggressive enough. I asked, "Have you told her that?" He said he hadn't, because he didn't think she wanted to change. Later, the department manager described a male subordinate in very similar terms and said that he was working with the man to help him become a supervisor.

The woman reporting this incident could not understand why the department manager would insure that the man was getting feedback on his shortcomings and allow his own unchecked assumptions to prevent the woman from getting the same constructive feedback.

Another explanation was presented by Kanter in her book, *Men and Women in the Corporation:*

> There were instances in which women trainees did not get direct criticism in time to improve their performance and did not know they were the subjects of criticism in the company until told to find jobs in other divisions. They were not part of the buddy network that uncovered such information quickly, and their managers were reluctant to criticize a woman out of uncertainty about how she would receive the information. (One man put quite simply how he felt about giving negative feedback to a woman: "I'm chicken.") Here, feelings that it is impossible to level with a different kind of person stood in the way.(4)

One of the men in our study had a different perspective on this issue. He said the male managers that he worked with complained that women always wanted more feedback than the men in the department. His view is that men and women both get the same amount of formal feedback, but the women are dissatisfied because they feel a need for more than they are receiving.

It is clear from the multiple explanations about why women aren't getting the kind of feedback they want, that the issue has many causes and influencing factors from all three levels. Those managers who want to effectively handle diversity will explore the issue of feedback beyond their own personal behavior to understand how stereotypes or policy interfere with this process.

IMPLICATIONS FOR ACTION

In our interviews, we often encountered attitudes which make it difficult to solve problems that stand in the way of women becoming productive engineers. One supervisor, for example, told us he didn't see what he could do about it. "I'm just a supervisor. I can't control what my subordinates say or change the policies of the company. The women will just have to prove themselves and then they'll be accepted."

We disagree with that view. In many of the examples described in this article, the first-line supervisor had adequate power and influence to improve the situation if he or she had only used that influence. Supervisors can do a great deal to create a climate where both men and women are given challenging job assignments, critical feedback, access to important job information, etc. They can also be allies for women in awkward situations or involve them in informal activities.

Another attitude that blocks progress in this area is the idea that we should let the men and women who are on the same work team deal with these problems. This implies that issues would only be addressed at the group level. Unfortunately, many men have not had experience in working with women as peers, and lack the skills to deal with problems that arise in this area. A group or interpersonal level problem often needs to be resolved with support from the large organization. In our research, we found several organizations that were not passive on this issue, but had taken the initiative to deal with many of the problems that we identified. Some concrete examples may illustrate what organizations can do.

A large research organization, which was praised by one woman employee for having a progressive outlook toward placing women in non-traditional jobs, has had a Women's Association for more than ten years. This association functions as an educational, discussion and action group that is primarily concerned with the problems women face in employment. The association sponsors monthly noontime programs for all women as well as a committee on science and engineering, which aids the company's scientists and engineers in forming a network.

Most companies are just starting to take an interest in networks and seminars for women. For example, one of the electronics firms in our study was interested in assisting men and women to understand and manage gender diversity. Therefore, they developed two seminars to address these issues. The first seminar was offered for professional women and was two days in length. It focused on the unique challenges facing women in the work place and discussed such issues as advancement, communication with men, etc. The most important aspect was the opportunity for women to meet and discuss common experiences. The second seminar focused on men and women working together. Ten men and ten women were assigned to each discussion group during the one-day seminar. The central issue was why women do not advance as fast as men in the organization when all other variables are equal. Male managers of the female engineers participated in the seminar. The major outgrowth of these seminars was increased awareness by both men and women of the organizational issues facing women.

For example, after one engineering manager participated in the seminar, he initiated a discussion with the women in his department to see if they were experiencing any of the problems he had heard about. His interest and openness encouraged them to speak candidly about things that were bothering them. Several of them admitted that they felt handicapped because of their lack of experience with some of the tools they were expected to know how to use. As a result of this discussion, the engineering department is planning to assess new engineers' skills with tools and offer a short training program for both men and women in the use of tools and equipment. This manager's willingness to listen and the company's willingness to change assumptions about engineers will benefit both men and women.

In the first example, we described a formal program of seminars, that was quite visible in the organization. But low-key activities that lack visibility can also be effective. One company with a small engineering department was seen as very supportive. We interviewed two women in the department who were hired a year apart. The first women hired reported being more frustrated by teasing than her co-worker, who was hired a year later. She said:

> When the men used to joke about women not being as smart as men, I felt they were making fun of me personally. Now that there are two of us, I feel more comfortable about joking back. The two women in our department are both on the same work team (4 people), so we have an equal vote in all of our work. It's a lot easier now that there are two of us.

Research indicates that a lone women in a professional organization often gets isolated. This company was sensitive to this issue and solved the problem by putting the two women in the department on the same work team.

This company was also willing to modify formal policies to meet special circumstances created by the presence of women in the organization. The company had a policy against family members working in the same department. When one of the women engineers married a man in the same department, that presented a problem. Rather than insisting that one of them leave the company or move to a non-engineering department, their supervisors counseled them about potential problems and then arranged for them to continue working for the same department, but on different projects and under different supervisors. These activities lacked the visibility of major programs or seminars, but they produced significant results. The women we interviewed in that organization were quite positive about the organization and its responsiveness to their needs.

In summary, those managers who learn to think critically about the dynamics which are occurring on each of the three levels of the organization will be far more effective in sorting out strategies that will contribute to employee effectiveness. By examining individual relationships between men and women, a manager can identify disruptive, prejudicial behaviors on the individual level and provide assistance to improve understanding and communication between employees. On a group level, a manger can become sensitive to the impact which stereotypical attitudes have on employee effectiveness. Finally, by examining organizational policies, the manager can sort out those practices which discriminate and be a catalyst in initiating the necessary changes.

In the next decade, engineering organizations will be hiring many more white women and women of color. Those organizations which encourage their employees and managers to develop the awareness and skills to manage a diverse work force will have the advantage in the competition for quality engineers.

REFERENCES

1. *Manpower Comments.* Scientific Manpower Commission, Vol. 18, No. 8, October 1981, p. 20.
2. *Employment and Earnings,* U.S. Department of Labor, Bureau of Labor Statistics, Vol. 29, No. 1, January 1982, p. 165.
3. For example, Kahne, Stephen, "A Crisis in Electrical Engineering Manpower." *IEEE Spectrum,* June 1981, pp. 50–52.
4. Kanter, Rosabeth Moss, *Men and Women of the Corporation.* New York: Basic Books, Inc., Publishers, 1977, p 227.
5. Rose, Clare, Sally Ann Menninger, and Glenn F. Nyre. "The Study of Women in Science and Engineering." Summary Report, Los Angeles: Evaluation and Training Institute, 1978, p. 21.

41

Rethinking Rewards for Technical Employees

LUIS R. GOMEZ-MEJLA
DAVID B. BALKIN
GEORGE T. MILKOVICH

At high-tech organizations, retaining key innovators can mean gaining a competitive edge. A responsive reward program can help keep them from jumping ship.

The scarcity of engineering and scientific talent is one of the most critical problems facing U.S. corporations today. Because of the difficulties that many companies face in retaining technical people, many also experience low rates of innovation and major delays in the marketing of new products. Rapid turnover at all levels for research and development (R&D) units is becoming the norm in such important industries as semiconductors and electronics. Technical employees behave as individual contractors, willing to change jobs with little remorse if their needs are not met by their current company.

Most disturbing to many of these firms is that an increasing number of top-level scientists and engineers are leaving corporate research labs to start their own companies. They are armed with venture capital and lured by the success stories of people such as Edson de Castro, who left Digital to start Data General, and Robert Noyce, a former Fairchild engineer who founded Intel. If successful, they could become major competitors eating away at the market share of their previous employers. But even if they fail, firms still suffer from the loss of some of their most valuable human resources.

One of the chief reasons that technical employees are so fickle about their employers is that they feel the contributions they provide their company are not adequately rewarded or recognized. Here are some actual examples of this syndrome:

• A research scientist for a large pharmaceutical corporation develops and patents a successful new drug that produces $100 million in revenue its first year on the market. The executives of the division receive large cash bonuses, and the top salespeople enjoy windfall commissions from the strong demand for the new product—but the scientist receives only a $500 honorarium for developing the drug.

• All of the engineers at a $7 billion electronics defense firm are either recent college graduates in their twenties with little work experience or plateaued engineers in their fifties who lack marketable skills and are merely waiting to retire. The shortage of experienced engineers with cutting-edge skills makes it more difficult for the firm to win important defense contracts and introduce new products to the market on time.

• Producing a major new memory chip takes enormous capital resources that only the largest firms such as Intel and Texas Instruments can afford. Yet top U.S. semiconductor companies have

Reprinted with permission of publisher, from *Organizational Dynamics,* Spring/1990 © 1990. American Management Association, New York. All rights reserved.

Luis Gomez-Mejia is Professor of Management at Arizona State University's College of Business. **David Balkin** is Professor of Management at University of Colorado's Graduate School of Business. **George Milkovich** is Professor at Cornell University's Center for Advanced Human Resource Studies.

been steadily losing world market share to Japanese competitors that produce better-quality and superior-performing chips. The most talented electrical engineers in the U.S. are leaving large U.S. semiconductor firms for "boutique" start-up companies that produce specialty chips for specific, limited markets. This trend hurts the large company's ability to compete in major semiconductor markets.

INEQUITABLE REWARDS

In each of the above cases scientists and engineers were compensated with a fixed salary and benefits package. This pay structure treats these innovators of new products as if they were generic employees. It does not reward them for the unique and indispensable contribution that they make to the organization. The traditional compensation systems that most organizations in the United States use were developed more than 50 years ago; they treat achieving "internal equity" and consistency across different employee groups as the ultimate goal. Under such a system, scientists and engineers, along with other employees, frequently are pigeonholed into predetermined grade levels with a standardized pay package.

These traditional pay methods are wreaking havoc with the morale and motivation of scientists and engineers in the 1990s. Research and development employees in technology-driven businesses are asked to produce innovations that are as critical to a firm's success as are the outputs of top salespeople or executives. Yet they operate under pay systems that often do not reward them accordingly. Top management in technology-intensive corporations needs to rethink reward policies for scientific talent, and to design pay policies that recognize their importance. Innovative ways to reward scientists and engineers should be based on strategic approaches to pay systems. Key contributor rewards, group rewards linked to company success, and increased budgetary discretion are examples of programs that can give technical innovators incentives to stay with their employer.

FLEXIBLE PAY SYSTEMS

How many times has a manager been frustrated when he or she loses a heavily-recruited engineer to a competitor because the human resources department refused to authorize a salary to match the competition? The HR manager typically justifies this refusal on the grounds that internal equity must be maintained: Other engineers would be dissatisfied and morale would suffer if pay guidelines were not followed. But as a result of his or her refusal, the company may lose rare and valuable technical talent.

Most firms face a dilemma between pressure to preserve equitable pay relationships among employees and the need to keep up with "going rates" in the labor market. When market forces are stable, it makes sense to develop a pay policy that gives high priority to salary equity among employees with jobs that require similar levels of effort, skill, and responsibility. The traditional, lock-step compensation system based on job evaluation does just that. Unfortunately, these systems often have difficulty adjusting to a changing economic environment. The market forces for technical employees are dynamic because of a severe scarcity of supply; therefore, it is more appropriate to develop a pay policy that permits flexibility and recognizes strategic and critical talent.

A flexible and adaptive pay system allows managers to respond to the jolts in the technical labor market. Under flexible pay systems, firms select a position in the market relative to their competitors for critical skill groups. The pay rate for a particular scientist or engineer is based more closely on his or her individual strategic importance than on "equitable" comparisons with the overall workforce. Managers must be supported with the necessary resources to put together an attractive pay package that becomes a competitive tool to bring scarce technical employees into the company where they are needed. Moreover, in addition to flexible pay systems, creative and innovative benefits and bonus packages can help firms to attract and retain technical talent.

A recent Peat Marwick survey found that 69%

of Silicon Valley high-technology firms used "sign-on" bonuses to attract scientists and engineers. The sign-on bonus can take the form of cash, stock options, or a combination of both. The cash sign-on bonus was in the $3,000–$4,000 range. The sign-on bonus gives a manager greater flexibility to attract a recruit without provoking anger among current employees.

At some firms, special relocation benefits are available to bring technical employees on board. The company may buy and sell the employee's house, provide a settling-in allowance for a temporary residence, and offer equity in a new house to a recruit. These benefits may not be available to employees in other job categories.

Many firms that employ scientists and engineers provide market adjustments to their pay. Thus the employees do not perceive themselves as underpaid with respect to the market and may be less likely to be pirated away by a competitor. The market adjustment is an across-the-board salary increase given to affected employees, and it is separate from annual merit pay increases. According to findings of a recent survey of companies in the Boston high-technology corridor, more than 70% of the firms made market adjustments to the pay of their technical employees, and each of these employees received on average a 10% market adjustment on top of merit pay.

REWARDING KEY PEOPLE

A major problem faced by most technical managers is how to reward their top performers in proportion to the value their contributions add to the company. According to recent surveys by the Hay Group, today's typical merit-pay plan provides only a 2% difference between an outstanding and a satisfactory performer. A top-performing scientist may develop a new drug or create a software program worth millions of dollars in revenues. Clearly, this individual would not be recognized adequately with conventional merit pay.

In the United States a company is under no legal obligation to share with employed inventors the profits it collects from their inventions. Under U.S. patent law, employers own any invention or discovery an employee makes while working for them. Some U.S. firms provide a cash bonus for inventors who receive a patent on a commercial product, but many offer no special recognition for these important contributions. By contrast, West Germany and the United Kingdom have laws that obligate the employer to share returns with an employed inventor in proportion to the commercial returns of the patented invention. In the United States, organizations that recognize key scientists and engineers gain an edge over their competitors in recruiting and retaining top talent.

KEY CONTRIBUTORS

A key contributor is an employee who has demonstrated special skills or proprietary knowledge, who has made a significant impact on the firm's performance, and whose loss would pose a threat to the company. These individuals are unique and virtually impossible to replace. For example, a scientist doing leading-edge work on superconductivity may possess unique skills that are critical for the success of a company that is trying to bring to market a ceramic material with superconductor properties. Loss of this individual would seriously disrupt the firm's research and development activity and threaten the survival of the business.

Companies that are in the vulnerable position of relying on the contributions of a few key technical people need to devise schemes to retain them, especially when they are most critically needed. Key-contributor pay policies are designed to recognize the achievements of these people and to provide the incentive for them to remain with their employer.

Cash Rewards
According to a Hay Group national survey, 76% of high-technology industries have some kind of special pay policy for key technical people. They usually provide top technical contributors with cash or equity rewards. Cash is the most common reward

and usually is given "after the fact" in recognition of an outstanding contribution.

To recognize the accomplishments of its top contributors, IBM offers cash bonuses at both the corporate and division levels. The IBM Corporate Award provides cash to the top technical people in the corporation each year during a special ceremony. IBM recently awarded $150,000 to each of two of its scientists who won the 1987 Nobel Prize in science for research in superconductivity.

At the division level, IBM gives Outstanding Innovation Awards to recognize individual achievements, such as important inventions or scientific discoveries. About 40 of these innovation awards, ranging from $2,500 to $25,000, are given each year.

Equity

Many companies also give equity to key technical people in the form of either a stock option or a stock grant. Restrictions placed on the exercise of the stock options allow the employer to retain the key person for several years before the restrictions lapse. The best opportunities to generate wealth from equity occur in small, private companies before the initial public offering of the stock. The IRS places tighter restrictions on the use of stock options on larger, public corporations. A technical employee, for example, may have to spend a considerable amount of personal cash to purchase stock when it is publicly traded, and he or she may be required to pay taxes on the gain before being permitted to sell the stock. As a result of the difficulties associated with stock options, some large, public corporations use unit performance shares or phantom stock to reward technical people in order to provide returns as great as those of venture-capital-financed start-ups.

Tektronix, a large, public, high-technology corporation, developed a unit performance shares program to reward key technical employees for the long-term commercial success of the venture unit in the corporation. Tektronix designed the payoff matrix of the unit performance shares to correspond to what would be available with equity participation in a small, private, start-up company. The

shares are tied to the commercial success of the product in the market.

Budgetary Discretion

Another, less widely used reward is increased budgetary discretion, which comes in two forms. First, key contributors are often given special budgets over which they have discretion outside of normal accounting controls. Some use their budgets to buy additional project equipment, attend special conferences, travel to visit colleagues in other firms or foreign countries, or purchase computer software.

The second form of budgetary discretion allows key contributors to grant salary increases to support staff and colleagues who may have contributed to their success. For example, one scientist was able to grant a 10% bonus to his technicians and secretary. The logic underlying the budgetary discretion award is that key contributors know who contributed to their past successes—and will choose to reward them—and that these top contributors will allocate extra resources in ways that will allow them to become even more productive.

PENALTIES OF HIERARCHY

Many U.S. firms, particularly large, high-technology organizations, establish an elaborate hierarchy of grade levels for employees—including scientists and engineers. For example, one company producing electronic components in Massachusetts employed 500 technical employees in a research and development unit. It has 48 grade levels, each with a separate pay bracket. Employees enter the firm at lower grade levels and move up through the ranks over time. The pay and degree of responsibility of scientists and engineers are predicated largely on successive advancement in grade. And although promotions are supposedly based on performance, more often they come with seniority. Within each grade, assessments of each individual's performance generally determine pay allocation. This system has been borrowed from a manufacturing environment where division of labor and design of work flows are associated with the use of mechanistic and bureaucratic human resources procedures. The theory is that by partitioning jobs into multiple components, and making rewards contingent on fine distinctions in the nature of the tasks being accomplished, management can create a predictable and controllable work environment.

Unfortunately, applying a strict manufacturing mentality in a technical environment can be highly counterproductive. This mechanistic approach may create artificial barriers among people, fragmentation, and an individualistic climate in the workforce. These behaviors and the resulting culture often run counter to successful research and development environments. A successful research environment requires intense team effort, integration of activities by many individuals, fluid tasks, exchange of knowledge, and minimal status barriers. Scientists and engineers working on common problems need to feel that they are not in competition against each other.

The disruptive effects of an inflexible hierarchical grade system on research and development work are evident in a medium-size firm located in the Denver-Boulder area. As the company grew from 100 to 800 employees during a three-year period, it hired a consulting firm to establish a formal compensation plan. This plan called for 20 grade levels for the research and development workforce. A year after the plan was implemented, management began to realize that something had gone awry. Senior scientists were looking down on their junior counterparts, and the design engineers made it clear in a number of public remarks that they felt superior to the production engineers whose job was to "carry out orders." Only limited communication was taking place between these groups, backbiting became common, and crucial information (e.g., design flaws) was being withheld from top management.

The myopic view and parochialism this pay approach engendered in the scientists and engineers developed in part because jobs and the status hierarchy were narrowly defined. Many scientists and engineers tend to be more loyal to their discipline than they are to their employer, and many are chauvinistic about their technical specialty. The hierarchical grade system reinforced these tendencies with predictably negative results. The eventual success of a research and development program requires a businesswide orientation that goes well beyond the lab. People within the organization need to be willing to channel scarce resources to research and development projects. And those outside the organization who are relied upon for support will give that support only if they perceive the firm as having a strong research and development program.

THE PRODUCTIVITY PARADOX

Obviously, research and development projects in private firms have little value unless they lead to commercial applications. Some observers see the United States as the envy of the industrialized world in research and development. But others see the U.S. falling behind its major competitors when it comes to reaping the commercial benefits of research and development. This paradox can be explained partially by American management techniques and by the use of conventional approaches to rewarding research and development that fail to exploit American research and development superiority. A managerial obsession with specialization and hierarchy runs counter to the need for interaction, coordination, reciprocity, and inter-unit teamwork involved in mass producing new innovations. It is not unusual to find companies where research and development is kept apart, both geographically and organizationally, from the rest of the firm. Findings of some surveys show that many employees in the production and manufacturing functions perceive research and development staff as being "weird" and disconnected from reality. On the other hand, those in research and development often view the former as drones who need close supervision in order to get things right.

Many human resources problems are difficult to solve because they seem to grow out of "human nature" and thus seem to be beyond management's control. People who do different kinds of work in separate departments may view each other with suspicion and contempt, and rivalries may develop between them. But, in fact, management has the ability to counteract this tendency. The pay system provides management with substantial clout to align the self-interests of scientists and engineers with those of other employees. Combining a conventional fixed compensation system with aggregate incentives can do much to create a unified workforce.

Promoting Team Elan

Many successful firms use team-based incentives as powerful tools to enhance the performance of research and development groups. They provide these incentives to an entire team of scientists and engineers working on a common problem when they achieve important milestones: reaching a scientific breakthrough, receiving a large government grant, obtaining a new patent, or finding a way to lower the costs of manufacturing a given product. These group-based incentives are remarkably instrumental in generating a tight and cohesive research and development team—a prerequisite for success. These rewards can also improve research and development performance by focusing employees' attention on high-priority tasks, bringing "free riders" into line, and encouraging people from diverse backgrounds to iron out their differences and work together for a shared goal and the common good.

One high-technology company in the Boston area offers a competitive bonus of 25% of an engineer's salary based on the performance of his or her entire team. Each team may submit a proposal to management explaining why it deserves a bonus based on costs saved or value added to the firm. Money for the bonus is generated by channeling into a special fund 1% of return on sales exceeding 5%. A companywide committee reviews the proposals twice a year. After consulting with supervisors, managers in other departments, and others who are involved with the teams in question, the committee makes a final determination. This special bonus fund may accumulate over time if only a few bonuses are awarded in a given year.

A company in Silicon Valley provides division managers with a pool of discretionary money that can be distributed to various research and development teams based on the difficulty of the work being done and its relative contribution to the firm. Confidential peer ratings are used to determine how the bonus is allocated among team members; in some cases the money is distributed equally among the members.

Fostering a Companywide Perspective

Successful start-up companies and mature high-technology firms have learned from experience that closely linking the fortunes of scientists and engineers to company performance is a powerful inducement to make them think like businesspeople rather than lab workers. Profit sharing leads to more variable compensation and requires the technical employee to share some of the firm's financial risks. As a result, scientists and engineers are forced to consider "bottom-line" commercial success as well as technical success. By focusing employees' attention on financial results, these plans pave the way for cooperation and integration of various units that might normally compete.

For example, every year that profitability goals are met, Hewlett-Packard awards a large cash bonus to each employee. Unlike many other high-technology firms, Hewlett-Packard has been in the black—and paying profit-sharing bonuses—for 25 years. In order to ensure that technical employees see a connection between their efforts and the firm's performance, and to make them feel that they share a common fate with others in the organization, Hewlett-Packard bases its profit-sharing plan at the divisional level. The company has a policy of splitting divisions soon after they exceed 1,000 employees.

Another example is provided by a Midwestern computer firm. The company gives employees involved in the development and manufacturing of a product 15% of any annual net profits attributed to the product whenever they exceed 1.6% of total sales.

Rewarding Long-Term Results

Perhaps no other activity in a corporation is more long-term oriented than research and development, both as an investment and as a process. It usually takes at least five years, and in many cases ten or more years, before the benefits of R&D efforts can be assessed. Because team-based bonuses and profit sharing are normally directed at short-term accomplishments (usually one year or less), successful high-tech firms often provide an additional layer of rewards designed to focus employees' attention on long-term results. These companies offer an extensive array of long-term incentives that treat research and development workers as executives by tying a portion of the income of scientists and engineers to the firm's stock values. Sharing equity with the employees enables management to use compensation as a form of communication: In this way management tells employees which outcomes the firm values. When they become part owners, technical employees may be more likely to understand the firm's perspective on their jobs. Long-term plans also encourage employees to share a vision of the firm's future financial success; research and development employees who share the vision may be particularly willing to initiate and sustain a common effort. Innovation relies on knowledge—a resource the resides in the employees themselves. Thus firms that base their success on continuing innovation are extremely vulnerable to the effects of attrition among R&D staff. Only by offering these employees incentives to remain with the firm can they hope to succeed.

THE SAIC EXAMPLE

Science Applications International Corporation (SAIC), a 20-year-old high-technology organization that employs some 9,000 workers in more than 200 offices throughout the United States, is one of the most profitable firms in the instrumentation and electronics industry. What is more, its turnover rate for scientists and engineers has a reputation for being well below the industry average. SAIC is a national leader in the use of equity compensation; it has offered an extensive menu of employee stock ownership plans (ESOPs) to its research and development employees for 20 years. The firm han-

dles these stock dealings through its wholly-owned broker dealership. Some of the plans employees can choose from include:

- Contribution of up to 10% of their salary, to be matched by SAIC dollar-for-dollar, to purchase company stock.

- A performance award program that provides company stock to selected research and development teams based on their contribution.

- Yearly allocation of a pool of stock options to division managers. The managers can distribute these stocks to individual research and development employees or teams who are deemed exceptional performers.

PROFESSIONAL REWARDS

Attitude surveys conducted since the 1930s have established that job satisfaction is closely correlated with occupational level and education. However, scientists and engineers working in industry represent an extreme deviation from this norm, showing satisfaction levels that are sometimes even lower than those of menial laborers. The most common complaint expressed by technical employees is that a few years after one enters the workforce, perhaps within five years of graduating from school, one reaches a dead end in terms of both professional challenges and financial progress. Boredom can easily set in after a scientist or an engineer has been on the job performing a narrow set of tasks for several years. Because of the fast rate of technical obsolescence that makes new graduates highly attractive to employers and helps create a tight labor market, pay compression is so severe in many organizations that a freshly minted engineer often commands a higher salary than a seasoned veteran does. Faced with an apparently bleak future in the organization, many senior scientists and engineers try to move into more lucrative and challenging management positions. Executive M.B.A. programs around the country enroll large numbers of scientists and engineers who hope that obtaining a business degree will help them make this transition. But the abilities and temperament of scientists and engineers are frequently quite removed from those of managers; thus an excellent engineer may turn out to be only a mediocre manager.

THE DUAL-CAREER LADDER OPTION

One solution to this problem, developed in the 1950s, is the use of dual-career ladders, which allow technical employees to move up in a grade hierarchy that is separate from but parallel to that of managerial employees. Consistent with the pay structures discussed earlier, this approach is often overly bureaucratic, and such attempts to solve the career stagnation problem for scientists and engineers have met with mixed results. One drawback of the dual-career ladder is that often it is based on the fragmentation of jobs, thus reinforcing pecking orders and impeding cooperation. A second, and perhaps greater, problem is that technical employees may not believe in the company line of "separate but equal." There is a widespread perception among scientists and engineers that parallel, dual-career ladders are a myth and that, in fact, upward mobility and influence in the organization, with their associated rewards, only come by moving into management ranks.

Alternatives to the dual-career ladder concept have blossomed in recent years at firms with successful research and development operations. These companies are experimenting with a wide variety of professional rewards that are valued highly by technical employees and that are not predicated on one's position in the organizational structure. Some of the most promising ideas are discussed below.

Expand the Nature of the Job
In order to prevent hierarchical barriers from arising, successful firms encourage the creation of large research and development teams composed of scientists and engineers from diverse areas in the organization. This allows technical employees to cross-fertilize ideas and experiment with a range of techniques, thereby reducing boredom and professional stagnation.

For example, one firm divides its technical people into teams of from five to thirteen employees guided by a leader. Each team is assigned a project. Team members have broad responsibility on a project and divide up the specific tasks themselves; each employee, theoretically, is able to do any job. By contrast with the dozens of job classifications for research and development personnel that exist in some other firms, under this system there is just one classification for all scientists and engineers. Moreover, more than half of these employees' pay is in the form of group and key contributor incentives.

Allow Technical Employees to Set Up New Ventures
One of the greatest fears in many high-technology companies is the potential loss of scientists and engineers who possess invaluable knowledge and who may become direct competitors by starting their own firms. Part of the motivation behind such a risky move by a scientist or an engineer is the wish to experience the thrills and challenges of entrepreneurship that they cannot feel in most large organizations. Firms with leading-edge research and development functions offer these employees the opportunity to start a new venture without incurring all the risks they would face if they went out on their own. After all, the mortality rate of such businesses is about 80% within a five-year period.

Firms such as 3M and Eastman Kodak have been enormously successful at setting up special "innovation banks" to fund internal enterprises. This not only allows a large venture to be supported inside the company as a separate business, but it also permits scientists and engineers to obtain resources that otherwise would find no place in a line manager's budget. At 3M, employees may request such funds from their division, from corporate research and development, or from the new venture division. These programs allow employees to satisfy their intellectual and entrepreneurial cravings without leaving the company. These programs also appeal to the employees' acquisitive side, since they receive large financial rewards if the new ventures succeed.

Support New Projects

Only a few technical employees may want to tackle the enormous task of starting a new business unit. But many may wish to develop their own projects of personal interest. Many firms with successful research and development staffs capitalize on these employees' interests by providing financial backing to scientists and engineers who choose to generate their own projects. Texas Instruments, for example, has an elaborate system that offers several options for funding projects, including a program called "wild hare grants" for ideas that are good but risky.

Allow Employees to Pursue Their Own Interests on Company Time

Another way to prevent career stagnation and alienation in the technical workforce is to allow a certain amount of discretionary time on the job, during which these employees may pursue their individual interests. This practice sometimes pays off handsomely when an employee comes up with a novel idea that eventually leads to a useful innovation. In one noteworthy example, 3M formalized its "15% rule"—up to 15% of an employee's time may be spent on projects of his or her own choosing.

REDUCING TECHNICAL OBSOLESCENCE

All organizations that employ scientists and engineers are concerned with maintaining state-of-the-art technical skills. Unfortunately, about five years after an engineer receives a university degree, half of his or her knowledge may be obsolete; in some fields, such as artificial intelligence, it may take only three years. As a result, it is not unusual for engineers to find that their careers have become plateaued by the time they reach their mid-thirties. The plateaued engineer may be a drain on company resources, since each additional year brings a de-

cline in technical productivity—while payroll costs steadily increase.

By fine-tuning the benefits component of the pay package for technical employees, management may reduce the damage that technical obsolescence does to the firm. Providing educational benefits and sabbatical leaves for employees can help the company stay on the cutting edge.

Educational Benefits

Most technical companies provide full-tuition reimbursement for employees who take university courses in technical disciplines. Many companies also encourage their scientists and engineers to pursue advanced degrees, and they fully cover the costs. Funds are provided for travel and expenses to scientific meetings, seminars, and workshops in emerging fields of study. Costs are covered for professional association memberships, journal subscriptions, books, and publishing fees for writing articles in scientific journals.

Bell Labs, a leading research firm, places a heavy emphasis on continuing education. It has a huge in-house education center that provides technical training in many advanced scientific and engineering disciplines.

Wang recently provided funds for a school called the Wang Institute, which offers a master's degree in a skill that is in critical demand—software engineering. Graduates are free to work for any company they choose, but the hope is that many will select Wang as their employer.

Merck also uses a variation on this theme. Believing that interaction with faculty and students will sharpen technical skills and stimulate creative thinking, the company encourages its scientists and engineers to teach at local universities.

Sabbatical Leaves

The sabbatical leave is another employee benefit that may be used to reduce technical obsolescence. Industry is starting to adopt this practice, which has been used for years in universities to provide time for faculty to renew their creative energies. A period of extended leave with pay, the sabbatical provides the opportunity for education or other meaningful activities that ultimately benefit both the employee and the firm. The educational sabbatical may be a good alternative for companies that do not have extensive in-house educational facilities and need to retrain their technical people. It also may be used to prevent job burnout, which develops frequently when scientists and engineers are working under high pressure to bring a new product to market on time.

At Intel, a technical employee who has worked at the company for seven years is entitled to take an eight-week sabbatical leave with pay in addition to his or her annual vacation. Employees also may apply for an additional six months off with pay to accomplish specified goals, such as doing service for the community, teaching, or continuing their education.

Xerox's technical employees may apply for management approval for sabbatical leaves that they use to perform social service for nonprofit organizations. If an employee's application is approved, he or she may take between three and twelve months' leave with full salary and benefits. This policy benefits both the employee and the firm. The community service performed by employees on sabbatical enhances the reputation of the company as a socially responsible employer. And the employee may return with a fresh perspective that may provide the inspiration for new innovations.

ENCOURAGING INNOVATIONS

All the reward programs examined in this article are designed to encourage technical employees to provide innovations that will lead to commercial success. Pay policies that treat innovators as "hired hands" and reward them according to inflexible methods clash with the interests of a firm and its scientists and engineers.

Executives who are interested in redesigning their reward systems for technical employees need to consider carefully the impact that any change will have on other organizational systems. The reward system is intimately related to job designs and organization structures, and changes in the rewards may result in some unpleasant surprises. Careful planning should precede the implementation of any new pay policy. Here are some suggestions for executives who may be considering making some adjustments to their technical reward systems:

• *Price the person, not the job, when rewarding a technical employee.* It is desirable to visualize each scientist and engineer as a unique individual with a unique market value. Executives and sales professionals are viewed this way in most organizations. A significant portion of the total earnings of the technical employee should come from variable compensation policies.

• *Provide a menu of pay incentives so that the total reward system for technical employees complements the goals and objectives of the organization.* Pay systems and policies should be compatible with other organization systems. The result is a multidimensional reward system that is in keeping with the goals of the organization and the interests of the technical employees.

• *Remove the professional reward system from the hierarchical structure.* Management needs to develop new ways of structuring jobs and building organizational units that meet more of the scientists' and engineers' needs.

• *Integrate the pay system for technical employees with the pay systems for other employee groups.* The more the pay system for technical employees is differentiated from that for other employees, the more buffering between the two clusters of employees is necessary. For example, because there is some interface between manufacturing and research and development, some of the production workers may feel that they are entitled to the same pay policies that apply to the design engineers. And, indeed, their demands should be considered. Where are the systems' lines drawn with respect to eligibility for a reward? One solution may be to allow production workers to share in the profit-sharing bonus (a share of company success) but restrict their inclusion in the team bonus (based on research and development success).

A PART OF THE TOTAL PICTURE

The pay system is a crucial element in research and development management. But it is only one part of the total picture in making the R&D operation effective. In some cases, variable pay systems succeed; in others, they fail. Success depends on fitting reward systems into a comprehensive and carefully integrated strategy. This strategy needs to include tough selection and hiring procedures, rigorous performance evaluation and feedback, increased discretion and flexibility for key contributors, and job designs that facilitate innovation.

42

Managing Dual Ladder Systems in RD&E Settings

RALPH KATZ AND THOMAS J. ALLEN

Organizations employing professional specialists, engineers, and scientists in particular face the dilemma of establishing reward systems that are both stimulating to the professional and productive for the organization. This problem stems in part from the notion that specialist groups bring to the organization a set of attitudes and career aspirations that are in conflict with the organization's work requirements and established career paths. It is often argued that many Research, Development, and Engineering (i.e., RD&E) professionals are socialized into their technical occupations with values and definitions of success that differ significantly from those prevailing in the traditional managerial setting [1]. In the typical organization, for example, management expects authority to be aligned with the hierarchical principle, discharged through a progression of well-ordered job positions. Technical professionals, on the other hand, value the freedom to pursue their own technical interests, the responsibility for making judgments in their areas of expertise, and the exercise of organizational control through knowledge, logical arguments, and collegiality.

For many years now, much has also been written about how professional needs clash with those organizational incentives normally available to managers [16, 22]. In theory, RD&E professionals are supposedly motivated by a desire to contribute to their disciplines and to establish a credible or distinguished reputation among their technical colleagues. In a sense, they are strongly oriented toward work in their professions, developing strong commitments to their specialized skills and outside professional reference groups [8]. And it is often this more "cosmopolitan" orientation that causes one to be seen as being less organization-loyal. For if publications, the production of knowledge for its own sake, or independence are the primary goals of scientists and engineers, then they will feel thwarted in achieving these goals when confronted by the economic realities and practical needs of the company. Managers, in contrast, desire upward mobility in the organizational hierarchy. In a sense, they are more committed to developing their own "local" organizational careers. They do this by focusing more on the achievement of company objectives and the acquisition of organizational approval and promotion. As one R&D professional recently framed it for us: "To have my ability recognized rather than my authority is far more rewarding." To the true professional, then, upward mobility in the managerial hierarchy is of little importance compared to autonomy in the practice of one's technical specialty. Success is, therefore, defined independent from managerial advancement. In short, the argument is that professionals acquire status and define success from the perspectives of their technical colleagues while managers build these same attributes from the perspectives of their organizational superiors.

These conflicts between professional and business-related goals can be very problematic for an organization as scientists and engineers try to uphold professional standards in the face of strong pressures for commercializable results [20]. Not all

Reprinted with the permission of the authors. Earlier versions of this research were published in T. J. Allen and R. Katz, "The dual ladder: motivational solution or managerial delusion?" *R&D Management,* vol. 16, no. 2, pp. 185–197, 1986; and T. J. Allen and R. Katz "Age, education, and the technical ladder," *IEEE Transactions on Engineering Management,* vol. 39, pp. 237–245, 1992.

Ralph Katz is Professor of Management at Northeastern University's College of Business and Research Associate at M.I.T.'s Sloan School of Management. *Thomas Allen* is Senior Associate Dean and Professor of Management at M.I.T.'s Sloan School of Management.

scientists and engineers are alike in their orientations toward career success, however. Whether engineers and scientists are more interested in peer recognition than they are in organizational advancement has been the subject of much debate. While some studies have suggested that engineers are very different in their professional and organizational orientations than their more scientific counterparts [1, 17], other studies question whether one can truly generalize within any professional occupation [6, 13]. Generally speaking, research studies have substantiated an important distinction between professionals who are either more "cosmopolitan" or more "local" in their career orientation [8, 7]. In contrast to the previously described cosmopolitan stereotype, many technical professionals are local in their overall perspectives and are, in fact, interested in working on the application of technology that achieves the business aims of the company. Local professionals, as a result, are more involved than their cosmopolitan counterparts in establishing organizational identities and careers through the successful commercialization of technical accomplishments. In a sense, the loyalties and work focus of locals are more strongly aligned with their organizations than with their professional peers. In any organization, there is generally some proportion of professionals who prefer technical problem solving and for whom management has very little attraction and vice versa.

THE DUAL LADDER REWARD SYSTEM

Despite these purported "professional/managerial" or "cosmopolitan/local" differences, the highest rewards in most business organizations are conferred on those who assume additional managerial responsibility. Advancement up the managerial ladder secures increases in status, recognition, salary, influence, and power. For many professionally oriented technologists, movement into management becomes the most viable career strategy simply because their opportunities to achieve success without undertaking such managerial responsibilities

are very limited. As a result, many productive engineers and scientists feel frustrated as they are "pressured" to take on managerial and administrative roles they really do not want in order to attain higher salary and more prestige.

The "dual ladder system of career advancement" is an organizational arrangement that was developed to solve these individual and organizational problems by formalizing promotions along two parallel hierarchies: one provides managerial progression, while the other provides opportunity for professional advancement [3]. The dual ladder system promises equal status and rewards to equivalent levels in the two hierarchies. In providing the more professionally oriented specialists with opportunities and incentives to remain active in their fields, without having to shift to management, the dual ladder aims to secure for the firm a highly motivated and creative pool of technical talent. It tries to establish a viable career track that maintains the productivity of highly innovative individuals who either see themselves or who are viewed by others as less interested in or less capable of carrying out managerial responsibilities by rewarding them with increased levels of prestige, freedom, and appropriate job perquisites as they are promoted up the technical ladder.

Although dual ladders have now been in use for some time, their success has been the focus of much debate [12]. Three generic kinds of problems seem to underly the concept. First, most cultures automatically associate prestige with managerial advancement. Titles of Department Head and Vice President convey images of success, while titles of Senior Researcher and Lead Engineer are considerably more ambiguous and therefore more subject to skepticism. Many organizations exacerbate these differences by not living up to their promised commitments of creating equal status, perquisites, resources, and other financial and symbolic rewards to those of equivalent levels in the managerial and professional hierarchies. Frequently too, management does a poor job of publicizing the technical ladder and little observable change takes place either in work activities or responsibilities after technical promotion. An additional problem arises when technical promotions are debated through justifications of past contributions while managerial promotions are more positively discussed in terms of future promise and potential.

A second set of problems concerns the nature of incentives associated with each ladder. Movement up the managerial ladder usually leads to positions of increased influence and power within the organization. The number of employees under a manager typically increases with promotion and such resources can be mobilized more easily to carry out the manager's needs and demands. In sharp contrast, advancement up the technical ladder usually leads to increased autonomy in the pursuit of one's technical interests but often at the expense of organizational influence and power. Neither the number of subordinates nor any visible means of power increase, fostering perceptions that the technical ladder might really be less important. The issue of relevance becomes even more difficult as the organization grants professionals enough freedom to select their work with little linkage between their activities and company objectives, returns, or paybacks. Such conflicts are aggravated even more as the organization chooses to either eliminate or deemphasize certain areas of interest. As a result, supervision of individual contributors becomes more difficult and feelings of isolation from the organization become more pronounced. The risk is that the technical side becomes a "parking lot" for bright technologists whose abilities to generate ideas easily outstrips the capability of the organization for dealing with them. The rewards of freedom and independence can also bring with them feelings of rejection and disconnection.

Finally, there is the inevitable tendency to "pollute" the technical side of the dual ladder. In addition to rewarding outstanding technical performers who choose to remain in the organization as individual contributors, the technical ladder becomes a repository for less successful, unnecessary, and even incompetent managers. Over time, the criteria for technical promotion are gradually corrupted to encompass not only technical contributions but also organizational loyalty, rewarding those individuals who have been "passed over" for managerial positions. Another common practice is to use the professional ladder primarily for pacifying individuals who are technically competent and who deserve to be rewarded, but who lack diplomatic skills or management ability. When any of this is done, it can make the technical ladder into a consolation prize, demotivating individuals who interpret technical promotions not as a reward but simply as a signal that they are "not good enough to be a manager." Certainly, such misuses undermine the integrity of the dual ladder system.

Much has been done over the past few years to improve the formal structures of dual ladder systems to alleviate these problems. Using internal and external peer reviews, organizations have begun "policing" their technical ladders to protect their purity and prevent the "dumping ground" abuses. They have tried to strengthen their commitment to the technical side through increased publicity, recognition, career counseling, and information dissemination; through making the ladders more comparable in numbers of people, and perquisites at equivalent hierarchical levels; through clearer job descriptions, qualifications, responsibilities, performance standards, and reporting relationships; and though greater involvement in organizational decision-making and in influencing technical strategy.

Despite these changes, there is still very little empirical research regarding the reactions of professionals for whom the technical ladder was originally designed. The present research, as a result, revolves around two key questions. First, what proportion of a laboratory's technical staff will find the technical ladder career an attractive one and to what extent do their perceptions change over time? This temporal investigation is critical since most technical professionals do not graduate with concrete notions of career success; instead they develop and change their orientations and perspectives over time as they encounter different work experiences [7, 19].

The second research question focuses on the characteristics of those scientists and engineers who indicate a preference or predisposition for the technical ladder. Were they to show a consistent set of characteristics, then knowledge of that fact could provide management with important guidance regarding the appropriate use of the dual ladder system for those types of people or situations. It is our initial contention that career orientations of technical professionals are strongly influenced by the nature of the work in which they are engaged and by their level of education.

One of the most important factors affecting one's work experiences lies in the nature of one's task assignments. Within an RD&E setting, projects can be categorized along a continuum ranging from research to development to technical service [21]. More importantly, empirical studies have revealed substantial problem-solving and information-processing differences among projects engaged in these kinds of activities [10]. Technical professionals with a more cosmopolitan orientation are more likely to be engaged in research projects since their problems and solution approaches are more universally defined and less constrained by organizational circumstances and boundaries [2]. Research projects are also more likely to involve the advancement of knowledge and are therefore less pressured by the business goals of the company. Development and technical service projects, however, require a more local outlook since the development or design of technology is without meaning if the technology is not successfully commercialized or otherwise put to use. As emphasized by Ritti [17], development or design projects are ultimately tested by competition in the marketplace and not by exposure to or review by one's technical peers and colleagues. We would expect to find, therefore, that technical professionals working in development and technical service projects are less cosmopolitan in their career and work orientations than their research colleagues. Based on this logic, the following hypothesis is suggested:

H1: The degree of preference for a technical ladder career will vary systematically with the nature of the work performed by an individual scientist or engineer, viz., those performing basic research will exhibit a stronger preference than those engaged in applied research, development, and technical service. Those doing applied research will show a stronger preference than those engaged in development or technical service, and so on.

Additional research also indicates that educational background strongly affects the values and career interests of scientists and engineers [17, 13, 6]. According to these studies, technical professionals with Ph.D.'s are not only more likely to prefer research work but they are also more likely to be interested in scientific and technical accomplishment rather than promotion within their organization. This is in sharp contrast to non-Ph.D.'s who have been shown to place greater emphasis on salaries and organizational advancement. Scientists and engineers with a Ph.D. degree have been shown to stress the importance of technical communication with their outside professional community while also striving to achieve greater autonomy within their organization [17, 1]. One explanation for these effects is that university education at the Ph.D. level is substantially more specialized and emphasizes more explicitly the values of fundamental knowledge and discovery. As a result of this exposure, Ph.D.'s often seek and expect upon graduation to be in positions that will allow them to continue to contribute to their technical disciplines. Our supposition is that the university experience of Ph.D.'s provides them with expectations and values that fit more directly with the goals of cosmopolitans than with local types of professionals. It is likely, therefore, that Ph.D.'s will develop a stronger preference for the technical side of the dual ladder than their non-Ph.D. colleagues. These educational differences lend themselves to the following hypothesis:

H2: The degree of preference for a technical ladder career will vary systematically with the level of education of the individual engineer or scientist, viz., those with a Ph.D. degree will exhibit a stronger preference than those with a Master of Science degree who in turn will show a stronger preference than those with a Bachelor of Science.

RESEARCH METHOD

The data were collected in a study of about 2,500 scientists, engineers and managers in nine U.S. and two European organizations. The selection of participating organizations could not be randomized, but they were chosen to represent several distinct sectors and industries. Two of the organizations are government laboratories, and three are not-for-profit firms doing most of their business with government agencies. The six remaining organizations are in private industry: two in aerospace, one in electronics, two in the manufacture of industrial equipment, and one in the food industry.

In each organization, short meetings were scheduled with the respondents to solicit their voluntary cooperation and to explain the purposes of the study. Each scientist or engineer received an individually addressed questionnaire at this time. The questionnaire included the usual demographic questions plus several questions about the ways in which the respondent viewed his or her future career and the ways in which the organization structured its reward system around career factors. There were also several questions addressing the way in which engineers viewed their jobs and the importance that they attached to various features in their jobs. The present paper is developed around the central questions shown in Table 42.1. These ques-

TABLE 42.1
Format of the Principal Questions

To what extent would you like your career to be:

		Not at all		Somewhat		To a great extent	
a)	a progression up the technical professional ladder to a higher-level position?	1	2	3	4	5	6	7
b)	a progression up the managerial ladder to a higher-level positon?	1	2	3	4	5	6	7
c)	the oportunity to engage in those challenging and exciting research activities and projects with which you are most interested, irrespective of promotion	1	2	3	4	5	6	7

tions ask engineers the degree to which they would prefer each of three alternative careers. They were asked to choose between progression on either the managerial or technical ladders or in lieu of these, the opportunity to engage in challenging and exciting projects irrespective of promotion. Using questions and definitions developed by the National Science Foundation and Pelz and Andrews [15], individuals also indicated how well the categories of research, development, and technical service represented the activities in which they were engaged.

Individuals were asked to complete their questionnaires as soon as possible. They were provided with stamped return envelopes so they could mail completed forms to the investigators directly. These procedures not only enhance data quality since respondents must commit their own time and effort but they also increase the response rate. The response rate across organizations was extremely high, ranging from 82 percent to 96 percent. A total of 2,199 usable questionnaires were returned.

RESULTS

Respondents (including staff technologists, managers, and professionals already promoted to technical ladder positions) ranged in age from 21 to 65, with a mean of 43 years. Individuals within this overall respondent sample were initially classified as being oriented toward a technical, managerial, or project-centered career if their response on one of the three scales exceeded the response on the other two by at least one scale point. Those who reported equally favoring any two of the three options were left out of the analysis. A total of 1,495 respondents indicated a preference for one of the three options. Of these, 488 (32.6 percent) preferred the managerial ladder over the two alternative career paths, 323 (21.6 percent) preferred the technical ladder and a surprising 684 (45.8 percent) reported a preference for having the, 'opportunity to engage in those challenging and exciting research activities and projects with which (they) are most interested, irrespective of promotion.'

Such a large proportion of respondents preferring a somewhat nontraditional form of reward arouses suspicions that the questionnaire's wording may have made the alternative more attractive than was intended. It would seem reasonable that, were this the case, the induced preference would not be as strongly felt as preferences based on a more substantial conviction. Increasing the margin of preference required in defining orientation did not, however, decrease the proportion of those preferring interesting projects. In fact, the proportions of respondents indicating a stronger preference for this third option over the managerial and technical ladder promotional options went from 45.8 percent to 48.4 percent to 51.4 percent as the margin of preference in scale points went from 1 to 2 to 3 (although the absolute numbers of individuals with this preference did of course decrease from 642 to 393 to 213 as the margin of scale preference was increased from 1 to 2 to 3).

Orientation as a Function of Age

Career preferences, as one might expect, are significantly related to age ($F = 18.25$; df = 2, 1399; $p < 0.001$). The proportion of engineers citing a preference for interesting projects increases almost monotonically with age (Figure 42.1). This may be due, partially, to a realization that advancement opportunities along the two traditional ladders are diminishing with age. This can be only partially true, since such a high proportion of those in their twenties indicate this preference. In fact, it is the most preferred alternative for all engineers, save those from 25 to 30.

The technical ladder career attracts the smallest proportion of engineers in all ages. The proportion indicating this preference hovers around 20 percent showing only a mild peak among those in their thirties. The proportion preferring a managerial career peaks in the late twenties and declines steadily thereafter.

Career Preference as a Function of Position

As one might expect, managers report a marked preference for a managerial career. There is some diminution with age (Figure 42.2) with a concomitant increase in preference for interesting projects. Only for a brief period in their late thir-

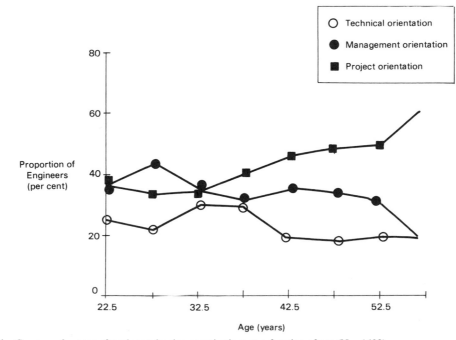

Figure 42.1   Career preferences of engineers in nine organizations as a function of age (N = 1402).

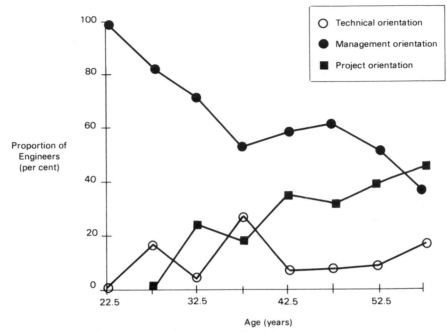

Figure 42.2 Career preferences of managers as a function of age (N = 374).

ties do managers show any interest in the technical ladder.

From the data displayed in Figure 42.3, it appears that most of the engineers who are on the technical ladder prefer one of the other two alternatives. The younger ones tend to show a slight preference for management over their own technical ladder. But the older technical ladder engineers indicate a strong preference for interesting work.

This increasing concern for interesting work among the older engineers in all of the figures is a very important and often misunderstood issue. Work assignments for older engineers are often made with the implicit assumption of the inevitability of technical obsolescence. That inevitability has been seriously questioned in recent years. Furthermore, such an assumption leads to work assignments that are inherently less challenging and thereby creates a self-fulfilling prophecy, guaranteeing obsolescence. Recent research [4] shows that instead of age being the cause of obsolescence, the failure of management to provide challenging work and to emphasize the need

for technical currency are the more likely causes. If older engineers seek more challenging work but seldom find it, can there be any wonder that they often allow themselves to sink into obsolescence? Our findings reinforce the importance of career growth for older engineers to prevent their movement into a career stage of stabilization [9]. Older engineers can be challenged by modifying job assignments and thereby forcing the acquisition of new knowledge. That they are interested and concerned about maintaining this type of challenge is quite evident in the data.

TECHNICAL LADDER ORIENTATION

Although career orientations vary with age, our data also show that a substantial proportion of the technical professionals have a preference for technical advancement within their organizations. The next question in our research, therefore, is to identify the characteristics of the respondents in this population. Toward that end, a three-way analysis of variance was performed on the data, with nature of the work (basic research; applied research; development; technical service), education level (B.S., M.S., Ph.D.) and position (manager or not)[1] as independent variables and the degree of technical ladder preference as the dependent variable. Since age was a significant factor influencing career orientation, it is used as a covariate in the analysis. Surprisingly, among this set of respondents, type of work does not affect the degree of technical ladder preference ($F = 0.78$; N.S.). The first hypothesis is not supported by the data (Figure 42.4).[2] Education level, on the other hand, has a significant effect ($F = 8.06$; $p < 0.001$), as does managerial position. As hypothesized, Ph.D.'s have a much stronger preference for the technical ladder than engineers without a doctorate. Managerial position, as one might expect, has an effect on attitudes toward the technical ladder (managers lose interest in technical ladder careers) so this variable is included as a control in the analysis. It is interesting that even among the managers, education has

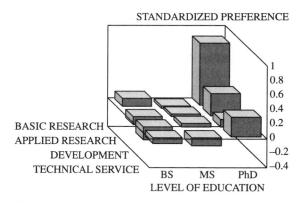

Figure 42.4 Degree of technical ladder preference as a function of education and the nature of the technical work performed.

an effect. While the average for all managers was below the population mean in desire for a technical ladder career, those managers with a Ph.D. degree scored much higher than those without (-0.02 vs. -0.29) and were very close to the overall mean.[3] There is no indication of significant inter-

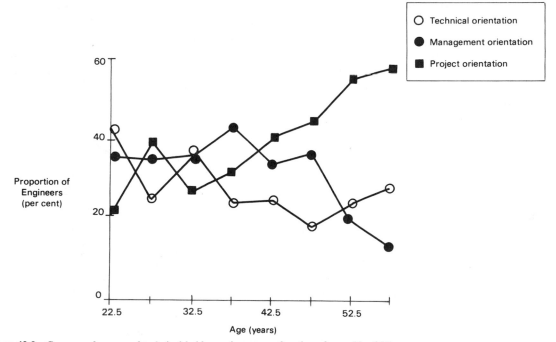

Figure 42.3 Career preferences of technical ladder engineers as a function of age. (N = 351).

action among any of three categorical variables. The effect of the covariate (Age) was not significant ($F = 3.76$; $p > 0.05$).

The analysis shows that the more education an individual has, the more likely that person is to choose or prefer a technical ladder career. This is particularly true of those with a Ph.D. degree. This information should be very helpful to organizations, since it indicates what circumstances would justify the cost of a dual ladder system and which people would feel more rewarded by promotion onto the technical ladder.

Since it is primarily those with a doctoral degree who fall into this class, it will be interesting to see in which other ways their motivations differ from those of their colleagues. If this were known, it could provide a deeper understanding of the reasons for choosing a technical ladder career and provide organizations with better guidance for its appropriate use.

One way of assessing an individual's work goals is to ask that individual for indicators of successful work outcomes. Fortunately, our questionnaire included a series of questions[4] that asked people to rate several possible outcomes on the degree to which, in their work, they would consider them measures of success. To simplify the analysis and reduce the number of variables, a factor analysis is performed on the responses to the questions, reducing them to two factors, one of which describes what one might consider academic/scientific measures of success, the other describing product-related commercial success (Table 42.2).[5]

An ANOVA was then performed using educational attainment (i.e., Ph.D. or non-Ph.D.) as the independent variable and each of the two factor scores as dependent variables (Figure 42.5). Age was again controlled as a covariate. It is no surprise that those with a Ph.D. degree attach importance to academic success criteria and are significantly less interested in commercial success. Adherence to success criteria, such as these, represent to some degree the way in which these individuals expect and want to be evaluated. Just who the anticipated evaluators are is not completely clear, nor does it matter. It is the internal self-eval-

TABLE 42.2
Factor Analysis of Questions Concerning Perceived Measures of Success

Question	Loading on factor 1	Loading on factor 2
Publishing a paper which adds significantly to the technical literature.	0.79	
Developing new theoretical insights or solutions.	0.84	
Developing concrete answers to important technical problems.	0.55	
Contributing to a product of high commercial success.		0.79
Contributing to a product of distinctly superior technical quality.		0.80
Coming up with a highly innovative idea or solution.	0.60	

uation that is important for our purposes. That these individuals evaluate themselves against particular external success criteria should provide insight into the nature of their career orientation and underlying value system. Those who are more inclined toward an academic career will measure their success according to appropriate criteria such as publication or theorizing (factor 1). Those inclined toward an industrial career will also choose appropriate criteria, in that case participating in the development of a successful product (factor 2).

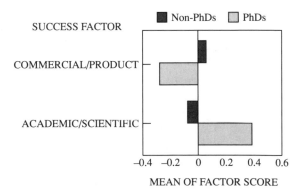

Figure 42.5 Factor scores relating to sucess criteria as a function of education.

It is clear from Figure 42.5, that educational level strongly influences the choice of success criterion. Those individuals with a Ph.D. degree are much more inclined toward the academic/scientific criteria ($F = 52.36$; $p < 0.001$) and less toward the commercial/product-oriented criterion ($F = 23.38$; $p < 0.001$) than are their colleagues who do not hold a doctoral degree. This is certainly understandable, although perhaps not desirable.

The long time which those with a Ph.D. degree spend in graduate school allows a degree of socialization into academic values that apparently persists even after these individuals have worked in industry for quite some period. In a sense one might argue that occupational socialization for these people is much stronger than their organizational socialization.

SOCIALIZATION AND RESOCIALIZATION

It should be interesting to see how long the effect of academic socialization persists. This can be examined by plotting the degree to which respondents cite, as a function of their age, the two types of success criteria. These plots are shown for those without a Ph.D. degree in Figure 42.6 and for those with the Ph.D. in Figure 42.7. It is startlingly clear from these figures that the effect of academic socialization is very persistent. It occurs for engineers and

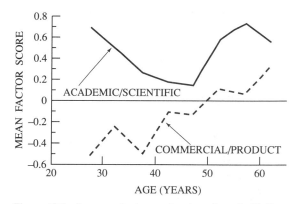

Figure 42.7 Success criteria as a function of age for Ph.D. engineers and scientists.

scientists, regardless of education level. They all enter industry with a much stronger orientation toward academic/scientific goals. For those without a doctorate, however, the commercial/product goals gradually increase in importance becoming more dominant at about age 30. This is a surprisingly long period of accommodation and would appear even more unusual, were it not for the situation among the Ph.D.'s, who appear never to reach a reasonable accommodation with industrial goals. Although the orientation toward commercial/product goals also increases in importance for those with a Ph.D., the magnitude of this success factor always falls below that for academic/scientific success.

To be certain, once again, that it is educational level and its concomitant socialization process that causes the effects shown in Figures 42.6 and 42.7, the same data were replotted after separating people who were working on basic and applied research activities from those working on development and technical service projects. Divided in this manner, the comparative plots for each of the two subgroupings were not very different in their overall patterns from those seen in Figures 42.6 and 42.7. Those without a Ph.D. degree begin their industrial careers with a stronger academic than commercial orientation. After a few years of experience, they shift and become more commercially oriented. The Ph.D.'s begin similarly but never lose

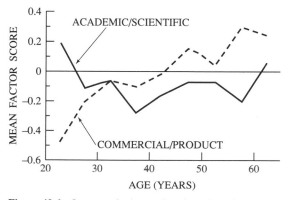

Figure 42.6 Success criteria as a function of age for non-Ph.D. engineers and scientists.

their academic orientation. Deep into their industrial careers, they are still concerned about academic success measures. This phenomenon appears for those with a Ph.D. degree whether they are working in research or in development or technical service.

RELATIONSHIP TO TECHNICAL LADDER PREFERENCE

To investigate further the interrelationships between educational attainment and perceptions of success, a two-way ANOVA was performed on preference for a technical ladder career, with education and success factors as independent variables. Although both effects are significant, that of education is greater[6] (Figure 42.8). What is more important, the standardized means clearly indicate that it is the combination of a Ph.D. degree and an academic/scientific orientation toward success that produces the strongest preference for the technical ladder. Non-Ph.D.'s with a commercial/product orientation have the lowest performance. It is also important to note that Ph.D.'s with a commercial/product orientation and non-Ph.D.'s with an academic/scientific orientation respond in a similar fashion concerning their preference for the technical ladder. Both are very close to the overall mean of zero.

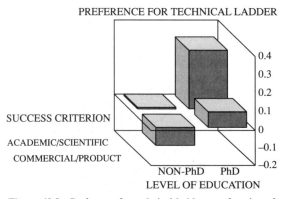

Figure 42.8 Preference for technical ladder as a function of education and criteria for success.

To investigate the degree to which academic or commercial success criteria are associated with education and managerial position, a logistic regression and categorical data analysis were performed on the data. This analysis shows Ph.D.'s, who are not managers, to be most likely to be academically oriented. Managers, who do not have a Ph.D. degree, are the most likely to have a commercial orientation toward success. Finally, those with neither a Ph.D. degree nor a managerial position are 1.32 times more likely to have a commercial orientation than are Ph.D. managers. Education, in other words, has a greater effect than organizational position on the chances of adopting a particular orientation.

If, in fact, the population groupings differ sharply in how they view the technical ladder, then it is important to know if they differ greatly in other work-related ways. Toward this end, a series of questions, previously used and described by Pelz and Andrews [15] were included in the study. These questions measure respondents' perceptions of important work-related opportunities and problem-solving approaches. The standardized mean responses to these items for the two extreme[7] subgroups are shown in Table 42.3. Not only do these subgroups differ sharply in their preference for the technical ladder, but they also differ significantly in the way in which they relate to their work environments.[8] Those who most prefer the technical ladder also prefer to work more conceptually and in greater depth on problems that are more important to their professional disciplines. In contrast, those who least prefer the technical ladder want to work on more immediate solutions to problems that are more relevant to the organization. Similarly, those preferring the technical ladder also value freedom and independence and prefer to work less collaboratively.[9] The groups did not differ on their need to work on challenging tasks or with competent colleagues.

DISCUSSION

Companies recruit engineers and scientists with a Ph.D. degree for their level of education and for

TABLE 42.3
Contrasting Perceptions of Work-Related Issues

Work opportunities and problem solving approaches	Means of standardized scores for:		
	Ph.D.'s with academic/scientific orientation	Non-Ph.D's with commercial/ product orientation	Difference
Preference for working toward immediate concrete solutions	−0.41	0.20	0.61*
Importance of working on organizationally significant tasks	−0.18	0.21	0.39*
Preference for working in collaboration with others	−0.21	0.14	0.35*
Importance of working on difficult and challenging assignments	0.18	−0.01	0.19
Importance of working with technically competent colleagues	0.14	0.02	−0.12
Importance of pursuing one's own ideas	0.16	−0.05	−0.21
Importance of having freedom to be creative	0.23	−0.16	−0.39*
Importance of working on professionally significant tasks	0.28	−0.13	−0.41*
Preference for deep probing of narrow areas	0.32	−0.19	−0.51*
Preference for working with general established principles	0.38	−0.14	−0.52*

*$p < 0.001$.

their demonstrated intelligence and perseverance, having survived a long and sometimes arduous educational career. They are also frequently recruited for their independence of thought. To the degree that this latter goal exists, industry may be getting more than they bargained for. Few firms can truly afford to support employees whose principal goals are publishing and theory development. Even in industry these may be fine as secondary goals. But the primary goal must be developing products that will allow the company to remain in business. Those without a doctoral degree are much quicker to see this. They begin their careers with a similar academic orientation, but after a few years they reorient themselves appropriately and become more commercially oriented. A real danger exists in that the Ph.D.'s are much more likely to be promoted onto the technical ladder. The risk is that they may have their academic values therefore reinforced and never become adequately socialized into the goals necessary to keep the firm in business. The Ph.D.'s in our study maintained a very strong academic and scientific orientation throughout their careers.

Education
If there were ever any doubt that the technical ladder reward system is better received by those educated to the level of the Ph.D., the present research should certainly remove that doubt. Over the several years required to achieve a doctoral degree, students are very strongly socialized into an academic system which has its own values and rewards. These are distinctly different from those of industry. The technical ladder reward system was originally designed to be more aligned with that view of the world. It attempts to emulate the academic reward system, based on a belief in the importance of peer recognition for technical professionals.

Those with a Ph.D. degree prefer it because they have been thoroughly steeped in the academic value system. Those without the Ph.D. degree, in contrast, are not as thoroughly socialized into the academic system. The technical ladder consequently does not have the same appeal or value in their eyes. The failure to recognize this fact has led to many problems in implementing the dual ladder system. It has also led to frustration on the part of personnel officers who cannot understand why so many engineers fail to see the wonderful benefits of their technical ladder.

About 80 percent of the 278 Ph.D.'s in our sample had a stronger academic/scientific focus than a commercial/product one. Based on the results of our study, it is these individuals who are especially likely to opt for technical ladder careers. It is important to recognize that this group of individuals differs from their organizational counterparts in many other important ways particularly with respect to work-related goals and problem-solving approaches. The establishment of two formal parallel career ladders creates added differentiation within the organization [14]. If the two ladders are also staffed with individuals who are significantly different from each other not only in terms of educational background but also in terms of values, attitudes, and work-related preferences, then the organization runs the risk of differentiating itself even more.

One of the more important forces affecting interaction patterns within organizations is the tendency for individuals to communicate more frequently with those who are most like themselves and whose ideas and viewpoints are most likely to agree with their own interest and perspectives [10]. Based on this notion of selective exposure and the strong differences emerging from our dual ladder study, it is not surprising that communication between technical and managerial groups may be severely strained. Promotional dynamics may even be exacerbating this problem. Prior research by Katz and Tushman [11] showed that individuals promoted on the technical ladder communicate less often and are significantly more isolated from organizational peers than those promoted to man-

agement. The results of our study indicate that organizations may be compounding this problem by promoting to the technical side individuals who not only have weaker communication ties to begin with but who also claim "they cannot do their best work in collaboration with others." They prefer, instead, the freedom to work independently and pursue their own ideas. Clearly, organizations need to build forces for integration that compensate for the structural and staffing differentiation that accompanies the dual ladder. Without establishing strong bridging mechanisms [18] to overcome the problems of coordination and communication, those on the technical ladder are likely to become decoupled from the rest of the organization. And as described by Allen [2] and others, such segmentation can be a strong barrier to effective technology transfer and innovation.

CONCLUSION

Although the Ph.D.'s, through their longer and more intense exposure, are more thoroughly indoctrinated in the academic values, all young people coming through the university system are to some degree affected. The views expressed by the younger people in the present sample show this. They feel that publication, theory building, and specialization are important. This culminates, after a few years on the job, in an attraction toward a technical ladder career. Shortly after that, however, reality begins to set in. They begin to understand that industry needs management as much as technology—that theories and publications don't put bread on the table and that commercially important projects are not necessarily those of the greatest scientific interest. This awakening occurs in the early to mid-thirties and results in a pronounced shift away from the technical ladder and increased interest in management. The initial state is found both among the research Ph.D.'s who are most interested in the technical ladder and among the other engineers and scientists not so predisposed. The degree to which the two groups adapt as time goes on differs considerably, however. Over time, the strength of the commercial focus among the non-Ph.D.'s greatly exceeds the strength of their academic interests. Although the commercial focus of Ph.D.'s also increases over time, it is always exceeded by their concern for academic and scientific success.

While many alternative personality and situational explanations could account for this strong difference, it is our contention that the separate organizational experiences of the two groups provide a stronger explanation of the observations than do differences in personality. Perhaps through the nature of their work assignments, their reporting relationships, or even the location of their offices, non-Ph.D.'s become more socialized into the value system of the organization and its management. The organizational socialization encounters and interactions of Ph.D.'s, on the other hand, may be very different. Perhaps they are given more independent activities, or research tasks that require little interaction, or they are co-located with each other, or they are assigned only to supervisors with similar academic values. Whatever the reasons, it may be that the organizational socialization experiences of these individuals are very different from their less highly educated colleagues.

Since whatever happens during organizational socialization dramatically affects one's performance, career, communication networks, and overall perspective, future research is clearly needed to understand and compare the organizational socialization process for engineers and scientists from differing backgrounds and educational environments. If the dual ladder is to work effectively in organizations, we must learn how to better organize and structure the early experiences of engineers and scientists to create better working relationships between those promoted technically and managerially, rather than estranging them from each other.

NOTES

1. Managerial position was included as an independent variable to control for its effect, since it would be expected to influence attitudes toward the technical ladder.

2. Although the means of the standardized preference scores of engineers in different types of technical work differ in the predicted direction, the differences do not reach statistical significance.

3. The overall mean is zero, since the data have been standardized.

4. Developed by Pelz and Andrews [15].

5. In line with our previous discussion, these two factors closely parallel the differences described by the local-cosmopolitan distinction.

6. For Education, $F = 17.72$, $p < 0.001$; for Success Orientation, $F = 5.80$, $p = 0.02$.

7. Ph.D.'s with an academic/scientific vision of success and non-Ph.D.'s with a commercial/product vision of success.

8. The items are listed in Table 42.3 by the magnitude of the disparities between the two groupings, not in the order in which they appeared in the questionnaire.

9. Interestingly enough, for each of the items, the mean standardized responses for the non-congruent (i.e., commercial/product Ph.D.'s and academic/scientific non-Ph.D.'s) groupings fell within the ranges reported in Table 42.3 and were not significantly different from the overall population means.

REFERENCES

1. T. J. Allen, "Distinguishing engineers from scientists," in *Managing Professionals in Innovative Organizations: A Collection of Readings,* R. Katz, Ed. New York: Harper Business, 1988, pp. 3–19.

2. T. J. Allen, *Managing the Flow of Technology.* Cambridge, MA: MIT Press, 1984.

3. T. J. Allen and R. Katz, "The dual ladder: motivational solution or managerial delusion?" *R&D Management,* vol. 16, no. 2, pp. 185–197, 1986.

4. T. J. Allen and R. Katz, "The treble ladder revisited: Why do engineers lose interest in the dual ladder as they grow older?" *International Journal of Vehicle Design,* vol. 12, nos. 5/6, 1991.

5. T. J. Allen and R. Katz "Age, education, and the technical ladder," *IEEE Transactions on Engineering Management,* vol. 39, pp. 237–245, 1992.

6. L. Bailyn, *Living with Technology: Issues in Mid-Career.* Cambridge, MA: MIT Press, 1980.

7. G. W. Dalton and P. Thompson, *Novations: Strategies for Career Management.* Glenview, IL: Scott Foresman, 1985.

8. A. W. Gouldner, "Cosmopolitans and locals—towards an analysis of latent social roles," *Administrative Science Quarterly,* vol. 2, pp. 281–306, 1957.

9. R. Katz "Managing creative performance in R&D teams, in *The Human Side of Managing Technolog-*

ical Innovation, R. Katz, Ed. New York: Oxford University Press, 1996.

10. R. Katz and T. J. Allen, Investigating the not invented here (NIH) syndrome," *R&D Management,* vol. 12, pp. 7–19, 1982.

11. R. Katz and M. L. Tushman, "A longitudinal study of the effects of boundary spanning supervision on turnover and promotion in R&D," *Academy of Management Journal,* vol. 26, pp. 437–456, 1983.

12. R. Katz, M. L. Tushman, and T. J. Allen, *Managing the dual-ladder: A longitudinal study.* Greenwich, CT: JAI Press, 1991.

13. S. Kerr and M. A. Von Glinow, "Issues in the study of 'professionals' in organizations: The case of scientists and engineers," *Organizational Behavior and Human Performance,* vol. 18, pp. 329–345, 1977.

14. P. R. Lawrence and J. M. Lorsch, *Organization and Environment.* Boston: Harvard Business School Press, 1967.

15. D. C. Pelz and F. M. Andrews, *Scientists in Organizations.* New York: Wiley, 1976.

16. J. Raelin, *Clash of Cultures.* Boston, MA: Harvard Business School Press, 1985.

17. R. R. Ritti, *The Engineer in the Industrial Corporation.* New York: Columbia University Press, 1971.

18. E. B. Roberts, "Stimulating Technological Innovations: Organizational approaches," *Research Management,* vol. 22, pp. 26–30, 1979.

19. E. H. Schein, "How 'Career Anchors' hold executives to their career paths," in *Managing Professionals in Innovative Organization: A Collection of Readings,* R. Katz, Ed. New York: Harper Business, 1988, pp. 487–497.

20. H. A. Shepard, "The dual hierarchy in research," *Managing Professionals in Innovative Organization: A Collection of Readings,* R. Katz, Ed. New York: Harper Business, 1988, pp. 177–187.

21. M. L. Tushman, "Technical communication in R&D laboratories: The impact of project work characteristics," *Academy of Management Journal,* vol. 20, pp. 624–645, 1977.

22. M. A. Von Glinow, *The New Professionals: Managing Today's High-Tech Employees.* Cambridge, MA: Ballinger Press, 1988.

15

Managing for Rapid
Product Development

43

A Six-Step Framework for Becoming a
Fast-Cycle-Time Competitor

CHRISTOPHER MEYER

The ongoing ability to deliver a quality product or service quicker than the competition yields a sustainable competitive advantage. At the expense of the U.S. Post Office, Federal Express created an entire business based on this principle. Citibank became the leader in home mortgage originations in part because it offered loan commitments within 15 minutes! Compaq computer established itself as more than a quality IBM clone manufacturer when it brought its 386 and 486 machines to market *be-fore* IBM. The bottom line is that when customers decide they want to buy, the first supplier who can fill that need with a quality product or service will flourish. These companies operate in Fast Cycle Time (FCT).

The benefits for FCT competitors are substantial. The first entrant into a market typically dominates that market in both share and profit margins. Pricing pressure does not exist when there is no competition. FCT leaders reinforce their posi-

Reprinted with permission from Meyer, Christopher.

Christopher Meyer is a Principal with Integral, Inc., a management consulting firm in Menlo Park, CA.

tion because they set the standards which others must follow. They secure the prime distribution channels which create additional entry barriers for the competition.

Becoming a FCT competitor is not easy. *FCT requires a systemic integration of new values, structures, and rewards into the core work process.* One can not simply accelerate the work pace without negative impact. First, people will make the same mistakes they always have, only quicker. Second, management will rapidly burn out the organization's most important resource: people. An image employees often have when they first hear about reduced cycle time is a cardiac stress test. They equate reducing cycle time to speeding up the organizational treadmill. Regrettably, they are often correct.

FCT is the ongoing ability to identify, satisfy and be paid for meeting customer needs faster than anyone else. There are several key words in this definition. The first one is *ongoing.* Although useful, single shot cycle time reductions do not provide a sustainable competitive advantage. In a competitive environment, the race is never over. Competitors who improve continuously will pass those who pause to relax. The next key word is *identify.* FCT is the responsibility of all organization functions from the start of the business cycle through the end. Some incorrectly consider cycle time an exclusively manufacturing or engineering issue. The firm that identifies the customer's need first, has a head start in filling that need. *Satisfy* means that one cannot sacrifice quality for time. The old rule was that if you required a product or service quickly, it would cost more and the quality couldn't be guaranteed. That thinking is dead. World class competitors such as Toyota have clearly demonstrated that speed does not have to sacrifice quality or cost. *Paid* refers to the attention FCT companies place on completing the business cycle. For example, while Toyota was able to reduce its manufacturing cycle time to 2 days, it still took 17 days to sell and deliver its cars. FCT companies view their organization as a value delivery system. As a system, the slowest sub-cycle limits the overall system's total cycle time. *Meet-*

ing customer needs declares that products or services which do not meet customer needs are not acceptable. And last, *faster than anyone else* reflects the reality of increasing competition. If there is a foreign or domestic competitor who is faster, it is only a matter of time before they will dominate that market. Detroit and the semiconductor industry have both learned the hard lesson of ignoring international competition.

Reducing product development cycle time requires a systematic strategy. This article defines the six key steps to becoming a FCT competitor and outlines how to implement them.

Step 1: Understand what your end customer regards as added value, and reflect that in every job and level within the organization.

An FCT strategy focuses the entire organization on work that adds value to the end customer while concurrently trying to eliminate anything that does not. Thus, product development managers in FCT companies structure and manage their organizations as value delivery systems focused on adding value for their customers. In order to do this, all employees must know who the end customers are and what is added value to them. Only people who *pay* for the product are end customers.

There may be more than one end customer. For example, consumer products have several end customers along the distribution chain, starting with the distributor and ending at the customer. To distributors, packaging may be a value added component of the product, whereas for the consumer, packaging adds little value. The main lesson here is to understand what is value added for each customer you serve.

This end customer view contrasts with the notion of internal customers popularized by quality programs. The internal customer concept suggests that each job has an upstream supplier and a downstream customer. For example, manufacturing is the customer of engineering's designs. While this approach improves understanding of mutual dependencies, calling internal groups customers can cause people to incorrectly equate internal definitions of value added with those of the end customer.

The difference is critical: End customers generate revenue while internal customers generate cost. For example, internal customers create 99 percent of the paperwork in organizations. Paperwork rarely adds value to end customers. Using the end customer's definition of value added exposes non-value added time and activities. Motorola, for example, no longer encourages the internal customer perspective.

After defining the end customer, one has to define what is value added in their eyes. A rule of thumb for determining value added is whether or not the end customer is willing to pay for the product, service or feature. If they are not willing to pay for it, then it is probably not value added. The information to make this determination comes from one place: the customer.

Traditionally, we have relied on sales and marketing to channel the customer's definition of value added into the organization. While efficient in the use of people, this approach limits the direct contact other functions have with the customer. It is increasingly evident that expanding the breadth of organizational contact with the end customer sharpens all employees' understanding of what is value added, as well as their motivation to deliver it.

For example, a leading manufacturer of electronic test equipment conducted a focus group in which customers compared their equipment to a competitor's. Invited to the focus group were several young engineers from the development team. Standing behind a one-way mirror, the engineers saw that most of the customers were attracted to their company's product before it was turned on. But after it was turned on, the customers drifted en masse to the competitor's product. Why? Simply because the display on the competitor's product was easier to read. Because display readability was not an issue for the engineers' young eyes, they had dismissed customer complaints. Seeing their competitor's "inferior" product surrounded by customers quickly changed their minds.

In another example, it was a Du Pont development technicians' visit to Reebok that generated a competitive response to Nike's "air cushion" heel. The technicians were there for another purpose; yet when they heard of this problem, they devised a solution involving implanted rubber tubes—made, of course, by Du Pont.

These examples illustrate that making customer needs visible to those who have traditionally been isolated or removed from the end customer can quickly reorient functional activities toward outcomes that are truly value added.

While end customers are the ultimate source of defining what is or is not value added, top management is responsible for defining the organization's value added focus and allocating resources accordingly. It does this by defining a *value proposition* for the organization. The value proposition is unique to each organization and defines that organization's value adding strategy.

A well-defined value proposition that is aligned with customer needs is critical for ensuring competitive advantage. For example, prior to 1989 Quantum Corporation, a computer disk manufacturer, had a value proposition that stressed quality and performance. Quantum's position in the marketplace grew accordingly. In contrast, a new competitor, Conner Peripherals, had an explicit value proposition to be first to market with their products. Conner's philosophy of "sell, design, build" focused on being first to market with products designed specifically for their customers' needs. In contrast, Quantum had been designing disk drives to meet market standards rather than a specific customer's needs. By carefully picking leading computer manufacturers as its customers, Conner was able to leverage the initial sales and development effort into a broader market opportunity. This was most graphically seen in Conner's relationship with Compaq Computer. Compaq was one of the initial investors in Conner as well as being the initial customer. Compaq's success in the PC market established a presence for Conner's drives.

As Conner's success grew, Quantum reexamined its value proposition of quality and performance relative to Conner's focus on custom designs done fast. Quantum determined that product performance was important, but availability of new products was even more so. In short, quality and performance value were insufficient without time to market. Even though many of Conner's customers complained about the quality of early models, one should not forget that these complainers were purchasing their drives from Conner, not Quantum. This is not to suggest that quality should be ignored in favor of developing products faster, but, rather, that a fanatical devotion to technical elegance can often undermine a company's ability to compete against those who can deliver their products faster. In sum, the value proposition focuses behavior and resources.

A good value proposition clarifies what is value added from what is not. As simple as this may appear, many organizations have value propositions that are not clearly stated. Management often assumes the value proposition is obvious and understood by all. Therefore, it concentrates on managing operations. Each element of the organization may have its own operating definition of the value proposition and act accordingly. The net result is that value adding efforts do not build on, but actually subvert one another. Ultimately, the customer becomes confused.

In the service sector, SAS Airlines provides another good example of how a clear value proposition guides behavior. Jan Carlzon, President of SAS, led that company's revival by defining SAS' value proposition as being the airline of the business traveler. SAS tuned its schedule, route structure and service to the needs of the business traveler. Since there are few business travelers on the weekends, SAS limits flights on Saturday and Sunday. During the initial implementation of this value proposition, employees frequently suggested ways to increase weekend aircraft utilization. Since aircraft utilization is a traditional measure of performance, this behavior was easily understandable. Under the new value proposition, however, weekend flights did not add value to the business traveler. Carlzon rejected these ideas and used weekends for maintenance and training to improve service during the week.

An organization must be aligned around its value proposition. When it is not, people may be working hard but the net force of their collective efforts will be significantly less. Alignment is more than a function of common understanding. Structural elements such as reward systems, policies, cultural norms, and organization design must be in alignment as well. To foster alignment, management should continuously communicate and test whether the value proposition is incorporated into each job. Like management, each employee has his or her own mental model of how they should add value for the customer. Without ongoing education efforts, employees may use outdated or conflicting models. Educational efforts minimally include exposing all employees to the corporate mission and value proposition on a regular basis. Additional methods may include:

- One-way briefings such as corporate video newscasts, "all hands" meetings, annual reports, and internal newsletters.
- Staff meetings where senior managers explicitly employ the value proposition as a criterion for decisions.
- Special meetings to describe *and* test the value proposition with key constituencies, including project reviews, new employee orientation, buzz groups, brown bag lunches, etc.
- Company symbols and giveaways such as desk accessories, T-shirts and coffee cups.

Step 2: Focus the entire organization on work that adds value to the end customer.

As we have stated, there are two types of work: value added and non-value added, the former being work for which the customer is willing to pay. For example, painting a car a specific color is value added work, whereas testing the paint for durability is not something a customer is willing to pay for. Surprised? Many might argue that untested paint could fade quickly, thus upsetting the customer. No question about that, but consider your reaction to a car's price sticker that showed below the $699 for optional leather seats a $45 charge for paint testing!

Non-value added practices such as testing are required because we do not fully trust the process being tested. This may be because the process is not well understood or developed or it may be due to poor operating practices. In either case, testing is a stop gap measure until the process is made stable. In the language of quality experts, testing quality into the product is inferior to designing it in. While one may argue as to when a process is stable enough to eliminate testing, the goal of doing so should always be present.

The only way to identify which work adds value is to study the organization's value delivery system. Constructing a high-level map can provide a macroview of the entire organization's value delivery system. Figure 43.1 is a generic example of such a map.

By limiting the amount of detail, it is easier to identify which steps are the most important value adding processes. For some, it may be steps in the process engineering or development process, while for others it could be the testing or prototype stages. Once identified, critical processes can be exploded in greater detail by flow charting and tracing the multi-functional processes and interdependencies,

as described in Meyer (1), chapter 7. At the least, this process map should identify the critical players, key tasks and the time required to complete them. In addition, it is also useful to specify the inputs and outputs of critical steps.

The map should accurately reflect how the process works today. During the mapping exercise, there is a strong urge to incorporate how the process ought to look or be changed. It is important to resist this urge and to defer these discussions until the map is completed. Until there is agreement on how the work flows are currently conducted, such discussions can become irrelevant. However, reaching agreement is not necessarily easy. Everyone has their own model of how the value delivery system works. Defined by personal experience, these models differ for each individual.

Similarly, senior management's models are frequently built on past experience that may no longer be valid. For example, a high technology company wanted to reduce new product development time and therefore mapped the entire development process. Management was shocked to dis-

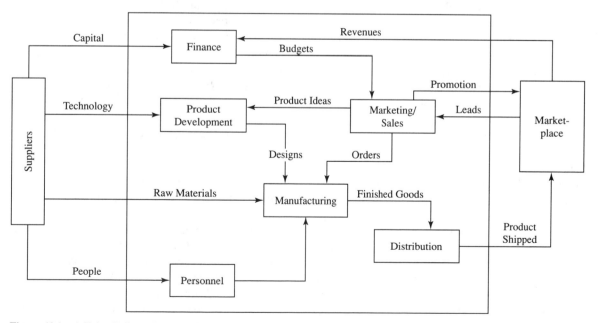

Figure 43.1   A Value Delivery Process Map

cover that the product definition phase often took as long as 12 months. Its mental model was based on experience gained when the company was much smaller and products were simpler. Management had lost contact with the impact of many small process changes made over time.

The mapping process does not require everyone to agree on each and every step. Rather, strive for general agreement that the map accurately reflects the most critical process steps. Once this is achieved, review the map and identify value added and non-value added steps. Test each non-value added task to eliminate or compress it. First efforts typically result in a "shrinkage" of the current process. A shrinkage has the same basic structure as the current process with many non-value activities removed. Shrinkages will often cut cycle time by 50 percent or more. But one should not stop here. Shrinkages are the results of picking the low-hanging fruit. These are efficiency improvements which do not fundamentally restructure the value delivery process or yield a *substantial* competitive advantage. Major breakthroughs come from insights that fundamentally restructure the core elements of the value delivery process. Clearly understanding the current delivery process, combined with seriously questioning and entertaining creative alternatives, generates such insights.

To become an FCT competitor, one must understand the value delivery process sufficiently to define and focus everyone's attention on value added work. It is curious that American business leaders love to invoke sports metaphors as competitive models yet rarely include the attention sports professionals pay toward process analysis and improvement. Specifically, world champions such as the San Francisco 49ers spend 100 hours off the field for every hour played. They use non-game time to analyze films about their value delivery process or for training. Yet in an informal survey that we conducted during a series of California Institute of Technology FCT seminars, we never found more than two executives per class who spend more than one day a month examining their organizations' work processes. One cannot expect dramatic breakthroughs without putting in more time.

Step 3: Redesign your organization so that it is flat and based on multi-functional teams, with blurred boundaries—inside and out.

By definition, large hierarchical organizations can never be quick. Every time an approval is required, there is a delay as the request is communicated, considered and responded to. The further the approval level is from the point of origination, the greater the time delay. When functionally organized, companies divide customer problems into pieces and channel each piece to the appropriate functional group. Inevitably, some needs fall in the cracks between functional specialties while others are miscast. In any event, internal functions never experience the complete problem or its ramifications as the customer does. Instead, all they see and attempt to remedy is a sub-set of the problem.

A further difficulty with this process is how solutions are defined. For the most part, solutions are *internally* defined within each function. To wit, engineering has its own design standards just as manufacturing has its quality standards. These standards are isolated from each other and most importantly, the customer. The customer is concerned about the total product or service while the functions are concerned with their piece of the action. The functional paradigm practically ignores the inherent interdependence between functions. The responsibility for cross-functional integration is concentrated in a single individual—the boss, who, in simpler times, might have been able to make all the integration choices wisely. Today's complex technologies and business conditions contain too many unknowns to expect any one person to know all the answers. The functional organization creates expectations that the boss should provide the answer when, in fact, he or she may be the least qualified to do so.

The multifunctional, team-based organization is an alternative. Composed of people from different functional disciplines, the teams have responsibility for the core value-added work processes of the business. Rather than operating as a coordinating body on top of the existing functional organization, the team focuses on delivering the organization's value proposition, and is allocated resources accordingly. Teams are typically organized around major product or market groupings.

Business teams are different from a classic matrix organization primarily in the breadth and scope of their responsibility. Theoretically, a matrix divides the power equally between project and functional bosses. In practice, the functional bosses wield more than 50 percent of the power. Because the core value adding process is within the team, the team-based organization keeps at least 51 percent of the power in the team.

Overly simplified, the teams become the line organization and the functions become staff. In contrast to the team itself, the team-based organization resists easy depiction. The supporting cast and connections to other teams are in constant flux. Teams are nodes in an organic network that continually adjusts itself in response to new customer demands. The role of the functions is to support the teams in the value-adding processes as defined by the teams.

Placing the core value delivery process into teams requires a fundamental shift in the organization's power structure. If management allows functional dominance to continue, employees will accurately perceive the teams as nice but not essential. The success of a multi-functional, team-based organization depends on creating a new organization *architecture*. The worst thing one could do would be to throw a group of people from engineering, operations and marketing together and call them a multi-functional team. They would find themselves struggling to define their role as they simultaneously tried to shift the organization's functional orientation. Well-designed team-based structures define the roles and responsibilities for those off the team as well as those on the team. Issues to be considered in the architecture include:

- Initial definition of team goals.
- Team charter.
- Team member responsibilities.
- Boundary conditions/limits of the teams.

- Linkages to other teams, functions and management.
- Team and personal rewards.
- Team support requirements from functions.

To work effectively, senior management must make certain that clear goals and chartered responsibilities are part of the team's design. This is management's control mechanism, and implementing the newly defined architecture is senior management's responsibility. They must demonstrate through their behaviors (and measures, as discussed later) the importance of teams. During implementation, the reality of the power shift becomes palatable as teams struggle to take control while some functional elements inevitably resist. Old habits will continue to dominate if senior management fails to publicly support the teams during the transition. Within well-defined parameters, teams need the power to take whatever actions are necessary to serve customers. And if teams contain the functional expertise required, there should be few cracks for issues to fall into.

In the same way that multi-functional teams blur boundaries within the organization, FCT competitors attempt to do the same thing between suppliers and customers. FCT companies consider suppliers and customers as partners in the value delivery effort. The fewer boundaries that exist in space or time, the more effective the value delivery process can be.

For example, Quantum Corporation designs application-specific integrated circuits (ASIC) for chip vendor manufacturers. Quantum now includes FCT in its vendor selection criteria. The net result is that a recent supplier placed two engineers plus their own engineering workstations at Quantum to speed the design of an ASIC. The cost to Quantum: nothing.

At the other end of the spectrum, customers are being included in the design phase of the value delivery process. For example, Conner Peripherals begins a product development effort only after they have a customer commitment for that product. Their senior technologist spends much of his time on the road meeting *and selling* customers.

The message is clear: to become fast, redesign your organization for speed. Just as one should not try to turn an oil tanker into a ski boat, one should not try to speed up a large, hierarchical organization. Overcoming the inherent structural limitations of centralized control and specialization is not possible. Flat, multi-functional, team-based organizations provide the architecture that enables locally informed and quick decision making.

Unfortunately, companies are often far more successful at launching these teams than they are at getting the teams *and* the functional areas to work together effectively. This occurs because the design of any performance-measurement system should reflect the basic operating assumptions of the organization it supports. But if the organization changes and the measurement system doesn't, then the latter is likely to be less than effective—perhaps even counterproductive. At many companies that have moved from control-oriented, functional hierarchies to a faster and flatter team-based approach, traditional performance-measurement systems not only fail to support the new teams; they often *undermine* them.

Ideally, a team-based management system should help get members from different functions on a team to focus their efforts and speak a common language. In many measurement systems today, however, each relatively independent function has its own set of measures, whose chief purpose is to keep top managers informed about its own performance. Marketing tracks market share, operations monitors inventory, finance watches costs, and so on. Such outputs or *"results measures"* tell an organization where it stands in achieving its goals but not how it got there or what it should do differently. Most results measures track what goes on within a function, not what happens across them, and most cross-functional results measures (such as gross margins or revenues) are limited to being financial in nature. What are needed, therefore, are *"process measures"* to track the various tasks and activities throughout the organization that are a responsible for producing a given result.

Teams must create the measures that support their mission, or they will not fully exploit their ability to perform the process faster and in a way that is more responsive to customer demands. A process measure that a product-development team might use, for example, is one that tracks staffing levels to make sure that the necessary people are on a given team at the right time. Another might be the number or percentage of new or unique product parts. One must also be careful not to burden and constrain teams with excess measures. All too often, I have seen organizations react to intensifying competition by piling more and more measures on their operations in the hope of encouraging them to work harder. The end result, however, is that team members often spend too much time collecting data, monitoring activities, and discussing minutia, rather than managing their projects and concentrating on what they really need to do together. Trying to run a team without a good, simple guidance system is like trying to drive a car without a dashboard. You might do it in a pinch but not as a matter of practice (see Meyer [2] for further discussion of "dashboards" and process measurement systems).

Although useful for keeping score on the performance of a business, results measures like market share, profits, and cost do not really help a multifunctional team monitor the activities or capabilities that enable it to perform a given process. Nor do these measures tell members what they must do to improve their team performance. Tracking staffing levels or years of experience in certain job categories during the course of a project, for example, might help explain why a program is 3 months late or over budget. A 10 percent rise in service costs combined with an 8 percent drop in quarterly profits does not tell a team what its service technicians should do differently on their next call. But knowing that the average time spent per service call rose 15 percent last month and that, as a result, the number of late or missed calls rose 10 percent might help explain why costs had risen and profits and customer satisfaction had gone down.

Finally, a team's reliance on traditional measures often causes its members to forget the team's goal and revert to their old functional way of working. Consider the case of a well-known automobile company during the development of its 1991 luxury model. The project was one of its first attempts to use multifunctional teams for faster product development. Unfortunately, the team's measurement system was still a collection of the individual measures that each functional area had used for years.

Shortly before they were to freeze the clay styling model and begin engineering the new body, a controversy erupted over a new door handle design. Purchasing and finance argued that it was too expensive, while the design and body engineering members responded that the new shape was integral to their styling theme and was affordable. Each came to the next meeting armed with data to support their respective functional perspectives. Design and body engineering presented their styling analysis and engineering model along with a vendor bid that showed the new handle would cost no more to manufacture than the old one. Purchasing and finance presented their figures that showed the new handle's warranty costs had not been taken into account. The current door handle was highly reliable and its warranty cost was extremely low. They asked body engineering to prove that the new handle could match that warranty cost. Body engineering responded that the part was not inherently any more complex than existing handles, but this didn't satisfy finance. Purchasing added that, while the bid came from an approved vendor, other approved vendors had historically achieved better warranty costs and presented their ranking list to prove it. After a short shouting match, design and body engineering gave up. The redesign minimally cost a week because going back to the old handle required changing its placement, which in turn required significant changes to the clay model.

While the above story is familiar to anyone who's worked within a traditional, functional organization, isn't this exactly what the multifunctional team was designed to address and if so, what happened? By using only their individual functional measures within the team, both parties quickly typecast each other in familiar functional roles and reverted to old, familiar behavior. Finance and purchasing was viewed as concerned only about cost and styling, and engineering was seen

to care only about performance. Regardless of who was right or wrong, because functional measures were the only ones used, they quickly channeled the discussion into a polarized, functional debate, rather than a team decision. *During the discussion, neither side asked the critical question: Would the new handle increase the car's ability to compete in the marketplace?* When a team hasn't created an integrated measurement system that tracks it's overall goal, its highly likely that during conflict, people will revert to their familiar roles. When cross-functional teams are established, organizations have to institute not only a measurement system that protects its functional excellence but also one that supports the company's basic strategy, prevents unpleasant and unexpected surprises, and truly empowers the teams to make appropriate decisions and trade-offs.

Step 4: Pursue process development as avidly as product or service development.

Process improvements can provide tremendous leverage. A single improvement can ripple across the product delivery system. For example, one of the major dilemmas in developing and manufacturing technology-intensive products is the ability to test them for functionality, reliability and quality. Frequently in their zeal to develop the product, development engineers do not focus on test development until late in the development process. In order to improve and innovate testing, the product development process must be changed. In short, test development must come earlier.

At Quantum, for example, managers realized that the bottlenecks that occurred downstream during testing were a significant impediment to rapid introduction of new products. Typically, drives were tested at the back end of the process using specially designed test equipment. The test hardware and software was developed after the product was well along in development. Early prototypes were typically tested by engineering and did not utilize any production test equipment because it was not readily available. In addition, there was always the issue of keeping the test equipment that was used up to date. Frequently, new drives would fail tests not because the drive was bad but because the test software was often a revision or two older than the drive it was testing.

Another factor that contributed to delays was the cost and number of testers. Testers represent one of the largest capital outlays required in drive development and manufacturing. For example, the more volume produced, the more testers that are required. Thus, testers came to be viewed as a significant bottleneck. And, when orders dropped, testers represented a very expensive and underutilized investment.

Quantum's approach to this problem was to incorporate "self-test" procedures within the drive itself. This required development engineers to design the test procedure into the product. It was an elegant approach. A more conventional approach would have been to persuade development engineers to pay more attention to test development earlier in the product development process. However, this approach has no real hook that grabs the development engineer. In contrast, development engineers had no choice but to focus their creative energies on process development when they were faced with the challenge that the product needed to be delivered without having to go through testing in downstream stages.

Why don't more organizations pay attention to process development? Three reasons stand out:

1. Because significant process improvements take time to design and implement, instant results are rare. In addition, it may take time for employees to learn and familiarize themselves with new work processes.

2. The second reason is embodied in the old development axiom that what you measure is what people pay attention to. The vast majority of organization performance measures are end results. While these measures tell us what we have accomplished, they provide little insight into how we did it. Because we don't measure the process itself, people don't pay much attention to improving it.

3. The third reason is closely related: We focus whatever measures we *do* use on those items that are easiest to measure. The dilemma created is

similar to the drunk who looks for his keys only under the lamp post because that is where the light shines. Most organizations limit their process measures to the tangible, linear work processes such as those found in manufacturing. Those processes are much easier to measure precisely than the non-linear work process found in design engineering, R&D, marketing, or sales. Non-linear work process measures are not as precise, nor do they need to be. What is most important is to develop measures that aid cycle time improvement efforts. Relative measures that compare current cycle time to past are sufficient.

Process improvement begins with allocating time to it in conjunction with the establishment of performance measures. Simple as this sounds, focusing on the "what" is so familiar that it takes effort to shift attention to the "how." Making process improvement routine requires improvement goals, dedicated time, appropriate rewards, forums for process improvement work, and skills to do it. This starts with top management since people take their cues from them.

An excellent starting point for the top team is to develop the macro map of the value delivery system that we described earlier. For each critical process, select a process champion from the top team. The champion is responsible for ensuring the continuous improvement of that process. This includes developing improvement goals and performance measures. Incorporating these goals into each executive's personal objectives and performance review makes process improvement very real.

Process champions do not work alone. They must involve those intimately familiar with the process in the diagnostic and improvement effort. A favorite tactic uses this enlarged group to create two additional maps. The first is the detailed map of the targeted process and the second proposes a new process architecture. The new architecture map becomes the foundation of the process improvement plan.

The mapping process creates a forum where people can engage in a dialogue around process improvements. Some firms find it useful to continue to segregate process improvement work from the mainstream in order to gain momentum. Others devote time to process improvement within their existing meetings. The point is that one must create, communicate and use clear forums for such process improvement dialogues.

Step 5: Set "stretch" cycle time goals and measure progress publicly.

Initial FCT goals should seek a minimum 50 percent improvement in cycle time. Setting goals lower than this does not achieve the cycle time reduction available or required to compete. Merely working harder within the existing process can reduce cycle time by 20 to 30 percent. When management sets a more aggressive goal, it signals the organization that everyone must consider new ways of working. This challenge in turn stimulates learning.

In the past, cycle time reductions were confined to manufacturing and were viewed in terms of incremental cost or efficiency improvements rather than as a competitive strategy. Knowledge work has received little attention, yet this is where the greatest leverage is (2). For example, the average design cycle of U.S. auto makers has been six years while production cycle time is less than a day. Until international competition in the auto industry made it clear that U.S. development cycles were double the Japanese, managers didn't realize that breakthroughs in excess of 50–200 percent were achievable. The reality is such improvements are now the minimum required merely to catch up!

When communicating stretch goals, expect people to respond with skepticism. Their response is entirely rational since they are being asked to make dramatic improvements without knowing exactly how they will do it. For this reason, it is essential that management have a strong FCT improvement vision that they agree to. Hewlett-Packard's CEO John Young asked all employees to cut in half the time it takes to break even on a new product. This vision provides a picture of the future to sustain people along the hard journey of getting there. Since the vision is only as effective as management's belief and enthusiasm in it, people will test it for holes as soon as it is communicated.

Defining the beginning and end of the cycle and sub-cycles is the first step in developing measures. This can be more difficult than it appears, since defining when a customer's need first exists is not easy or precise. Recognize that beginning and end points are inherently arbitrary choices. One can always mount a rational argument for other points. Select points that make sense for your industry and organization. If there are any sub-cycles that you will be focusing on, such as new product development, define that cycle as well. Once completed, establish the organization's initial FCT goal by benchmarking total current cycle time against your best competitor worldwide. Recognize that their current capability is the *minimum* target you can set since they won't be standing still. Only if the gap between you and them is enormous should an interim goal be selected.

Hewlett-Packard starts the new product development cycle when applicable technology exists within H-P Labs. The end of the cycle is when the profits from the product equal the total investment in the product. They call this break-even time (BET). The primary reason for using break-even time is to discourage quick introduction of products that fail to meet customer's needs. Quantum begins its new product development cycle with the first approved specification and ends at the passage of a process maturity test. Pick what works for your business.

Defining the cycle and sub-cycles permits internal comparison to past efforts and external comparison to competitors. For example, pick the last three products in a given area and see how long they took to develop. In doing so, it is quite easy to examine what contributed to FCT and what impeded it. This can also occur with key components required to build those products. Quantum has analyzed the time it has taken to develop firmware on every disk drive the company has made. The beauty of this approach is that it quickly moves the FCT conversation to the operating level and stimulates quality improvement discussions.

It is highly advantageous to distribute and display cycle time measures. A lack of feedback regarding results limits the possibility for initiating improvements. Research demonstrates that major breakthroughs frequently come from people who are less familiar with the process. As functions and teams develop their own FCT goals, display them. Graphics are far superior to tables and words.

One cannot understate the importance of aggressive FCT goals and publicly displayed measurements. Perhaps a colleague of mine describes this best using what he calls Management's Apparent Interest Index. Employees throughout an organization take action based on what they believe interests management. If management frequently discusses FCT, sets clear goals and consistently updates public measures, employees will recognize and act on management's attention. Without these factors, management's apparent interest will not be visible.

Step 6: Create an environment that stimulates and rewards continuous learning and action.

Increasing the rate of organizational learning is the heart of an FCT competitive strategy. As a relatively new area, organizational learning deserves special attention. Learning in organizations is a re-iterative process by which individual insights and discoveries are converted into organizational knowledge (3). Thus, organizational learning involves the building of a knowledge base that can be made accessible to others, shared, evaluated, and codified—rendering the knowledge independent of the inventor or person who originally generated the insight. Moreover, access to a shared knowledge base in organizations is critical; a lack of knowledge can result in major product errors and delays (4).

By reducing the time it takes to learn, fast-cycle organizations internally benefit from a parallel reduction in the time it takes them to detect and correct errors in the product development process. Many development efforts have been delayed, or have failed, because errors in the early stages of development were either ignored or went undetected.

Failure to detect errors in product development is costly, since problems are usually not seen until prototypes have been scaled up or advanced into manufacturing—usually with disastrous results (5). Similarly, product development efforts are thwarted when problems take too long to fix. Knowing what caused a problem (error detection) is useful only when someone acts to prevent its recurrence (error correction). Hence, the ability to correct errors in a timely manner once they have been detected is also critical to organizational effectiveness. Fast cycle companies are intent on increasing the rate of organizational learning.

Organizational learning is an organizational *process,* as opposed to merely the collection or summation of individual insights. Further, there are two critical differences between organizational and individual learning. First, organizations have a collective purpose, and to be useful, learning in an organization must be in line with that purpose. Second, organizations are social systems. While individual learning can be entirely personal, organizational learning requires that employees at large have access to the learning process and understand the new knowledge created.

Learning in public presents major dilemmas, however. Consider the following: Organizations reward technical competence, which drives people to speak out only when they know the right answer. According to this definition, learning is equated with competence. Thus, if the behavioral norms of the organization reward people who demonstrate competence, it would be wise to be quiet if one didn't know something. *Yet, if people cannot be public about what they don't know, how can we expect them to learn?* The logic of this model is as frightening as it is clear. FCT organizations and leaders begin by rewarding the right questions as much as they do the right answers.

A further dilemma is that the knowledge we have gained to date blocks the path to organizational learning. These established mental models are deeply entrenched and act as walls: they support what we are doing today *and* they act as barriers to thinking and doing differently (6,7). The older our organization is, the more we must "unlearn" in order to learn. The process of learning requires letting go of existing beliefs about current organizational practices, technologies and existing power relationships. To become a FCT competitor, it is essential that senior management embrace organizational learning as a strategic objective. The executive's job is to define a *strategy and system architecture* that increases the speed of learning throughout the firm. Because organizational learning is a social activity, it requires an architecture that creates forums where ideas and experience can be exchanged. The multi-functional team creates such a forum for task-related interactions between people of diverse background and experience. When combined with a clear team goal and rewards, individuals enthusiastically engage in both dialogue and discussions of differences that functional organizations usually evade or ignore. Insights that could not have been attained by individuals acting alone inevitably result from these interactions. In sum, team members gain invaluable experience by being actively engaged in the process of organizational learning.

While organizational learning is a new area of strategic focus for corporations, there are no hard and fast templates to follow. Leading FCT competitors are writing the rules right now by defining both a strategy and an architecture that supports learning in their organizations. The shift to a process-sensitive, learning organization requires time and effort. New values and structures take hold only as old ones are retired. FCT yields a sustainable competitive advantage because it is woven into the cultural fabric of the entire organization's value delivery process. World-class quality has become the "ante" required to be a global competitor, but it does not ensure leadership. Any organization that couples world-class quality with an FCT capability will have a competitive edge.

REFERENCES

1. Meyer, Christopher. *Fast Cycle Time: How to Align Purpose, Strategy, and Structure for Speed.* New York: The Free Press, 1993.
2. Meyer, Christopher. "How the right measures help teams excel." *Harvard Business Review* 72, No. 3 (1994): 95–103.
3. Nonaka, Ikujiro. "The Knowledge-Creating Company." *Harvard Business Review,* November–December (1992): 96–104.
4. Shrivastava, Paul. "A Typology of Organizational Learning Systems." *Journal of Management Studies* 20, No. 1 (1983): 9–25.
5. Purser, Ronald, Pasmore, William, and Tenkasi, Ramkrishnan. "The influence of deliberations on learning in new product development teams." *Journal of Engineering and Technology Management* 9 (1992): 1–28.
6. Purser, Ronald. "Redesigning the Knowledge-Based Product Development Organization: A Case Study in Sociotechnical Systems Change." *Technovation* 11 No. 7 (1991): 403–416.
7. Senge, Peter. *The Fifth Discipline: The Art and Practice of Organizational Learning.* New York: Doubleday, 1990.

44

Shortening the Product Development Cycle

PRESTON G. SMITH AND DONALD G. REINERTSEN

OVERVIEW: As techniques like cross-functional development teams and concurrent engineering become widespread, these approaches to shortening development cycles lose their competitive edge. Decisive advantage is likely to come from the techniques competitors are *not* using. The authors explain that there are other untapped sources of cycle time reduction for R&D managers to exploit. These include opportunities to accelerate the "fuzzy front end," in which half of a typical development cycle vanishes before the team even starts work. The authors caution against structuring a development process around a company's largest projects because this can excessively delay smaller ones. They also question the use of phased development systems, which often cause delays in their attempts to standardize control of projects.

The demands on product developers have never been greater. Product life cycles have shortened and continue to shrink. Product technologies, particularly in the electronics and materials areas, are changing faster than ever. As a consequence, the pressure is on to shorten product development cycles.

Frequently, the R&D manager becomes the focal point of efforts to cut development time. To deal effectively with this challenge, the technical manager must look beyond popular but limited solutions to see the breadth of the problem. Such techniques and tools as quality function deployment (QFD), simultaneous engineering, and computer-aided design (CAD) still leave many time-saving opportunities untouched (1).

Great reductions in cycle time are obtainable by applying various techniques blended to suit a particular company's needs. Fortunately, the R&D manager is in a strong position to initiate and foster many time-saving approaches. This article covers 10 such approaches in which such managers play a particularly important role.

1. BE FLEXIBLE ABOUT PROCESS

There are many sound approaches to managing R&D projects. Each method has its advantages and shortcomings. The correct approach can only be selected when one has a clear vision of which advantages are critical in a particular situation. For example, consider the tradeoff between managing development time and technical risk. Most product development systems, such as phased systems (see Authors' Addendum at end of article), are designed to monitor and control technical risk. Such systems are effective and appropriate where reducing technical risk is the paramount concern. Yet managing technical risk is not always the prime objective. Speed can be more important when trying to head off an emerging competitor, and cost can dominate our concerns in a mature market.

The most effective organizations have different development systems available and tuned to suit these distinct objectives. Without alternative processes, all projects tend to get sent through the same process, a common denominator that suits no

Reprinted with permission from *Research-Technology Management,* May–June, 1992, pp. 44–49.

Preston Smith is a management consultant in West Hartford, CT. ***Donald Reinertsen*** is a management consultant in Redondo Beach, CA.

objective well. In practice it usually errs on the side of minimizing technical risk at the expense of speed. This one-size-fits-all mentality usually creates a system tailored to the largest, most complex projects to the detriment of simpler ones. If the R&D manager is successful in minimizing product complexity, simpler systems can be used.

2. LET ECONOMICS BE YOUR GUIDE

You need a yardstick to decide which development goal to stress for a particular project, and in business the time-tested yardstick is marked in dollars. It is both simple and valuable to develop financial yardsticks for the development process. Such yardsticks tell you the relative financial impact of project delay versus a product cost overrun. They guide you toward choosing the most productive development goal and applying a development process that facilitates this goal.

In addition to these strategic decisions, there are countless daily tactical decisions where yardsticks help to make accurate, fast, low-level decisions on tradeoff issues. For example, is it worth spending $100 on air freight to get a sample into a customer's hands for evaluation two days sooner? How about buying an extra microscope for $2000 if it will cut a week off of the schedule? Or $50,000 for temporary tooling that will allow you to start production two months early while permanent tooling is being made? Without sound decision rules these decisions are likely to be made both incorrectly and slowly.

The financial model that provides the yardsticks is not hard to build (2), but it requires cross-functional effort. The finance department may have the greatest expertise in financial model building, and marketing has important data. But R&D should probably initiate this activity because it will obtain the greatest benefit from the model. For instance, it is not unusual to discover that the product's development expense has far less impact on its life cycle profitability than development delay. When this is the case, R&D managers who spend much of their time massaging the budget are concentrat-

ing on a low-leverage area. (See Editor's Addendum for additional discussion.)

3. WATCH OUT FOR COMPLEXITY

The degree of complexity in a project determines the effort needed and thus the length of the development cycle. Although this is not surprising, product development people are frequently startled to discover how quickly complexity mounts.

For example, consider the experience of a company that makes industrial process controls. They made ambitious plans to use a microprocessor in their product for the first time, figuring that this is hardly a new technology anymore. To make full use of the new capability, they tapped a new market they had been unable to serve previously, and they added new product features that had been unavailable to them before. In retrospect, they realized that complexity had multiplied on them. Microprocessors may have been familiar components to others, but this firm had to learn how to procure them, design for them, test and assemble them—everything. In addition, they had to master the new features and establish the new market. This project was slow and fraught with other difficulties.

Complexity is insidious because it multiplies quickly and its effects are indirect and often not apparent. It increases the risk—both technical and market (discussed later). It increases workloads because many more interactions among elements must be considered. It tends to draw in more people, often specialists, which complicates communication and decision making. All of this necessitates a more complicated—thus slower—management process.

The way to get new products out quickly is to minimize complexity by moving in short, simple steps, sampling customer response along the way by selling intermediate models (2). This incremental innovation strategy involves two roles for the R&D manager. First, as manager of technical people who generally enjoy experimenting with new technologies, the R&D manager needs to temper others' desires to put the latest technologies into new products by applying his or her accumulated wisdom. In particular, stress the use of carryover parts and standard components, such as fasteners and connectors. Emphasize inelegant but clean architectures (2). Rechannel the technical brainpower toward solving those problems that will provide more substantial benefit for the customer.

These days the Japanese are often held up as innovation leaders, particularly companies like Honda. In fact, these companies control their pace of innovation carefully. Even their "all new" products are often far from all new. For instance, the initial Acura automobile models which made their debut in 1986 were advertised as "new automobiles . . . designed and engineered from the driver out." However, inspection of the Acura Integra revealed that the skin was indeed new, but many functional components—the most highly engineered ones like the engine, brake, door latches, and panel instruments—were carryovers from Honda Civics and Accords.

4. MANAGE THE INVENTION PIPELINE

Complexity is minimized by moving into new areas in a planned and evolutionary way, as just covered. This does not mean that newness is avoided. Quite the contrary, newness and invention must be embraced and managed.

Invention presents a dilemma to rapid product development. On the one hand, invention is essential to innovation: continual repackaging is a dead-end strategy. On the other hand, invention is a notoriously unpredictable activity. It cannot be scheduled into a normal project, must less an accelerated one. Any attempt to schedule this wild card into a project just adds uncertainty to the schedule, and in some markets schedule uncertainty is more detrimental than a longer but certain schedule.

Resolving this dilemma falls to the R&D manager. The solution is to invent off-line in a separately scheduled program that is tightly integrated with your market and product plans. Companies like Canon, Honda and Sony are innovation lead-

ers because they devote considerable resources to maintaining a storehouse of developing technologies basic to their businesses. Both the invention track and the product development track are market driven, and both are given resources adequate to keep projects moving swiftly. The difference is that the former is loosely scheduled while the latter is tightly scheduled. When a technology reaches the point that much of its schedule uncertainty is eliminated, it switches tracks.

Consider the two types of failures that occur when this type of system is short-circuited. Many companies try to avoid the invention track by integrating it with the product development track. Then, schedule uncertainty is high in development projects, which ultimately causes both employees and customers to have little regard for development schedules. Every project proceeds at its own pace, unable to be accelerated.

The other failure is even worse. In this case a company simply does not invent. Its development schedules are predictable, but so is its demise.

5. AVOID THE "THINKING STAGE" TRAP

Other departments are often quick to blame R&D for slow product development, but the fact is that half of the typical product development cycle has vanished before development is even authorized (2). What we call the fuzzy front end is frequently one of the largest and cheapest opportunities to shorten the development cycle.

The front end of a development project starts when the need for a new product is first apparent, whether the company acts on it or not. Product need could be mandated by the enactment of a new government regulation, the emergence of a new technology, or certainly, the appearance of a competing product. The front end terminates when the firm commits significant human resources to development of the product.

We are not suggesting that the front end is unimportant; it is more like the heavens—mostly empty. Some crucial decisions are made during this period regarding the size of the market opportunity, the target customer, alignment with corporate strategy, and availability of key technologies and resources. In fact, research on the market success of new products suggests that products fail because companies don't do enough of this "homework" (3). Nonetheless, front-end time is still mostly a vacuum, largely because managers who haven't calculated the dollar value of development delay believe that time is free until people are assigned to the project.

As an R&D manager, your role in this phase is to be hard-nosed about using your people on product concepts. Resist the attempts of marketing or general management to have one of your people "look at" an idea in their "spare time." Remind them that delay erodes product profitability, and offer to assign one of your people immediately at full- or half-time to reach a certain decision by a definite date. If you aren't this serious about using your resources, then the company isn't serious about the product concept.

6. STAFF TEAMS ADEQUATELY

Our experience, and that of many others, suggests that product development proceeds most quickly and effectively with a team of six to ten full-time members. Although some products, like automobiles, computers or aircraft, require more effort than this, far more common is the development project that seems too small to justify this level of commitment. It receives perhaps a full-time person, a couple of part-timers, and a flock of bit-part participants. Given the heavy load of projects underway at a typical company, this appears to be the best that can be done. No single project has enough importance to command adequate resources.

The solution to this situation is simple in principle. If each project requires a certain number of person-years of effort, consider doubling the staff on half of the projects and complete them in half the time. Then do the other half of the projects similarly. Fewer projects will be underway at any point in time, but the same number will be completed each year.

Although the annual output is the same, the shorter, more intense project option has several benefits. The projects started first get to market sooner, giving them a competitive advantage and a longer sales life. The ones started later are completed no later than before, but they enjoy the advantages of a late start, such as better market information and more recent technologies. Both the early starts and the late starts reap the advantages of a short cycle: fewer opportunities for the market or the project objectives to shift, which means less redesign.

The shorter, more intense option is a valid model if project pacing is primarily dependent on labor availability, that is, project tasks typically sit waiting for people to work on them. In our experience, this is a frequent occurrence. Occasionally, project pacing depends primarily on outside events, like tooling lead time or prototype testing time, in which case it may not be possible to save appreciable time through heavier staffing.

A common objection here is that a more intense effort suggests large teams and thus a greater communication burden, which negates part of the anticipated benefit. However, we can obtain the extra effort without extra people by staffing teams with full-timers rather than part-timers.

Although it is possible to overstaff a team, our experience suggests that American development teams suffer much more from fragmented understaffing than from overstaffing.

7. STAFF WITH GENERALISTS

Often teams are fragmented, having many part-time members, because people are viewed too narrowly, and they in turn often mold themselves as narrow specialists. Some people indeed must be highly trained in a specific technical area in order to advance the state of the art, but the need for such skills is limited in most product development, which instead stresses application and integration. Having a narrow person on a development team causes the R&D manager three problems:

• First, it is difficult to keep such people fully occupied on the project. They tend to split their time commitment among one or more other projects. They drift in and out of a project as their particular skills are needed or as they have the time. They may shift to another project when the going gets tough on a particular project. Consequently, the team leader is consumed by simply keeping the team together and communicating with the part-timers, not on the primary task of developing the product.

• The second difficulty with specialization on the team is that good products require balance to provide value to the customer. This balance is achieved most quickly and with the least communication burden if everyone involved has a solid appreciation of the customer, the economics, the various technologies involved, and the manufacturing methods.

• Third, a high degree of specialization inhibits the manager's ability to redeploy people within a development team to match the workload, which leads to queues and delay.

There are a couple of implications for the R&D manager. First, staff teams with generalists or those willing to become generalists. This will give the team a more comprehensive view, which will allow them to move quickly and precisely. It will also strengthen the team if team members can shift to various secondary team jobs rather than dropping off of the team for a while.

Second, encourage and develop generalists. We recently saw a manufacturing engineer take on the company's cost accounting system when the manufacturing costs for his product weren't coming out to his liking. He didn't overhaul the corporate system, but he did negotiate a more equitable way of costing his product, a more creative one than a cost accountant was likely to have proposed. He learned a lot about cost accounting in the process, and he is now more valuable to his organization.

Deliberately expose people to new areas, either by transferring them to new departments or through outside training. Send your engineer to an accounting course or your draftsperson to a production machine programming course; encourage a marketing person to enroll in a microwave fundamentals course. Just by staying on a development team from start to finish, people will broaden, but this process can be accelerated through deliberate training.

8. LET THE TEAM MANAGE THE TEAM

Product development is just a succession of problems to be solved, so development speed depends on the speed of the problem-solving process, which in turn depends on how tightly problem-solving loops are connected. Every time the team has to go outside of itself to obtain a decision, additional delay is incurred. The farther it has to go, geographically or organizationally, the greater the delay is likely to be.

A Boston-area computer peripherals firm attacked the problem-solving-loop issue directly. The vice president observed that their development team was wasting time because designers weren't getting good enough guidance at their weekly meetings. They would design what they thought was desired, only to find out a week later that they were off track and most of the week had been wasted. So the vice president organized short, daily team meetings at the ten o'clock coffee break. Not only was there less waste of design talent, but everybody moved faster and more surefootedly because progress was now measured on a daily basis.

Just as important as the fivefold shortening of the loop is the vice president's role in this process. He recognized the problem, got the group to meet daily, and even attended many of the meetings. But he didn't run the meetings or participate in their content. He only made sure the group got together daily and left each meeting with a clear idea of what they would be doing next. The team ran the team, and if the company had had a team leader, the vice president's involvement would have been unnecessary.

Getting the team to run itself involves a couple of difficult organizational challenges. In typical organizations, managers of R&D and other functions typically control pieces of development projects, which are completed as these managers coordinate their efforts—often slowly. These roles must shift as the team assumes control of the project. The functional managers now act as advisors and coaches, assisting their colleagues on the team but not using the colleagues as conduits to carry information back to the functional manager for a decision. If this occurs, the organization has just installed a group of puppets as an additional level in the decision-making process. The R&D manager will still have plenty to manage, but his or her role changes with respect to a fast development team.

Frequently the team is also uncomfortable with its new role of making final decisions. If it tries to toss the decision back to management, management must simply toss it back to the team. Before long the team will rely on management as a source of decision-making information, not as a source of decisions.

9. MANAGE BOTH TECHNICAL AND MARKET RISK

Risk management has always been a large part of the technical manager's job. As cycle length shrinks, this job becomes even more essential. Faster projects employ a greater amount of task overlapping, which creates loose ends and, in turn, more opportunities for key steps to be omitted accidentally (2). If the team is managing itself, as just suggested, there is less formal opportunity for the management hierarchy to apply its considerable experience to averting past mistakes. Finally, there is less time available in a compressed schedule to recover from problems.

Fortunately, there is a great deal the R&D manager can do to manage risk in an accelerated project. Sensitivity to risk comes in part from years of experience, which managers are more likely to possess than are the members of the team. Through frequent informal interactions with the team, management can see potential pitfalls and inject insight

to cope with them, all without infringing on the team's charter to make its own decisions.

One area where the manager's experience is most valuable is in balancing testing and analysis. Many technical people are prone to analyze an issue profusely before building something and testing it. Just making a model seems like an unprofessional expedient, but expedients are often just what we are looking for as we try to shrink tasks. Others, who may lack the analytical skills or discipline, do the opposite. They build and test repeatedly before thinking much about what the underlying issues may be, so they waste time in resolving risk, too.

The trick is in knowing when to test and when analysis would get the answer faster, or better yet, how test and analysis can be blended to get the best of both. The R&D manager's accumulated wisdom can be invaluable in raising and helping to resolve these issues. The manager also must make sure that analytical and testing resources, such as an open lab, are easily available to the team for this hands-on work.

Risk is of two types: technical risk, which is the inability to satisfy the product specification, and market risk, which is the inability to sell the product assuming it meets specifications. We tend to concentrate on technical risk, ignoring market risk, because we have better techniques for resolving technical risk, it is easier to identify and measure, and its symptoms usually appear sooner.

The R&D manager's job here is to teach the rest of the organization that market risk is just as real as technical risk and that the same general risk management techniques apply to it, although the two should be managed independently (2).

10. DEVELOP A RESERVE

We have saved the toughest topic until last. As suggested in 6, above, development projects are slow largely because they spend most of their lives waiting to be worked on. Projects are abundant but resources are tight. One reason for this predicament is that we use the popular development funnel concept where it doesn't apply.

For some products, often chemical products, the concept of a development funnel does make sense. The failure rate in the initial feasibility stages of a project is high, and the cost of these stages is low. So we start lots of projects at the top of the funnel, and a few winners flow from the bottom through a natural selection process.

Ironically, the development funnel doesn't work well for many products because the failure rate isn't high enough. Such projects are more likely to succumb to market causes either before or after development than to fail on technical grounds during development. Nevertheless, companies load the funnel with plenty of new-product ideas, and marketing is in fact encouraged to overstock the funnel (2). Because few projects actually fail, projects languish in the funnel awaiting resources. R&D managers must discourage application of the development funnel mentality where it does not apply. Applying it under low failure-rate circumstances generates a glut and demoralizes technical people whose perfectly acceptable projects get shelved in midstream for lack of resources.

However, eliminating just the glut is not going far enough. There actually has to be some slack because unplanned new product ideas will arise unexpectedly. The time-competitive firm needs some reserve development capacity to respond to these customer needs quickly, just as they retain reserve manufacturing capacity to fill unanticipated production orders responsively.

This presents a difficult challenge for the R&D manager. At planning time, don't accept a full load and then a bit more to cover fallout. Instead, leave some unused capacity for the really new projects.

This completes our tour of 10 areas where the R&D manager can shorten development time dramatically. You obtain the greatest benefit by making all of these improvements, because they all reinforce one another. But this is a long-term goal because no company we know of does all of these things well yet. So get started with some of them, perhaps by using a pilot rapid development project to initiate several of the changes immediately (2). Finally, get the non-R&D parts of the company in-

volved compressing development time too. Even those apparently removed from the process, like corporate planners, have essential parts to play (4).

REFERENCES

1. Reinersten, Donald (1991); "Outrunning the Pack in Faster Product Development," *Electronic Design,* 39, 1, pp. 111–118.
2. Smith, Preston, G., and Donald G. Reinersten (1991); *Developing Products in Half the Time* (New York: Van Nostrand Reinhold).
3. Cooper, Robert G. (1988); *Winning at New Projects* (Reading, Mass: Addison-Wesley).
4. Reinertsen, Donald G., and Preston G. Smith (1991); "The Strategist's Role in Shortening Product Development Cycles," *The Journal of Business Strategy,* July/Aug. pp. 18–22.
5. Rosenau, Jr., Milton D. (1990); *Faster New Product Development* (New York: AMACOM).
6. Reinertsen, Donald G. (1983); "Whodunit? The Search for the New-Product Killers," *Electronic Business,* July, pp. 62–66.
7. Reinertsen, Donald G. (1992); "The Mythology of Speed," *Machine Design,* March, pp. 95–98.

AUTHORS' ADDENDUM

Beware of Phased Development

The concept of dividing a project into phases and funding each phase only if its satisfies certain prerequisites would appear to be a good management tool. Yet, as consultants, we see an oil-and-water relationship between phased systems and accelerated development.

Developed by NASA as the PPP (phased project planning) process, phased development systems are designed to control technical risk. But when speed is important, market risk becomes more critical: even if the product is designed according to spec, there is a significant possibility for market failure if it is introduced late. When technical risk must be balanced with market risk, a monolithic PPP-type system is no longer the clear choice. Adaptation and balance are needed in the project management system, and the balance shifts toward empowering the people and away from depending on formal control systems.

The question is really where the balance should lie. We advise some companies, usually fast-growing small ones, to formalize their review systems because with the product line and the staff growing rapidly, more formal management checks are needed to avoid technical failures. Yet in the majority of cases we see phased control systems that are overly cumbersome for a firm's needs. Sometimes a company will just adopt another's phase process, as we once observed when a 100-person instrument manufacturer adopted Hewlett-Packard's phase process, figuring that HP was also an instrument producer—a very good one indeed. But HP's process, fine-tuned for a large company with dozens of divisions, was excess baggage for this small firm.

Fundamental Limitations

Phased systems have a number of fundamental limitations that restrict the ability to shorten development cycles. They often preclude employing one of the most fundamental time-shrinking tools: overlapping activities. Often a particular stream of activities could be overlapped to advantage, but a phase review breaks the chain by requiring that all activities be finished up for review before the next phase can start.

Moreover, the very act of discovering overlapping opportunities requires a new attitude for an organization long indoctrinated in a sequential phased review process. It is that much more difficult to get people thinking creatively about overlapping dissimilar activities when their mindset is built around established phase gates.

Overlapping is enabled by employing partial, fragmentary information that evolves in a stream (2). Phased systems fight against partial information, providing credit and passage to the next phase only when the information package is complete. Here again, the time-saving opportunities must be discovered in a particular circumstance by thinking creatively about inching forward with the information at hand. A tidy phase framework discourages these discoveries.

Exploiting system architecture opportunities is another means of compressing development cy-

cles (2). By dividing a product into subsystem modules with relatively clean interfaces and ample performance margins, these modules can be developed concurrently by different teams. For example, a transceiver might be divided into a power supply, a transmitter, a receiver, and an audio amplifier. There is no reason to believe that these four modules will have the same timing. One module might require more conceptual design or technology exploration, while another might need a great deal of prototype testing. Putting all modules in a lockstep phase review process stretches the overall cycle.

Moreover, a phased system encourages queues. Queue reduction is a huge and inexpensive opportunity to shorten cycles simply because most development projects spend the majority of their time sitting in queue somewhere. With phases, queues build up in preparation for a review. (Remember that only a complete package is acceptable for a review, so some items wait while the package is completed.) Then, when the review is complete, a flood is released into the next stage of the system, swamping it.

For example, upon final approval of the design, purchasing may be faced with simultaneously ordering a million dollars of capital equipment from a dozen suppliers. Or in one case we observed, the chief engineer signed and released into manufacturing nearly 500 drawings in a single day when his project passed a milestone. You could actually observe the glut passing through the manufacturing transition process.

A phase process also causes problems when, as is often the case in practice, "the product" is really a line of products in different sizes, materials or colors. Then, forcing all variants into synchronization for convenience in review creates both pre-review delays and post-review gluts unnecessarily.

Responsibility Belongs to People

In short, phased approaches are attempts to build judgment into the process rather than into the people. It is reactive, it is slow, and it removes the responsibility from the people doing the work, where the responsibility belongs.

Shifting away from a phased process is difficult. There is a great deal of management comfort involved in taking a thorough, formal look at a project periodically and making an explicit decision whether or not to proceed. Unfortunately, the cost can be high when time is at stake. A balance must be struck between comfort and speed, and all too often, comfort wins out even when speed is the key competitive factor.

Some rapid product development specialists suggest that the phased approach should remain the foundation but that the phases should be compressed and "dead time" between phases should be eliminated (5). Our observations of how development projects actually proceed in industry suggests that the greatest opportunities for improvement lie in eliminating the delays associated with synchronization and queueing. This requires a fundamental departure from the phased approach, not fine-tuning it.—D.R. and P.S.

EDITOR'S ADDENDUM

In Reinertsen's (6) original publication of the trade-off between speed and costs, he emphasized that the key to winning lies in a company's flexibility in adapting a product's development to its specific market conditions and strategy. Based on a relatively simple economic model of new product development and commercialization, Reinertsen compared the effects of a product delay, a product-development expense overrun, and a product cost increase on total life cycle profits in two different kinds of market situations: (1) a high-growth, price-eroding market and (2) a low-growth, non-price eroding market. After examining the comparative results of his model, Reinertsen drew the following three conclusions:

1. Development expense overruns have little effect on total life cycle profits. In both high- and low-growth market conditions, overrunning development cost budgets by 50 percent had less than a 4 percent impact on total life cycle profits before tax.

2. Speed is not always the most critical factor. In

a high-growth market with short product-life cycles, shipping a product six months late can decrease its cumulative profits by 33 percent. On the other hand, in a slow-growth market with long product-life cycles, a six month delay creates only a 7 percent decline in overall profits.

3. In many market situations, the single most important factor may be product cost. A product cost overrun of only 9 percent reduced total life cycle profits by 22 percent in a fast-growth market and resulted in a devastating 45 percent decrease in profits in a slow-growth market.

In general, Reinertsen stresses that the art of managing product development depends on making well-informed trade-offs between the four possible objectives of (1) development speed, (2) product cost, (3) product performance, and (4) development expense. He urges managers to build some simple economic models and tools to show the profit impact of the trade-offs they are making, often even unconsciously, between these objectives in their specific competitive situation. Based on his experience working with companies to improve and speed up their development processes, Reinertsen (7) offers a number of additional suggestions as follows:

1. Don't wait until all plans and schedules are in place. Design can always begin before planning is complete. Do just enough planning to begin design and then complete it early enough to support key design decisions.

2. Be careful in drawing up elaborate schedules with very long lists of supposedly predictable activities that then force developers to waste effort explaining why they're off schedule. Engineering is stochastic and is, therefore, extremely hard to schedule. Microscheduling can be a huge drain on design resources. Focus instead on a handful of critical high-level milestones. Find ways to set and communicate priorities so that top management does not have to intervene to accelerate one program at the expense of others.

3. Don't get bogged down waiting until all the

specifications are complete, accurate, and frozen. Keep the specs adaptable throughout the design process. Progressively finalize them after compromises have been made on features. Concentrate on making product specifications fit customer requirements to control risk.

4. Don't believe that the key to rapid product development is designing things right the first time, and that too much time is spent correcting mistakes. Early testing is critical for rapid development. Instead, quickly implement a partial solution and then keep working to test and improve it. Pay more attention to how fast you can arrive at an answer, not just the number of mistakes made along the way.

5. Don't implement control and measurement systems that end up disempowering people. Rapid development relies on motivating teams rather than imposing top-down plans.

6. Too much time is often spent planning and rehearsing for formal review meetings. Instead, improve informal monitoring of development programs and strengthen informal channels of communication. Manage by "wandering around" for faster and more timely information.

7. Don't concentrate on defining the perfect development process that avoids all possible problems. It encourages the compliance of people rather than their initiative to find new ways of solving old problems. Well-trained people armed with information and the means to choose and implement appropriate approaches can outperform most systems in a fast-changing environment.

8. Be careful of the "do-it-try-it-fix-it" mentality. While managers get frustrated with too many analyses, make sure that analysis plays a strong role, as it is the only practical means for uncovering problems in complex systems.

9. Establish autonomous teams carefully to avoid the disadvantages of not using the organization's existing designs, solutions, and technologies.

10. The slowest portion of most organizational processes is deciding to get started. Running fast is good, but starting early is better!

45

The Hidden Costs of Accelerated Product Development

C. MERLE CRAWFORD

Rarely has a strategic management option captured American industry as has the thrust of accelerated product development. When accompanied by the goals of lowered cost and increased new product quality, it seems almost unstoppable. However, industry may have been swept up in the enthusiasm. Any strategic option so tempting (with long lists of advantages and no suggested limitations) needs to be viewed critically. Crawford reveals several "hidden costs" of accelerated development. He does not oppose the new strategy, and indeed endorses it highly, but urges that it be considered carefully before application.

Over the past five years we have seen widespread trial and adoption of what is call *accelerated product development* (APD). The focus is the entire process of product innovation, not just the R&D/design/engineering/manufacturing phases that are sometimes equated with the term *development*.

Though not yet subjected to serious critique by the academic researchers, word through the business press is exciting. Reductions of development time from 36 months to 18 months are common. Who can fault that? Users of the approach imply that they are extending the techniques of acceleration to many other projects. (The better reports on recent activities in this field are given in Refs. 6, 7, 19, 21, 29, 32, 40-42, 44, 46.) Specific benefits are summarized by a member of the Boston Consulting Group staff as higher prices, opportunity to incorporate the latest technology, more ac-

curate forecasts of customer needs and increased market share [37]. All of us who work on product innovation welcome new ideas for the development process, and most of what we've heard about APD makes sense. Much of it will find a permanent home in our tool kits, partly because we are already familiar with the techniques in selective settings. People in the fast-paced food industry yawned when Digital shocked its managers by giving a team *only* 12 months to develop a lower-cost mouse. Now might be a good time to drop the other shoe. Accelerated product development has a price tag, a much larger one than most of its eager (and very busy) practitioners talk about. The purpose of this article is to take a hard look at that price tag.

An awareness of the costs, especially the hidden ones, will help direct the acceleration to its proper applications. Otherwise, the innocent and uncritical acceptance of speed will lead to misuse, frustrated team players and a reduction in other types of product development that also are badly needed.

THE SOURCES OF HIDDEN COSTS

The hidden costs of speeded-up development are of five types:

1. Low-profit, trivial innovation tends to drive out the more profitable breakthrough types. Gresham's law about "bad money driving out the good" works on innovation.

2. Many mistakes happen when skipping steps sacrifices necessary information [10].

Reprinted by permission of the publisher from "The Hidden Costs of Accelerated Product Development," by C. Merle Crawford, *Journal of Product Innovation Management*, 1992, Vol. 9, pp. 188–199. Copyright 1992 by Elsevier Science Co., Inc.

C. Merle Crawford is Professor of Marketing at the University of Michigan's Business School.

3. A surprisingly negative and disruptive side to new styles of small-team management sometimes appears. It can boost people costs.

4. Unexpected inefficiencies result when the process of innovation warps under pressure; the various steps don't respond evenly to cuts in the time budget.

5. A firm's complex set of support resources can get chewed up by pressure from players on speeded-up teams.

After looking at the costs, we will see what steps managers can take to capitalize on the new approach without being overcome by those costs.

Hidden Cost #1: Low-Profit, Trivial Innovation Tends to Drive out the More Profitable Breakthrough Types. Gresham's Law about "Bad Money Driving out the Good" Works on Innovation.

Managers are usually skeptical of strategic myopia—the commitment to one strategy above all others. (For good reason. McKinsey & Company's Krubasik [30] made clear the need for a mix of strategic options based on a matrix of opportunity costs and entry risk.) Unfortunately, APD seems to fit only incremental innovation and actually may threaten other types. A research report from Arthur D. Little [34, p. 16], a leading consultant on technological innovation, said "One of the critical choices in innovation strategy is whether to seek major breakthroughs or smaller, incremental innovations. Our answer is that in most cases, if you know roughly where you want to go, incremental innovation is faster and cheaper." *Incremental innovation* is that which advances a product or product line in little steps—small changes, made often. *Breakthrough* (pioneering) *innovation* creates entirely new products, and new markets as well. Most firms need both (and a middle ground too), and spend their money in an effort to get them. The relative emphasis may, of course, shift across various businesses within these firms. In the process there is healthy, built-in competition for resources.

We should be careful to note that incremental and breakthrough innovation can both be consistent with today's emphasis on core technologies.

DuPont, Merck and others certainly have breakthrough products within their core technologies. Generic copiers in the same pharmaceutical industry have minuscule incremental innovation, often totally outside any core technology restrictions. (For more on core techologies, see Prahalad and Hamel [36].)

Ralph E. Gomory, former technical head at IBM, and Roland W. Schmitt, his counterpart at GE, have recently argued that we have historically weighted the scales toward breakthrough innovation but need to push now for more incremental innovation. They favor speeding up the process [20].

Gresham's Law about bad money is relevant here. Economist Gresham noted many years ago that if a monetary system contains a mix of sound and unsound paper, the bad money will always tend to drive out the good. It's not appropriate to use the terms good and bad for new products, but many people feel that emphasis on incremental projects will inevitably lead to less emphasis on the breakthrough type. There is only so much "emphasis" to spread across the portfolio, just as when a laser concentrates light it leaves surrounding areas in the dark. Resources devoted to incrementalism may be more highly protected in the short run, leaving breakthrough projects to lag.

Edwin Land, founder of Polaroid, insisted that any R&D project had to be almost impossible, or he would not allocate money to it. APD would probably have been anathema to him, though some suggest that his later years with the firm would have been more productive had there been more incremental work to balance his blockbusters. This might suggest that APD is a better strategy for larger, established firms than for younger, growing ones.

Even APD users say one sometimes has to decide what the firm wants to deemphasize. Several recent articles suggest that Xerox may have so concentrated on copiers that it hurt its work beyond copiers [24,47,48]. Xerox's stated mission now emphasizes document handling.

Some firms tell us their first criterion in screening a new product concept is: How long will it take? One example, from many, is Honeywell's

Building Controls Division, where managers stopped the tracking of costs on new product projects and implemented a milestones system [18]. They apparently felt that it was more valuable to control time than money within the context of their overall approach to development. If slow, screening is insensitive to sales potential. Apparently there is little consideration given to opportunity costs, and strong efforts are made to achieve a company-wide commitment to speed.

It seems that by the very nature of the process, APD works best on incremental projects, in practice, even if not in theory. It may not be a coincidence that several recent articles on APD have mentioned cars, textiles, software, an improved air grinder, a new thermostat, a desktop microfilming machine, later versions of workstations, motorcycles, mid-size and small computers, toilet fixtures, hand tools and small kitchen appliances. These are rather clearly markets that are in, or nearing, their mature phase, a time when incremental product development takes over from the more innovative and expansive phases. We occasionally hear promoters of APD warning managers to "avoid technological leaps" [2].

APD also takes sides in the struggle between strategies of technology and of market. Which side to depend on doesn't seem to matter; there is usually one ready to go, and the other is left to scurry along in a necessarily minor role. As many people now think that *dual* drive (a solid market opportunity *and* an available technology) is best, speed may tempt managers to make the weaker choice of a single drive [14].

Critical here, of course, is risk and the company attitude toward it. To some managers, doing nothing is less risky than doing something later shown to be clearly wrong, so the mindset favors small changes. The breakthrough project is not only delayed but often destroyed (the scientist leaves the firm, the technology is sold, a competitor discovers it).

Is there any evidence that APD is reducing major innovations? Here's a list.

1. Expenditures on R&D have had trouble holding their own lately [27]. In spite of annual predictions of increasing spending, actual expenditures have been disappointing. Moreover, expectations are that spending on basic research will actually fall, as funds go to "new business projects."

2. As stated above, some proponents of speed have gone so far as to argue that speed is the only game. As one division general manager put it, "A speed-based system doesn't work if you're tracking it by the amount of money spent." (John Bailey, Honeywell Building Controls, See Gerber [18].) Under these conditions, managers may find it difficult to defend spending money (and time) on projects whose finish dates fall off the tracking system. Such a strategy, of course, may not be appropriate for other operating units within the same company.

3. Arguments for faster new product development include lower product cost and improved manufacturability, descriptors that clearly are associated with incrementalism. With exceptions, of course, cost and manufacturability contribute mainly to current market competitiveness; breakthrough projects (more likely offering significant product differentiation) offer cost and manufacturing advantages only as a by-product.

4. Integrated manufacturing systems (especially Just-in-Time arrangements) are high on managements agendas today, and such systems are noted for using process innovations that work against product innovation (e.g., supplier plants located next door, long-term supply and/or sales contracts, volume accounts, major process capital investments). Suppliers locked up in integrated manufacturing systems may degenerate into external workbenches, expensive new equipment (beyond a point) becomes inflexible, and the locking of arms may be good for insiders but keeps out some firms (especially smaller ones) that may have new product contributions to make. Japanese firms are apparently rethinking the immobility of capital brought about by supplier plants "next door" [1, 16, 23].

5. To gain speed it is necessary to avoid projects that require lots of learning. APDers must stick to what they know well. Some people find they can have it both ways be designing families of products; later members of the family may be imperfectly understood at the beginning when the APD effort is initiated. (From personal correspondence with Milton D. Rosenau, Jr.) This, of course, puts some pressure on the later stages, especially marketing. Arthur D. Little reported a similar variation from their research: Sony (and others) have found that by breaking their R&D into small projects and opting for a high frequency of product introductions, each new product can incorporate just a few technological innovations. If a promising innovation has to be deferred, it is no matter; there is another new product coming down the line soon [34]. These modifications show that there are ways for a firm to have its (speed) cake and good bites of innovation too, but managers have to accept the need to be creative. The key is that speed is achieved within the constraints of an overriding vision of innovation.

6. Many honored innovators have extolled the value of product champions, but champions are unwanted (and said to be unnecessary) in APD. They tend to fight the rejection of their product/technology, and people on a tight timetable have no need for troublemakers. The enthusiasm of a whole team presumably makes a single champion redundant, but some people forget that champions are not needed just for radical innovations; they are needed anytime there is internal opposition to a new program, and such opposition may come from manufacturing, purchasing or sales, even if the new product is at best a modest product improvement. A project that needs no champion is virtually certain to be bringing about very little institutional change.

7. We often hear about how the use of small teams lets the product innovation work proceed without the "interference" of top managments. Such interference is apparently helpful in avoiding the slowdowns associated with bringing management up to date, but it is widely recognized that top managements play a major role in product innovation. This suggests that much APD is focused on projects whose product innovation charters call for risks low enough that top managements can stay hands-off.

8. It might be no coincidence that top managements are adopting APD during the same period when they are slashing middle managements.

I've seen no research on the subject, but it would seem likely that skeleton crews and wide spans of control are associated with lesser innovativeness.

9. Lastly, the food industry has used speeded-up product innovation for many years. New product failure rates there are very high (some reports show 90 percent, versus an all-industry rate of around 35 percent), and true innovation is rare [13].

Hidden Cost #2: Many Mistakes Happen When Skipping Steps Sacrifices Necessary Information.

The key steps omitted in APD seem to be ones that involve the acquisition of information. There is less technical R&D/engineering, no basic market studies, a bare minimum of concept testing and other pretechnical work, most product requirements written from current staff knowledge and experience and little if any product use testing or market testing [4]. There is no attempt to study options at decision points. Even if each of five information rejections has an 80 percent chance of being right, the probability of being right on all five is 33 percent. Information rejection, defendable when done once, becomes very risky when repeated as policy down the line.

Research shows there are three major causes of new product failure: no need for the item, a need wasn't met or the item was not marketed wisely [5, 8, 25]. All three causes can be overcome by widely accepted market research during development, but with APD there is rarely time. Some are now asking whether skipping testing may actually *add* time to the project, given the iterations otherwise required later [2]. What this amounts to is false economy of time.

Many firms do something comparable to what is called Beta testing in the computer industry—give a few customers some of the product and see if it "works." It takes just a few weeks, but it doesn't settle a key issue: Does the new item actually meet the customer's *need?* That takes longer, and APD doesn't have longer.

Frito-Lay had an interesting experience when, upon acquiring a new CEO, a well-established and successful new products program came under the stopwatch. Launches were speeded up, and key information-gathering steps were skipped or misused. In just a few years there was evidence that product failures helped cause the ousting of the new CEO, and replacement leadership said there would be a "return to the basics" [17].

A similar story with another very large consumer packaged-goods firm involved a management that threw out their formal new product process in the late 1970s and promptly lost $1.5 billion on new products. Current (1990) thinking in the firm was to get back to basics by reintroducing the new product process [9].

Lest this article give the impression that skipping field market research is a weakness only of packaged-goods firms, recall that General Electric also had a product quality problem on a new compressor for refrigerators. This product failure may well cost GE a half billion dollars before all the dust settles [33, 35]. Amdahl had a similar experience in marketing an incompletely tested new mainframe computer that just didn't work: their next venture, three years later, was with a thoroughly field-tested model that succeeded very well [3].

These examples suggest the dangers of skipping steps in the product innovation process, action that usually results in loss of key information. Though these examples are anecdotal, research data support them. (Cooper and Kleinschmidt [11]. Cooper, in personal correspondence, says his research proves that the best way to save time is to do the job right the first time.)

During the entire product development process decisions are calculated risks. We lack certainty in everything. Risks by definition are occasionally costly, yet proponents of APD claim speed is associated with *lower* costs. Speeding up must be used only in those cases where experience permits *reduction* of risk.

We went through the same thing early in the life of Critical Path Scheduling, where parallel processing was used to squeeze the time dimension; but we only overlapped steps when we were quite sure there would not be a problem (or where there was no interdependence between the steps and thus shouldln't have been sequenced in the first place). This means information already in hand.

APD requires that at many steps in the process the natural desire for additional information must be squashed, even if that one piece of information is customer acceptance. So one critical hidden cost is the cost of failure; and it will be there, unless the projects are so safe there is no risk.

Hidden Cost #3: A Surprisingly Negative and Disruptive Side to New Styles of Small-Team Management Sometimes Appears. It Can Boost People Costs.

Accelerated product development apparently demands interfunctional teams as the mechanism by which traditional bureaucratic encumbrances are overriden; but a team system can by tricky. For example, teams are used to gain added flexibility (outside the bureaucracy) yet teams also may be very *in*flexible. The team's assignment has to be unidirectional, and we know a strongly commissioned team will indeed market a new product, whether ready or not. After all, that was its assignment, and promotions and salary increases will come accordingly. Team members with fire in their bellies don't dally.

This is myopia within flexibility, the same as discussed earlier in connection with integrated manufacturing systems. One technique that aids APD is the early elimination of options—reducing the number of alternatives kept open in the development process. This increases one's vulnerability to the moves and countermoves of competitive firms, thus weakening the accuracy of demand forecasts.

APD teams are necessarily small if they are to move fast. The operating style is that fringe people are invited into the clubhouse from time to time, but mainly it is team members who make forays outside the clubhouse when they need some specific help. Thus it is not surprising that small teams sometimes report rejection and noncooperation by support groups. Smallness also leads to elitism, especially on venture teams. What is the effect on the attitudes and work habits of people just not quite on the team? What do they think when the team members get the big rewards—the ones associated with successful APD projects?

Teams also have leaders, and we're seeing impressive new methods of team leadership—healthy, positive, dynamic, indirect. Yet when published accounts of team actions part the curtains, we often see the shadow of a dictator. When push comes to shove, democracy is weak. That Frito-Lay CEO (above) was described by one of his staff: "When he stepped things up he didn't care who he stepped *on*." What are the hidden costs of 14-hour days? Many readers, for example will recall the vivid and devastating personal pains disclosed in *The Soul of a New Machine,* the story of a new minicomputer development at Data General [28]. Some team members suspect *speeding*-up is the old-time assembly line *speed*-up in a new costume. It will be interesting as researchers get into this new type of team and find out what participants really think, and more important, what personal risks and added efforts they are willing to put out, and for how long. Sustainability is suspect.

Some team leaders have already had multiple success stories and eagerly seek new team assignments. Others can't wait to get off the team. How many 12-month projects can the average manager survive? Assuming that the damage is mental, how can it be assessed? Isn't there burnout, and if so, isn't the manager under pressure not to show it, especially if the rewards go to the hare, not the tortoise? Such practice is questionably cost-effective. Too, we are entering an era of limited supply of skilled workers: is this the best way to use them?

Even where team leaders want to avoid excessive pressure, and know full well how to generate positive teamwork, there are costs that managements may object to. Digital Equipment Corporation, for example appointed an experienced leader for their computer-mouse project (mentioned above) who immediately asked for a 30-day orientation period; team members would get acquainted, socialize and prepare to work together. He got his wish, and the project was more than successful, but how many managements would cut normal time from two years to one, and then allow the first month to be spent in backyard barbecues and hikes in the woods?

Of no less significance, and still hidden, are the indirect costs of teams—such as people being pulled off other work, special handling by top management, reintegrating team members back into the regular organization upon failure or completion of the team's assignment and forcing the solo players to live a loner's life in a team world. Steve Sakoman, Apple hardware developer, indicated the problems such people may face when he said that today's rugby players (on fast teams) should not be the "stereotypical engineer who sits off in a corner, never goes home and sleeps on a mat" [47].

Hidden Cost #4: Unexpected Inefficiencies Result When the Process of Innovation Warps under Pressure; the Various Steps Don't Respond Evenly to Cuts in the Time Budget.

In recent years we have seen great progress in creating an effective and efficient product innovation process. (Several such studies have already been cited. One in particular involves the concept of stage-gate [9].) That process is still evolving, and needs experimentation; it can be warped and distorted under pressure. When pushed, we tend to make do with what we have, rather than developing the right tools and other resources. The new product may call for a special sales force, distributed field service capability, a stand-by plan if anticipated problems come up during launch so on. These are obstacles to be overcome, and any one may kill chances to hit the deadline. When so, it is difficult to resist the temptation to proceed as though these needs do not exist.

Even ideation can suffer. Active, purposeful ideation is at the heart of successful innovation. Nothing, absolutely nothing, beats having an important customer problem to deal with—new products people want to market solutions to problems, not solutions looking for problems or solutions that aren't quite solutions. Teams in a hurry tend to work from suggestions already on the table (from the sales force, product management, engineering or wherever).

Innovation is a process of defining an objective (performance, feature, customer saving or the like) and then evolving something that will achieve the objective. The process is *focused creativity,* not shooting in the dark. A push for speed early in a project tends to diffuse our picture of the objective—if we don't take the time to make it clear, requirements will change constantly under pressure, and scientists and engineers have to shoot at moving targets. Thus almost all people offering advice on APD urge that time be spent at the beginning to make sure the target is clear and achievable. To save time, we either have to make the target very simple (incremental innovation) or accept partial innovation. Some call this *continuing compromise* (e.g., dropping from three forms of the new item to just one, with the others to follow "soon"). Unless the followers are well into development when the first one is launched, this is not a valid process [12].

Hidden Cost #5: A Firm's Complex Set of Support Resources Can Get Chewed up by Pressure from Players on Speeded-up Teams.

Teams make use of many other people and systems. Even within a team, there will occasionally be scientists who are forced to cave in or get out. There are others for whom there isn't adequate training and orientation time, and others whose inability to handle risk makes them a psychological mismatch. Teams also require people who are good communicators and effective teammates, but there is a worldwide shortage of such people. What does intense team participation do to people who are simply not good team people?

Even if there are no basic attitude changes by the participants, we can certainly expect behavioral ones. Players will learn how to survive; messengers who carry bad news do indeed get shot. Where, for example, were the top executives at Frito-Lay who felt they had no recourse but to let the new CEO overhaul a well-functioning product innovation system? We don't know the internal dynamics, of course, and perhaps they tried, but given threatening environments, some managers with good potential find those places in the firm where there is less pressure, or they begin giving management and the team what it wants, hiding the real costs as necessary.

Once an operation really commits to acceleration, would it be "bad news" that an exciting longer-term discovery was made in the lab, and would this information have to be squelched? Managers may opt against becoming a champion for it—indeed, may purposely distance themselves from it.

Then we have the people who work in staff service departments (packaging, legal, government, human resources, quality and so on) who find it difficult to charge off the "costs" of speed. For example, we really don't know what behavioral changes rapid introduction of incremental products brings about in a sales force.

What has just been said is speculative. We lack good research in this area, but the nature of the speeded-up system is such that many of the human costs will for a long time be hidden.

Perhaps more obvious, but also costly, are the negative effects on suppliers, who often must cooperate closely in these accelerated programs. (This includes suppliers of R&D, as well as of materials and parts. See Souder and Nassar [45]. IBM seeks finished software this way [26].) Must they write off the added costs associated with speeding up by giving less service and assistance to other lines and developments and by coming up with fewer improvements on their own initiative? One answer is that the APD supplier must in turn seek more innovativeness in its suppliers, but that assumption is fraught with many questions.

Lastly, we cannot forget the customer, where effects can be similar to those on suppliers. Resellers are wary of joining manufacturers' systems, and often are strong enough to force adaptation the other way (Wal-Mart recently made Procter & Gamble bend its logistics system to meet that of the chain). End-users may be happy with short-term incremental innovation, but unwilling to commit to a supplier whose contributions are primarily line extensions. They may want true innovation to help them solve their bigger problems and also to avoid the substantial switching costs associated with this steady "stream of improved products" (such as with office computer systems).

Some of the Arguments for Accelerated Product Development Are Very Weak

The opening sections of this article cited the very real and valid reasons for APD. However, much of the talk surrounding this topic verges on hype. Here are four arguments that are very weak indeed.

1. *APD must be good; the Japanese use it.* Auto industry executives and engineers have heard this so much they must have dreams in which their 5's (for years) are magically converted into Honda-Toyota 3's. Most of the Japanese projects done using intensive APD appear to be incremental, but, of course, one person's incrementalism is another person's breakthrough. The developments of the Japanese auto companies demonstrate well the strategic interest many managements put on core technologies [36]. Second, the Japanese gain time by freezing specs early, and then immediately beginning a follow-on project for the improvements delayed by the freezing. They don't reject options, only when they are to be used.

2. *APD must be good; look how XYZ Company did it.* The fact that XYZ did something is worthwhile to know, and many such examples are given in this article, but we need to look at their total experience. For example, reports from firms active in APD often are laced with phrases like "be realistic," "don't be overly ambitious," "don't try to make advances in too many areas at once" and "our worst disasters have come when we rushed out with a product in time to hit the show." All of these suggest rather major cost problems just below the surface. Further, there is no evidence that anyone has bothered to look at what was postponed or dropped in order that the favored project could be rushed to market, and it is impossible to assess the long-term consequences (good or bad).

3. *APD must be good; look at the close teamwork, the customer involvement and so on.* In this reasoning, APD writers tend to take credit for any innovations in the innovation process. For example, we now hear that R&D directors are asking their staffs of scientists to scout out around their firms and find applications for their new technolo-gies. This is fine; there are many ways of "selling" R&D, and there will be more, but they should be used regardless of the speed dimensions of particular projects.

Another example concerns involvement of the customer: proponents of APD claim that faster development equals higher quality, but along the way they have the teams work closely with the customer. It is a pity that speed has to be the lever to get us to do what we should be doing all the time, on all of our projects—that is, building new products on the solving of customer problems.

Other APD programs have included selling all participants on the importance of the project and getting top management to personally order cooperation by all parties. These efforts will almost guarantee a launch, but pulling out all stops means overriding budgets and other programs. The costs become hidden only because we don't calculate them; and we sometimes don't look too closely at the failure rates of such "top-down" products.

4. *APD must be good; order-of-market-entry data show it pays to be first.* There are no such data, except those that assume the second and third entries have comparable products. Given second tier adaptive innovation (which second and third entries should always have) shares are determined by the quality of those improvements. The literature is full of testimony to this. (Two of the better articles on this subject are Lilien and Yoon [31] and Robinson [39]. The latter article has an excellent bibliography. Readers should note that definitions in this area of study permit seemingly conflicting interpretations of the data.) Moreover, don't confuse order-of-entry with speed. Order-of-entry studies imply that to be first, one must be fast, but this isn't necessarily true. Speed is probably most essential to early followers, as they jockey for shares and try to overtake the pioneer. We talk a lot about famous pioneers (3M's Post-it Notes, Birdseye frozen vegetables, and Federal Express overnight delivery), but we forget such winning nonpioneers as IBM computers, Texas Instrument transistors and hand calculators, Matsushita VCRs, Kimberly Clark Huggies, Bartles & James wine coolers and hundreds more. The picture is a mix: Who would have thought that Anheuser Busch couldn't overtake Miller Lite; who would have expected RCA to lose its pioneering position in color TV [22]?

Research data here yield little truth, given the vagaries of business conditions, regulation, competitive product differentiation, price ploys and the like.

APD success stories from industry have almost all concerned early attempts. They are very encouraging, and so were the experiments at Western Electric's Hawthorn plant 65 years ago. The "Hawthorn effect" is widely documented, so we should be sure the fifth, 10th, and 20th APD projects work out before we jump to conclusions. There may be added costs of keeping teams dedicated after the novelty and attention have worn off. Also, what works on a limited scale can fail badly when applied on a larger scale. We should be careful not to evaluate strategically what is essentially a tactical tool.

Recently we have been reading McKinsey & Co. data which show that to be late, but on budget, loses more money than to come in on time and over budget. (The original report on this study was by Reinertsen [38] but more recent sources are Dumaine [15] and Smith [43].) What we read are citations of the original publication and they are incomplete. The author of the report, Donald Reinertsen, a McKinsey Associate, actually used his findings to warn the reader: "The new product race does not always go to the swift. Speed is sometimes secondary and, if unduly emphasized, can lead to disaster."

The commonly cited data about lateness costing more profits than being over budget and on time applies only to "high-growth markets, and short product life-cycles." For example, in slower-growth markets, a 9 percent product-cost overrun "resulted in a devastating 45 percent decrease in [life-cycle] profits." In addition, Reinertsen warned, "A company that stresses speed above all else indeed can manage to achieve early profit gains, but the crash program inevitably results in

high product costs, [and] early profits dissolve as margins are squeezed by high costs and rapidly dropping prices." The data were apparently derived in one particular product setting, and with one particular accounting, and the "costs" of being on time included only the amount the project was over budget: researchers excluded the costs sunk in other projects that had to be dumped or permanently delayed while the subject one was being rushed to market. The study also excluded most of the costs discussed in this article.

My point is this: so far we have seen too much specious reasoning and hoopla and not enough hard data from experience over time. It is interesting that Reinertsen is now a leader in urging *responsible* accelerated product development [44].

Some Actions That Will Let a Management Capitalize on a Worthy New Concept Yet at the Same Time Help Hold Down the Hidden Costs

• First, spell out new products strategy clearly, and get understanding and agreement on it. If primarily incremental innovation is desired, say so, but otherwise, what mix of incremental, expansion and breakthrough projects is desired? Should the mix vary by market, by company profitability level and so on? Under the stress of day-to-day business the APD projects carry big sticks—other projects need firm management support to stay on their course. APD fits especially well with lines that have short life-cycles, low switching costs, ease of customer understanding on new features and reduced barriers to entry.

• Second, review constantly to see if the innovation mix desired is being achieved. Study progress reports, time schedules, and people's feelings. There may be more hidden "bad news" than realized, especially if the organization has given a lot of publicity to its adoption of accelerated product development. Changes in the firm's accounting system may be necessary [32].

• Third, select two typical APD projects that have run their course and hold post-mortems. Postmortem is an unfortunate term, as technically it applies to products that fail, but there may be "failure" even in what appears to be a winner, so the process is the same. In addition to the most important issue of method, check specifically for burnout, repressions and dictators. This may be tough to do, given the pressurized environment of APD, but it is relevant information.

• Fourth, keep asking for evidence that APD projects offer genuine benefits to the customer. Does the customer agree there is usable value added? This protects against the tendency for speeded-up projects to compromise on key benefits.

• Fifth, pick one project and have an independent party try to assess the true hidden costs. This effort will defy the accounting system, but judgments can be made if the proper investigator can be found.

• Sixth, taking into consideration the hidden costs discussed in this article, manage the APD program in a way to avoid the biggest problems. This means (1) keep one eye clearly on the slower-moving breakthrough programs and ask about their problems, (2) keep asking for evidence that key speeded-up decisions are information-based, (3) have someone on staff who understands product innovation and is independent of the time pressures faced by the teams and (4) check to see that suppliers are not being asked to pay too high a price to play on your teams.

• Seventh, if contemplating putting an accelerated program into action, be sure the overall product innovation system to be changed is itself a good one. Several recent research studies indicate that more time may be saved by having a good overall system than by trying to fine-tune a defective system [10, 21, 42]. As one report put it, "The most common mistake made in product development programs is failing to execute all the steps." The report added that skipping steps and doing them in illogical order will "produce a large percentage of false starts, program delays, budget overruns, late product introductions and program cancellations" [42].

CONCLUSION

This article has taken as given that accelerated product development is virtually a revolution in product innovation management. We have seen the practice spread, and the reports are generally encouraging. Taking unnecessary time out of a development project strengthens the overall competitiveness of an organization. Product innovativeness offers a long list of advantages.

Unfortunately, the APD revolution is spreading too fast. Adherents are overlooking research reports that warn about its limitations. One bundle of limitations relates to what are here called hidden costs. These are sometimes just hidden in an accounting sense (data on them are not usually available), sometimes they are indirect and sometimes they are opportunity costs.

The potential payoff for speeding up the product innovation process is too great to have success riding on what so far has been mainly anecdotal evidence and on management's hope that there are no significant hidden costs. This article has attempted to spell out the various types of hidden costs that exist, and proposes some actions managements can take to reduce the chances of a major blind siding.

REFERENCES

1. Arnold U, Barnard KN: Just-In-Time: some marketing issues raised by a popular concept in production and distribution. *Technovation* 9(5):401–431, 1989.
2. Barr V: Six steps to smoother product design. *Mech Engng*, pp 48–51, Jan 1990.
3. Beauchamp M: Learning from disaster. *Forbes*, pp 96–97, Oct 19, 1987.
4. Bertrand K: New product success starts with homework. *Bus Marketing*, pp 36–38, Aug 1988.
5. Booz-Allen and Hamilton: *New Product Management for the 1980s*. New York, 1982.
6. Bower JL, Hout TM: Fast-cycle capability for competitive power. *Harvard Bus R* 66(6):110–118, Nov–Dec 1988.
7. Bylinsky G: Turning R&D into real products. *Fortune*, pp 72–77, Jul 2, 1990.
8. Cooper RG: New product success in industrial firms. *Ind Marketing Mgt* 11:215–223, 1982.

9. Cooper RG: Stage-gate systems: A new tool for managing products. *Bus Horizons* 33(3):44–54, May–Jun 1990.

10. Cooper RG, Kleinschmidt EJ: An investigation into the new product process: steps, deficiencies and impact. *J Prod Innovation Mgt* 3(2):71–85, Jun 1986.

11. Cooper RG, Kleinschmidt EJ: Resource allocation in the new product process. *Ind Marketing Mgt* 17(3):261–262, Aug 1988.

12. Crawford CM: How product innovators can tore-close the options of adaptive followers. *J Consumer Marketing* 5(4):17–24, Fall 1988.

13. Crawford CM: New product failure rates: a reprise. *Res•Tech Mgt* 30(4):20–24, Jul–Aug 1987.

14. Crawford CM: The dual drive concept of product innovation. *Bus Horizons* 34(3):32–37, May–Jun 1991.

15 Dumaine B: How managers succeed through speed. *Fortune,* pp 54–59, Feb 13, 1989.

16. Emshwiller JR: Suppliers struggle as big firms slash their vendor rolls. *Wall St J, p B1, Aug 16, 1991.*

17. Fannin R: Frito-Lay: The binge is over. *Marketing & Media Decisions,* pp 54–60, Apr 1987.

18. Gerber B: Speed: where the people fit in. *Training* 27, Aug 1989.

19. Gold B: Approaches to accelerating product and process development. *J Prod Innovation Mgt* 4(2):81–88, Jun 1987.

20. Gomory RE, Schmitt RW: Step-by-step innovation. *Across the Board,* pp 52–56, Nov 1988.

21. Gupta A, Wilemon DL: Accelerating the development of technology-based new products. *Calif Mgt R* 33(2):24–44, Winter 1990.

22. Haines DW. Chandran R, Parkhe A: Winning by being the first to market ... or second? *J Consumer Marketing* 6(1):63–69, Winter 1989.

23. Hall, Jr. EH: Just-in-time management: a critical assessment. *Academy of Mgt Exec* 3(4):315–317, Nov 1989.

24. Hooper L: Xerox tries to shed its has-been image with big new machine. *Wall St J,,* pp A1, Sep 20, 1990.

25. Hopkins DS: *New Product Winners and Losers.* The Conference Board, New York, 1980.

26. IBM extending its reach. *Software M,* pp 21–23, Mar 1988.

27. Industrial Research Institute's Annual R&D Trends Survey. *Res•Tech Mgt* 34 (1):12–14, Jan–Feb 1991.

28. Kidder JT: *The Soul of a New Machine,* Little Brown, Boston, MA, 1981.

29. Kleinfield NR: How "Strykeforce" beat the clock. *NY Times,* Sect 3, p 1, Mar 25, 1990.

30. Krubasik EG: Customize your product development. *Harvard Bus R* 66(6): 46–52, Nov–Dec 1988.

31. Lillien GL, Yoon E: The timing of competitive market entry: an exploratory study of new industrial products. *Mgt Sct* 36(5): 568–584, May 1990.

32. Main J: The winning organization. *Fortune,* pp 50–60, Sep 26, 1988.

33. Naj AK: GE's latest invention: A way to move ideas from lab to market. *Wall St J,* p A1, Jun 19, 1990.

34. Nayak PR: Planning speeds technological development. *Planning R* 18(6): 14–19, Nov–Dec 1990.

35. O'Boyle TF: GE refrigerator woes illustrate the hazards in changing a product; firm pushed development of compressor too fast, failed to test adequately. *Wall St J,* A1, May 7, 1990.

36. Prahalad CK, Hamel G: The core competence of the corporation. *Harvard Bus R* 68(3): 79–91, May–Jun 1990.

37. Reiner G: Winning the race for new product development. *Mgt R* 78(8):52–53, Aug 1989.

38. Reinertsen DG: Whodunit? The search for new-product killers. *Electronic Bus,* pp 62–66, Jul 1983.

39. Robinson WT: Product innovation and start-up business market share performance. *Mgt Sci* 36(10): 1279–1289, Oct 1990.

40. Rosenau, Jr. MD: Faster new product development. *J Prod Innovation Mgt* 5(2): 150–153, Jun 1988.

41. Rosenau, Jr. MD: *Faster New Product Development,* AMACOM, New York, 1990.

42. Rudolph SE, Lee WD: Lessons from the field. *R&D M,* p 119+ , Oct 1990.

43. Smith PG: Winning the new products rat race. *Machine Design,* pp 95–98, May 12, 1988.

44. Smith PG, Reinertsen DG: *Developing Products in Half the Time,* Van Nostrand Reinhold, New York, 1991.

45. Souder WE, Nassar S: Choosing an R&D consortium. *Res•Tech Mgt* 33(2):35–41, Mar–Apr 1990.

46. Stalk, Jr. G, Hout TM: Competing against time. *Res•Tech Mgt* 33(2): 19–24, Mar–Apr 1990.

47. Uttal B: Speeding new ideas to market. *Fortune,* pp 62–66, Mar 2, 1987.

48. Vogel T: At Xerox they're shouting "once more into the breach." *Bus Week,* p 62 + , Jul 23, 1990.

6

MANAGING TECHNOLOGICAL INNOVATION

16

Managing the Marketing/ Technology Interface for New Product Development

46

Managing Relations between R&D and Marketing in New Product Development Projects

WILLIAM E. SOUDER

INTRODUCTION

Research and development (R&D) and marketing personnel depend on each other for the creation of new product innovations. Yet R&D and marketing departments have frequent misunderstandings and conflicts.

Many managers have first-hand experience with R&D/marketing interface problems and behaviors between R&D and marketing groups have been carefully studied [3,5,7–11]. However, much more information is needed about this complex and important topic. This paper examines the R&D/marketing interface conditions found at 289 new product development innovation projects. Based on these findings, strategies and guidelines are presented for improving the relationships between R&D and marketing groups.

Reprinted by permission of the publisher from "Managing Relations Between R&D and Marketing in New Product Development Projects," by William E. Souder, *Journal of Product Innovation Management*, 1988, Vol. 5, pp. 6–19. Copyright 1988 by Elsevier Science Co., Inc.

William Souder is Professor of Management at the University of Alabama Business School.

About the Data Base

Data: Life cycle data were collected on 289 new product development innovation projects at 53 consumer and industrial product firms [7–10]. The data collection focused on project events, with detailed attention given to organization structures, environments, climates, behavioral processes and project success/failure factors. The ultimate objective was to understand development processes for new product innovations.

Sample of Firms: Using published statistics, an industry by industry compilation was made of firms with significant new product activities in either consumer or industrial goods. Target firms were then randomly selected from this list, based on a compromise design that carefully considered the cost of traveling to distant sites and the need to maintain representivity on several important dimensions [7–10]. Approximately five firms were selected from each of the following ten industries: metals, glass, transportation (includes automotive and mass transit), plastics, machinery, electronics (includes computers and instruments), chemicals, food, aerospace and pharmaceuticals.

Sample of Projects: Using carefully specified definitions, the population of new product innovation projects initiated during the preceding five years was assembled at each firm. A random sampling of equal numbers of success and failure outcome projects was taken from these populations at each firm, while maintaining a range of types of technologies, types of innovations, degrees of difficulty of projects, central vs. divisional R&D efforts, and several other important dimensions [7–10]. Several ongoing projects whose success or failure outcomes were unknown at that time were intentionally included in this sampling. Following these procedures, approximately 10% of each firm's portfolios were selected into the 289 project sample studied here.

Data Collection: A total of 27 instruments, numerous telephone interviews and 584 in-depth face-to-face interviews were carried out on each project to record the life cycle histories and extract the relevant data on each of the 289 projects [7–10]. A cascading interview procedure was used to cross-validate information collected from each marketing, R&D and other subject on each project [7–10].

Methodology of This Study

This study was carried out on a comprehensive data base of life cycle information on 289 new product development innovation projects. The data were collected through ten years of intensive field research at 56 consumer and industrial products firms [7–10]. The Box "About the Data Base" and Table 46.1 present the methodology and the project outcome measurement scales used in collecting that data base.

The 289-project data base contains numerous detailed descriptions and ratings of key events, activities, attitudes and behaviors of the R&D and marketing personnel who worked on each project. As part of the content analyses, statistical reduction and factor analyses of this large data base [1,2,4], these items were reduced to 42 attitudinal and behavioral descriptors of the R&D/marketing interface. Some examples of these descriptors are "Frequency of Joint Meetings," "Frequency of Joint Customer Visits," "Degree of Perceived Need to Interact," and "Degree of Regard for the Other Party's Competency."

Each of the 289 projects was rated on each of these descriptors. Some of these ratings came directly from the instruments, while others were developed through content analyses of the interviews [1,2,7–10]. Redundancies were built in at several points. For example, the "Frequency of Joint Meetings" was primarily measured by questionnaire items that asked for the number of times per year that joint meetings were held. Details about these joint meetings were solicited during the interviews. Differences greater than 10% in the questionnaire responses of the marketing, R&D and other personnel on the same project were reconciled during the interviews. As another example, the "Degree of Perceived Need to Interact" was primarily measured by asking pointed questions of the respondents during the interviews. The information from the interviews was then checked against the Likert-type scale ratings supplied on the questionnaires. Apparent disparities were resolved by returning to the subjects to clarify their responses and ratings. This type of multi-method, multitrait measurement approach is commonly used to maximize the validity of social science measurements [4].

A profile of ratings was thus developed for each of the 289 projects. Some of these profiles appeared to be very similar; others appeared to be very dissimilar. Statistical cluster analyses techniques were then applied to the profiles in order to exhaustively cluster the projects by the various types of profiles that were found [2,4].

SEVEN R&D/MARKETING INTERFACE STATES

Using a 95% statistical significance level, seven different clusters were found from the cluster analysis. Each cluster was then labeled according to its observed items. For example, a review of the items in one cluster showed that it was characterized by a low frequency of meetings between the R&D and marketing personnel, highly specialized and organizationally separated R&D and marketing functions, and a low degree of perceived need to interact. Therefore, the label "Lack of Interaction" was coined to describe this R&D/marketing interface state of affairs. Twenty-two of the 289 projects, or 7.6% of the sample, exhibited this state. Similarly, the other states and percentages shown in Table 46.2 were found and accordingly labeled.

TABLE 46.1
Project Outcome Measurement Scale

| | Success outcomes | |
| | Descriptors | |
Degrees of success	**Technical outcomes**	**Commercial outcomes**
High	Breakthrough	Blockbuster
Medium	Enhancement	Above expectations
Low	Met the specs	Met expectations

| | Failure outcomes | |
| | Descriptors | |
Degrees of failure	**Technical outcomes**	**Commercial outcomes**
Low	Learned a lot	Below expectations
Medium	Gained some technology	Protected our position but lost money
High	Complete dud	Took a bath we won't forget

Other outcome

SE = Stopped the effort early due to poor progress

TABLE 46.2
Incidence of Harmony and Disharmony States

States	Percentage of projects experiencing each state
Mild Disharmony	
Lack of interaction	7.6%
Lack of communication	6.6
Too-good friends	6.3
Subtotal	20.5
Severe Disharmony	
Lack of appreciation	26.9
Distrust	11.8
Subtotal	38.7
Disharmony total	59.2
Harmony	
Equal partner	11.7
Dominant partner	29.1
Harmony total	40.8
Overall total	100%

Several firms that experienced the Lack of Interaction, Lack of Communication and Too-Good Friends problems on the projects studied here avoided these states on some subsequent projects. Follow-up studies with these firms showed that they overcame these states through modest efforts. These efforts included more frequent joint meetings, joint involvements in planning proposed projects and increased sharing of information. Moreover, though these problems often lowered the organization's new product development effectiveness, they were not totally disruptive and they seldom led to major project failures. Therefore, as shown in Table 46.2, these problems were labeled 'mild'. By contrast, the Lack of Appreciation and Distrust problem states were labeled 'severe'. Follow-up studies showed that these types of problems were not easily overcome, they usually caused operating disruptions, consumed many hours of managerial talent in moderating disputes, delayed key actions and important decisions and led to project failures.

Many other projects were found that did not exhibit either mild or severe disharmonies. As shown in Table 46.2, these projects were considered to be in a 'harmony' state.

CHARACTERISTICS OF THE MILD DISHARMONY STATES

Lack of Interaction

In this state of affairs, there were very few formal and informal meetings between the R&D and marketing personnel. Both parties were deeply concerned with their own narrow specialties and neither saw any reason to learn more about the other's work. Neither party saw the need for close interaction. R&D expected marketing to use whatever they gave them, and marketing expected R&D to create useful products.

This state resulted more from simple neglect than from any strong animosities between the parties. For example, one subject noted: "You get busy and you don't stop to think about whether or not they should know about this or that. . . . when you have to get your part of the job done." Another subject said: "If you don't get used to seeing each other you don't miss each other, and if you don't think about each other you don't make any effort to get together. And you always have to make an effort." It may be noted that several projects experiencing the Lack of Interaction state were in older, commodity product firms that were attempting to develop new product lines. Most of these firms had no histories of close R&D/marketing interactions.

Lack of Communication

In this state, the two parties purposely maintained verbal, attitudinal, and physical distances from each other. R&D purposely did not inform marketing about their new technologies until very late in the development cycle. Marketing purposely did not keep R&D informed about market needs. This occurred because neither party felt the other had much information of significant value. And neither felt it was important to inform the other of the details of their own work. This state was aptly summed up in the comments of one respondent. "If we told them all this, they wouldn't know what to do with it. . . . We know more about it than they do. Our best source of information comes from right here, from ourselves." Note how this state of affairs is different from the above Lack of Interaction syndrome, where the perceived urgency of pursuing their own activities caused the parties to neglect each other. Here, both parties harbored negative feelings about the worth of the other that stood in the way of interaction.

Though various causes of the Lack of Communication state were observed within the data base, two experiences repeatedly lead directly to this problem. One was the perceived theft of credit. When either party took what the other thought was undue credit for meritorious project achievements, this inevitably led to a Lack of Communication problem. The impression that the other party had taken unfair advantage was long remembered. Another experience that frequently led to the Lack of Communication state was top management's uneven use of accolades. If top management praised one party and did not praise the other, rivalry invariably developed that shut off some future communication. As one subject noted: "If we don't tell them anything, they can't go to management and take credit for it."

Too-Good Friends

In this state of affairs, the R&D and marketing personnel were too friendly and maintained too high a regard for each other. They enjoyed each other's company so much that they frequently met socially, outside the work environment. These social affairs often included the individual's families, e.g., family picnics and Sunday afternoon socials were common. In most of the Too-Good Friends cases, work and social aspects were commingled, e.g., joint visits to customer facilities might also involve a round of golf and the Sunday afternoon socials always included some informal discussion of business. Each party felt that the other had their own area of exclusive expertise, and that the other was beyond reproach. This inhibited each party from challenging the other's assumptions and judgments. Consequently, important information and subtle observations were overlooked that were significant for the project.

What factors led to this type of problem? Surprisingly, past successes sometimes led the team members to become too-good friends. Teams of R&D and marketing personnel who had worked together successfully for long periods of time often became complacent. Their potency appeared to decline once they had achieved complete harmony. Apparently, they needed some conflicts or the challenge of building harmonious relationships to maintain their alertness. A related factor was a kind of blind faith in the correctness of the counterpart person. As one respondent observed: "You are always sort of reluctant to challenge and question what your colleague tells you. He's the expert in that area. And you don't expect that he'll play politics with you, so there's no reason to question his integrity. And you figure he's the best man you've got, so he probably won't steer you wrong."

A detailed examination of the other clusters of projects showed that past successes and great faith in each other also characterized effective R&D/marketing interfaces, i.e., the Equal Partner Harmony state in Table 46.2. What were the distinguishing factors? The answer appears to be a matter of interpersonal dynamics. The parties to an effective interface always challenged and penetratingly questioned each other. They appeared to enjoy and thrive on this aspect, sometimes with impish good humor. When one partner found a gap in the other's logic, both partners were suddenly energized to close that gap. Such experiences further strengthened their relationship. The partner who committed the logic gap never seemed to suffer any loss of prestige in the other's eyes. Rather, the ambience was described by one partner as "a climate where we look for flaws, and it's not important who committed the flaw. We just want to find it and work together to fix it." This is clearly a different climate from the above Too-Good Friends state.

It should be noted that such professional disagreements and challenging behaviors, that often characterize effective R&D/marketing interfaces, may give the outside observer the mistaken impression of disharmony and strife. Professional disagreement appears to be a very healthy and enlightening climate for its members. At times, such disagreements may seem to become very heated and destructive. Yet if these discussions are confined to the issues and do not become personally threatening to the participants, they can actually strengthen the R&D/marketing interface. Thus, it is the lack of professional disagreement (Too-Good Friends) that constitutes disharmony, and not its presence.

CHARACTERISTICS OF THE SEVERE DISHARMONY STATES

Lack of Appreciation

This state was characterized by strong feelings that the other party was relatively useless. Marketing felt that R&D was too sophisticated, while R&D felt that marketing was too simplistic. Marketing felt that R&D should be prohibited from visiting customers because they would talk over their heads. R&D felt that marketing did not have a good grasp of the market needs. In this state, the marketing groups often purchased their R&D work outside the firm rather than use the in-house R&D group. R&D often independently moved ahead with its own ideas, by-passing marketing and attempting to launch their own new products. These efforts seldom succeeded, and the failures were usually rationalized by the R&D personnel as marketing's fault for failing to assist them!

What caused the Lack of Appreciation? No single cause was identified. Some cases had long remembered histories of ineffectiveness by one party, e.g., R&D failed to develop the promised product or marketing failed to correctly identify the market. Sometimes, the organizational climates fostered a lack of appreciation. For example, several respondents indicated that they "never see any signals from management that collaboration is desired." Other respondents noted that "management has not indicated that we are expected to cooperate with them." It is interesting that management must make a special effort to encourage cooperation: it does not seem to be automatic.

The organization of R&D and marketing into separate departments with separate budgets and op-

erations often fostered a lack of appreciation. As evidence, consider the following sampling of statements from personnel at five firms in the Lack of Appreciation state. "We don't have any inputs into their plans and budgets". "They have their own operations and so do we". "We get our rewards from doing our things and they get theirs from something else". "No one is responsible for how it all comes together". "We just go our separate ways."

Distrust

Distrust is the extreme case of deep-seated jealousies, negative attitudes, fears and hostile behaviors. In this state of affairs, marketing felt that R&D could not be trusted to follow instructions. R&D felt they were blamed for failures, but marketing was credited for successes. Several R&D groups in this state feared that marketing wanted to liquidate them. R&D lamented that marketing often attempted to dictate exactly what, where, when and how to do the project, allowing no room for rebuttal and no tolerance for their suggestions. Marketing lamented that when R&D got involved the project disappeared and they never saw it before it was completed, at which point it was seldom what they wanted. Several cases were found where R&D initiated many projects and kept them secret from marketing "so marketing wouldn't kill them before they gained enough strength to move along on their own." Cases were found where marketing brought R&D into the picture only after the product specifications had been finalized "in order to avoid any arguments from R&D about how to do it".

What caused the Distrust state? Though no single cause was found, several important contributing factors were isolated. All the Distrust cases began as either a Lack of Appreciation or a Lack of Communication problem that evolved into Distrust. Many of the Distrust cases were characterized by personality conflicts that top management had allowed to exist for a long time. In some cases, these conflicts had become so institutionalized that even personnel who had not been involved harbored feelings of Distrust. As an example, note the following quote from one respondent, referring to his counterpart in another department. "He once did some things to us. I'm not sure what they were. It all happened before I came into this group. So, you see, you really have to watch out for him." This type of institutionalized Distrust was found surprisingly often.

CHARACTERISTICS OF THE HARMONY STATES

Equal Partner Harmony

In this state, each party appeared to share equally in the work loads, activities and rewards. Each party felt free to call joint meetings on almost any issue. These meetings were characterized by an open given and take of facts, opinions and feelings. No issues were left unresolved and consensus was sought by everyone. Study committees and task forces with joint memberships were common, with the task force chairmanships rotated between the R&D and marketing personnel. Moreover, it was part of the Equal Partner culture to involve R&D and marketing personnel jointly in all customer visits, customer follow-ups, customer service, new product planning and forecasting, project selection and product strategy formulation activities.

Three features were common to all the Equal Partner cases. One, the marketing personnel were technically trained. They all had undergraduate degrees in science or engineering. Two, the marketing personnel had prior careers in R&D. Thus, personnel were often successfully exchanged or rotated between the R&D and marketing functions. Three, the R&D and marketing personnel had a strong sense of joint partnership. As evidence, note the following sampling of quotes collected from R&D and marketing personnel in Equal Partner states. "We couldn't get along without them". "We're on the phone with each other constantly". "I feel like I've known them a long time". "We've been through 'thick and thin' together."

Dominant Partner Harmony

In this state, one of the parties was content to let the other lead. Both R&D-dominant and marketing-dominant cases were found. For example, one

R&D subject in a marketing-dominant case noted: "We have no idea at all what the market needs are. But if they'll tell us what they want and supply the specs we can sure make it for them." A marketing respondent in an R&D-dominant case said: "We can usually sell what R&D gives us. We don't really know what they are able to come up with. They know what it takes to make a good performing product better than we do."

It may be noted that the dominant partner cases seldom involved complex technologies, exacting customer needs or large R&D efforts. Most of these cases involved developmental efforts as opposed to research efforts. This reinforces the notion that problems at the R&D/marketing interface escalates as the technology or the user's environment become more complex.

INCIDENCE, SEVERITY AND CONSEQUENCES OF DISHARMONY

As the percentages in Table 46.2 show, a surprisingly high incidence of R&D/marketing disharmony was found. Nearly two-thirds (59.2%) of the projects studied here experienced some type of R&D/marketing interface disharmony. Moreover, it is especially disconcerting that over one-third (38.7%) of the projects studied here experienced severe disharmonies. These results are statistically significant at the 99.9% level of confidence (using the binomial statistical test [6]). That is, a statistically significant number of projects were found to be experiencing disharmonies. And a statistically significant number of these projects had severe disharmonies.

But is disharmony disruptive to project success? Table 46.3 responds to this question. Most of the Harmony projects succeeded. Partial success characterized the Mild Disharmony projects. And most of the Severe Disharmony projects failed. As noted in Table 46.3, these results evidence a statistically significant relationship between the degree of harmony/disharmony and the degree of project success/failure. This relationship is significant at greater than the 99.9% confidence level. Thus,

TABLE 46.3
Distribution of Project Outcomes by Harmony/Disharmony States

States	Percentage of projects in each state exhibiting each outcome[a]		
	Success	Partial success	Failure
Harmony	52%	35%	13%
Mild disharmony	32	45	23
Severe disharmony	11	21	68

χ^2 statistic = 88.84, significant at <.001

[a]The following definitons are used, based on Table 46.1:

Success =	High plus Medium Degrees of Commercial Success (Blockbuster plus above Expectations)
Partial Success =	Low Degree of Commercial Success plus low Degree of Commercial Failure (Met Expectations plus Below Expectations)
Failure =	Medium plus High Degrees of Commercial Failure (Protected Our Position But Lost Money, plus Took a Bath We won't Forget)

these results demonstrate that the quality of the R&D/marketing interface effects the degree of success of new product development efforts.

A case-by-case examination of the data base revealed many informative details underlying the results in Table 46.3. In many of the projects experiencing the Too-Good Friends problem, important information was overlooked that severely diminished the effectiveness of the end products. In many of the projects experiencing the Lack of Communications problem, the new products either did not match the market needs or failed to meet some important customer specification. In about half of the projects with Lack of Interaction problems, the end products either did not perform as originally planned or arrived too late to capture a rapidly changing market. Thus, Mild Disharmonies generally depreciated the degree of success of the end products. But they seldom resulted in dismal product failures.

By contrast, in a majority of the projects experiencing Lack of Appreciation problems, the end products either failed to perform or they were not cost-effective. In many of the projects where Dis-

trust occurred, the products did not perform at all. Thus, Severe Disharmonies resulted in a high frequency of rather dramatic failures. Moreover, it should be noted that Severe Disharmonies were very difficult to overcome. Attempts by management to ameliorate them through negotiation, reorganization, bargaining or personnel transfers often left deep scars and sowed the seeds for a renewed outbreak of similar problems elsewhere. Thus, the prognosis for firms experiencing Severe Disharmonies is unusually pessimistic. Once they appear, their persistence can doom the firm's new product success rate for a long time.

Thus, these results show that the incidence and seriousness of R&D/marketing interface problems are distressingly high. Moreover, many of these problems are chronic, persistent, difficult to correct and seriously detrimental to new product success. These results are both surprising and disappointing. In spite of previous awareness and study of these problems [3,5,7–11], they still persist.

The reader is cautioned to use some care in interpreting these results. As mentioned above in connection with the discussion of the characteristics of the various R&D/marketing interface states, disharmony is a complex facet of human behavior. Professional disagreements, that may appear disharmonious to a casual observer, are often a sign of a very healthy and harmonious interface. The strong statistical relationships found here between disharmony and success do not mean that every disagreement and all apparent disharmonies are bad. One must be very careful in defining what constitutes real disharmony. In fact, the results show that a lack of professional disagreement (Too-Good Friends) may indicate disharmony. Thus, the reader is cautioned to use these results in the context of the definitions of the R&D/marketing states set forth here.

EIGHT GUIDELINES FOR OVERCOMING DISHARMONY

An analysis of the projects in the data base revealed eight practices that alleviated R&D/marketing interface problems. These practices are summarized in the Box of guidelines.

Guidelines for Improving Relations between R&D and Marketing

1. *Break Large Projects into Smaller Ones.* Three-fourths of the projects with nine or more persons assigned to them experienced interface problems. By contrast, projects with five or fewer persons assigned to them seldom experienced problems. The smaller number of individuals and organizational layers on the small projects permitted increased face-to-face contacts, increased empathies and easier coordination.

2. *Take a Proactive Stance toward Interface Problems.* In those cases where potential interface problems were avoided and actual problems were overcome, the parties maintained a posture of aggressively seeking out and facing such problems head-on. They openly criticized and examined their behaviors. As one individual noted: "We don't treat it like a social disease and sweep it under the rug. If we got it, we want to know about it so we can get rid of it."

3. *Eliminate Mild Problems before They Grow into Severe Problems.* All the cases of severe (Lack of Appreciation and Distrust) problems studied here began as mild problems at some earlier points in time. As noted elsewhere in this paper, severe disharmonies were extremely difficult to eliminate. Mild disharmonies were much easier to overcome. Thus, it is wise to eliminate mild problems while they are still mild.

4. *Involve Both Parties Early in the Life of the Project.* Much has been said and written about the benefits from participation and early involvement of the R&D and marketing parties in decision processes [3,5,10,11]. The results here reinforce the conclusion that when R&D and marketing are joint participants to all the decisions, from the start of the project to its completion, Lack of Appreciation and Distrust are lessened.

5. *Promote and Maintain Dyadic Relationships.* A dyad is a very powerful symbiotic, interpersonal alliance between two individuals who become intensely committed to each other and to the joint pursuit of a new product idea [10,11]. Dyads are fostered any time persons with complementary skills and personalities are assigned to work together and given significant autonomy. Dyads are worth promoting not only because they encourage innovation in particular cases, but because they can become the kernel of a much wider circle of interrelationships between R&D and marketing. A successful dyad composed of an R&D person and a marketing person will draw other R&D and marketing personnel onto their bandwagon.

6. *Make Open Communication an Explicit Responsibility of Everyone.* This was dramatically illustrated by the Open Door policy at one of the firms in the data base that had a history of poor R&D/marketing interfaces. This policy consisted of quarterly information meetings between R&D and marketing, day-long and week-long exchanges of personnel, periodic gripe sessions, and the constant encouragement of personnel to visit their counterparts. Every employee was formally charged with the responsibility of playing a role in this Open Door policy. Moreover, each employee's success in meeting this responsibility was formally evaluated at the end of each quarter. The open-door policy survived the initial skepticism that surrounded it, and the examples set by a few diligent individuals eventually spread.

7. *Use Interlocking Task Forces.* A vivid illustration of the use of interlocking task forces was provided by one firm in the data base. The top-level task force or steering committee consisted of the company president, the vice presidents of R&D, marketing, and finance, the project coordinator, the R&D task force leader and the marketing task force leader. The marketing and R&D task force memberships changed as the project metamorphosed over its life cycle. In the early stages of the project, phenomenological research work was carried out by Ph.D. scientists. Application oriented scientists gradually replaced them as the project aged. Finally, engineering personnel replaced them. This interlocking task force structure was repeatedly successfully used by this firm to foster R&D/marketing harmony and new product development success.

8. *Clarify the Decision Authorities.* The decision authority is a kind of charter between R&D and marketing. It governs and guides the R&D/marketing venture by detailing who has the right to make what decisions, under which circumstances. For example, at one firm the policy specified that marketing had the sole authority and responsibility for defining the user's needs.

R&D had the ultimate authority and responsibility for selecting the technical means to meet these needs. R&D and marketing were given the joint responsibility for deciding when an adequate product had been defined. Complaints and appeals to top management could not be made unilaterally by either party. Top management only entertained an audience composed of both parties. A decision authority policy, as well as the group process of developing such a policy, can contribute enormously to clarifying the roles between R&D and marketing. Well-developed decision authority policies were observed at several firms. They fostered a sound foundation for the avoidance of many time-consuming conflicts.

Each of these eight practices reflects an actual experience of one or more firms in the data base. The users contended that the practice significantly increased the harmony of their R&D/marketing interface. In every case, these contentions were borne out by the data. The firm's interface became more harmonious after the practice was implemented.

Each guideline in the Box is effective for managing innovations because it pushes the R&D and marketing parties into a more collaborative, partnership role. The guidelines create conditions in which disharmonies are discouraged and harmonious behaviors are encouraged. Unfortunately, the guidelines do not provide much information about where and when they should be used. For example, when is it best to use guideline #8 (decision authority clarification)? Should guideline #8 always be used, on every project? In order for managers to intelligently apply the guidelines, a framework is needed for analyzing the role needs of the situation and for selecting the guidelines that best meet that need. An attempt to present such a Customer-Developer-Conditions (CDC) framework can be found in Souder (10) and in the original source publication of this article.

SUMMARY AND CONCLUSIONS

Nearly two-thirds of the 289 projects in the data base examined here experienced one of five types of R&D/marketing disharmony. The severity of disharmony was found to be statistically significantly related to the degree of success of innovation projects. Since the data base showed that severe disharmonies were extremely difficult to overcome, it is essential to prohibit their formation.

The results of this research indicate that R&D and marketing managers should jointly work together to help avoid disharmonies in seven ways. First, they should make all their personnel aware that R&D/marketing interface problems naturally occur. Second, they should encourage their personnel to be sensitive to the emergence of R&D/marketing interface problems by watching for the appearance of any characteristics of five types of disharmonies, as discussed above. Early detection is the key to their elimination. Third, managers should be especially careful to give equal credit and public praise to their R&D and marketing personnel in order to eliminate jealousies that might form a basis for severe disharmony. Fourth, R&D and marketing managers must make special efforts to reinforce in words and deeds their desire that the R&D and marketing parties collaborate. They must constantly send signals to their personnel that cooperation is essential. Fifth, managers should use teams of R&D and marketing employees at every opportunity. This will help avoid the natural impression that R&D and marketing are two separate organizational entities and cultures. Sixth, managers must not let personality clashes and other problems remain for so long that they become institutionalized into extremes of distrust. Finally, managers must also be aware that there is such a thing as too much harmony: R&D and marketing personnel can become too complacent with each other.

Outdated role concepts appear to be a major obstacle to achieving R&D/marketing harmony. This study encountered a surprising number of organization structures, organization behaviors, organizational reward systems, product strategies and new product development processes that emphasized a clear separation of roles and specialization of functions between R&D and marketing. This separation was only effective for handling simple technologies, simple markets and well defined customer needs, i.e., the Dominant Partner Harmony case. To successfully develop many types of new product innovations, R&D and marketing must work closely together. In some cases, they must work jointly with the customer in a trial and error fashion, trying various prototypes as a means to discovering the customer's real needs and the appropriate product. In other types of innovations, a true creative process is required in which new information and concepts are generated on the basis of the information shared between members of the R&D/marketing team. In still other cases, it is essential that the parties feel a strong sense of joint responsibility for setting new product goals and priorities, generating and selecting new product ideas, researching and analyzing customer wants, setting product performance requirements, and defining the new product's performance and cost trade-offs.

It appears that the institutionalized roles between R&D and marketing must be radically changed before new product development success rates can significantly increase. The only effective means to permanently avoid disharmonies is for the R&D and marketing parties to fully understand and appreciate their reciprocal roles, and to play out these roles in a true team setting. Moreover, it is essential that the R&D and marketing parties establish a team relationship that permits them to flexibly swap roles in response to evolving technologies, markets and customer needs. Unfortunately, there is as yet no recipe for such role swapping. Each R&D/marketing team must discover what works best for them. The point is: this discovery process can only unfold when the R&D and marketing parties act like a true team.

These conclusions and recommendations are all too familiar. Many firms are not implementing the team approaches and organizational techniques that this research has once again shown to be effective. Disharmonies between R&D and marketing continue to be surprisingly prevalent, chronic and disruptive to successful new product development. These findings are discouraging, in view of the obvious importance of the topic and an emerging awareness of it.

As noted above, the lack of detailed experimental knowledge of R&D/marketing interface problems remains a barrier to their prevention. Far too little is known about what constitutes real disharmony, the distinctions between professional disagreement and disharmony, how to alter the institutionalized roles between R&D and marketing and how to implement new team approaches between R&D and marketing personnel. It is hoped that this broadbased, ex post exploratory field study may provide a convincing basis for more advanced experimental research. Perhaps these results can serve as a basis for deriving empirically based propositions and operational hypotheses, that can then be tested through interventions and administrative experiments in real organizations. The results from these experiments should eliminate the last barrier to informed actions for reducing R&D/marketing interface problems.

REFERENCES

1. Berelson, B. *Content Analysis in Communication Research.* New York: Free Press, 1952.
2. Crollier, D. J. *Pattern Recognition Methods for the Social Sciences and Economics.* Cambridge Press: Cambridge, 1986.
3. Gupta, A. K., Raj, S. P. and Wilemon, D. The R&D-marketing interface in high-technology firms. *Journal of Product Innovation Management.* 2: 12–24, March 1985.
4. Kerlinger, F. N. *Foundations of Behavioral Research.* New York: Holt, Rinehart and Winston, 1973, pp. 514–535, 659–692.
5. Shanklin, W. L. and Ryans, J. K. *Marketing High Technology.* Lexington Books: Lexington, MA, 1984.
6. Siegel, Sidney. *Nonparametric Statistics for the Be-*

havioral Sciences. McGraw-Hill: New York, 1956, pp. 36–42, 175–179, 196–202.

7. Souder, Wm. E., et al., *An Exploratory Study of the Coordinating Mechanisms Between R&D and Marketing as an Influence on the Innovation Process.* Final Report, National Science Foundation Grant 75-17195 to the Technology Management Studies Institute, August 26, 1977.

8. Souder, Wm. E., et al., *A Comparative Analysis of Phase Transfer Methods for Managing New Product Developments*, Final Report, National Science Foundation Grant 79-12927 to the Technol-

ogy Management Studies Institute, August 15, 1983.

9. Souder, Wm. E. *Technology Management Studies Institute Field Instruments Package.* Technology Management Studies Institute, University of Pittsburgh, Pittsburgh, PA 15261, 1987 edition.

10. Souder, Wm. E. *Managing New Product Innovations.* Lexington Books: Lexington, MA, 1987.

11. Young, H. C. *Product Development Setting, Information Exchange, and Marketing-R&D Coupling.* Unpublished Ph.D. dissertation. Northwestern University, Evanston, IL 1973.

47

Engineering's Interactions with Marketing Groups in an Engineering-Driven Organization

JOHN P. WORKMAN, JR.

I. INTRODUCTION

Successful new product development requires firms to link their technical capabilities with products or services which customers want. While many researchers have called for better cross functional integration [11], field researchers have found that marketing and R&D personnel in high-tech firms frequently have difficulties in communicating with one another [4], [7], [35]. There has been relatively little inductive research into the underlying reasons why marketing and R&D groups have a hard time communicating and working with each other. The research reported in this paper was motivated by the desire to better understand the communication issues as seen by people in marketing and R&D groups.

One approach to innovation management, popular in the technology management literature, has used surveys to understand development practices and to identify those practices which lead to more successful development. One of the earlier studies by Dean [6] found that slightly more R&D projects originated in "research and engineering" rather than "sales, marketing, and planning" (33 versus 30), however he did not relate the source of the idea to success. Later work by Myers and Marquis [23] and Utterback [32] presented evidence that most successful new products came from market needs rather than technical opportunities. More recent research has argued that the source of the innovation is less important than the interactions between the groups in product development [2], [3].

Organizational researchers who have studied innovation by using field interviews [15], [24] have also argued for a greater focus on organizational forms to promote creativity and continuous innovation and have been less concerned with where ideas originate.

Another stream of research on organizations and innovation has focused on cross functional communication and "integration" between marketing, R&D, and manufacturing groups. While many studies have focused on theoretical constructs such as integration [21], [27], [36] and conflict between marketing and R&D [12], [28], there has been less study of the actual organizational processes involved in product development. Rather most of the papers on integration have been either conceptual reviews or have used surveys from single informants in the organization and they have not probed social constructions [1] and social processes within firms.

There has been a greater use of field interviews and observation to study organizational processes for product development in the management and strategy fields. Dougherty [7], drawing on field interviews with 80 people on 18 new product teams in five firms, argues that people in various functional groups (such as engineering, production, planning, and the field organization) have different information about customer needs, technical possibilities, and financial consequences. However, these groups tend to focus just on their part of the new product development process, dismiss the contributions of the other groups, and de-

© 1995 IEEE. Reprinted with permission from *IEEE Transactions on Engineering Management*, Vol. 42, No. 2, pp. 129–139, May 1995.

John Workman Jr. is Assistant Professor of Marketing at University of North Carolina's Business School.

fine the entire process from their own perspective. She uses the term "thought worlds" to characterize these varying sense-making contexts and claims that the problem is not really one of conflict:

> ". . . the collaboration problem runs deeper than conflicts over personality types or goals. Indeed, to attempt to resolve the problem through negotiation over goals may only begin to touch on the divergent understandings which lay at the heart of the problem. Nor is the problem like the proverbial blind men touching a different part of an elephant. It is more like the tales of eye witnesses at an accident, or of individuals in a troubled relationship—each tells a 'complete' story, but tells a different one." [7].

A similar portrait of different cultures emerges in one of the few ethnographic accounts of marketing and R&D perspectives in high-tech firms— Dubinskas' [8] account of scientists and managers in biotech firms. Dubinskas uses fieldwork conducted over several years to explore the cultural gap between scientists and managers. In his study, biologists typically have technical backgrounds and work experience in university or private labs while "managers," who represent the business or marketing perspective, typically have MBA's and a background with other entrepreneurial start-ups or with venture capital firms. He explores how the professional training and career socialization of the molecular biologists and the business managers leads to very different "culture-worlds" and different ways of thinking about planning time and development time. Dubinskas' account has a similar theme to Dougherty's—that the technical and business people have different perspectives and the problem is less one of direct conflict over goals but rather that the groups talk past one another.

Recent work in technology management has also focused on the organizational system within which product development takes place. For example, Schmidt and Freeland [29] note that much of the work on project selection has been at the level of individual projects. They argue for studying the overall organizational context and the actual processes by which projects are selected and

note that "the systems approach represents a fundamental shift in emphasis from 'decision events' toward 'decision processes.' " McGuinness [19] has also emphasized that product development should be viewed as "a system of social activities" and that "managers need to be less concerned with such things as formal checklists for idea screening than with the overall health and effectiveness of the social processes that make up the search system."

In summary, while there has been growing interest in decision processes and activities within engineering management, there have been few studies which have inductively explored in-depth the types of interactions that occur between R&D and marketing personnel. Many studies of development practices have used either mail surveys [9], [18] or interviews with managers in a range of firms [4], [5], [10], [17], [19], [22]. The research reported in this paper sought to understand the interactions between functional groups during product development. The paper begins with an overview of the research method and the processes by which decisions are reached. Next, the descriptive body of the paper presents engineering complaints about information they receive from marketing groups, followed by marketing's complaints concerning engineering. The paper concludes with a discussion assessing the implications of these observations on research on how marketing and R&D groups interact.

II. METHOD

Given my interest in the organizational processes and the cultural perspectives of engineers and marketing personnel, I chose to spend nine months on a full time basis observing the new product development activities within one firm in the computer systems industry. "Zytek" (a pseudonym) is an established supplier of computer systems, offering a full line of computing equipment, systems software, and a range of services. Zytek is reported to be an "engineering-driven" company and most marketing, field, and engineering people within Zytek generally agree that engineering has the most power in the firm, particularly in regard to new product decisions. Most of the VP's and senior managers have technical backgrounds and many have come up through the engineering ranks. Zytek had historically sold to technical customers but as Zytek grew in size, they increasingly sold their computers to managers in departments outside of MIS and engineering.

The fieldwork took place in 1988 and 1989 and I was provided with a "contractor badge" allowing access to Zytek facilities, an electronic mail account I could access from my PC at home, and was assigned to the "Low End Systems" group. I initially attended the weekly design review meetings for two different projects at differing stages of development and in engineering groups with differing track records of success. Over the next few weeks, I attended meetings for these projects, set up interviews with managers on my sponsor's staff, and read various documents and material that explained the product development process. During the fieldwork, I kept records of how I allocated my time. Of the 577 documented hours spent observing or interacting with people, I spent 33 percent of my time attending meetings, 28 percent in scheduled interviews, 24 percent in (unscheduled) informal discussions, and 15 percent attending formal presentations. I attended 68 meetings including weekly design review meetings, daily "war room meetings" of engineering for an approaching introduction, marketing and engineering staff meetings, announcement planning meetings, and numerous committee meetings that review product and marketing plans. I had 144 formally scheduled interviews.

After the completion of the fieldwork, all of the field notes were systematically analyzed and categorized. The primary subheadings in the engineering and marketing sections of this paper reflect the categories of comments that were heard most frequently during the field work concerning problems of marketing and R&D in working with each other. In ethnographic terms, these are *emic* categories—those used by people in the field. In order to provide structure and analytic critique of these comments (my own *etic* perspective), I use two

strategies. First, under each of the subheadings in the next two sections, I have inserted a commentary section which provides my own views and interpretations of the "native" comments. Secondly, in the discussion section, I suggest limitations to the traditional focus on integration and harmony in the relationship between marketing and R&D.

III. OVERVIEW OF ORGANIZATIONAL STRUCTURE AND PRODUCT DEVELOPMENT PROCESS

New product development at Zytek is a highly iterative process, with customers on the one hand, technical capabilities on the other, and numerous mechanisms used to link the two. The merger of "possibilities" with "applications" is frequently achieved by engineering managers or product managers directly interacting with customers. Information from customer surveys is viewed as having limited usefulness, as is information received from marketing groups. The engineers claim that marketing people lack the expertise and the appropriate time horizon to make the "translations" from what customers are doing in their business, to what that means in terms of the technology. Their response is to seek out forums that allow interactive discussions directly with customers, allowing them to test out many different ideas.

The VPs in engineering have a profit-and-loss statement and typically have a number of engineering group managers reporting to them along with a base product marketing (BPM) manager. People in BPM groups focus on the products produced within the engineering group and take responsibility for producing the product-specific marketing literature and sales plans. Also within the engineering side of the company are the product marketing groups (PMG's) which focus on the applications the products are used for. In contrast to the BPM groups, the product marketing groups consider all of the hardware, software, services and support requirements for various types of applications such as engineering applications (e.g., CAD/CAM, fault analysis), office applications (e.g., database, work processing, desktop publishing), or manufacturing (e.g., factory information systems, robotics).

A third major set of marketing groups are the Industry marketing groups who report up through the field sales, service, and support side of the organization. While the number of industry marketing groups vary over time, they are broadly organized by the sectors of the economy (manufacturing, service, government). These groups are further broken down to specific sectors such as financial services, aerospace, telecommunications, state and local government, and automotive. The industry marketing groups are primarily responsible for working with the sales force in developing marketing and sales strategies for their respective industry sectors. They also may play a key role in identifying third party hardware and/or software needed for applications in the industry sector which are not provided by Zytek engineering groups.

Since each engineering group manager has a Profit and Loss statement, they are expected to understand their business. Most of the engineering group managers I interacted with did seem to have a substantial amount of interaction with customers, either through trips to the field or by meeting with or making presentations to customers who visited Zytek facilities. Other Zytek systems and processes tend to funnel customer input directly into engineering, frequently bypassing the marketing groups altogether. On several occasions I heard people who had transferred from marketing to product management positions in engineering say that they had more contact with customers in engineering than in marketing. Others noted that since engineering has most of the political power and makes most of the decisions around new products, the best way to influence engineering is to either be included in their organization or to use a label other than marketing or sales.

While there is value in having engineering groups directly interact with customers and make key decisions on product attributes, there are limits to this approach. Marketing groups claim that engineers tend to focus just on their piece of the system. Another limit of direct information is the lack of context and prioritization. Direct interaction does not address such questions as whether a given customer's needs are broad-based and whether the product should be optimized for a few market segments or should be more modular to address a broad range of market segments. With this background on the organizational structure, I now turn to complaints people in engineering have with the information they receive from marketing.

IV. ENGINEERING COMPLAINTS ABOUT INFORMATION RECEIVED FROM MARKETING

While textbooks call for firms to carefully study customers, to segment customers into relatively homogenous groups and to test new product concepts, the reality I found was that things were not so clear cut. Engineering tended to dominate decisions about new product specifications as well as the selection of new products; marketing had to exert influence in indirect ways, and the overall corporate culture was technology-focused with marketers being looked down upon. Interviews I had done with more than 30 people in a dozen other high-tech firms before beginning the fieldwork reported here suggest that Zytek is not atypical of high-tech firms. In this section, I present the most commonly heard complaints engineers have concerning the information they receive from marketing.

A. Customers Don't Know What They Want

The most frequent reason engineers give for not making more use of market research was some variation on the theme, "Customers don't know what they want." Frequently, people in engineering say that customers want "the past extended into the future." One manager phrased it, "Customers just extrapolate from current concepts and ideas they are familiar with." An engineer gave an example:

> "Customers typically can't visualize completely different approaches. A person using a teletype can't visualize the usefulness of a full screen monitor. They just want a faster, cheaper, quieter tele-

type. If you were to show them the interactive monitor, they wouldn't know what to do with it and might not like it."

On at least 15 occasions, people noted that no amount of market research would have come up with the Sony Walkman. I eventually discovered that Zytek's CEO had used the story in a large meeting of managers and it had diffused throughout the organization. In this speech he said:

> "The biggest danger to us is market surveys. When my friend came up with the Sony Walkman, he said in his book don't ask marketers for surveys . . . Marketers will never come up with a new idea. They are taught formally you ask the customer what he wants. But he only wants what he's seen. And nothing will come out of it. One of the most serious dangers is if we say 'here it is black and white, the market survey says this.' That's almost as bad as 'the consultants predict this.' "

1) *Commentary:* The comment that "customers don't know what they want" was heard repeatedly, both in my fieldwork in Zytek and in other firms. To the extent that the technology is changing rapidly and customers value innovative new products over compatibility with existing products or processes, there may be some truth to the statement that they cannot articulate what they want in terms of the specifications that engineers desire. However, these comments are somewhat self-serving for engineers to make, since they provide justification for not listening to the marketing groups and gives them license to be "technology driven." When these comments come from the CEO (as in the quote above) and are continually reinforced by an engineering-driven organizational culture, they become self-reinforcing. The risk is that once an industry begins to mature and competitive advantage shifts from innovativeness to cost-effectiveness and lower cost distribution, firms such as Zytek may be unable to change their organizational cultures and have engineers start listening to what customers want.

Some of the ways to address this limitation are to identify "lead users" [33] who are more familiar with the new technology, to use "information acceleration" to educate users up to a knowledge state they will be in when the product reaches the market [34], and to encourage interactive forums between people who understand potential customer applications and people who understand the technical capabilities. These interactive forums can consist of either contact by engineering personnel directly with customers (e.g., customer visits, focus groups, interactions at trade shows) or with intermediaries (e.g., consultants, distributors, marketing and sales personnel) who are familiar with customer business practices and potential applications.

B. Marketing Doesn't Have the Needed Expertise

Another factor making communication between engineering and marketing difficult is their varying levels of expertise and understanding of what is technically feasible. The engineers often complain that marketing people provide simplistic "product requirements" and that the information is not very useful: "Marketing wants everything right now at no cost—they have no concept of feasibility—they want a $5000 Cadillac tomorrow." They say the marketing input is reflective of what customers are asking for today and based on what the competition is doing.

An example of marketing's perceived limitations is the ability to identify the design assumptions inherent in competitor's products. The image most engineers had of marketing was of "technical incompetents" that generated a lot of "fluff, hype," and paper. Engineers claim that a high level of expertise is needed to unravel the design assumptions made by competitors. For example, at one day long design session with 20 people in attendance (only one from marketing), a manager of the power and packaging design group spent 35 minutes taking apart a competitor's system, explaining their design decisions along the way. By having the "top notch engineers" together at the same time in the meeting, it is thought possible to quickly identify the design assumptions made by competitors. The analysis of competitor's approaches helps to generate new ideas, and with expertise from all the relevant groups present, it is possible to quickly make tradeoffs, discuss interdependencies, and rule out alternatives that are not technically feasible within the time horizon for the product. This generally is not possible with marketing people, since they do not have the same level of technical expertise as the engineers. Rather marketing people focus more on benchmarking performance levels (e.g., MIPS, vectors per second), feature and benefit claims, and pricing information.

    1) *Commentary:* With the technology changing at a rapid rate, many engineers claimed even they found it difficult to stay abreast of what was technically feasible and the technical approaches adopted by the competition. Since it typically takes 18–36 months before leading edge technology shows up in products and since marketing groups spend most of their time working with products that either have been or are about to be introduced, it is inevitable that they will know less about the leading edge technology than engineering.

    The varying levels of expertise between engineering and marketing is compounded by a self-selection bias. That is, the most technical people tend to take jobs in engineering rather than marketing—particularly in an engineering-driven firm where the power and rewards are perceived to be in engineering, not marketing. Much of what went under the "marketing" label in Zytek was the external, communication activities involved in introducing, positioning, and getting third party software for the waves of products continuously rolling out of engineering. In sum, there are structural reasons why marketing will know less about the state-of-the-art technology than engineering. However, this does not mean that they cannot be effective at providing information to engineering. It only implies that engineers should not expect detailed implementation and design trade-offs to be made by marketers. Rather, engineers should look to marketing for what they can provide—information on underlying customer needs, competitor actions, and general trends in the market.

C. Marketing's Time Horizon Is Too Short

Another of the engineers' most frequent complaints about input from marketing is that they tend to provide information on what customers are saying today or what competitors are offering today. Since these products reflect design decisions made years earlier, the feedback is of limited usefulness. For example, one product manager said:

> "The marketing groups tend to have pretty short time horizons—3 to 6 months out. Thus, they don't tend to provide much input into the REAL design decisions which are made 12 to 24 months before introduction . . . it's really hard to get them to come to the design meetings and have their say."

An engineering manager offered the following assessment:

> "The problem with Product Marketing and Industry Marketing is they only tell us what customers are telling us now—they're not looking out two years at what customers will want then . . . they are reactive . . . they have blinders on, see only their set of customers, and don't have the big systems perspective."

One design engineer spoke of the limited usefulness of the information received from customers:

> "The problem with asking customers what they want, is that the design cycles are significantly longer than the foresight of customers. I'm a customer for logic analyzers, and if you ask what I need in a logic analyzer two years from now—I don't know! I couldn't help other engineers design that product."

One product manager complained, "Marketing tends to think only in terms of concepts customers are already used to; they can't provide good advice about break-through types of products." Similarly, a Systems Task Force member mentioned "If you build what they want, you're always several years behind the times. You want to build what they're GOING to want." Finally, another

Systems Task Force member commented on how he tries to get around the time horizon problem:

> "Marketing doesn't have good info on competitors. I need to know where they'll be in three years. What are their strategic relationships? What are their technology directions? . . . Marketing works too much on positioning the products . . . they typically give me feedback on what the market needs, in terms of what today's customers are saying. I need it 18 to 30 months out."

1) *Commentary:* This "time horizon" complaint is related to the first one—"customers don't know what they want." The key difference is that the first is a claim that customers cannot express what they want while this one is a claim that marketing cannot translate what customers express in terms of today's competitive conditions into the level of information needed for the next generation of products. One of the factors that may prevent this translation is the second point above—the limited technical expertise of marketing. Engineers complain that people in marketing do not understand the technical capabilities and trends well enough to look beyond today's product implementations.

Possible ways to remedy this situation are to hire more technical people in marketing, transfer people between engineering and marketing, increase the amount of interaction between marketing and engineering, establish positions such as product or technology managers who are an integral part of the engineering organization, or encourage direct interaction between engineering managers and key customer accounts. Zytek tended to favor the latter two approaches which have the effect of reinforcing engineering's control over product decisions versus increasing the power and capabilities of the marketing groups. In sum, marketing's time horizon might have been too short because they had not been provided with the capabilities they needed to effectively translate expressed customer needs into next generation technology.

D. We Don't Have Time to Wait

One dominant aspect of life within the hardware engineering groups is the time pressures induced by the continual march of semiconductor technology down the "Price Performance" trend lines. The incessant pressure to "move on" leads to short time spans within which product decisions can be made and typically does not allow time for customized market research projects. Engineers often cite these time pressures as reasons that they do not have time to wait for input from the marketing groups. As an illustration of this pressure, in a videotaped presentation reviewing the development history of one project, the engineering manager for the project commented:

> "The first priority on this project was time to market. The second priority was time to market. The third priority was time to market . . . Time to market really drove the project . . . you have to institutionalize time to market . . . Get a stable spec quickly, and don't change it . . . Throw a stake in the ground and leave it there . . . if the juggernaut is rolling, people will have less time to try to kill it . . . We managed to the schedule, not to budget."

This project turned out to be one of the most successful products in Zytek's history—thus reinforcing the myth that engineers shouldn't wait around for marketing to decide on what to do. As a product approaches introduction, marketing and sales groups receive training on the products and strategy, invite customers to announcement events, reserve hotel rooms and announcement facilities, brief the consultants, press, and financial analysts, buy advertising space, and make other commitments that are hard to change without public embarrassment. These commitments make it difficult to slip the schedule, thus increasing the time pressure on engineering.

This dynamic environment leads to many complications. Customers complain of confusion and product obsolescence; account reps complain that it is impossible to keep up with so many new products; marketing people spend all their time with the logistics of "getting products out the door" and "training the field"; engineers "get burned out." One marketing manager commented on the difficulty customers face: "The products are coming every six months, the customer design cycles are 10 months—it's a fundamental problem we've got." Another manager summarized, "It's tough when your technology cycle is shorter than your customer's decision making cycle."

1) *Commentary:* The statements above have to be taken with the caveat that there are hundreds of projects under development at any given time and specific projects often do not map into a single marketing group, but rather span many industries and applications. Often, the engineers were complaining about a specific marketing group trying to hold up development in order to make changes for its own market segment. In other cases, one specific marketing group might identify a limitation of a proposed design, but it might take weeks or months of lobbying to build enough consensus among the other marketing groups in order to get a change made. In the meantime, the engineers might have already made decisions and didn't want to revisit them later.

One of the central issues raised here is that the types of on-going market research done by the marketing groups may not directly relate to specific engineering groups or be in a form that is useful to the development team. For example, Zytek had a market research group of approximately 30 people which performed an annual mail survey of existing customers with several thousand replies being received. They additionally did dozens of custom projects on market trends and industry sector needs as well as research projects on specific products. However, given the hundreds of project development efforts underway in engineering and only a handful of *product-specific* market research projects it was rare for the internally collected market research information to correspond to a specific project. Additionally, formal market research was only a small part of the information collected on customer needs and market trends. Additional sources were purchased market research studies from firms such as IDC, Gartner Group, and Dataquest, information received from the sales force, as well as on-going interactions between key customer accounts and personnel throughout

Zytek. As will be discussed later, marketing groups were most concerned with understanding trends affecting their respective market segments and given the variety of ways of segmenting the market, the concerns of the marketing groups did not directly translate into the information engineering needed to make design decisions. It was very time intensive for engineering to collect the "market needs" from all the possible marketing groups affected by their project and then make the trade-offs of optimizing the design for a few of these groups versus designing a modular system architecture that could be adapted to a wider variety of segments through value-added activities of marketing groups and third party external suppliers. The result was engineers often said they didn't have time to wait and instead tried to turn out "base platforms" which incorporated the state-of-the-art technology.

V. MARKETING'S COMPLAINTS ABOUT ENGINEERING

With this background on the complaints engineers have of the information they receive from marketing, I now turn to marketing's view of engineering. Since these comments are organized around the categories that emerged from the systematic analysis of the field notes, many of marketing's comments do not directly address the issues raised by the engineers. However, as Dougherty [7] has pointed out, people in marketing and engineering have differing "thought worlds," see different sets of issues, and talk past each other more than they directly conflict with each other. Thus the categories below are more a synthesis of marketing complaints and reactions to what their role in product development was rather than a point-for-point reaction to engineering's complaints.

A. Engineers Lack Perspective

The single greatest complaint marketing people have with engineers is that the engineers are too detail-oriented and lack perspective. Many marketing people complain that engineers are fascinated by the technology, yet have little appreciation for what customers do with the products. "They turn out products looking for markets" is a common complaint. Others complain that engineering can be very insular and not open to new approaches; said one base product marketing person, "It's the Not Invented Here Syndrome." One woman in product marketing who had recently transferred out of engineering commented, "Engineers put their priority list together based on what they think will be fun to do. Engineers have a strange sense of fun."

Perhaps out of frustration, there is no lack of creativity in coming up with names to call the engineers. A few terms overheard include "tech-weenies," "pinheads," "tech-heads," "tech-nerds," "propeller heads," "techno-dweebs," "technoids," and the most frequently used, "techies." Some of the words used to criticize engineers are "narrow," "parochial," "insular," "literal," "rational," "focused," "technology driven," "analytic," and "social incompetents." One sales manager claimed that within engineering, "They're rewarded for analytic abilities, so the most analytic people rise to the top" while in sales, "empathy" and understanding of what customer are trying to do is required, and the "analytic" engineering mind set is unable to communicate with "empathetic" sales and marketing mind set.

Marketers also complain that engineers focus on specific components, leave gaps in the product line, and do not deliver the "solutions" that customers want. For example, one product marketing manager claimed, "They see their products as products in and of themselves, rather than as components in a larger system being sold to solve some problem or change the way a customer does business." One strategic planner in a base product marketing group spoke of this emphasis on "products:"

> "We spend so much time on the products—and then leave it up to marketing and sales to go do it—engineering washes their hands of it. But you have to communicate it, train people on it, differentiate it, have a marketing campaign to roll it out, and worry about all the other stuff—availability, distribution, third party software . . . engineering

builds devices and relies on separate groups to do their part. . . . It's difficult to get all the pieces in place."

1) Commentary: Many researchers studying marketing/R&D interaction across different firms [7], [12], [20], [30] have reported similar complaints by marketing people. Within Zytek, these complaints revolve around both engineering's focus on technical details as well as a perceived lack of social skills of engineers. The fact that the Zytek culture and organizational structure gives engineers more power than marketers no doubt makes people in marketing envious and frustrated. However, in spite of the criticism, most people in marketing have a high level of respect for the engineers and their abilities and generally acknowledge that engineering produces good products.

B. Engineers Don't Appreciate Prior Customer Investments

People in marketing also complain of engineers being arrogant and ignoring the investments customers have already made in software, training, and peripherals for other vendor's equipment. Several marketing people talked of engineers being "belligerent" with customers and getting into arguments over the "best" technical approach. One industry marketing specialist provided an example:

> "Customers criticize us for being arrogant. They can't throw out their [*Competitor T*] investments. We aren't good at being nondisruptive . . . we just lost a proposal at [*Bank X*]. They had the feeling Zytek wanted to get in and throw out [*T*] . . . [*Bank Y*] has [*over £2 billion*] invested in [*T*]'s equipment. [*T's system architecture*] can't be replaced. One of the Zytek people doing a demo said they should replace it. The guy from [*Bank Y*] was a little upset. It's so typical of the engineering mind set—that our products are superior . . . They very well may be, but they don't understand that they have to deal with the here and now of what customers have."

Marketing people often pointed to the market success of products that may not have had the most features, but were rather compatible with prior purchases. In many meetings, marketing people argued for being more concerned with how new products fit with customer work practices and less concerned with using the latest technology.

1) *Commentary:* Rogers [25] lists compatibility as one of the key factors which can affect the adoption of new innovations and Jackson [14] has focused on switching costs as a major factor affecting computer purchases. Marketing's complaint was that engineers underestimated the inertia of "the installed base" and thought customers would switch to leading edge technology quicker than they typically did. I found that these complaints particularly came from the industry marketing groups that dealt with more mature, "commercial computing" environments. They argued that Zytek had historically sold to technical customers (scientists and engineers) who valued state-of-the-art technology and wanted the "latest and greatest technology." However, as Zytek increasingly penetrated commercial markets, there were a different set of customer needs. For industry segments where customers had built business processes around computer systems from competitors, it was impossible to penetrate these accounts without providing for a migration path or somehow reducing the switching costs.

C. Engineers Don't Appreciate the Diverse Market Segments We Represent

People in marketing often said that engineers ask very detailed questions, don't appreciate the varying customer needs between different market segments, and expect a consensus response from the marketing groups. One product marketing manager said:

> "Engineers have a very simplistic view of the world—what do customers need? Well it's not that simple. The world isn't homogeneous. [a lot of times] they ask us for is a prioritized list of needs from marketing—they want everyone in marketing to agree. The unanimous opinion of marketing. They don't realize the diverse sets of markets we represent."

Marketing input may be coming from not only the Base Product marketing group associated with an engineering group, but also from the five product marketing groups and the dozens of industry marketing groups. This organizational structure had evolved over time to serve the diverse information needs and differing customer needs of various groups both in the distribution channel (e.g., VAR's, OEM's, retail stores, systems integrators) and in customer accounts (e.g., MIS groups, departmental managers, senior managers, end users). While the product managers in engineering attempted to synthesize and make tradeoffs between the diverse marketing inputs, such a task was often impossible given the heterogeneity of the market segments represented.

One committee that sought to facilitate the coordination of marketing input to engineering was the "Marketing Advisory Board." This ad hoc group, composed of roughly 20 people from various marketing groups, met on a biweekly basis and had engineering group managers and projects managers present their product development plans. While this committee was sometimes able to make changes in product plans, it was not perceived by engineering to be very powerful and sign-offs from this committee were not required to proceed through development phases. However, an important role was to provide a single forum where engineering groups could come and hear feedback from the various market segments that a product might be trying to reach.

1) *Commentary:* It seems that much of the tension between engineering and marketing arises over the level and type of information each wants from the other. Engineers must make very detailed design and implementation decisions and they go to marketing asking for help with these decisions. As Section IV of this paper indicates, the engineers generally feel that marketing doesn't provide the information they need. However, the marketing groups at Zytek do not deal with single, isolated products or with individual customer accounts, but rather with aggregate groups of each. Most engineers only see a small part of the world—their part of the system. In a similar way, most people in the field see only a small slice of customers—the account(s) they are assigned to. People in marketing deal with larger abstractions and attempt to "bridge the gap" between the hundreds of components and systems coming out of engineering and the set of customers within each of their respective market segments. However, because they deal with these abstractions, they seem to operate in a no man's land, where they typically don't know the technology as well as the engineers, nor do they know the "needs" of specific customers as well as the field sales personnel calling on those customers. As in Dougherty's field research [7], people in marketing have a difficult time connecting with engineering because of their differing "thought worlds." However, what is different between the firms in Dougherty's field research and Zytek, is engineering interacts not with a single marketing group but rather with many groups representing differing ways of segmenting the market.

D. Our Role Is To Refine Technically Driven Ideas

Finally, many people in marketing argued that it was not appropriate for marketing people to tell engineers what to do. Rather, they believed the ideas should be technology-driven, but with feedback from marketing, customers, and the field to determine both the usefulness of various product concepts and the relative size of the market. The chairwoman of the Marketing Advisory Board (the group which coordinated feedback from marketing groups to engineering), reacted to my question of how marketing provided input to engineering in the following way:

> "Have you been in any forums where there WAS input to engineering? . . . At Zytek we look at it from the technology out. If we could build this, what could you do with it? It means marketing input is used to refine the concepts . . . Our crystal ball isn't very good—all we see is the past extended . . . it has to be iterative—here's what we can do, could you use it?"

While there were several groups scattered around Zytek that conduct market research studies on a full time basis, they were relatively small in relation to the number of people in other marketing and sales positions. One marketing manager mentioned that these studies are "just one data point:"

> "The quantitative methods and tools are just a footnote in the appendix. They aren't that important—the decisions and business plans are much more complex and are focused on a broad understanding of what customers could do with a given set of capabilities."

Others emphasized the usefulness of focus groups, given the rapid changes and dynamics of the computer industry and the confusion over terminology. For example, one product marketing manager said:

> "The meaning of terms is different to people . . . everyone wants 'open systems'—but just what are 'open systems?' Only 2% of the people really understand the issues . . . it's very complex . . . so surveys are pretty limited. That's why focus groups are so useful—to get at language and meaning. They allow you to move beyond the simplistic statements to a real probing of the issues."

Many of the focus groups were done by a group called the "Customer Information Group" which was not officially part of marketing, but rather reported directly to an engineering vice president. The head of this group was quite aware of the negative stigma associated with marketing ("we don't use the M-word around here") and said that they had shifted away from large scale surveys toward more focus groups in order to get a better understanding of what customers wanted.

1) Commentary: I was somewhat surprised that many of the marketing people argued for this "refinement" rather than "initiation" role for marketing. However, after my nine months of field work, I came to appreciate the logic of it. Most of the people in marketing spent the majority of their time on "outbound" marketing tasks—preparing for product introductions, doing demos, training the sales force, preparing merchandising material, and working with other various types of business partners such as third-party hardware and software firms, systems integrators, and value-added resellers. They realized they didn't know the technology as well as the engineers and claimed that they shouldn't be initiating the new products or providing all the detailed answers such as "telling engineers where to put the switches." Furthermore, the people with more experience with the firm appreciated that Zytek's development processes and corporate culture did not give the leading role to marketing for product development decisions. However, they did feel they had a significant role to play in providing reactions to the concepts put forth by engineering.

I found that there were differing views within engineering as to whether marketing's role should be primarily one of refining engineering-driven ideas. Some engineering managers had very close working relationships with their counterparts in marketing and looked to them to provide reactions on design ideas and stories and summaries on trends in the market. On the other hand, other engineering managers had more adversarial relationships with marketing groups and complained that marketing could not provide a stable spec for them. However, in general I believe that the top managers in both engineering and marketing thought the ideas should originate in engineering.

VI. DISCUSSION

Since much of the literature on marketing/R&D interaction has acknowledged differing perspectives between the two groups [4], [7], [12], [20], [28], [30], the descriptive body of this paper is organized around the perspectives of people in engineering and marketing. Similar to other empirical studies of new product development practice in high-tech settings, my fieldwork found relatively little use of formal market research techniques [10], [16], [18], [19]. This is no doubt partially due to engineering-

driven culture and the lack of power and status of marketing groups. However, one of the general themes that runs through the engineering complaints is that when technical capabilities are rapidly changing and when the technology is complex, customers may not anticipate what they can do with a given capability. Furthermore, information that passes through marketing and sales groups is often filtered and misinterpreted due to the technical complexity.

Some of these points have been made by prior research on product development in high-tech environments. For example, Von Hippel [33] has recognized the limitations to input from customers who do not have experience with a new type of product and he recommends identification of "lead users." An empirical example of using lead users to help design a new product is presented in Urban and Von Hippel [31]. Others have focused on the personality and translation problems between marketing and R&D. For example, Moenaert et al. [20] use a mail survey of 386 people to identify differing information styles of communication and identify four dimensions (relevance, novelty, comprehensiveness, and credibility) which affect the usefulness of the information. What this study adds to this prior research is a detailed description of problems marketing and R&D have in working with each other in one engineering-driven organization. While I am limited in my ability to generalize from these observations to other settings, I am able to use these observations to critique the existing literature on marketing and R&D interactions and to suggest directions for future research. I focus my discussion of the theoretical implications of this work on how the nature of the products produced by Zytek and the organizational structure prevented a dyadic interaction between marketing and R&D.

1. Modular Systems Prevent Dyadic Interaction between Marketing and R&D. Much of the prior work on marketing/R&D interactions [12], [13], [28] has implicitly assumed: 1) There is a dyadic relationship between one engineering group and one marketing group, 2) marketing has information that engineering needs and should represent the needs of customers to engineering, and 3) the problems are primarily ones of conflict, integration, or translation of customer needs to engineering specifications. However, computers are modular products which are customized and configured in different ways for different market segments and there are typically many marketing groups that an engineering group has to listen to. In Zytek there were many marketing groups representing a variety of ways of segmenting the market.

While I often observed engineering personnel trying to address the concerns of marketing groups, this was often difficult given Zytek's unusual organizational structure. A design team in Zytek has to deal not only with its own Base Product Marketing group, but also with five Product Marketing groups and roughly two dozen Industry marketing groups. Even if engineers are predisposed to cooperate with marketing, it is impossible to accommodate the varying needs of over 20 different marketing groups. The critical design decisions often revolve around whether to optimize a system for specific applications or specific industries or whether to design more flexible, modular systems that can later be customized by marketing groups or external third parties to a broader range of applications.

Within Zytek, these decisions of how modular and flexible to make a product were made within engineering. The annual R&D funding was allocated by a committee called the Systems Task Force and there were biweekly review meetings throughout the year between this committee and various engineering groups. A critical role of this committee was to plan and monitor compliance with an overall system architecture for Zytek's systems. Such an architecture helped ensure interconnectivity among the various systems and components under development within engineering.

There has been relatively little research exploring marketing/R&D interactions for such complex systems where multiple marketing groups interact with R&D project teams. However, Rothwell [26], [27] has pointed out some of these issues re-

lating to modular products, economies of scope, and "robust designs." Additional research is needed to relate the design trade-offs between general purpose and specialized machines to organizational structure and communication processes. Do firms typically have a formalized system for collecting requirements of different market segments and analytically making trade-offs between the varying customer needs or is the chaotic, coalitional adhocracy seen within Zytek more common? Is a complex network organizational form more appropriate for dynamic, technology-driven environments with more systematic procedures appropriate in more stable environments? These and other questions relating organizational structure and processes to environmental conditions are in need of additional research.

VII. SUMMARY

While single site participant observation studies are useful for inductively developing insights into issues such as organizational structure, culture, and decision making processes, follow-up studies are needed to test the generalizability of the findings. Two obvious questions that arise from this descriptive account are: 1) Do engineering groups have similar levels of power over product development decisions in other high-tech firms? 2) Is it appropriate for engineering to have control of product development decisions? Zytek is an engineering-driven firm producing modular systems and the nature of the interactions between marketing and R&D may be a function of this specific organizational context. Other computer firms give greater power and stature to marketing and specialize in narrower market segments than Zytek, thus it is probably not appropriate to generalize to all computer firms based on these observations. Additionally, this study does not attempt to assess organizational outcomes such as product development success or improved organizational performance. Future research is needed to assess both how generalizable these observations are and to assess the impact of various ways of structuring the marketing/R&D on organizational and product development performance.

In conclusion, this study has provided greater insight into problems in the interactions between marketing and R&D groups in an engineering-driven firm than has been provided in prior research. One of the key points made is that marketing groups may not have all of the information that engineers need and may not be structured in a way to easily help engineering make design decisions. Thus, some interaction directly between engineers and key customers may be desirable. However, marketing groups should help provide context and strategic prioritization for this direct input.

REFERENCES

1. P. L. Berger and T. Luckmann, *The Social Construction of Reality*. Garden City, NY: Doubleday, 1966.
2. K. Brockhoff and A. K. Chakrabarti, "R&D/marketing linkage and innovation strategy: Some West German experience," *IEEE Trans. Eng. Manage.*, vol. 35, pp. 167–174, Aug. 1988.
3. R. G. Cooper, "The dimensions of industrial new product success and failure," *J. Market.*, vol. 43, pp. 93–103. Summer 1979.
4. R. G. Cooper and E. J. Kleinschmidt, "An investigation into the new product process: Steps, deficiencies, and impact." *J. Prod. Innovation Manage.*, vol. 3, no. 2, pp. 71–85, 1986.
5. R. G. Cooper and E. J. Kleinschmidt, "New product processes at leading industrial firms," *Ind. Marketing Manage.*, vol. 20, pp. 137–147, 1991.
6. B. V. Dean, *Evaluating, Selecting, and Controlling R&D Projects*, Amer. Manage. Assoc., 1968.
7. D. Dougherty, "Interpretive barriers to successful product innovation in large firms," *Organiz. Sci.*, vol. 3, pp. 179–202, May 1992.
8. F. A. Dubinskas, "Janus organizations: Scientists and managers in genetic engineering firms," in *Making Time: Ethnographies of High-Technology Organizations*, F. Dubinskas, Ed. Philadelphia, PA: Temple Univ. Press, 1988, pp. 170–232.
9. L. Dwyer and R. Mellor, "New product process activities and project outcomes," *R&D Manage.*, vol. 21, no. 1, pp. 31–42, 1991.
10. L. P. Feldman and A. L. Page, "Principle versus practice in new product planning," *J. Prod. Innovation Manage.*, vol. 1, pp. 43–55, 1984.
11. A. Griffin and J. R. Hauser, "Patterns of communication among marketing, engineering, and manufacturing: A comparison between two new product teams," *Manage. Sci.*, vol. 38, pp. 360–373, Mar. 1992.
12. A. K. Gupta *et al.*, "A model for studying R&D—Marketing interface in the product innovation process," *J. Marketing*, vol. 50, pp. 7–17, Apr. 1986.
13. J. R. Hauser and D. Clausing, "The house of quality," *Harvard Bus. Rev.*, vol. 66, pp. 63–73, May/June 1988.
14. B. B. Jackson, *Keeping and Winning Industrial Customers*. Lexington, MA: Lexington Books, 1985.
15. M. Jelinek and C. B. Schoonhoven, *The Innovation Marathon: Lessons from High Technology Firms*. Cambridge, MA: Basil Blackwell, 1990.
16. A. Johne and P. Snelson, "Auditing product innovation activities in manufacturing firm," *R&D Manage.*, vol. 18, no. 3, pp. 227–233, 1988.
17. R. M. Knight, "Product innovatin by smaller, high-technology firms in Canada," *J. Prod. Innov. Manage.*, vol. 3, pp. 195–203, 1988.
18. V. Mahajan and J. Wind, "New product models: Practice, shortcomings, and desired improvements," *J. Prod. Innov. Manage.*, vol. 9, pp. 128–139, 1992.
19. N. McGuinness, "New product idea activities in large technology based firms," *J. Prod. Innov. Manage.*, vol. 7, pp. 173–185, 1990.
20. R. K. Moenaert *et al.*, "Information styles of marketing and R&D personnel during technological product innovation projects," *J. Prod. Innov. Manage.*, vol. 9, no. 1, pp. 21–39, 1992.
21. R. K. Moenaert and W. E. Souder, "An information transfer model for integrating marketing and R&D personnel in new product development projects," *J. Prod. Innov. Manage.*, vol. 7, pp. 91–107, 1990.
22. W. L. Moore, "New product development practices of industrial marketers," *J. Prod. Innov. Manage.*, vol. 4, pp. 6–20, 1987.
23. S. Myers and D. Marquis, "Successful industrial innovations," *Nat. Sci. Found.*, pp. 69–97, 1969.
24. H. Nystrom, *Technological and Marketing Innovation: Strategies for Product and Company Development*. New York: Wiley, 1990.
25. E. M. Rogers, *Diffusion of Innovations*, 3rd ed. New York: Free Press, 1993.
26. R. Rothwell and P. Gardiner, "Re-innovation and robust designs: Producer and user benefits," *J. Market. Manage.*, vol. 3, no. 3, pp. 372–387, Spring 1988.
27. R. Rothwell and T. G. Whiston, "Design, innovation, and corporate integration," *R&D Manage.*, vol. 20, no. 3, pp. 193–201, 1990.
28. R. W. Ruekert and O. C. Walker, Jr., "Marketing interaction with other functional units: A conceptual framework and empirical evidence," *J. Market.*, vol. 51, pp. 1–19, Jan. 1987.
29. R. L. Schmidt and J. R. Freeland, "Recent progress

in modeling R&D project-selection processes," *IEEE Trans. Eng. Manage.*, vol. 39, pp. 189–201, May 1992.

30. W. E. Souder, "Managing relations between R&D and marketing in new product development projects," *J. Prod. Innov. Manage.*, vol. 5, no. 1, pp. 6–19, Mar. 1988.

31. G. L. Urban and E. von Hippel, "Lead user analyses for the development of new industrial products," *Manage. Sci.*, vol. 34, pp. 569–582, May 1988.

32. J. M. Utterback, "Innovation in industry and the diffusion of technology," *Science*, vol. 183, pp. 620–626, 1974.

33. E. von Hippel, "Lead users: A source of novel product concepts," *Manage. Sci.*, vol. 32, pp. 791–805, July 1986.

34. B. Weinberg, "An information acceleration based methodology for developing preproduction forecasts for durable goods: Design, development, and initial validation," unpublished dissertation, MIT Sloan School of Manage., 1992.

35. J. P. Workman, Jr., "Marketing's limited role in new product development in one computer systems firm," *J. Market. Res.*, vol. 30, pp. 405–421, Nov. 1993.

36. B. J. Zirger and M. Maidique, "A model of new product development: An empirical test." *Manage. Sci.*, vol. 36, pp. 867–883, July 1990.

48

Examining Some Myths About New Product "Winners"

ROBERT G. COOPER

Overview: Too many myths prevail about how to manage new product projects. This article probes what truly separates winners from losers in the new product game. It reports the results of a study of 103 new product cases from 21 major firms and divisions in four countries. Key success factors are identified—factors that distinguish the successful projects from the commercial duds.

New products continue to fail at an alarming rate. Although numerous studies have probed the reasons for failure, or what distinguishes winners from losers, many pundits appear to have ignored their conclusions and prescriptions, clinging to old beliefs, even myths, about how new products ought to be managed. Could some of these traditional beliefs underlie what is wrong with new product management? Consider the following 8 myths:

1. First into the market wins!
2. Analysis means paralysis ... let's just get out there and do it: "Ready, fire, aim!"
3. Company reputation, a strong brand name, and a good selling effort will make almost any new product a success.
4. Having a low price is critical to winning.
5. We just can't afford the time to do market studies, customer tests, and a trial sell. Speed is of the essence!
6. If you're large, powerful, and strong enough, you don't need synergy to win. Diversify anywhere ... any product, market, or technology arena is "fair game."
7. Don't try to pin down the definition of the product before development begins. This thwarts the creativity of scientists.
8. The competitive situation makes all the difference between winning and losing. If you don't succeed, blame it on a highly competitive market.

You may not believe all of these, but if one looks at the way many new product initiatives are managed, it is clear that these myths have many adherents. Our research team set out to gather data that would either prove or disprove these and other popular tenets of new product management (1). To do so, we selected one industry—the chemical industry—with a long tradition of science-based product development, and one in which there are many recognized leaders in innovation. Twenty-one major firms and divisions in four countries, including companies such as Du Pont, Dow, Shell-UK, Exxon Chemicals, ICI and Rohm & Haas, provided 103 case histories of significant and recent new products for in-depth study. New products covered a wide range of specialty products, including polymers (e.g., a modified polyethylene, a clarity film resin, an extrusion coating resin and a silicone rubber acoustic), as well as chemicals (e.g., a non-ionic surfactant, a pigment dispersant, an industrial heat transfer fluid, and an inorganic ultraviolet absorber).

The results reported here are from the New-Prod studies, an ongoing research investigation into

Robert Cooper is Professor of Industrial Marketing and Technology Management at McMaster University's Business School. For an earlier version of this paper and for more discussion of the issues covered, see Cooper, R. G. "Debunking the myths of new product development." *Research-Technology Management*, July–August, 1994, pp. 40–50; and Cooper, R. G. *Winning at New Products*, 2d ed. Reading, MA.: Addison-Wesley, 1993, respectively.

factors that separate new product winners from losers (2–6). A conceptual framework or model of new product outcomes formed the basis for the study (7,8). Thirteen blocks of variables or *dimensions*—such as Synergy, Market Attractiveness, and Product Advantage—were identified from this model, along with 95 variables that comprised these dimensions. Of the 103 new product cases, 68 were commercial successes and 35 were failures. All were fairly major products of their type; all had been launched and had been on the market for three years. Data on each product were collected via detailed questionnaires administered to members of the project teams. For each project, the 95 descriptor variables were measured on 10-point anchored scales along with a number of key performance measures: profitability, market share, and others.

By observing what separated the winners from the losers in this sample, we were able to shed light on what makes a winner, and which myths really are founded on fact. Although undertaken in only one industry, the results appear to have face validity generally; hence, they are likely to apply to a broader range of moderate-to-high technology industries.

SUCCESS VS. FAILURE

New product success was measured in a number of ways, including profitability, impact on the firm, current sales and market share, and timeliness. Some performance measures were in percentages, others in dollars and many gauged on zero-to-ten scales. Timeliness measures included time efficiency (whether the project was done in a time-efficient manner) and adherence to the time schedule (both were scaled, perception measures).

Two-thirds of the projects were rated as successes, based on profitability. Indeed, this two-thirds did much better on every performance dimension we measured save one. Winners did not differ from losers in terms of costs. The mean development cost for both successes and failures was about $2.25 million.

What then were the main drivers of new product success? To answer the question, we developed *major dimensions* or *indexes*, each based on a number of different measures. New product projects were then split into thirds—the top, middle and bottom third—on each dimension or index; we then looked more closely at the performance of each third. Here are the keys to new product success:

1. PRODUCT SUPERIORITY IS NUMBER ONE

Having a high-quality, superior product that delivered real value to the customer made all the difference between winning and losing. The most superior products—the top third on this dimension—achieved a success rate of 90.6 percent, 61 percentage points higher than the 29.6 percent success rate of products in the bottom third, most of which were "me-too" types of products. These superior products scored high on seven key items:

- Excellent *relative product quality*—relative to competitors' products, and in terms of how the customer measures quality.
- Good *value for money* for the customer.
- Superior *price/performance* characteristics for the customer relative to competitors' products.
- Superior to competing products in terms of *meeting customer needs*.
- Product *benefits* or attributes easily perceived as being *useful by the customer*.
- *Unique attributes* and characteristics for the customer—not available from competitive products.
- Highly *visible benefits*—very obvious to the customer.

There are two messages for managers:

1. Use these seven key elements of product advantage as screening criteria. If your new product projects don't score high on these items, then maybe you should be spending your money elsewhere!

2. These seven items become project objectives. No effort should be spared building these key elements into your next new product. The first step is to listen to the voice of your customer; only then can you fashion a product that truly does deliver these seven winning elements. Key customer questions include:

- What is "quality" in the customer's eyes?
- What is "value" to him?
- What are desired price/performance characteristics?
- What are her needs, wants and preferences?
- What are useful and unique product benefits, attributes and characteristics?
- What benefits will be highly visible—will really jump out at the customer?

Answers to these questions are central to developing that superior product that yields a 91 percent success rate.

That Product Superiority is the number one success factor should come as no surprise. Apparently it does to some people, though, including many project teams in these large, well-run chemical companies.

About one-third of these project teams developed and took *very mediocre new products* to market—products that scored poorly on this Product Superiority index. The results were predictable: This one-third had a 70 percent failure rate!

One element noticeable for its absence is having a low price. Low price was measured, but it was not related to either new product performance, or to the items that comprise Product Superiority. A low-price strategy is not key to winning at new products in the chemical industry.

2. QUALITY OF MARKETING ACTIONS IS CRITICAL

How well the marketing activities were executed from idea through to launch was the second key success factor. Note that "marketing activities" include a lot more than merely the launch. In fact, five marketing actions had almost equal impact on success. In rank order of impact, these activities were:

1. Undertaking *customer tests* or field trials of the product proficiently: the right number and location of test sites, good controls, appropriate metrics, etc.

2. Building in a *trial sell* or test market phase, and executing it well—where the product was sold to a limited number of customers in order to test the product, production and marketing, and to confirm market acceptance.

3. Executing the *launch* well: a solid launch plan, properly resourced, and executed proficiently.

4. Undertaking a *detailed market study* before Development begins: face-to-face interviews with potential customers/users to determine needs, wants, preferences, likes and dislikes, competitive weaknesses, and purchase intent.

5. Carrying out a *preliminary market assessment*—a quick scoping of the market in the *earliest* stage of the project.

Those new chemical products, for which these five marketing activities were executed—in a quality way—were far more successful. They had a success rate of 88.6 percent (versus only 37.5 percent for projects where these actions were poorly handled or not taken at all); and they also scored significantly higher on our other measures of performance (see Cooper [10] for actual data tables).

Sadly, many projects were found lacking in these five pivotal marketing actions. For example, there were many doubtful omissions: 57 percent of projects featured no detailed market study; 46 percent omitted the trial sell; and 28 percent did not even have a *formal* launch. Further, one-third of projects had quality-of-execution ratings for marketing actions below 5.0 out of 10—a dismal score. Not surprisingly, these same projects suffered a failure rate of 63 percent!

No doubt there are good and valid reasons why

certain commonly recommended actions may be omitted. Not every project needs a market test or trial sell, for example. But the frequency of omission of too many activities was substantial, certainly more than one would have expected from the occasional skipping over a step in the development and commercialization process. Moreover, most of the excuses for omission were fairly lame. For example, we heard from marketing that "they had a limited window of opportunity, so they had to move fast and that meant cutting out a few of the normal steps." From R&D we heard, "We didn't do a user study because we didn't have the budget—and besides, there was nobody to do it—the marketing folks were too busy doing other things." Project members would also claim that, "We don't usually do a detailed financial analysis prior to development—the numbers really aren't too reliable." Or, "We didn't do 'beta tests' or field trials because we didn't want competitors to find out about the new product." While confidentiality is important, it is also imperative to make sure that the product really does perform under live field conditions in a manner acceptable to the customer.

It is also important to point out the impact of these marketing actions on cycle time. Projects that featured well-executed marketing activities fared much better on both measures of timeliness—time efficiency and adherence to the time-line. Contrary to myth, taking a little extra time to execute the customer test, trial sell, product launch, and detailed market study in a quality fashion *does not add extra time*; rather, it pays off, not only with higher success rates but in terms of staying on schedule and achieving better time efficiency.

The message is clear: Marketing actions are critical to both new product success and cycle time reduction. If these actions are not done, or are carried out in a sloppy fashion, then watch out: Expect a drop in success rates, profitability, market share, and company impact—and watch time efficiency and time-lines suffer. Marketing actions, executed in a quality fashion, must be an integral facet of your firm's product development game plan. Unfortunately, they often are not!

3. DON'T SKIP UP-FRONT HOMEWORK

Homework undertaken before the project proceeds into Development is critical. Projects that boasted superb up-front homework achieved a 43 percent higher success rate and were rated significantly more profitable; they were more likely to be successful technically, and they had a greater impact on the company. Most important, better homework reduced cycle time; such projects were undertaken in a more time-efficient manner, and stayed on-schedule.

Five critical activities comprise the homework phase of the project. In rank order (some of which overlap the marketing actions above) that precede the Development phase are:

1. Initial screening: the first decision to get into the project (the idea screen).
2. The detailed market study or marketing research (described above).
3. The business and financial analysis held just before the decision to "Go to Development." (Some people call this "building the business case.")
4. Preliminary market assessment—the first and quick market study.
5. Preliminary technical assessment—the first and quick technical appraisal of the project.

While the wisdom of doing these tasks may be apparent, good homework certainly was missing in too many new product projects. Indeed, one-third of the projects had a homework quality-of-execution rating of less than 4.5 on the ten-point scale—an indictment of the quality of homework here.

Once again the message is obvious: Don't skimp on the homework. If you find yourself making the case that, "We don't have time for the homework," you are heading for trouble on two counts: First, cutting out the homework drives your success rate way down; second, cutting out homework to save time today will cost you in wasted time tomorrow. It's a "penny-wise, pound-poor" solution to saving time. Make it a rule: No significant project should move into the Development phase without the five actions described above completed, and in a quality way.

4. PICK ATTRACTIVE MARKETS

This sounds a bit like saying, "Buy low and sell high"; except that with new products, the choice is much more apparent—there are *evident market characteristics to look for*, characteristics that most often result in success.

Here are the ingredients of this winning market situation:

- The product type (category) represented an essential one for the customer;
- The market was growing quickly;
- There was a positive economic climate for the new product;
- The market demand for this type of product was stable over time (as opposed to cyclical and unstable);
- Potential customers were innovative adopters, amenable to trying new products;
- Potential customers were relatively price-insensitive;
- The market was a large one;
- Potential customers themselves were very profitable.

Note that few of these characteristics on their own were predictive of success, but when taken together as an "index of market attractiveness," they were strongly linked to performance. For example: Those projects in the top third on this index achieved an enviable success rate of 87.5 percent; they were rated significantly more profitable; they had a higher market share (by 20 share points); and they were executed in a more time-efficient manner.

The implications for management are evident: Create an "index of market attractiveness," perhaps using the eight characteristics cited above, and use this index in scoring or rating projects when determining your project priorities.

5. GET PRODUCT DEFINITION RIGHT—FIRST

Defining the product sharply before proceeding to the Development phase closely parallels the need for homework. Sharply defined projects were decidedly more successful: 85 percent successful versus only 47 percent for those without good, early definition. Sharply defined projects also had significantly higher profitability ratings.

Good definition leads to success in other ways too: technical success, impact on the company, and market share (20 share points higher). Staying on schedule was also tied to good definition. Projects that lacked sharp, early definition had dismal adherence-to-schedule ratings.

Management must make certain that significant projects are clearly defined when they are released for development. Here are the ingredients of this definition (again, in rank order of impact):

1. The product benefits to the customer are clearly defined.
2. The target market is precisely spelled out.
3. The product's requirements, features and specs are clearly defined.
4. The product concept—what the product will be and do—is conceptually laid out.
5. The positioning strategy—how the product will be positioned in the minds of users and vis-a-vis competitors' products—is mapped out.

Unless these five items are clearly defined, written down and agreed to by all parties prior to entering the Development phase, then your project will face tough times downstream: Your odds of failure have just skyrocketed by a factor of three!

6. PLAN AND RESOURCE THE LAUNCH PROPERLY

Whoever said, "Build a better mousetrap and the world will beat a path to your door" was a poet, not a businessman. Not only must the product be a superior one, but it must also be launched, marketed and supported in a strong and proficient manner. This was not always the case for the sample of chemical products studied, and most often the result was failure.

The "goodness of launch" index consisted of eight elements. In rank order of impact, they were:

1. Service quality: the quality of the service and technical support aimed at the customer (e.g., the right people, qualified, responsive, etc.).

2. Reliability of product delivery—on-time shipments.

3. Product availability—the product supply was adequate.

4. Sales force quality: quality of the selling effort (the right people, properly trained, etc.).

5. Promotional quality: quality of the promotional effort (trade shows, events, etc.).

6. Promotion magnitude—enough promotional effort.

7. Service magnitude—enough support resources.

8. Sales force magnitude—enough sales people and effort.

Although advertising, both quality and magnitude, was measured, it did not impact strongly on success; consequently, it was dropped from this index of "goodness of launch." Apparently advertising is not a critical component of the launch of products (at least in this sample) in the chemical industry; it may, however, be more critical in other industries such as consumer goods.

The launch clearly had an impact on performance. New products scoring in the top third in terms of "goodness of launch" achieved an admirable performance: 78 percent success rate, versus only 41 percent for the poorly launched products. They also had significantly higher ratings on profitability, technical success, and impact on the company; and closer adherence to the time schedule (although one is not sure what is the cause and what is the result here; perhaps an "on-schedule" project resulted in a better launch).

The message is this: Don't assume good products sell themselves, and don't treat the launch as an afterthought. Never underestimate the importance of this final step in the process. Plan for the launch early (some chemical firms' divisions require a *preliminary launch* plan to be delivered as part of the "business case" before the Development phase even begins), and make sure that sufficient resources are allocated to this launch.

7. SYNERGISTIC PRODUCTS DO BETTER

The old adage, "Attack from a position of strength" certainly applies to these new chemical products. Where synergy with the base business was lacking, new products fared poorly on average. Synergistic products, by contrast, achieved an 81 percent success rate (versus only 49 percent for the non-synergistic one-third of products); they had significantly higher profitability ratings and impacts on the company; and they achieved a higher market share—about 19 percentage points higher than for products without synergy.

In the context of the chemical industry, here are some of the more important ingredients of a "synergistic" new product. There was a strong fit between the needs of the new product project and the resources, skills and experience of the firm/division in terms of:

- Management capabilities;
- Technical support and customer service skills/resources;
- Market research and market intelligence skills/resources;
- Selling (sales force) skills/resources;
- R&D (product development) skills/resources (for example, the new product could leverage internal, existing technical skills);
- Manufacturing skills/experience;
- Distribution skills/resources.

These seven synergy ingredients become obvious checklist items in a scoring or rating model to help prioritize new product projects. If your synergy score is low, then there must be other compelling reasons to proceed with the project.

8. NATURE OF PURCHASE HAS STRONG IMPACT

The *nature of the purchase* is often overlooked; yet it constitutes an important body of literature in the field of buyer behavior, namely literature on the *adoption-of-innovation process*.

Our study concludes that many of the characteristics that capture the nature of the purchase—specifically, the level of risk, ease of adoption, and purchase importance from the customer's perspective—are indeed important considerations in the success equation. These adoption characteristics, in rank order of importance, are:

1. Projects where customer tests or trials could be used as valid predictors of ultimate product performance (low risk to the customer);
2. Products that represent important purchases to the customer, with a significant impact on her operation;
3. Products whose adoption holds little risk for the customer;
4. Products for which the customer is certain about the outcome of the purchase;
5. New products that the customer can test or try out easily and inexpensively before adoption;
6. New products that require little change to the customer's own product or process.

Taken together, these characteristics indicate the likelihood of product adoption, and hence have a profound impact on new product performance. For example, new products in the top third on this "adoption likelihood index" achieved an admirable success rate (79 percent); they had a higher profitability rating; they were more likely to be technical successes; and they had a greater sales and profit impact on the firm. Although these purchase characteristics are unfamiliar to many product developers, they deserve to be built into your checklist

of items to consider when evaluating the odds of winning.

9. RIGHT ORGANIZATIONAL DESIGN IS AT HEART OF SUCCESSFUL PROJECTS

"Rip apart a badly developed project and you will unfailingly find 75 percent of slippage attributable to (1) 'siloing' or sending memos up and down vertical organizational 'silos' or 'stovepipes' for decisions, and (2) sequential problem solving," according to Peters (9). Our study concurs: Good organizational design was strongly linked to success. Projects that lacked good organizational design—the bottom third on this dimension—fared poorly, with much lower success, profitability, technical success, and timeliness ratings. Good organizational design in this study meant (in rank order of impact) projects:

1. Organized as a cross-functional team (as opposed to each function doing its own part independently);
2. Where the team was dedicated and focused (i.e., devoted a large percentage of their time to this project, as opposed to being spread over many projects);
3. Where the team was accountable for the entire project from beginning to end (as opposed to being accountable for only one phase);
4. Led by a strong champion;
5. With top management committed to, and strongly supporting, the project.

While the ingredients of "good organizational design"—"good O.D."—should be familiar, it is surprising that many projects lacked good O.D. For example, one-third of the projects scored below 6.5 on this ten-point metric or dimension. This is not a particularly admirable score, given that a dedicated, accountable cross-functional team approach is such a well-known success ingredient!

Interestingly, performance for the top third and the middle third of projects in terms of O.D.

was essentially the same; it appears that there are diminishing returns to O.D., and that only when O.D. is poor (bottom third) are the effects felt.

The implication is that careful thought must be given to how the project team is structured and led. Strive toward a cross-functional, dedicated and accountable team, led by a champion and supported by top management. Although some of these concepts are not new, it is reassuring to find concrete evidence that this team approach *really does deliver better results*; it is equally provocative to find that despite the pleas to move to a team approach, many firms/divisions have yet to get the message.

10. STEP-OUT PROJECTS TEND TO FAIL

Some projects took the firm into unfamiliar territory: a new product category, new customers, unfamiliar customer needs served, new competitors for the firm, unfamiliar technology, new sales force, channels and servicing requirements, and an unfamiliar manufacturing process. These step-out projects into unfamiliar territory had a lower success rate (by 26 percentage points); achieved a lower market share (by 8 percentage points); and were rated lower in terms of both profitability and impact on the company.

The encouraging news is that the negative impact here was not as strong as for most factors. New and unfamiliar territory certainly results in lower success rates and profitability, on average; but the rates were not dramatically lower. The message from our study is that sometimes it is necessary to venture into new and unfamiliar markets, technologies or manufacturing processes. Do so with caution, and be aware that success rates will suffer; but note that the odds of disaster are not so high as to justify not making the move altogether.

11. QUALITY OF EXECUTION PAYS OFF

The great majority of new product resources—people and money—goes to technological activities in these new chemical products. Not surprisingly, how well these activities were executed also impacted on success. As for other activities, we developed a quality-of-execution index for technical actions: preliminary technical assessment; product development; in-house or lab testing; pilot or trial production; and commercial production start-up.

Projects where these five technical activities were well executed out-performed the rest, and by a considerable margin on some performance dimensions. The top third of projects, in terms of quality-of-execution of technical actions:

- Had a higher success rate (73 percent versus only 49 percent for the bottom third);
- Had a higher technical success rating (but not a significantly higher profitability rating);
- Did significantly better on the two time metrics: time efficiency and adherence to the time schedule.

While quality-of-execution of these technical activities did not have the dramatic impact on new product performance that either marketing or homework activities did, the good news is that proficiency was much better here: The top third of projects' technical actions scored over 8.0 on this ten-point quality-of-execution index, considerably higher than for other activities; even the middle third scored reasonably well—a score of 6.8 or better.

12. NON-PRODUCT ADVANTAGES HAVE LESS IMPACT

Some firms seek competitive advantage via elements other than product advantage; for example, through superior customer service, a strong company reputation or a better sales force. Does such a non-product strategy work in the new product arena? Yes, but not as well as gaining advantage via the product itself.

Non-product advantage was gained from six key elements (in rank order of impact):

1. Superior customer service and technical support for the new product;

2. High level of technical competence (as perceived by the customer) for this type of product;

3. Superior sales force (e.g., larger, better qualified);

4. Positive company image or reputation;

5. Faster or more reliable product delivery;

6. A well-known brand name.

One other possible element of non-product advantage included advertising and promotion, but it failed to impact on success, and hence was dropped from this list.

Non-product advantage, as gauged by these six elements, certainly did influence new product outcomes, but not nearly as dramatically as for the other success factors described so far. For example, the top third of products on this dimension had a success rate of 80 percent (versus 57 percent for the bottom third); and they also had significantly higher profitability and impact-on-the-company ratings.

The message is evident: By all means, strive for advantage via non-product elements—superior service and technical support, a reputation for technical competence, a quality sales force, product availability, and a positive company image and brand name. Every advantage helps. But don't pin your hopes on these elements alone; whenever you hear yourself saying "Our company's reputation, brand name or sales force will make this product a winner," be on guard. If these are your only elements of advantage, you may be overestimating your chances of winning!

The competitive situation has surprisingly little impact on new product outcomes: 64 percent of new products were successful in the highly competitive markets while 74 percent were successful in the less competitive markets. Other performance measures showed similar tendencies. The one exception was timeliness: Highly competitive markets meant closer adherence to the time schedule.

One message is that the markets for these chemical products were *all quite competitive*, and there was not much dispersion along this dimension. In short, there is no such thing as a "non-competitive, comfortable market"—they are all tough! Hence, a difficult competitive situation is most often a given. Second, look to other factors as the key to success: New products succeed *not so much because of their external environment, but because of what project teams and leaders do*—because they conceive and develop superior products, execute pivotal activities in a superb fashion, do solid up-front homework, have a strong customer focus, get sharp and early product definition, and plan and execute a good launch.

13. NATURE OF INNOVATION HAS SURPRISING IMPACT

Innovativeness can be measured in one of two ways: whether or not the product is truly new to the marketplace, and how new the product is to the developing firm. The new products studied fit into one of five categories of product innovativeness (percent breakdowns are given):

1. Innovation: a totally new product to the world (18.8 percent of cases);

2. New to market, new to company—a totally new product to the company that also offered new features to an existing market (33.7 percent);

3. New line: a totally new product or line to company, but an existing market and similar products in that market (16.8 percent);

4. A new item in an existing product line for the company (11.9 percent);

5. A modification of an existing company product (18.8 percent).

Surprisingly, success and failure were not strongly connected to the nature of the innovation. For most measures of performance, there was no significant connection, but there were trends and some significant impacts, including some surprising U-shaped impacts (see Table 48.1):

TABLE 48.1
Impact of the Nature of the Innovation

Nature of innovation	True innovation	New to company and to market	New line for company	New item in existing line	Modification
Category:	1	2	3	4	5
Percent breakdown	18.8%	33.7%	16.8%	11.9%	18.8%
Percent successful	63.2%	68.6%	47.1%	83.3%	70.0%
Tech success rating (0–10)	8.32	7.69	6.39	7.75	7.56
Impact on company (0–10)	6.11	5.46	5.72	7.08	6.37

- New items in an existing company line (category 4 above) had the highest success rate (83 percent), while new lines for the firm (category 3) had the highest failure rate (53 percent). Note that highly innovative products had a respectable 63 percent success rate.

- Technical success ratings were greatest for true innovations (category 1), and least for new lines.

- Closer-to-home new products and highly innovative products had the greatest sales and profit impact on the company: new items in an existing line (category 4) followed by true innovations (category 1). Products *new to the company* had the least impact.

The message is that highly innovative products (category 1), in spite of all their perceived risks and pitfalls, achieved an admirable track record in this study. Perhaps there is less to be feared from being bold and innovative than we had imagined. Note that *innovativeness* is not the same dimension as developing step-out products (item 10 above). The latter is measured *relative to the firm*; products that represented new territory for the company did poorly. Product innovativeness, by contrast, is measured *relative to the marketplace and competition*; new products high on this dimension did very well.

Near the other end of the innovativeness spectrum, much less innovative products—new items in an existing company line, category 4—also achieved a high performance, indeed the best *overall*: the highest success rate, highest technical success rat-

ing, and greatest sales and profit impact on the firm. By contrast, the "middle of the road" or "fairly safe" strategy of launching a new product line, where there is already a market with very similar products in it (category 3), may not be so safe after all. Such products yielded the lowest success rates (47 percent) and the lowest impacts on the firm.

ORDER OF ENTRY MAKES LITTLE DIFFERENCE

One of the drives of today's quest for cycle time reduction is the belief that "being first into the market spells success." The evidence from our study does not support this contention, however. True, products that were first into the market were more successful than those that followed (71 percent versus 60 percent), but this difference was not significant; nor were the profitability rating differences significant. Being "first-in" should not be one's ultimate goal. Many of our new product failures were first into their markets—"fast failures"; an ill-conceived product, developed in haste, often leads to disaster. The lesson is that it may be better to be a fast second with a superior product that has real customer benefits than simply being first.

SO MUCH FOR MYTHS!

None of the 13 success factors discussed in this article come as a total surprise. Indeed, many have been reported or hinted at in previous studies or articles. The success factors we identified are totally consistent with our previous NewProd conclusions (6). Therefore, these results and the ensuing message for managers can likely be applied to a wider range of industries. The disconcerting evidence is that many managers and project teams apparently have failed to get the message.

I began the article with eight well-known myths. Here's how they stack up against the evidence:

1. Being first into the market is only marginally more successful. Being "best in" is far more profitable.

2. Up-front homework really does pay off, not only in terms of higher profits and success rates, but it saves time as well.

3. While a company reputation, a strong brand name, and a good selling effort do help, they are not nearly as decisive as gaining advantage via the product itself.

4. Low price is not the key to winning; rather, good value for money and superior price/performance characteristics are.

5. You cannot afford not to do market studies, customer tests, and a trial sell. High-quality marketing actions yield a double payoff: they drive up profitability and drive down the cycle time.

6. Even for large and powerful firms, synergy is important. The ability to build on in-house resources and capabilities is central to success.

7. Pin down the definition of the product before development begins; it may limit the scope of the developer or designer somewhat, but it certainly drives profits up and time-to-market down in a major way.

8. New products succeed in spite of the market's competitiveness; the competitive situation per se is not that strongly linked to winning and losing. You cannot blame competitiveness for your ills.

So much for myths!

REFERENCES

1. The research team consisted of the author, Professor Robert G. Cooper, and his colleague, Professor Elko Kleinschmidt, together with graduate student research assistants. Professor Kleinschmidt has co-authored a number of research reports on the NewProd studies with Cooper.

2. Cooper, R. G. "Why new industrial products fail." *Industrial Marketing Management*, 4, 1975, pp. 315–26.

3. Cooper, R. G. "The dimensions of industrial new product success and failure." *Journal of Marketing*, 43, Summer 1979, pp. 93–103.

4. Cooper, R. G. and E. J. Kleinschmidt. "An investigation into the new product process: steps, deficiencies and impact." *Journal of Product Innovation Management*, 3, 2, 1986, pp. 71–85.

5. Cooper, R. G. and E. J. Kleinschmidt. "New products: what separates winners from losers." *Journal of Product Innovation Management*, 4, 3, 1987, pp. 169–184.

6. Cooper, R. G. and E. J. Kleinschmidt. *New Products: The Key Factors in Success*. Chicago: American Marketing Assoc., 1990, monograph. See also: Cooper, R. G. "New products: what distinguishes the winners." *Research • Technology Management*, Nov.–Dec. 1990, pp. 27–31.

7. Cooper, R. G. and E. J. Kleinschmidt. "Major new products: What distinguishes the winners in the chemical industry." *Journal of Product Innovation Management*, vol. 2, no. 10, March 1993, pp. 90–111.

8. Cooper, R. G. and E. J. Kleinschmidt. "New product success in the chemical industry." *Industrial Marketing Management*, vol. 22, no. 2, 1993, pp. 85–99.

9. Peters, Tom. *Thriving on Chaos*. New York: Harper & Row, 1988.

10. Cooper, R. G. "Debunking the myths of new product development." *Research-Technology Management*, July–August, 1994, pp. 40–50.

11. Cooper, R. G. *Winning at New Products*, 2d ed. Reading, MA.: Addison-Wesley, 1993.

17

Managing the Dynamics of Innovation

49

Product and Process Concept Development
Via the Lead User Method

ERIC VON HIPPEL

The field experiment reported in this paper addresses an important problem facing all innovative organizations, which is, how can one effectively determine user needs for developing new products (processes and services, too) in markets that are strongly affected by rapid changes in technology? This paper begins by exploring some of the difficulties faced by traditional methods of market research. It then presents and tests a "lead user" methodology that I propose as a useful managerial solution for dealing with this problem.

ROOT OF THE PROBLEM: MARKETING RESEARCH CONSTRAINED BY USER EXPERIENCE

One important function of marketing research is to accurately understand user needs for potential new

Eric von Hippel is Professor in the Management of Technology Group at M.I.T.'s Sloan School of Management. Reprinted with permission from von Hippel, Eric.

products. Such understanding is clearly an essential input to the success of the new product development process. Nevertheless, users selected to provide input data to consumer and industrial market analysis have an important limitation: their insights into new product (and process and service) needs and potential solutions are constrained by their real-world experiences. Users steeped in the present are, therefore, unlikely to generate novel product concepts that conflict with the familiar.

The notion that familiarity with existing product attributes and uses interferes with an individual's ability to conceive of novel attributes and uses is strongly supported by research into problem solving. Extant studies have shown, for example, that when experimental subjects are familiarized with a complicated problem-solving strategy, they are unlikely to devise a simpler one even when this is appropriate. Moreover, subjects who use an object or see it used in a very normal and familiar way are strongly blocked from using that object in a new or novel manner. In fact, the more recently these objects or problem-solving strategies were used in a familiar way, the more difficult it was for the subject to employ them in a more innovative way. In an R&D setting, Allen and Marquis showed that the success of a research group in solving a new problem was strongly dependent on whether the solutions and experiences it had used in the past fit the demands of the new problem.[1] All of these research studies suggest that typical users of existing products—the type of customer or userevaluators usually chosen in market research—are poorly situated with regard to the difficult problem-solving tasks associated with assessing unfamiliar product and process needs.

The constraint of users to the familiar pertains even in the instance of sophisticated marketing research techniques such as multiattribute mapping of product perceptions and preferences. Multiattribute (multidimensional) marketing research methods, for example, describe users' (buyers') perception of new and existing products in terms of a number of attributes (dimensions). If a complete list of attributes is available for a given product category, the users' perceptions of any particular product in the category can be expressed in terms of the amount of each attribute they perceive it to contain, and the difference between any two products in the category can be expressed as the difference in their attribute profiles. Similarly, users' preferences for existing and proposed products in a category can in principle be built up from their perceptions of the importance and desirability of each of the component product attributes.

Although these methods frame user perceptions and preferences in terms of known attributes, they do not offer a means of going beyond the experience of those interviewed. First, for reasons discussed earlier, users are not well positioned to accurately evaluate novel product attributes or accurately quantify familiar product attributes that lie outside the range of their real-world experience. Second, and more specific to these techniques, there is no mechanism to induce users to identify all product attributes potentially relevant to a product category, especially attributes that are currently not present in any of the given categories.

In similarity-dissimilarity data techniques, for example, users are asked to characterize a product category by comparing products in that category and assessing them in terms of their similarity and dissimilarity. Sometimes the user specifies the ways in which the products are similar or different. In others, the user simply provides similarity and difference rankings or ratings, and the market researcher determines (through his personal knowledge of the product type in question) the important perceptual dimensions that must be motivating the user's data comparisons.

Such similarity-dissimilarity methods clearly depend on the analyst's qualitative ability to interpret the data and correctly identity all the critical dimensions. However, this method can only explore perceptions derived from attributes that exist in, or are associated with, the actual products being compared. Thus, if a group of evaluators is invited to compare a set of cameras and none has a particular feature—say, instant developing—then the possible utility of this feature would not be incorporated in the perceptual dimensions generated. That is, the method would have been blind to the possible value of instant developing prior to Edwin Land's invention of the Polaroid camera.

While other market research techniques, focus group methods for example, need not be limited in principle to identifying only attributes already present in existing products, most of the discussions and associated data are nominally focused on these. Generally speaking, it is very unlikely that these methods can be used to identify attributes not present in the actual set of products being studied, much less a complete list of all relevant attributes. Conventional market research methods simply do not contain an effective mechanism for encouraging these kinds of outcomes, and discussions with practitioners indicate that in present-day practice, identification of any novel attribute is improbable. In sum, then, marketing researchers face serious difficulties when they attempt to determine new product needs that fall outside of the real-world experience of the users they analyze.

LEAD USERS AS A SOLUTION

In many product categories, the constraint of users to the familiar does not lessen the ability of marketing research to evaluate needs for new products by analyzing typical users. In the relatively slow-moving world of steels and autos, for example, new models often do not differ radically from their immediate predecessors. Therefore, even the "new" is reasonably familiar and the typical user can thus play a valuable role in the development of new products.

Contrastingly, in high technology industries, the world moves so rapidly that the related real-world experience of ordinary users is often rendered obsolete by the time a product is developed or during the time of its projected commercial lifetime. For such industries, I propose that lead users, who *do* have real-life experience with novel product or process needs, are essential to accurate marketing research. Although the insights of lead users are as constrained to the familiar as those of other users, lead users are more familiar with conditions that lie in the future and so, are in a position to pro-

vide accurate data on needs related to such prospective conditions.

Lead users of a novel or enhanced product, process, or service are defined as those who display two characteristics with respect to it:

1. Lead users face needs that will be general in a marketplace, but they face them months or years before the bulk of that marketplace encounters them, *and*

2. Lead users are in a position to benefit significantly by obtaining a solution to those needs.

Each of the two lead user characteristics provides an independent contribution to the type of new product need and solution data that such lead users are hypothesized to possess. The first specifies that a lead user will possess the particular real-world experience that the manufacturers must analyze if they are to accurately understand the needs that the bulk of the market will have "tomorrow." Users "at the front of the trend" typically exist simply because important new technologies, products, tastes, and other factors related to new product opportunities typically diffuse through a society over many years rather than impact all members simultaneously.[2]

The second lead user characteristic is a direct application of the hypothesis that the greater the benefit a given user expects to obtain from a needed novel product or process, the greater his investment will be in obtaining a solution. Users who expect high returns from a solution to a need they are experiencing should have been driven by these expectations to attempt to solve their need. This work in turn will have produced insight into the need and perhaps useful solutions that will be of value to inquiring market researchers.

In sum, then, lead users are users whose present strong needs will become general in a marketplace months or years in the future. Since lead users are familiar with conditions that lie in the future for most others, it is hypothesized that they can serve as a need-forecasting laboratory for marketing research. Moreover, since lead users often attempt to fill the need they experience, it is also hypothesized that they can provide valuable new product concept and design data to inquiring manufacturing organizations in addition to need data. As a result, lead users may have a great deal more to contribute than data regarding their unfilled needs; often, they may contribute insights regarding solutions as well. Such "solution" data can range from rich insights to actual working and tested prototypes of the desired novel product, process, or service.

This lead user method was developed by von Hippel, based on his 12-year study of the innovation process.[3] Von Hippel's research traced the role of users in product innovation. The most striking finding was that *users* were often the actual developers of original prototype solutions to what eventually became successful commercial products. In some industries, users had been responsible for most of the important product or process innovations. Users were found, for example, to be the actual developers of 82% of all commercialized scientific instruments studied and 63% of all semiconductor and electron subassembly manufacturing equipment innovations studied. These findings go against conventional wisdom, which holds that manufacturers are typically the developers of new products. It is also a major challenge to the common belief that users can provide market researchers only with data on market need. What von Hippel's research evidence demonstrates convincingly is that often innovative users also have valuable new product information to offer design engineers and product developers.

TESTING THE METHOD

To test the usefulness of the lead user concept, a prototype lead user market research study was undertaken in the rapidly changing field of computer-aided-design (CAD) products.[4] (Over 40 firms compete in the $1 billion market for CAD hardware and software. This market grew at over 35% per year over the period 1982 to 1986 and the forecast is for continued growth at this rate for the next several years.) Within the CAD field, we decided

to specifically focus on CAD systems used to design the printed circuit (PC) boards used in electronic products, PC–CAD.

Printed circuit boards hold integrated circuit chips and other electronic components and interconnect these into functioning circuits. PC–CAD systems help engineers convert circuit specifications into detailed printed circuit board designs. The design steps that are, or can be, aided by PC–CAD include component placement, signal routing (interconnections), editing and checking, documentation, and interfacing to manufacturing. The software required to perform these tasks is quite complex and includes placement and routing algorithms and sophisticated graphics. Some PC–CAD manufacturers sell only such software, whereas others sell systems that include both specialized computers and software. (Important suppliers of PC–CAD in 1985 included IBM, Computervision, Redac, Calma, Scicards, and Telesis.)

The method used to identify lead users and test the value of the data they possess in the PC–CAD field involved four major steps: (1) identify an important market or technical trend, (2) identify lead users with respect to that trend, (3) analyze lead user data, and (4) test lead user data on ordinary users. I will discuss each in turn.

Identifying an Important Trend

Lead users are defined as being in advance of the market with respect to a given important dimension that is changing over time. Therefore, before one can identify lead users in a given product category of interest, one must specify the underlying trend on which these users have a leading position.

To identify an "important" trend in PC–CAD, we sought out a number of expert users. We identified these by telephoning managers of the PC–CAD groups of a number of firms in the Boston area and asking each: "Whom do you regard as the engineer most expert in PC–CAD in your firm?" "Whom in your company do group members turn to when they face difficult PC–CAD problems?"[5] After our discussions with expert users, it was qualitatively clear to us that an increase in the density with which chips and circuits are placed on a board was, and would continue to be, a very important trend in the PC–CAD field. Historical data showed that board density had in fact been steadily increasing over a number of years. And the value of continuing increases in density was clear. An increase in density means that it is possible to mount more electronic components on a given size printed circuit board. This in turn translates directly into an ability to lower costs (less material is used), to decreased product size, and to increased speed of circuit operation (signals between components travel shorter distances when board density is higher).

Very possibly, other equally important trends exist in the field that would reward analysis, but we decided to focus on this single trend in our study.

Identifying Lead Users

To identify lead users of PC–CAD systems capable of designing high-density printed circuit boards, we had to identify that subset of users: (1) who were designing very high-density boards now and (2) who were positioned to gain especially high benefit from increases in board density. We decided to use a formal telephone-screening questionnaire to accomplish this task, and we strove to design one that contained objective indicators of these two hypothesized lead user characteristics.

Printed circuit board density can be increased in a number of ways and each offers an objective means of determining a respondent's position on the trend toward higher density. First, the number of layers of printed wiring in a printed circuit board can be increased. (Early boards contained only 1 or 2 layers but now some manufacturers are designing boards with 20 or more layers.) Second, the size of electronic components can be decreased. (A recent important technique for achieving this is surface-mounted devices that are soldered directly to the surface of a printed circuit board.) Finally, the printed wires, vias, that interconnect the electronic components on a board that can be made narrower and packed more closely. Questions regarding each of these density-related attributes were included in our questionnaire.

Next, we assessed the level of benefit a respondent might expect to gain by improvements in PC–CAD by means of several questions. First, we asked about users' level of satisfaction with existing PC–CAD equipment, assuming that high dissatisfaction would indicate expected high benefit from improvements. Second, we asked whether respondents had developed and built their own PC–CAD systems rather than buy the commercially available systems such as those offered by IBM or Computervision. (We assumed, as we noted previously, that users who make such innovation investments do so because they expect high benefit from resulting PC–CAD system improvement.) Finally, we asked respondents whether they thought their firms were innovators in the field of PC–CAD.

The PC–CAD users interviewed were restricted to U.S. firms and selected from two sources: A list of members of the relevant professional engineering association (IPCA) and a list of current and potential customers provided by a cooperating supplier. Interviewees were selected from both lists at random. We contacted approximately 178 qualified respondents and had them answer the questions on the phone or by mail if they preferred. The cooperation rate was good: 136 screening questionnaires were completed. One third of these were completed by engineers or designers, one third by CAD or printed circuit board managers, 26% by general engineering managers, and 8% by corporate officers.

Simple inspection of the screening questionnaire responses showed that fully 23% of all responding user firms had developed their own in-house PC–CAD hardware and software systems. Also, this high proportion of user-innovators that we found in our sample is probably characteristic of the general population of PC–CAD users. Our sample was well dispersed across the self-stated scale with respect to innovativeness: 24% indicated they were on the leading edge of technology, 38% up-to-date, 25% in the mainstream, and 13% adopting only after the technology is clearly established. This self-perception is supported by objective behavior with respect to the alacrity with which our respondents adopted PC–CAD.

We next conducted a cluster analysis of screening questionnaire data relating to the hypothesized lead user characteristics in an attempt to identify a lead user group. The two cluster solution is shown in Table 49.1.

Note that this analysis does, indeed, clearly indicate a group of respondents who combine the two hypothesized attributes of lead users and that, effectively, all of the PC–CAD product innovation is reported by the lead user group.

In the two-cluster solution, what we term the lead users cluster is ahead of nonlead users in the trend toward higher density. That is, lead users report more use of surface-mounted components, use of narrower lines, and use of more layers than do members of the nonlead cluster. Second, lead users appear to expect higher benefit from PC–CAD innovations that would allow them even further progress. That is, they report less satisfaction with their existing PC–CAD systems (4.1 vs. 5.3, with higher values indicating satisfaction). Strikingly, 87% of respondents in the lead user group report building their own PC–CAD system (vs. only 1% of nonlead users) in order to obtain improved PC–CAD system performance.[6] Lead users also judged themselves to be more innovative (3.3 vs. 2.4 on the four-statement scale with higher values

more innovative), and they were in fact earlier adopters of PC–CAD than were nonlead users. Note that 28% of our respondents are classified in this lead user cluster (which is a far higher percentage than I have since found in other lead user studies).

A discriminant analysis indicated that building one's own system was the most important indicator of membership in the lead user cluster. (The discriminant analysis had 95.6% correct classification of cluster membership. The standardized discriminant function of coefficients were: build own .94, self-stated innovativeness .27, average layers .25, satisfaction −.23, year of adoption −.16, surface mounting .15.)

Analyzing Lead User Insights

The next step in our analysis was to select a small sample of the lead users identified in our cluster analysis to participate in a group discussion to develop one or more concepts for improved PC–CAD systems. Experts from five lead user firms that had facilities located near MIT were recruited for this group. The firms represented were Raytheon, DEC, Bell Laboratories, Honeywell, and Teradyne. Four of these five firms had built their own PC–CAD systems. All were working in high-density (many

TABLE 49.1
Cluster Analyses Revealing Lead and Nonlead User Groups

	Two-cluster solution	
	Lead users	Nonlead users
Indicators of user position on PC-CAD density trend		
Use surface mount?	87%	56%
Average line width (mils)	11	15
Average layers (number)	7.1	4.0
Indicators of user-expected benefit from PC-CAD improvement		
Satisfaction[a]	4.1	5.3
Indicators of related user innovation		
Build own PC-CAD?	85%	1%
Innovativeness[b]	3.3	2.4
First use of CAD (year)	1973	1980
Number in cluster	38	98

[a]7-point scale—high value more satisfied.
[b]4-point scale—high value more innovative.

layers and narrow lines) applications and had adopted the CAD technology early.

The task set for this group was to specify the best PC–CAD system for laying out high-density digital boards that could be built with current technology. (To guard against the inclusion of "dream" features impossible to implement, we conservatively allowed the concept the group developed to include only features that one or more of them had already implemented in their own organizations. No one firm had implemented all aspects of the concept, however.)

The PC–CAD system concept developed by our lead user creative group integrated the output of PC–CAD with numerically controlled printed circuit board manufacturing machines; had easy input interfaces (e.g., block diagrams, interactive graphics, icon menus); and stored data centrally with access by all systems. It also provided full functional and environmental simulation (e.g., electrical, mechanical, and thermal) of the board being designed and could design boards of up to 20 layers, route thin lines, and properly located surface-mounted devices on the board.

Testing Product Concept Perceptions and Preferences

From the point of view of marketing research, new product need data and new product solutions from lead users are only interesting if they are preferred by the general marketplace.

To test this matter, we decided to determine PC–CAD user preferences for four system concepts: the system concept developed by the lead user group, each user's own in-house PC–CAD system, the best commercial PC–CAD system available at the time of the study (as determined by a PC–CAD system manufacturer's competitive analysis), and a system for laying out curved printed circuit boards. (This last was a description of a special-purpose system that one lead user had designed in-house to lay out boards curved into three-dimensional shapes. This is a useful attribute if one is trying to fit boards into the oddly shaped spaces inside some very compact products, but most users would have no practical use for it. In

our analysis of preference, we think user response to this concept can serve to flag any respondent tendency to prefer systems based on system exotica rather than practical value in use.)

To obtain user preference data regarding our four PC–CAD system concepts, we designed a new questionnaire that contained measures of both perception and preference. First, respondents were asked to rate their current PC–CAD system on 17 attribute scales. (These were generated by a separate sample of users through triad comparisons of alternate systems, open-ended interviews, and technical analysis.) Each scale was presented to respondents in the form of five-point agree-disagree judgment based on a statement such as "my system is easy to customize."[7] Next, each respondent was invited to read a one-page description of each of the three concepts we had generated (labeled simply, J, K, and L) and rate them on the same scales. All concepts were described as having an identical price of $150,000 for a complete hardware and software workstation system able to support four users. Next, rank-order preference and constant-sum paired comparison judgments were requested for the three concepts and the existing system. Finally, probability-of-purchase measures on an 11-point Juster scale were collected for each concept at the base price of $150,000, with alternate prices of $100,000 and $200,000.

Our second questionnaire was sent to 173 users (the 178 respondents who qualified in the screening survey less the 5 user firms in the creative group). Respondents were called by phone to inform them that a questionnaire had been sent. After telephone follow-up and a second mailing of the questionnaire, 71 complete or near-complete responses were obtained (41%) and the following analyses are based on these.

CONCEPT PREFERENCES

Our analysis of the concept questionnaire showed that respondents strongly preferred the lead user group PC–CAD system concept over the three others presented to them: 78.6% of the sample selected the lead user's creative group concept as their first choice. It was strongly preferred by users over their existing systems. Respondents maintained their preferences for the lead user concept even when it was priced higher than competing concepts. The effects of price were investigated through the probability of purchase measures collected at three different prices for each concept. Even when the lead user concept was priced twice as high as that of competing concepts, the lead user concept was still strongly preferred and more likely to be purchased.

The needs of today's lead users are typically not precisely the same as the needs of the users who will make up a major share of tomorrow's predicted market. Indeed, the literature on diffusion suggests that in general the early adopters of a novel product or practice differ in significant ways from the bulk of the users who follow them. However, in this instance, the product concept preferences and the probability of purchase measures of lead users and nonlead users were very similar. Furthermore, a comparison of the way in which lead and non-lead users evaluated PC–CAD system attributes showed that this similarity was deep-seated.

Even though this field experiment supports the usefulness of the lead user method, there are certain problematic issues that must be further explored. One problem is accurate trend identification. Currently we rely on a skillful analyst to select an important trend on the basis of judgement (much as product attributes for use in multi-attribute analysis are selected by market research analysts on the basis of judgement and qualitative data). Clearly, it would be useful to improve this method. A second problem is the tacit assumption that the product perceptions and preferences of lead users are or will be similar to non-lead users as a market develops. When this is true, evaluation of the eventual appeal of a lead user product or product concept is straightforward. But what if lead users like the product and non-lead users do not? In this case there are two possibilities: (1) The concept is too novel to be appreciated by non-lead users—but it will later be preferred by them when their needs evolve to resemble those of today's lead users; (2) the concept appeals only to lead users and will

never be appreciated by non-lead users even after they "evolve."

And finally, this study focused on the identification and study of naturally occurring lead users. Perhaps lead users can also be created? It is possible for manufacturers to stimulate user innovation by acting to increase user innovation-related benefit. If they can also place users in environments which they judge to foreshadow future general market conditions, they may be able to create lead users. Market research studies which allow users to experience prototypes of proposed new products and then test their reactions are a possible step in this direction.

IMPLEMENTING THE LEAD USER CONCEPT

Over the past years, we have done successful lead user studies in many different industries both in the U.S. and in Europe. For example, at Hilti, a leading European manufacturer of components, equipment, and materials used in the construction industry, we conducted a lead user study to develop a concept for a novel "pipe-hanger" system.[8] This is a type of fastening system used to hang pipes on walls and ceilings in commercial and industrial buildings. By working with lead users. Hilti personnel developed a new pipe-hanger system that was commercially very successful and that also won them an industry achievement award for outstanding product development work. Listed below are the steps they went through in their study.

The Hilti research team first identified a few important need-related trends by conducting telephone interviews with experts in the field of study. Based on their trend analysis they came up with these three market needs:

1. Pipe hangers that are very easy to assemble (the reason being that education levels among installers are going down in many countries);

2. A more secure system of connecting hanger elements together and attaching them to walls and ceilings (the reason—more stringent safety requirements in the industry);

3. Pipe-hangers made from lighter, noncorrodible materials (e.g. plastics rather than commonly used steel elements).

Next they found 22 expert users by surveying co-operating firms throughout Europe. The users were all tradesmen who had actually designed, built and then installed hangers that were not commercially available. The list of 22 was paired down to 12 lead users who had the richest information to offer. They participated with 3 Hilti engineers and the marketing manager in a 3-day creative problem-solving workshop to develop a system for a novel pipe-hanging system that had the characteristics identified in the trend analysis. The final step in their study was to ask a small sample of "routine" users to evaluate the concept that came out of the workshop. The majority of those surveyed preferred the new concept and indicated they would be willing to pay a 20% higher price for it, relative to existing systems.

As another example in a much different industry, Lee Meadows (a fellow market research consultant) and I undertook a lead user study for a major manufacturer of food products. The company was seeking a new kind of snack. In this study, lead users, nutrition experts, and internal scientists developed a concept for a performance-enhancing cookie designed to appeal to the amateur athlete market. Prior to the study, the client company's market research groups had identified several trends that suggested opportunities for new snack foods. One, for example, was a trend towards more interest in ethnic foods. Another was a growing public interest in healthy foods. A third trend was an increasing interest in workout activities and sports by "weekend athletes." Based on the interests expressed in discussions with Management, it was decided to focus on the trends toward an increasing interest in nutrition and weekend sport activities.

At the start of the study, it was known that nutrition was obviously connected in some ways with athletic performance, but they did not know if nutrition in the form of "snacking" could actually help performance in any way. Thus, they began their work by reading a range of sport magazines (e.g. those aimed at serious amateur runners and weight lifters) and articles by "sport nutrition" experts to determine if there was evidence of a link between certain forms of snacking and improved performance. In their reading they found there was a real basis for the performance-enhancing value of eating some kinds of snacks before, during and/or after athletic activities (e.g. eating certain nutrients after athletic performances could speed recovery of muscles).

We then conducted telephone interviews with a number of elite athletes, prominent coaches and nutrition scientists to identify an appropriate group to participate with internal scientists in a concept development workshop. Some of those interviewed were olympic athletes, coaches, and scientists associated with their training. The workshop group they assembled included a nutrition scientist who was involved in work with elite Navy fighters, a competitive bike racer, and a winner of national events in weight lifting. Through the interviews, we found that knowledge about performance enhancing snack foods was segmented between the nutrition scientists and athletes. The scientists knew what ingredients the snacks should contain and something about dose timing. The athletes knew how the cookie should be formulated for easy consumption. To be able to clearly focus on first one and then the other type of information, they decided to run two concept development workshops. One was composed mainly of nutrition scientists and the other was made up primarily of elite athletes.

Workshop participants succeeded in developing a concept for an "olympic cookie" which specified what it should contain and how it should be formulated and packaged. Of course, lead users and the nutrition scientists could only comment on what they cared about and knew. They did not care much how the cookie tasted so the company experts added the taste dimension based on previous studies of more routine snack consumers. Management of the company was very pleased with the concept that came out of the study and planned to introduced it in a line of "healthy snacks."

Typically, our lead user studies are carried out

by a team composed of both technical and marketing people. It is done before the start of formal product development work. The research process includes four stages, with each stage defined by activities that move the research team forward to a more refined understanding of market needs *and* possible solutions to these needs. The essence of the four stages is described below:

Stage 1: Planning the Lead User Project—Management selects the focus of the innovation effort and determines the resources needed to carry out the lead user study.

Stage 2: Identifying an Important Trend—The core research team identifies a promising need-related trend (by scanning trade literature and interviewing experts in the field of study).

Stage 3: Screening for Lead Users—The team locates a small group of sophisticated users (e.g. 4–6) who "lead" the trend.

Stage 4: Learning from Lead Users—The lead user group and in-house experts co-develop a concept for a new product in a 1–2 day workshop and the appeal of the concept is tested in the general market.

It is my strong belief that there are certain advantages of the lead user method over traditional research approaches. By "traditional" approaches, I mean methods designed to collect data on the *needs* of typical users prior to product development. First, I see the lead user method as enabling research teams to collect more accurate and richer data on future market needs than is possible to get with traditional methods. Recall that by definition, lead users have product needs that are ahead of the general market. Thus, by focusing on this type of user, teams are likely to uncover information on *emerging* product needs—ones that are latent for the majority of the market. The limitation of traditional methods stems from the fact that the "average" user—the type usually selected for analyses—does not have the real work experience required to know or even imagine what products others will want in the future. Lead users are also limited in a similar way. However, because they lead the market in

terms of their experiences with existing products, they are in a better position than most users to have insights into future market needs.

Secondly, lead user research typically enables manufacturers to speed up the new product development process. One reason for this is that the output of a lead user study is an actual new product concept, thus cutting down the work required by design engineers. In addition, the whole innovation process is more integrated because technical and marketing people are working collaboratively throughout the lead user study and they maintain their interaction with the external environment as well. As a result, there is much less chance of having product development slowed up later in the process because of misjudging or disagreeing about what the customers want. This heavy involvement with external people is very different from what commonly goes on during front-end market research. Other than one or two focus groups, there is usually no *systematic* interaction with users or experts. Moreover, R&D personnel are typically not directly involved in gathering needs data from users. Even after product development is under way, user contact is likely to be hit and miss, at best. The net effect of the holistic approach employed in a lead user study is to greatly reduce the total expense of new product development. For example, management from Hilti estimated that they were able to cut in *half* both the expense and time of new concept development with the lead user method, versus when they used their traditional methods.

Finally, despite my confidence in the lead user method, I recognize that, for many managers and research teams, it is a very new and therefore, suspect way to go about market research. The "newness" isn't so much in the specific techniques. We find that often teams are familiar with the procedures involved in doing a lead user study. The main difficulty many marketing and R&D personnel have is one of *mindset* about how market research "should" be done. One key aspect of the lead user method that is unfamiliar to many personnel is the idea that sophisticated users can be a source of design data and product ideas, as well as needs and information. Doing a lead user study also requires some managers of the innovation process to make a shift in resource allocation for pre-development market research. Often, managers are skeptical of the value of in-depth market research at the front-end of an innovation project and therefore, do not want to invest much time and money in it. A typical market research reaction is "We can't afford to tie up our best people for this." Unfortunately, many managers still see the "real and important" work as starting with formal product development. They fail to realize that in-depth exploratory market research done early in an innovation project is one of the key ingredients of new product winners.

NOTES

1. T. J. Allen and D. G. Marquis, "Positive and Negative Biasing Sets: The Effects of Prior Experience on Research Performance," *IEEE Transactions on Engineering Management* EM-11, no. 4 (December 1964): 158–614.

2. For example, when Edwin Mansfield (*The Economics of Technological Change* [New York: Norton, 1968], 134–35) explored the rate of diffusion of 12 very important industrial goods innovations into major firms in the bituminous coal, iron and steel, brewing, and railroad industries, he found that in 75% of the cases it took over 20 years for complete diffusion of these innovations to major firms. Accordingly, some users of these innovations could be found far in advance of the general market.

3. Much of this research is reported in E. von Hippel, *The Sources of Innovation*, New York: Oxford University Press, 1988.

4. See G. Urban and E. von Hippel, "Lead User Analyses for the Development of New Industrial Products," *Management Science*, 1988.

5. PC–CAD system purchase decisions are made primarily by the final users in the engineering department responsible for CAD design of boards. In this study we interviewed only these dominant influencers to find concepts and test them. If the purchase decision process had been more diffuse, it would have been appropriate to include other important decision participants in our data collection.

6. The innovating users reported that their goal was to achieve better performance than commercially available products could provide in several areas: high routing density, faster turnaround time to meet market demands, better compatibility to manufacturing, interfaces to other graphics and mechanical CAD systems, and improved ease of use for less experienced users.

7. The 17 attributes were: ease of customization, integration with other CAD systems, completeness of features, integration with manufacturing, maintenance, upgrading, learning, ease of use, power, design time, enough layers, high-density boards, manufacturable designs, reliability, placing and routing capabilities, high value, and updating capability.

8. C. Herstatt and E. von Hippel, "From Experience: Developing New Product Concepts via the Lead User Method: A Case Study in a 'Low-Tech' Field," *Journal of Product Innovation Management*, Vol. 8, 1992, pp. 213–221.

50

Technology Maturation and Technology Substitution

LOWELL W. STEELE

I have always argued that establishing, and modifying over time, the appropriate balance between the application and extension of conventional technology and the development and introduction of new technology is the most important and difficult task in managing technology. This paper will explore additional characteristics of technology, its life cycle, and factors that influence its introduction and use, which we must understand and take into account in establishing this critical balance between conventional and new.

Most candidate new technologies will prove unworthy. Moreover, a manager of technology lacks the in-house skills to pursue every candidate that comes along. He or she must understand the dynamics of technology, how it advances, and what hurdles new technology must pass in order to be accepted. The endgame is application. I learned long ago that R&D managers do not and should not get Brownie points for elegant new technology that somehow does not make it. One CEO, in instructing the new vice president of R&D of a laboratory that had this problem, said, "Get that damned place hooked to the company!"

TECHNOLOGY IS LIKE A JIGSAW PUZZLE

A particular technology does not function in isolation; it is part of a complex system of knowledge of how to do things. In considering whether to continue to rely on present technology or to opt to develop new technology, it is important to understand the process by which a new technology enters the system. I find that it helps to think of the edifice of technology as a complex jigsaw puzzle—a puzzle that has literally been created over centuries. The fit between the pieces, each representing a particular technology, is exceedingly intricate and precise. Occasionally, an invention, e.g., instant photography, antibiotics, lasers, or television, leads to a new capability which actually extends the puzzle, but this is a rare event that cannot form the basis for management principles and priorities. Even the continuing advances in microelectronics, information, and biotechnology, which in the aggregate will have enormous impact and extend the puzzle, will as single entities have a limited impact on the management of most businesses. The difference between a micro- and a macroperspective is important. An individual management team cannot act as though all possible dramatic advances will be important to it.

Even the rare discontinuities, however, cannot be brought into use independent of the existing body of technology. They will have to be made of materials that can be produced in adequate quantities and fabricated with tolerances that can be achieved. They must not introduce undue hazards or side effects and must be amenable to operation by ordinary humans.

A more typical situation, however, occurs when a potential new technology provides a capability that overlies that of one or more pieces in the puzzle. The present corpus of technology represents a capability of enormous power, which is by no means yet fully exploited. Therefore, the new piece (technology) must enter by demonstrating attributes that are in some way superior to those of the present pieces. Even such dramatic advances as

Reprinted with permission of the McGraw-Hill Companies from *Managing Technology: The Strategic View* by Lowell Steele, 1989, pp. 41–52.

Lowell Steele was General Electric's Corporate Vice President for R&D.

the transistor and jet engine had to run the gauntlet of competitive evaluation.

The existing puzzle is both intricate and unforgiving. A new piece must fit the present configuration with great fidelity or else demonstrate enough promise to energize a reconfiguration of the puzzle—a requirement that few advances satisfy. Unfortunately, the fit cannot be determined by inspection, analysis, or simulation—it actually must be tried. This demand imposes so many constraints on a new technology that most prove deficient in some crucial respects. Even more unfortunately, the new technology may exhibit a potential fit with several different pieces of the puzzle, but only trial will demonstrate which, if any, can in fact be replaced.

The situation is even more intractable because several different new pieces may appear at roughly the same time—witness the recent competition in laser disks between electronic and mechanical scanning or the earlier competition between Kevlar, steel, and fiberglass in radial-tire belt cord. None may prove successful in entering the puzzle, but the first one to succeed will usually foreclose the acceptance of any other contestant. (The success of the VHS system of video recording over Betamax is an interesting example of an exception.)

Finally, the puzzle itself is not passive. It recognizes the potential threat of new technology and busily tries to improve its existing structure so as to resist replacement. The manufacturers of photo flashbulbs managed to delay the adoption of electronic flash for widespread amateur use for approximately twenty years by creative invention of lower-cost, more convenient flashbulb systems. The threat to their business proved to be a powerful stimulus to innovation that succeeded in holding off electronic flash despite continuing important advances in the latter. Vacuum tubes were thought to be doomed by the transistor over twenty-years ago, but by virtue of emphasizing cost reduction and identifying niches where they had special advantages, they managed to remain profitable long after they had been written off as finished.

Thus new technology is chasing the constantly moving target of conventional technology, which is goaded to accelerated improvement by the threat.

Frequently, the new technology never catches up. In fact, I would argue that one of the most important economic benefits of a high level of innovative activity is the stimulus it provides for improving conventional technology. The continuing advances in magnetic tape for audio and video recording prevented thermoplastic recording from ever becoming established, and analogous advances in magnetic disks represent a dynamic challenge to optical memories. In a similar fashion, advances in existing technologies for interrupting high-power circuits proved to be an insurmountable barrier to vacuum interrupters despite their technical elegance and many attractive features. Steel manufacturers, threatened by aluminum, found ways to resist corrosion and use thinner sheets and lighter shapes.

Videotape and videodisk are examples of competing new technologies. The advances of the tape cassettes in recording length, ease of use, and miniaturization, together with the advantage of home recording and reusability, proved a formidable—and moving—obstacle to the success of videodisk.

Fortunately, the circumstances that discourage the incorporation of a new "piece" also stimulate an active search for additional applications once a new piece is accepted. I have seen a number of situations in which the most enthusiastic supporters of a fledgling technology failed by an order of magnitude to foresee the success it would achieve over the next ten to fifteen years.[1] Many of the new applications were ones they never even imagined.

The pioneering user of a new technology runs two risks. The technology may not be successful, but that can happen with conventional technology too. With a new technology, however, the pioneer can look silly as well, and be criticized for having tried something unproven. Once the technology has been demonstrated to perform successfully, the second risk evaporates. After the credibility of a new technology has been established, one may have thousands of "helpers" seeking additional uses. Their aggregate impact is frequently grossly underestimated.

THE TECHNOLOGY PARADOX

Given the power and complexity of the existing edifice of technology, it is not surprising that most attempts to replace existing elements are doomed to fail. Evolutionary advances that require adjustments among present pieces are much more likely to succeed. Since the failures usually disappear quickly, while the successes receive wide attention, we often underestimate the failure rate. Starting with the beginning step—a bright new idea—those that survive all the way to successful application are probably less than 1 percent. The director of one lab in a company renowned for its success in innovation says you need 2000 tries to get a hit.[2] Even those that survive long enough to compete for entry probably fail 95 percent of the time.

Fortunately, human nature manifests the duality of seeking security and predictability, but at the same time, of being fascinated and excited by change and the uncertainty of the unknown. Managers face a perpetual trap in technology. If you say no, most of the time you will be right, but that other 5 percent can kill you. I repeat, the price of survival is to wear a hair shirt of wariness.

Thus a manager of technology is left with a threatening paradox. If you examine the history of technology, you are forced to conclude that all technologies are fated to be replaced—eventually; however, most attempts to replace them will fail. That "eventually" is like Russian roulette: when will it fire?

Achieving a sound balance between continued concentration on conventional technologies and diverting effort to bring on a new technology means understanding the process by which a new technology arrives and appreciating the barriers to introduction that an aspiring new technology must overcome. One must remember that a perception of the conditions which foster innovation comes from observing failures as well as successes and that failures are more common, though less amenable to study.

TECHNOLOGY LIFE CYCLES

Interestingly enough, despite the intense interest in technological innovation, much insight has been gained by studying the process of technology maturation. If we understand how and when a technology becomes vulnerable as well as the issues involved in technological substitution, we are more likely to achieve a sound balance of effort.

Understanding the maturation of technology is important for three reasons. The kind of advance that is made in a technology tends to change as it matures, and work that continues to focus on objectives which were appropriate at an earlier stage is likely to become progressively less productive. Second, this change in the nature of technical progress is a signal that a technology is maturing and therefore may—I emphasize, *may*—be becoming vulnerable to attack by a new technology. Third, accompanying the maturation of the technology is a change in the nature of the management focus that is needed and in the business strategy that should be pursued.

Maturation of Industries

Two lines of inquiry have given much better insight into the dynamics of maturation. One line of study has examined the history of particular industries from birth to maturity. The other has looked at individual technologies, their characteristics during the early years, how those characteristics shift over time, and the events that occur as they are replaced by new technologies. Although the specifics of the two types of studies differ, their findings are compatible.[3]

Study of industries indicates that at the beginning an industry is characterized by a great variety of product features and a large number of product offerings from many different suppliers. Gradually, a dominant configuration of product features and attributes emerges. Figure 50.1 shows this change graphically.

As this occurs, the driving forces that shape the industry begin to change. Initially the rewards

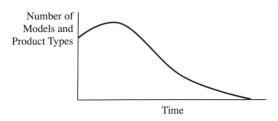

Figure 50.1 Industry maturation of product and model diversity.

go to those innovations that contribute to the further proliferation of products and features in the search for the dominant survivor; i.e., successful innovations tend to keep an industry in flux. Eventually, the rewards go to those innovations that stabilize the industry and contribute to the strength and penetration of the dominant configuration. As the sequence progresses, extensions and refinements of the dominant attributes and configurations become more and more prominent. As the product stabilizes, process improvement and contributions to improved productivity become increasingly important, as shown in Figure 50.2. As the industry moves toward maturity, product differentiation becomes more difficult to establish, and total business effectiveness largely determines competitive success—breadth of product line, strength of distribution, quality of service, and so forth.

Persistent efforts to introduce destabilizing innovations when a young industry, for example, personal computers is moving toward a dominant configuration—as Apple attempted with its Apple II, Apple III, Lisa, and Macintosh, each of which largely ignored prior history—are unlikely to be effective. Conversely, when an industry is far advanced in maturity, its modes of operating and of competing become a kind of security blanket that is increasingly vulnerable to a destabilizing attack—remember the problems encountered by the U.S. auto industry and the tire industries' persistence in ignoring radial tires. This process is not immutable, however. Sometimes an industry headed into maturity can be revitalized by the in-

troduction of new technology or new design concepts that greatly enhance its value. The introduction of the self-cleaning oven is an example of new technology that induced many owners of gas or electric ranges to buy a new product. In analogous fashion, in-the-hood microwave ovens markedly enlarged the market beyond that for countertop ovens.

Maturation of Technologies

The life history of particular technologies reflects an analogous pattern. When a technology first emerges, there is a sense of wonder about the new capability, e.g., jet engines, semiconductors, or integrated circuits. At that point the technology is relatively primitive and many of the paths for improvement are evident to those working in the field. Since no inventory of the product is in the field, there are almost no constraints on what can be tried. During the early years, progress is rapid and nearly all the effort is focused on improving the raw physical capability of the technology. Also, during those early years a business seeking to capitalize on the new technology is dominated by engineers. A sophisticated understanding of the potential of the new technology and an aggressive pursuit of key advances are critical to success. An engineer whose career coincided with the development of jet engines commented of the early days, "Hell, it was a miracle that the things flew at all. Nobody had any preconceived expectations, so you felt free to try anything."

As the technology is applied, constraints begin to emerge. Advances in technology must be ap-

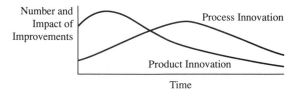

Figure 50.2 Industry maturation.

plied in ways compatible with equipment already being used. Basic geometries and configurations become standardized. Preferred materials and components begin to dominate. Unrecovered investments in facilities encourage adoption of advances that make use of those same facilities. In many respects, the price of progress in a technology is to take the fun out of it. In part, this is because nature does impose limits. As an example, the melting point of tungsten has been a constraint on incandescent lamps for more than 75 years. As the gap between natural limits and reliable practice narrows, the effort to achieve additional advances becomes more difficult, and advances are likely to be smaller and less frequent. More and more attention shifts from improvements in capability to improvements in processes that lead to lower cost. Thus manufacturing effectiveness rises in importance and visibility for management as well.

This neat sequence is more complicated in cases where product and process technology must be developed together. This has been obvious in the so-called process industries, especially chemicals and petroleum, for many years. It is becoming more prevalent in other industries as well, e.g., instant photography, integrated circuits, liquid crystal displays, and compact disks. In each of these cases, there could have been no product without parallel sophisticated process development. Furthermore, the success of the new product was dependent as much on advances in the process technology to reduce the initially high cost as it was on advances in product features and performance.

As processes become more sophisticated, they become more expensive and specialized, and the technology becomes more capital intensive. Concurrently, the effective management of assets increasingly determines competitive success. Inevitably, management becomes more financially oriented. It is not unusual to have a shakeout in an industry as capital intensity becomes more important, and this heightens the role of capital investment in competitive advantage. Figure 50.3 illustrates this dynamic process.

This work on life cycles has been extended by applying microeconomic analysis of marginal cost

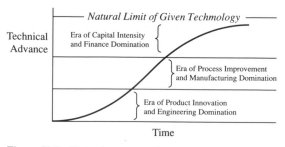

Figure 50.3   Technology maturation.

and marginal utility.[4] Every technology has a theoretical upper limit of performance imposed by nature. As technological progress accumulates, at some point the marginal cost of developing an additional increment of improvement increases. Hence, a company seeking to retain a competitive advantage from this technology must invest larger and larger sums in R&D. If a new technology is invented that has the potential of replacing that technology, a competing firm will have an economic advantage because the investment required to create an increment of improvement will be less, as shown in Figure 50.4.

This view, or course, assumes a more or less constant field of applications. As our technology base grows, however, the application of old technology in new fields becomes an important source of innovation and can return the technology to a lower point on the curve. For example, the use of electrical motors—a very old technology—in tape drives imposed extraordinary new demands for acceleration and precision in control, which suddenly made engineering of improved product attributes much more important.

The slope of the improvement reaches its maximum at some inflection point of the S curve. The inflection point on the curve is difficult to predict in advance. R&D people, deeply involved in developing the technology, tend to become zealots and to anticipate continued advance beyond the point when progress will in fact begin to diminish, as suggested in Figure 50.5.

When a new technology begins to supplant the present state of the art, we are confronted with a

Figure 50.4 Marginal impovement in technology per unit cost.

discontinuity that places us at a much lower point on the S curve for the new technology (Figure 50.6). As we have noted, the new technology is often developed by outsiders who have no commitment to the present state of the art. Since the young new technology yields much larger increments of improvement for a given level of effort, the conventional technology faces a growing and eventually insuperable handicap in attempting to compete. The intrinsic limits imposed by nature, of course, represent the ultimate limit on technological performance—a limit that is approached asymptotically. Obviously, the speed of development varies markedly from one technology to another, e.g., lasers required years to begin to find uses and thus remained as intriguing technological curiosities, whereas microprocessors moved very rapidly to begin to ascend their maturation curve.

A. D. Little (ADL) also emphasizes the S curve as a representation of the maturation and replacement of technologies and the need to pursue different strategies for technologies at different stages of maturity.[5] ADL divides the S curve into four segments, as shown in Figure 50.7. ADL divides technologies into three categories:

1. *Base technologies.* Those that are the foundation of the business, but are no longer critical to competitive success because they are widely available to all competitors, e.g., keyboards and power supplies for computers, landing gear for aircraft, shock absorbers and batteries for automobiles, and picture tubes for television.

2. *Key technologies.* Those that currently have the greatest leverage on competitive position, e.g., very large-scale integration (VLSI), operating systems, and applications software in computers; composite materials, propulsion, and electronic controls in aircraft; electronics and aerodynamic design for automobiles; and digital and stereo television.

3. *Pacing technologies.* Those in an early stage of development with a clear potential for changing the competitive equation, e.g., gallium arsenide or vector and parallel processing for computers, the unducted fan engine for aircraft, ceramics for automobile engines, and high definition for television.

ADL asserts that companies tend to overinvest in base technologies relative to the competitive leverage which further progress in those technologies can provide. In addition, companies often are insufficiently aware of new technologies having the potential to replace present key technologies as important competitive weapons.

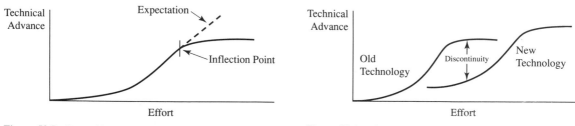

Figure 50.5 Rate of improvement of technology.

Figure 50.6 Discontinuity created by a new technology.

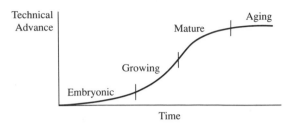

Figure 50.7 Technology maturation sequence.

Technology Substitution

Perhaps the earliest rigorous analysis of techno-logical substitution was done by Fisher and Pry.[6] They discovered that the percentage of penetration of a new technology (and therefore its level of sub-stitution for present conventional technology) also takes the shape of a classical S curve. They exam-ined many different examples and found that the time scale for substitution varies widely, but the characteristic S shape always holds. They also noted that—at least historically—once the first 10 to 15 percent of substitution had occurred, the process could be regarded as self-sustaining, as in-dicated in Figure 50.8.

Retrospective studies help to illuminate the generality of the process, but they may do little to help predict the course of specific technologies. For example, color television appeared well before black-and-white had achieved full saturation. Sub-sequently, black-and-white sets were sold princi-pally as lower-cost second sets—an application that had not existed before; therefore, sale of one ver-sus the other was not a straightforward substitution.

These various studies demonstrate some gen-eral historical principles of technological matura-

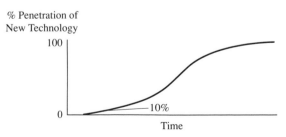

Figure 50.8 Technology substitution.

tion and substitution and the tension that exists be-tween conventional and emerging technologies. Unfortunately, the future course of events remains murky. At a minimum, awareness that a technol-ogy is maturing should alert managers of technol-ogy to its growing vulnerability and lead them to an increased monitoring of potential threats from new fields that may supplant conventional tech-nology. The third section of my referenced book includes a critical examination of these concepts and the techniques for applying them.

Clearly, the most important strategic techno-logical judgment is to determine not only the like-lihood, but also the timing, of the emergence of a candidate new technology as a genuine threat. A company cannot afford to fritter away its resources in pursuing every potential threat that appears—es-pecially considering the poor rate of success for new technologies. However, a company risks ex-tinction or severe trauma if it misses the emergence of a new winner.

Thus, as I previously mentioned, the most im-portant single task in managing technology is to maintain the proper tension between effort devoted to conventional technology and work that seeks to replace it. Implicit in this tension is the existence of effective programs in each category of work. There can be no tension if all the effort is devoted to conventional technology and one only bemoans the absence of candidate replacements. Companies must innovate in order to survive. Yet technology managers and general managers have an in-escapable responsibility to understand the realities of the process.

NOTES

1. John H. Dessauer (in *My Years with Xerox*, Dou-bleday, Garden City, N.Y., 1978, p. 30) notes the same phenomenon even among the most enthusiastic Xerox pioneers.

2. Steven Greenhouse, "An Innovator Gets Down to Business," *New York Times*, Business Section, Octo-ber 12, 1986, pp. 1, 8.

3. There is an extensive body of literature on this subject. An excellent review article by James M. Utter-back provides an authoritative overview and bibliography ("Innovation and Industrial Evolution in Manufacturing Industries," *Technology and Global Industry*, National Academy Press, Washington, D.C., 1987, pp. 16–48).

4. Richard Foster, *Innovation: The Attacker's Advantage*, Summit Books, New York, 1986.

5. *The Strategic Management of Technology*, Arthur D. Little, Cambridge, Mass.

6. J. C. Fisher and R. H. Pry, "A Simple Substitution Model of Technological Change," *Technology Forecasting and Social Change*, Vol. 3, 1972, pp. 75–88.

51

Managing Invention and Innovation:
What We've Learned

EDWARD B. ROBERTS

When the Industrial Research Institute was founded in 1938, industrial research in the United States had experienced 20 years of dramatic growth, despite the shock of the Depression, and was poised on the brink of World War II expansion that gave it the form and scope we see today. MIT historian Howard Bartlett reported that from 1921 to 1938 the number of U.S. companies with research staffs of more than 50 persons grew from 15 to 120 [1].

Despite continued rapid increases in industrial R&D involvement and resource commitment over the following 25 years, in 1962, when we founded the MIT Sloan School of Management's Research Program on the Management of Science and Technology, we encountered an academic tradition that for the most part had paid little attention to the organization and management of large-scale technology-based programs. Indeed it was for the purpose of bringing academic research-based insights to bear on such technological enterprises that James Webb, the visionary administrator of the National Aeronautics and Space Administration, urged us with exhortation and funds to begin our research program.

Prior to our start, academics had concentrated largely on two themes: historical romanticism about the lives and activities of great "creative inventors," like Edison and Bell, and psychological research into the "creativity process." While those writings made interesting reading, in my judgment neither track contributed much usable knowledge for managers of technical organizations. Indeed with such rare exceptions as Jewkes et al. [2], the few university researchers who were focusing at

that early time upon issues of R&D management were not paying much attention to organizational variables or to innovation as a multistage, multiperson, complex process. Perhaps not surprisingly, industry in the early 1960s appeared rather unenthusiastic about social science attempts to probe the underpinnings of effective research, development, and technology-based innovation. In contrast, I sense broad acceptance in the 1980s of the results of many academic studies of RD&E, with the Industrial Research Institute especially noteworthy in its efforts to advance collaboration in the field of management of technological innovation.

INVENTION AND INNOVATION

Roundtable discussions at the 1970 annual IRI spring meeting provide a useful starting point for this review—a set of definitions of the invention and innovation process:

> Innovation is composed of two parts: (1) the generation of an idea or invention, and (2) the conversion of that invention into a business or other useful application.... Using the generally accepted (broad) definition of innovation—all of the stages from the technical invention to final commercialization—the technical contribution does not have a dominant position. [3]

This leads me to a simple definition of my own, but nonetheless one that I feel is critical to emphasize:

Reprinted with permission from *Research-Technology Management*, Vol. 31, January–February, 1988, pp. 11–29.
Edward Roberts is Professor in the Management of Technology Group at M.I.T.'s Sloan School of Management.

Innovation = Invention + Exploitation

The invention process covers all efforts aimed at creating new ideas and getting them to work. The exploitation process includes all stages of commercial development, application, and transfer, including the focusing of ideas of inventions toward specific objectives, evaluating those objectives, downstream transfer of research and/or development results, and the eventual broad-based utilization, dissemination, and diffusion of the technology-based outcomes.

The overall management of technological innovation thus includes the organization and direction of human and capital resources toward effectively: (1) creating new knowledge; (2) generating technical ideas aimed at new and enhanced products, manufacturing processes, and services; (3) developing those ideas into working prototypes; and (4) transferring them into manufacturing, distribution, and use.

Technologically innovative outcomes come in many forms: incremental or radical in degree; modifications of existing entities or entirely new entities; embodied in products, processes or services; oriented toward consumer, industrial, or governmental use; based on various single or multiple technologies. Whereas invention is marked by discovery or a state of new existence, usually at the lab or bench, innovation is marked by first use, in manufacturing or in a market.

Most organized scientific and engineering activity, certainly within the corporation, is beyond the idea-generating stage and produces not radical breakthroughs but rather a broad base of incremental technological advance, sometimes leading cumulatively over time to major technical change. Academic research in the area of technology management has focused primarily on incremental product innovations oriented toward industrial markets. (Interestingly, academic marketing research has focused primarily on incremental product innovations aimed at consumer markets.) Neither the less frequently arising areas of radical innovation nor process innovation has received much systematic attention from academic, unfortunately.

One of my favorite visual aids is Figure 51.1, portraying a process view of how technological innovation occurs, and emphasizing two key generalizations. First, technological innovation is a multistage process, with significant variations in the primary task as well as in the managerial issues and effective management practice occurring among these stages. Figure 1 presents six stages, but the precise number and their division are somewhat arbitrary. What is key is that each phase of activity is dominated by the search for answers to different managerial questions.

At the outset, for example, emphasis is on finding a motivating idea, a notion of possible direction for technical endeavor. Coming up with one or more technical and/or market goals that stimulate initiating a research, development, and/or engineering (RD&E) project is the task undertaken during Stage I. The relevant managerial question for this stage is, How do more and better targets get generated? Which people, which structures, which strategies can be employed toward more effective idea generation for these objectives? Good managerial practice at this stage frequently involves loose control, "letting many flowers bloom," pursuing parallel and diverse approaches, fostering conflict or at least contentiousness, stimulating a variety of inputs. Critical at this early stage is ready access to small amounts of R&D financing, free of heavy and discouraging evaluative procedures. A major mistake is to set up stringent formal processes for approval of the small sums needed to try out an idea. Distributing small "pots of gold" for first- or second-level R&D supervisors to dispense at their discretion, akin to Texas Instruments' heralded "$25,000 money," makes good sense.

Later, the Stage 5 commercial development for example, the task involves in-depth specification and manufacturing engineering of ideas that have by now already been reduced to an acceptable working prototype. The managerial issues in this stage involve coordinating a number of engineers of different disciplinary backgrounds toward achieving, within previously estimated development budget and schedule, a predefined technical output ready for manufacture in large volume, re-

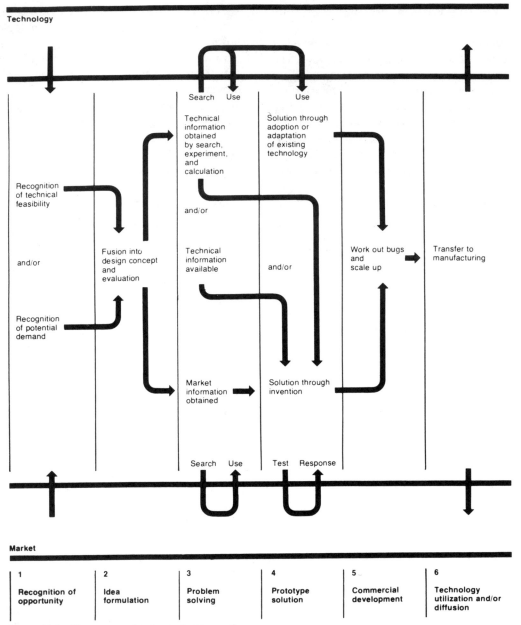

Figure 51.1   The process of technological innovation.

liably, and at competitive production costs. Effective managerial practice in this stage might well involve tight control, elimination of duplication, strong financial criteria for resource use accompanied by formal evaluation, single-minded even

somewhat rigid adherence to plan, especially in regard to those resources—in many ways the opposite of what is encountered in Stage 1!

The next generalization embodied in Figure 51.1 is that innovation occurs through technical efforts carried out primarily within an internal organizational context, but involving heavy interaction with the external technological as well as market environment. Proactive search for technical and market inputs, as well as receptivity to information sensed from external sources, are critical aspects of technology-based innovation. All studies of effective innovations have shown significant contributions of external technology and have found success heavily dependent upon awareness of customer needs and competitor activity. Indeed one of the most important trends in industrial innovation activity during the 1980s is the continuing increase in the use of external sources of technology as critical supplements to internal R&D efforts.

The details of Figure 51.1 specify a set of key flows and decision points that occur during the process of innovating. A number of major managerial elements that are embodied in those details will be treated in the remainder of this article. Two aspects of the diagram, however, are potentially misleading and deserve immediate mention. First, for ease of presentation all stages are shown at equidistant intervals, inappropriately suggesting perhaps the similarity of these phases from a time duration and/or consumption perspective. This is by no means true. In particular, while each technical field is characterized by quite different schedule and resource requirements, Stage 5, commercial development, usually takes as long as the several earlier stages combined and requires more resources than most of the other stages together. That is the reason for tight financial standards being properly applied immediately prior to a project's entry to this stage.

Second, for simplicity's sake no feedbacks are pictured in Figure 51.1 from later stages back to earlier ones. Yet, inevitably, these feedbacks exist and cause reiteration to occur among the stages. For example, involvement in the problem-solving process, Stage 3, generates new insights as to alternative idea formulations, Stage 2; and efforts at transfer into manufacturing as part of technology utilization, Stage 6, often create new requirements for problem-solving, Stage 3. Indeed a recent article by Kline [4] argues that the multiple feedback loops are the essence of the innovation process. Thus the real process of technical innovation involves flows back and forth over time among differing primary activities, internal and external to the dominant innovating organization, with major variations arising throughout the process in regard to specific tasks, managerial issues, and managerial answers.

Beyond my descriptive perspective on how innovation occurs is Peter Drucker's [5] prescriptive advocacy as to how it ought to happen: "Systematic innovation . . . consists in the purposeful and organized search for changes, and in the systematic analysis of the opportunities such changes might offer for economic or social innovation." Drucker identifies seven sources for innovative opportunity. Most challenging to those of us committed to the development and use of new science and technology is Drucker's assertion that "contrary to almost universal belief, new knowledge—and especially new scientific knowledge—is not the most reliable or most predictable source of successful innovations." As with most Drucker "truths," this one is intuitively attractive, as well as unverified in any systematic manner. Whether or not new science is a critical "source" of successful innovations no doubt depends on how you define both *science* as well as *source*. But there is no doubt that advances in science and technology are instrumental to the development and implementation of almost all successful product and process innovations. It is the rare case that a success stems from merely a repackaging of previously existing science and technology.

Rather than focusing at this point on the claimed sources from which innovations arise, the remainder of this article concentrates on three dimensions—staffing, structure, and strategy—each subject to managerial influence and/or control. (I will discuss innovation sources much more in the section on structure.) . . . Taken together, improved management of these dimensions contributes critically to achieving successful institutionalized innovation. Throughout the article I shall be seeking to blend the findings from academic research on the management of invention and innovation with the experiences and observations of successful industrial and government technology managers.

STAFFING CONSIDERATIONS

Two primary issues arise in regard to staffing the technological organization: what kinds of people need to be involved for effective technical development, and what managerial actions can be taken to maximize their overall productivity. In regard to people requirements, as explained by Roberts and Fusfeld [6], a number of "critical behavioral roles," not just technical skills, must be practiced by the people involved in a technical development. By combining the management of technological innovation literature with our own consulting experiences, we identified five key roles for achieving successful innovation, which we have been able to use to enhance RD&E organizational performance. Following us, others have since added to this list, generating as many as 12 key roles needing separate monitoring and support.

Critical Innovation Roles

First are *idea generators*, the creative contributors of new insights that both initiate projects and contribute to problem solutions throughout technical projects [7,8]. Ideas can be drawn from the "market pull" of sensing real or potential customer needs or demands, or from the "technological push" of envisioning the possible extension of technological performance of a material, component, or system. Ideas include not just those which lead to project initiation, but also the many throughout an innovation-seeking endeavor which contribute importantly toward invention or innovation outcomes. Thus idea generators for technical projects may be scientists or engineers, sales or marketing persons, or even managers! The rare but valuable idea generators are those who come up with multiple ground-breaking ideas over their careers, such as S. D. Stookey at Corning Glass Works who among other successes came up with key ideas for photosensitive glass and Pyroceram [9]. Individual differences that are either innate or developed over

long periods no doubt account for many of the distinctive characteristics of effective idea generators. But many sources of heightened idea creativity arise from managerial influences, for example, from the internal organizational climate or environment and especially from supervisory practices. These are discussed in greater detail in my later section on individual and organizational productivity.

There are, however, significant differences between "idea-havers" and "idea-exploiters"—those who come up with ideas and those who do something with the ideas they have generated [10,11]. This holds true whether the ideas are born in universities, government labs, or in industry. The generally low rate of energetic pursuit of newly created RD&E ideas mandates the requirement for the second key role in technical innovation-seeking activities, that of the *entrepreneur* or *product champion*. Entrepreneurs advocate and push for change and innovation; they take ideas, whether their own or others', and attempt to get them supported and adopted. Most major studies of factors affecting product success have found the active presence of a product champion to be a necessary condition for project success [12]. For example, in recent years the late Ken Estridge gained widespread repute as the product champion behind IBM's successful development and launch of its personal computer. Lew Lehr rose to the presidency of 3M as an eventual outgrowth of his own championing of 3M's health products business [13]. And despite not being a family member of the closely-held Pilkington Glass company, Alistair Pilkington became "process champion" for the revolutionary float-gass process which dramatically changed the company and the industry and again, not incidentally, led this "champion" into the chairmanship of the firm.

As I reported in my first *Research Management* article, the entrepreneurial "role" is the same, whether carried out internally in existing organizations or "externally" in their own newly founded companies [14]. But the mode of behavior and what is needed for "internal" versus "external" entrepreneurial success may well be different, as expanded by Maidique [15]. My own studies of "internal entrepreneurs" found that they needed to be sensitive to company politics and the latest corporate "buzzwords" in order to gain internal support, and as indicated below required a high-level "sponsor" to lead them through the corporate jungle. Lehr [13] argues that strong entrepreneurial efforts are needed even within companies that have long traditions of fostering entrepreneurship, in order to overcome inevitable managerial resistance.

A third required role in effective innovative activities is the *program manager or leader*, sometimes strangely called the "business innovator," supplying the support functions of planning, scheduling, monitoring and control, technical work supervision, business and financial coordination relating to the R&D project [16,17]. This is the one "role" which is also usually an assigned job in the organization, the other roles being incidental to an individual's specific work assignment.

Gatekeepers, or special communicators, are the fourth critical role identified, the link-pins who frequently bring information messages from sources outside of a project group into that group [18]. These human bridges joint technical, market, and manufacturing sources of information to the potential technical users of that information. Gatekeepers may bridge one technical group to another within the same company, or may link university research activities to a corporate advanced technology center, or may tie customer concerns into a supplier's design team.

Tom Allen's pioneering empirical studies of the functioning of the technical gatekeeper have been extended by many other academics and broadly accepted and applied throughout industry and government. For example, a study of so-called bridge scientists at Stanford Research Institute found that such individuals are rare but easily identified [19]. Effective "bridgers" were found to be interpersonally able (e.g., good listeners), have depth in at least one discipline, have a wide range of interests, and be oriented toward problem solving. As I have argued repeatedly [6], a vital extension of the concept is the recognition that some gatekeepers can "bridge" to market or manufactur-

ing inputs, rather than just technical information, often bringing in raw or processed information, or points of view, that are otherwise lacking within the R&D organization itself.

The final key role is that of the *sponsor* or *coach*, performed usually by a more senior person who is neither carrying out the R&D itself nor is directly and personally aggressively championing the change. The role is one of providing encouragement, psychic support, facilitation to the more junior people involved in the task implementation, often including important help in "bootlegging" the resources needed by those trying to move technological advances forward in an organization [14]. My research data affirmed the logical—the higher up in an organization a sponsor was located, the higher the probability of success of internal efforts to generate new product lines. Sponsors are often needed for idea generators, project managers, and especially for entrepreneurs. A good example of the effectiveness of the "ultimate sponsor," the corporate chief executive officer, is Chapman's sponsorship of Gorman's work on "available light motion pictures" at Eastman Kodak [20]. But CEOs as project sponsors can be organizationally dangerous too! Who is to turn off the CEO's pet project when it runs amok?

These several critical roles are all needed within or in close contact with each internal working group in order for it to achieve successfully the goals of an innovative outcome. But in addition, the effective development and maintenance of a technical organization requires recognition of these differentiated roles in order to create and implement appropriate people management processes, including recruiting, job assignment, personnel development and training, performance measurement, and rewards.

Individual and Organizational Productivity

Beyond the people and role behaviors needed for effective staffing are the principal managerial acts that can affect staff creativity, inventiveness, and productivity. The 30 years of *Research Management* reveal plentiful discussions of approaches for stimulating creative idea-generating among scientists and engineers, including such techniques as brainstorming, Synectics, and morphological analysis. (See 21 and 22 for extensive reviews.) Despite the enthusiastic testimony in the various articles, I remain unconvinced that systematic evidence supports the use of these methods, which, frankly, I view as mainly gimmicks. As documented below, effective individual and group supervision, including proper maintenance or group diversity and task challenge, seem to me more likely to produce usable ideas.

Stages of a scientist's or engineer's career, and the composition of his/her immediate work group are primary influences upon technical productivity (or creativity or inventiveness, if you prefer). This generalization rests upon a broad foundation of research into the performance of technical people and project groups. Katz [23] has demonstrated that technical professionals evolve through three career stages, which he labels socialization, innovation, and stabilization. As with the different stages of a project cycle, each stage of an individual's career provides a new set of managerial challenges for maximizing personal productivity. The setting of work norms, providing task direction, and joining new employees into the internal technical communications network are managerial issues confronted during the socialization or job "break-in" stage. In contrast, maintaining the employee's earlier motivation and renewing technical skills are among the very different sort of questions needing treatment in the stabilization or job maturity phase.

But personal and group productivity are not just influenced by the individual's job cycle. The nature of the immediate work group, its composition and supervision, matter greatly. In general what Kuhn [24] called creative tensions, a mix between comfort-reinforcing stability and conflicting challenge, seems desirable. For example, multidimensional diversity among technical colleagues in a project team heightens technical performance [71]. Variations in age, technical background, even personal values, correlate with enhanced group productivity. This need for internal challenge is further reflected in the findings that the average years a group has worked together significantly impacts

upon that group's technical productivity [25]. The long-term stable technical group apparently becomes too self-secure, diminishes its outside technical contacts, and decreases its performance. Supervisory intervention at the technical group or RD&E project level seems able to affect this performance, however. For example, technical skills of the first-level group leader, and not human relations skills, enhance a group's effectiveness [26]. And even the stable technical team can be moved to high-performing status with proper leadership, in this case requiring strong direction and control by the project manager [17]. Thamhain and Wilemon [27] support the importance of the project manager's technical expertise and reliance upon work challenges as major sources of effective technical performance.

ORGANIZATION STRUCTURE

The design of organization structures that will enhance technological innovation requires focusing on both the organization's inputs and its outputs. Effective RD&E organizations need appropriate technical and market information inputs, and their outputs need to be integrated toward mission objectives and transferred downstream toward their ultimate users.

Market Inputs
Managerial research has repeatedly demonstrated that 60 to 80 percent of successful technical innovations seem to have been initiated by activities responsive to "market pull," that is, forces reflecting orientation to perceived need or demand [28–30]. Of particular note is the recent IRI study of basic research in industry [31], which among many other interesting conclusions produced the unsought finding that "most innovations come about as a result of the recognition of a market need or opportunity. While the push of new technology is also important, it plays a distinctly secondary role." These studies less frequently indicate how technical organizations uncover these needs. Sometimes one person's personal "hobby-horse" forces "mar-

ket" consciousness to initiate and sustain a technical program, especially when coupled with that individual's entrepreneurial drive and skills, as in Peter Goldmark's successful pursuit of the long-playing record. As Goldmark exclaimed, "My initial interest in the long-playing record (LP) arose out of my sincere hatred of the phonograph . . . it seemed to violate what I thought the quality of music should be" [32].

In organizations less dominated by one key figure, "market gatekeepers" or customer liaison personnel frequently aid the technical organization to better understand its customers' requirements, priorities, or preferences. For example, Corning Glass supposedly discovered the need for optical waveguides as a result of one of its staff visiting the British Post Office. Organizing to gain meaningful market inputs for research and engineering use may depend upon explicit assignments of such responsibilities to cooperating marketing staff or to RD&E people themselves. The product development cycle should be organized, as suggested in Figure 51.1, to bring market inputs into design repeatedly, during the early product specification stage and again during prototyping, through active involvement of selected customers. As a sharp contrast to desirable practice, in one consulting project for a major chemical company I found the sales organization prohibiting R&D people from visiting "their" customers, lest the R&D people agree with customer complaints!

A special prospective customer for innovations, often overlooked when R&D does occasionally seek market inputs, is the company's own manufacturing activity. Yet depending on the company and industry, the manufacturing organization turns out to be the eventual "customer" of anywhere from one- to two-thirds of the company's technological developments. Manufacturing, similar to an outside unrelated potential product customer, has to decide whether or not it wants to "buy" an internally developed improvement in materials, components, manufacturing equipment, or overall production process, for its own internal "consumption." That prospective in-house manufacturing "customer" deserves at least the same degree of involvement

with the design and development process as does an outside firm or individual. If R&D's "market-oriented" ties to its own manufacturing group can be improved, the potential for significantly impacting company performance is high, especially given the recent IRI study results that show R&D aimed at process innovation as far more likely to succeed than that targeted toward new and improved products [33]. But I am convinced that overcoming the gap between the central lab and a major plant installation usually needs special efforts and sometimes creative organizational designs, in particular when important process changes are contemplated.

Rather than seeking collaboration to provide market information to the RD&E process, many companies have ill-advisedly substituted marketing-oriented control of RD&E. Organizational subordination of research and engineering to "product managers" (inevitably marketing or sales people) or tight budgetary control of RD&E by these units may force market-based criteria to dominate technical project selection. But this is usually accompanied by a short-term quick-fix orientation, erosion of technical capability, and gradual destruction of product/process competitiveness. Analyses by Souder [34] have demonstrated that strong and positive relations between R&D and marketing organizations significantly improve the track record on new product introductions. In my experience this is best achieved by welding partnerships among equals, rather than by extracting compliance from subordinates. Good examples of such R&D/marketing partnerships are evident in the team structures used by both Hewlett-Packard and 3M in their new product pursuits.

Market research techniques have long been used to help define consumer preferences in new product designs [35]. These methods have been less helpful for developing industrial goods. Recently von Hippel [36] has demonstrated that potential industrial customers whose needs place them at the leading edge of technological demands can be used to specify detailed desired performance characteristics and features for as yet non-existing products. Military or space research requirements are frequent sources of such "leading edge" requirements. Fusfeld [37] has long used this insight in developing forecasts of the rate of market penetration of new technologies. The problem, however, is to distinguish a customer demand that is truly in the vanguard of future broader market needs from the "cry for help" from what amounts to the "lunatic fringe" that exists in almost every technical field. That fringe also has needs that are real and extraordinary, but unfortunately not representative of future growth opportunities.

Technical Inputs

Despite the presumed dominant role of "market pull" as a source of innovative projects, "technology push," that is, undertaking projects for advancing the technical state-of-the-art in an area without anticipation of the specific commercial benefits to be derived, is also the critical source of many significant product and process successes. The many studies cited earlier still show these technology-push successes to be in the minority, but unfortunately do not clearly indicate the relative worth of the two approaches. One confusion leading to arguments is to assert that if market pull is the key, then market research should be more effective than it has proven to be! Collier [38] for example quotes Barnes' listing of "Neoprene, nylon, polyethylene, silicones, penicillin, Teflon, transistors, xerography, and the Polaroid Land camera" as not resulting from "a market research study of what people *said* they wanted." While market research is not the only or even the primary indicator of market pull, many research directors especially sympathize with Collier's point of view. Guy Suits [39], long-time leader of General Electric's research efforts, cites Langmuir's work on hydrogen dissociation, leading to a new type of welding, as a good example of technology push. Indeed, Casey [40] goes further, arguing that misleading market research was a contributor to the long period required for commercial development of high-fructose corn syrup. More logs are heaped on this fire when one cites the supposed market research studies (often claimed to have come from the same large consulting organization!) that demonstrated no mean-

ingful market prospects for computers, instant photography, or the dry copier.

When technical advancement is the goal, managers have long understood that professional depth in an organization is achieved by grouping people together in their own area of specialization, with work assigned and performance supervised by a more accomplished person of the same specialization [41]. This approach is called functional or discipline-based or specialty-oriented organization. It is the traditional organization structure of the craft guild and of the university. Multiple specialists working together interact comfortably, using the same general knowledge base, analytic skills and tools, and vocabulary. When technical people are organized in functional arrays, their natural interplay brings depth of specialized capabilities to bear on technical problems. Indeed, Marquis and Straight found that technical groups organized in functional forms have the highest technical excellence [42].

But in any nontrivial technical field the vast majority of applicable technical knowhow exists outside of a performing technical organization. For technical effectiveness even a strong functional team needs to draw upon the preexisting technical knowledge that is in the outside world, whether in the technical literature, in already developed products and processes, or especially in the minds of other technical professionals. For example, in summarizing his review of major studies of innovation, Utterback pointed out that, for innovations eventually developed within a firm, about 60 percent of the sources of the initial technical ideas had outside origins [28]. Allen [43] has demonstrated the relative differences among channels for technical information input to an organization, distinguishing what is readily accessed from what is used most effectively in coming up with high-rated problem solutions. His work, as well as that of others [44, 45], indicates the minor role played by the literature, especially in contributions to engineering and development, in contrast with personal contacts, experience, and training.

One factor that inadvertently has significant effect on technical inputs to RD&E groups is the architectural layout of their work space. Early observations by Jack Morton, then vice president of semiconductor research at Bell Laboratories, led to his concern for the physical separation between technical organizations that were intended to relate to each other [46]. Research at MIT by Muller-Thym in the early 1960s empirically established spatial effects on the frequency of communication among engineers and scientists in the same laboratory. These concepts have been well developed by Allen [18] into careful findings on specific design elements of RD&E architecture. The distance between two potential communicators, vertical separation, walls, and other architectural features importantly influence technology flows.

Thusfar I have addressed what affects technical inputs in support of an organization's internal invention activities, the first element of the two-step innovation process I defined initially. What about technical inputs not aimed at invention but rather at innovation directly? Clearly, technological solutions (inventions) already exist elsewhere, and an innovating organization might merely adopt or adapt them by slight modification for a new purpose. This would permit skipping the first stage of invention and going directly to the exploitation stage. An early U.S. study determined that 22 percent of key successful innovations had been adopted or adapted [44] while comparable U.K. data indicated a 33 percent adoption rate [45]. Japanese data on license fee payments for foreign technology show a long-established pattern of heavy use of outside technology. A small study of Taiwanese innovations found adoptions to have accounted for the bulk of successes [47]. While specific percentages no doubt have changed in recent years, adoption or adaptation of prior outside inventions is a major source of innovation worldwide, but apparently still substantially underutilized by U.S. firms. In recent years the growth of research consortia, effective or not, and the rapidly growing number of "strategic alliances" between large corporations and new firms in areas of emerging technologies indicate that more looking to the outside for technology is taking place, even by U.S. companies. I will discuss

this development further in the section on strategy.

One unique source of potential adoptions is the user. Von Hippel [48] has shown that users frequently create and implement innovations for their own use, followed later by manufacturer adoptions of those innovations for large-scale production and distribution. His research on scientific instruments and several areas of manufacturing equipment demonstrated that heavy percentages of new products had been user-developed.

Technical organizations need to be designed to facilitate accessing these several different sources of technical information inputs, whether as contributions toward internal inventions or as sources for adoption more directly as innovations. A variety of approaches are suggested, ranging from such simple considerations as ensuring that at least some salespeople have technical skills and/or incentives so that they bring back a customer's ideas in addition to his orders. Much more ambitious are the IBM marketing department's several "applied science centers" across the United States, established adjacent to concentrations of innovative users to learn about new software and hardware developments and transfer that technical information back into IBM's product development groups. IBM's Cambridge operation in Technology Square, working closely with MIT's pioneering Project MAC, thus became the source of IBM's first commercial computer time-sharing system, a field adaptation of an innovative user's development. As one approach to overcome biases against outside sources of technology, increasingly corporations are establishing the position of chief technical officer or vice president of technology, with broad responsibility for both internal technology development as well as external technology acquisition. Organizational experiments to enhance both technical and market information inputs are underway across a broad front.

Output-Focused Organization

Just as the functional organization structure maximizes technical inputs, the project, program, mission, or product organization is intended to integrate all inputs toward well-defined outputs. By placing in the same group, under a single leader, all the contributors toward a given objective, the project organization maximizes coordination and control toward achieving output goals. The Marquis and Straight study [42] cited earlier supports these findings. But project structures have a fundamental flaw that seriously affects many technical organizations. The project form tends to remove technical people from organizational groups in which they interact with colleagues of their own scientific or engineering discipline. Furthermore, the project manager may be technically expert, but inevitably in only one of the disciplines of his or her subordinates, not all of them. If the project has long duration, especially when the technology base is rapidly changing, the technical skills of the project members erode over time due to lack of stimulating technical reinforcement and supervision.

This dilemma has led to the creation of an organization that is intended to be a "compromise"—the "matrix" structure in which technical performers are supposed to maintain active membership in two organizations, their original discipline-based functional group as well as the focused project group. In theory the "matrixed" person thus has two bosses, one functional and one project, each of whom will extract his appropriate "due," thereby attempting simultaneously to maintain the technical skills and performance of the individual, more or less, while orienting his loyalty and contributions toward the project's output goals, more or less! However, most technical "matrix" organizations are only "paper" matrices, not "real" matrices—they appear to be matrices on organization charts but do not strongly pull the engineer between two conflicting masters.

If one wanted to obtain truly matrixed individuals, the influences that push a technologist's time and attention toward competing sets of objectives (e.g., functional excellence versus project schedule demands) would have to be roughly balanced between those objectives. A technical contributor's priorities are influenced by: (a) who is responsible for his/her performance evaluation and reward distribution, (b) who makes the individual's specific task assignments, (c) where is the individual physically located relative to the two "competing" managers, (d) what is the longer-term career relevance of the competing groups, and (e) what is the relative persuasiveness (whether based on personality or power) of the two managers. Achieving even a rough balance among these influences would be practicable only by dominance of the functional manager on some of these dimensions, dominance of the manager on others, and perhaps rough evidence of the two managers on still other influences upon matrixed persons. The absence of reasonable balance in most "paper matrixed" cases leads the actual situation to its "default" condition, with the achieved results reflecting the characteristics of the dominant organization form, either functional or project but seldom both. Recent studies suggest that certain patterns of dominance among these contending influence sources achieve better performance of matrix organizations [25].

Output Transfers

But in addition to generating outputs, the technical organization needs to be designed to enhance output transfer downstream toward eventual customers and users. Downstream is where innovation takes place and where benefits are realized! A consulting survey of prestigious major corporate research laboratories has indicated a high degree of dissatisfaction with the extent and effectiveness of transfer of results to potential recipient groups [49, 50]. Three different clusters of bridging approaches were found helpful in increasing transfer in those labs—procedural, human, and organizational. Most organizations used a variety of these approaches, often several simultaneously. My findings have been reaffirmed by recent comparative case studies by an internal task force at IBM [51] and by a consulting project at Union Carbide [52], among others.

Procedural methods include: joint planning of RD&E programs by the performing group and the organization that is expected to be the receiver, often resisted by R&D as an "invasion" of its turf;

joint staffing or projects, especially pre- and post-transfer downstream; and joint project appraisal after project completion, done cautiously if at all after failures in order to avoid destructive finger-pointing.

Human bridges are the most effective transfer mechanisms, especially the upstream and downstream transfers of people. Movement of people upstream: (a) brings with them information on the context of intended project use, (b) establishes direct person-to-person contacts that will be helpful in later posttransfer troubleshooting, and (c) creates the image that the project eventually being transferred has involved prior ownership and priority inputs from the receiving unit. Later movement of people downstream: (a) carries expertise for post-transfer problem-solving, and (b) not unimportant, conveys the risk-reducing impression that the receiving unit will not be stuck with solving post-transfer problems by itself. Other human bridges that are widely used include rotation programs, market gatekeepers, joint problem-solving sessions, and other formal and informal meetings.

Organizational techniques for enhancing transfer are usually more complicated to design and implement than procedural or human bridge approaches. "Integrators," sometimes named transfer managers, or integrating departments are frequently appointed to tie together the sending and receiving organizations. This person or unit is given the responsibility for moving the project from the sender into operating condition in the receiver organization, either lacking authority in one or the other organization or being matrixed between both.

More ambitious organizational approaches include dedicated transfer teams, established solely for the period during which technical results are being transferred to their "customers," done especially for moving purchased process technology. Venture teams, discussed further below, are also employed to reduce functional organizational transfer issues, shifting leadership responsibility among the many-disciplined team members as the primary phase of the project shifts from research to engineering to manufacturing to sales.

STRATEGY

Strategic management of technology includes both strategic planning and strategic implementation aspects at either of two levels: (a) overall, for the entire technology-dependent firm, government agency, division or product line, or (b) more focused, for just the technology development/acquisition process/department/laboratory of the entire organization. As recently as 10 years ago neither of these levels of strategy was the subject of much serious scholarship, or even management consulting practice. Few researchers carefully studied the overall management of the technology-intensive company. And fewer still addressed the questions of how to incorporate technological considerations into overall business strategy.

Strategic planning focuses upon the formulation of an organization's goals and objectives, and upon developing the policies needed to achieve those objectives, including identification of the organization's primary resources and priorities. But developing corporate strategy with such a global perspective, including technological dimensions, is quite new. Indeed the evolution of corporate strategic planning as a field of practice is divisible more or less into three decades: the 1960s, during which multiyear budget projects became the earliest forms of financial planning, sometimes mislabelled *long-range planning*: the 1970s, when market growth/share matrices and market attractiveness considerations added a new dimension to strategic analysis; and the 1980s, during which technology as a strategic factor became so widely acknowledged as to cause firms and even countries to realize that financial, marketing, and technological considerations needed to be integrated in overall strategy development [53].

Strategic Thinking and Planning

Horwitch and Prahalad [54] provided an early set of perspectives at the overall strategic level, differentiating the key issues of technology-oriented strategic management among three modes: the small, usually single-product, high-tech firm; the large, multimarket, multiproduct corporation; and the multiorganization, even multisector societal program. For each of these, Horwitch and Prahalad find a primarily nonoverlapping set of strategic issues and priorities. More recent writing has focused upon similarities between the first two "modes," the entrepreneurial smaller firm and the successfully innovative larger corporation [55–58; see also 14]. Maidique and Hayes conclude that to be innovative the large corporation needs to manage the "paradox" of chaos versus continuity, similar to the "creative tensions" required for the innovative technical person [7, 24].

In moving from strategic thinking toward strategic planning we need principals for developing more detailed technology strategies. But what are the underpinnings of technological change, especially as it relates to the corporation, upon which overall technology strategy should be based? Three general observations seem critical here, all linked to the dynamics of technological innovation processes: (1) there are characteristic patterns over the life cycle of a technology in how frequently product versus process innovations occur; (2) each stage of a technology has differing critical implications for innovation, including type, cost, degree of invention, and source; and (3) an organization's efforts to generate technological innovation create almost inevitable internal dynamics in the allocation of R&D efforts, generating multiple management problems. Each of these is discussed more fully below, with suggestions of related technology planning and strategy development approaches.

Utterback and Abernathy [59] demonstrated that a technology tends to evolve in three stages. Most technologies move from an early "fluid stage," dominated by frequent product innovations, through a "transition stage," characterized by significant process innovation and the emergence of a dominant product design, into a "specific stage," featuring lower rate of and more minor product and process innovations. While variations in this pattern of course occur, some of which are already well understood [60, 61], this generalization becomes one important basis for developing a company's or a product line's technology strategy.

One of the most significant findings from this research has been the reaffirmed role of the smaller firm as the dominant source of innovation during the earliest emerging stage of a technology, with the locus of innovation shifting toward larger companies in the transitional and more mature stages of a technology [59]. Most studies that have sought to find differences in R&D productivity as a function of company size have not made this critical distinction as to the stage of technology or type of innovation. Consequently, the findings of these economic analyses have varied unconvincingly all over the lot, from some that have asserted the large company is most productive of innovations to others that have claimed the exact opposite, to still other studies that have found nonlinear ties between size and R&D results.

The potential stability or predictability in patterns of technology evolution is the rationale for attempting to use technological forecasting techniques as part of technology planning and strategy development. Most technology forecasting methods are simple, often inadequate for the task [62, 63]. Indeed, despite recent "rediscovery" by some consultants of technology S-curves for forecasting and planning [64], the intellectual development of the technology forecasting field more or less stopped over a decade ago [65, 66]. Yet some corporations have benefited enormously from thoughtful application of technology forecasting methods to their strategic analyses. Tracy O'Rourke, the chief executive officer of Allen-Bradley, for example, cites a comprehensive technology forecast as the basis for planning his company's successful transition from electromechanical to solid state electronic devices [67].

Each stage of a technology is associated with different strategic implications. The earliest stage in a technology's life cycle tends to feature frequent major product innovations, heavily contributed by small entrepreneurial organizations, often closely tied to lead user needs. The development of frozen orange juice concentrate by the National Research Corporation and its spinoff companies is one such example [68]. The present rash of biotechnology discoveries is coming primarily from university laboratories directly or from young small enterprises, leading irresistibly to the explosion of biotech alliances between large companies and the new start-ups. The same alliance pattern has evolved in the areas of machine vision and artificial intelligence.

The intermediate stage of a technology's life cycle may include major process innovation, with continuing but lessened product variation occurring, with increasing numbers of competitors, both large and small. To achieve the dominant product–process design during this stage, large corporations sometimes undertake longterm development programs that combined many elements of applied research and engineering. For example, General Motor's successful efforts in developing its two-cycle diesel engine included more than 10 major developments needed for the final system [69].

The late stage of a technology features less-frequent minor product and process innovations, contributed primarily by large corporations, motivated mostly by cost reduction and quality improvement operational objectives. As illustrated by Hollander's [70] careful analysis of Du Pont rayon innovations, these numerous minor innovations can produce dramatic cumulative impact upon costs. In fact the so-called learning curve (i.e. decreasing unit manufacturing cost as cumulative production increases) results primarily not from the volume itself but rather from the usual continuing allocation of engineering efforts to incremental cost reduction projects as a product line's volume increases. Management of the technical investment is the primary source of the so-called learning curve competitive advantage, not the share of market.

These key dimensions of a technology described above should strongly influence choices made by a firm or government agency in developing its technological strategy. A company's detailing of its "product innovation charter" [71], or its application of project selection principles or techniques [72] as part of technology planning, ought to reflect at least general consideration of the current stages of its principal technologies. In particular, the late stage of one technology usually corresponds to earlier stages of other potentially threatening technologies. Most corporations fail to anticipate or even appropriately respond to these technological threats [64, 73].

Technology life cycles occur in an industry as a whole, thus providing an "environmental" set of influences upon a single organization's strategy. A different kind of cycle, however, is produced within a firm by its own attempts to develop and commercially exploit technology. As a major project moves downstream through a multistage research-design-development-production engineering-field trouble shooting technical organization, decisions on acquisition and allocation of technical resources can cause major instability in overall performance, including in the rate and character of new product releases and resulting sales and profits [74, 75]. For many small firms the resulting "boom then bust" often spells disaster. Similar though less-evident problems arise at the product line level of large corporations and government agencies. Self-induced cycles of primarily discovery followed then by primarily exploitation seem to have plagued the growth years of Polaroid Corporation, for example, contributing to its financial crises of the late 1970s.

Large-scale and realistic computer simulation models have been developed and increasingly employed in recent years for helping to cope with this aspect of technology and overall organizational strategy development [65, 74–76]. While these computer modeling methods are primarily strategic support tools, the technological forecasting and project selection techniques that were mentioned principally enhance tactical and operational aspects of technology planning and management. Other approaches to technology planning have been developed and successfully applied at both the tactical and strategic levels. For example, Crawford [71] has conceptualized a "product innovation charter" that contains five major areas for inclusion in a formal strategy statement, with each of the five subdivided into finer categories. Crawford argues for taking into account explicitly the company's target business arenas, objectives of product innovation, specific program of activities, the degree of innovation sought, and any special conditions or restrictions on the strategy.

Another most impressive technique for technology planning is "competitive product profiling," in which an organization's product line is compared to its key competitors in terms of seven technology-based measures: functional performance, acquisition cost, ease of use, operating cost, reliability, serviceability, and system compatibility [77]. IBM adds "availability" to this list of competitive measures, making "reliability, availability, serviceability" (RAS) a critical element of its internal technology planning. Extending this approach to analysis of competitive manufacturing processes has been attempted, but with less success due to relative lack of competitor data. Fusfeld [77] has tried to overcome this limitation and bring technology planning to the level of assessment of overall organizational capability. He uses in his analytical framework the "technology planning unit," the level of generic technology in the organization as it is being applied to a particular market opportunity, and tries to evaluate relative technical strength. Further developments of technology planning approaches, especially at the strategic level, are needed and can be expected during the coming decade [78].

Strategic Implementation

But beyond strategic planning must come strategic implementation. Tactics and operations are the means of implementation of strategy. Not much has yet been written about specific implementations of technology strategies. At the national level, Johnson [79] has concluded that, relative to American firms, Japanese industry has more heavily invested in applied rather than basic research, adopting and improving on preexisting products and technologies, in already well-developed market areas. He cites government policies in regard to patents, subsidies, and tax incentives as important in both countries. In his recent survey studies while at MIT, Hirota [80] has developed strong empirical evidence on U.S.–Japanese technology strategy differences, supporting but going beyond Johnson's observations. However, recent Japanese pioneering efforts in such areas as compact-disk technology and more advanced semiconductor memories suggest that

Japanese R&D strategy may be in transition toward what has been a dominant U.S. approach [81].

Although now also of increasing interest to nontechnical industries, the so-called venture approaches have been a unique means for implementing overall strategies seeking accelerated technology-based new business development for growth and/or diversification. These venture approaches involve larger organizations in attempts to emulate or couple with smaller entrepreneurial units. The spectrum of possible strategic and organizational alternatives includes venture capital investments in young "emerging technology" companies, sponsored spin-offs of new product development-commercialization groups, "new-style joint ventures" that feature alliances between large and small companies, internal ventures, and integrated venture strategies [82]. Collaborative undertakings among U.S. firms are growing dramatically, involving new linkages with universities and especially new investment/development/commercialization ties with young high-technology companies [83, 84].

A subject of active study and industrial practice off and on since the early 1960s, venture approaches have recently become increasingly attempted by companies and even countries as part of their strategies for intensifying their technological industrial base. Venture strategies require long-term persistence for effective implementation and dramatic differences in management style and policies from traditional mainstream approaches. These demands for "managerial innovation" are seldom adequately met, producing high failure rate among corporate ventures [85, 86]. Yet the occasional dramatic success, such as Texas Instruments' entry into the semiconductor business [87] or IBM's Personal Computer venture or 3M's "Post-Its," offer sufficient upside attraction to keep companies making new venture attempts.

The variety of venture alternatives for entering new businesses has raised issues as to means for selecting among them. Roberts and Berry [88] have devised a research-based matrix reflecting primarily the organization's "familiarity" with the market and technology aspects of the new business.

The Roberts/Berry framework, supported by a field test in a large diversified U.S. firm, concludes essentially that the further the new area is from the firm's base "familiar" business, the less resource-intense the venture approach to be taken. An unpublished Japanese analysis of corporate venture success and failure and a host of studies performed by members of my mid-career MIT Management of Technology Program have strengthened the data support for "familiarity" as a powerful determinant of business development. Further reaffirming this emphasis upon "familiarity" as a key variable for eliciting strategic direction are the recent findings by Meyer and Roberts [89] that the more successful small high-technology companies pursue product development strategies that are focused upon moderate degrees of technological and market change. Much more research is needed to test the applicability of these results in other industries and with larger companies.

With the exception of its brief mention above in regard to U.S. and Japanese R&D investments, the role of government policies and actions in affecting technology strategy has been ignored thusfar. Yet government regulatory activities in regard especially to health and safety have had significant positive and negative influences on technological innovation [90–92]. But, as pointed out by Abernathy and Chakravarthy [93], government's strategic role has also included actions to create technologies directly (via the Horwitch/Prahalad Mode III, for example, 54) as well as indirectly through market modifications [94]. In a sense the variety of alternatives facing governments for influencing technological change are equivalent to the corporate venture alternatives described previously.

IN CONCLUSION

Recent work by Gobeli and Rudelius [95] provides a fitting basis for finishing this article. In their integrative comparative analysis of five firms in the technology-intensive cardiac-pacemaker industry they observe the differing competitive impacts that have come from the multiple stages of the innovation process. Managing at the creativity phase is not enough, nor even is managing manufactured quality sufficient, nor is managing that is focused primarily upon any other single aspect of innovation. They reaffirm the importance of key innovation-supporting people roles. Gobeli/Rudelius describe the importance of market–technology linkages, effective program management, government intervention, and appropriate goal setting, planning, and risk taking for firms in this medical electronics industry.

Technological innovation can provide the potential for altering the competitive status of firms and nations. It can contribute to increased corporate sales and profits, as well as individual and national security and well-being. But its purposeful management is complex, involving the effective integration of people, organizational processes, and plans. Only recently have some companies undertaken bold and broad action steps to try to institutionalize an effective product and process innovation program. Two firms in particular, long known for effective innovation, have publicized ambitious multifaceted endeavors. 3M has based its attempts heavily upon a so-called intrapreneurship approach, while Corning Glass has developed a more broadly based effort, including redesigning organization structures, changing incentive programs, and undertaking widespread management involvement and educational change activities. In both cases leadership for these multiyear institutional change programs came from the CEO's office. Other companies would be wise to consider whether top-down companywide commitments to accelerate and enhance effective innovation might not also apply to them.

This article has argued a host of generalizations about managing the process of invention and technological innovation, each supported by literature, empirical research, and practitioner experience. Some of these generalizations have already been widely diffused into practice, such as recognition of the gatekeeper's importance to information flow and nearly everyone's efforts to stimulate internal entrepreneurship. Some of my other contentions may still be subject to debate, modification, and even rejection as we learn more.

Both academics and technology managers need to join in this continuing search for clearer managerial insights about technological invention and innovation and more effective organizational performance. The National Research Council's recent report, *Management of Technology: The Hidden Competitive Advantage*, summed up the goals: "Effective work in the field of management of technology can play a crucial role in devising the strategies and imparting the skills and attitudes to U.S. engineers and managers that they will need in the future technology-dominated economy" [96]. It listed eight challenges of critical importance to industrial competitiveness: how to integrate technology into the overall strategic objectives of the firm; how to get into and out of technologies faster and more efficiently; how to assess/evaluate technology more effectively; how best to accomplish technology transfer; how to reduce new product development time; how to manage large, complex, and interdisciplinary or interorganizational projects/systems; how to manage the organization's internal use of technology; how to leverage the effectiveness of technical professionals. Hopefully, more light will be shed on these key industrial needs prior to the IRI's Diamond Jubilee!

SUMMING UP

- Technological innovation is a multistage process, with major differences needed for effective management of each stage of activity.
- To achieve effective innovation, an organization requires that "critical role-players" collaborate in a formal or informal team relationship. These critical roles include the idea generator, the entrepreneur, the program manager, several types of gatekeepers, and the sponsor.
- Group diversity is a major influence upon technical performance. A group that stabilizes its membership for too long not only decreases its productivity but tends to become insular and to evidence "Not Invented Here' behavior.
- Highest product development success rates are produced when marketing and R&D organizations work in close collaboration.
- "Market pull" far more frequently leads to successful innovations than does "technology push," although both sources of initiating projects account for success and failure alike.
- Users not only furnish critical "market needs" input data to designers, but in some industries supply the actual innovations that manufacturers later adapt, improve, and commercialize.
- Downstream transfer of RD&E results can be improved through use of multiple procedural, human, and organizational "bridges." Human bridges are the most effective transfer mechanism, and people movements, rotations, and face-to-face meetings should be used routinely and frequently.
- Most technologies move through evolutionary stages: an early one dominated by frequent product innovations, a transition characterized by increased process innovation and the emergence of a dominant product design, and a mature stage featuring much lower rate and more minor degree of both product and process innovation. A firm's innovation strategy and technological resource allocations should differ markedly depending upon the stage of its primary technology.
- "Competitive product profiling" is a useful method for initiating technical planning in a company, comparing the key technical performance characteristics of a product line with competitors' related products.
- Recent growth of venture capital and alliance methods reflects increasing recognition of the need to link external technologies with internal capabilities.
- Top management commitment is essential to assure success of broad-based programs aimed at institutionalizing the development of effective product and process innovations.

REFERENCES

1. H. R. Bartlett, *The Development of Industrial Research in the United States* (Washington, D.C.: National Research Council, 1941).

2. J. Jewkes, D. Sawers, and R. Stillerman, *The Sources of Innovation* (London: Macmillan, 1958).

3. "Top Research Managers Speak out on Innovation," *Research Management*, November 1970.

4. S. J. Kline, "Innovation Is Not a Linear Process," *Research Management*, 1985.

5. P. F. Drucker, *Innovation and Entrepreneurship: Practice and Principles* (New York: Harper & Row, 1985), pp. 35–36.

6. E. B. Roberts and A. R. Fusfeld, "Staffing the Innovative Technology-Based Organization," *Sloan Management Review* 22, no. 3 (Spring 1981).

7. D. Pelz and F. M. Andrews, *Scientists in Organizations*, rev. ed. (Ann Arbor, MI: University of Michigan Press, 1976).

8. F. M. Andrews, "Innovation in R&D Organizations: Some Relevant Concepts and Empirical Results," in E. B. Roberts et al., eds., *Biomedical Innovation* (Cambridge: MIT Press, 1981).

9. S. D. Stookey, "History of the Development of Pyroceram," *Research Management*, Autumn 1958.

10. D. Peters and E. B. Roberts, "Unutilized Ideas in University Laboratories," *Academy of Management Journal* 12, no. 2 (June 1969).

11. E. B. Roberts and D. Peters, "Commercial Innovation from University Faculty," *Research Policy* 10, no. 2 (April 1981).

12. A. H. Rubenstein, A. K. Chakrabarti, R. D. O'Keefe, W. E. Souder, and H.C. Young, "Factors Influencing Innovation Success at the Project Level," *Research Management*, May 1976.

13. L. W. Lehr, "Stimulating Technological Innovation: The Role of Top Management," *Research Management*, November 1979.

14. E. B. Roberts, "Entrepreneurship and Technology: A Basic Study of Innovators," *Research Management* 11, no. 4 (July 1968).

15. M. A. Maidique, "Entrepreneurs, Champions, and Technological Innovation," *Sloan Management Review* 21, no. 2 (Winter 1980).

16. D. G. Marquis and I. M. Rubin, "Management Factors in Project Performance," MIT Sloan School of Management Working Paper, 1966.

17. R. Katz and T. J. Allen, "Project Performance and the Locus of Influence in the R&D Matrix," *Academy of Management Journal* 26 (1985).

18. T. J. Allen, *Managing the Flow of Technology* (Cambridge: MIT Press, 1977).

19. J. Gartner and C. S. Naiman, "Overcoming the Barriers to Technology Transfer," *Research Management*, March 1976.

20. L. J. Thomas, "Available Light Movies—An Individual Inventor Made It Happen," *Research Management*, November 1980.

21. W. E. Souder and R. W. Ziegler, "A Review of Creativity and Problem-Solving Techniques," *Research Management*, July 1977.

22. H. Geschka, "Introduction and Use of Idea-Generating Methods," *Research Management*, May 1978.

23. R. Katz, "Managing Careers: The Influence of Job and Group Longevities," in R. Katz, ed., *Career Issues in Human Resource Management* (Englewood Cliffs, NJ: Prentice Hall, 1982).

24. T. S. Kuhn, *The Structure of Scientific Revolutions* (Chicago: University of Chicago Press, 1963).

25. R. Katz and T. J. Allen, "Investigating the Not Invented Here (NIH) Syndrome: A Look at the Performance, Tenure, and Communication Patterns of 50 R&D Project Groups," *R&D Management* 12, no. 1 (1982).

26. G. F. Farris, "The Technical Supervisor: Beyond the Peter Principle," *Technology Review*, 1973.

27. H. J. Thamhain and D. L. Wilemon, "Leadership, Conflict, and Program Management Effectiveness," *Sloan Management Review* 19, no. 1 (Fall 1977).

28. J. M. Utterback, "Innovation and the Diffusion of Technology," *Science* 183, no. 4125 (February 15, 1974).

29. A. Gerstenfeld, "A Study of Successful Projects, Unsuccessful Projects, and Projects in Process in West Germany," *IEEE Transactions on Engineering Management* EM-23, no. 3 (1976).

30. R. Rothwell, C. Freeman, A. Horsley, V. T. P. Jervis, A. B. Robertson, and J. Townsend, "SAPPHO Updated-Project SAPPHO Phase II," *Research Policy* 3 (1974).

31. W. C. Fernelius and W. H. Waldo, "Role of Basic Research in Industrial Innovation," *Research Management*, July 1980.

32. P. C. Goldmark, "How the LP Record Was Developed—Or the Case of the Missing Fuzz," *Research Management*, July 1974.

33. N. R. Baker, S. G. Green, and A. S. Bean, "The Need for Strategic Balance in R&D Project Portfolios," *Research Management*, March–April 1986.

34. W. E. Souder, "Effectiveness of Product Development Methods," *Industrial Marketing Management* 7 (1978).

35. G. L. Urban and J. R. Hauser, *Design and Marketing of New Products* (Englewood Cliffs, NJ: Prentice Hall, 1980).

36. E. A. von Hippel, "Lead Users: A Source of Novel Product Concepts," *Management Science*, July 1986.

37. A. R. Fusfeld, "How Not to Fall on Your Face in

Technological Forecasting," *Inside R&D* 7, no. 2 (January 1978).

38. D. W. Collier, "More Effective Research for Large Corporations," *Research Management* 12, no. 3 (May 1969).

39. C. G. Suits, "Selectivity and Timing in Research," *Research Management* 5, no. 6 (1962).

40. J. P. Casey, "High Fructose Corn Syrup—A Case History of Innovation," *Research Management*, September 1976.

41. P. R. Lawrence and J. W. Lorsch, *Organization and Environments* (Boston: Harvard Business School, 1967).

42. D. G. Marquis and D. L. Straight, "Organizational Factors in Project Performance," MIT Sloan School of Management Working Paper #133-65, 1965.

43. T. J. Allen, "Performance of Information Channels in the Transfer of Technology," *Industrial Management Review* 8, no. 1 (Fall 1966).

44. S. Myers and D. G. Marquis, *Successful Industrial Innovation* (Washington, D.C.: National Science Foundation, 1969).

45. J. Langrish, M. Gibbons, W. G. Evans, and F. R. Jevons, *Wealth from Knowledge* (London: Macmillan, 1972).

46. J. A. Morton, *Organizing for Innovation* (New York: McGraw-Hill, 1971).

47. A. Gerstenfeld and L. H. Wortzel, "Strategies for Innovation in Developing Countries," *Sloan Management Review* 19, no. 1 (1977).

48. E. A. von Hippel, "Has a Customer Already Developed Your Next Product?" *Sloan Management Review* 18, no. 2 (Winter 1977).

49. E. B. Roberts, "Stimulating Technological Innovation: Organizational Approaches," *Research Management* 22, no. 6 (November 1979).

50. E. B. Roberts and A. Frohman, "Strategies for Improving Research Utilization," *Technology Review* 80, no. 5 (March/April 1978).

51. H. Cohen, S. Keller, and D. Streeter, "The Transfer of Technology from Research to Development," *Research Management*, May 1979.

52. J. J. Smith, J. E. McKeon, K. L. Hoy, R. L. Boysen, L. Shechter, and E. B. Roberts, "Lessons from 10 Case Studies in Innovation," *Research Management* 27, no. 5 (September–October 1984).

53. E. B. Roberts, "Strategic Management of Technology," in *Global Technological Change: Symposium Proceedings* (Cambridge: MIT Industrial Liaison Program, June 1983).

54. M. Horwitch and C. K. Prahalad, "Managing Technological Innovation—Three Ideal Modes," *Sloan Management Review* 17, no. 2 (Winter 1976).

55. J. B. Quinn, "Technological Innovation, Entrepreneurship, and Strategy," *Sloan Management Review* 20, no. 3 (Spring 1979).

56. T. J. Peters and R. H. Waterman, *In Search of Excellence* (New York: Harper & Row, 1982).

57. M. A. Maidique and R. H. Hayes, "The Art of High-Technology Management," *Sloan Management Review* 25, no. 2 (Winter 1984).

58. J. Friar and M. Horwitch, "The Emergence of Technology Strategy: A New Dimension of Strategic Management," *Technology in Society* 7, nos. 2 and 3 (Winter 1985/1986).

59. J. M. Utterback and W. J. Abernathy, "A Dynamic Model of Product and Process Innovation," *Omega* 3, no. 6 (1975).

60. J. M. Utterback, "Systems of Innovation: Macro/Micro," in W. N. Smith and C. F. Larson, eds., *Innovation and U.S. Research* (Washington, D.C.: American Chemical Society, 1980).

61. J. M. Utterback and L. Kim, "Invasion of a Stable Business by Radical Innovation," in P. R. Kleindorfer, ed., *The Management of Productivity and Technology in Manufacturing* (New York: Plenum Press, 1986).

62. E. B. Roberts, "Exploratory and Normative Technological Forecasting: A Critical Appraisal," *Technological Forecasting* 1, no. 2 (Fall 1969).

63. A. R. Fusfeld and F. C. Spital, "Technology Forecasting and Planning in the Corporate Environment: Survey and Comment," in B. V. Dean and J. L. Goldhar, eds., *Management of Research and Innovation*, TIMS Studies in the Management Sciences, vol. 15 (North-Holland, 1980).

64. R. N. Foster, *Innovation: The Attacker's Advantage* (New York: Summit Books, 1986).

65. E. B. Roberts, *The Dynamics of Research and Development* (New York: Harper & Row, 1964).

66. J. P. Matino, *Technological Forecasting for Decision Making* (New York: Elsevier, 1972).

67. T. O'Rourke, Presentation at Pugh-Roberts Associates, Inc., Workshop on Critical Issues in Technology Management, April 15, 1986.

68. D. H. Peters, "The Development of Frozen Orange Juice Concentrate," *Research Management* 11, no. 1 (January 1968).

69. R. A. Richardson, "Research toward Specific Goals: Development of the Light-Weight, Two-Cycle Diesel," *Research Management*, Summer 1958.

70. S. Hollander, *The Sources of Increased Efficiency* (Cambridge: MIT Press, 1965).

71. C. M. Crawford, "Defining the Charter for Product Innovation," *Sloan Management Review* 22, no.1 (Fall 1980).

72. M. R. Baker and W. H. Pound, "Project Selection: Where We Stand," *IEEE Transactions on Engi-*

neering Management EM-11, no. 4 (December 1964).

73. A. C. Cooper and D. Schendel, "Strategic Responses to Technological Threats," *Business Horizons* 19, no. 1 (February 1976).

74. E. B. Roberts, "Research and Development System Dynamics," in E. B. Roberts, ed., *Managerial Applications of System Dynamics* (Cambridge: MIT Press, 1978).

75. H. B. Weil, T. A. Bergan, and E. B. Roberts, "The Dynamics of R&D Strategy," in E. B. Roberts, ed., *Managerial Applications of System Dynamics* (Cambridge: MIT Press, 1978).

76. K. G. Cooper, "Naval Ship Production: A Claim Settled and a Framework Built," *Interfaces* 10, no. 6 (December 1980).

77. A. R. Fusfeld, "How to Put Technology into Corporate Planning," *Technology Review* 80 (May 1978).

78. M. E. Porter, *Competitive Advantage: Creating and Sustaining Superior Performance* (New York: Free Press, 1985).

79. S. B. Johnson, "Comparing R&D Strategies of Japanese and U.S. Firms," *Sloan Management Review* 25, no. 3 (Spring 1984).

80. T. Hirota, "Environment and Technology Strategy of Japanese Companies," MIT Sloan School of Management Working Paper #1671-85, June 1985.

81. M. A. Cusumano, "Diversity and Innovation in Japanese Technology Management," in R. S. Rosenbloom, ed., *Research on Technological Innovation, Management, and Policy* (Greenwich, CT: JAI Press, 1986).

82. E. B. Roberts, "New Ventures for Corporate Growth," *Harvard Business Review* 59, no. 4 (July–August 1980).

83. D. Dimanescu and J. W. Botkin, *The New Alliances: America's R&D Consortia* (Cambridge: Ballinger Publishing, 1986).

84. "Strategic Alliances: New Competitive Muscle," *Business Week*, October 6–7, 1986.

85. E. B. Roberts and A. Frohman, "Internal Entrepreneurship: Strategy for Growth," *Business Quarterly* 37, no. 1 (Spring 1972).

86. N. Fast, "A Visit to the New Venture Graveyard," *Research Management*, March 1979.

87. P. E. Haggerty, "Strategy, Tactics, and Research," *Research Management* 9, no. 3 (1966).

88. E. B. Roberts and C. A. Berry, "Entering New Businesses: Selecting Strategies for Success," *Sloan Management Review* 26, no. 3 (Spring 1985).

89. M. H. Meyer and E. B. Roberts, "New Product Strategy in Small Technology-Based Firms: A Pilot Study," *Management Science* 32, no. 7 (July 1986).

90. W. M. Capron, ed., *Technological Change in Regulated Industries* (Washington, D.C.: The Brookings Institution, 1971).

91. T. J. Allen, J. M. Utterback, M. S. Sirbu, N. A. Ashford, and J. H. Hollomon, "Government Influence on the Process of Innovation in Europe and Japan," *Research Policy* 7, no. 2 (April 1978).

92. O. Hauptman and E. B. Roberts, "FDA Regulation of Product Risk and its Impact upon Young Biomedical Firms," *Journal of Product Innovation Management* 4, no. 2 (June 1987).

93. W. J. Abernathy and B. S. Chakravarthy "Government Intervention and Innovation in Industry: A Policy Framework," *Sloan Management Review* 20, no. 3 (Spring 1979).

94. J. M. Utterback and A. E. Murray, "The Influence of Defense Procurement and Sponsorship of Research and Development on the Development of the Civilian Electronics Industry," MIT Center for Policy Analysis Working Paper CPA-77-2, June 1977.

95. D. H. Gobeli and W. Rudelius, "Management Innovation: Lessons from the Cardiac-Pacing Industry," *Sloan Management Review* 26, no. 4 (Summer 1985).

96. National Research Council, *Management of Technology: The Hidden Competitive Advantage* (Washington, D.C.: National Academy Press, 1987).

INDEX